Eyes Upside Down

EYES UPSIDE DOWN

Visionary Filmmakers and the Heritage of Emerson

P. Adams Sitney

OXFORD
UNIVERSITY PRESS

2008

OXFORD
UNIVERSITY PRESS

Oxford University Press, Inc., publishes works that further
Oxford University's objective of excellence
in research, scholarship, and education.

Oxford New York
Auckland   Cape Town   Dar es Salaam   Hong Kong   Karachi
Kuala Lumpur   Madrid   Melbourne   Mexico City   Nairobi
New Delhi   Shanghai   Taipei   Toronto

With offices in
Argentina   Austria   Brazil   Chile   Czech Republic   France   Greece
Guatemala   Hungary   Italy   Japan   Poland   Portugal   Singapore
South Korea   Switzerland   Thailand   Turkey   Ukraine   Vietnam

Copyright © 2008 by P. Adams Sitney

Published by Oxford University Press, Inc.
198 Madison Avenue, New York, New York 10016

www.oup.com

Oxford is a registered trademark of Oxford University Press.

Library of Congress Cataloging-in-Publication Data

Sitney, P. Adams.
   Eyes upside down : visionary filmmakers and the heritage of Emerson / P. Adams Sitney.
      p. cm.
   Includes index.
   ISBN 978-0-19-533114-1
   ISBN 978-0-19-533115-8 (pbk.)
   1. Experimental films—United States—History and criticism.
   2. Emerson, Ralph Waldo, 1803–1882—Influence. I. Title.
   PN1995.9.E96S49 2008
   791.430973—dc22   2007031171

9 8 7 6 5 4 3 2 1

Printed in the United States of America
on acid-free paper

To Tony Pipolo and Jeffrey Stout

Preface

In 1992 I began taking notes for a book on avant-garde filmmakers that would focus on the heritage of Ralph Waldo Emerson and Walt Whitman. For Marie Menken, Stan Brakhage, and Jonas Mekas, the relationship to both seemed to me uncannily apt, while Ernie Gehr's affinities appeared to be dominantly Emersonian and those of Warren Sonbert and Andrew Noren Whitmanian. As I slowly worked on the book, its range expanded. The films of Ian Hugo and Su Friedrich began to take on new meaning for me when I considered them in this tradition. Eventually, the more remote filmographies of Hollis Frampton, Abigail Child, and Robert Beavers were drawn into the expanding circle of these considerations. Their writings on cinema first alerted me to their Emersonian aesthetics. When I examined their films in this light, I was rewarded with a clearer sense of the ways in which they simultaneously resist and participate in the native tradition.

I also found that many of them, like Whitman, assembled individual films into complex series, sometimes even projecting a single serial film as the work of a lifetime. So, embedded within this long study of the Emersonian heritage in the American avant-garde cinema is a sustained consideration of the role of the film sequence. I had considered extending the range of filmmakers even further. I would have liked to include chapters on Saul Levine, Nathaniel Dorsky, and Peter Hutton, and perhaps others, but the manuscript grew unwieldy at seven hundred pages. By the time this book is published I hope the gist of my reflections on their films will have appeared elsewhere.

In writing this book I have benefited enormously from a fellowship at the Getty Research Institute (2004–2005), where for the first time in my career I had an entire year to devote to a book. I am deeply grateful to Thomas Crow and Charles Salas for inviting me, and to Rani Singh for tirelessly providing me with facilities and research materials while I was in Los Angeles. Without her help, I would not have been able to complete the book at that time. I had the good fortune to have Genevieve Yue as my research assistant at the Getty. She is a distinguished young scholar of the avant-garde cinema in her own right. When I could not catch words from the soundtracks of Beavers's *Plan of Brussels* and *Palinode*, my colleagues Howard Bloch and Tom Levin helped me with the French and the German.

In the three decades since I wrote *Visionary Film*, there has been a spectacular growth in the criticism and scholarship of the American avant-garde cinema. My frequent citations and footnotes indicate how indebted I am to the insights of other scholars. No one has done more for the field than Scott MacDonald. His five volumes of *The Critical Cinema* have become essential references for us all. MacDonald was particularly generous to me, sharing unpublished tapes from older interviews, and including questions that I had in interviews he was conducting as I was writing this book. Fred Camper, Martina Kudlacek, Robert Haller, David James, Paul Arthur, Tony Pipolo, Marie Nesthus (whose work on Brakhage's serial films preceded my own), John Pruitt, Amy Taubin, Keith Sanborn, Gerald O'Grady, and Marilyn Brakhage have shared their insights and learning with me.

All of the filmmakers discussed in this book have been extraordinarily generous to me, in making films and stills available, providing me with manuscripts, and answering my tiresome questions. All of them are, or were, my friends. I regret than nothing I can write will ever do justice to their films, which have irradiated my life. The deaths of Hugo, Menken, Frampton and Sonbert before I started writing the chapters on their films, and of Brakhage while I was still at work on this book, have impoverished those sections, insofar as I was unable answer questions about their films and their reading for which no documentation survives.

The Princeton University Committee on Research in the Humanities and Social Sciences gave me a series of grants to pursue aspects of this work. The Stanley Seeger fund of the Program in Hellenic Studies also helped me in my work on Robert Beavers. Marilyn Brakhage (and the estate of Stan Brakhage), Andrew Noren, Jonas Mekas, Jon Gartenberg, Abigail Child, Robert Haller,

Su Friedrich, Robert Beavers (and Temenos), Fred Camper and Anthology Film Archives provided me with stills. Arunas Kulikauskas made other stills especially for this book. Sandi Milburn and Rick Pilaro, at Princeton University, helped me digitalize the stills and lay them out.

A secular miracle gave me Shannon McLachlan as my editor at Oxford University Press. No one in the world of publishing knows the films I write about better than McLachlan. She had been a supporter of my work long before she came to Oxford. Paul Hobson, who copyedited the book, has been extremely helpful. My agent, Georges Borchardt, Inc. has been, as ever, encouraging and very helpful. My dear friend, Jeffrey Stout, meticulously read every page of the manuscript, correcting errors, offering suggestions, and sharing his vastly superior knowledge of Emerson with me. In acknowledgement for the unremitting kindnesses he and Tony Pipolo have shown me for many years, this book is dedicated to them.

Acknowledgments

I am grateful to the following individuals, presses and estates for permission to quote texts: Wesleyan University Press (John Cage: *Silence*); University of Alabama Press (Abigail Child: *This is Called Moving*); Marian Faller and the estate of Hollis Frampton (Frampton); Marilyn Brakhage and the estate of Stan Brakhage (Brakhage); New Directions (William Carlos Williams); Barbara Stuhlmann, Lilace Hatayama, The Charles E. Young Library of UCLA, and the Anais Nin Trust (Nin and Ian Hugo); University of Chicago Press (Gertrude Stein: *Narration*); Melissa Watterworth and the Thomas J. Dodd Research Center, University of Connecticut (Charles Olson); Georges Borchardt, Inc. (John Ashbery: "Tapestry"); W.W. Norton and Company (Rilke).

John Cage, pp. 73, 75, 100, and 111 in *Silence: Lectures and Writings* © by John Cage and reprinted by permission of Wesleyan University Press.

"To and Dog Injured in the Street" (excerpt), from *Collected Poems 1939–1962*, Volume II, copyright © 1953 by William Carlos Williams. Reprinted by permission of New Directions Publishing Corp.

Contents

Eyes Upside Down

Introduction: Emersonian Poetics

The art of the first British settlers of America was literary, originating in the severe rhetoric of New England divines. Absolutely convinced of their election, and often ferociously excoriating the heresy of toleration, they theologized the very idea of America as a redemption from Europe according to God's plan and covenant. Consequently, the great flowering of American literature and painting in the first half of the nineteenth century arrived with the secularization of that rhetoric and theology. The turning point in our native tradition from an art in the service of Christian theology to an orphic theology of art may be symbolically represented by Ralph Waldo Emerson's resignation in 1832 from the Second Church of Boston (the pulpit of the author of *Magnalia Christi Americana*, Cotton Mather). In the following two years, Emerson gradually transferred the locus of his teaching from Unitarian pulpits to the public lecture halls, such as that of the Society for the Diffusion of Useful Knowledge in Boston's Masonic Temple. His essays that both predict and inform American artistic discourse retain "in the optative mode" (as he said of all of our literature) the fervor and conviction of the founding divines.

American artists—poets, composers, painters, filmmakers—have largely perpetuated Emerson's transformation of the homiletic tradition in their polemical position papers. Sometimes they have even implicitly acknowledged their awareness of that tradition, as when Charles Ives published his *Essays before a Sonata* (1920) to accompany his "Concord Sonata." More often they have been unwitting Emersonians, or even Emersonians in spite of themselves. Gertrude Stein is an example of the former, John Cage and Charles Olson of the latter. I shall focus on them as significant figures in the transmission of Emersonian aesthetics to the filmmakers at the core of this book, although they are by no means the only exemplars that might have been chosen. They represent a sufficient variety of responses to Emerson (and his disciple Walt Whitman) to chart the array of variations on Emerson that the filmmakers will demonstrate.

Museum lectures, program notes, exhibition catalogs, interviews, and, in cinema, introductions to film screenings (since Maya Deren pioneered that mode in the late 1940s) have been the means through which American artists have continued this fundamentally oral tradition. Often they have spoken of their work with the absolutist confidence of the seventeenth century elect, and just as often have extirpated the heresies of those fellow artists who deviated from their convictions. All of Gertrude Stein's theoretical work took the form of public speeches. The title of her most comprehensive series, *Lectures in America* (1935) attests to this. *Narration* was presented as four lectures at the University of Chicago, and she delivered "What Are Masterpeices and Why There Are So Few of Them" at Oxford. John Cage turned the lecture format into another art form, at times interweaving (on tape) at least four different lines of argument at once. Maya Deren began the practice of lecturing with her films as an economic necessity and a proselytizing tactic. Since her death in 1961, this has become a common practice for avant-garde filmmakers. Parallel to the oral style runs an epistolary mode (corresponding to Emerson's journals) in which public polemic takes the guise of a correspondence between artists, as in many of the polemical writings of Ezra Pound and Charles Olson. Among the filmmakers, Stan Brakhage, Hollis Frampton, Jonas Mekas, and Abigail Child are exemplars of this mode.

Throughout this book, I identify American aesthetics as Emersonian. I want to include in this sweeping claim Emerson's disciples Thoreau and Whitman, and even those such as Melville who set themselves in opposition to him, insomuch as Emerson comprehensively set out the terms of the argument and defined the terrain on which the Americanness of our native art would be determined.

Emerson himself knew that the mutually opposed artistic positions and the variety of styles, in a given nation at any one time, participate in a coherent system. Near the beginning of his essay "Art," he described the way in which the air an artist breathes "necessitates" an "ineffaceable seal on [his] work":

> [T]he new in art is always formed out of the old. The Genius of
> the Hour sets his ineffaceable seal on the work, and gives it an

inexpressible charm for the imagination. As far as the spiritual character of the period overpowers the artist, and finds expression in his
work, so far it will retain a certain grandeur, and will represent to
future beholders the Unknown, the Inevitable, the Divine. No man
can quite exclude this element of Necessity from his labor. No man
can quite emancipate himself from his age and country, or produce a
model in which the education, the religion, the politics, usages, and
arts, of his times shall have no share. Though he were never so original, never so willful and fantastic, he cannot wipe out of his work
every trace of the thoughts amidst which it grew. The very avoidance
betrays the usage he avoids. Above his will, and out of his sight, he is
necessitated, by the air he breathes, and the idea on which he and his
contemporaries live and toil, to share the manner of his times, without
knowing what that manner is.[1]

Gertrude Stein virtually repeats Emerson's terms when she begins the
fourth lecture of *Narration*: "After all anybody is as their land and air is....
It is that which makes them and the arts they make and the work they do
and the way they eat and the way they drink and they way they learn and
everything."[2]
It is characteristic that an avowed anti-Emersonian poet such as Charles
Olson, who deliberately aligned himself with Melville's rejection of the
Sage of Concord, would recast this passage in a polemical essay, ignoring its
Emersonian source because he found something similar in Carl Jung's study
of synchronicity and the aleatoric *Book of Changes*. But Olson was never more
Emersonian and less Jungian than in asserting the prime point of his episto-
lary essay, that wisdom cannot be detached from poetic form:

> We are ultimate when we do bend to the law. And the law is:
> / whatever is born or done this moment of time, has
> the qualities of
> this moment of
> time/[3]

The peculiarly Emersonian inflection of this commonplace would be the
invocation of Necessity or Ananke under the guise of "law."
The transformation of Necessity into a category of poetics is one of the
dominant Emersonian features of American aesthetic theory that I shall

---

1. Ralph Waldo Emerson, *Essays and Lectures* (New York: Library of America, 1983), pp. 431–32.
2. Gertrude Stein, *Narration* (Chicago: University of Chicago Press, 1969), p. 46.
3. Charles Olson, "Against Wisdom as Such," *The Human Universe* (New York: Grove Press, 1967), p. 70.

emphasize in this book. Others are the primacy of the visible and the transformative value of vehicular motion.

The great ode to Ananke concludes Emerson's late essay "Fate":

> I do not wonder at a snow-flake, a shell, a summer landscape, or
> the glory of the stars; but at the necessity of beauty under which the
> universe lies; that all is and must be pictorial; that the rainbow and
> the curve of the horizon and the arch of the blue vault are only results
> from the organism of the eye....
>   Let us build altars to the Beautiful Necessity, which secures that all
> is made of one piece; that plaintiff and defendant, friend and enemy,
> animal and planet, food and eater are of one kind... to the Necessity
> which rudely or softly educates him to the perception that there are
> no contingencies; that Law rules throughout existence; a Law which
> is not intelligent but intelligence,—not personal nor impersonal,—it
> distains and passes understanding; it dissolves persons; it vivifies
> nature; yet solicits the pure in heart to draw on all its omnipotence.[4]

In the second half of the twentieth century, the aesthetics of the Beautiful Necessity animated the debate on the function and value of chance in making art. The expansiveness of the Emersonian heritage makes John Cage, who tirelessly sought to erase the distinctions between art and life, and Stan Brakhage, the orphic filmmaker whose poesis was a religious vocation, coequal heirs of the Beautiful Necessity, although they invoke it to opposite ends. Cage's systematic disruptions of continuous discourse often make it difficult to isolate his version of Ananke in a succinct quotation. However, the concluding paragraph of his "History of Experimental Music in America" offers the following reflection:

> History is the story of original actions.... That one sees the human
> race is one person (all of its members parts of the same body,
> brothers—not in competition any more than hand is in competition
> with eye) enables him to see that originality is necessary, for there
> is no need for eye to do what hand so well does. In this way, the
> past and present are to be observed and each person makes what
> he alone must make, bringing for the whole of human society into
> existence a historical fact, and then, on and on, in continuum and
> discontinuum.[5]

4. Emerson, *Essays and Lectures*, pp. 967–68.
5. John Cage, *Silence* (Middletown: Wesleyan University Press, 1961), p. 75.

In an interview with Roger Reynolds at the time of the publication of *Silence*, he restated this idea, again linking necessity to originality:

> I'm devoted to the principle of originality—not originality in the egoistic sense, but originality in the sense of doing something that is necessary to do. Now, obviously the things that are necessary to do are not the things that have been done, but the ones that have not yet been done. This applies not only to other people's work, but seriously to my own work.[6]

For Brakhage, Ananke animated his vocation. He was unembarrassed by what Cage calls egoism:

> OF NECESSITY I BECOME INSTRUMENT FOR THE PASSAGE OF INNER VISION THRU ALL MY SENSIBILITIES, INTO ITS EXTERNAL FORM. My most active part in their process is to increase all my sensibilities (so that all films arise out of some total area or being or full life) AND, at the given moment of possible creation to act only out of necessity. In other words, I am principally concerned with revelation. My sensibilities are art-oriented to the extent that revelation takes place, naturally, within the given historical context of specifically Western aesthetics. If my sensibilities were otherwise oriented, revelation would take an other external form— perhaps a purely personal one.[7]

In the early short book *Nature* (1836), Emerson set forth a hyperbole for the primacy of the visible in his and our world. In response to it, Christopher Cranch famously caricatured him as an enormous eyeball on spindly legs:

> Crossing a bare common, in snow puddles, at twilight, under a clouded sky, without having in my thoughts any occurrence of special good fortune, I have enjoyed a perfect exhilaration. . . . There I feel that nothing can befall me in life,—no disgrace, no calamity, (leaving me my eyes,) which nature cannot repair. Standing on the bare ground,—my head bathed by the blithe air, and uplifted into infinite space,—all mean egotism vanishes. I become a transparent eye-ball; I am nothing; I see all; the currents of the Universal Being circulate

6. Richard Kostelanetz, *Conversing with Cage, 2nd Edition* (New York: Routledge, 2003), p. 221.
7. Stan Brakhage, *Metaphors on Vision* (New York: *Film Culture* no. 30, 1963), pages unnumbered, fourth letter of "Margin Alien."

through me; I am part and parcel of God.... In the tranquil landscape,
and especially in the distant line of the horizon, man beholds somewhat as beautiful as his own nature.[8]

In that same book, Emerson provides a scenario for the quickening of
visual experience that is central to the argument of this book, as my title
suggests. I shall return to it again and again in the succeeding chapters:

> The least change in our point of view, gives the whole world a picto-
> rial air. A man who seldom rides, needs only to get into a coach and
> traverse his own town, to turn the street into a puppet-show. The men,
> the women,—talking, running, bartering, fighting,—the earnest me-
> chanic, the lounger, the beggar, the boys, the dogs, are unrealized at
> once, or, at least, wholly detached from all relation to the observer, and
> seen as apparent, not substantial beings. What new thoughts are sug-
> gested by seeing a face of country quite familiar, in the rapid movement
> of the rail-road car! Nay, the most wonted objects, (make a very slight
> change in the point of vision,) please us most. In a camera obscura, the
> butcher's cart, and the figure of one of our own family amuse us. So the
> portrait of a well-known face gratifies us. Turn the eyes upside down,
> by looking at the landscape through your legs, and how agreeable is the
> picture, though you have seen it any time these twenty years![9]

If this passage sounds familiar, it may be because Whitman so thoroughly
took over its catalog of the puppet show of city life and made it his own in
Leaves of Grass. However, before the invention of cinema it was not possible
to make visual art directly following most of the cues in this catalog. We shall
see the various ways in which all the filmmakers I discuss followed Emerson's
suggestions without knowing the source.

For the American visual artists who inherited the exhilaration of the transparent eyeball, the dissolution of the self within a divine afflatus often entails
the hypothetical silencing or disengagement of language. In particular, the
temporary suspension of the substantive, name-giving activity of the mind
assumed a redemptive status for the Abstract Expressionists. Furthermore, the
primacy of vision always contains a dialectical moment in which visibility is
effaced by whiteness. The monumental expression of that threatening void at
the core of vision also can be found in Emerson's *Nature*:

> The ruin or the blank that we see when we look at nature, is in our
> own eye. The axis of vision is not coincident with the axis of things,

8. Emerson, *Essays and Lectures*, p. 10.
9. Ibid., pp. 33–34.

and so they appear not transparent but opake. The reason the world lacks unity, and lies broken and in heaps, is because man is disunited with himself.[10]

The polar stasis at the end of Poe's *Narrative of Arthur Gordon Pym* and the chapter "The Whiteness of the Whale" in *Moby Dick* are examples of this national obsession with the "blank" (or etymologically, white) of nature that Wallace Stevens called "an ancestral theme" in "The Auroras of Autumn":

> Here, being visible is being white,
> Is being of the solid of white, the accomplishment
> Of an extremist in an exercise...[11]

One extremist, Gertrude Stein, absorbed Emerson through her teacher at Radcliffe College, William James, who, as Richard Poirier has shown, owed more to Emerson than he cared to acknowledge.[12] Quoting the following passage from "The Stream of Thought," the cornerstone chapter of James's *Principles of Psychology*, Poirier points to "the emphasis on action, on transitions" in both James and Emerson and the skeptical rejection of false substantives and illusionary ends in the frozen meaning of words:

> We ought to say a feeling of *and*, a feeling of *if*, a feeling of *but*, and a feeling of *by*, quite as readily as we say a feeling of *blue* or a feeling of *cold*. Yet we do not: so inveterate has our habit become of recognizing the existence of the substantive parts alone, that language almost refuses to lend itself to any other use.[13]

One might even say that Stein took this as a literary program. In the lecture "Poetry and Grammar" she discussed her reluctance to depend upon nouns in her writing:

> As I say a noun is a name of a thing, and therefore slowly if you feel what is inside that thing you do not call it by the name by which it is known. Everybody knows that by the way they do when they are in

---

10. Ibid., p. 47.

11. Wallace Stevens, "The Auroras of Autumn." in *The Palm at the End of the Mind: Selected Poems and a Play*, ed. Holly Stevens (New York: Knopf, 1971), p. 308.

12. Richard Poirier, *The Renewal of Literature: Emersonian Reflections* (New Haven: Yale University Press, 1987).

13. Ibid., p. 16. From William James, *The Principles of Psychology* (New York: Dover, 1950), vol. 1, pp. 245–46.

love and a writer should always have that intensity of emotion about whatever is the object about which he writes.[14]

By dislocating syntax, she foregrounded conjunctions and prepositions in her writings of the second and third decades of the twentieth century. For example, "If I Told Him: A Completed Portrait of Picasso" (1923) lays stress on *if* and *as* in exposing the infrastructure of portraiture.[15] James's chapter "The Stream of Thought" also resonates in the thought of Stan Brakhage and Ernie Gehr, both avid readers of Stein.

In *Narration* (1935), Stein interrogated the nature of American literature, poetry, and prose, the differences between literary narratives and newspapers, and the status of an audience. Several Emersonian topoi occur in these talks. I begin with the vehicular perspective.

A sign glimpsed from a train became the exemplum of the second lecture:

Let's make our flour meal and meat in Georgia.

    This is a sign I read as we rode on a train from Atlanta to Birmingham and I wondered then and am still wondering is it poetry or is it prose let's make our flour meal and meat in Georgia, it might be poetry and it might be prose and of course there is a reason why a reason why it might be poetry and a reason why it might be prose.

Does let's make our flour meal and meat in Georgia move in various ways and very well and has that to do really to do with narrative in poetry, has it really to do with narrative at all and is it more important in poetry that a thing should move in various kinds of ways than it is in prose supposing both of them to be narrative.[16]

These "new thoughts" excited by the fast-moving perspective turn on the puns embedded in the advertising sign. Stein's method is circular; examples are displaced; later lectures suggest ways of reading earlier ones. Thus, when she distinguishes between English and American narratives in the opening lecture, she offers no examples to illustrate her contention that "English literature...has been determined by the fact that England is an island and that the daily life on that island was a completely daily life"[17] but in a different context

14. Gertrude Stein, "Poetry and Grammar," *Lectures in America,* (New York: Random House, 1935), p. 210. Tony Tanner points to a direct Emersonian source for this rejection of nouns and sees in her use of repetition "Emerson's wisdom of wondering at the usual." Tony Tanner, *The Reign of Wonder: Naivety and Reality in American Literature* (Cambridge: Cambridge University Press, 1965), pp. 198–201.
15. See P. Adams Sitney, *Modernist Montage: The Obscurity of Vision in Cinema and Literature* (New York: Columbia University Press, 1992), pp. 151–52.
16. Stein, *Narration*, p. 16.
17. Ibid., p. 3.

in the third lecture she gives her example: Defoe's *Robinson Crusoe*. Similarly, in the lecture following the description of the sign seen from a moving train, she gives an oblique clue to her reading of how it "moves in various ways":

> I love my love with a b because she is peculiar. One can say this. That has nothing to do with what a newspaper does and that is the reason why that is the reason that newspapers and with it history as it mostly exists has nothing to do with anything that is living.[18]

The seeming nonsense of "I love my love with a b because she is peculiar" becomes an erotic epigram when we read "a b" as her companion and lover, Alice B. [Toklas]. Looking back to the earlier lecture with this in mind, we may note that the train was moving from A[tlanta] to B[irmingham] and the prosaic advertisement for Georgia products can be read as a call to assignation (*meat* as *meet*). This confirms Stein's definition of the American difference in literature in the opening lecture:

> In the American writing the words began to have inside themselves those same words that in the English were completely quiet or very slowly moving began to have within themselves the consciousness of completely moving, they began to detach themselves from the solidity of anything, they began to excitedly feel themselves as if they were anywhere or anything, think about American writing from Emerson, Hawthorne Walt Whitman Mark Twain Henry James myself Sherwood Anderson Thornton Wilder and Dashiell Hammitt [sic] and you will see what I mean, as well as in advertising and in road signs, you will see what I mean, words left alone more and more feel that they are moving and all of it is detached and is detaching anything from anything and in this detaching and in this moving it is being in its way creating its existing. This is the real difference between English and American writing and this then can lead to anything.[19]

The play of movement and detachment here redeploys terms from Emerson's essay "The Poet," where he balances "the intellect, which delights in detachment" and "the quality of the imagination [which] is to flow."

Stein's most startling evocation of the uniqueness of the American dynamic contributes a theory of what has come to be called "hanging out" as a native posture:

> I always remember during the war being so interested in one thing in seeing the American soldiers standing, standing and doing nothing

18. Ibid., p. 37.
19. Ibid., p. 10.

standing for a long time not even talking but just standing and being
watched by the whole French population and their feeling the feeling of the whole population that the American soldier standing there
and doing nothing impressed them as the American soldier as no soldier could impress by doing anything. It is a much more impressive
thing to any one to see any one standing, that is not in action than
acting or doing anything doing anything being a successive thing,
standing not being a successive thing but being something existing.
That is then the difference between narrative as it has been and narrative as it is now.[20]

These soldiers are unconsciously collective followers of Whitman, who
chanted, "I lean and loaf at my ease," celebrating themselves by doing
nothing. Many of the filmmakers I discuss here have been intensely aware of
the excitement of doing nothing, although they may not have realized their
antecedents in Stein or Whitman.

As I analyze the work of eleven filmmakers in this book, I treat images and
film shots as Stein treats road signs (some of those images may even be road
signs), looking at the poetry of their movement and detachment. I also point
out elements in their films that might be viewed as implicit responses to themes
and tropes in the major essays of Emerson and the central poems of Whitman.

The objective of Stein's *Narration* is the displacement of narrative as "a telling of what is happening in successive moments of its happening" and poetry as
"an intensive calling upon the name of anything" to a modern mode of knowledge of "things moving perhaps perhaps moving in any direction," which has
been the discovery of American literature.[21] Stein has reinterpreted Emerson's
doctrine of the oversoul in literary terms, fashioning a new definition of *audience* from his mystical concept of the eternal One. Emerson wrote:

> We live in succession, in division, in parts, in particles. Meanwhile
> within man is the soul of the whole; the wise silence; the universal
> beauty, to which every part and particle is equally related; the eternal
> ONE. And this deep power in which we exist, and whose beatitude is
> all accessible to us, is not only self-sufficing and perfect in every hour,
> but the act of seeing and the thing seen, the seer and the spectacle, the
> subject and the object are one....
>
> If we consider what happens in conversation, in reveries, in remorse,
> in times of passion, in surprises, in the instruction of dreams, wherein

20. Ibid., pp. 19–20.
21. Ibid., pp. 17, 25, 28.

often we see ourselves in masquerade,—the droll disguises only magnifying and enhancing a real element, and forcing it on our distant
notice,—we shall catch many hints that will broaden and lighten into
knowledge of the secret of nature.[22]

In the fourth lecture, Stein comes to her definition of an audience from
a darker moment of solipsism than Emerson will allow here. It is one of her
versions of his earlier noncoincidence of the axes of vision and of things:

That is to say can does any one separate themselves from the land so
they can see it and if they see it are they the audience of it or to it. If
you see anything are you its audience and if you tell anything are you
its audience, and is there any audience for it but the audience that sees
or hears it.[23]

Still, the act of recognition that occurs in the process of writing, in which
something beyond intention originates, convinces her that the apperceptive
audience the writer becomes to her own writing is a model for the wider
audience of readers:

That is what mysticism is, that is what the Trinity is, that is what marriage is, the absolute conviction that in spite of knowing anything about
everything about how any one is never really feeling what any other one
is really feeling that after all after all three are one and two are one. One
is not one because one is always two that is one is always coming to a
recognition of what the one who is one is writing that is telling.[24]

Her uncharacteristic evocation of theological language is itself Emersonian. In "The Over-Soul" he wrote: "In all conversation between two
persons, tacit reference is made, as to a third party, to a common nature.
That third party or common nature is not social; it is impersonal; is God."[25]
Curiously, Stein is at her most Emersonian when she interiorizes all three
parties and comes almost to identifying narrative with the Beautiful Necessity that keeps on generating the mystical marriage of reader and writer,
or the trinity of reader, writer, and text. But this is the step the filmmaker

22. Emerson, *Essays and Lectures*, p. 386.
23. Stein, *Narration*, p. 51. In an early notebook she had written another version of Emersonian blankness:
"Great thinkers eyes do not turn in, they get blank or turn out to keep themselves from being disturbed."
Quoted by Ulla E. Dydo, "Gertrude Stein: Composition as Meditation," *Gertrude Stein and the Making of
Literature*, ed. Shirley Neuman and Ira B. Nadel (Boston: Northeastern University Press, 1988), p. 43.
24. Stein, *Narration*, p. 57.
25. Emerson, *Essays and Lectures*, p. 390.

Hollis Frampton will take, completing Stein, as I show when I discuss his narrative theory in chapter 7.

Since the late 1960s, John Cage has expressed his Emersonianism largely through the mediation of Emerson's first disciple, Henry David Thoreau. Cage wrote in his "Preface to 'Lecture on the Weather'": "No greater American has lived than Thoreau. Emerson called him a speaker and actor of the truth. Other great men have vision. Thoreau had none. Each day his eyes and ears were open and empty to see and hear the world he lived in. Music, he said, is continuous; only listening is intermittent."[26] Cage said he composed his *Empty Words* (1974) by "subjecting Thoreau's writings to *I Ching* chance operations to obtain a collage text." However, I understand this radical enthusiasm for Thoreau to have been primed by the Emersonian aesthetics already evident in his crucial first book, *Silence* (1961), an anthology of many of his articles and lectures since 1937, in which a sometimes chronological arrangement interacts in a thematic collage with short narrative anecdotes and interspersed parables.[27]

Stein exerted a great influence on Cage early in his career. In college he played the smart aleck, answering test questions in her style, winning thus alternately As and Fs. He quotes her in his most elaborate statement of the American uniqueness in music: "Actually America has an intellectual climate suitable for radical experimentation. We are, as Gertrude Stein said, the oldest country of the twentieth century. And I like to add: in our air way of knowing nowness."[28]

In his "Lecture on Nothing" (first delivered in 1949 or 1950 at the Abstract Expressionists' Artists' Club) he presented the core of his negative, necessitarian teaching ("I have nothing to say / and I am saying it / and that is poetry / as I need it"). He urges his listeners to think of the lecture itself as if it were a sight glimpsed from a moving vehicle:

                                                             Re-
gard it as something   seen   momentarily   ,   as
though   from a window   while traveling   .
If across Kansas   ,   then, of course,   Kansas
.   Arizona   is more interesting,
almost too interesting   ,   especially   for a New-Yorker   who is
being interested   in spite of himself   in everything.
. . .
Or you may leave it   forever   and never return to it   ,
     for we pos-sess nothing   .   Our poetry now

---

26. John Cage, *Empty Words: Writings '73–'78* (Middletown: Wesleyan University Press, 1973), p. 3.

27. I believe Annette Michelson was the first critic to note the importance of Emerson for Cage in her *Robert Morris* (Washington, DC: Corcoran Gallery of Art, 1969), p. 27.

28. Cage, "History of Experimental Music in America," *Silence*, p. 73.

is the reali-zation   that we possess nothing
    Anything   therefore   is a delight
(since we do not   pos-ses it)   and thus   need not fear its loss
    We need not destroy the past: it is gone;
at any moment,   it might reappear and   seem to be   and be
    the present
    Would it be a   repetition?   Only if we thought we
owned it,   but since we don't,   it is free   and so are we[29]

Behind this passage lie not only the aesthetics of movement from *Nature*, but also one of Emerson's most eloquent moments in his most powerful essay, "Experience": "All I know is reception; I am and I have: but I do not get, and when I fancied I had gotten anything, I found I did not. I worship with wonder the great Fortune. My reception has been so large, that I am not annoyed by receiving this or that superabundantly."[30]

The "Lecture on Nothing" invokes as well the doctrine of the Beautiful Necessity:

What I am calling   poetry   is often called   content.
I myself   have called   it form   .   It is the conti-
    nuity   of a piece of music.   Continuity   today,
when it is necessary   ,   is a demonstration   of dis-
interestedness.   That is   it is a proof   that our delight
lies in not pos-sessing anything   .   Each moment
presents what happens   .[31]

Charles Olson encountered Cage and felt his influence when they were both on the faculty of Black Mountain College in the 1950s. But his own relationship to Emerson owed nothing to Cage. It was profound and went back to the origins of his vocation; it has been commented upon extensively. His friend the poet Robert Duncan first noted it; Sherman Paul examined it extensively; Stephen Fredman devoted a study to it; I discussed it in my *Modernist Montage*, and Tom Clark's biography firmly established the dominant role played by Emerson's writings in Olson's undergraduate career at Wesleyan.[32]

29. Cage, *Silence*, p. 110.

30. Emerson, *Essays and Lectures*, p. 491.

31. Cage, *Silence*, p. 111.

32. Sherman Paul, *Olson's Push: Origin, Black Mountain, and Recent American Poetry* (Baton Rouge: Louisiana State University Press, 1978); Stephen Fredman, *The Grounding of American Poetry: Charles Olson and the Emersonian Tradition* (Cambridge: Cambridge University Press, 1993); Sitney, *Modernist Montage*; Tom Clark, *Charles Olson: The Allegory of a Poet's Life* (New York: Norton, 1991).

At that time, he confessed in his journal that Emerson made him feel like "an intellectual pigmy."

After Wesleyan, Olson became absorbed in the work of Herman Melville and he largely took upon himself Melville's anxiety and discomfort with Emerson. In fact, much of our direct knowledge of Melville's reaction to Emerson is the result of Olson's remarkable enacting of his own Herodotean principle: "History" is, etymologically, what one finds out for oneself; for as a young graduate student, he searched for and found much of Melville's library. He turned Melville's copy of Emerson over to his teacher, F. O. Matthiessen, who discussed the annotations in his *The American Renaissance*, and he reserved the elaborately marked Shakespeare for himself, drawing from it important points of his first book, *Call Me Ishmael*.

The gist of his Melvillean position can be gleaned from his 1958 review, "Equal, That Is, to the Real Itself":

> Melville couldn't abuse object as symbol does by depreciating it in favor of subject. Or let image lose its relational force by transferring its occurrence as allegory does. He was already aware of the complementarity of each of two pairs of how we know and present the real—image & object, and action & subject—both of which have paid off so decisively since. At this end I am thinking of such recent American painting as Pollock's, and Kline's, and some recent American narrative and verse; and at his end, his whale itself for example, what an unfolding thing it is as it sits there written 100 years off, implicit intrinsic and incident to itself.
>
> Melville was not tempted, as Whitman was, and Emerson and Thoreau differently, to inflate the physical: take the model for the house, the house for the model, death is the open road, the soul or body is a boat, etc.[33]

This insistence on the irreducible particularity of things, one of the cornerstones of Olson's aesthetics, would seem to be a repudiation of the "transparent eyeball" and the opacity of "the axis of things." The desire to be a disembodied eye and the fantasy of seeing through things by an Emersonian redemption of the soul are the inflations of the physical he shuns.

At the core of Olson's teaching there is an affirmation of the inescapable centrality of the poet's body, a thoroughly Whitmanian revision of Emerson. The body is forever in contact with the particularity of things so that (a) poetics must be based on the respiration patterns of the individual poet, for his words emerge "projected" from his breath; (b) the body is always in a particular

---

33. Charles Olson, *The Human Universe and Other Essays*, ed. Donald Allen (New York: Grove Press, 1967), p. 121.

locality, for which the poet must account; and (c) the body is never static; it is always in motion, dancing even when sitting down, breathing, pumping blood. Finally, (d) at each interfacing of body and things, history intervenes. The history of language, of poetry, of localities, and of the human species since the Pleistocene era become areas for the poet "to investigate for himself."

Yet for Olson, Emerson's influence is inescapable. His Herodotean definition of history is a gloss on "Self-Reliance," and Emerson's essay "History" might well be a source for his argument, in *The Special View of History*, that history itself "is the *function* of any one of us,"[34] as well as his equation of mythological and historical narratives. Emerson's essay "The Poet" plays an even more potent role behind Olson's theoretical writings. He mined it for several of his most important theoretical texts. In the most condensed statement of his poetics, "Letter to Elaine Feinstein," he responded to her inquiry about the status of imagery in his concept of the poem:

> You wld know already I'm buggy on say the Proper Noun, so much so I wld take it Pun is Rime, all from tope/type/trope, that built in is the connection, in each of us, to Cosmos, and if one taps, via psyche, plus a "true" adherence of Muse, one does reveal "Form"[35]

Packed into this sentence are several dimensions of Olson's aesthetics as he articulated them in the late 1950s and early 1960s. First of all, he stressed the poetic importance of the proper noun and of the etymology of *proper* (from *proprius*, "one's own") as the stamp of a writer's activity. Narrative, as he understood it, was the elaboration of a proper noun into a story. The trinity *tope/type/trope* (more often named by him in Greek *topos/typos/tropos*) elliptically encodes Olson's scattered claims that the poet begins in a specific place—which is always historically conditioned—and, by turning or troping through the shifting of his attention and the figuration of his language, he types a type of poem. The pun on *type* fuses the printed letters of the resulting text to its generic limitation and to the persona invoked by the poet's voice. The articulation of this situation entails the interaction of the personal history of the poet (psyche) with his language in its historical-etymological density (Muse).

We find in Emerson's "The Poet" vestiges even of Olson's aesthetic diction, as we had found Stein's use of motion and detachment:

> [T]he poet is the Namer or Language-maker, naming things sometimes after their appearance, sometimes after their essence, and giving

---

34. Charles Olson, *The Special View of History*, ed. with intro. by Ann Charters (Berkeley: Oyez, 1970), p. 17.
35. Ibid., p. 97. See Sitney, *Modernist Montage* for an extended reading of "Letter to Elaine Feinstein."

every one its own name and not another's, thereby rejoicing the intellect, which delights in *detachment* or boundary. The poets made all
the words, and therefore language is the archives of history, and, if we
must say it, a sort of tomb of the muses....The etymologist finds the
deadest word to have been once a brilliant picture. Language is fossil
poetry. [emphasis mine][36]

Another passage from "The Poet" may be the precursor of Olson's essay,
"Against Wisdom as Such":

But the quality of the imagination is *to flow*, and *not to freeze*. The poet
did not stop at the color, or the form, but read their meaning; neither
may he rest in this meaning, but he makes the same objects exponents
of his new thought. Here is the difference betwixt the poet and the mystic, that the last nails a symbol to one sense, which was a true sense for a
moment, but soon becomes old and false. For all symbols are fluxional;
all language is *vehicular* and transitive, and is good, as ferries and horses
are, for conveyance, not as farms and houses are, for homestead.[37]

"Against Wisdom as Such" attacks the mystical and cultic dimensions of
Robert Duncan's work, denying the metaphor of wisdom as light, substituting instead a notion of poetic heat:

Rhythm is time (not measure, as the pedants of Alexandria made it).
The root is "rhein": *to flow*. And mastering the flow of the solid, time,
we invoke others. Because we take time and *heat* it, make it serve our
selves, our, form.

...One has to drive all nouns, the abstract most of all, back to
process—to act.[38]

In his observations on the dynamics of the noun in his lecture series "The
Chiasma," he comes close to Gertrude Stein's concept of American language.
Clearly Whitman was on his mind:

Why, in short, a noun is so vital is not at all that it so much differs
from a verb (does not have motion) but because it is a motion which
has not yet moved.

---

36. Emerson, *Essays and Lectures*, pp. 456–57 (emphasis mine).
37. Ibid. 463. (emphasis mine).
38. Olson, *The Human Universe*, p. 70 (emphasis mine).

... [Do] we not have to leave compulsions on the other side of syntax, no matter how much syntax does give us the means to indicate all stages of propulsion, including that quietist of all movements, doing nothing—contemplating a leaf of grass?

...All I want to do is to beat you into the recognition that *things*—the hard things—are, wherever,...changeable because they are already moving, sitting down.[39]

Thus, even though there is no direct expression of the Emersonian concept of motion as a key to a new aesthetic perspective in Olson aside from that implicit in the opening of *Call Me Ishmael* ("I take SPACE to be the central fact to man born in America, from Folsom cave to now....Some men ride on such space, other have to fasten themselves like a tent stake to survive"[40]), his protracted reflections on naming instantiate Emerson's idea of "vehicular and transitive" language.

Perhaps because of his encounter with John Cage at Black Mountain College, chance came to play an important role in his theory of poetry. For him it was a version of the Beautiful Necessity. (In "The Poet" Emerson wrote: "The beautiful rests on the foundations of the necessary.") In *The Special View of History*, Olson lectured:

> *Coincidence* and *proximity*, because the space-time continuum is known, become determinants of *chance* and *accident* and make possible *creative success*....And man's order—his powers of order—are no longer separable from either those of nature or of God. The organic is one, purpose is seen to be contingent, not primordial: it follows from the chance success of the play of creative accident, it does not precede them.[41]

In reformulating the concepts of chance and purpose, he suggests that poems, or works of art generally, are the necessary consequences of an aesthetic process of natural selection rather than exclusively the willed acts of conscious individuals. The individuals respond to "instruction" by bringing the energies of their conscious and unconscious histories to the service of a "true adherence" to language. Charles Stein has written the most lucid analysis of these ideas:

> The emphasis on the inclusion of purpose and chance, accidence and necessity, form and chaos, as being *within* actual process, is the

---

39. Charles Olson, "The Chiasma, or Lectures in the New Sciences of Man," ed. George Butterick, *Olson*, no. 10 (Fall 1978), pp. 83–84.
40. Charles Olson, *Call Me Ishmael* (New York: Grove Press, 1947), pp. 11–12.
41. Charles Olson, *The Special View of History*, p. 49.

cosmological justification for Olson's "concretism," his insistence that words be treated as solid objects, and poems be treated as force fields. As events in the new cosmology are neither determined purposively nor given form by powers outside of process, so words must not be treated as if their functions could be limited by either abstract definitions or canons of usage. Similarly poems must not take models from forms extrinsic to the forms emergent in *their* emergence; symbols must not subsume the material of the work in literary reference, but must be allowed to emerge as local centers of force within the field of the poem.[42]

By *process* Stein means how the poet "must map (i.e. project) the movement of the mind in the heat or calm of composition."[43]

Olson's project suggests a possible convergence of Gertrude Stein and John Cage's positions (although that was never his intention). Her imputation of a dynamics within American language and immanent in apparent stasis and Cage's attention to the beauties of unwilled reception correspond to Olson's poetics of bounded force fields.

My insistence on the Emersonian sources of these positions is not an effort to elevate the Sage of Concord at the expense of his most lively twentieth-century heirs. Emersonian aesthetics is so radical, so diffuse, and even so contradictory that it elicits perennial refocusing. Our strongest filmmakers are less likely to attend to Emerson himself than to Stein, Cage, or Olson. When they are unmoved by any of these three and invent theoretical positions from whole cloth for themselves, they are usually reshaping a number of Emersonian stances they have absorbed from the native air they breathe.

---

42. Charles Stein, *The Secret of the Black Chrysanthemum* (Barrytown: Station Hill, 1987), p. 107.
43. Ibid., p. 104.

CHAPTER I

Marie Menken and the Somatic Camera

The artists of the American avant-garde cinema not only inherited the massive legacy of Emersonian aesthetics, they assumed as well the major native revisions and dilations of Emerson's thought. The most formidable and pervasive of these was Whitman's insistence on the centrality of the body—not solely the transparent eyeball, but the complete corpus with a strong emphasis on binocular vision, as well as an utterly un-Emersonian celebration of genital sexuality. The persona he invents for *Leaves of Grass* emphasizes his somatic presence:

Walt Whitman, an American, one of the roughs, a kosmos,
Disorderly fleshy and sensual...eating drinking and breeding,
...

Through me forbidden voices,
Voices of sexes and lusts...voices veiled, and I remove the veil,
Voices indecent by me clarified and transfigured.

I do not press my finger across my mouth,
I keep as delicate around the bowels as around the head and heart,

Copulation is no more rank to me than death is.
I believe in the flesh and the appetites,
Seeing hearing and feeling are miracles, and each part and tag of me is a
    miracle.[1]

Yet vision holds a unique place in his doctrine of purification by sensual experience. This is most summarily expressed in "There Was a Child Went Forth":

There was a child went forth every day,
And the first object he looked upon and received with wonder or pity or
    love or dread, that object he became,
And that object became part of him for the day or a certain part of the
    day...or for many years or stretching cycles of years.[2]

Tony Tanner summarized Whitman's poetics of vision thus:

Not to be blasé, not to receive the world sieved through classes and
genres and types; rather to note each item as a small miracle, to regard
the diversity of particulars with a lucid awe, to let the eye travel from
apple-blossom to a drunkard with no diminution of wonder and no
access of moral judgment; this is the required facility. And Whitman
thought that the child and the uneducated vernacular figure were
gifted with this facility. To some extent so did Emerson and Thoreau
but where Whitman advances on them is in trying to formulate a style
mimetic of this response to the world....Whitman practices what Emerson and Thoreau preached: visual capitulation to the benign tyranny
of the material world.[3]

Although the most blatant extension of the Whitmanian supplement to the American avant-garde cinema would be its historical obsession with the human body, especially the naked body, there is actually a more pro-found inflection that can be traced back to Walt as the visionary child, in motion, going forth each day; for a central element in the stylistics of the American avant-garde cinema is the handheld camera, although that

---

1. Walt Whitman, "Leaves of Grass," *Selected Poems 1855–1892: A New Edition*, ed. Gary Schmidgall (New York: St. Martin's, 1999), pp. 34–35. I have used this edition for the texts of the poems as they were first published.
2. Walt Whitman, "There Was a Child Went Forth." *Selected Poems 1855–1892*, p. 105.
3. Tony Tanner, *The Reign of Wonder: Naivety and Reality in American Literature*, (Cambridge: Cambridge University Press, 1965), pp. 70, 71 (ellipsis mine).

term is somewhat misleading in this context; perhaps the walking camera or the somatic camera might more vividly convey the identification of the mobile frame of the ultimately projected image with the movements of the filmmaker.

Marie Menken pioneered the radical transformation of the handheld, somatic camera into a formal matrix that would underpin an entire work in the films she made between 1945 and 1965. By the end of the 1950s her reputation among filmmakers was split between those who cited her as the height of inept fumbling and amateurishness and those for whom her style was revolutionary and a liberating influence. Stan Brakhage wrote:

Marie Menken opened for me (1) a sculptured and very heavy filmic door (in *Visual Variations on Noguchi*) by "swinging" it, (2) a garden gate (in *Glimpse of a Garden*) by "swinging" on it, and (3) my microscopic or "inner" eye (in *Hurry! Hurry!*) with a kind of lid-swinging technique. The heavy door, which was at the time (around 1956) weighing very heavily on this young film-maker, was the influence of Hollywood in dealing with its ponderous technical equipment which almost automatically (a well-chosen word) forced the most individual film-makers to make "smooth" pans, dollies, etc. even tho' they were economically forced to accomplish this with hand-held equipment.... Marie Menken's "Open Sesame" to me was that *Visual Variations on Noguchi* was the first film I had ever seen which completely not only admitted but capitalized on the fact that the camera was hand-held. She was at that time the purest disciple of Jean Cocteau's advice to young filmmakers to take advantage of the freedom of the hand-held camera.... This was, in one sense, a very simple contribution by Marie, but it led me to begin questioning the entire "reality" of the motion picture image as related to a way, or ways, of seeing.[4]

The turning point in her reputation occurred near the end of December 1961 when the Charles Theater in New York showed two evenings of her work, finished and in progress. In the January 4, 1962, edition of the *Village Voice*, Jonas Mekas led the critical acclaim for her work as among "the very best of our contemporary poetic cinema." But by that time Mekas himself was already among the many filmmakers working with the somatic camera who did not even then quite fully realize the extent of her precedence. In fact, it took the widespread emergence of a spectrum of handheld strategies, at the end of the 1950s, from the work of Stan Brakhage to that of Leacock and

---

4. Stan Brakhage, "Letter to Gerard Malanga," *Filmwise* 5–6 (1964), pp. 19–20.

Pennybaker (who were probably unaware of her existence), to make visible Menken's remarkable achievement.

Menken described the origins of her filmmaking, responding in 1962 to questions I sent her for an interview by mail:

> The twittering of leaves when I was bored in class as a child, and the delights of moving my feet in silhouette against the lights of the window when I was being punished and sent to my room in "solitary" led me to believe in private and personal dramas. Later, I made flip books out of the corners of my textbooks while I listened to a drone in school. All of this came into my work when I finally got Francis Lee's camera. He went into the Army, bequeathing me the pawn ticket for his camera. I made good use of it exploring, along with Willard Maas, my husband, when he made *Geography of the Body* with George Barker. There is no why for my making films. I just liked the twitters of the machine, and since it was an extension of painting for me, I tried and loved it. In painting I never liked the staid static, always looked for what would change with source of light and stance, using glitters, glass beads, luminous paint, so the camera was a natural for me to try—but how expensive!...
>
> As a painter of some experience, I can frame immediately with no deliberation of arrangement. As a painter one does that for composition. In film-making every frame is a picture and what a joy that is!...
>
> I was working on something...for Noguchi, some special effects for *The Seasons*, a ballet by Merce Cunningham with music by John Cage, and while I was experimenting around I had the advantage of looking around Isamu's studio with a clear, unobstructed eye. I asked if I might come in and shoot around, and he said yes. I did that. And when he saw that footage, he was entertained and delighted. So was I. It was fun. All art should be fun in a sense and give one a kick.[5]

Geography of the Body was made in 1943. Menken's published filmographies list *Visual Variations on Noguchi* as a film of 1945, but Cunningham staged *The Seasons* with sets and costumes by Noguchi early in 1947; he did not bring Noguchi into the project until the summer of 1946. Yet the film was shown in the amateur division of the Cannes Festival in the spring that year.

5. P. Adams Sitney, "Interview with Marie Menken," *Filmwise* 5–6 (Maas and Menken issue, ca. 1965), pp. 10–12.

There are several reasons for the difficulty of ascertaining accurately the dates of Menken's films: In the first place, there is no archive of her papers. Shortly before she died late in 1970 a flood destroyed her studio; then vandals looted it. Maas died a few days after her, so that all of her property passed to Maas and then to his son by his first marriage before provisions could be made for her effects. Menken's sister, Adele, salvaged a small fraction of her papers that Anthology Film Archives obtained in 2005, but they had not been cataloged when this book went to press.

Aside from the loss of documentation, the problem of accurate dating is complicated by the fact that Menken herself seldom made definitive versions of her work. Her film *Notebook*, first publicly screened in 1961, contained fragments, sketches, and the embryonic versions of films she later expanded into autonomous units. The segments are undated, but they probably range from her earliest work to her latest, and the film itself underwent changes after the initial screening. At the triumphal screening in which it was premiered, several other films were shown in progress. Willard Maas may have been responsible for forcing her to "complete" them. Maas had a strong classicizing tendency; he was forever nagging her to make titles and have musical soundtracks made for the films. Eventually two of his protégés, Gerard Malanga and John Hawkins, made titles for some of her films. Teiji Ito composed and performed a soundtrack for *Arabesque for Kenneth Anger* after the otherwise finished film had been shown in 1961. He also scored and performed the music for *Moonplay*.

Actually, it seems as though many of her films reached their final or penultimate stage under the impetus of the 1961 screening. Both *Arabesque for Kenneth Anger* and *Bagatelle for Willard Maas* had been shot in 1958 when Menken visited Europe following the Belgian Cinémathèque's Second International Experimental Film Competition. Her *Glimpse of a Garden* was shown there, and it may actually have been completed under the impetus of the competition deadline, although she submitted it as a film of 1956 (rather than 1957 as later filmographies indicate). Thus the published filmographies that show a gap of twelve years between her first film and her second, *Hurry! Hurry!* (1957) may be very misleading.

The most useful and insightful writing on Menken's cinema is the chapter devoted to her work in Stan Brakhage's *Film at Wit's End*. Even though Brakhage reproduces for the most part the filmography Menken herself supplied for the special issue of *Filmwise* devoted to herself and Maas, he implies that *Hurry! Hurry!* was not her second film, when he describes witnessing the visit to the Maas-Menken penthouse of a scientist who ran a film society in Delaware: "He liked Marie's work so much, and was so confident that the other members of his film society would be as charmed by them, that he asked if there was anything he could do for her."[6] Brakhage recounted how she asked him for the stock footage of spermatozoa she would use in *Hurry! Hurry!* But he does not tell us what films, presumably in addition to *Visual Variations on Noguchi*, she showed that night in the mid-1950s.[7]

There is some scanty evidence that she concentrated her energies on paint-ing in the late 1940s and early 1950s. She had two shows at the prestigious Betty Parsons Gallery during that period. The first, in 1949, was a two-person show with Ad Reinhardt; the next a one-woman show in 1951. During those years Parsons was exhibiting the major Abstract Expressionists (Newman, Rothko, Still, etc.); Jackson Pollock's 1951 show followed immediately after Menken's. Furthermore, Maas's collaborator, Ben Moore, included a portrait of Menken in his *Four American Artists*, made in the mid-1950s and usually dated 1957; it shows her completing a painting, incorporating, as she usually did, sand and thread; there is no hint in the portrait that she is also a filmmaker.

The early films *Geography of the Body* and *Visual Variations on Noguchi* demonstrate different aspects of the Whitmanesque fascination with the body. Menken's contribution to the former, which is clearly Maas's film, was twofold: as the female model, and as one of the cinematographers. The idea of attaching a magnifying glass to the lens for some of the disorienting close-ups seems to have been hers. The visual principle of the film was to select and frame corporeal details in violation of the conventions of anatomical repre-sentation to the point of rendering mysterious and allusive contours of flesh, folds of skin, and pillar terrains. George Barker's neosurrealist commentary orients the leisurely montage of close-ups and occasional torsos in the direc-tion of an exotic travel narrative (e.g., a close-up of the texture of the tongue is accompanied by the following: "With the aid of mirrors we made our way down the mountain. Here we found oversize lizards wallowing into and out of oil paintings in Spanish frames").

It is unlikely that Menken associated the imagery of *Geography of the Body* with her somatic approach to camera movement in *Visual Variations on Noguchi*. In his memoir "The Gryphon Yaks," Maas says that Menken used to deny that she was the female model for his film until the 1960s.[8] Never-theless, her entry into cinema involved the convergence of several affirma-tions of the body. In addition to the accident that her work with Noguchi

---

6. Stan Brakhage, *Film at Wit's End: Eight Avant-Garde Filmmakers* (Kingston, NY: Documentext, McPherson, 1989), p. 39 (emphasis mine).

7. An application Menken submitted to the Ford Foundation in 1963 for a grant she did not receive lists *Glimpse of a Garden* as her second film and *Hurry! Hurry!* as the third, made the same year: 1957. It is just possible that she screened *Visual Variations on Noguchi* and *Glimpse of a Garden* to the scientist and then made *Hurry! Hurry!* later that year out of the materials he sent her.

8. Willard Maas, "The Gryphon Yaks," *Film Culture* no. 29 (Summer 1963), p. 49.

occurred in conjunction with Cunningham's dance *The Seasons*, she claimed, convincingly, that the schema of Maya Deren's *A Study in Choreography for Camera* (1945) was her idea, which she presented to Deren as a hypothetical illustration of a theoretical argument Deren was expounding to Maas and Menken's guests at their Montague Street penthouse; and that she showed Deren how the final leap in that film could be filmed from the picnic table on the penthouse terrace, where it was eventually shot.

Menken could not have realized when she playfully moved amid Noguchi's sculptures, filming them in defiance of their gravitational orientation, that she was initiating a visionary project which would slowly elaborate itself over the next two decades of her filmmaking and thus profoundly change the way avant-garde films were made in America. The factors involved in Menken's self-evaluation and self-presentation as a filmmaker are rather complex and open to speculations such as Brakhage's: "Marie knew perfectly well who and what she was, but her way of dealing with the inattention was to treat her own works more lightly than they should have been treated.... Marie avoided posing as 'the artiste' in her lifetime, with the result that she could be an artist."[9] As Brakhage lucidly illustrates, Maas postured as the original and polished filmmaker, monopolizing the very limited limelight the field could provide. Although Menken was genuinely modest, playful, and kindly, there was an aggressive dimension to her posture: In her anecdotes and her repartee there was a consistent needling of all artistic posing—of Deren's relentless theorizing, the young Brakhage's earnest mythologizing, Warhol's affectations, and the vatic seriousness of many of the painters of her generation who became celebrities. She had a finely tuned sense of humor that she often directed at the pretensions of artists who had negotiated an escape from the neglect shown to her own work. Several of her strongest films benefit from a tension between versions of this comic rivalry and sincere acts of homage.

This tension is minimal in *Visual Variations on Noguchi*. The rapid pace of the film prohibits contemplation of the sculpture; instead of the slow, reverential camera movements usual in films depicting sculpture, Menken's rapid sweeps, tilts, and pans affirm her presence and her maneuvering at the expense of Noguchi's objects so that at times the film seems to represent the open space bounded and shaped by the sculpture rather than the works themselves. Lucia Dlugoszewski's musique concrète, with repeated whispers of women's names from Gertrude Stein's play *Dr. Faustus Lights the Lights*, emphasizes the active role of the somatic camera. From the opening Menken exploits the gray ranges of her black-and-white film stock, abetting the confusion of objects with their shadows. By withholding any establishing shot that would provide

---

9. Brakhage, *Film at Wit's End*, pp. 46–47.

an overview of the studio, and even by suppressing images that would frame a whole, autonomous piece of sculpture, she makes it impossible to predict the purposiveness of her camera movements. The editing takes up the logic of those movements, abstracted from the objects encountered in them, to elongate, in an additive manner, sweeping gestures in one direction or to bring about oppositional shifts of direction.

Menken's title for the film suggests a musical model: One of the oldest continual traditions in Western music is the melodic and harmonic ornamentation of a theme taken from another composer. Noguchi's sculpture provides the static theme for her virtuoso transpositions into a temporal medium. Many of her subsequent films will take their titles from music: *Eye Music in Red Major*, *Arabesque for Kenneth Anger*, *Bagatelle for Willard Maas*, and even *Mood Mondrian*, if the title echoes, as I believe it does, Duke Ellington's "Mood Indigo."

In both style and title, *Hurry! Hurry!* marks a different direction for her work. She superimposed what she called "murky fire"—orange flames presumably from a gas source—over black-and-white microscopy of spermatozoa with the aural accompaniment of aerial bombardment. Menken called *Hurry! Hurry!* both her favorite and her saddest film. Brakhage is at his best, bordering on the outrageous, in his discussion of the film:

> It is the flame's rhythms and their variety—achieved by Marie's keen splicing—that gives the film life. Against this flame image, then, are the images of the spermatozoa and their rhythms, which involved more detailed splicing.
>
> The little spermatozoon that is "Willard" can be seen as a note of music, an eighth-note, say. Wherever this little eighth-note pauses or whirls around, she would make a cut to place it rhythmically in the following scene. That is, if the next scene is a cluster of spermatozoa, then the lone spermatozoon from the preceding scene is—bang! just like that—in its place, through what is called the plastic cut...
>
> ...
>
> The flame pulses, but obviously never *exactly* repeating either its rhythms or its shapes; and in this regard *Hurry! Hurry!* is kindred to an essential aesthetic of Gertrude Stein: Marie often seems to be repetitive but, like Stein, she never is.[10]

In Brakhage's strong reading of the film, craft, intention, and personal narrative come to the fore. At most moments in the four-minute film, sper-

10. Ibid., p. 40 (ellipsis mine).

matozoa are in frenetic movement desperately searching for an egg. To see in this swarm the quest of a single spermatozoon and to identify it with Willard Maas is his most daring interpretive gesture. The biography he gives of Menken stresses the tragedy of her stillborn baby and Maas's homosexual promiscuity as the background to the narrative he finds depicted in the film.

Brakhage's interpretation is a brilliantly clever recuperation of his own aesthetic allegiance to nuanced editing and personal narrative in the face of a particularly resistant film. Yet the film can also be seen as the precursor of the conceptual projects that came to dominate the American avant-garde cinema a decade later. The fusion of three independent tracks, two visual and one aural, two found objects and one—the flames—apparently a random (unless we grant Brakhage's sensitivity to their intentionality) recording by the filmmaker, gives to their aleatoric cohesion both fascinating dynamics and the sense of purposiveness. *Hurry! Hurry!* then becomes the first monument to the Beautiful Necessity in our native cinema. At this point it may be productive to remember that one of Menken's cherished projects, executed by Maas and John Hawkins in 1966, was *Sidewalks*, a film of found patterns in the pavement. Menken may have known that John Cage predicted the scenario of her film in describing an aesthetic epiphany after first seeing Mark Tobey's paintings:

> I remember a particular walk with Mark Tobey from the area of Seattle around the Cornish School downhill and through the town toward a Japanese restaurant—a walk that would not normally take more than forty-five minutes, but on this occasion it must have taken several hours, because he was constantly stopping and pointing out things to see, opening my eyes in other words—which, if I understand it at all, has been the function of twentieth-century art: to open our eyes.... [T]here was an exhibition at the Willard Gallery that included the first examples of white writing on the part of Mark Tobey. I liked one so much that I began buying it on the installment plan.... This one had nothing [representational]. It was completely, so to speak, abstract. It had no symbolic references. It was a surface that had been utterly painted.... [W]hen I left the Willard Gallery exhibition, I was standing on a corner on Madison Avenue waiting for a bus and I happened to look at the pavement, and I noticed that the experience of looking at the pavement was the same as the experience of looking at the Tobey. Exactly the same. The aesthetic enjoyment was just as high.[11]

It is the signal achievement of Menken's cinema to accommodate both the poles of the aesthetic enjoyment of chance discoveries and meticulous craftsmanship. She was the first American filmmaker to invent a range of automatisms capable of sustaining convincing films. She gave herself unusual freedom in moving with her camera; she incorporated hesitations, awkwardnesses, and even "mistakes" in the mesh of her editing rhythms. The borderline between the intentional imposition of order and the discovery of unexpected orders in what she shot (or even was given, in the unique instance of *Hurry! Hurry!*) frequently dissolves in her films, leaving the work open to criticism as maladroit amateurism as well as connoisseurship of the most refined sophistication.

Sidewalks illustrates the subtle elegance of Menken's art, but by a negative route. After she announced that she wanted to make a film of the sidewalks she walked on her way to work, she put off filming the project for years. Eventually Willard Maas and John Hawkins undertook the execution of the film from her conception. The black-and-white film they made is a competent, even-paced work, made up of something under thirty shots of sidewalks—mostly well-worn and cracked concrete, but including tiled and cemented brick surfaces—filmed from a height of about three feet, looking straight down, with a steadily moving camera. Generally the image sways slightly from left to right and back and the surface passes from the top of the screen out the bottom; sometimes the movement follows large cracks. The sudden appearance of gutter drains and manhole covers give a strong graphic punctuation to the firm, even pace. Yet the Menken magic is utterly lacking. Missing are the minute shifts of attention in response to what the camera sees, the unpredictable changes of rhythm and even of subject, the uninhibited confidence of bodily motion; in short, the signs of a sensibility looking through the camera have been repressed by Maas's and Hawkins's smooth tracking, which owes more to the opening hopscotch scene of Sidney Peterson's *The Lead Shoes* than anything in Menken's work.

Both the strengths and the awkwardnesses of Menken's cinema are evident in her *Notebook*, which seems to span her filmmaking career. The nine sections may be in chronological order: "Raindrops," "Greek Epiphany," "Moonplay," "Copy Cat," "Paper Cuts," "Lights," "Night Writing," "The Egg," and "Etcetcetc." The first three are black and white; "Copy Cat" is a hand-painted film in the style of Norman McLaren; the last five are in color. "Raindrops" predicts the form of her early *Glimpse of a Garden* (1956); "Paper Cuts" seems a primitive version of *Dwightiana* (1957); "Lights" and "Night Writing" look like sketches for *Eye Music in Red Major* (1961) and *Lights* (1966) respectively; "The Egg" bears a distant relationship to *Watts with Eggs* (1967); and "Etcetcetc" is a sketch in the stop-motion style of *Go!Go!Go!* (1963) and *Excursion* (1968). A further argument for chronological arrangement is my distant and dubious memory that only the end of "Etcetcetc" was added after the Charles Theater retrospective of 1961.

Although "Raindrops" probably dates from the beginning of Menken's filmmaking, it ranks among her highest achievements. Two ducks appear in the opening images of a pond's surface, at first delineated by the slightest of movements at the upper edge of the screen, to establish the natural setting. The pond serves as a sensitive plane (almost identical with the screen itself) for registering the rainstorm that follows in approximately thirty short shots. In the ensuing crescendo and diminuendo, the images alternate between the concentric circles brought into play by the rainfall on the pond and beads of water accumulating on leaves and buds.

At one point, the camera dwells on a drop at the tip of a leaf as it slowly gathers sufficient mass to drop of its own weight. We can sense the filmmaker's impatience and anxiety lest the hand-wound camera run down before the drop falls. Offscreen she shakes the branch with too much force to pass for the level of wind intensity apparent in the rest of the film. Then, again and again, she shakes the water from the trees whose leaves are before her lens. The culmination of this sequence is a bit of sequential montage: A drop gathers and falls (again impelled by her manipulation); a subsequent close-up records only the gravitational fall of a single droplet, fictively the same, through the frame. In a conventional nature film, with its fiction of impersonal and passive objectivity, shots such as these would have been eliminated because of their crudity. But in Menken's subtle cinematic poem, such attempts to hasten and narrate the natural processes redirect the energy of the film from its ostensible subject to the subjectivity observing and intervening in it. She whimsically deflates the "transparent" decoupage she would have projected onto her material by exposing the film director's and editor's heavy hands: Having set in motion the fragile project, she traps her own will-to-shape in the act and offers it as the fragment's negative moment. By contrast, the elliptical skipping from the first drops to the erratic rhythms of the full rain falling on the pond, and then to the beaded leaves and twigs, attests to the irrevocable discontinuity in her process of sighting, winding the camera, and filming, and the compensatory synthesis of nonnarrative montage. Spoofing both the organic totality of an event occurring within a shot and the illusion of seamless temporal continuity across shots, she decides in favor of a multiplicity of discrete visual events constellated by the intricate tensions among their microrhythms and textures. Thus in her framing, offscreen intrusions, camera movements, and editing she makes her sensibility the theme of the film: The very ephemerality of the meteorological representations lends itself to this authorial transcendence.

In the Greek Orthodox Church, the feast of Epiphany corresponds to the Baptism of Jesus by John. The blessing of water on the eve of Epiphany acknowledges the sanctification of the created world. Menken's inclusion of this candlelit ceremony in her *Notebook*, between her celebration of rain and the dance of the moon, intimates her theological vision of the holiness of all things. She was a Roman Catholic by birth and practice, and a religious liberal by temperament. The most ambitious of her incomplete film projects was *The Gravediggers of Guadix*, a film about Spanish monks devoted to burying the dead. She shot approximately fifty minutes of it in 1958 but never edited the work. Like the monks she filmed, Menken conscientiously performed the Corporal Works of Mercy.

Both "Moonplay" and "Lights" were sketches for eponymous films she completed after 1963. The thirty-second sketch became the conclusion of the four-minute *Moonplay*. However, I cannot identify any of the material of the ninety-second *Notebook* section in the six-minute *Lights*. To make the longer film, Menken must have returned a different year to the Christmas tree in Rockefeller Center, where she repeated some of the sketch's camera gestures (most blatantly rotating her camera so that the tree seems to circle in the air clockwise). To this she added other Christmas displays and fast-motion shots of traffic and boats at night. Some of the fast-motion imagery approaches the calligraphy of colored lines of whipped light we see in the gorgeous fifteen-second fragment, "Night Writing." The brevity and incisiveness of these *Notebook* sketches give them a power that the elaborations tend to relax. Furthermore, the lucid fragments of the *Notebook* benefit from the abrupt shifts of materials and rhythms dictated by the original and daring form of the film. Their very brevity, their autonomy, and the elusive complexity of the authorial presence (or series of such) that they project are indices of this originality.

Menken's authorial presence can be illuminated by an examination of two of her crowning achievements: *Arabesque for Kenneth Anger* (1961) and *Go!Go!Go!* She called the latter, "My major film, showing the restlessness of human nature and what it is striving for, plus the ridiculousness of its desires. I am dedicating it to Jonas Mekas because he knows more than anyone else what it is not about." I may be alone in preferring *Arabesque for Kenneth Anger* above all her films. Menken herself, filmmaker Charles Boultenhouse, and Brakhage gave preference to *Bagatelle for Willard Maas*,[12] which she shot on the same European trip, although Brakhage's enthusiasm is tainted by the extraordinary error of his description of the film as intercutting "scenes of Versailles with images of their home," for all the images come from the French palace and its grounds.

---

12. In the *Film-makers' Cooperative Catalogue No. 7* (New York: Film-makers' Cooperative, 1989), p. 369, Boultenhouse quotes Menken: "A more serious film than *Arabesque*, *Bagatelle* attempts to synchronize into a lyric statement some observations on Versailles."

Arabesque for Kenneth Anger records a walk through the Alhambra of Granada that Menken took with Anger while she was in Spain to shoot *The Gravediggers of Guadix*. It is an homage to and parody of Anger's own *Eaux d'artifice* (1953). (The spirit of Menken's playful treatment of fellow artists is embodied in the title "Copy Cat" from her *Notebook*, in which she admits to imitating Norman McLaren while accusing him of copying Len Lye.) She treats the Moorish pools and fountains as if they were the waterworks that Anger used in his fugal evocation of a woman in a baroque gown flitting through the D'Este gardens at Tivoli at night until she is transformed into a fountain herself.

Arabesque for Kenneth Anger too ends with an image of a fountain jet, but whereas Anger filmed in black and white and printed the film on color stock, filtered to produce a deep blue saturation, Menken shot in color with a comparatively rich range of blues and whites, as if to tease Anger by showing that she could casually achieve what he got through meticulous calculation.

Premiering the film at her Charles Theater retrospective, she called the audience's attention to the doves flying around the Alhambra in the opening shots: "That's me," she claimed, identifying her freely handled somatic camera with the mobility and perspective of the birds. To a Lithuanian Roman Catholic fascinated by saints, monks, and religious iconology (whose visit to Granada was incidental to her pilgrimage to Guadix to make her most explicitly religious film), the emblem of the Holy Ghost would not have escaped her, nor would the irony of such symbolism in an Islamic palace in the company of her Luciferian friend. Yet if her capacity for invention brings the suggestion of the Holy Ghost descending into a Moorish monument and finding in the up-flowing fountain that concludes the film a figuration of baptism, she knows it as a reflection of the tenacity of her Catholic heritage rather than a pious epiphany.

Following the pattern she established with *Glimpse of a Garden* (and already foreshadowed in "Raindrops"), Menken exhibits at once the exhilaration she feels at the site of filming and the details that attract her attention. The dynamic matrix of sweeping and whirling camera gestures, as if an action painter's preconception of the spatial purview, makes the shimmering delicacy of the minutiae over which she pauses all the more poignant in their power to arrest her balletic energy; for they absorb the kinetics of her movement through the palace and refract it, almost muted, in the reverberations of drops in an otherwise still sluice, or in the respiratory hovering of the camera over a pattern in the tiles.

She sweeps so quickly over the high arabesque windows through which a bluish white light pours that they seem to take wings. Then, pushing the avian metaphor, she suggests the image of flocks of birds zigzagging in flight by rocking the camera over the field of tiles. As the film moves to its conclusion,

the camera becomes decidedly ambulatory, quickly traversing the ambit of a
square colonnaded courtyard, then circling the leonine fountain at its center
before framing the fountain's jet against the sky. In these rapid circuits of the
courtyard, she filmed at a slower camera speed to accelerate the image. Although the increased pace pushes the presentation of the embodied camera
hastening around the atrium to a point where the fountain almost seems to
pirouette of itself, there is no suggestion of a magical transformation as in
Anger's model. Menken's film cultivates bright daylight, recording spontaneous discoveries and even fanciful analogies as the happy encounter of camera
consciousness and irreducibly concrete visible facts, while Anger's cultivates
night, flight, mystery, and transfiguration. She refuses to disguise the fact that
she is a frisky tourist at an exotic site; instead, she finds that to be an interesting situation insofar as it is a quickened occasion for her to take the measure
of her sensibility.

Brakhage identified the films she made dedicated to other artists (or filming their works) as examples of "portraiture." He quoted an interview she
gave me: "I have a feeling about these people and have somehow created,
cinematically speaking, . . . what I thought was an insight into their own creative work." He interprets this in the light of the completed films: "Marie
made portraits of her subjects by photographing the things that these people
would love, or did love, and she did so in ways which, being at her desper-
ate wit's end, betray her thoughts of their character—always with humor."[13]
That Anger, who painstakingly decorates his own dwellings with exotica and
venerates Valentino in his arabesque stances, should love the Alhambra is
convincing, but Menken uses Anger's "character" as she uses the Alhambra
itself to quicken her Emersonian afflatus. If indeed the film is haunted by
Christian icons, hinting at the descent of the spirit to the fount of baptism,
its unorthodox point is a wholly orphic confirmation of Menken's election
as an artist: the American free spirit flying into a gorgeous Old World birdbath.

Perched on top of a Brooklyn apartment, with a fine view of New York
Harbor, married to Maas, a poet and professor of English as well as a filmmaker, Menken would have been familiar with the poetic history of that view,
especially with Whitman's great chant of vehicular motion, "Crossing Brooklyn Ferry," and Crane's minor epic, *The Bridge*. Early in *Go!Go!Go!* the cream-
ily smooth, unnaturally swift crossings of ferries, barges, and liners (filmed
in steady time-lapse) offers visual and emotional relief from the opening on-
slaught of images filmed, from a vehicle crossing the Brooklyn Bridge into

13. Brakhage, *Film at Wit's End*, p. 45–46.

Manhattan and by the filmmaker walking the city streets shooting one frame at a time. Although the technique is essentially the same, the sudden transition from the frantic participatory opening to the tripod-steady contemplation of a swifter world signals an antithesis at the heart of the film between a sensibility attacked by an overwhelming torrent of observations hovering on the threshold of assimilation and a detached vision of the rhythms of human temporality that project into a repeating future. Her instinctive recognition of the heightened subjectivity of handheld pixilation would have a decisive influence on Jonas Mekas's art in ways Menken could hardly have suspected when she dedicated the film to him. The combination, or rather the contrast, of stop-motion modalities so early in the film is a trope for the interplay of present and future, self and community, which drives Whitman's poem and which he registered with a shift of sense within his parataxis:

> Crowds of men and women attired in the usual costumes, how curious
>   you are to me!
> On the ferry-boats the hundreds and hundreds that cross are more
>   curious to me than you suppose,
> And you that shall cross from shore to shore years hence, are more to me,
>   and more in my meditations, than you might suppose.
> . . .
> I too lived,
> I too walked the streets of Manhattan Island, and bathed in the waters
>   around it;
> I too felt the curious abrupt questionings stir within me.
> . . .
> I too had received identity by my body,
> That I was, I knew was of my body, and what I should be, I knew should
>   be of my body.[14]

Menken's note on the film in the *Film-makers' Cooperative Catalogue* copiously addresses the technical production of the film, but merely implies its central dialectic:

> Taken from a moving vehicle, for much of the footage; the rest using
> stationary frame stop-motion. In the harbor sequence, I had to wait
> for the right amount of activity, to show effectively the boats darting
> about; some of the sequences took over an hour to shoot, and last

---

14. Walt Whitman, "Sun-Down Poem," *Selected Poems 1855–1892*, pp. 134, 137.

perhaps a minute on the screen. The "strength and health" sequence was shot at a body beautiful convention. Various parts of the City of New York, the busy man's engrossment in his busyness make up the major part of the film... a tour-de-force on man's activities.[15]

The key negative term here is *engrossment*, which is often used aesthetically to describe illusionistic seduction, as in saying that one is engrossed by the plot of a commercial film. The stop-motion technique makes a comedy of engrossment: Herds of people glide through the city streets as if on a conveyor belt; the alternations of traffic and pedestrians on a corner, filmed from high above, reveal a rhythmic rite invisible to those who participate in it; the black-and-white parade of muscle men, which Brakhage convincingly notes she "photographed, no doubt, to tease Willard"[16] for his promiscuous homosexuality, predicts the antic theater of exhibitionism in her film *Wrestling* (1964); a graduation ceremony (another comment on her husband, who earned his living as a professor) reduces the degree recipients to translucent ghosts and the conferring officials to automatons. At the conclusion of this deflation of the busy solemnities that absorb and distract its engrossed participants (including a wedding and a formal dance), the scene returns to her penthouse roof, where Maas moves between his alfresco typewriter and the roof ledge, apparently gazing at the view awaiting inspiration as he writes a poem. His creative enterprise is the dramatic equivalent of the filmmaker's patient acceleration of the ships near the beginning and the sunset at the very end of the film. Through their arts they are able to escape momentarily and give meaning to the engrossments of the world in which they work, play, superficially celebrate, and even experience sexual stimulation.

The structure of the film insists upon the iterative return to the inassimilable stimuli of the hyperactive world. I perceive seven movements to the film, each lasting one or two minutes. It opens with a trip over the Brooklyn Bridge into Manhattan, a rapid tour of the city, and a return via another bridge. This hyperbole of subjective vehicular movement contrasts with the luscious second movement, in which the pixilated view of the harbor orchestrates the angular dance of liners, tugs, ferries, and barges. Sometimes Menken follows a vessel, keeping it trembling in the frame as the coastline moves; then with a rock-steady camera she manufactures an Olympian view of the glossy harbor surface on which the boats make elaborate turns. A transition

---

15. *Film-makers' Cooperative Catalogue No. 7*, p. 370.
16. Brakhage, *Film at Wit's End*, p. 43.

of traffic patterns brings her to the third movement: the college graduation. Recalling her account of her election as an artist by ignoring the instructions of school in favor of the twittering of leaves and turning the textbook pages into a protocinematic flip book, we can see her vision of industrialized degree production as the consequence of the systematic repression of imagination in the mechanical standardization of formal education.

Another transition resolves into the fourth movement, which effaces the individuality of gaits, rhyming the flow of pedestrians through a revolving door, with construction workers seen from high above their site, and matching young women in a formal dance with wedding guests entering a church. In the midst of these fluid collective movements, Menken has introduced the black-and-white footage shot from the balcony of a male physique contest. The speed of the contestants replacing one another on a podium where they strike poses denies to each of them the very uniqueness that generates a competition. The short fifth movement is the antithesis of the body builders: Alone on their penthouse rooftop, Willard Maas composes at a typewriter. Beside him a bust of Hermes, after Praxiteles, offers an ironic echo of the bare-chested muscle men. The fast motion caricatures the poet's struggle with his muse: He scratches his head, takes deep puffs of cigarette smoke, rushes three times to the edge of the roof until he throws up his hands as if inspired by a new notion, throws away one sheet, and rolls another into the typewriter. He is the center of the film, both the object of affection and the stand-in for the filmmaker.

In the film's sixth movement, recreation at Coney Island becomes as tumultuous and compulsive as the collective movements seen earlier. The camera arrives by elevated train, glimpses roller coasters and rides, watches couples sunbathing and kissing, then tours the avenues of food stalls. Young men trying to form human pyramids recall the theatrical physique contestants. Then the finale joins elements of the teeming life previously seen in the city, until views of a ferry departing and the Brooklyn Bridge—the film's starting point—conclude the film with two gorgeous shots of the sun sinking. By embedding her moments of transcendence within the rhythmic convulsions of city life, Menken declares her participation in the very ceremonies and engrossments she sees through. Again the analogy of Whitman's "Crossing Brooklyn Ferry" is apt, all the more so as it was originally titled "Sun-Down Poem" (just as Menken concludes her film with a return to the swiftly gliding boats at sunset); for Whitman wrote as if riding the ferry in the last half hour of daylight, thinking prophetically of those like Menken who would follow him:

Others will see the shipping of Manhattan north and west, and the
heights of Brooklyn to the south and east...

Fifty years hence, others will see them as they cross, the sun half an hour
    high,
A hundred years hence, or ever so many hundred years hence, others will
    see them,
Will enjoy the sun-set, the pouring-in of the flood-tide, the falling back
    to the sea of the ebb-tide.

. . .

It avails not, neither time or place—distance avails not,
I am with you, you men and women of a generation, or ever so many
    generations hence,
I project myself, also I return—I am with you, and know how it is.[17]

Menken too projects herself in the frame; for the opening and end titles
of *Go!Go!Go!* are unlike any others in her work: We see her through a mirror
on which the film's title has been painted in red, gesturing as if urging the
engrossed masses on, or simply waving, to them and to us. She has masked
out the camera with a black rectangle. As she waves her outstretched hand,
it briefly crosses between the camera and the mirror, miming a shutter effect and punctuating the word "GO!" seven or eight times. When the subsequent mirror title "By Marie Menken" appears, the waving arm does not
cross in front of the camera but only appears in reflection. This too is a
Whitmanesque gesture, the unique insertion of her own image into her
film, equating her hand gesture with the mechanism of the camera and
projecting herself into the future and waving to us, now from beyond the
grave.

Pixilation for wonder and comic effect is as old as the cinema itself. Historically the measure of its success had been the illusionism achieved by rigorously anchoring the camera and controlling the rhythm of shooting so that
people and objects seemed to move smoothly at incredible speeds. Menken
does this when she films boats in the harbor. But the steady camera serves
especially as a foil to its opposite—the somatic rhythms and complex, instantaneous shifts of tempo she brings to the screen by daring to hold the pixilating camera in her hands.

One of Menken's last completed films, *Excursion* (ca. 1968), returns to
pixilation to produce a much simpler and ultimately tenebrific echo of
Go!Go!Go! Like the earlier film, it begins in celebration of vehicular motion
and ends with a version of sundown: In its final minutes the scene darkens,
presumably from the dying of the light rather than from a shift of exposure.

---

17. Whitman, *Selected Poems 1855–1892*, p. 135

That is uncertain insofar as chance plays a larger role in *Excursion* than in any other work of Menken's except, perhaps, *Hurry! Hurry!*; for its reduction of a three-hour trip around Manhattan on the Circle Line to four and half minutes may have had the unintended consequence of effecting a diminuendo of light if the afternoon's ride ended near dusk. It is even possible that this monument to the Beautiful Necessity emerged from the camera with little or no editing. It breaks off without the clearly articulated finale of *Go!Go!Go!*

For the most part, Menken stands on the deck of the crowded tourist boat, filming a few rows back from the prow; often she pans to either side and occasionally even seems to be shooting through a window from inside the boat. Just in front of her is a party of three: Willard Maas and her sister, Adele, with distinctive black hair and black glasses, flank a blond young man whom I believe to be John Hawkins, the young filmmaker who collaborated on projects of both Menken and Maas. Menken befriended, virtually adopted, many of the young men in whom Maas showed a passionate interest. Adele Menken lived in the same apartment building as Marie in Brooklyn and was her constant companion. So, as the ark of the Circle Line circumnavigates the island, she films at the circumference of her own circle of affection, accompanied by her intimates.

The fast-motion photography animates the anonymous passengers into a quivering restless throng. Maas himself is the most restless of Menken's party; he stands up early in the film as the boat swings past the Statue of Liberty. He sometimes blocks Menken's sight of it, becoming himself a temporary figure of "liberty." The impulsive rhythm of the pixilation suggests that Maas has been transformed, absorbed into a collective American persona as the excursion passes the symbol of a national melting pot. With similar playfulness, she catches sight of the Chrysler Building through the curls of Adele's hair, as if it were a barrette she stuck in it.

As fatigue sets in and the surrounding cityscape grows dim, two children near the prow seem to be the focus of attention, as if Menken were trying to experience the tour through their eyes. But even here the passing of other tourist vessels reminds us that the experience is multiplied and will continue to be. After the boat turns, undramatically, into wider expanse of the Hudson River and passes under the George Washington Bridge, the three companions reoccupy the center but the light grows progressively dimmer. The filmmaker continues to show fatigue: The bridge passes without the attention she had given to those on the other side of the island.

It is difficult to know how much weight to put on the opening and end titles, written on animated boats of folded newsprint. The concluding boat bearing the title "The End" does not make it across the screen, but turns downward instead, sinking before the frame. I believe John Hawkins may have made these titles, perhaps at Maas's behest rather than Menken's. Although their cuteness does a disservice to the subtlety of the film, the cartoon shipwreck is consistent with the film's evolving tone, even if its exaggeration works against the filmmaker's tonal nuancing.

In my 1962 interview with her, Menken said that her audience consisted of:

> Mostly people I love, for it is to them I address myself. Sometimes the audience becomes more than I looked for, but in sympathy they must be my friends. There is no choice, for in making a work of art one holds in spirit those are receptive, and if they are, they must be one's friends. . . . There is love, and it is everywhere.[18]

The titles of her films often revealed the centrality of friendship and love in her art: (Isamu) Noguchi, Dwight (Ripley), Willard Maas, and Kenneth Anger are named in them. When she wrote of *Go!Go!Go!*, "I am dedicating it to Jonas Mekas because he knows more than anyone else what it is not about," she intimated that Mekas is one whose daily labor is neither a vanity nor a habitual routine.

In *Excursion* she actually gathers "people I love" into the film. Furthermore I believe that her friendship with Stan Brakhage operates somewhat more remotely throughout it. She had accompanied Brakhage and Kenneth Anger to Paris in 1958 after the International Experimental Film Competition in Brussels, where they all showed new work. They were together when Brakhage smuggled his camera into Père Lachaise cemetery to shoot some of the footage that would go into *The Dead* (1960). I do not know whether she accompanied him when he filmed from a bateau mouche on the Seine. In any case, she would have seen the results in the finished film.

Making *The Dead* was Brakhage's act of resistance to European culture, tradition, and history. He saw Paris as a tomb and Parisians as the walking dead. Brakhage's film is only incidentally a portrait of Anger, who appears briefly in the opening shots: Anger and his exploration of the death instinct serve as the pretext for Brakhage's preoccupation with his own mortality, projected through his ambivalence about Europe as a museum and a sepulchre. The film's central trope, the superimposition of the same positive and negative images, with a delay of a few seconds between them, has a retardation effect that is matched by what appears to be slightly slow-motion photography from the tourist boat. I believe Ian Hugo's *Melodic Inversion*, premiered

18. Sitney, "Interview with Marie Menken," pp. 9, 11.

at the same film competition, inspired his use of negative superimpositions (see chapter 3).

In the introduction to *Metaphors on Vision*, Brakhage described his crisis making the film:

> I had to find, realize re: *The Dead* that somehow all images of death or all concepts of it are structured here in life. Then I knew the answer as to why I'd shot in the same day, and out of the same needs, material in the graveyard of Père Lachaise and on the Seine.... Then I could structure *The Dead* by way of a concept of the future as that through which we can't live.... So the question becomes one of all that is pitched out of life; how the walking dead come to be that... and how living people do relate to that, and how even trees, shaped that way and so ordered and structured, become living dead and like the walking dead, who are people so dead on their feet you can't even use the word "living" in relationship to them.... The graveyard could stand for all my view of Europe, for all the concerns with past art, for all involvement with symbol.... The action of making *The Dead* kept me alive.[19]

On the other hand, Menken was describing her aspirations in cinema (several years before making *Excursion*) when she said:

> I want to impart hilarity, joyousness, expansion of life with an uncontrollable mirth. I try. Get it? While we have life we are superior to death, but watch out: death might be closer than you know. And that is our end. If I can postpone death even for one minute, I have been successful in my art and so is all art, for art postpones death.[20]

This early text could be a hypothetical scenario for *Excursion*, where death threatens to turn the casual trip around Manhattan into an allegorical journey beyond the limits of experience. In fact, one of the meanings of *excursion* is to transgress a limit. At the core of the word's etymology is an act of running (Latin: *ex* [from, out of] *currere* [to run]). At one time the term covered sallies of wit and outbursts of feeling. For the most part, we take the title in a conventional modern sense to refer to a trip that implies a quick return home. But the film ends at its crepuscular apogee before the Circle Line can complete its orbit. The pixilation literalizes the running tempo of "ex-cursion"; it

19. Stan Brakhage, *Metaphors on Vision* (New York: *Film Culture* no. 30, 1963), pages unnumbered.
20. Sitney, "Interview with Marie Menken," p. 11.

both hastens "our end," by rushing forward, and postpones it, by making a diversion. At the beginning of the film, as in *Go!Go!Go!, Wrestling*, and parts of *Andy Warhol*, the speeded-up movement is a trigger for "hilarity, joyousness, expansion of life." Such a quickening of vitality is antithetical to Brakhage's vision of *The Dead*, where the living (of Paris) are possessed by mortal lassitude.

If Menken is responding to Brakhage with this film, she is drawing his attention to the teeming life around him and to the power of companionship to raise the coefficient of joyousness. In fact, the very experience they shared in Paris, as baroquely described in *Metaphors on Vision*, is to be found in *Excursion*; but its systematic elimination was central to Brakhage's conception of *The Dead*. For him, sharing an experience with friends requires a submission to the mediation of language that, he feared, threatened the integrity of his vision. The convoluted account of his shooting in Paris was the last text he wrote for *Metaphors on Vision*. It reflects his ambivalence toward both the original event and his impulse to write about it. At twenty-five, Brakhage was the youngest and decidedly the least urbane of the company; Anger, thirty-one, had lived in Paris for several years; Menken was then forty-eight. I shall try to preserve the sense of his difficult text while eliminating several sentences:

> I was twice in the Graveyard of Père Lachaise, first in the company of friends, myself and Marie Menken as American tourists, Kenneth Anger our guide, the three of us, as film-makers, eye-orienting ourselves [...] so as to say "There?", the first quest shunning one's own vision [...] to say "There!", the drawing of all gestures to oneself, a play of planes wherein one makes marionette of one's eye's sight for the vanishing of lines into perspective, to say "O!", to have x-changed one's owned sight for the first ring of a chain of other vision.
>
> And we e-voked, x-changing each vis for viz: this for that, here for there, wording our ways a-way to haunts in which the ghosts of our children-selves could hunt as we were used [...]
>
> [...] I was there in Père Lachaise, for the first time, being where I was and imagining, vis-a-vis, some hypothetical where-with-all to include *we* of a three-part there-with-all, a fix to invent *were* or, more uni-vers-ally, a development to invert *re* for some sense of the invisible as *members* of a child(who-dead?)-scene, played grave-stonely with no thought for the mo-or-monu-meant [...]
>
> With this word-wrest went all de-corum; and while we did not actually dance, we moved as if I, and he, and she, had each been aware of the dance we three were image engendering [...]

> In that state (you'll have to take my word for it) I became aware of
> (as if it clothed my eye's sight) and wary of (as if it were) a whitening
> of all objects seen.[21]

On the one hand, Brakhage struggled against the friendly hilarity Menken espoused while, on the other hand, he was seduced by the regression to a sense of childlike adventure she inspired. Out of his frustration at the dilemma between wanting to capture on film their unconscious communal dance and to attend solely to the supralinguistic dimensions of his eyesight, he had the visionary glimpse of an anxiety-provoking "whitening of all objects seen" that became the basis for his film. Evidently, in *Excursion* Menken felt none of Brakhage's epistemological anguish. Aloof, she holds fast to her autonomy, yet she comfortably remains within the circle of her extended family, observing them and observing for them.

---

21. Brakhage, *Metaphors on Vision*. The ellipses I have made in the complete text of this convoluted statement are indicated by [...]. I have made some speculative emendations in the published text, which Brakhage noted contained many errors, although he did not leave a corrected copy:

> but (of Orient) creating the exotic (in comp.) prehension re: childhood—(the tour) nascence meant to be (re: our guy): follow the leader—(membering: the first) game: to see as the other— to see "other," by direction, to see "over there," where the lines of many gestures converge, to see "O—there,["] the vanishing point, to see "O" the point, to see "There," its vanishing...
>   to say then "Oh, there!", the cognition which gears one's sight to the other's gesture, to say "Oh?,["] the second question{"} being of the other's gesture wherein it vanishes at the point, ...each search con(tracted to) struct (the) tour (re: turn)ing. And cats were *there*, where here *lost* flowers to *their* eyes, where this lost (sun) flowers to *that* (moon) cat's eyes, wherein un-sound symbols flourished (to the x-pense of papier-maché) paying out a fee line space-wise (trans parent flesh), governing the person (all) sight, as any G-host (spirit) will will will within such con-(struct-tour)-text:—as here, all Wo-Rds.
> [at least one line seems to be missing in the text] sentence at similar points, periodically, and vanish into space for para-graphing:—and there we were, not where we were, but having been there where we were–tho', as Creeley points out (a parent thesis): "We is not the plural of I:"— And we saw The City of The Dead as ave-newed, more alive than the spooking words "Rue de la Reste," et set, or as if "Here lies" were to be taken literally as comment upon all tombstone writing.
> viz-a-viz:
> WISHING TO HELL—
> (Epstein's Wilde little penis which wasn't there again to-(that)-day.)
> SMELLING TO HIGH HEAVEN—
> (The Polish roses on Chopin's grave being Stein's "is a—is a—is a—is a" ad-infinitum.)
> PURSUED TO EARTH ENDS—
> (Each crypt-door hinging on Bottom's pit, each crack-of-tomb light's abcess.)
> FORE ALL TIME—
> (Tears and tiers of imaginable coffins of descendencies x-tending Roman-tick-tock-ally thru monks to monster monkies.)
> SENSUALITIE'S MEASURE—
> (All angel, and other-mother-death-sculpture, per-as-con-ceived sexually x-citing symbol's oh-and-ah-bayence.)

The distinctive features of Menken's somatic camera movements can be seen most clearly in the films she made with static subjects: *Eye Music in Red Major* and *Mood Mondrian*. In the first of these, Menken pointed her camera at colored lightbulbs against a black background where, as the title tells us, red bulbs predominate over green, blue, and purple. The complex rhythms of the film derive from her subtle movements toward and away from individual bulbs, in rather soft focus, so that the intense light of the filament often appears as an amorphous yellowish white hot spot within the red sphere. By substituting a green bulb, perhaps underexposed so that it forms a circular corona of greenish blue light, for the pulsating red, she can fuse changes of hue and movement instantaneously.

She alternates this central motif with sweeping shots of groups of three or four bulbs in different colors that follow all the vectors of screen movement: left, right, up and down, in the first minute of the five-minute film. Then she tilts these movements toward the diagonal and eventually orchestrates arcs and nearly circular orbits within the frame. By the third minute, the pulsing spheres and now jittery movements begin to give way to pencil-thin short white lines of light and even a glimpse of the moon. In the final minute and a half, she points the camera through a kaleidoscope. (Presumably it is the same instrument she used to make the recently recovered film, *Here and There with My Octoscope*, which she had included in the Charles Theater program. In both films the kaleidoscope is positioned delicately off center.) In *Eye Music in Red Major* the kaleidoscopic effect gives the film its diminuendo; its predominantly pink and red points of refracted light form a single circle, or concentric circles, as if absorbing into an epicenter of the screen the dynamics of the previous movements. On the other hand, *Here and There with My Octoscope* uses the full circle of eight mirrors to generate a rapidly changing cascade of colors in a full spectrum.

Less successful, but more daring than *Eye Music in Red Major*, *Mood Mondrian* provides the template against which we can observe Menken's camera gestures most clearly. In this film she paid homage to Piet Mondrian's *Broadway Boogie-Woogie* by filming it. The flatness of the canvas prevents the camera movement from creating the illusion of objects in motion, and of course it does not allow her to move within it as she did in the architectural precinct of the Alhambra, so that the similarities of the film's movements to both *Eye Music in Red Major* and *Arabesque for Kenneth Anger* point out the consistency and autonomy of Menken's style.

Harry Cooper wrote of Mondrian's importation of musical ideas into *Broadway Boogie-Woogie*:

> The sound of good boogie-woogie, as early critics recognized, is a single mesh whose elements...seem to eat away at one another....

Boogie-woogie is the very model of a collapsed dualism, or rather
a collapsing one, since the two hands remain distinct despite their
similarities: the left hand is (more) repetitive, the right hand (more)
discursive.

Mondrian takes an uncharacteristic stab at illustrating this music in
Broadway Boogie Woogie, with its Albers-like blocked chords (pound-
ing right hand) and, at lower center, its similar patterns of alternating
colors that run along parallel horizontal tracks at different rates (poly-
rhythm of simultaneous lines)....

Whatever the particular bass-line motif chosen by the pianist,
boogie-woogie nearly always had an eight-note rhythmic feel...hence
the nickname "eight to the bar."[22]

Although Menken planned to put on the film the music of Pinetop Smith,
who first recorded the boogie-woogie style in the 1920s, there is no recognizable reflection of the collapsing dualism of that style in its camera rhythms.
In "translating" Mondrian's static mapping of music back into a temporal
art of film, Menken did not seek a cinematic equivalent of the right- and
left-handed articulation.

Quickly edited graphic films are particularly susceptible to apparent synchronization with randomly selected music. The domination of the auditory
rhythm influences the visual perception of the film. Harry Smith exploited
this phenomenon when he periodically changed the accompaniment to his
collection Early Abstractions even though most of those films were initially
created in response to specific jazz pieces. I have tried playing recordings of
Pinetop Smith's boogie-woogies randomly while projecting Mood Mondrian.
In many places the film seems as if it had been edited to the music no matter
which composition I played. The eight-to-a-bar pulse fits both the montage
of static details and the swings of the camera so that the two-handed interplay
corresponds both to the way the camera movements alternate with quickly
edited details and the back-and-forth panning in passages with no stops.

The addition of music gives Menken's films a more polished, "professional," and conventional look. Even the score Teiji Ito composed for Arabesque for Kenneth Anger undermines the visual-kinetic subtlety of the film. It
deemphasizes the awkward split-second hesitations at the beginning of shots
and the tiny shifts of direction and rhythm that may first strike us as accidents
but which become the core of Menken's art on repeated viewings. If they
were accidents in the first place, her stroke of genius was to leave them in the

---

22. Harry Cooper, "Mondrian, Hegel, Boogie," October 84 (Spring 1998), pp. 135–36, 137.

finished film. Menken cheerfully and self-confidently grounded her cinema in a space where originality and mastery could be taken for ineptitude. The hesitations and split-second adjustments inherent in the process of making a film without a scenario became the foundation of her cinematic poetics. Her heirs, Stan Brakhage and Jonas Mekas, taught us to see this from the lessons they learned watching her films and making her poetics their own.

In *Mood Mondrian*, Menken represents the movements of her eyes and her acts of attention as she stands before *Broadway Boogie-Woogie*. Only once, very early in the film, does she make a zigzag gesture with her camera to follow the path of Mondrian's gridwork. In effect, this sole acknowledgment of the mesh of perpendiculars highlights the disjunction between Menken's camera movements and Mondrian's geometry, even though she favors horizontal and vertical movements (rather than diagonals) more in this film than in any other. She does not provide us with a view of the whole painting until one of the film's five minutes has elapsed. She builds her rhythms from the alternation of directional movements and the sudden interjection of static details (often individual rectangles or squares within rectangles). These usually appear in a short series, as if slamming the brakes on her panning camera. She cuts the shots of the painted rectangles closer with each new image, in short series, as she does the montage of tiles in *Arabesque for Kenneth Anger*. Then for half a minute she rocks the camera back and forth across the painting.

A montage of static details precedes each new strategy of camera movement. She pans quickly from left to right about ten times in a row, almost giving the impression of a long horizontal extension of Mondrian's checkered line as if it were a strip of film. A return to a view of the whole canvas initiates the concluding diminuendo of details.

The glory of Menken's cinema is its openness and attention to stochastic rhythms. Early in *Notebook* she discovered a way to make the random patterns of rain falling on a pond an occasion of excitement and wonder. In the late *Drips in Strips* the gravitational pull on daubs of thin paint running in rivulets down a vertical sheets of paper generates the film's rhythms. In six or seven takes, from three to twenty strips of color run down the frame. Some of the lines halt midway and others merge or divide as they flow through the frame. The different rates of descent control the rhythm of this very simple film.

The corporeal aesthetics of Menken's somatic camera align her photographic style with her thematic exploration of human physicality, which is especially evident in several fast-motion films she made at the end of her career that exemplify her overall desire "to impart hilarity, joyousness, expansion of life with an uncontrollable mirth." In *Wrestling*, a black-and-white film that evidences her "uncontrollable mirth" at watching the sport on television, she reduces the cathode image to a frenzy of bands and pixels in which the individuality of the wrestlers and referees dissolves; wild arm motions blend into unheard interviews; in tumbling violence men hurl and sit upon one another.[23] The outrageous physicality of the bodies on the television screen finds its counterpart in the handheld camera of the seated artist-observer; for the pixilation of single-frame filmmaking necessarily amplifies the slight alterations in the viewer's perspective. *Andy Warhol* (1965) is indeed a portrait of the Pop artist as a frenetic producer of multiple objects. At the comic apex of this film she cuts from fast-motion scenes of Warhol's assistants making Brillo boxes and a crowded gallery celebrating their exhibition to trucks at a Brillo storage depot loading boxes onto train cars. The creation and consumption of art, in this film, become functions of mad hyperactivity and herd stampedes. Finally, *Excursion* directly enacted the Emersonian scenario that impels all of her films in one way or another: With her single-frame technique she "gave a pictorial air" to a trip on the Circle Line around Manhattan. Each of these three films explores an aspect of her earlier and more elaborate *Go!Go!Go!* It is as if she isolated the ritual theater of gymnastic exhibition in its bodybuilder episode to create *Wrestling*; or transformed the comedy of artistic creation as manic movement in her portrait of Maas trying to write into a parody of mass production in *Andy Warhol*; and extended its exhilaration of turning the world "into a puppet-show" from the vantage of a moving vehicle with *Excursion*.

The extraordinary cinematic style that I have been calling Menken's somatic camera has been her most influential gift to the American avant-garde cinema. It is an embodiment of the Emersonian invention of a pictorial air, the spiritual emancipation automatically brought about by "certain mechanical changes, a small alteration in our local position." It is also analogous to the equally Emersonian somatic theory of poesis Charles Olson was developing at nearly the same time: his emphasis on breath and proprioception corresponds to Menken's identification of the camera with the body in motion and her cultivation of the respiratory and nervous agitation of the handheld camera even in its quietest moments.

23. On the film itself the title appears as *Wrestlers*, although Menken always called it and advertised it as *Wrestling*.

CHAPTER 2

Ian Hugo and Superimposition

"Ian Hugo" was the pseudonym of Hugh Parker Guiler. His films *Bells of Atlantis* (1952) and *Melodic Inversion* (1958) were significant in establishing the centrality of superimposition in the rhetoric of the American avant-garde cinema. In this chapter, I show that both films were virtually collaborations with his wife, the writer and diarist Anaïs Nin. She acted in them and made crucial directorial, editing, and sound suggestions. Hugo's artistic dependence on her was nearly pathological. At the same time, those two films reflect the complexity and tensions of their marriage. His anger at his dependence on her animated his subtle distortion of her text that is the basis of *Bells of Atlantis*, just as he projected his anger and humiliation at her infidelities as a fantasy of her jealousy in *Melodic Inversion*. In his tectonic use of superimposition, he invented an extraordinary vehicle for subtly exploring the nuances of his crises.

Guiler worked as a banker until his retirement in 1949, supporting Nin from the time of their marriage in 1923 until her last years, when the income from the sales of her expurgated diaries exceeded his dwindling assets. He had followed her lead into psychoanalysis with her own doctors, René Allendy in Paris in the 1920s and Inge Bogner in New York, from the late 1940s at least through the 1950s. His analysis with Bogner facilitated his decision to make films and supported his persistence in the medium despite his massive insecurities as an artist. She brought him to recognize his childlike dependence on Nin and his anger because of it. Yet he never freed himself of Nin's domination. He confessed that to her in a long letter written near the start of his filmmaking career: "Bogner has this week broken the news to me that I have been deceiving myself into thinking that I am an artist. She says that I am primarily a businessman, and on the side, an artist."[1] This and his other letters to Nin are included in the archive of her diaries at the Young Research Library of UCLA. The collection is particularly extensive after 1947, when Nin lived more than half of every year in California with Rupert Pole, her lover (and after 1955 her bigamous husband, although he did not know she was still married to Hugo), without Guiler acknowledging, or perhaps even knowing, the situation. The letters reveal his unremitting quest for legitimation and recognition as a filmmaker. He quoted to her virtually every phrase of critical or even audience praise he heard and repeatedly complained of the failure to win festival prizes. Throughout his career he turned obsessively to other filmmakers to help him achieve mastery. In 1949 he hired Alexander Hammid to give him lessons in handling his expensive 16 mm camera. Soon after that he enlisted the help of James Broughton. He met both of these filmmakers through Nin. She had met Hammid and Maya Deren, who fascinated and intimidated her, in 1944 when they were making *At Land*. In 1948 she met a number of filmmakers in California: Curtis Harrington and Kenneth Anger in Los Angeles, and Broughton in San Francisco while she and Pole were living in those cities. When she introduced Hugo to Anger that year, the younger, yet more experienced filmmaker urged him in vain to stop seeking teachers and to pursue filmmaking intuitively, self-taught, as he himself had since he was an adolescent.

In 1949 Hugo engaged the puppeteer Eugene Walter to work with him on a script for a film around an idea he had of an erotic triangle set in a tower. At Nin's insistence, Hugo quickly abandoned the plan of using marionettes for some scenes, but he did shoot several episodes of what they called *The Dangerous Telescope*—"a phallic joke" according to Walter—with Robert DeVries, a painter who was Walter's neighbor, and Nin herself as a jealous "siren." At first Hugo wanted to hire Hammid to photograph the film, but eventually

---

1. Hugh Guiler to Anaïs Nin, December 4, 1949, Young Research Library of UCLA. Ian Hugo's letters are included within the unpublished diaries of Anais Nin in the Special Collections of the Young Library, printed here by permission of the Anais Nin Trust and the Young Library.

he decided to handle the camera himself. More than forty years later Walter told Katherine Clark:

> But Anaïs came back and was directing Hugo how to direct the film. I can still see his horn-rimmed specs as he was looking down and figuring something out about the camera. And she would say, "Well, let's do this, and why don't I come down this path?" He said, "Now wait, Anaïs, we are not making the film yet. I've got to figure out the camera." You know, "Let me get this right."
>
> There was one great party scene where I assembled thirty actors at this Rhenish Castle [on the Hudson River]. He filmed the whole day but forgot to put film in his camera. She was so busy doing Anaïs that he got rattled...
>
> So afterwards I sat at a little Moviola with him and made a new story using what footage there was.[2]

Hugo himself had a much more productive experience of technical errors. On September 26, 1949, he wrote to Nin about *Ai-Ye*, which he was making at the same time:

> I had some trouble filming a number of Acapulco shots, but the accident worked a little miracle with the church and certain other scenes, giving a ghostly appearance I would like to be able to control. Others were spoiled by the accident due to a mistake I made several times in looking (Sascha [Hammid] had not had time to teach me that), but on the whole I would prefer to lose what I lost and gain what I did.

In San Francisco Nin met the electronic composers Bebe and Louis Barron and sent them to look up Hugo when they relocated to New York that year. He engaged them to make a soundtrack for *The Dangerous Telescope* but he abandoned the project shortly after he and Walter showed a rough cut to DeVries, Broughton, and some friends. He would return to this footage ten years later, but the Acapulco material he had been collecting commanded his attention. Thus *Ai-Ye* became his first completed film.

In the fifth volume of her *Diary*, Anaïs Nin describes Ian Hugo's birth as a filmmaker:

> As a result of several trips to Mexico, Ian Hugo made the transition from engraver to film maker. He followed the process of free

---

2. Eugene Walter, *Milking the Moon: A Southerner's Story of Life on This Planet, as told to Katherine Clark* (New York: Crown, 2001), pp. 117–18.

association: he filmed whatever touched him or appealed to him, trusting to an organic development of themes. The results were an impressionistic interpretation of the universal story of mankind's voyage told without words through a kaleidoscope of color, through sound and images. Beginning while he and the animals sleep and dream of the past, man is taken through tropical lagoons from birth, through childhood, adolescence, pain, struggle, old age, death, and burial in the mouth of a volcano in the clouds. Ozzie Smith improvised drumming and chanting as he watched the film unroll. Ian Hugo called the film *Ai-Ye*.

At about the same time he filmed some footage of a shipwreck on the beach, of the sea's constant tumult, which he later edited, inspired by the prologue to my House of Incest and the line: "I remember my first birth in water." The film [later called Bells of Atlantis] evoked the watery depths of the lost continent of Atlantis. It is a lyrical journey into prenatal memories, the theme of birth and rebirth from the sea.[3]

More of a blurb than a diary entry, it was almost assuredly written after 1952 when *Bells of Atlantis* was completed, rather than in the winter of 1950–51 as the published diary indicates. Nevertheless, this diary passage is also the best interpretive commentary written on *Ai-Ye* in the forty-three years since it was made and released.

In *Ai-Ye*, a montage of images clusters around the organizing trope of a boat passage through a tropical environment. Thus in his self-incarnation as a filmmaker Hugo rehearses one of the founding strategies of our Emersonian aesthetics: The camera, planted securely in the center of the small, oar-propelled vessel, often frames the triangle of the prow in the lower center of the frame. However, images are by no means limited to the boat's perspective. Nin's diary entry provides a convincing master narrative for the successive matrices of images as they progress from sleeping animals and people through images of village life that include rites—first communion, perhaps a wedding, a funeral—and images of the maimed and dead. Nin's synopsis draws a cyclical meaning from them and leaps to understand the juxtaposition of aerial views of a volcano with the slow-motion repetitions of a man diving from cliffs as "burial in the mouth of a volcano." Another prominent cluster of the varieties of work—cooking, spear fishing, archaeologists excavating—escapes her commentary.

Between 1936, when Nin published *The House of Incest*, and 1966, when the *Diary* began to appear in print, her underground reputation had been

---

3. Anaïs Nin, *The Diary of Anaïs Nin, Vol. 5 (1947–1955)*, ed. with a preface by Gunther Stuhlmann (New York: Harcourt Brace Jovanovich, 1974), pp. 59–60.

precariously sustained by a series of poetic novels she published herself with engravings by Hugo under the general rubric of *Cities of the Interior*. The reanimation of her work brought about by the republication of these novels by the small Swallow Press in the early 1960s was negligible compared to the international acclaim that almost immediately followed Harcourt Brace Jovanovich's major distribution of the *Diary*. The diaries owed their success largely to the vivid portraits of the literary celebrities Nin knew intimately: Henry Miller, Lawrence Durrell, Antonin Artaud, Otto Rank, Edgar Varese, Timothy Leary, Ossip Zadkine, and so on.

Following Nin's death in 1977 and Guiler's in 1985, volumes of the *Unexpurgated Diary* began to appear, throwing a wholly new light on the previous reticences. In two of the volumes so far available, *Henry and June* and *Incest*, Nin records her extended adulterous affairs—with Henry Miller, with his wife, June, with both her psychoanalysts of the period, René Allendy and Otto Rank, and a passionate incestuous relationship with her father. All this sexual questing entailed elaborate deceptions of Guiler, including an implausible persuasion that the diary—into which he peeked and from which he recoiled—was an elaborate fantasy: "to compensate for all I don't do," she boldly lied.

I dwell on this dramatic detail of their married life because it is pertinent to my interpretations of *Bells of Atlantis* and *Melodic Inversion*. Nin writes of her "demoniac elation" at taking the risk of leaving the diary open in a room where Guiler is working: "I desire the catastrophe, and I dread it…I want him to chase me away." When he forgives her and asks only for the truth, she lies: "I wanted Hugh angry, but he said, 'I will forgive you.' So even if he knew the truth he would forgive me, and I would remain here—here. Protected, loved, forgiven. It was the word forgive which set me off lying, playacting."[4]

From the beginning of his filmmaking career, Hugo aligned himself with the American avant-garde. James Broughton's autobiography offers a perspective on both Hugo's complicity in Nin's sexual promiscuity and the making of *Ai-Ye* and *Bells of Atlantis*:

> He had acquired expensive camera equipment on which to learn filmmaking and he sought my collaboration. Wanting to enjoy a holiday while filming he invited me to accompany him to Mexico. There we traveled extensively and photographed randomly. In time we reached Acapulco where Anaïs awaited us.

4. Anaïs Nin, *Incest/ From a Journal of Love/ The Unexpurgated Diary of Anaïs Nin: 1932–34* (New York: Harcourt Brace Jovanovich, 1992), pp. 268–89.

...Each day Hugo took me into nearby jungles where I helped him film swamps and birds and natives in hammocks which eventually he shaped into his first completed picture, *Ai-Ye*. We also shot scenes of Anaïs rocking in a hammock underwater for a fanciful portrait of her called *Bells of Atlantis.*....

Evenings at the hotel, as we sat watching young divers plunge into the sea from perilous cliffs, Anaïs would ask Hugo to proposition any young man in the bar who caught her fancy. Being the most generous cuckold I have ever known, Hugo did her bidding without protest and withdrew into the background of her flirtations. He truly adored her.[5]

Two subsequent biographies of Nin indicate that Hugo—as he came to be called both in the diary and in the world—knew with certainty of some of his wife's extramarital affairs by the time he came to make *Bells of Atlantis*.[6] (But he did not learn until her death of her bigamous relationship to Poole that began in 1947 and lasted thirty years.) However, even if he were improbably free of suspicions that the diary confessions he had seen in 1932 were more than compensatory fantasies, he would have realized that those fantasies (or acts) were the basis for her prose poem, *The House of Incest* (begun in 1923 but published in 1936), from which he adapted his film.

The House of Incest is a prose poem in seven chapters with a prologue. The Swallow Press edition, with photomontage illustrations by Val Telberg, extends its forty-three pages of text over seventy-two pages. Thus it is approximately one third the length of its primary literary ancestor, André Breton's *Nadja*. Breton poses the question "Who am I?" in the opening sentence of his book. His initial proposal of an answer parodies the Cartesian *cogito*: he defines himself as one who "haunts." Thus haunting Paris as a *flaneur*, he narrates the extraordinary series of fortuitous encounters that brought together the Surrealist company (Eluard, Desnos, Peret, et al.) as *Acta apostolorum*. Amid this company he arrives at a more elaborate definition of his identity: punning on *verre* as glass and poetry (*vers*), he announces:

I myself shall continue living in my glass house [maison de verre] where you can always see who comes to call; where everything hanging from the ceiling and on the walls stays where it is as if by magic, where

5. James Broughton, *Coming Unbuttoned* (San Francisco: City Lights, 1993), pp. 72–73. Since Broughton always used a cameraman or technical assistant when making his own films, he was an odd choice for this role. His version of Hugo's erotic generosity contradicts most of the published testimony.

6. Deirdre Bair, *Anaïs Nin: A Biography* (New York: Putnam's, 1995); Noel Riley Fitch, *Anaïs: The Erotic Life of Anaïs Nin* (Boston: Little, Brown, 1993).

I sleep nights in a glass bed, under glass sheets [sur un lit de verre aux draps de verre] where *who I am* will sooner or later appear etched in diamond.[7]

This image, like the pun that subtends it, is open to multiple readings: Breton asserts his refusal to hide, his openness in the metaphor of the glass house, but he takes it away at the same time; for, if he is dreaming, the essential visionary scene is lost to those of us looking into the glass house; if he is dead and the etched words are "André Breton," the book is merely a tomb; if, however, "who I am" [qui je suis] is the answer to the opening question, "Who am I?" [Qui suis-je?], in the form of the entire text of *Nadja*, the etching of that text over the walls of the glass house, and over the bed and the sheets, would deface the transparency; finally, the literal possibility must be considered; for, if the words "qui je suis" are etched into the glass, then language, the glass medium, and the biological being, André Breton, retain their autonomy.

The central chapter of *Nadja* presents Breton's diaristic account of a series of meetings with a somewhat mad free spirit who has named herself Nadja: "because in Russian it is the beginning of the word for hope, and because it is only the beginning." Their meetings involve a series of coincidences and correspondences between the author's poetic activities and readings, on the one hand, and Nadja's unpredictable acts and claims on the other. Nadja herself disappears from the narrative when she is committed to an insane asylum, but the associations of the places they visited and the disjunctions between the visual and verbal illustrations Breton assembles for his book continue to provide him with provocative variations on the gulf between names and things or persons, in the final section of the book.

The pattern of *Nadja* is characteristic of the Surrealist myth of inspiration: A chance encounter with a mysterious woman quickens the poet's imagination to the point of defining who he is. The disappearance or rejection of the poet by the woman is an important element in the allegorical pattern. The films *L'etoile de mer* (1928), *Un chien andalou* (1929), and *L'age d'or* (1930) offer variations on this pattern. Its roots go back to Marian visions and the courtly love of troubadour poets.

The most important of Nin's many revisions of this allegory in *The House of Incest* was her inscription of the female protagonist. The Surrealist mythology emphatically registers the questing poet as a male. The first-person narrator of Nin's prose poem is a siren: "My first vision of earth was water veiled." The brief preface suggests she makes a musical instrument, the quena, of bones of her lover, savagely incrementing its mythic origin: "Only I do not wait for my love to die." Like the threatening figure Odysseus outsmarted, she seduces and destroys men: "I awoke at dawn, thrown up on a rock, the skeleton of a ship choked in its own sails…the sea anemones will float over my head, and the dead ships will end their voyages in my garden." However, it takes a sexual encounter with another woman, Sabina, to initiate the poetic quickening that brings about her version of Breton's opening question: "DOES ANYONE KNOW WHO I AM?" The first answer, also printed in capitals, is directed to Sabina: "I AM THE OTHER FACE OF YOU…THIS IS THE BOOK YOU WROTE / AND YOU ARE THE WOMAN / I AM."[8]

This is another decisive swerving from the Surrealist model. The otherness and the reality of Nadja are qualities essential to emphasizing the uncanniness of the coincidences she provokes. But *The House of Incest* takes place in an oneiric world where the boundaries between selves break down and fusion is possible. The documentary actuality of Breton's Paris has no place in Nin's poetic landscape, nor is there the suggestion that its inhabitants—the narrator, Sabina, Jeanne and her brothers, and the modern Christ—are autonomous beings, even though we now know they were drawn from Nin's relationships with June Miller, the aristocratic Louise de Vilmorin and her brothers, and Antonin Artaud. The speed and ferocity with which the self of the narrator finds a mirror image in the figures she encounters and absorbs them indicate the American inflection of her writing.

Naturally, some readers will object to my identification of Anaïs Nin as an American writer. Her parents were Cuban by birth; her father a Spanish pianist, her mother a Danish-French singer. She herself was born in Neuilly, outside of Paris, and lived in Europe for her first eleven years. From 1914 until 1922 she lived and studied in New York. Her childhood diaries were written in French in New York, but she soon adopted English as her written language and stayed with it until her death. Her early discovery of Emerson's "Self-Reliance" confirmed her dedication to writing and to her diary. Finally, her long, intense intellectual and sexual affair with Henry Miller, himself an American avatar of her elected artistic mentor, D. H. Lawrence, brought her to her first aesthetic maturity.

For the author of *The House of Incest*, Emerson's essay "Circles" may be a more relevant starting point than "Self-Reliance," the diarist's point of origin. In it Emerson begins: "The eye is the first circle; the horizon which it forms

---

8. Nin, *The House of Incest*. Chicago/Athens, Ohio: Swallow, 1958) pp. 15, 11, 17, 32, 26, 28 (in order of quotations).

is the second; and throughout nature this primary figure is repeated without end. It is the highest emblem in the cipher of the world."

And he concludes:

> The one thing which we seek with insatiable desire is to forget ourselves, to be surprised out of our propriety, to lose our sempiternal memory, and to do something without knowing how or why; in short to draw a new circle. Nothing great was ever achieved without enthusiasm.... Dreams and drunkenness, the use of opium and alcohol are the semblance and counterfeit of this oracular genius, and hence a dangerous attraction for men. For like reason, they ask the aid of wild passions, as in gaming and war, to ape in some manner these flames and generosities of the heart.[9]

Whitman mediates Nin's Emersonianism, as he does for many of the poetic exhibitionists of the twentieth century in America. Along with the Whitman of "The Sleepers" Nin will contradict Emerson on one point, denying that dreams are merely counterfeits of oracular genius. The new circle Nin attempts to draw for herself in *The House of Incest* is to sustain the surprise of an autonomous questing selfhood through sexual excess. Emerson would have been shocked at the libidinous reading of his rejection of limitation: "The only sin is limitation. As soon as you come up with a man's limitations, it is all over with him.... Infinitely alluring and attractive was he to you yesterday, a great hope, a sea to swing in; now you have found his shores, found it a pond, and you care not if you ever see it again." Yet his poetic mask in this instance, the "circular philosopher," discovers "the saccharine principle" in nature, and boldly declares the "inundation of the principle of good into every chink and hole that selfishness has left open, yea into selfishness itself and sin itself; so that no evil is pure, nor hell itself without its extreme satisfactions."[10] *The House of Incest* studies the extreme satisfactions of hell from the point of view of a siren mesmerized by her own sexual destructiveness. Only in the final passage do she and the other constrained inhabitants of "the house of incest" see a vision of escape in the Dance of the Woman without Arms.

For Emerson's conjunction of eye and horizon, Nin substitutes eye and water, as if the sea extended the aqueous humor:

> My first vision of earth was water veiled. I am of the race of men and women who see all things through this curtain of sea, and my eyes are the color of water.

---

9. Emerson, *Essays and Lectures*, (New York: Library of America, 1983), pp. 403, 414.
10. Ibid., pp. 406, 412.

I looked with chameleon eyes upon the changing face of the world, looked with anonymous vision upon my uncompleted self.

I remember my first birth in water. All round me a sulphurous transparency and my bones move as if made of rubber. I sway and float, stand on boneless toes listening for distant sounds, sounds beyond the reach of human ears, see things beyond the reach of human eyes. . . .

Loving without knowingness, moving without effort, the soft current of water and desire, breathing an ecstasy of dissolution.[11]

My singling out "Circles" should not imply that other Emersonian echoes have been silenced. Obviously the transparent eyeball of Nature has been recast here, and the vitalism of "Self-Reliance" is always central to Nin's writing that strives, often too breathlessly, for its "hour of vision" when "the way, the thought, the good, shall be wholly strange and new." Yet the last lines of the prose poem—the evocation of the Dance of the Woman without Arms—resounds with Emerson's "circular philosopher":

And she danced: she danced with the music and with the rhythm of
the earth's circles; she turned with the earth turning, like a disk,
turning all faces to light and to darkness evenly, dancing toward
daylight.[12]
And it echoes an ecstasy in Whitman's "The Sleepers":
I go from bedside to bedside. . . . I sleep close with the other sleepers, each
in turn;
I dream in my dream all the dreams of the other dreamers,
And I become the other dreamers.

I am a dance. . . . Play up there! the fit is whirling me fast.[13]

Such is the Whitmanesque scenario of *The House of Incest*: A series of confessional encounters excite varieties of psychic crises in the narrator after she emerges from the narcissistic pansensorium of the sea. These episodes are largely monologues, printed without quotation marks to accent the ambiguity of the speaker and prepare the agonies of fusion between the listening "I" and her lovers and guides. In the penultimate encounter, "the modern

---

11. Nin, *House of Incest*, pp. 15, 17.
12. Ibid., p. 72.
13. Walt Whitman, "The Sleepers." *Selected Poems 1855–1892: A New Edition*, ed. Gary Schmidgall (New York: St. Martin's, 1999), p. 70.

Christ," a paralytic, articulates the medieval Church's interpretation of incest as narcissism, as the addictive paralysis motivating the prose poem:

> If only we could all escape from this house of incest, where we only love ourselves in the other, if only I could save you all from yourselves, said the modern Christ.
> But none of us could bear to pass through the tunnel which led from the house into the world on the other side of the walls, where there were leaves on trees, where water ran beside the paths, where there was daylight and joy. We could not believe that the tunnel would open on daylight: we feared to be trapped into darkness again...[14]

The trajectory of *The House of Incest* is first an oscillation from sea to land, sea to land, and then an exploration of the infernal architecture of the house of incest. The oceanic passages evoke synesthesia in depicting a self-reliant oracular consciousness. The descent from the pansensual opening to the interior gallery of progressively more crippled amorists, from "the colors of the Atlantide" to night and fearsome darkness, gives the Dance of the Woman without Arms its charge.

Hugo's cinematic interpretation of this text virtually reverses its meaning without changing a word. He manages to do this by almost exclusively representing and quoting from the opening, oceanic passage, and by systematically replacing the prose poem's infernal progression with images connoting flight and ascent. Seen in terms of its literary origins, his version of the text isolates the Emersonian selfhood at the expense of the Whitmanian sexuality; it utterly divests itself of the emulation and revision of Breton's *Nadja*.

The juggling display of Hugo's editing is most evident in the final utterance of the film, the only quotation not to be found in the first chapter of the prose poem. It is from the opening paragraph of the third chapter. In the second, the narrator experienced a crisis of identity in her lesbian encounter with Sabina analogous to the tense fusion of two women Ingmar Berman would film decades later in *Persona*. Yet the only traces of this chapter in Hugo's film are images of a ship and a palm tree from its conclusion: "I was in a ship of sapphire sailing on seas of coral.... My singing swelled the sails and ripped them.... I saw the glass palm tree sway before my eyes.... Green leaves withered for me, and all the trees seemed glassily unresponsive while the glass palm tree threw off a new leaf on the very tip and climax of its head."[15]

14. Nin, *House of Incest*, p. 27.
15. Nin, Ibid., p. 33.

I mark with italics the one sentence Hugo culls from the third chapter:

I am floating again. All the facts and all the words, all images, all passages are sweeping over me, mocking each other. The dream! The
dream! The dream rings through me like a giant copper bell when I
wish to betray it. It bruises me with bat wings when I open human
eyes and seek to live dreamlessly. When human pain has struck me
fiercely, when anger has corroded me, I rise, I always rise after the
crucifixion, and I am in terror of my ascensions. THE FISSURE IN
REALITY. The divine departure. I fall. I fall into darkness after the
collision with pain, and after pain the divine departure.[16]

Instead of Nin's crystalline reduction of "As I Ebbed with an Ebb of the
Ocean of Life," in which Whitman walking on the Paumonok beach is hu-
miliatingly depleted and mocked, "Because I have dared to open my mouth
to sing at all," Hugo turns her words into an apotheosis, anger superceded by
divine afflatus, an ascension without a fall. This underscores the visual trajectory of *Bells of Atlantis*: It moves progressively from under the sea to a fusion
of sea and sunlit air and finally into the sky with aerial photography of the
Mexican coastline.

From the opening shots, Emerson's circular motif enriches the film's multilayered texture. The expanding chain of analogies with which Emerson
opened "Circles"—eye, horizon, God—were tropes for his moral interpretation that "every action admits of being outdone" in our fluid, impermanent
universe. The circles superimposed over the initial watery imagery of *Bells of
Atlantis* invoke an eye, the sun, and the expanding concentric reverberations
made by an object dropped into water, while Nin's narration suggests, at first
at least, that we are sharing the narrator's perspective through a "curtain of
sea" with her visionary power of drawing a new circle "beyond the reach of
human eyes." Such a reading of the remorseless siren-narrator as a circular
philosopher can be sustained for the whole film, just as one can read *Meshes
of the Afternoon* as a film in the first person, although it moves from an opening identification of camera and editing with the heroine's point of view to
a symbolical drama in which the camera observes her. In such a reading, the
final aerial superimposition of the coastline would be a projection of the matrix of resurrection images, in the outstretched arms of the sunbathing Nin
and in the voice-over text.

However, in addition to the structural progression of *Meshes of the Afternoon* reflected in Hugo's film, the husband's cinematic portrait of his wife

16. Ibid., p. 37.

drives a parallel psychodrama, although Hammid's appearance as an actor at the end of *Meshes of the Afternoon* makes explicit what is obfuscated in *Bells of Atlantis* since Hugo remains behind the camera. Thus, an intersubjective reading of the film must identify Hugo as the photographer, editor, and superimposer expanding his own circle around and beyond Nin's braggart siren. This interpretation makes us recast the humble, adoring filmmaker's homage to his wife's poetic gifts and erotic power as an enlarged emblem of his own capability of poetic transcendence. In its most extreme catachresis such a reorganization of the film's images would trope the filmmaker as the solar eye of the opening that dives for the siren and as the "monster" who "brought [her] up to the surface" in the penultimate utterance, artfully culled for new emphasis from the first chapter of *The House of Incest*.

Apparently Hugo and Broughton filmed Nin in the hull of a wrecked boat, walking about, swinging in a hammock, silhouetted against a sheet, and sunbathing spread-eagled against an upraised plank. The materials superimposed over these banal shots of vacation leisure are often harder to discriminate: reflections on water, reefs, gentle waves, and the coastline from an airplane. Just as he had enlisted Broughton's help in making *Ai-Ye* and filming some of *Bells of Atlantis*, Hugo considered working with Francis Lee before he called upon the talents of the veteran avant-garde filmmaker Len Lye, a pioneer of hand painting and stenciling multilayered images on film, to help him orchestrate dramatic color tints and vivid abstract—mainly circular—patterns in the superimposed images. According to James Leo Herlihy, who was staying with Hugo at the time, he ran to Lye's studio "two and three times a day," trading raw film for Lye's advice and help.

Nin was troubled by Lye's influence on the film. An extraordinary diary passage, as yet unpublished, outlines her frustrations with Hugo during the completion of the film:

> People feel such compassion for the victims of domination. I domi-
> nated Hugo artistically—I started this film [*Bells of Atlantis*] in
> Acapulco by posing in a ship wreck and suggesting super impositions
> of sea—We unconsciously turned out Part one of *House of Incest*.
> Hugo was defeated by the technicalities—just before his illness—
> When I left the film was complete except for smoothing and polishing
> all technicalities. Immediately Hugo turned to Len Lye, who, being an
> artist did not give him technical help but superimposed his abstrac-
> tions over Hugo's film so that when I returned Hugo's film—simple
> and clear at first was almost entirely obliterated. Barrons were in
> despair but found that the slightest criticism made Hugo angry—So
> that when I returned I had to take the brunt of saying: your own
> film was perfect before Len Lye's abstractions. You should have

confidence in yourself as an artist—Hugo was angry but I smoothed
him down and we continued to work—Slowly we rescued some lost
passages from the original concept. Barrons created a very original
music—electronically—Film, began to emerge. The abstractions
were better integrated. But how we worked! Hugo leaned on Louis
technically. They stayed up all night—Bebe and I gave out and fell
asleep all dressed—At 6am I would get up and make breakfast. Hugo
withstands strain amazingly—but his temper is worse than ever. He
has no friends. He treats everyone not as an equal—he demands—
Bebe finds he has changed. I am losing all my love for Hugo, all my
sympathy. I find him hard and he uses people He—
    Stop Anaïs...
    Guilt makes you hate someone—I hate Hugo most of the time...[17]

The continual motif of superimposition that gives the film its peculiar character cannot be reduced to an agon between an unseen and unheard filmmaker
and the speaking siren any more than it can be accounted as a representation of subaqueous vision, although at moments it assumes an environmental
function and at others it suggests a dialogue. In either case, by ceaselessly
thickening the film's texture, the superimposition quickens the invention of
an imaginary space in which the images resonate with the quoted poetry.

Beyond that, Hugo creates a new subtext foreign to *The House of Incest*. The
image of Nin wrapped in the hammock suggests a cocoon. By timing the appearance of the hammock with the first instances of direct sunlight in the film,
he introduces a charged movement from water into air and light. The white
hammock becomes a hot spot of light in the filmic web, as if the sun were maturing the chrysalis within. At this very moment, the circular panning movement around the decaying hulk in which the hammock is strung transfers the
opening emblems of disks and spheres to the intelligence behind the camera,
as if it were an extension of the heliotropic drawing forth of the figure that
next appears in silhouette against the screen of a cloth or sail.

This crucial development occurs with purely musical accompaniment:
Louis and Bebe Barron's exotic electronic score of eerie tremulous and ominous crescendos. Then, just before the clearest image of Nin in the film, as she
explores the hulk in sunlight, she declares the oneiric mode of the film: "This
Atlantis could only be found at night by the route of the dream." Literalizing
this claim, images of Nin supine as if sleeping in water effect a transition to
the finale where she climbs the phallic plank and stretches out her arms and

17. Anaïs Nin, unpublished diaries, UCLA, August 11, 1952.

legs to receive the sun. Hugo has not only drawn his own expanding circle around the erotic odyssey of *The House of Incest*, he has converted it to a version of Apollo's conquest of a sea nymph, illuminated by allegorical references to the creative power of cinema: the focusing light, the screen silhouette, the inventive energy of superimposition and camera movement.[18]

Through Lye and Broughton, Hugo aligned himself with the central tradition of the avant-garde cinema, and one of the most vital artistic phenomena in America when he relocated from Paris. At that time Maya Deren was its dominant spokesperson. I have already suggested that the development from the point of view of the unseen siren to the images of her as a dreamer recapitulated the structure of *Meshes of the Afternoon*. A more complex bond links *Bells of Atlantis* to Deren's *At Land* (1944), as the title suggests. It is just possible that a reading of *The House of Incest* (privately printed first in 1938) influenced Deren's vision of an alienated Aphrodite figure who comes out of the sea and experiences quasi-erotic adventures with several men and at least one woman in a quest for self-definition. But I have found no corroborating evidence of Deren's knowledge of Nin's text that early. In any case, Hugo returned the compliment by working in Deren's genre, filming Nin's oneiric emergence from the sea along with other unacknowledged debts to the film she and Hammid made together.

Nin so hated the way Deren depicted her in *Ritual in Transfigured Time* (1947) that she wanted to be cut from the film. Her narcissistic wound was so intense that it bothered her for years. Hugo thought of *Bells of Atlantis* as a redemption of Nin's cinematic image. Immediately following the premiere at the 1952 Venice Film Festival, he cabled her: "GREAT SUCCESS OLDEST ITALIAN CRITIC SAID INTERVIEWING ME TELEVISION MOST BEAUTIFUL IN FESTIVAL YOU REDEEMED FROM MAYA LOVE HUGO."[19]

---

18. In July 1952, Hugo wrote to Nin describing how the search for a title for the film inspired a crucial development in its structure: "Jim [Herlihy] had suggested 'Nativity' as a title & this gave me the idea of showing at the end the figure of the plank & across forming a cross, with a new superimposition I have made of the cocoon hammock seen through the plank away down below. I will show the arms climbing up before that but I think this makes a more dramatic and meaningful ending, followed probably with more water & recitation. We will see how it works out. But I do want your definite idea on the title." Herlihy also suggested the title *Bells of the Atlantyde*, which Nin revised to *Bells of Atlantis*.

19. His lifelong antipathy to Deren can be heard in the remarks he made at SUNY Buffalo in a public interview with Stan Brakhage. Describing the dissolution of the Independent Film Association over which he had presided, he remarked that Maya Deren was the only one who could raise funds, "which she did through young [James] Merrill whose father was the president of Merrill, Lynch, [...] and through him she got a grant for a foundation [The Creative Film Foundation] and she was the only beneficiary of the grant; so it helped her but it didn't help anybody else and that's what really broke it up because it became a Maya Deren affair, you know, which most things became when she became associated with them." Gerald O'Grady generously provided me with a tape recording of this session, recorded May 1, 1973.

In 1958, six years after *Bells of Atlantis*, the influence of *Meshes of the Afternoon* reasserted itself in Hugo's *Melodic Inversion*, which seems to be equally indebted to Kenneth Anger's *Fireworks* (1947) and *Eaux d'artifice*. In the intervening time, Nin had acted in Anger's *Inauguration of the Pleasure Dome* along with several of her closest friends in Los Angeles.

These echoes are not obvious, but they help us to establish the genre of Hugo's film as psychodrama despite the reticence and evasions that set him apart from his models in the work of Deren, Broughton, and Anger. Hugo was older, more conservative, much wealthier, and utterly lacking in the exhibitionism that characterized most of the leading artists of the emerging American avant-garde cinema of the late 1940s. In each instance, he followed up Nin's initiating contacts with them and, unlike her, kept an emotional distance from them. She elaborately orchestrated Hugo's contacts with her close friends, including these filmmakers, in order to keep her life with Pole a secret.

Bells of Atlantis had brought Hugo a mild degree of conventional success. Although it was minimal in filmmaking terms, it was sufficient to arouse Nin's jealousy—her own writings had almost no recognition before the publication of her diaries in the 1960s—and the disdain of some avant-garde filmmakers. *Bells of Atlantis* circulated as a theatrical short film for several years, in fact, until that practice died out in the early 1960s; and Hugo was a frequent guest of international film festivals, where he could pay his own way as a "producer" as well as director. There was an exotic, picturesque gloss to his films that abetted their acceptance by festival organizers and audiences otherwise alienated by the moral and aesthetic challenges posed by his more radical contemporaries.

Hugo followed *Bells of Atlantis* with *Jazz of Lights* (1954), in which he orchestrates the lights of Times Square to another electronic score of Bebe and Louis Barron as the blind street musician Moondog and Nin wander through the New York cityscape. Subsequently he had the idea of a superimposition film, made by projecting two films on top of each other, before he knew what he would film. Thinking to pursue the abstract elements of *Jazz of Lights*, he borrowed a reflecting sphere and recorded the light patterns.[20] Over the next two months, he filmed Tiffany windows and worked with Val Telberg, a photographer and filmmaker who had made collage images for an edition

---

20. Anaïs Nin (unpublished diaries, UCLA, January 18, 1957): "When I had arrived Hugo had borrowed from the window display artist of Bergdorf Goodman a sphere—one piece all mirror, like a half of a sun, and within it, rotating, a plastic planet—the concave mirror creating a thousand reflections. On this was spotted a changing color spotlight. The first night, after we had dinner, we worked on photographing this—"

of Nin's *House of Incest*, building a device to synchronize two projectors in order to refilm the superimposition of the lights and the windows. It seems as though he never considered using A and B rolls to have the superimpositions done in a laboratory. This is probably because he had intended from the beginning to project the footage through anamorphic lenses before refilming it. Unsatisfied with the experiments in Telberg's studio, he asked Hilary Harris and Leo Lukianoff to help him. Eventually he hired a young filmmaker, Allan de Forest, as a technical collaborator.

By April 1957, he decided to return to the very origins of his filmmaking. He would use the footage that survived of *The Dangerous Telescope*, which he supplemented with some new shots he took of DeVries, whom he had not seen in the intervening decade. He even commissioned Nin to have some shots taken of her in California.

De Forest thought the film should be silent. But that idea did not appeal to Hugo. He had used the Barrons' music for his previous two films, but this time he wanted something different, perhaps Haitian flute music. (Deren was an authority on Haiti; she often had Haitian musicians staying at her apartment.) Characteristically, Nin wrote in July 1957 as the film was near completion, urging that he listen to Berg, Schoenberg, and Bartók. Just as characteristically, he followed up her suggestion immediately: He thought Bartók's *Concerto for Orchestra* would be perfect until he listened to Schoenberg and developed a passion for his *Fourth Quartet for Strings*. He even considered hiring a composer to imitate it when he was temporarily stymied in his efforts to get the rights to use it in his film. This scrupulousness about music rights was unusual for avant-garde filmmakers of the 1950s. It indicates an aspect of Hugo's commercial aspirations, or fantasies, for his work.

In his August 7, 1957, letter to Nin, we can see the origin of the film's title: "I am in love with that music for this film. It is a music of "*Melodic Inversion*," & "retrograde motion", expressing perfectly all the neurotic elements of the film & it may make Schoenberg's music more understandable to some."

His immersion in the music stimulated the structural elaboration of the film by the end of the year:

> Have been using my time in listening over & over again to the
> record & have made notes of many key passages which would fit
> well. Am more and more impressed with the richness of Schoenberg's
> music & how perfectly so much of it extends the meaning of the
> images. It is almost as if he wrote it for me, or that I wrote the music.
> This is the first time I have taken charge of the music & it probably
> makes a significant opening out of my emotional sense to complement
> the purely visual that I have up till now let myself practice. This also
> corresponds to the present place of my analysis, which is concerned

with direct feeling instead of with my old habit of relying on silent images, objects and postures. A break from the "shoe on the book" to say what I mean and from the expectation that others will be expected to understand my sign language. Instead of a cry on the screen it is a sound that I make, and the chords are my own vocal chords.[21]

According to Eugene Walter, when he had helped Hugo edit a rough cut of *The Dangerous Telescope* ten years earlier, he emphasized narrative coherence over the association of images:

Of course it's very spotty. I did not have in mind a surrealist film. I had in mind a legend. A magic tale, with logical development. Even though it was fantastical, it was logical. It wasn't juxtaposed images. So often those early surrealist films are surrealist only because they never had enough money to finish the story, or weather went bad the day they wanted to finish it. So they just made something that jumps, you know, like a flea on goat.[22]

Yet, after working with Walter, Hugo had become a filmmaker who knew that the automatisms of anamorphosis and superimposition as well as the rhythms of editing could generate a more profound film than the "legend" he had abandoned. The very juxtapositions Walter scorned became the cornerstones of Hugo's art. In fact, its central limitation was the filmmaker's timidity in placing his confidence in the power of those automatisms. In the published version of her diary Nin, writing as if Hugo had full confidence in his discoveries, provided what is surely another program note or blurb for the completed film:

When Antonin Artaud first became involved with films he was exhilarated because it would be such a perfect medium for the depiction of dreams. His wish was not fulfilled. But Ian Hugo has used film to depict exactly the atmosphere, the symbolism, the lure of dreams.
Melodic Inversion is a perfect example of a haunting dream. Inversion—the process of reality unmaking itself as it makes itself, as in an hourglass. This film is a visual melodic study of transposal in which brilliantly diffused colors with fluid movements are constantly revealing moods embedded in its theme. With imaginative boldness it stands alone. Images from dreams are often too diffuse to be captured,

21. Hugo to Nin, unpublished diaries, UCLA, December 27, 1957.
22. Walter, *Milking the Moon*, p. 118.

but Ian Hugo achieves this. The passage from one image to another is accomplished almost mysteriously, as it is in dreams. Haunting footage uncoils in a special world of shimmering lights and colors.[23]

Hugo used most of this passage as a catalog entry without citing Nin. While stressing the oneiric, it discreetly avoids mentioning both the dominant techniques of the film—anamorphic distortion and superimposition—and the theme—erotic jealousy. It tells us nothing about the central ambiguity of its narrative: whether there are two or more characters in the film. We can look at its cast as one man and two women (both played by Nin), or two aspects of the same woman. Likewise, there may be two aspects of one man, underlined by the alternation of color with black-and-white negative.

At the start of *Melodic Inversion* we see a man, supine and shirtless, stroking a cat at his waist as if he were masturbating. (Anger's *Fireworks* had opened with a similar image of a young man holding a phallic fetish in the sheets of his bed.) Through a telescope he spies a woman (Nin) on a stone tower. When he climbs up to join her, she gives him something wrapped in a blue cloth. He leaves her, descending to the beach, where he seems to compose a woman's face out of jewels or stones, probably her gift. Then he spots her again in the tower, to which he ascends. She is simultaneously in the tower with him as he looks through the telescope and on the beach as the object of his observation, examining and rearranging the objects he laid out there. (In the doubling of the female figure the influence of *Meshes of the Afternoon* can be felt.) In a jealous fury the woman in the tower seizes and tramples the telescope. The man (in negative) rushes back to the empty beach. From there he watches the woman suddenly disappear from the tower. He makes a final gesture of rage and again looks through the telescope.

The synopsis I am proposing, the result of several viewings of the film, is necessarily tentative: The continual superimposition, the frequent use of negatives, and the stippling and anamorphosis of the images obfuscate the narrative.

The glowing blue cloth of Nin's kerchief becomes a fetish object in the film, suggesting both the tint and the use of fans in Anger's *Eaux d'artifice*. Behind the allusions to American avant-garde films there may be an even more substantial debt to Man Ray's surrealistic evocation of fetishism and erotic jealousy, *Etoile de mer*, in which anamorphic distortion plays a prominent role.

23. Nin, *The Diary of Anais Nin, Vol 6 (1955–66)* ed. with a preface by Gunther Stuhlmann (New York: Harcourt Brace Jovanovich 1977), p. 119.

The "inversion" of the film's title acknowledges the formal influence on the film of dodecaphonic music, where the substitution of a corresponding descending interval for every ascending interval, and vice versa, eliminates tonality. Nin's hourglass metaphor aptly describes the inversion of actors and actions in the film's dreamscape. Psychologically, the scenario of the dream inverts or defensively projects his erotic jealousy onto the figure played by Nin.

Hugo sent her a letter with an intriguing, admittedly ad hoc, interpretation of the film:

> You were concerned that I might be putting in the shot of Bob emerging from the father figure merely under the influence of the analysis. I don't think so. I think it fits artistically also & that such a shot is necessary to explain why or how the boy comes to see the woman as she is, without the super-impositions, of which the most important is the father.
>
> Actually I got the idea on Thursday when Katrina invited me to meet a young Japanese filmmaker who wanted me to explain to him what I was attempting to convey by my film. I had to talk to him through a teacher of Japanese at Columbia (very intelligent) and in trying to do this I said that the underlying theme was that of the male principle, of what it means to be a man, & that is to be able in a positive way to attain the goal he sets for himself—whatever that may be. Whether a man is successful in representing & living out this principle depends on the role he assigns to the image of his father—that of a horse or rider. If the father is to be like a strong horse whose strength he can use & direct—there is no limit to the goals he can attain. If the father is like a rider & the man is the horse that is ridden, with spurs & whip—the man, as in the film, will fail as a man by frustrating his own desires, because they will be dually directed. So I think it is of great importance for the point of view of the story itself to at least show that the young man understands that the father is not his father in reality, but only the father *in himself*, to show the dissolution of this ghost, and the emergence of himself from the mask. By then, after looking at himself as he is, he can see the woman as she is.[24]

Even with this prompting it is not clear what Hugo means by "Bob [De-Vries] emerging from the father figure." He seems to be referring to one of

24. Hugo to Nin, unpublished diaries, UCLA, February 15, 1958.

the penultimate moments of the film when the superimpositions briefly disappear to reveal the male figure in negative. That is when he looks to the tower to see the woman disappear or fall.

A passage in Nin's unpublished diaries from the same period on the psychodynamics of triangulation does not refer to the film but offers some insight into the allusion to a father figure and the allegory of the horse and whip:

> In New York Hugo was working with success, but still depressed. And I was investigating for both of us it seemed the theme of the TRIANGLE.
>
> In neurotic relationships there are never *two*—*There is always* a third person.
>
> ...It is not the other man, for Hugo, the rival, the younger man (in his dreams). This is a mask for the true triangle of our lives. Anaïs and her father and mother. Hugo and his father and mother. He is the young man fearful of defeat, crushed by the union of the other two, jealous, seeking to divide them and possess one.... *He* is the young man who tried to get rid of his father (he tried to horsewhip him when his father came from Puerto Rico) and possess his mother. So when I appear, he has already been defeated. A young man will arise to punish him in the same way.[25]

Additionally, Nin left a passing comment on her influence on the editing of *Melodic Inversion*:

> He wanted to put my name on his new film because it was I who suggested representing reality and the present in color, and the past and ghostly fantasies in black and white negative printing.
>
> I said such a mere suggestion or inspiration "was not enough"—I had merely started him—[26]

In his 1971 interview with Stan Brakhage, Hugo elaborated on the meaning he attributed to the black-and-white negative, as he employed it, without any reference to a father figure: "I wanted the effect of death there, and the bloodlessness of this young man...a sudden...a kind of death, where the blood runs out of him: he's left white...in the face of required action. That's where the woman dies, over the tower."[27]

---

25. Nin, unpublished diaries, UCLA, 1957.
26. Nin, unpublished diaries, UCLA, May 29, 1957.
27. Stan Brakhage, interview with Ian Hugo (see note 19, above).

That an action is "required" or even that "the woman dies" is far from evident in the film. The central event of *Melodic Inversion* is the destruction of the telescope. Clearly the machine of vision is a symbol of male sexuality here. This "phallic joke," as Eugene Walters had called it, had a contemporary narrative exfoliation in Alfred Hitchcock's *Rear Window* (1954). We do not know if Hugo ever saw the film or if he did, whether it reminded him of *The Dangerous Telescope*. However, it is clear in Hitchcock's film that the power and violence of a "father figure" excites the protagonist's masturbatory fascination with looking at his neighbors through the lens of his still camera, arousing the jealousy of his girlfriend.

Hitchcock's plot carefully orchestrates a climactic scene of "required action" in which the spying photographer must fend off his murderous neighbor. But Hugo radically displaced his version of the Oedipal scenario into the rhythmic structure of his film—the variations on the ascent and descent to and from the tower—and into the visual texture of the superimpositions and the negative. The penultimate shot of single-layered negative gets its emphasis from its context: After the destruction of the telescope, the man rapidly descends to the beach, in negative with superimpositions. Then as he gazes at the ground where the jewel or pebble design had been, in a posture somewhat reminiscent of Caravaggio's *Narcissus*, his negative image reappears as a superimposition. When he looks up, the superimpositions disappear, leaving, for the only time in the film, a vivid white negative of his head. In the brief sequence that follows it, the man relapses into his voyeurism. Apparently Hugo believed the meaning of the film depended on this moment, which he shot with DeVries in 1957. His two glosses—emergence from the father to see the woman as she is (1947); the morbid bloodlessness of paralysis in the face of a necessary action (1971)—attempt to explicate the graphic power he discovered immanent in the figurative language of the cinematic materials. The conjunction of the interiorized father and "the effect of death there" suggests that Whitman's inescapable sea chant, "As I Ebb'd with the Ocean of Life," haunts this film too, yet so massively disguised that we need Hugo's scattered commentaries to reveal it despite the littoral location and the image protagonist "baffled, balk'd bent to the very earth."

CHAPTER 3

Stan Brakhage's Autobiography as a Cinematic Sequence

Stan Brakhage was the youngest of the great generation of American avant-garde filmmakers who came to cinema during and after the Second World War. Deren, Anger, Peterson, Broughton, Markopoulos, Harry Smith, Harrington, Maas, and Menken had made their mark before him, but he was quick to catch up. Between 1952 and his death in 2003, Brakhage made approximately 350 films, some shorter than a minute long and one more than four hours. Naturally in this immense oeuvre the short films predominate; the majority fall between ten and forty minutes. Until 1964 he completed one or two films a year (that he made four in 1959 was an exception and a sign of a major breakthrough in his art); subsequently the norm was closer to five annually. In the 1990s he sometimes made ten or more a year. Even Andy Warhol's astonishing fecundity is dwarfed in comparison when we consider that his work was largely over once he photographed a film—for he never edited and rarely even had to assemble or order reels—and that his most intense productivity was limited to five years (1963–68).

The scale of Brakhage's filmography requires some division into periods to facilitate discussion. In proposing a periodization here, I am merely offering a crude framework.[1] I take the first six years, from *Interim* (1952) to *Anticipation of the Night* (1958), his first major work, to be Brakhage's apprenticeship to his art. These initial works were predominantly psychodramas: often fantasies of suicide motored by sexual frustration and adolescent despair. He employed a limited version of the bodily camera movement Menken perfected before he ever knew her work; but it was a commission from Joseph Cornell to film New York's Third Avenue El before it was torn down that inspired his recognition of the rhythmic and structural potential of vehicular motion (*The Wonder Ring*, 1955). The experience of making *The Wonder Ring* seems to have revealed to him how he might use and expand upon Menken's visual rhetoric, which became the basis of *Anticipation of the Night*. Within a few years he began to explore the syntactical use of superimposition, which he learned from Ian Hugo. He so thoroughly mastered somatic camera movement and superimposition that they became the hallmarks of his style, along with a mode of rapid editing suggestive of peripheral vision.

His marriage to Jane Collom at the end of 1957 coincided with a surge of invention and increased authority from the four films of 1959 (*Wedlock House: An Intercourse*, *Window Water Baby Moving*, *Cat's Cradle*, and *Sirius Remembered*) in which he explored the possibilities of the cinematic crisis lyric, which he had largely invented himself, to *Dog Star Man* (1961–64) and its four-and-a-half-hour exfoliation, *The Art of Vision* (1965). He abandoned what he had called *drama*, a complex term that included the use of actors and staged fantasies, to concentrate on sights he encountered in his routine daily life. Eros and death (but no longer suicide) continued to be his central themes, along with a new preoccupation with childbirth—he filmed the arrival of the three children Jane bore during that period. Animal life (and death) too became the focus of several films, inspired by Jane, a passionate naturalist. During this time of fervor and enthusiasm he completed and published his most important theoretical volume, *Metaphors on Vision* (1964).

When Emerson extolled poverty in "Experience," he wrote of a spiritual divestment that would underwrite a self-reliant, utterly American, mode of vision:

> And we cannot say too little of our constitutional necessity of seeing things under private aspects, or saturated with our humors. And yet is the God the native of these bleak rocks. That needs makes in morals

---

1. Paul Arthur has questioned the viability of "even a cursory attempt to summary the trajectory" of Brakhage's career in "Qualities of Light: Stan Brakhage and the Continuing Pursuit of Vision," *Film Comment* 31, no. 5 (September–October 1995), p. 69.

the capital value of self-trust. We must hold hard to this poverty, however scandalous, and by more vigorous self-recoveries, after the sallies
of action, possess our axis more firmly.[2]

Brakhage, the most Emersonian of our filmmakers, struggled to make a
virtue of his self-trust and of the technological poverty forced on him by his
dire economic situation in the next phase of his career (1964–70). When the
theft of his 16 mm equipment from a car in New York City curtailed the flood
of highly original short lyrical films in 1964, he turned to inexpensive 8 mm
filmmaking and a series of thirty *Songs* (1964–69), until his elaborate editing
and printing drove him into serious debt. One solution to these costs was
painting on film: *The Horseman, The Woman, and the Moth* (1968). By the
end of the 1960s his severe poverty was slightly eased by minuscule production grants and exhausting lecture tours. To the abiding subjects of birth, sex,
death, and animals he added a vigorous exploration of cinematic portraiture
and an increasing attention to landscapes.

He was living with his wife and then five children in a very small cabin,
purchased by his in-laws, high in the Colorado Rockies, initiating a large-scale
autobiography in 16 mm, of which the four-part *Scenes from Under Childhood* and *The Weir-Falcon Saga*, itself in three parts, were completed by 1970.
His project, tentatively called *The Book of the Film*, was to have been, he
half-humorously predicted, a twenty-four-hour film. Initially he conceived
the autobiography as generalized and emblematic: His observations of his
young children would provide the visual materials for an allegory of the
growth of his mind, as well as stimulate his buried memories.

The economic, professional, and political tensions of his life in the first
half of the 1970s forced him into even greater spiritual loneliness than he
had known as a beginning filmmaker or subsequently as an impoverished
pioneer. Institutional interest and support for avant-garde cinema increased
greatly but superficially during this period. Although Brakhage did benefit
from the newly opened teaching positions, regional programming initiatives,
state and federal endowments, and critical attention in academic journals,
his rewards were not commensurate with the relative scale of his achievement
and influence. Yet conversely his work drew disproportionate criticism. The
incessant teaching and lecturing he had to do to keep his family together
brought him into frequent contact and conflict with audiences in ideologi-
cal opposition to his films and his aesthetics. His vehement insistence that
there was no place for propaganda or partisan argument in works of art made

2. Ralph Waldo Emerson, *Essays and Lectures* (New York: Library of America, 1983), pp. 489–90.

him a target for left-leaning theoreticians, feminists, and the critics of canon formation.

With the help of the Carnegie Institute in Pittsburgh he made three films he thought of as documentaries, very personal views of a day in a police patrol car, another in a hospital operating theater, and the most startling, a day at the morgue (*eyes, Deus Ex, The Act of Seeing with One's Own Eyes*, 1971). A series of *Sexual Meditations* (1970–72) pictured his erotic fantasies when he slept in motels on lecture tours; in making these too he had indirect institutional help: Students in the colleges he visited willingly served as nude models. During the same years he made his first personal autobiography: *Sincerity (reel one)* (1973) uses childhood photographs, the environs of Dartmouth College (which he attended for a semester before quitting to make films), and filmed snippets of the making of his first film. He also created a number of "tone poems" that embodied his emerging theory of "moving visual thinking," the cinematic mimesis of elusive cognitive acts.

The harsh irony of this period, from 1970 to 1974, was that institutional support transformed but did not alleviate substantially his marginal economy. It is true that he was asked by the Art Institute of Chicago to give courses every spring semester: They paid his travel expenses and a rather high salary for the eight trips—every other week—he made from Colorado. But it added up to less than a poorly paid full-time teaching position. A sputtering trickle of grants and the distribution of his films through the filmmakers' cooperatives in New York and San Francisco helped sustain his impressive productivity only with dramatically increasing debts to film laboratories. This period culminated in the completion of his long abstract film, *The Text of Light* (1974)—wholly composed of luscious splays of light refracted through a crystal ashtray. It was the paradigm of his inward turn at the time.

Brakhage provided the following catalog note for *Duplicity: Reel No. 1* (1978):

> A friend of many years['] acquaintance showed me the duplicity
> of myself. And, midst guilt and anxiety, I came to see that duplic-
> ity often shows itself forth in semblance of sincerity. Then a dream
> informed me that *Sincerity IV*, which I had just completed, was
> such a semblance.... I saw that the film in question demonstrated
> a duplicity of relationship between the Brakhages and animals
> (Totemism) and environs (especially trees), visiting friends...and
> people-at-large.[3]

---

3. *Film-makers' Cooperative Catalogue No. 7* (New York: Film-makers' Cooperative, 1989), p. 56,

Again he refracts Emerson, who wrote in his essay "Friendship": "Every man alone is sincere. At the entrance of a second person, hypocrisy begins."[4] This note, with its Emersonian echo, suggests the inward and self-critical turn Brakhage's cinema took in the late 1970s.

The autobiographical series *Sincerity I–V* (1973–80) and *Duplicity I–III* (1978–80) dominate the next period, in which he sustained for the most part the tensions and aspirations of his films of the early 1970s. Within the tiny audience for avant-garde films, interest in his work began to ebb; younger spectators were more excited by eccentric narratives, political messages, and the use of language both on soundtracks and as a structuring principle. Brakhage had insisted on the aesthetic purity and visual intensification of silence since 1956, experimenting with soundtracks merely four times until a change of stance in the late 1980s. In an extreme and problematic extension of his confidence in the truth of vision, by making *The Governor* (1977), an hour-long silent scrutiny of Colorado Governor Richard Lamm at work and at home, he tried to apply the experience of his Pittsburgh films to "a study of light and power" as an optical examination of politics, personally observed. Finally, a number of quarrels with colleagues and rivals were making Brakhage in his forties the Isolato of moving visual thinking.

Most of his energetic output of films in the 1980s reflected the prolonged crisis culminating in the end of the marriage in which he had been so invested as an artist and polemicist. The key documents representing aspects of that agony would be *Tortured Dust* (1984), a four-part film of sexual tensions surrounding life at home with his two teenage sons; *Confession* (1986), depicting a love affair near the end of his marriage (1987); and the *Faust* series (1987–89), four autonomous sound films reinterpreting the legend that obsessed Brakhage throughout his career. He had begun the 1980s with two related series of silent "abstract" films—modulations of color and light without identifiable imagery—*The Roman Numeral Series* (1979–81), nine films "which explore the possibilities of making equivalents of 'moving visual thinking', that pre-language, pre-'picture' realm of the mind which provides the physical grounds for image making (imagination), thus the very substance of the birth of imagery,"[5] and *The Arabic Numeral Series* (1980–82), nineteen "abstract" films "formed by the intrinsic grammar of the most inner (perhaps pre-natal) structure of thought itself."[6] In using the metaphor of prenatal vision, Brakhage continued to arouse the opposition of some feminists who read an antiabortion polemic into these imageless films. These films would

---

4. Emerson, *Essays and Lectures*, p. 347.
5. *Brakhage Films* (print sales catalog) (Boulder, CO: Stan Brakhage, 1989), p. 18.
6. *Film-makers' Cooperative Catalogue No. 7* (New York: Film-makers' Cooperative, 1989), p. 58.

also be seen, perhaps more cogently, as the response to the trend of converting to video by a filmmaker utterly committed to the nuances and subtleties of the chemical image.

The last phase of Brakhage's filmmaking spanned from 1989, the year he married Marilyn Jull and published *Film at Wit's End*, until 2003. In the 1989 book, his most lucid and coherent since *Metaphors on Vision*, Brakhage offered his analysis of the sensibilities of eight of his contemporaries in the avant-garde cinema.

Suranjan Ganguly has extensively interviewed Brakhage on his early and late career. I quote him at length on the filmmaker's development since the mid-1980s:

> At a number of points, Brakhage re-engaged with modes of filmmaking he had earlier abandoned for personal or philosophical reasons. Thus, the four-part collaborative *Faust* project (1987–1989), which Brakhage made with a group of young Boulderites, came as a surprise from one who had always upheld the sovereignty of the artist as maker. The project also led to a revival of interest in film sound which he had virtually written off as an aesthetic error.... There was also a reversion to story and narrative in the *Faust* films.... And, finally, Brakhage turned to psychodrama after many years, because it offered him a chance to confront the psychic drama of his own mid-life crisis. Thus, not only the *Faust* films, but films like *Nightmusic* (1986), *Confession* (1986), *Kindering* (1987), *The Dante Quartet* (1987) and *I...Dreaming* (1988) are rooted in the events and emotions of this period....
>
> But already by 1988 this phase was drawing to a close and Brakhage had begun a cycle of films inspired by Marilyn: *Marilyn's Window* (1988), *[A] Child's Garden and the Serious Sea* (1991) and *Untitled Film (For Marilyn)* (1992) in which there are allusions—especially in *[A] Child's Garden*—to earlier concerns with childhood, primal sight, the beginning of consciousness, and the phenomenological discovery of the world. It is in these films that Brakhage finally frees himself from "all melodramatic self-imaginings."
>
> Brakhage was also at work on films that reflect his life-long obsession with modes of seeing.... [T]he most extensive study of this subject resulted in a multiple series Brakhage began in 1979 and completed in 1990: *The Roman Numeral Series, The Arabic Numeral Series, The Egyptian Series*, and *The Babylon Series*....
>
> Since then, Brakhage has used the camera less and less, preferring to paint on film, but without reference to his own life or his thought process or that of others. As he likes to say, film should be "about nothing

at all," and in the very short films that he's now making, sometimes at a
rate of four per month, there is a sense of an opening into the ineffable.[7]

Painting on film has been one of Brakhage's privileged strategies since 1961,
but it did not assume a dominant place in his filmography until the 1980s.
Not only did he call upon earlier options from his filmmaking for further
exploration, but he measured and questioned his development and its modes
of consistency by returning to previously fecund themes, locations, and image
associations. So the periods I have tentatively outlined are traced within a
palimpsest of filmic revisions.

In the early 1970s, when Brakhage announced that he seemed to be engaged in a long autobiographical film in many parts and series, he tended to
speak of *The Book of the Film* as an aesthetic entity he was slowly coming to
understand, in distinction from a drafted schema to be executed over years;
so he occasionally wondered aloud and publicly if a particular film of the
1970s was a piece of *The Book of the Film*, such as the following suggestively
Hegelian perspective on the first three subsections:

> It might be said that chapter 1 (*Scenes From Under Childhood*) set
> [*sic*] forth birth and being, Chapter 2 [*The Weir-Falcon Saga*]—
> consciousness, Chapter 3 (*Sincerity*)—*self*-consciousness; thus *Soldiers
> and Other Cosmic Objects* begins the strictly philosophical task of dis-
> tinguishing from, in this case, the rituals and trials of public school).[8]

However, in the 1989 catalog of his films for sale, *Brakhage Films*, he retitled the sequence *The Book of Family*, running thirteen hours and seven
minutes, and reserved the title *The Book of Film* [*sic*] for an utterly different
on-going compendium of *The Art of Vision*, the *Roman*, *Arabic*, and *Egyptian
Series*, the then just begun *Visions in Meditation* and future work. Here is his
note for the former:

> *The Book of Family* (as I think it should be called) consists of *Scenes
> From Under Childhood, Songs*, the trilogy of *The Weir-Falcon Saga*,

7. Suranjan Ganguly, "Stan Brakhage—The 60th Birthday Interview," *Film Culture* no. 78 (Summer
1994), pp. 18–19.
8. *Film-makers' Cooperative Catalogue No. 7*, p. 57. There is no evidence that Brakhage was reading Hegel's
Phenomenology of Spirit at this time. However, there is an interesting linguistic as well as formal coincidence in A. V. Miller's translation (Oxford University Press, 1977) of the dialectic of "duplicity" (Chapters
V/C.a. and VI/C.b). The "Sincerity/Duplicity" opposition occurred in a dream of 1975 [Stan Brakhage,
I. . . . Sleeping (Staten Island, NY: Island Cinema Resources, 1989), p. 19]. The earlier, Baillie translation of
the *Phenomenology* (1910) translated "dissemblance."

Sincerity and *Duplicity* (in this order: *Sincerity (reel one)*, II, *III*, *Duplicity*, I, *II*, *Sincerity IV*, *Duplicity III*, *Sincerity V*) and *Tortured Dust*. This "book" of films, following the evolving lives of the Brakhage family, has never before been screened in its entirety.[9]

The inclusion of *Songs* is even more surprising than the exclusions: *The Trip to Door* (1971, "originally intended to be a continuation of *Scenes From Under Childhood*"), *Soldiers and Other Cosmic Objects* (1977, which similarly could be considered a continuation of *The Weir-Falcon Saga*) and *Confession* ("the most extremely autobiographical documentation given me to do") which was probably left out because it represents an affair partly instrumental in the breakup of the family. Principally, the inclusion of the thirty *Songs* and their subdivisions in this cycle redefines its center away from the traditional forms of autobiography—the subject reconstructing a narrative of his history—and toward an anatomy of the Brakhages's family life in their home in mountains above Boulder Colorado, where they lived from 1964 to 1987; that is, emphasizing a site as much as a selfhood. This late, retrospective, insight into a large body of his work may resolve some of the problems posed by the *Sincerity/Duplicity* series as "autobiography." It is consistent with Brakhage's long-standing commitment to Charles Olson's poetics in which the triad "Topos/Tropos/Typos" constitutes the generative matrix of poetry. Thus *The Book of Family* would find its "topos" in Lump Gulch (Rollinsville, Colorado) as *The Maximus Poems* do in Gloucester, Massachusetts.

Nevertheless, still embedded in this monumental cycle of cycles is the three-part autobiography or "song of myself"—to impose its appropriate Whitmanian analogue on Brakhage. In *Scenes from Under Childhood, The Weir-Falcon Saga*, and the *Sincerity/Duplicity* films he approaches the problem of the education of a sensibility from three similar angles, often reusing the same archival photographic images in different contexts. The four-part *Scenes* takes as its given the daily life of a household with five children. Fusing acute observation to expressionist mimesis, it traces and projects the growth of infant perception and childhood affections while at the same time representing that developmental schema as the source of memories for the filmmaker and his wife (indicated by their childhood photographs). The autobiographical moments, then, occur as if in spontaneous, automatic memories triggered by sights, textures, and gestures from the world of the children.[10]

9. *Brakhage Films*, p. 23.

10. Phoebe Cohen, "*Scenes from Under Childhood*," *Artforum* (January 1973), pp. 51–55; Marjorie Keller, *The Untutored Eye: Childhood in the Films of Cocteau, Cornell, and Brakhage*; P. Adams Sitney, "Autobiography in Avant-Garde Film," *The Avant-Garde Film: A Reader of Theory and Criticism* (New York: NYU Press, 1978), pp. 199–246.

The Weir-Falcon Saga recapitulates the organization and socialization of consciousness as a three-part study of the illness, convalescence, and recovery of Brakhage's fifth child, Rarc. The first film, *The Weir-Falcon Saga*, alternately presents the filmmaker's anxiety and the child's fevered consciousness when he falls ill and requires hospital care. *The Machine of Eden* takes advantage of spots of light on the camera lens, blurring swish pans of the landscape of the Rockies, and the optical phenomena in the room where the child lies in bed (featuring a loom) to suggest a myth of creation. *The Animals of Eden and After* continues this trope, articulating a theory of metaphor in which the child regains his strength as he unconsciously differentiates himself from the animals he sees, making them emblems of his emotions, and eventually generalizing these emblems into an abstraction of the state. In order to return to school he must recover from the visionary dissolution of boundaries between self and other, put off cosmological fantasies, and master the hierarchical distinctions that make a symbolical currency of things at the cost of their sensual uniquenesses.

Then in the eight *Sincerity/Duplicity* films Brakhage focuses on first himself and then himself and Jane as fictive constructions of cinema and memory. The series is so complex, difficult, and nuanced that it challenges synopsis; the problem of identifying some of the characters who appear in it or even of catching Brakhage's attitude toward them contributes to their moments of obscurity; but above all the visual and rhythmic tonalities of the last four sections—a masterful ascesis with enigmatic ellipses and charged synecdoches—suggest a drama of referential allusions and conflicting affects that almost makes the films hermetic. These are the very obstacles Brakhage had complained made reading Blake and Pound, two poets he venerated, daunting to him.

The first reel utilizes a visit to Dartmouth College as the occasion for an attempt to remember and re-create the psychic crisis that drove him from the college and made him a filmmaker. It culminates in glimpses of the production of *Interim*. The second reel reconstructs his relationship with Jane Collom from the first images he had taken of her as a student in a filmmaking class he taught through their marriage and their cross-country movements until they acquired their home in Rollinsville. By the end of *Sincerity V* it is apparent that Jane is the object and focus of the whole series; Brakhage's love, and its betrayals, the subject. The cycle begins with the making of *Interim* (a psychodrama of erotic longing) and it analyzes, sometimes ruthlessly, the growth and countercurrents of the filmmaker's capacity for love: first as an Oedipal longing sublimated into filmmaking, then fixed on Jane (mediated by filmic images), and next its vicissitudes as it extends to their five children, who dominate the three *Duplicity* films.

Brakhage told Gerald Barrett and Wendy Brabner, the authors of *Stan Brakhage: A Guide to References and Resources*, that a friend said, "his biography stopped after he and his family settled in Lump Gulch."[11] The third part of *Sincerity* reflects this notion: The diachrony constructed and critically exposed in the first two reels gives way to a synchronous portrait of family life with the filmmaker centered at his editing table; that is, he reveals himself constructing the synchrony as artificially as he had made up the diachrony.

The tour-de-force editing of this segment utilizes the full musical range of Brakhage's style in the 1970s: He fluidly passes through black and white and color, positive and negative, slow motion and stop action, enriched with swish pans, flares, fades, and minute shifts of focus, giving a wholly unique rhythmic signature to his work—a Brakhage rubato. Early in the film, one can discern traces of a debt to Peter Kubelka's use of negative and positive in *Adebar*, and, as if in acknowledgment of it, one can even discern a shadow image of Kubelka himself. But the differences between their rhythms are more distinctive than their affinities. Kubelka mastered an isometric montage, with serial rigor, in his three metrical films, *Adebar*, *Schwechater*, and *Arnulf Rainer*. In order to give the strongest possible accent to every change of shot in his microrhythmic system, Kubelka reduced his images first to rigid graphic outlines, and then to mere black and white frames. Brakhage, however, maximized the possibility of contracting and expanding thematic phrases with imperceptible boundaries, so that images, often difficult to discern, surge, glimmer, halt, or barely emerge from a constantly throbbing visual magma. In *Sincerity III* he shares Kubelka's consistent rejection of diachronrous editing, but even here with different interpretation. Kubelka's cinema posits a denial of history, asserting the identity of contemporary and Neolithic man. Brakhage's diachrony reflects his "sincere" allegiance to moving visual thinking, the product of his apperceptive study.

The intensity of his effort to acknowledge with "sincerity" the cinematic illusion of the self as an envisioned character or the family members as personae opened up the negative recognition of the "duplicity" of his project and its psychological detriments. The first *Duplicity* reel heaps together glimpses of foolish, hypocritical, and painful activities in the Brakhage household and menagerie. After exhaustively cataloging these subtle humiliations, Marie Nesthus concluded: "Here must lie the most devious because most intimate duplicity—that of Brakhage toward his own family. The inescapable duplicity for him as an artist is to use those he loves most as the objects of his art, to

11. Gerald R. Barrett and Wendy Brabner, *Stan Brakhage: A Guide to References and Resources* (Boston: GK Hall, 1983), p. 37.

construct his truth from their faces and lives, implicitly subordinating their truths in the process."[12] His note on the second part of *Duplicity* would direct our attention to a much more subtle matter altogether, pointing out that the reel "is composed of superimpositions much as the mind 'dupes' remembered experience into some semblance of, say, composed surety rather than imbalanced accuracy—as thought may warp 'scene' into symmetry, or 'face' into multitudinous mask."[13] Brakhage is again imbuing a familiar cinematic trope with a new meaning: here slowly dissolving superimpositions as the duplicity of remembered scenes.

After the marriage itself had ended, Brakhage reflected:

> [A]fter the second marriage, I felt strong desire to *have* my life rather than photograph it.... I underestimated the historical flypaper I was stuck in. I didn't realize until much later how people in their daily living imitate the narrative-dramatic materials that infiltrate their lives through the radio, TV, newspapers, and, certainly, the movies....
> Despite all the evolutions of my film grammar and my inclusion of hypnogogic and dream vision, [my films] were still tied to the more traditional dramatic-narrative framework. Moreover, while shooting I would ask Jane and the children to keep quiet to be still, very basic things, but that pushed everything back toward drama. And then, although they were used to being photographed, they knew, like most people, when their picture was being taken, and that became a factor in what they did before the camera.... As a result, their childhoods were distorted in subtle and dangerous ways.... when an artist mixes his working process with his daily life then there is a psychological imposition on other people who are involved.... So while I certainly achieved a better relationship vis-à-vis the children in the act of making those films than what I had inherited, it didn't go as far as I would have hoped—all of which goes to show why the 29-year-old marriage, much celebrated in print and constant point of reference within my art-making, finally collapsed.[14]

By making *Sincerity IV* the next segment, Brakhage suggests that the truth of self-reflective duplicity is a return to sincerity, just as the self-reflexive truth of sincerity had been duplicity. In ever-optative terms derived from Emerson, we could say that with each acknowledgment of duplicity and self-recovery, he

12. Marie Nesthus, *Stan Brakhage*, Filmmakers Filming 1 (St. Paul, MN: Film in the Cities, 1979), p. 11.
13. *Film-makers' Cooperative Catalogue No. 7*, p. 56
14. Ganguly, "Stan Brakhage," pp. 19–21.

repossesses the axis of sincerity more firmly. Both thematically and formally, *Sincerity IV* recapitulates the oscillation by which Brakhage extended the *23rd Psalm Branch* of *Songs* in its second part, "To Source." There the section "My Vienna" had been an alternative to the preceding portrait of Peter Kubelka and his daughter, Marille ("Kubelka's Vienna"), and a mediation-at-a-distance on the first part of the film's representation of family life during the Vietnam War. In a reductive effort to find minimal equivalents to the filmmaker's moving visual thinking about his home as he travels to lecture, *Sincerity IV* enforces a radical cessation of the modes of cinematic knowledge invoked in the five previous sections: diachronous memory stirred by a place, diachrony constructed of home movie clips, polyrhythmic synchrony, denunciation of the self, and doubt cast on the possibility of sincere cinematic knowledge. First from the welter of shadows, silhouettes, and partial objects he grasps some clear images of Jane and her animals and then the children gradually become differentiated. They all look older than before; the stark, ascetic tone of the film hints that the filmmaker desperately needs to see them as they are, free even of the earlier images he made of them, and separated from a mysterious association through montage with black-and-white images of young women and men not seen previously in the series. Within the overall context of the series' meditations on the inescapable, intrusive presence of the filmmaker, these images project a fantasy of seeing his home when he is not present. Then Brakhage turns the suddenly anchored camera unflatteringly on himself, sometimes naked, in a Chicago hotel room where, it seems, he has an affair with an unidentifiable woman.

The third *Duplicity* returns us to the social environment of the end of *The Animals of Eden and After*: the routines of school, banal theatricals, imitative play with masks, and the observation of animals. In this context, the familiar prophetic energy Brakhage often directed against the institutions of socialization implicitly condemns himself, as a parent who lets his children endure the formation he deplores. Even the note he supplies could be read as itself a duplicitous evasion, or an excuse for the inevitability of all the duplicity he found in his project: "Obvious costumes and masks, Drama as an ultimate play-for-truth, and totemic recognition of human *animal* life-on-earth dominate all the evasions duplicity otherwise affords."[15]

Sincerity V seems at first to continue *IV*. Brakhage is still traveling, but gradually it becomes clear that much time has passed: We can see that the children have entered their teens. The filmmaker borrows a trope from Jonas Mekas's *Reminiscences of a Journey to Lithuania* to end the film and the series

---

15. *Film-makers' Cooperative Catalogue No. 7*, p. 56.

with a symbolic conflagration. However, he precedes the images of a burning house and forest fire with glimpses of another disaster: an overturned car
being hoisted from the rapids of a river. Flood and fire, suggestions of apocalyptic destruction that show up in daily life, announce the (premature) closure of the autobiographical project with imagery complementing the Edenic
allusions of *The Weir-Falcon Saga.*

In shaping *Sincerity IV* and *Sincerity V,* Brakhage returned to one of the
most basic, and dynamic, of montage structures operating in the American
avant-garde cinema: the sustained propelled camera. He links the two parts
across the intervening space of *Duplicity III* with a song of travel, shot from
cars and airplanes. This form-giving propulsion records the factual centrality
of travel to his economy in the 1970s, but more significantly, it brings into
his ambitious and innovative autobiographical work a generic option that
had grounded some of his strongest films and linked them through precursor
works such as Hugo's *Ai-Ye* and Menken's *Excursion* to the Emersonian aesthetics of the coach rider's liberation of the "puppet-show" of the townscape
into a spectacle of apparent being.

The eight films, taken together, form a paradigm for Brakhage's extension
of intimacy into epic, in which each element offers an unanticipated response
to the previous inspiration. For instance, in the early 1960s he thought he
would make something of the footage others had shot of him and Jane, particularly Bruce Baillie's footage of their departure from San Francisco. He was
waiting for the appropriate film. Then, in 1968 Dartmouth College invited
him to lecture; on that occasion, his first return since dropping out in 1952,
he filmed details of the campus that excited his memories. Five years later,
those images became the matrix of his autobiographical *Sincerity.* Only after
completing it did he realize that it might be continued and that he had found
the place for his collection of images of himself and Jane, but he did not know
that it would make up a separate unit until he completed it, calling it *Sincerity II;* so he renamed the Dartmouth film *Sincerity (reel one).* That, in turn,
revealed the form *Sincerity III* would take. In a like vein, the fourth part was
finished as *Sincerity IV* before he realized it was a new direction, requiring a
new title: *Duplicity.* Yet it was not then clear to him that there would be more
films of that subseries.

The major poetic sequences or minor epics produced by Americans in the
twentieth century grew in similar organic patterns: Eliot's *The Waste Land,*
Crane's *The Bridge,* Pound's *The Cantos,* Williams's *Patterson,* and Olson's *The
Maximus Poems.* More precisely, since the last three are composed of individual books, completed and published before the whole design was fashioned, the *Sincerity/Duplicity* films constitute the equivalent of one of their
component books.

CHAPTER 4

Jonas Mekas and the Diary Film

Like any grownup, he has lost his childhood; like any American, he has lost a nation and with it the God of the fathers. He has lost Walden; call it Paradise; it is everything there is to lose. The object of faith hides itself from him. He knows where it is to be found, in the true acceptance of loss, the refusal of any substitute for true recovery.[1]
— Stanley Cavell

Jonas Mekas, the great champion of the American avant-garde cinema and the founder of several of its key institutions, is the one filmmaker discussed in this book who began his filmmaking career with a 35 mm, feature-length dramatic film: *Guns of the Trees* (1962). Actually, as a critic and editor he even evinced hostility to some aspects of the native experimental cinema—in fact, the very aspects he would later risk prison promoting and defending. He has often said, with some irony, that he was driven to his diaristic mode of filmmaking because his work on behalf of other filmmakers left him no time to prepare and shoot the dramatic feature films he had initially dreamed of making. He had to photograph in spare moments, wherever he was, with no preparation. Often the footage he shot in that way would sit for years unedited. Driven in extremis by looming deadlines for a public presentation to which he had committed himself, he would assemble a film, working night after night while keeping to his daytime schedule at

1. Stanley Cavell, *The Senses of Walden* (New York: Viking, 1974), p. 50.

the Film-makers' Cooperative, *Film Culture* magazine, or Anthology Film Archives.

Since his youth, he has been an important poet in his native Lithuanian language. While assisting his brother, Adolfas, as he shot his first film, *Hallelujah the Hills* (1962) in Vermont, he used his spare moments studying William Blake's poetry and exploring the possibility of adapting the haiku form to film, as his friend Maya Deren had tried (in a work that she left incomplete and unseen when she died in 1961).

So it was during the shooting of what he would eventually title *Rabbitshit Haikus*, that Peter Beard gave him a copy of Henry David Thoreau's *Walden*. Mekas was familiar with a German translation of Thoreau he had picked up in the Displaced Persons Camps in Wiesbaden some sixteen years earlier, but the original would soon strike him with the power of a discovery. Recently graduated from Yale, Beard was about to publish *The End of the Game*, a book of African wildlife photography. Shortly after Jerome Hill, Beard's uncle, had introduced him to the Mekases, Adolfas asked him to play a leading role in *Hallelujah the Hills*.

There are images of Mekas reading Blake in the *Haikus*, just as he had shown himself studying Shelley's *Prometheus Unbound* in *Guns of the Trees*. In fact, he would even run the camera over a page of his book, aware that the focus of a few words from several vertical lines could not be read in sequence by the film viewer, but to emphasize the importance of the text without isolating a legible passage. Indirectly, these moments affirm the centrality and privacy of reading, its refractive preservation from the intrusions of cinema. He eventually would do the same with Thoreau's text in his own *Walden*.

Diaries, Notes, and Sketches (1969), Mekas's continuing film of many autonomous parts, his life work in cinema, began neither as *Walden* nor as a volume of film diaries. When he started shooting it, he had the idea of representing New York through the eyes of an adolescent girl. He studied some of the letters and diaries of teenagers and filmed a few girls—the daughters of friends and colleagues, babysitters who worked for producers David and Barbara Stone—in Central Park. He also had in mind subsequent films of the fictional diaries of men and women ten, twenty, thirty years older than the initial fifteen-year-old girl. All that remains of this project, his final fantasy of cinematic ventriloquism, are the screen tests of the young women in the park, which nearly bracket the completed *Walden*. The adolescent girl ceded her place as the protagonist of the film to the filmmaker himself, first seen playing his accordion-like boyan, then heard on the soundtrack. Her diminished status resulted initially from the multiplicity of adolescent figures: All the tests were used, so that these women become the fleeting objects of the filmmaker's attention, rather than the figures through whom he views New York. Because they are not identified by intertitles, they have less stature in the film than his named colleagues and friends. Nevertheless, they haunt the film as weighted charges, nodes of emotional investment for which the filmmaker does not account.

A similar instance of apparently hermetic encrypting can be explicated easily in retrospect. At the climax of the central "VISIT TO BRAKHAGES" an intertitle exclaims "I FIND RABBIT SHIT!" The release of *Lost, Lost, Lost* (1976) seven years later glossed this odd climax doubly, by bringing to light *Rabbitshit Haikus* and by telling the parable of the quest for the end of the road.

The allusion, then, is an outcropping of the autobiographical narrative Mekas excluded from *Walden* in order to ground the film in the rhythms and fluidities of daily life. However, the viewer of 1968, knowing nothing of this history, would be confronted with a sprawling, paratactic film so long its overall argument, its very shape, would be difficult to ascertain. Thoreau's *Walden* was an account of an experiment, a new life; the description of an isolated place as scenery for the acts of the self; the meditations of an obsessive journal keeper in one diffuse but well-contained essay. Mekas's film follows its nameskae metaphorically in chronicling the author's daily life, making New York (and emblematically its Central Park) the focus of observations for an isolato lodged in a single room at the Chelsea Hotel, and recasting the diary form as an essay on life as art, identifying just enough of the events and the characters to keep the roiling superabundance of what remains unnamed an issue.

Here the filmmaker represented himself as bold and cheerful, with melancholic moments. At times he would clown, play the fool (but never as blatantly as in *Lost, Lost, Lost* or *In Between*, 1978). Early on, he chants his mock cogito: "I live, therefore I make films. I make films, therefore I live. Light. Movement. I make home movies, therefore I live. I live, therefore I make home movies," and then sings:

> They tell me I should be searching.
> But I am only celebrating what I see.
> I am searching for nothing.
> I am happy.

That this euphoria is defensive had already been hinted by an intertitle, "MORBID DAYS OF NEW YORK & GLOOM," and a recorded conversation with Barbara Stone in which she told him she had dreamed he died. He replied: "What's this? I won't, not even thought of it. I never felt better in my life!" Over the long exfoliation of the film, Mekas's verbal interventions gradually turn more somber. His final speech, ten minutes from the end, returns to morbid gloom: "I wanted to take the subway. They don't take five-dollar bills now. I walked into the Hector's. They have a minimum. I took a pie, a terrible pie.... The place was so sad my whole body trembled. The pie stuck in my mouth."

Here as elsewhere in the film, Mekas counters his dejection with flights of exhilaration: a visit to Yoko Ono and John Lennon in Montreal holding a pajama party for peace, the birth of Blake Sitney—my son and Mekas's godson—and a finale with a girl in Central Park studying a blade of grass. His formal models are the major American autobiographical chants and reflections: *Walden,* "Song of Myself," Emerson's *Journals.* The dilations and deflations of the spirit occur suddenly, unpredictably, in these expansive works.

David James reads the end of the film as rejection of the norms of avant-garde cinema:

> In the last movement of the film, after returning from the Brakhages' home, he clarifies his own practice as one of personal perception defined not against Hollywood, but against the avant-garde, which is now revealed to be debased, commercialized, and sensationalized. The countertheme is dramatized in a longish sequence in which Adolfas directs scenes for *Hallelujah the Hills* for the benefit of a German TV crew making a documentary about underground film.... [B]itterly ridiculing and scorning what have become clichés of the underground, he returns to the photography of his daily life, asserting he shoots only for himself, and ends the film with a woman friend on a beautiful autumn day in Central Park.[2]

Although he astutely realized that the late sequence on the German TV crew is crucial to understanding the shape and tone of *Walden,* James overstated Mekas's irony and thereby skewed its focus. It is not just any German producer, but Gideon Bachmann, Mekas's collaborator from his first days in New York, who had revisited America, after spending the 1960s working in Europe, to document the movement he had missed and Mekas had guided. The filming excursion to New Jersey, in fact, replicates events from the mid-1950s Mekas will give prominence in *Reminiscences of a Journey to Lithuania* (1972) and show briefly in *Lost, Lost, Lost.*

Mekas's satyr play of an "underground movie"—"Who knows in Germany!" he says, "Let them believe that's how an Underground movie is being made, and we are having a good time"—is a metalepsis for his own obtuseness toward the native avant-garde cinema when he had been Bachmann's collaborator.

2. David E. James, *To Free the Cinema: Jonas Mekas and the New York Underground* (Princeton, NJ: Princeton University Press, 1992), p. 176.

He even worked on an aborted parody of avant-garde films with Edouard de Laurot at that time. So, we are more than two hours into *Walden* when the filmmaker indirectly represents his critical stance prior to his conversion to the avant-garde cinema. Yet all through the film there are portraits of his mentors—Marie Menken, Stan Brakhage, Hans Richter—and the filmmakers he admires: Ken Jacobs, Gregory Markopoulos, Andy Warhol, Naomi Levine, Shirley Clarke.

If we view *Walden* as a film about artistic election, these portraits play a critical role in defining the filmmaker's lineage, none more so than the central visit to the Brakhage home in the Colorado mountains where Mekas finds the icon of his unique signature, the gift of his muse, rabbit shit, even though its meaning was occult to others at that time. In his excursion to the Brakhages' he has "come to the end of the road," where he recognizes his autobiographical enterprise is a shaggy dog story. Like all shaggy dog stories, its point is the prolongation of its narrative, not its telos.

Early in *Metaphors on Vision*, which Mekas published, Brakhage wrote of Georges Méliès:

> One may, out of incredible courage, become Méliès, that marvelous man who gave even "the art of film" its beginning in magic. Yet Méliès was not witch, witch doctor, priest, or even sorcerer. He was a 19th-century stage magician. His films *are* rabbits.... In the event you didn't know "magic" is realmed in "the imaginable," the moment of it[sic] being when that which is imagined dies, is penetrated by mind and known rather than believed in. Thus "reality" extends its picketing fence and each is encouraged to sharpen his wits. The artist is one who leaps the fence at night, scatters his seeds among the cabbages, hybrid seeds inspired by both the garden and wits-end forest where only fools and madmen wan[d]er.[3]

However, in the last chapter of the same book, he criticized Mekas for using the same commonplace metaphor of artist as fool:

> Even tho' you said it was a joke, I could not help but be bothered by your referring to the Co-Op as a "monastery of fools." ... I think the time has come to abandon this Neanderthal form of pardon for insistence upon support for creative endeavor. I think the time has come to throw off The Fool's Cap.[4]

3. Stan Brakhage, *Metaphors on Vision* (New York: *Film Culture* no. 30, 1963), pages unnumbered.
4. Ibid.

In many of his self-representations in *Diaries, Notes and Sketches* (not just *Walden*), Mekas plays the fool. Pointing out the rabbit shit so emphatically is just such a gesture. Doing it at the climax of the "VISIT TO BRAKHAGES" is an act of self-assertion and poetic autonomy in the face of his most powerful precursor.

The chant about home movies is a fool's cogito. *Home* is the complex word in that formula; for when Mekas raises making intimate, amateur films to an existential principle, he is also confessing that making films of home is his mode of living. But what does *home* mean in this film? The second use of the word in *Walden* initiates a dramatic cut: After an opening invocation of spring that included a portrait of filmmakers "TONY CONRAD AND BEVERLY GRANT AT THEIR SECOND AVENUE HOME," he shows himself in bed, unable to sleep; the title, "I THOUGHT OF HOME," suddenly introduces an idyllic scene of boats on a pond (actually in Central Park), followed immediately by the title "WALDEN" and the first of the adolescent girls fondling a flower in the park. The editing equates home and Walden, suggesting they conjoin in a remote, inaccessible, or lost place, radiated by an idealized light of memory (and yet illustrating that it is a mere forty blocks away from his room in the Chelsea Hotel).

The passage from Emerson's *Nature* to which I return again and again in this book occurs in the chapter "Idealism." In a five-tiered analysis of "the delicious awakenings of the higher powers," nature blossoms into thought. The first tier, nature's conspiracy with spirit, entails the series of kinetic exercises, democratically available to artist and layman, I have read here as fundamental to our native aesthetics: views from a balloon, a moving carriage, a railroad car, in a camera obscura, or with your head between your legs. (Poetry, philosophy, science, and religion are Emerson's four subsequent stages in this process of idealist education.) But of the first and most accessible stage, he writes:

> In these cases, by mechanical means, is suggested the difference between the observer and the spectacle,—between man and nature. Hence arises a pleasure mixed with awe; I may say, a low degree of the sublime is felt from the fact, probably, that man is hereby apprized, that, whilst the world is a spectacle, something in him is stable.[5]

In the montage fragment beginning with "I THOUGHT OF HOME" Mekas achieves "a low degree of the sublime," realizing and demonstrating

---

5. Ralph Waldo Emerson, *Essays and Lectures* (New York: Library of America, 1983), p. 34.

the flexibility of titles and images ready to hand in negotiating the transfer from sensual immediacy to reflection.

Much later in the film, he addresses the viewer on an aspect of this exchange:

> And now, dear viewer, as you sit and watch and as the life outside in
> the streets is still rushing.... The images go, no tragedy, no drama, no
> suspense. Just images, for myself, and for a few others... these images,
> which I figure, as life will continue, won't be here for very long.... No
> boats in the morning, and maybe not even trees, nor flowers, at least
> not in such an abundance. This is Walden, this is Walden, what you see.

If Walden is a name for home, and for what you see, it is a state of mind, an investment in the present moment just as it is undergoing revaluation under the threat of destruction. In later volumes of the film diary, he will sometimes call this state paradise. The staccato cinematography, orchestrating abrupt changes in the apparent pace of things, is the "mechanical means" for suggesting "the difference between the observer and the spectacle," a difference that turns the spectacle of the world into "image, for myself and for a few others."

But nowhere in the film is home explicitly associated with the Lithuania of his childhood. In fact, there is no mention of Lithuania per se in *Walden*. The Lithuanian word for meadow appears in an intertitle in the long episode "A TRIP TO MILLBROOK": at Timothy Leary's rural retreat he films a girl playing in a meadow with the title "LAUKAS, A FIELD, AS WIDE AS CHILDHOOD." An hour later we read "AT TABOR FARM LITHUANIANS DANCED TILL SUNRISE," while the voice-over, beginning to find the somber tone that will dominate the end of the film, remarks on his lack of dreams and fear of walking barefoot: "Am I really losing slowly everything I had brought with me from the outside?" "The outside" is a remarkable periphrasis for his Baltic youth and an unstated structuring principle in the film. The filmmaker does not inform us that Tabor Farm, near Chicago, is the site of an annual Lithuanian festival. *Reminiscences of a Journey to Lithuania* and *Lost, Lost, Lost* will gloss many of these covert allusions.

The very absence of explicit autobiographical information becomes a trope of intimacy. The first of several weddings, eight minutes into the film, is the only one utterly unidentified, yet it is the most important one for the film. His brother, Adolfas, married Pola Chapelle in 1965. "AL MOVES OUT" follows the wedding. There is an image of an empty apartment, and then an abrupt jump to the filmmaker in France, "BREAKFAST IN MARSEILLES." Thus he elliptically and antidramatically represents the change in his life that is the fundamental ground for the whole film: For the first time Mekas begins to live alone.[6] Thus, his *Walden* begins with this almost tacit, certainly stoical acceptance of a mode of solitude. Adolfas had shared his flight from Lithuania, forced labor and displaced person camps, and emigration to America, where they were briefly separated by Adolfas's curtailed army stint and a sojourn in Mexico. According to the associative logic of the film, Jonas's orphic vocation as a maker of home movies coincides with the dissolution of the home in exile he and his brother had made for themselves.

The peculiarity of this solitude is that it is presented as the reflection of an unusually active social life amid a welter of acquaintances and in the company of some illustrious and glamorous people. He told Scott MacDonald that he had been and still was exceptionally shy, and that he had very little social contact and "no friends, nobody" for the two years Adolfas was in the army and Mexico, but that he acquired "techniques to cover" his shyness.[7] In a sense, the most radical and successful of those techniques was to film the society he encountered. He manages to intimate in *Walden* that the camera acts as a shield, defending his shyness from the very milieu it records. Furthermore, by stripping the social ambience of its sounds and its conversation, and substituting music and noise, and above all capitalizing on the disjunction between pictures and sounds, he stimulates a series of tropes for the solitude of an observer who is seldom at home in society.

Although Mekas never portrays himself leaving New York, we often see him away or returning. Corresponding to the two appearances of the substantive "home" as a mental image in the title "I THOUGHT OF HOME" at the start and close of the film, the directional adverb *home* occurs twice: once read—"COMING HOME FROM ST. VINCENT COLLEGE" early in the film—and heard once much later: "The other day on my way back home from Buffalo, early in the morning, coming back from long distances, coming back to New York by train, the train always pulls in at sunrise." Both times, filming the sunrise from the moving train, he gives the city the pictorial air Emerson prophesied. He further repeats this trope several times in the film without the reinforcement of the adverb *home*; for the propulsion itself and the consequent pictorial quickening turns New York into home for the filmmaker. Yet the most elaborate application of Emerson's program appears very late in *Walden* as he returns from his visit to Ono and Lennon in Montreal. As if literalizing the perspectival renewal for which Emerson recommended balloon travel, he filmed traffic in his own speeding and halting rhythms

---

6. He had spent two months on a visit to Los Angeles by himself and he lived alone in New York while Adolfas was in the U.S. Army. But it was only when Adolfas married that his solitary life became definitive.
7. Scott MacDonald, *A Critical Cinema 2: Interviews with Independent Filmmakers* (Berkeley: University of California Press, 1992), p. 89.

from the window of the singers' skyscraper hotel; then superimposing the dawn from a moving train, he dissolved to a bus ride in New York, mimicking and exaggerating the tempi of public transport by single-framing traffic from the rear window while the bus was moving and by shifting to real time for the halts. Here he reveals his signature single-frame style as an extension of this moving vehicle dynamic. In an optative mood he takes up residence in a figurative topos of the American transcendental heritage. His *Walden* is the terrain where he is at home making movies. The film's accumulation of weddings repeatedly underlines Mekas's homely solitude and his determination to celebrate it, and in so doing to elevate it, as if to put into visible form Thoreau's metaphor in the chapter "Where I Lived and What I Lived For":

> I know of no more encouraging fact than the unquestionable ability of man to elevate his life by a conscious endeavor. It is something to be able to paint a particular picture, or to carve a statue, and so make a few objects beautiful; but it is far more glorious to carve and paint the very atmosphere and medium through which we look, which morally we can do. To affect the quality of the day, that is the highest of arts. Every man is tasked to make his life, even in its details, worthy of the contemplation of his most elevated and critical hour.[8]

At Princeton University, Mekas offered the following account of the origin of his characteristic diary style:

> There was a tree in Central Park that I wanted to [film]. I really liked that tree, and I kept filming at the very beginning—when I began. And then I look on the viewer and it's not the same. It's just a tree standing there: it's boring.
>
> And then I began filming the tree in little fragments: I fragmented; I condensed...and then you can see the wind in it; then you can see some energy in it. Then it became something else. Ah, that's more interesting! That's my tree! That's the tree that I like, not just a tree that is naturalistic and boring, not what I saw in that tree when I was looking.
>
> I'm trying to get to why I'm looking at what I'm filming, why I'm filming it, and how I'm filming. The style reflects what I feel....I'm trying to understand myself, what I do....I'm totally ignorant of what I'm doing.[9]

8. Henry David Thoreau, "Where I Lived and What I Lived For," *Walden* (New York: Penguin, 1983), p. 134.
9. Jonas Mekas, untitled lecture, (John Sacret Young Lecture, Princeton University, February 18, 2004).

The three stages of the story of the tree—observation, fragmentation, and revelation—go to the core of Mekas's enterprise. The effort to mold the cinematic material into some kind of conformity with experience initiates a dialectic of self-analysis. Starting off in ignorance of his own intentions, he transforms the image and its context to make it both more interesting and more his own. But it is the later editing phase that pushes him to understand why he has fixed upon the original object. Often the random juxtaposition of shots taken at different times and in different places on the original roll of film reveals unanticipated meaningfulness:

> From [John Cage] I learned that chance is one of the great editors. You shoot something one day, forget it, shoot something the next day and forget the details of that.... When you finally string it all together, you discover all sorts of connections. I thought at first that I should do more editing and not rely on chance. But I came to realize that, of course, there is no chance: whatever you film you make certain decisions, even when you don't know what you do. The most essential, the most important editing takes place during the shooting as a result of these decisions.[10]

In November 1970, responding to Jacqueline Kennedy Onassis's request to instruct her children in the rudiments of filmmaking, he wrote an Emersonian textbook without realizing how close he was to the author of *Nature*. Its first lesson is, emblematically, the energizing of a tree:

> Home Movie Textbook
>   For Caroline & John
>   Chapter One
>   EXERCISES IN TIME
>   1.
>   Shoot a tree in wind, for ten seconds, continuously.
>   Shoot a tree in wind, in brief spurts of frames, in order to condense one minute of actual time to ten seconds of filmed time.
>   See what happens.
>   2.
>   a. Shoot a face of a person, for ten seconds, continuously.
>   Shoot the same face, in brief spurts, in order to have ten seconds of filmed time.
>   See what happens.

10. MacDonald, *A Critical Cinema 2*, p. 91.

3. Shoot fire (or candle) for ten seconds. Keep the camera focused on fire, steadily.

See what happens.

4.

Point a camera at the horizon and turn around fast.

Point a camera at the horizon and turn around very slowly.

See what happens.

5.

Shoot a brief spurt (two seconds) of a face; then shoot a brief spurt of a colorful flower, any color; then shoot the face again, briefly; then the flower again. Do this about ten times.

See what happens.

6.

Shoot a street (you could do it from a window) busy with traffic. Shoot continuously for ten seconds.

Shoot the same street and traffic in very brief spurts of frames. Get ten seconds of footage.

See what happens.[11]

In 1969, when he finished and released *Walden*, the fragmentary style had become characteristic of his diary signature. The film incorporated the lesson of the tree in Central Park. Later, in 1971, during the filming of *Reminiscences of the Journey to Lithuania*, Mekas discovered a defect in the camera he was using. At the beginning of every shot the third or fifth frame (sometimes even later) was overexposed with a light flash. He found he could avoid this by taking a few single frames every time he started to film. Upon his return to America he discovered an unanticipated expressive energy and power in the single frames themselves; so he incorporated the technique into his film even when using cameras without the defect. However, he had used single-frame montage with slowly increasing frequency since the very beginning of his filmmaking.

The first part of *Reminiscences* drew upon footage Mekas had shot in the 1950s: It freely mixed short static shots with handheld pans and swishes, and included brief superimpositions, but it did not fragment successively images of a single object or person. This material seems to have antedated the revelation of the tree. So the shift to the second part of the film, "100 Glimpses of Lithuania," where the single-frame technique first appears in Mekas's work, marks a dramatic introduction of his mature style to correspond to his first

11. Jonas Mekas, *"This Side of Paradise": Fragments of an Unfinished Biography* (Paris: Galerie du jour Agnès B., 1999), pages unnumbered.

visit to Lithuania after twenty-five years of exile. In the first part, his sustained voice-over commentary (as well as intertitles) inflects the archival footage with melancholy. In the middle part, uninterrupted Lithuanian music, played over the first six of the numbered glimpses, emphasizes the contrast of styles as a contrast of moods. It culminates in the seventh glimpse with the return of voice as Mekas sees his mother for the first time in a quarter century.

The combination of styles also underlines a shift of genre. Whereas *Walden* is an encyclopedic lyric, one of the several cinematic heirs of Whitman's "Song of Myself," *Reminiscences* structures similar material into an autobiography, primarily through the diachrony of the first section. In *Lost, Lost, Lost* the older footage dominates the two-and-a-half-hour film. It turns the autobiographical mode into a reflection on poetic origins in six reels. The first presents the filmmaker as a solitary, alienated walker, newly arrived in Brooklyn; the second narrates his attempts to locate himself in the community of Lithuanian exiles. In the third, he and Adolfas move to Manhattan and turn away from exilic politics to cinema and a new set of friends among whom (in the fourth reel) he witnesses another form of political activism. At this point, Mekas incorporated into his work the aborted *Rabbitshit Haikus* which he had shot in Vermont in the winter of 1962. It consists of fifty-six very brief sections, often a single shot usually accompanied by a simple sound—boyan music, bells, or a word repeated three times. For example, the passage numbered 30 shows a tree trembling in the wind and clouds moving behind it, probably filmed in stop-motion. During this shot we hear Mekas recite: "The clouds the clouds the clouds. The wind the wind the wind."

Across haikus 38 to 41 (each composed of one or two shots, half of them of Mekas himself) he tells a parable:

> Do you know the story of the man who couldn't live anymore without the knowledge of what's at the end of the road, and what he found there when he reached it? He found a pile, a small pile of rabbit shit at the end of the road. And back home he went. And when people used to ask him, "Hey, where does the road lead to?" He used to answer: "Nowhere, the road leads nowhere, and there is nothing but a pile of rabbit shit at the end of the road." So he told them. But nobody believed him.

Over the final, fifty-sixth, haiku he takes up the story again as if it were about him:

> He used to work, like everybody else, and then stop and look at the horizon. And when people used to ask him, "Hey, what's wrong with you? Why do you keep looking into the distance?" he used to tell

them, "I want to know what's at the end of the road."...No, he found nothing, nothing at the end of the road when later, many years later, after many years of journey he came to the end of the road, there was nothing, nothing but a pile of rabbit shit, not even the rabbit was there any longer, and the road lead nowhere.

In the same reel, thirteen "Fool's Haikus" mark the transition from the black-and-white poems shot on the set of *Hallelujah the Hills* to color haikus made in New York with the companionship of Barbara Rubin, a central presence in the final, sixth reel. Maya Deren had attempted to find a filmic equivalent to the haiku shortly before her death. She left the project incomplete. Brakhage too used the analogy to the haiku in discussing his 8 mm *Songs*. By including the two haiku series in *Lost, Lost, Lost,* Mekas contextualized them as steps in the development of his poetic incarnation as a filmmaker. There they become documents of the period in which they were made and of the company the filmmaker kept. They aspire to create a new cinematic genre of autonomous serial illuminations of the time, place, and mood of a fleeting moment. But in compensation for their failure to do so, they clarify the fundamental temporality of Mekas's diary project.

The fragmentary style, speeding up action through single-frame photography or doubling temporal referents with brief superimpositions, continually reminds the filmmaker and the viewer of the superabundant, ungraspable welter of events surrounding him and us. While affirming the reality of the external world, this style posits a mode of time that escapes the categories of past, present, and future. Whereas the time of a written diary is serially retrospective (a string of essays on the events of the days just past), the temporality of the film diary, as Mekas came to fashion it, can color each scene with the ecstasy or the anxiety of the act of capturing it on film.

Walden begins in the teeming world: There is no setting up of the immediate environment, no identification of the significant personae, who are rarely even named. When they are, it is often only by first names, as in the very first title of the film, "Barbara's flower garden," which precedes shots of producer David Stone and his wife, Barbara, in their New York apartment as she waters plants on her windowsill. Before that, there had been a shot of Mekas in his room at the Chelsea Hotel playing his boyan. Throughout the diaries, these self-portraits of the filmmaker, alone, playing the boyan, serve as icons of his orphic incarnation. The world he invokes and represents, however, is not the product of his imagination. It is already there, fully constituted when Mekas's diary begins: it is full of familiar people and of unknown persons; he is one among them—he readily passes his camera to his companions for shots of himself, or he inserts shots other filmmakers have taken of him without drawing attention to the authorial signature of the person behind the camera or, as in the case of the image of him playing the boyan, sets it up on a tripod and films himself remotely. Even the bracketing images of the young women in the park must wait three minutes before appearing as if in a mental picture; for when we see the filmmaker tossing in his bed and read "I Thought of Home," the sound stops suddenly, and then we see rowboats full of people on the lake in Central Park and read again "Walden" before the first of these girls appears.

Yet again, I turn to David James's fundamental essay on *Walden* for his description of the dialectic of shooting and editing at the point when Mekas first articulated a completed film from his amassing of diary footage:

> [E]diting replaced shooting as the moment of crucial perception; fragments of film replaced the visual texture of daily life as the privileged object of sight; the inscription of subjectivity took the form, not of somatically attuned single-framing and iris manipulation of in-camera visualization, but in cutting, and adding titles and soundtracks in the editing room.[12]

In *Paradise Not Yet Lost a/k/a Oona's Third Year* (1979), Mekas offers a gnostic myth of fragmentation. The scene is idyllic. He had made a second visit to his mother in Lithuania, this time with his wife and baby. The sequence, titled "Later that afternoon," had begun with Hollis and Oona resting by a window; it continues outdoors with children playing, women drawing water from the well (just as the voice-over uses the metaphor of rain), and a group of men, Mekas prominent among them, cutting grain with scythes. Over these images we hear:

> But there is this tale I was told once that when Adam and Eve were leaving the paradise and Adam was sleeping in a shadow of a rock, Eve looked back and she saw the globe of paradise exploding into millions of tiny bits and fragments. And it rained. It rained into her soul and that of the sleeping Adam: the little bits of paradise. The rest was gone. The paradise was gone. I don't think Eve ever told this to Adam.

From the beginning, the diary style that Mekas invented suggested that the shots of the film, from a fraction of a second to many seconds long, were glimpses of the world and triggers to memory. Here the secret theology of fragmentation sublimates those glimpses into "millions of tiny bits

12. David E. James, *Power Misses: Essays across (Un)popular Culture* (London: Verso, 1996), p. 137.

and fragments" of an otherwise lost paradise. Lest we miss the implication, the filmmaker inserts an intertitle in the midst of this sequence: "These are the fragments of Paradise."

The frequency and fluidity with which Mekas incorporates images of himself, without calling attention to how those images were made, contribute to the singular epistemological stance of his project. Mekas evades the egotistical sublime and its attendant threat of solipsism that marks Brakhage's work and in differing degrees affects those Brakhage has influenced. There is hardly any place in Mekas's work for dreams, fantasies, problems of perception and recognition. He relegates the central issue of memory to the voice-over soundtrack and the intertitles. Even when he cuts from "I Thought of Home" to an idyll of rowboats, there can be no doubt that he is using an image from contemporary New York as a trope for Lithuania in the past. Through all his figurations of subjectivity, Mekas remains a realist.

Curiously, Mekas's studied indifference to psychology is one of his many radically Emersonian positions. (His professed contempt for travel is another.) Certainly, there is no direct figuration of guilt, erotic disappointment, or regret in the many, many hours of his completed film diaries. His evasion of psychology sustains his self-presentation as a realist. In "Just Like a Shadow," he wrote of filming his friends and his family:

> Why did I film it all? I have no real answer. I think I did it because
> I was a very shy person. My camera allowed me to participate in the
> life that took place around me. My film diaries are not like the diaries
> of Anaïs Nin... [who] agonized about her psychological adventures.
> In my case, the opposite, whatever that opposite may be. My Bolex
> protected me while at the same time giving me a peek and a focus on
> what was happening around me. Still, at the very end, I don't think
> my film diaries are about the others or what I saw: It's all about myself,
> conversations with my self.[13]

Despite his professed contempt for travel, Mekas continually represents himself in foreign places or en route to and from them. Ancient literary criticism called the genre describing what one encounters in travel *periegeten* or, rhetorically, *topographia* and *topothesis*. Whereas Menken's *Arabesque for Kenneth Anger* and *Bagatelle for Willard Maas*, Hugo's *Ai-Ye*, and Brakhage's *The Dead* might be examples of topographia, insofar as they each isolate a single location for examination, Mekas integrates the periegeten into his diaries. For almost all of the filmmakers in this study, topographic cinema or versions of the periegeten are crucial modes of conversation with themselves.

13. Jonas Mekas, "Just Like a Shadow," *Logos* (Spring 2004), www.logosjournal.com.

CHAPTER 5

Hollis Frampton and the Specter of Narrative

I n this book I am concerned with three waves or generations of filmmakers. The first all began to make films before 1960: Marie Menken, Ian Hugo, Stan Brakhage, Jonas Mekas, and Larry Jordan (whom I consider in the conclusion, Perfect Exhilaration) benefited in different degrees and in different ways from the aura of newness associated with the American avant-garde cinema in the 1940s and 1950s. They felt impelled and free to invent new automatisms (what Emerson called "mechanical means") for generating a new kind of cinema. Of course, they struggled with the rivalry of other filmmakers, especially with Maya Deren, who aggressively asserted her aesthetic and theoretical primacy, and in some measure with each other. Nevertheless, the advantage they had in feeling the freshness of their enterprise in the morning of the American avant-garde cinema registers in the directness with which they responded to the optative mode of the Emersonian tradition. The next wave of filmmakers I treat in this book—Hollis Frampton, Andrew Noren, Robert Beavers, Warren Sonbert, and Ernie Gehr—all exhibited their first films in the late 1960s. They were keenly aware of the achievements of the earlier generation, even when their debts were not primarily to the artists I have named as the chief representatives of the Emersonian tradition. They reinvented, analytically questioned, parodied, or purified the tropes and themes of those precursors. Of this generation, Frampton was the most formidable ironist (a successor of Sidney Peterson and Bruce Conner). Through irony he sought to distance himself from the previous generation of avant-garde film-makers and from the Emersonian legacy. I shall later discuss the work of two figures of a third wave—Abigail Child and Su Friedrich—who started to make films in the late 1970s and hit their stride in the subsequent decade. Their relationship to the Emersonian tradition was yet another step removed, for they had to contend with the work of their immediate antecedents. They are both ironists themselves who found that Frampton, more than any other figure of the middle generation, had changed the landscape for them. In fact, he might be seen as a bridge between the great filmmakers of the 1950s and early 1960s and many of those who came in their wake.

Frampton dated the start of his filmmaking career from 1962, but he has left two slightly different accounts of this myth of origination. He told Scott MacDonald that he shot *Ten Mile Poem* from an elevated section of a Brooklyn subway, mostly with a telephoto lens, "always in motion." This alternative would be the perfectly Emersonian version, unconfirmable because the film was lost or destroyed. However, the film does appear in his filmographies as a work from 1964. Instead, he lists the similarly destroyed *Clouds Like Sheep* as his only film of 1962. Making the matter even more obscure, he described to MacDonald an unnamed long film of cloud patterns dissolving into one another, in negative, printed in a blue tint, from 1964. Frampton identified the monochrome of the film as "all in Mallarmé azure," thus aligning this alternative point of origin with European modernism. If these films were never actually photographed, Frampton would not be unique among filmmak-ers who have antedated their empirical filmographies with unrealized projects as if they actually had been completed and lost. Their significance remains as Emersonian projects—the poem of vehicular motion and the meditation on the changing, tinted clouds, recalling the passage in *Nature* where the Orpheus of Concord contemplates "long slender bars of cloud" and the sea "seem[s] to partake its rapid transformations; the active enchantment reaches my dust, and I dilate and conspire with the morning wind."[1]

Brakhage absorbed Emerson's aesthetic legacy through his embracing of Gertrude Stein, and Mekas sought a channel to it through Thoreau, but Frampton distanced himself from it by choosing James Joyce as the idealized precursor of his cinema, even more than Ezra Pound, for whose tutelage he quit college and moved to Washington, DC, in 1957. After a year of faithful attendance at his ad hoc seminar in St. Elizabeth's Hospital, where Pound was

---

1. Ralph Waldo Emerson, *Essays and Lectures* (New York: Library of America, 1983), p. 15.

confined as a mental patient, Frampton moved to New York, recognized that poetry was not his vocation, and concentrated his energies on photography, first, and then cinema.

Frampton's affinities were with the modernist canon: Along with Joyce, he frequently cited his alternative models, Beckett and Borges, virtually identifying modernism with irony. But more crucially, he claimed the rhetoric of science and mathematics (especially set theory) as his distinguishing stamp. His theoretical essays and the titles of his films are marked by allusions to axioms, theorems, and classic experiments, although his films actually have fewer traces of "scientific" filmmaking than Brakhage's.

This cultivation of metaphors and analogies from mathematics and science, his fascination with systemic models for aesthetic inventions, and his persistent evocation of James Joyce as a precursor and guide would, apparently, make Frampton the least Emersonian of the major American avant-garde filmmakers. Yet he himself invokes Emerson as an enlightened forebear who had "no problems" fusing art and science.[2] If we change the word *ethics* to *aesthetics*, Emerson's assertion in chapter 4 ("Language") of *Nature*, "The axioms of physics translate the laws of ethics," might stand as a motto for Frampton's use of mathematics and science in *Circles of Confusion*.

In "Circles," Emerson's "circular philosopher" articulates a theory of perpetual flux that Frampton will find at the heart of Duchamp's enterprise: "There are no fixtures in nature. The universe is fluid and volatile. Permanence is but a word of degrees."[3] What sort of circular philosopher is the author of *Circles of Confusion*? At first Frampton would seem antithetical to Emerson. He utterly eschews many of the fundamental Emersonian terms and concepts: There is no place for "spirit," "soul," "the Poet," or "self-reliance" in his essays. Nonetheless, an American artist cannot sidestep Emerson so easily. The *Essays* (First and Second Series) pervade Frampton's writings: "Ox House Camel Rivermouth," the preface to *Circles of Confusion*, is a meditation on the hieroglyphic language of "The Poet"; the conclusion of "A Pentagram for Conjuring the Narrative" coincides with the first principle of "Art": "Now that which is inevitable in the work has a higher charm than individual talent can ever give, inasmuch as the artist's pen or chisel seems to have been held or guided by a gigantic hand to inscribe a line in the history of the human race...the whole extant product of the plastic arts has herein its highest value, as history."[4] Even the insight into an aesthetic of time that animates "Eadweard Muybridge: Fragments of a Tesseract" is a transposition of the

---

2. Scott MacDonald, *A Critical Cinema: Interviews with Independent Filmmakers* (Berkeley: University of California Press, 1988), pp. 56–57.
3. Emerson, *Essays and Lectures*, p. 403.
4. Ibid, p. 432.

ethics of time Emerson articulated at the start of "The Over-Soul": "Our faith comes in moments; our vice is habitual. Yet there is a depth in those brief moments which constrains us to ascribe more reality to them than to all other experiences."[5] The echoes are distorted and diffused because Frampton seems to have filtered his Emersonianism through reluctant and oblique conduits: Ezra Pound, John Cage, and even Brakhage.

Frampton's Emerson would be fundamentally the author of "Nature," not the short book to which I refer again and again in these pages but the essay of 1844. Even a quotation as long as the one that follows, skipping quickly over several paragraphs, merely hints at the resonances a reading of the whole essay would have for one familiar with Frampton's writings:

> Motion or change, and identity or rest, are the first and second secrets of Nature: Motion and Rest. The whole code of her laws may be written on the thumbnail, or the signet of a ring. The whirling bubble on the surface of a brook admits us to the secret of the mechanics of the sky.... Compound it how she will, star, sand, fire, water, tree, man, it is still one stuff, and betrays the same properties.... Space exists to divide creatures; but by clothing the sides of a bird with a few feathers she gives him a petty omnipresence. The direction is forever onward, but the artist still goes back for materials, and begins again with the first elements on the most advanced stage: otherwise all goes to ruin. If we look at her work, we seem to catch a glance of a system in transition.... Things are so strictly related, that according to the skill of the eye, from any one object the parts and properties of any other may be predicted.... This guiding identity runs though all the surprises and contrasts of the piece, and characterizes every law. Man carries the world in his head, the whole astronomy and chemistry suspended in a thought. Because the history of nature is charactered in his brain, therefore is he the prophet and discoverer of her secrets...And the knowledge that we traverse the whole scale of being, from the centre to the poles of nature, and have some stake in every possibility, lends that sublime luster to death, which philosophy and religion have too outwardly and literally striven to express in the popular doctrine of the immortality of the soul. The reality is more excellent than the report.... Nature is the incarnation of a thought, and turns to a thought again, as ice becomes water and gas.[6]

5. Ibid, p. 385.
6. Ibid., pp. 547, 548, 555.

The overriding conceits of Frampton's essays turn on parables of scientific experiment, and reorient filmic poetics away from intuitive expression toward systemic matrices for generating individual works. He theorizes that "[t]he infinite film contains an infinity of endless passages wherein no frame resembles any other in the slightest degree, and a further infinity of passages wherein successive frames are as nearly identical as intelligence can make them"; from this a complex but rational history of cinema can be derived resembling "the Knight's tour in chess"; and he discovers literature and music guiding the filmmaker in four modes of productively reading his tradition and an unspecified number of contingent "axioms derived by misreading."[7]

Along with several of the other filmmakers I shall treat here, Frampton follows Whitman's revisions of Emerson in sexualizing the vital principle (as Hugo and Brakhage had), but he is paramount among them in subscribing to Whitman's fixation upon death as a determining factor of aesthetic production. In "A Pentagram for Conjuring the Narrative," narrative is born among the "animal necessities of the spirit" because we are "waiting to die." Art making itself, in "Incisions in History/Segments of Eternity" turns out to be "a recent adaptive mutation aimed at assuring mental continuity, through historic time, to a species whose individual experiences constitute a testament to the notion of disjunction." As such, it is something man "superimposes upon animal sexuality."[8] The allusion to Venus Genetrix in the Muybridge essay shows that Frampton traced the genealogy of this notion back to Lucretius. He and Andrew Noren were the primary Lucretians among the filmmaking descendents of Whitman.

Photography and cinema are the epicenters of Frampton's *Circles of Confusion*, the most important work of film theory in the American avant-garde cinema published after Brakhage's *Metaphors on Vision*, and surely the most masterfully written work of its kind. These essays are brilliant, serious fun, and reading them makes it clear, clearer than in his films despite his frequent protestations, that Frampton aspired to recognition as a "stoic comedian" in Hugh Kenner's categorization of Flaubert, Joyce, and Beckett.[9]

The theoretical power of *Circles of Confusion* comes from the clarity with which Frampton has located the issues crucial to the history and evolution of the American avant-garde cinema. The initiator of this branch of theory was Maya Deren. In the chapter "For a Metahistory of Film," he pinpoints the

7. Hollis Frampton, *Circles of Confusion: Film, Photography, Video, Texts 1968–1980* (Rochester: Visual Arts Studies Workshop, 1983), pp. 114, 116, 121.

8. Ibid., p. 90.

9. See Federico Windhausen, "Words into Film: Toward a Genealogical Understanding of Hollis Frampton's Theory and Practice," *October* 109 (Summer 2004), for a discussion of the relationship between Frampton and Kenner's work.

origin of cinema as an independent art with the beginning of her filmmaking career: "The notion that there was some exact instant at which the table turned, and cinema passed into obsolescence and thereby into art, is an appealing fiction that implies a special task for the metahistorian of cinema."[10] The turning point, which made cinema obsolete and therefore ready to become an art, he wittily suggests, was the advent of video and radar, which made the nineteenth-century mechanics of the filmmaking apparatus obvious. Significantly, he added, "Its introduction coincides quite closely with the making of Maya Deren's *Meshes of the Afternoon*."

For Frampton, the highest aspiration of film theory might be to win the title of "appealing fiction." His own tests continually bring fiction, history, parody, analysis, polemics, and speculation into intimate contact. Nowhere is this more direct than in his central statement on film, "A Pentagram for Conjuring the Narrative," with which he chose to open the book. It is a five-part essay on the ineluctability of narration. Although we might expect such an argument from a theoretician hostile to the American avant-garde cinema, it seems odd from the pen of a man who never made what one could reasonably call a narrative film. The displacement of expectations is deliberate, of course; for the aim of the essay is to replace the notion of narrative as a finite sequence of events represented within a film with an ontology of human temporality that refuses to credit the distinction between events depicted in a film and the narrative of the film's creation within the implicit story of a filmmaker's career.

Of the five alternative approaches to this matter that make up the "Pentagram," the first is the funniest and perhaps the most obscure. It is a fiction. The author claims to have heard a friend tell him a nightmare in which he is first the rich daughter of an eccentric who films every moment of her life, and then after death and reincarnation, the obese, asthmatic, homosexually inclined male heir to her fortune who must spend his life watching the film of hers. If we did not get the earlier clues, then the description of the asthmatic viewer yelling "focus" identifies the heir, and by extension the dreaming friend, as Stan Brakhage, at least to readers aware of the personalities in the American avant-garde cinema.

Obviously, the real Brakhage was a very different sort of eccentric father. He filmed the birth and many intimate moments in the lives of his first five children, not so much to document their histories but to visualize his experience of them and his relationship to seeing them. The fiction of the double nightmare provides one narrative context for every possible film of the sort Brakhage makes, and intimates that we are all narrators in our sleep.

---

10. Frampton, *Circles of Confusion*, p. 113.

The second part of the "Pentagram" focuses on Mt. Fujiyama as "a stable pattern of energy" inevitably visible throughout the Japanese landscape. Frampton deduces that every inevitable condition engenders "a supreme metaphor." Narrative, it will turn out in the third part, is such an inevitable condition of all films. In a reductive temper, Frampton makes it the third such condition, the first two being the frame and the "plausibility of photographic illusion." The first two play no active roles in the opening essay but return later in the book to claim their acknowledgments. "The plausibility of photographic illusion" is a nuanced version of Deren's central claim: "As a reality, the photographic image confronts us with the innocent arrogance of an objective fact, one which exists as an independent presence, indifferent to our response."[11] In the same essay, her final theoretical text, "Cinematography: The Creative Use of Reality," she had dismissed the challenge of the then-emerging Brakhage:

> [T]he camera itself has been conceived of as the artist, with distorting
> lenses, multiple superimpositions, etc., used to simulate the creative
> action of the eye, the memory, etc. Such well-intentioned efforts to
> use the medium creatively, by forcibly inserting the creative act in
> the position it traditionally occupies in the visual arts, accomplish,
> instead, the destruction of the photographic image as reality.[12]

Frampton's formulation of the second inevitable condition purposely avoids the metaphysics of Deren, which would make the film instrument a superior epistemological tool, directly capturing reality. Although later in the book he will again echo Deren's arguments by suggesting that animation is a separate art from filmmaking, thereby brushing aside the major challenge to the issue of photographic plausibility, Frampton's substitution of "plausibility" for "reality" shifts the argument to the semiotic habits of film viewers. His competence in Latin suggests that he was playing on the etymology of plausibility, from *plaudere* (to applaud)—we applaud the photograph only insofar as we appreciate its successful trickery. The figura etymologica suggests that the illusion retains vestiges of a theatrical performance and, therefore, would be anything but "indifferent to our response" as Deren would have it.

Frampton ironically called the postulation of the inevitability of narrative "Brakhage's Theorem," claiming that Brakhage, acting as "avocatus diaboli" had proposed it to him, and that it had been tested against such difficult cases

---

11. Maya Deren, "Cinematography: The Creative Use of Reality," *Daedalus* (Winter 1960), reprinted in P. Adams Sitney, ed., *The Avant-Garde Film: A Reader of Theory and Criticism* (New York: Anthology Film Archives, NYU Press, 1978), p. 65.
12. Ibid., p. 68.

as Kubelka's *Arnulf Rainer* and Conrad's *The Flicker*. The issues at stake in the essay were very much on the filmmaker's mind when he went to England in May 1972 to show what he had completed of *Hapax Legomena* and to film material for what would become *Ordinary Matter*. That was three months before he submitted the text of "A Pentagram for Conjuring the Narrative" to the Vancouver Art Gallery for its initial publication. Frampton neglected to mention that his encounter with Peter Gidal, the British filmmaker and theoretician, was crucial to the elaboration of this thesis. Gidal challenged Frampton's apparent lapse into narrative in parts of *Hapax Legomena*, which he contrasted with *Zorns Lemma*, claiming that Kubelka and Conrad retain narrative and "authoritarian" elements in their flicker films but that *Zorns Lemma*, as well as films by Sharits and Snow, avoid the those pitfalls.[13] Additionally, Frampton publicly articulated for the first time the theory of myths with which "A Pentagram" concludes in an interview with Simon Field and Peter Sainsbury the same month: "There was this thing called the plot, and down underneath the plot which is as it were the musculature of an entertainment film, you have a kind of armature in the terms of which, for instance, *Hamlet* and *The Odyssey* are the essentially same story, one written from the point of view of the son, one written from the point of view of the father."[14]

The formulation of "Brakhage's Theorem" is purely Frampton's language:

For any finite series of shots ["film"] *whatsoever there exists in a real time a rational narrative, such that every term in the series, together with its position, duration, partition, and reference, shall be perfectly and entirely accounted for.*[15]

I understand the unusual term *partition* to be an adaptation from set theory, where it would mean the decomposition of a set into disjoint subsets.

In the fourth section of "A Pentagram," Frampton invokes Samuel Beckett's *Malone Dies* to explore the fundamental principles of narration, circling back to the opening dream or parable in which the self is both performer and observer. So he defines the first person:

"I" is the English familiar name by which an unspeakably intricate network of colloidal circuits—or, as some reason, the garrulous

13. Peter Gidal, "Interview with Hollis Frampton," *October* 32 (Spring 1985), pp. 106–7.
14. Simon Field and Peter Sainsbury, "*Zorns Lemma* and *Hapax Legomena*, Interview with Hollis Frampton," *Afterimage* [London], no. 4 (Autumn, 1972), p. 50.
15. Frampton, *Circles of Confusion*, p. 63.

temporary inhabitant of that nexus—addresses itself...in time it convinces itself, somewhat reluctantly, that it is waiting to die.[16]

As it waits to die, the garrulous self divides into speaker and listener, telling itself stories; for storytelling is among "the animal necessities of the spirit," he concludes, quoting an unspecified source.

The fifth and final part of the essay opens with its most memorable moment:

> One fine morning, I awoke to discover that, during the night, I had learned to understand the language of birds. I have listened to them ever since. They say: "Look at me!" or: "Get out of here!" or: "Let's fuck!" or: "Help!" or "Hurrah!" or: "I found a worm!" and that's *all* they say. And that, when you boil it down, is about all we say.
>
> (Which of those things am I saying now?)[17]

I take it that the final question is so funny because it points to the self-interested claims the theoretician would make on different readers. This parabolic distillation of linguistic motives prefaces Frampton's reduction of narratives to mythic archetypes and pairs the archetypes on the bifurcated model of the "I" as speaker and listener. Thus the story of Odysseus narrates the father-son story from the father's point of view; *Hamlet* tells the same story from the son's. Malone joins Scheherazade and the storytellers of Boccaccio's *Decameron* to wait for death or to evade it.

In large part, the theoretical discussion of the tripartite nature of cinema in "A Pentagram for Conjuring the Narrative"—frame, photographic illusion, and narrative—reflects Frampton's filmmaking in the early 1970s, particularly in a remarkable sequence of seven films called *Hapax Legomena*. Before Frampton, the practice of combining several avant-garde films into a poetic sequence had been one of Brakhage's signature gestures: *Dog Star Man, Songs, Scenes from Under Childhood, Lovemaking* (1968), *Sexual Meditations,* and *The Weir-Falcon Saga* (1970) are composed of between three and thirty autonomous films. Jonas Mekas began to release his ongoing *Diaries, Notes and Sketches* in 1968. Saul Levine's open-ended series of 8 mm films with the word *Note* in their titles began to appear at the same time; Brakhage's *Songs* inspired them. Frampton, however, drew some of his inspiration from the same sources as Brakhage, most evidently Pound's serial poem, *The Cantos.* Furthermore, Frampton had written poetic sequences himself and more recently had made several photographic series. In fact, he had initially chosen

16. Ibid., p. 64.
17. Ibid., p. 66.

the title *Hapax Legomena* for a projected volume of poetry. Similarly, he salvaged the titles *Clouds of Magellan* and *Straits of Magellan* from photographic
sequences to use for serial film projects.

Having recently completed his longest film so far, *Zorns Lemma* (1970),
the seven-part series was his most ambitious project before the monumental
Magellan, which he left uncompleted at his death in 1984. Each of the seven
parts addresses the tension between the flat graphic arrangement of tonally
varied chemicals on the filmstrip and the illusions projected by them. Additionally, several of the parts deal autobiographically, but tangentially, with
the filmmaker's personal crisis as his six-year marriage to historian Marcia
Steinbrecher came to an end. They separated in 1971, shortly after he completed the first film of the series. "*Hapax Legomena* really came from a year
in which I wasn't feeling all that trustful[,] you know; it was something of a
black time," he told Simon Field and Peter Sainsbury.[18]

Frampton provided the *Film-makers' Cooperative Catalogue* with a useful
note about the sequence:

> *Hapax legomena* are literally, "things said once." The Greek scholarly
> jargon refers to those words that occur only a single time in the entire
> *oeuvre* of an author, or in a whole literature. The title brackets a
> cycle of seven films, which make up a single work composed of
> detachable parts, each of which may be seen separately for its own
> qualities. The work is an oblique autobiography, seen in stereoscopic
> focus with the phylogeny of film art as I have had to recapitulate it
> during my own fitful development as a film-maker. *Hapax Legomena*
> incorporates what I could learn along the way of making it, and
> includes my own false starts and blind alleys...what T.E. Hulme
> once called "the cold walks, and the lines that lead nowhere." Such
> "double-vision"—that is, the superimposition of a personal myth of
> the history of one's art upon a factual account of one's own *persona*—
> certainly does not originate with me. At least, I believe I see ample
> precedent in the last two books of James Joyce.[19]

The first film of the cycle, *Hapax Legomena: (nostalgia)* (1971), delineates
the filmmaker's career as a still photographer and dramatically alludes to
his transition to cinema through a series of burning photographs. The next
two parts focus on connubial discord: *Hapax Legomena: Poetic Justice* (1972),
the first silent film of the sequence, allows us to read a handwritten film

18. Field and Sainsbury, "*Zorns Lemma* and *Hapax Legomena*," p. 52.
19. *Film-makers' Cooperative Catalogue No. 7* (New York: Film-makers' Cooperative, 1989), p. 170.

script about voyeurism and sexual jealousy; in the third film of the cycle, the ritualized, looped sound of a couple arguing when the male refuses to explain or apologize for a night away from home makes *Hapax Legomena: Critical Mass* (1971) a hyperbole of domestic friction. More remote vestiges of an autobiography can be found in the two subsequent parts: *Hapax Legomena: Traveling Matte* (1971), also silent, surveys a bleak academic landscape where Frampton hoped to find a teaching position; *Hapax Legomena: Ordinary Matter* (1972) would reflect the filmmaker's life only insofar as the inclusion of images of crossing the Brooklyn Bridge recalls a similar sequence in his earlier film *Surface Tension* (1968) and images of Stonehenge mark his invitation to England to show his work. Frampton has referred to the two monuments as instances of the primary aesthetic experiences of his life. The sequence concludes with the silent *Hapax Legomena: Remote Control* (1972), composed largely of loops of television images, and *Hapax Legomena: Special Effects* (1972), a meditation on the empty rectangle of the screen. These films seem to have no autobiographical content; as such, they signal a movement beyond the personal identification of the filmmaker with his work.

The cycle recapitulates the phylogeny of the art by beginning with photographic cinema (which often had an offscreen commentator in the first years of the invention), introducing the written intertitle, incorporating sound, and opening the possibilities of videotaping. More obscurely, the final three parts may be seen as developing systemic modes of montage and exploring a fundamental unit or inevitable condition of cinematic ontology; that is to say, they schematize a history of the avant-garde cinema since *Meshes of the Afternoon*, to which we might crudely attach the names Deren or Brakhage (*Ordinary Matter*), Kubelka or Sharits (*Remote Control*), and Snow or Frampton (*Special Effects*).

Aside from one loop of television images in *Remote Control*, the entire cycle is in black and white. Most of the elements enact radically minimal strategies: *(nostalgia)* maintains a single, overhead camera position to depict thirteen photographs serially burning on a hotplate. Even more minimally, the camera of *Poetic Justice* looks down on a table with a small cactus plant, a mug of coffee, and a sheaf of papers on which the filmmaker has hand printed, in bold magic marker, a film script. Over the course of the film's thirty-one minutes, he allows us six seconds apiece to read the 240 pages of the unrealized, and perhaps unfilmable, text. Only the concluding film, *Special Effects*, offers less visual variation: We see a black rectangle made up of a broken white line just within the rectangle of the film frame. He filmed this with a telephoto lens, holding the camera by hand, so that its "action" is the jittery nervous tension of his hands trying to hold the spring-wound machine steady, magnified by the leverage of the telephoto image.

In contrast, the drama of *Critical Mass* consists of a young couple arguing in front of a blank background, elaborately reedited into an asynchronous canon. In *Traveling Matte*, Frampton transferred to film an uncut videotape he made by walking for twenty minutes on the State University of New York at Binghamton campus with his hand partially covering the lens of the camcorder. *Ordinary Matter* and *Remote Control* present the most extensive and varied visual material in the series—the former, moving camera images of landscapes and architectural monuments, the latter apparently random television images, looped in repeating cycles, interrupted by graphic numbers and a graphic sign. Yet in both instances, pixilation almost reduces the moving images themselves to graphic signs.

The cycle alternates between sound and silent films. *(nostalgia)* builds voice-over descriptions of the photographs (displaced so that we hear about the photograph to follow while we watch one burn) into an autobiography of poetic election; *Critical Mass* creates a quasi-musical composition, reminiscent of Steve Reich's 1965 tape "It's Gonna Rain," by repeating and overlapping snippets of its fierce argument; on the accompanying tape of *Ordinary Matter*, Frampton recites the Wade-Giles Mandarin syllabary without the tonal distinctions that would make it intelligible to a speaker of Chinese, thus creating an incomprehensible but coherent language. Finally, at the University of Pittsburgh he used a Buchla synthesizer to generate the electronic sound he used for *Special Effects*, which has the only nonverbal soundtrack in the cycle.

On November 20, 1971, at the Millennium Film Workshop he presented four parts of *Hapax Legomena* as a work in progress. At that time it had a different order: He referred to its first three sections then, *(nostalgia)*, *Critical Mass*, and *Traveling Matte*, as "an extended sonata-allegro form" in which the first was the andante, the second allegro vivace, and the third a largo. Later, Warren Sonbert would use a similar musical analogy to connect several films he had made into a composite cycle. At the same Millennium screening Frampton gave the working title *Poetic Justice* to what would evolve into *Special Effects* by playing the Buchla synthesizer tape while projecting the empty white rectangle of the projector without a film. He told the audience that the words "A photograph of your face" would appear at the beginning of the film. Introducing this performance, he proposed a radical revision of the history of the art:

[T]he aural cinema was discovered first and then later pictures were added to it. By which I mean definitely to imply that there's a cinema of the ear. The cinema is the whole universe of sound ordered to aesthetic ends which subsumed music, among many other things.

And music, of course, has a considerable history. If you are willing to entertain the conceit, then of course, cinema is not the youngest of the arts, but the oldest.[20]

Even if the frame, the plausibility of photographic illusion, and narrative—the three "inevitable conditions of film art"—compose the central triad of thematic concerns uniting the parts of *Hapax Legomena*, they do not fully account for its organization. The cycle contains several sets of interlocking subjects and themes: *(nostalgia)* and *Poetic Justice* tells stories about photography; *Traveling Matte* and *Remote Control* illustrate aspects of video and television—the one demonstrates the transfer of video onto film, and the other largely recaptures film images after they have been transformed by television. *Poetic Justice* and *Critical Mass*, along with the fourth story in *(nostalgia)*, illuminate aspects of sexual jealousy. The handheld vibrato of *Special Effects* recalls the hands in front of the lens in *Traveling Matte*, while the somatic camera of the latter film anticipates the jitters of *Ordinary Matter*. Even the rubber glove that suddenly appears on top of the sheaf of papers to signal the end of *Poetic Justice*, itself probably an homage to Duchamp and his 1964 *Pocket Chess Set with Rubber Glove*, is a metonymy for the absent hand that wrote the script.[21] In turn, those hands are synecdoches for the body of the filmmaker, the focus of recurring ironies in the cycle: We hear in *(nostalgia)* (while we are watching a portrait of his friend the sculptor Carl Andre burn):

> I take some comfort in realizing that my entire physical body has been replaced more than once since it made this portrait of its face. However, I understand that my central nervous system is an exception.

Here the deictic adjective *this* would deliberately confuse a viewer so early in the film—it is only the second description of thirteen—into thinking that it refers to the image on the screen at the time of hearing the text. The asynchronous structure is just one of several strategies in the serial work for foregrounding the nature of indexical representation and emphasizing that reference (including, primarily, photographic illusionism) is merely "plausible," that is, tricks to elicit our applause, or perhaps ways of saying "'Look at me!' or: 'Get out of here!' or: 'Let's fuck!' or: 'Help!' or: 'Hurrah' or: 'I found a worm!'" Photographs, camera movements, and deictic words are the most prominent indices in *Hapax Legomena*. Furthermore, Frampton suggests

---

20. Hollis Frampton, "Three Talks at Millennium," *Millennium Film Journal* 16/17/18, p. 277.
21. See Allen S. Weiss's erudite and provocative essay "*Poetic Justice*: Formations of Subjectivity and Sexual Identity," *Cinema Journal* 28, no. 1 (all 1988) for an extensive discussion of the relationship between Frampton and Duchamp. Weiss also discusses *Poetic Justice* in "Cartesian Simulacra," *Persistence of Vision* 5 (1987).

that the principle of synchronization, exemplified under negative signs in *(nostalgia)* and *Critical Mass*, implies a reciprocal indexicality in the imaginary notion of the speaker.

He told Simon Field and Peter Sainsbury:

> My own turning away from narrative, or from what is called narrative, really had to do with how suppositious I felt it to be.... It is riddled with conventions that are precisely as much artifices, they are precisely as much man-made things that are agreed upon, as the notion that c-o-w corresponds to something that weighs 800 pounds and gives milk...I was interested, and I'm still interested, in eliminating such suppositions, eliminating automatism, eliminating the idea, or the suspicion, that the "culture" is responsible for the film.[22]

One supposition would be that there is a causal or automatic connection between an index and its referent. Without completely eliminating that connection, Frampton qualifies it as merely plausible in "A Pentagram for Conjuring the Narrative" and plays with it to generate the parables and paradoxes in *Hapax Legomena*.

Starting from the claim: "This is the first photograph I ever made with the direct intention of making art," the sequence of immolated photographs and their displaced descriptions purports to chronicle the maker's career from 1959 until 1966, when the deictic dislocations culminate in a narrative of uncanny referentiality for which there is no subsequent, confirming image unless we view the film as cyclical. But even in that case, the opening image of a darkroom (presumably the maker's) could hardly correspond to the "hopelessly ambiguous" image, grainy from successive enlargements that lead the narrator to conclude:

> Nevertheless, what I believe I see recorded in that speck of film, fills me with such fear, such utter dread and loathing, that I think I shall never make another photograph again.
> Here it is!
> Look at it!
> Do you see what I see?

The excess of affect both entices and frustrates the viewer's complicity in the quest for the uncanny referent. In this regard, Frampton reenacts the semiological mise en abyme of Stéphane Mallarmé's "Le demon de l'analogie."

22. Field and Sainsbury, "*Zorns Lemma* and *Hapax Legomena*," p. 50.

The four tableaux of *Poetic Justice* ring the changes on indexical shifters by making "you," "your lover," and "me" the protagonists of the script in which photographs are repeatedly said to be taken and torn up. The first tableau opens with a tacit acknowledgment of Walt Whitman's domination over elegies for erotic and imaginative loss in the American tradition:

> #2
> (LONG SHOT)
> A BLOOMING LILAC IN EARLY LIGHT. SCENE BRIGHTENS
> SLOWLY. (SLOW DISSOLVE TO...)
> ...
> #13
> (CLOSE-UP)
> A LILAC. A BLUEJAY LANDS.
> #14
> (MIDDLE SHOT)
> YOU RAISE A CAMERA TO YOUR EYE.

Whitman had set the scene of "Out of the Cradle Endlessly Rocking" thus:

> Once Paumanok,
> When the lilac-scent was in the air and the Fifth-month
> grass was growing,
> Up this seashore in some briers,
> Two feathered guests from Alabama, two together...

Whitman preceded Frampton in awaking "to discover [he] had learned to understand the language of birds"; it is a common topos of poets. In the song of the he-bird who lost his mate, Whitman heard the repeated word, "Death, death, death, death, death." Although death is not mentioned in *Poetic Justice* and is not one of the six expressions Frampton claims encompasses the entire avian vocabulary, it is a central term in "A Pentagram for Conjuring the Narrative," where narrators tell themselves stories because they are "waiting to die." The prevalence of corpses in the subsequent *Magellan* project more than compensates for the displacement of the imagery or allusions to death in *Hapax Legomena*. In the essay on Muybridge in *Circles of Confusion*, Frampton attributed his subject's obsession with the atomization of time to the ecstatic moment in which he shot and killed his wife's lover. Significantly, he uses the very word for the sections of *Poetic Justice* when he writes, "Time seems, sometimes, to stop, to be suspended in tableaux disjunct from change and flux. Most human beings experience, at one time or another, moments of intense passion during which perception seems vividly arrested: erotic rapture, extremes of rage or terror came to mind."[23] Here the very title *Poetic Justice* is a name for irony, with overtones of retribution. In the erotic triangle between the three essentially grammatical persons of the film, at the conclusion of the third tableau, the "first person" shoots with a camera, not a gun:

#179
(MIDDLE SHOT)
BEDROOM. LOVE MAKING.
OUTSIDE THE WINDOW I AM AIMING A CAMERA.

Ironically, that would be one of the few easily realizable shots in the section; for the entire tableau is a phantasmagoria, plausible only in the etymological meaning of the term, as the filmmaker slyly reveals in

#160
(MIDDLE SHOT)
BEDROOM. LOVE MAKING. OUTSIDE THE WINDOW IS A
SEATED AUDIENCE APPLAUDING.

Pointing to the confluence of the Muybridge essay, *Poetic Justice*, and *Critical Mass*, Annette Michelson noted "the crystallization of the thematics of a double violence within language and the erotic."[24] Michelson pointed out the element of performance in this film, which by extension applies to Frampton's analysis of photography and temporal ecstasy in general: The act of taking an image and the consciousness of being photographed turn the cameraman and his subject into performers in a plausible mimesis of voyeurism and exhibitionism. Subsequently, in 1982, Frampton made the nexus of eros, violence, and performance the basis of his lecture "The Pornographic and the Erotic Image—Toward Definition and Implication" at the International Center of Photography. In that text he insisted that "eroticism depends very heavily on exactly the supposed plausibility" of images of "that swarm of events we are accustomed to call the real world."[25]

To make *Critical Mass*, Frampton enlisted two students of filmmaker Larry Gottheim at SUNY Binghamton to improvise a fight under the pretext that the young man has just returned from two nights away from the young

23. Frampton, *Circles of Confusion*, p. 79 (italics mine).
24. Annette Michelson, "Frampton's Sieve," *October* 32 (Spring 1985), p. 160.
25. Hollis Frampton, "Erotic Predicaments for the Camera," *October* 32 (Spring 1985), p. 56. The lecture consisted of four dramatic monologues ventriloquizing F. J. Moulin, Lewis Carroll, an anonymous crime photographer of one of Jack the Ripper's victims, and Leslie Krims.

woman with whom he lives, refusing to explain where he has been or to apologize for not contacting her while he was away. The composition of the two one-hundred-foot-long takes, showing the couple posed closer to one another than would seem natural for their conflict, dressed in black, in front of bright lights, up against a white wall, resembles an improvisational exercise in an acting studio. The brilliance of the film lies in the editing strategy that extracts musicality from the sometimes hysterical explosions of the woman and the angry resistances of the man.

Frampton acknowledged the influence of Ken Jacobs's aesthetics in the conception of the film: "Ken has had, for a long time, a fantasy of a form that keeps trying to get itself together, and does so for a little while, and then keeps breaking down again, falling apart, goes staggering along.... [T]he seeds of perfect coherence and the seeds of chaos would follow with utter inexorable logic from the nature of the material itself..."[26]

The film corresponds to his adoption of a version of Jacobs's idea by beginning in blackness with the voices edited in rhythmic repetitions. We hear the woman answering the barely audible "How are you?": "Just/ Just fine. Where/ fine. Where the hell were you?/ fine. Where the hell were you?/ were you?" After two minutes of this exchange in growing intensity, there is a sudden pause followed by the first appearance of the image showing the coded punch holes of the start of the camera roll. For the next five minutes they argue in synchronous sound, with jump cuts in the same three- or four-part stages of repetitions into which he gradually introduces new words and gestures. Woman: "...to go. There are plenty of guys/...to go. There are plenty of guys I could live/ plenty of guys I could live with/ plenty of guys I could live with. I don't/ I could live with. I don't need your shit/...your shit." Man: "And probably have been/ probably have been/ have been..."

The argument continues in waves of intensity, sometimes out of synch, for more than twenty minutes. Nothing could be further from Jacobs's sensibility, however, than Frampton's precision and attention to quantitative editing rhythms and the harmonic phasing of overlapping voices. Jacobs has spent his entire career exploring the nuances of the humilis style, redeeming popular detritus with an extraordinary sensitivity to moments of uncanny beauty in unexpected places and situations. Frampton, by contrast, was an intellectual committed to the canons of high modernism. His films seem to be organized by sets of rules even when the rules are not immediately perceptible. Jacobs, on the other hand, gives his works the appearance of having been spontaneously intuitive. They often seem to be expandable, as if the filmmaker imagined that an ideal film would be assembled even while it was

26. Field and Sainsbury, "*Zorns Lemma* and *Hapax Legomena*," p. 61.

being projected.[27] Not surprisingly, Jacobs had an intensely negative reaction to *(nostalgia)* and *Critical Mass* when he first saw them. Larry Gottheim believes that this resulted in foreclosing the possibility of Frampton becoming a member of the Cinema Department at SUNY Binghamton.[28]

During the week when he shot the original material for *Critical Mass*, Frampton also recorded the basis for the subsequent film in the cycle, *Traveling Matte*:

> I'd gone up there [Binghamton] to show some films and... to make
> the lip-synch footage for *Critical Mass*. ... I started thinking about
> being kind of trapped in this motel room, and trying to look out, as a
> metaphor for part of the human condition, which is being trapped in
> this little round bone room (the skull) and trying to see *out*. ... There
> were two students there, who were part of an experimental video lab,
> and they were very hot to have anybody who came there make a video
> tape piece; and they were going to put the camera in my hand and tell
> me what buttons to press. So I thought about doing something about
> that feeling of being locked up in a room. ... So I went out, having got
> an image that I thought would make some sense in that very sparse,
> scummy sort of penal institution of a university landscape covered
> with mud and slush and snow. ... I wanted to emphasize the graphic-
> ness that the TV image has. ... It is really like a crude engraving; it's
> not like a photographic image.[29]

During the question and answer period following a presentation of the film at the Millennium Film Workshop, Frampton added:

> I wanted the action of the film to be a kind of larger metaphor for the
> transition in my mind from photographic to graphic images. ... The
> film begins, I think, quite simply, as peeking through a hole *at*
> something, and it ends quite simply as looking at the shape of the
> hole. ... Within the context of the larger form of this five-part [*sic*]
> thing (which I would rather call Pentecost than Pentality), if you think
> about the pretext given for the content of *Critical Mass*, a title which

27. Jacobs once recounted to me his thrill in the early 1960s, during a screening of Ron Rice's films, when a reel of film fell off the projector at the Film-makers' Cinematheque, unraveling as it rolled from the balcony into the audience (without hurting anyone); he dreamed of safely incorporating such an event into one of his works.

28. Letter from Larry Gottheim to Scott MacDonald, read by MacDonald at Princeton University during the conference Gloria! The Legacy of Holly Frampton, November 6, 2004.

29. Field and Sainsbury, "*Zorns Lemma* and *Hapax Legomena*," pp. 64–65; some of the ellipses were in the original interview, most are mine. I have also slightly revised the punctuation.

of course is a pun in itself, then *Traveling Matte* is about something quite personal. Whether it is about being lonely or not is strictly my business. It is most assuredly about being alone and about having not very much but your eye and two hands at a particular time of life.[30]

In preferring the religious metaphor for the five-part structure, Frampton is suggesting that the whole cycle concerns both inspiration and the extraordinary acquisition of new languages. That is congruent with the theme of the five-part "Pentagram for Conjuring the Narrative," where the metaphor is theurgic and the sudden gift of tongues is that of the birds. In fact, the metaphor of consciousness as a prisoner in the body closely echoes the "supreme metaphor" of the self Frampton derived from Beckett in the fourth part of that essay.

Brakhage singled out the wordless *Traveling Matte* for praise. He must have realized that by using his hand as a mask in front of the lens, Frampton was repeating his own innovation in *Song 8* (1965), where he used his fingers to shape the frame as he filmed underwater life in an aquarium. He may also have intuited the regression to childhood Frampton felt "making a telescope out of [my] fist, which is a little child's gesture."[31] Brakhage wrote, "This film metaphors an entire human life: birth, sex, death—the framing device is the fingers and palm of the maker's hand, wherein others only attempt to read the future."[32] A return to childhood is also implicit in the structure of the companion piece, *Ordinary Matter*, as Frampton described it to Mekas:

> [A]nd finally the eye that was trying to see out, through the little hole—through the fist, in *Traveling Matte*, opens up and does, to an extent, really see out, and end with something that is a very old image in my eye, of running through corn fields as a child, with the leaves slapping me in the face, and the sun hitting me, and so forth.[33]

As late as May 1972, Frampton spoke of *Hapax Legomena* as a six-part sequence with a slightly different order: *(nostalgia)*, *Critical Mass*, *Traveling Matte*, *Ordinary Matter*, *Poetic Justice*, and *Special Effects*. He had not completed *Ordinary Matter*, which he predicted would be "a more or less continuous time lapse journal, a dolly from Stonehenge on Salisbury Plain to the kitchen of my farmhouse in central New York State via a number of other landmarks. The dolly will come to rest on a still photograph of my face, lying on a small table, between a potted cactus and a coffee cup lying next to a

30. Hollis Frampton, "Three Talks at Millennium," pp. 277–78.
31. Jonas Mekas, Movie Journal, *Village Voice*, January 11, 1973.
32. *Film-makers' Cooperative Catalogue No. 7*, p. 171.
33. Jonas Mekas, Movie Journal, *Village Voice*, January 18, 1973.

window."[34] Apparently as a metahistorian of the cinema he was preparing to ironize the structure of Michael Snow's *Wavelength* in which he had appeared, by substituting the props of *Poetic Justice* and *(nostalgia)* for Snow's photograph of waves. On the soundtrack he proposed to edit twelve one-sentence descriptions of Marcel Duchamp's *Given: (1) the waterfall, (2) the illuminating gas*, six written by men, six by women, and recited by voices of the opposite genders. The title, like that of *Critical Mass*, puns on a term from physics. Ordinary or baryonic matter—as solids, liquids, or gases—makes up less than half of one percent of the universe. The part of the Mass that does not change from day to day is called "ordinary." The Latin words *ordo* (order) and *mater* (mother), by way of *materia* (timber, building material) are at the etymological sources of the expression. Similarly, at the root of "critical mass," the expression physicists use to denominate the fissionable material needed to sustain a chain reaction, we find *krinein* (Greek: to separate, discern, judge) and *massa* (Latin: bread dough, from *mag*—the Indo-European radical for *soften* or *knead*). Clearly, the explosive, unstoppable argument at the core of the film is such a chain reaction. Frampton has massaged the raw sound and visual tracks of *Critical Mass*, separating their discernible elements into combustible particles from which he orchestrated the film. But the title of *Ordinary Matter* seems more remote from the film to which it was given. The solids and gases it depicts are the landforms, monuments, and atmosphere of Stonehenge, Salisbury Cloister, the Brooklyn Bridge, and the filmmaker's farm in Eaton, New York; wood shingles, megaliths, carved marble, granite blocks, and steel cables are the building materials surveyed.

Camera movement is, indeed, an ordinary matter in the history of the American avant-garde cinema. The first word of the earlier title, *Traveling Matte*, also refers to this trope. (A traveling matte was an element in creating special effects before the advent of computer graphics in film production: It was a mask to block out a mobile element of a shot so that a foreign image might be embedded in its place.) Together *Traveling Matte* and *Ordinary Matter* instantiate the stage of somatic camera movement in Frampton's metahistorical scheme. The latter film even mimics a more arcane movement:

> It happens to contain mirror reflections that wind and unwind on the rotary sections of the film involving Stonehenge and Salisbury Cloister. . . . I have built into *Ordinary Matter* a montage that equates a set of connections among different kinds of space with a film projector. The film goes from rotary to reciprocating to rotary motion, like a projector. . . . A cloister is, by definition, an enclosure that one sees only from the inside: one looks inward. Stonehenge only appears

34. Peter Gidal, "Interview with Hollis Frampton," *October* 32 (Spring 1985), p. 102.

to be that way. Instead of looking inward entirely, it also very much
looks outward, first, towards the larger geographical place in which
it's situated—Salisbury Plain; ... then, historically, towards the sites in
England where the stones were brought from; and finally, because it
is an astronomical observatory, towards very large astronomical spaces
with long periodicities. Brooklyn Bridge, of course, is a monument—
one that I've always had a special predilection for—to connecting
places otherwise inaccessible to each other. ... The first time I walked
across Brooklyn Bridge was unquestionably one of the grand aesthetic
experiences of my life—and Stonehenge, indeed, was another.[35]

The intricacy of *Ordinary Matter* arises from its shifting sites and the
variations of its rhythms. Often the breakneck movement created through
pixilation will transfer its momentum for a brief moment to a static shot
of running water or decelerate to the pace of a brisk walk. The "vision of a
journey, during which the eye of the mind dives headlong through Salisbury
Cloister (a monument to enclosure), Brooklyn Bridge (a monument to connection) Stonehenge (a monument to the intercourse between consciousness
and LIGHT... visiting along the way the diverse meadows, barns, waters
where I now live; and ending in the remembered cornfields of my childhood"
makes reference to a large number of avant-garde films that explore camera
movement.[36] To MacDonald, Frampton said, "In a jittery way, it does a little
bit of what [Michael Snow's] machine in *The Central Region* does: namely,
it presents a kind of deanthropomorphosized vision, by traversing the space
in a manner and at a speed that a human being could not."[37] The restless
camera incarnates the Emersonian topos at the mythic origins of Frampton's
cinema—the lost *Ten Mile Poem*. Yet the handheld, humanized quality of the
pixilation seems to owe something to Jonas Mekas's film diaries. The movement over the hayfields echoes Ernie Gehr's blurred striations of vegetation
in *Field* (1970); the circling of Salisbury Cloister recalls Menken's movement
around the courtyards of the Alhambra in *Arabesque for Kenneth Anger*; the
walk across Brooklyn Bridge may allude to Menken's *Go!Go!Go!* but it un-
doubtedly recapitulates Frampton's own *Surface Tension*; there is a debt to
Brakhage's movement through Père Lachaise cemetery in *The Dead* and to
several other Brakhage films in the representation of Stonehenge; and finally,
the sensual movement through the cornfields may pay homage to the country
excursion in Andrew Noren's *Adventures of the Exquisite Corpse: Huge Pupils*, a
work Frampton repeatedly praised for founding a tactile cinema.

35. MacDonald, *A Critical Cinema*, pp. 68–70.
36. *Film-makers' Cooperative Catalogue No. 7*, p. 171.
37. MacDonald, *A Critical Cinema*, p. 69.

Remote Control was a late addition to the cycle. The filmmaker told Mekas that it was the one film in the cycle that might not be considered an autonomous, self-sufficient work.[38] He made the film by shooting single frames from a television set, one frame for each shot in the sequence of programs that he watched over two evenings. (It is noteworthy that he tentatively assigned it the Duchampian title, *Given:*.) He used the two-and-three-quarter-minute in-camera montage that resulted from this exercise as a loop that ran ten times through the whole length of the film. In counterpoint to this, he inserted numbers from 0 to 40 in five different sets, accompanying 0 and 1 with a graphic figure: a "solid" pyramid of broken lines representing the projection of a light beam, from left to right with 0, and right to left with 1.

His note for the *Film-makers' Cooperative Catalogue* exemplifies his most arcane style:

> A "baroque" summary of film's historical internal conflicts, chiefly
> those between narrative and metric/plastic montage; and between illu-
> sionist and graphic space. It incorporates 3 apposite "found" narratives,
> condenses 5 ways of making, and includes a "surprise" out of Hayden
> (or S.M. Eisenstein's IVAN, II).[39]

I had no idea what he meant by the three "apposite 'found' narratives" until I read in Scott MacDonald's interview that the rapid-fire montage included televised stories of a murderer who could pass through matter, killing his victims by squeezing their hearts; a police series marked by illusionary continuities of disparate locations; and an espionage drama in which a central controller could see what the spy he controls sees and thereby can send him instructions.[40] In an unpublished portion of the interview, Frampton emphasized the epistemological dimension of these found narratives:

> There is a Gertrude Stein opera that I've always been extremely
> fond of called *Blood on the Dining Room Floor*, which was a kind
> of Agatha Christie weekend in which the crux of the fiction is that
> the...personae only know what the audience knows and people keep
> dying—they're murdered—until finally there is only one woman left
> and she decides that she must be the one who did it....[The television

38. Scott MacDonald, "Hollis Frampton's *Hapax Legomena*," *Afterimage* 4, no. 4 [Rochester, N.Y.] (January 1978), pp. 8–13. MacDonald generously shared with me the elaborate notes he took on *Remote Control*. Shortly after Frampton completed *Hapax Legomena*, Jonas Mekas interviewed him about the unity and meaning of the cycle: Jonas Mekas, Movie Journal columns, *Village Voice*, January 11, January 18, 1973.
39. *Film-makers' Cooperative Catalogue No. 7*, p. 172.
40. MacDonald, *A Critical Cinema*, p. 70.

dramas represented] various narrative modes which had to do with essentially the relationship between some sort of active consciousness and the space in which it found itself and the things in that space and how much was known or not known about them.[41]

The five ways of making refer to the five systems of enumeration: The first appears to be irrational until we realize that there is a fixed progression from one to forty, although a random series of numbers—none equal to or higher than the next in the series—can intervene in the ordinal sequence. This system may correspond roughly to the editing of *Critical Mass*. The second mode had no numbers at all. Instead, the third loop switches from black and white to color (as in the conclusion to Eisenstein's *Ivan the Terrible, Part Two*). When the fourth loop reaches the same point, it reverts to black and white. As the only color portion of *Hapax Legomena*, this constitutes a surprise, motivating the allusion to Franz Josef Hayden's Symphony no. 97, known as the *Surprise Symphony*. The color loops reveal that the imagery had to be in color originally and therefore that the black-and-white repetitions of the loop had to have been made by a transfer to monochrome tonalities. This surprise implies a mystery of origins for all of the black-and-white photography in the cycle.

Frampton marked the third mode by repeating eleven times in a row, at regular intervals, the number and graph for 1. That would correspond, again approximately, to the structural organization of the thirteen burning photographs of *(nostalgia)*. The fourth, a nonsequential passage of unrepeated numbers, might be construed to schematize intuitive editing such as Frampton practiced in *Ordinary Matter*. Finally, the fifth, descending from 40 to 0, evenly paced one number every five seconds, would account for any purely rational fixed order, ironically even that of *Poetic Justice*, where the numbered pages ascend rather than decrease.

Remote Control's permutations on a loop of single frames suggest that Peter Kubelka's metric films, especially *Schwechater* (1958), were among his models and objects of contestation here. Similarly, the graphic image of the projection beam alludes to the graphic light bulb in *N:O:T:H:I:N:G* (1968), the flicker film of his friend Paul Sharits. The reduction of modes of filmmaking to sequences of numbers may also be linked to the hilarious schematization of narrative strategies with algebraic equations in "A Pentagram for Conjuring the Narrative."

41. Scott MacDonald, unpublished interview with Frampton, "*Hapax*, tape 5," p. 2. Mss supplied to author by MacDonald.

With *Special Effects*, Frampton returns to the first of his three inevitable conditions for cinema:

I wanted to affirm and honor the film frame itself. Because so much of what we know now, so much of our experience is something that comes to us through that frame. It seems to be a kind of synonym for consciousness. I have only seen the Pyramids of Egypt within that frame. I have only seen—endless things—most of what I believe I have experienced I have in fact seen at the movies, I've seen it inside that frame. But then, it's just my frame too, it's not everyone's. So that rather than filming it as a rock-steady monument, I did the film hand-held, with a long lens, and put myself in a physical position where it would be impossible to hold the camera steady....

That is my own frame, that is the vibration, let's say, of my own imagination and my own body, in relation to that bounded possibility of consciousness. Then you can imagine whatever you want inside of it.[42]

Here the "mechanical changes" hardly effect the "low degree of the sublime" Emerson invoked and Menken's somatic camera evoked. If, at the end of *Hapax Legmonena*, Frampton was finally fulfilling one of the aesthetic aspirations of the handheld telephoto lens of his lost *Ten Mile Poem*, it was in a severely ironic mode. When Emerson's spectacle of the world is reduced to the outline of a frame, the corresponding stability within the selfhood, or what Frampton here calls "the vibration of my own imagination and my own body," becomes an empty ("bounded") field of pure possibility, or "a kind of void," as he described it in the interview in which he said these words about the conclusion of his cycle. There he reluctantly consented to Mekas's request that he give a narrative account of the whole film, distancing his subject as "someone who resembles me in some ways." A paraphrase of the story he invented would be: A "non-poet" whose "first interest in images probably had something to do with what clouds of words could rise out of them" becomes a photographer before he attempts, with limited success, to destroy his work in the effort to become a filmmaker; he tries to write a script ("a fairly mundane kind of love story"), until the image first takes on movement and then sound, at which time "the primacy of the eye" emerges, creating the need to make some sense out of the ineluctable experience of vision. After tentatively peeking through the imaginary telescope of his hand with a mobile camera, he ceases to worry about words and still photographs and accelerates his

---

42. Mekas, Movie Journal, January 18, 1973.

embrace of vision in an "ecstatic, headlong dive." That accelerates further and further until "the person is no longer myself...the protagonist had gone hurtling out into a kind of void."[43]

This ad hoc scenario valorizes a trajectory that runs counter to Frampton's strength and originality as a filmmaker; for it is precisely his masterly engagement with spoken and written language that makes the first three parts of *Hapax Legomena* so fascinating. The concluding four are disappointing precisely insofar as they fail to achieve the ecstatic visuality to which they aspire.

Furthermore, the "spiritual biography" he invents for the person "who resembles me in some ways, and in others doesn't resemble me at all" represses the psychosexual allusions in the cycle's first three parts. Frampton seems to be struggling to give birth to a new protagonist disconnected from the trauma of his failed marriage. There are, as well, even more covert echoes of an earlier anguish. Frampton sometimes spoke, but never publicly as far as I know, of the terrible effects of his mother's psychosis on his childhood and adolescence. He said she would sit with a typewriter recording the often obscene messages sent into her head from outside forces. He claimed he went to Philips Academy at Andover (where he won a scholarship) largely to escape from her. Insofar as *Ordinary Matter* culminates in an "ecstatic" return to the cornfields of his remembered childhood, the title of the film could be read as a pun in English and Latin on the wish to have had an "ordinary mother." Following the same logic, we might hear in the words "remote control" an allusion to Nellie Cross Frampton's paranoia.

Hapax Legomena is a Menippean satire, a form as suited to Frampton's comic genius as it had been to Sidney Peterson's in the 1940s. Its allegorical structure describes the escape from psychic anguish, or from the dynamics of spiritual biography in all its forms, as the aesthetic achievement of systemic reductions. Each of the seven parts of the series posits a normatively creative subject and a system for voiding whatever intimations of a stable selfhood might be apprised by "certain mechanical changes" in the application of cinematic rhetoric. Emerson calls it the apprising of "a dualism...between the observer and the spectacle—between man and nature." Frampton postulates the polar oppositions of language and images, speaker and listener, frame and energy pattern, presence and memory, left and right hemispheres of the brain, only to generate filmic structures that question their stability. *Remote Control* points to the arbitrary nature of those very structures by abstracting them and imposing them upon a random selection of banal television dramas. That leaves us with *Special Effects'* dualism of a jittery camera and an empty frame as Frampton's reduction of the Emersonian cinema of Menken, Hugo, Brakhage, and Mekas.

---

43. Ibid. The synoptic story of the "non-poet" comes from the January 11, 1973 installment of the interview.

CHAPTER 6

Robert Beavers's *Winged Distance/Sightless Measure:* The Cycle of the Ephebe

I n *Circles of Confusion*, Hollis Frampton postulated four modes of composition for postsymbolist art. For the mode he called *constriction*, the reduction of a canon to a single author, he chose the example of James Joyce: "the works from which he derived the laws that govern his writing were those of one author, Gustave Flaubert."[1] Surely this is a hyperbole, but an instructive one. A similar case in the history of the American avant-garde cinema would be that of Robert Beavers; a parallel hyperbole might usefully claim that he constricted the history of the cinema to the films of Gregory Markopoulos, the Greek American avant-garde filmmaker whom he met in 1965 and with whom he lived until Markopoulos's death in 1992.

At thirty-seven, when he met Beavers, Markopoulos was at the height of his creative powers and artistic reputation. At that time, he was pushing his signature editing style of single-frame clusters to its limits with *The Illiac Passion* (finished 1967) and returning to the in-camera editing of his precocious

1. Hollis Frampton, *Circles of Confusion: Film, Photography, Video, Texts 1968–1980* (Rochester: Visual Arts Studies Workshop, 1983), p. 120,

youth for sections of that film and especially for his portrait series, *Galaxie* (released 1966), and the remarkable short tone poems *Ming Green* (1966) and *Bliss* (1967). He taught by example, encouraging the sixteen-year-old Beavers to begin making films right away, to learn the craft in the process of making his own works. Beavers's apprenticeship began with watching Markopoulos shoot several of the portraits and in posing as the sole subject for the forty-five minute film *Eros O Basileus* (1967).

Markopoulos had favored mannerist compositions: intense colors, beautiful and elegant men with expressive postures and gestures; he directed *Eros O Basileus* in this way. He possessed an extraordinary confidence in the aesthetic infallibility of his intuitions. In turning to portraits of people and places in the late 1960s, he put his faith more and more in the power of cinema to reveal the genius loci of the sites to which he was drawn and the character of his sitters through the rhythms of in-camera compositions.

At the start of his career, many of Beavers's fundamental attitudes toward his art were molded by Markopoulos's tutelage. Although he had decided to leave Deerfield Academy, an elite prep school, convinced that a traditional university education would not enrich but perhaps detract, and certainly distract him, from his artistic vocation, even before he learned that Markopoulos had dropped out of the cinema program at the University of Southern California in the late 1940s (after independently completing *Psyche*, the film that immediately established his importance as an avant-garde filmmaker), Beavers, an unusually determined, reserved, meticulous young man, was very far from the typical dropout of the 1960s. In his manner and his erudition he resembled the urbane, Ivy League–educated poets of an earlier generation who chose to live in Europe—James Merrill, John Ashbery, and Harry Matthews. When he and Markopoulos left America, the older filmmaker permanently withdrew all his films from distribution. Instead, he conceived the Temenos, a visionary exhibition space in central Greece, where he hoped eventually to build a theater and archive, a pilgrimage site devoted solely to the cyclical screenings of his and Beavers's films. Consequently, Beavers's whole career had been focused on preparation for the eventual exhibition of his work at the Temenos, until Markopoulos's death in 1992 led him to seek support for the Temenos project by showing his and Markopoulos's films internationally in museums, festivals, and other institutions.

From Markopoulos's films Beavers derived his predilection for montage, meticulous and often static compositions with clean, geometrical modeling and deeply saturated colors, and the rhythmical use of isolated sounds. Yet from the very start of his career, Beavers manifested a style and an atmosphere wholly his own: rigorous intellectual detachment, disdain for all anecdotal or narrative development, and an unwavering confidence in the truth of details and the poetic power of metonymy. Custom-designed masks and partial color filters were often central to his stylistic signature in his work of the 1970s. Several of his early films are self-portraits; he often represents himself as a filmmaker reframing and altering the colors of his empirical observations.

After making eight impressive films between 1967 and 1970, Beavers attained a new level of assurance with *From the Notebook Of...* (1971/1998). Inspired by Da Vinci's notebooks, and Valéry's *Introduction à la Méthode de Leonardo da Vinci*, he filmed undramatic views of Florence with marginal glimpses of himself crafting his images. Here Beavers declares an abiding theme of his work, the examination of the creative imagination. His subsequent films, *The Painting* (1972/1999), a Flemish triptych; *Work Done* (1972/1999), a "book of hours"; and *Ruskin* (1975/1997), the Alpine and Venetian studies of Ruskin, mediate between the contemporary perceptions of the filmmaker and the aesthetic past. In his films of the 1980s and afterward, the self-reflexive gestures become more oblique and subtle; montage and sound evoke the filmmaker's sensibility.

Within the projected Temenos, his films to date would be shown in three cycles under the rubric *My Hand Outstretched to the Winged Distance and Sightless Measure*. (Markopoulos's *Eniaios* spans a staggering fifty-two cycles.) The first cycle would consist of most of his first films, the second of *From the Notebook Of...*, *The Painting*, *Work Done*, and *Ruskin*. The third cycle includes *Sotiros* (1976–78/1996), *AMOR* (1980), *Efpsychi* (1983/1996), *Wingseed* (1985), *The Hedge Theater* (1986–90/2002), *The Stoas* (1991–97), and *The Ground* (1993/2001). If "winged distance" can be read as a metonymy for the optical infinity of the focus of the film camera, "sightless measure" might similarly refer to the musical or poetic rhythm of the soundtrack. Nevertheless, the long title Beavers gave the series inescapably evokes, and even defines, the American sublime, since it combines a hyperbole of personal expansion and a metonymy for the canon of artistic permanence; for the literal translation of *kanon* would be "measuring rod."

Although Beavers, of all the filmmakers I consider in this book, is the least Emersonian in his cinematic rhetoric, his aesthetics so often correspond to Emerson's "Circles" that I am tempted to read the title as a derivation from its first two paragraphs, where we find:

> Our life is an apprenticeship to the truth, that around every circle another can be drawn; that there is no end in nature, but every end is a beginning, that there is always another dawn risen on mid-noon, and under every deep another lower deep opens.
>
> This fact, as far as it symbolizes the moral fact of the Unattainable, the flying Perfect, around which the hands of man can never meet, at once the inspirer and condemner of every success, may conveniently

serve us to connect many illusions of human power in every department.[2]

"Sightless measure" even nearly echoes a passage in Whitman's "Song of
Myself," merely five lines after the first great climax where Whitman had
vaunted, "Dazzling and tremendous how quick the sunrise would kill me, / If
I could not now and always send sunrise out of me." Where Whitman wrote
"speech," "film" would be appropriate to Beavers's version of this sublimity:

Speech is the twin of my vision. . . . it is unequal to measure itself.
It provokes me forever,
It says sarcastically, Walt, you understand enough. . . . why don't you let it
    out then?[3]

Of course, Beavers's tone is much cooler, guarded, and therefore closer
to that of Ashbery, when he concludes "Tapestry" with his own version of a
"sightless measure":

It proposes: sight blinded by sunlight.
The seeing taken in with what is seen
In an explosion of sudden awareness of its formal splendor.[4]

In two of his rare polemical broadsheets, the filmmaker defended his reticence to accent the emotional contours of his films and, in so doing, defined
his relationship to viewers and to language:

The spectator must discover why an image was chosen to be represented; the silence of such a discovery becomes a moment of release.
It is not the film maker's work to tell you: his work is to make the
film and to protect what he does, in the serenity of a thought without
words, without the quality in words which would destroy what he in-
tends to represent.[5]

2. Ralph Waldo Emerson, *Essays and Lectures* (New York: Library of America, 1983), p. 403.
3. Walt Whitman, "Leaves of Grass," *Selected Poems 1855–1892: A New Edition*, ed. Gary Schmidgall (New York: St. Martin's, 1999), p. 37.
4. John Ashbery, "Tapestry," *Selected Poems*, (New York: Penguin, 1986), p. 269.
5. Robert Beavers, "Em.blem." [Originally distributed as a broadsheet published by Temenos and distrib-uted at Temenos screenings in Greece in the 1980, the original version was also published as a note to Bea-vers screenings at the New York Film Festival, 1999.] In editng *The Searching Measure* (Berkeley: Berkeley Art Museum and Pacific Film Archive, 2004), pages unnumbered, Beavers made many changes in the texts that had been published earlier. I give the early version here and its revision in the following chapter.

I have named these projections, *Hautprobe*, in order to reflect towards the spectator the ambiguity of his awareness,

Strictly speaking there is no film audience...

The point from which to begin...then, is with the eye of the spectator, the first sense, and proceed to the others, as he recognizes the presence which becomes awareness. This is not a matter of understanding a film's content in one way or another; rather the viewer creates an order within himself, and this order is as conscious as Language.[6]

This sounds more like Hugo von Hofmannstahl's "word-skepticism" than Brakhage's imagining of preverbal seeing. For Beavers, the orphic film artist isolates an image as an autonomous entity of thought; that image points back to the filmmaker as well as to the object of contemplation ("The seeing taken in with what is seen"). He writes of displacing verbal elaboration with an intuitive optical intensity—"Sustained by the awakening of emotion united to strength, I reach beyond the life-likeness of the actor and the shadow of performance to the figure gathering the life that is in the light of the image"[7]—to the end that the viewer must reimagine the film in all its musical tensions and qualifications, at times bringing this subjective order into being through language. Thus Beavers anticipates the limitations and inevitability of efforts, such as this chapter, to tease into critical language a response to the style and implications of each of his films.

Around and between the gorgeous still-life shots Beavers mastered from Markopoulos's example—an open suitcase in a beautiful humble room, the details of a youthful male body—he orchestrated a wide range of movements: typically, the nervous vibration of a pod, shot in close-up with a handheld camera; fast panning back and forth over the landscape; abrupt vertical tilts; the trembling hairs on a man's leg. For the most part, these movements terminate abruptly, unexpectedly, carrying their suspended energy into the shots that follow them. When those subsequent images are static, the suddenly arrested propulsion accents and intensifies their richness and, in the filmmaker's terms, "harmony," soliciting our attention to their connotations. Beavers's montage manifests extraordinary restraint as if his rhythmic inspiration distilled and crystallized a musical idea, impeding viewers' anticipation of a figure of cadence, while again and again surprising us with new variations from the repertoire often exhibited in the first moments of a film.

---

6. Robert Beavers, "Hautprobe for a Spectator," (Milan: Temenos, 1978), pages unnumbered.
7. Robert Beavers, "Editing and the Unseen," in *The Searching Measure*.

The cutting on varieties of camera and object movement is so sophisticated that I might be tempted to say that Beavers has learned as much from Brakhage in this respect as from Markopoulos, and that his style is a wonderfully urbane synthesis of the two. But Beavers, working solely in Europe and sharing, at that time, Markopoulos's disdain for most American avant-garde cinema, probably had less contact, after an initial exposure in 1965, with Brakhage's art than any other major American avant-garde filmmaker of his generation. In fact, it is actually the difference between Brakhage's sense of moving visual poetry and Beavers's poetics that can help us define Beavers's style. Brakhage's chosen affinities in literature are largely American, Emersonian, with a predilection for modern poets who stress the rhetoric of energy and dynamic renewal: Stein, Pound, Olson, Duncan, McClure, Kelly, Johnson. But Beavers has self-consciously shuffled off his native muse—nothing is more American than his fascination with the monuments of European culture. He disciplined his sensibility with an intense reading of modern European poets: Valéry, George, Saba, Cavafy, Rilke, and perhaps Hofmannstahl. Their aesthetic nostalgias, negating arrests, and epistemological ironies—which portray poetic craft as an inspired construct to transform things and events into acts of the mind—inform his poetics of the cinematic image as the fusion of observation and action, seeing and directing: "I am aware of the way in which 'observing' becomes 'directing,' aware of the power that exists in Seeing. The making of a film allows one to move back and forth, observing-directing."[8]

Whereas Brakhage's moving camera usually represents the bodily presence of the unseen filmmaker (virtually synonymous with the empirical Brakhage), so that in the film we see what he sees as he moves through space, Beavers's rhythms, isolating images as nodes of thought and memory, goad us to give as much weight to their disparities as to their fusions. His images are monads, irreducibly simple and real, yet their author's mental images as well, loaded with the history of poetic iconography. The poets to whom he seems closest often substitute masks or ventriloquize voices to compensate for a felt discontinuity of identity. In the many films that show him manipulating filters or masks, Beavers sketches his idealized persona—the Filmmaker—without pushing its identification with the empirical self into a confessional mode. In the later films, the images and the harmonic editing bear the burden of the evoking of that persona; the masks, filters, and brief self-portraits disappear.

However, some of the distinctions between his earlier and later films became obscured in the late 1980s and early 1990s when the filmmaker systematically reedited the images (sometimes even including new shots) and remade the soundtracks of nearly all his films. He no longer shows his first film,

---

8. Beavers, "Em.blem."

Spiracle (1966), or his third, *On the Everyday Use of the Eyes of Death* (1967). Instead, at the premiere screening of *Winged Distance/Sightless Measure*—his abbreviation—at the Whitney Museum of American Art (October 7–30, 2005), he began the first cycle by showing *Winged Dialogue* (1967/2000) and *Early Monthly Segments* (1968–70/2002). The latter is an anthology of exercises Beavers disciplined himself to shoot so that more than a month would not pass without him recording images. Several of the segments show him making one or another of the films of the first cycle. Others offer glimpses of daily life with Markopoulos and their travels in Europe. Beavers abandoned the discipline after two years: His work on *From the Notebooks Of...* entailed the incorporation of such material in the film itself.

In assembling the first cycle for its premiere at the Whitney Museum, Beavers retrospectively followed the example of *From the Notebooks Of...*; he inserted the segments chronologically into the series of six films he made between 1967 and 1970, so that after we see *Winged Dialogue* and the collection of *Early Monthly Segments*, we see the former film again as the start of a sequence that includes five other films and the monthly segments in the order in which they were shot. The removal of individual titles that had been at the head of each film often obscures the transition between a previously autonomous film and a segment, especially in those instances when the segment describes a moment in the making of the film we have been viewing. This reorganization greatly enhances the impression of that the first cycle is one long, complex film.

Winged Dialogue is a portrait Beavers made of Markopoulos (and himself) on the Greek island Hydra. It is an epithalamium and conversation lyric, enthusiastically conflating his intense passion for the art form he was learning with the pleasures of his new conjugal relationship. Its interior serial organization, segmented into stanzas by passages of pure blue as if images of the sky, suggests a lyric sequence of variations on a theme, such as Whitman's Calamus poems in *Leaves of Grass*, but from the perspective of the enthralled ephebe rather than the older lover. Whitman, imagining himself in both roles in "Whoever You Are Holding Me Now in Hand," fantasized a scenario similar to that realized in this film:

> ....on the beach of the sea,or some quiet island,
> Here to put your lips upon mine I permit you,
> With the comrade'.s long-dwelling kiss, or the new husband's kiss,
> For I am the new husband, and I am the comrade.[9]

---

9. Walt Whitman, "Whoever You Are Holding Me Now in Hand," *Selected Poems 1855–1892*, p. 226.

The tactility of the cinematic image plays a central role in all of Beavers's films. He frequently portrays the filmmaker as a hand craftsman, focusing the lens, pushing a filter across the plane of vision, making a splice. Even more often, he films hand gestures, clapping, touching, and shaping imaginary spaces. In all these references to the sense of touching there is a double acknowledgment of the power of the filmic caress and the impossibility of actually touching anything in cinema: Even the metaphors of the light touching the raw film stock or the projector beam hitting the screen reveal both the desire for a greater substantiality and its impossibility.

Where Whitman apotropaically warned his companions and interlocutors in the Calamus sequence of "the real reality," elusively signified by the juncture of love and death in "Scented Herbage of My Breast"—"Death is beautiful from you—(what indeed is more beautiful, except Death and Love?)"[10]—Beavers intimated the threat posed by the solitude and uncertainty of the erotic imagination as if it were an ontological condition of the film medium, although that problem and the idea of death preoccupy him more directly and intensely in the subsequent three films of the first cycle.

The threat or limitation of the erotic imagination is more clearly articulated in the two hundred revisions of *Winged Dialogue* than it had been in the initial editing: Images of Beavers and Markopoulos superimposed, or their shadows meeting, or reaching out from distinctly autonomous spaces through montage mark both their union and its threatened stability. A typical instance of this would be the stretch of Beavers's breast stroke as he swims, seeming to reach for Markopoulos's hand or body as he in turn extends his hand through the window of an island chapel or sunbathes naked in a ruined mill.

Beavers tacitly acknowledged the importance of *Winged Dialogue* as the locus of his poetic origination when he conceived the title for the whole series: He not only transfers "winged" from *dialogue* to *distance* but indicates that from the very start of his career the "outstretched hand" was the synecdoche of his incarnation as a filmmaker acutely sensitive to the elusive tactility of cinematic subjects; for in this film he repeatedly reaches into the frame, stretching his hand or hands toward the image, as if reaching for it or caressing it. At times he seems close to the Calamus poet in "Of the Terrible Doubt of Appearances" whose epistemological doubts are temporarily quieted "When he whom I love travels with me, or sits a long while holding me by the hand."[11] Yet Beavers' hand outstretched to a distance is one that can never grasp; it remains a gesture of signification and a trope.

10. Walt Whitman, "Scented Herbage of My Breast," *Selected Poems 1855–1892*, p. 224.
11. Walt Whitman, "Of the Terrible Doubt of Appearances," *Selected Poems 1855–1892*, p. 231.

Marie Menken: *Notebook*

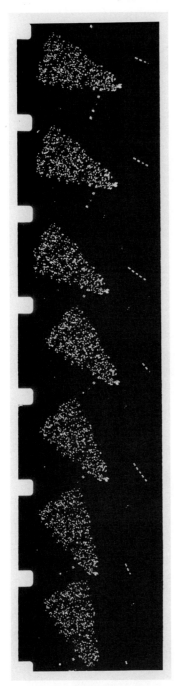 

Lights. Upside-down view
of the Christmas tree

Night Writing. Calligraphic
camera movement

Stills courtesy of Anthology Film Archives

Marie Menken: *Arabesque for Kenneth Anger*

The descent of the dove
into the Alhambra

Filmstrip courtesy of
Arunas Kulikauskas

Stills courtesy of
Anthology Film Archives

Marie Menken: *Go!Go!Go!*

Willard Maas writing
on the penthouse roof

Stills courtesy of
Anthology Film
Archives

Sunset over the
harbor

Sunset filmstrip made
by Arunas Kulikaukas

Ian Hugo: *Bells of Atlantis*

Anaïs Nin superimposed over wrecked ship
Still courtesy of Robert Haller

"I always rise after the crucifixion . . ."
Still courtesy of Anthology Film Archives

Ian Hugo: *Melodic Inversion*

Filmstrips made by Arunas Kulikaukas
Still courtesy of Anthology Film Archives

Stan Brakhage: *Duplicity III*

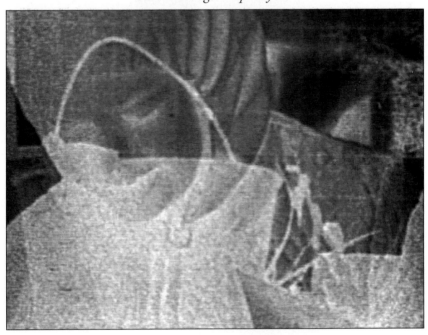

Still courtesy of the estate of Stan Brakhage

Stan Brakhage: *Sincerity IV*

Filmstrips made by Arunas Kulikaukas

Stan Brakhage: *Duplicity III*

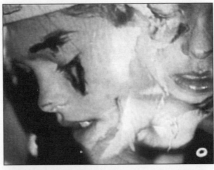

Stills courtesy
of the estate of
Stan Brakhage

Jonas Mekas: *Diaries, Notes and Sketches (Walden)*

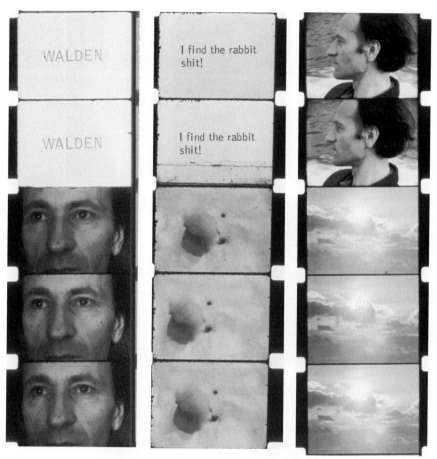

Filmstrips made by Arunas Kulikaukas
Stills courtesy of Jonas Mekas

Hollis Frampton: *Hapax Legomena*

(nostalgia)

Poetic Justice

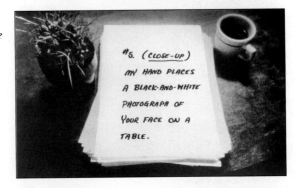

Critical Mass

Traveling Matte

Hollis Frampton: *Hapax Legomena*

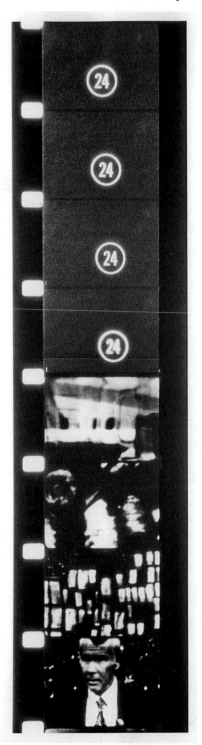

Remote Control

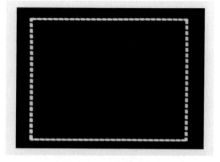

Special Effects

Stills courtesy of Anthology Film
Archives

Robert Beavers: *My Hand Outstretched to the Winged Distance and Sightless Measure: Cycle One*

The image of Markopoulos superimposed on the tower of Hydra in *Winged Dialogue*

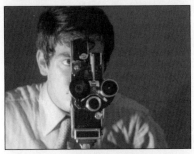

Beavers filming himself in *Early Monthly Segments*

Consecutive images of *Diminished Frame*

Stills © Robert Beavers, courtesy Temenos

Robert Beavers: *My Hand Outstretched to the Winged Distance and Sightless Measure: Cycle One*

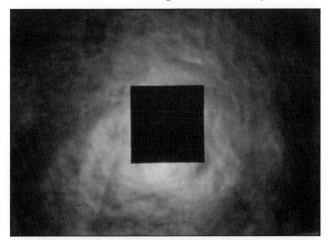

Count of Days

Still Light

Robert Beavers: *My Hand Outstretched to the Winged Distance and Sightless Measure: Cycle Two*

Markopoulos
and Beavers
in *From the
Notebook Of* . . .

Beavers in
*From the
Notebook Of* . . .

The torn
photograph
of Beavers in
The Painting

Stills
© Robert Beavers,
courtesy Temenos

Robert Beavers: *My Hand Outstretched to the Winged Distance
and Sightless Measure: Cycle Two*

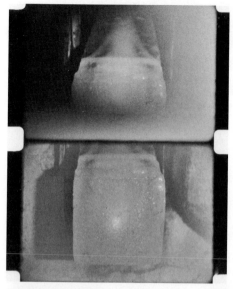

Work Done

Ruskin

Stills
© Robert Beavers,
courtesy Temenos

Andrew Noren: *The Adventures of the Exquisite Corpse*

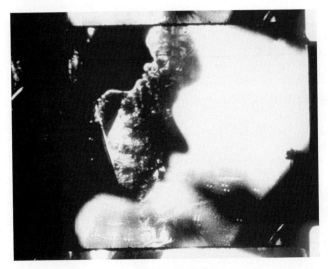

Charmed Particles

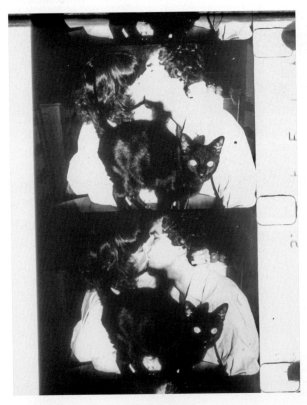

Lighted Field

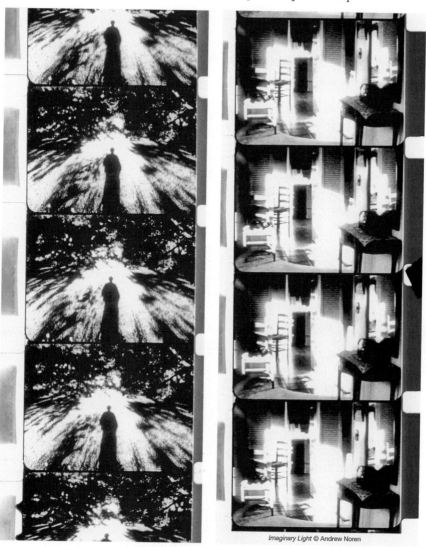

Imaginary Light © Andrew Noren

Imaginary Light
Stills © Andrew Noren, courtesy of the filmmaker

Ernie Gehr: *Side/Walk/Shuttle*

Stills courtesy of Ernie Gehr

The montage of body and hands shows the influence of Markopoulos's *Himself as Herself* (1966), which depicts its protagonist caressing himself as if with the hands of another, just as late in the film a rapid recapitulation of shots suggests the signature editing strategies of Markopoulos's *Swain* (1950), or *Twice a Man* (1963). More indirectly, Beavers manipulates the images through unusual framing and superimposition. Holding the camera sideways, he filmed Markopoulos walking (his upper body almost invisible in the superimposition because he was wearing a black shirt); then, after rewinding the film, he shot him from the other side, to create a four-legged being. Another repeated superimposition shows Markopoulos as if holding his own head at his waist. Like the riddle of the sphinx, as Freud understood it, these composites are hyperboles of his mentor's sexual power. Sometimes there are three images of the older filmmaker on the screen at once; in many of these shots (and many others) Beavers uses the rectangle of a door or window to frame him. In the films that follow he will explore the Bolex filter holder, and eventually homemade matte boxes, to reduplicate the foundational rectangle in different areas of the image.

In the revision of *Winged Dialogue*, the splash of Beavers's swimming is spread out through the shortened film, as if the gestures of his swimming strokes were acts or attempts at touching Markopoulos in the separated spaces in which he appears, often superimposed, on the frame. Touch is the central issue here. Beavers explores the illusion of touching, either as shadows seem to touch each other, or hands come nearer or apparently touch although the spaces they occupy clearly indicate that the conjunction is the illusion of the filmmaker. Thus the film acknowledges the failure of physical contact as it extols touching.

The first of the *Early Monthly Segments* immediately follows the revised *Winged Dialogue*. In it Beavers holds a white sheet of paper or cardboard before the camera. A circular hole has been cut in it, rhyming with the circle of the camera lens, through which we see a self-portrait of the young filmmaker-ephebe with his Bolex. He is at once self-circumscribed and "filled with the new wine of his imagination," as Emerson described the poet in "Circles":

> Then cometh the god and converts the statues into fiery men, and by a flash of his eye burns up the veil which shrouded all things, and the meaning of the very furniture, of cup and saucer, of chair and clock and tester, is manifest....
>
> He smites and arouses me with his shrill tones and breaks up my whole chain of habits, and I open my eye on my own possibilities. He claps wings to the sides of the solid lumber of the world, and I am capable once more of choosing a strait path in theory and practice.[12]

---

12. Emerson, *Essays and Lectures*, pp. 231–32

With the image of a body hitting the water at the conclusion of the film, Beavers invoked the moment in Jean Cocteau's *Le sang d'un poet* when the poet dives through a mirror to enter the domain of his imagination. His next film, *Plan of Brussels* (1968), made when he was nineteen, owes an even greater conceptual allegiance to Cocteau's film, which had been the fountainhead of lyric visions of the narcissistic imagination for Deren, Anger, and Brakhage as well as for Markopoulos. Beavers filmed himself alone in a hotel room, both at his work desk and lying naked on the bed, while in rapid rhythmic cutting, and sometimes in superimposition—inspired by his recent acquaintance with Dreyer's *Vampyr*—the phantasmagoria of people he met in Brussels and images from the streets flood his mind. Fragments of Ghelderode's *Duvelor* can be heard on the soundtrack, cuing the viewer to the Faustian theme of this twenty-eight-minute film, which he has said was inspired by James Ensor's paintings. He included geometrical masks—moving rectangles, circles, triangles against iridescent colors—in the fast alternation of images. As punctuation, lubrication, and percussion, these abstract elements shape and formalize the film. In the subsequent films of the cycle, colored masks and filters will become dominating stylistic traits.

Ghelderolde's puppet play dramatizes the last hours of the devil Duvelor as he attempts in vain to hang himself in order to return to hell. He bemoans his existence: "Here I am alone in the world...And I am sick to death of it!...What a profession [Quel metiér]! There aren't many more souls for me to lose—nowadays most mortals manage to lose themselves..." Each time there is a knock on the door, he kills his visitor and stashes the body in his cellar. In the last moment of the film he is about to die: "Somebody go get a confessor, a confessor. I am dying!!! Arise, my soul."[13]

The new soundtrack of *Plan of Brussels*, giving more centrality to the sinister and military imagery embedded in the film, makes the influence of Ensor more transparent. We hear Duvelor's invocation of Lucifer and Satana several times early on; crowd noises, drum rolls, thunder, bells, and the repeated knocking on the door combine with the montage of faces and the rhythmic geometrical figures to trouble the repose of the autobiographical figure, clearly modeled on the ghostly, superimposed image of the self in *Vampyr*.

The programming of *My Hand Outstretched* at the Whitney premiere underscored the significance of pairs of films in the first and second cycles. Together *Winged Dialogue* and *Plan of Brussels* contrast two sides of the film-

---

13. For a discussion of the play and an English translation of the text, see Antoinette Botsford, *The Toone Marionette Theater of Brussels* (Dissertation, University of California, Los Angeles, 1980). I have made some slight adjustments of her translation to correspond to the fragments used in Beavers's film. See Robert Guiette, *Marionettes de tradition populaire* (Bruxelles: Editions Cercle d'Art, 1950) for the original text.

maker's erotic imagination. Without Markopoulos, he is invaded by fantasies of military parades, murders, and seductions. In fact, the whole first cycle poses the problem of the Self and the Other: In *Winged Dialogue* and *Plan of Brussels* the Self is literalized, as Beavers appears in both films. He disappears from the previously completed films of the first cycle to reemerge in *From the Notebook Of...*, but by incorporating the *Early Monthly Segments* into *My Hand Outstretched*, the filmmaker reiterated the representation of the Self and of Markopoulos as the central Other. The segment immediately following *Plan of Brussels* is emblematic of the whole cycle: Markopoulos, holding a mirror, flashing light into the camera lens; we can glimpse images of Beavers in the mirror too. The following segment focuses on the filmmaker's tools, and the one after that shows him naked, performing his morning ablutions. Subsequently, the second pair, *The Count of Days* and *Palinode*, proceeds from a withdrawal of the presence of the filmmaker from the screen and his consequent effort to articulate the film in terms of the intersubjectivity of others. Then in the final pairing, *Diminished Frame* and *Still Light*, the lyrical self, as the unseen observer behind the camera, comes to the fore.

Plan of Brussels was the first of three films Beavers made in 1968 and 1969 reflecting his engagement with the psychodramatic genre that had been the dominant part of the American avant-garde cinema when Markopoulos made his *Psyche* (1947). That film was at once more narratively complex and more ambiguous than the psychodramas of his contemporaries Deren, Anger, Harrington, and Maas. Yet by the 1960s the narrative dimensions of Markopoulos's cinema had become much more elliptical and hermetic. Beavers, in turn, radicalized the strategies of these later works when he made *Plan of Brussels* and especially the subsequent pairing, *The Count of Days* (1969) and *Palinode* (1969). From the beginning, his films were built out of minimal events; he concentrated his attention on nuances of color, sound, editing, and, eventually, camera movement rather than narrative; for, in the whole of Beavers's oeuvre, there is hardly a single continuous passage in which two events follow in a sequential or causal timeline.

In the obscure psychodrama of *The Count of Days*, we can perceive the rudiments of a triangular conflict: A middle-aged man reads from a book and talks to a young woman. There is a younger man apparently waiting at the Zurich train station. Later, we see the men struggling with each other in the street. Amid these events there regularly and festishistically appear images of underwear, of a dead white rat on sheet of paper and, separately, a still life of a scalpel, tweezers, and scissors. Eventually, we come to see the rat dissected and pinned. At the time, Beavers felt he had a "cruel" interest in dissection. The University of Zurich turned down his request to film an autopsy, but he was able to film the dissection of an eye at that time. Spurred by Markopoulos's interest in Jung, he approached a psychoanalyst for treatment at the C. G. Jung-Institut who dismissed him because she did not think he required analysis. During this period he discovered Freud's 1909 "Notes Upon a Case of Obsessional Neurosis" (the Rat Man case), from which he derived the images of the rat—Freud's patient was pathologically disturbed by a story of torture in which a rat bore into a man's anus—and the train station—the patient behaved obsessively in taking trains. Beavers even considered his filming of the gold decoration on the train station as a transmutation of the symbolic obsession with money in the case history.

Freud analyzed the Rat Man's obsessions as symptoms of a profound ambivalence toward his dead father. He speculated that a forgotten scene of punishment or severe reproof for masturbation crystallized the tension between love and hatred that became displaced in the adult patient as compulsion and doubt. There is nothing in the film to indicate if the filmmaker associated his feelings for his own father, who died when he was ten, with those of Freud's subject, or identified the Rat Man with the writer Stefan Sadkowski, the older man in the film who reads fragments from his text, "Petermann in Hinterland," on the soundtrack.

While he was making *The Count of Days*, he was learning how Markopoulos prepared a film. His earlier experiences had been acting in his *Eros O Basileus* and accompanying him on the shooting of some of the portraits in *Galaxie*. Now he observed how the older filmmaker organized his footage without using an editing table. In 1998 he told Tony Pipolo how he prepares his own films:

> I usually start with just a few notes; the notes develop further as I am filming and continue while I edit. Once the filming is completed, or sometimes before it is completed, I project the footage and then separate the shots, noting each shot and its details. And I usually snip one or two frames from the shot and place it on a piece of paper. While editing, I have all the footage before me wound onto cores and I have these sheets with the film frames, and I have a set of rewinds with the reel onto which I wind the pieces of film as I choose them. When it is finished or nearly finished, I then look at it on a steenbeck table or project it. It is *important* to have the space between editing—and the *special quality of memory that is involved*—seeing the actual film in front of one. It is to a certain extent how Gregory edited some of his films although he was thinking in smaller units.[14]

14. Tony Pipolo, "Interview with Robert Beavers," *Millennium Film Journal* no. 32/33 (Fall 1998), p. 21. (emphasis mine).

In a monthly segment shown as a coda to *The Count of Days*, Robert Beavers sits at a table, without any visible film equipment, assembling and taping together shots of a 16 mm film, presumably the one we have been watching. I understand the imagery of the film and the allusions to Freud's case history fundamentally in terms of the young filmmaker's relationship to his art. In the first place, he has said that he used the dissecting instruments seen in that work to cut and scratch film. If dissection is a metaphor for filmmaking, it applies not just to disfiguring the photographic emulsion, or even to separating and editing shots, but to the basic configuration of events and characters as well as to the represented persona of the filmmaker. The dynamics of Freud's model for the evolution of infantile sexuality into obsessional structures can be considered as an allegory of the poetics of filmmaking, particularity if we view the dogged, repetitive work of film editing as the sublimation of an obsessional compulsion. From the beginning of his career, Beavers had sexualized the acts of filmmaking. In this allegorical schema the filmmaker becomes the vessel for generating images that represent a conflict between opposing impulses; his instinctual strategies for the repression of the associations of these images would channel displacements as the associations force their return within the obsessional structures of aesthetic composition—meticulous note taking, attentions to framing and focus, sundering and reorganization of shots, synchronization of sounds. Even "the special quality of memory" that comes from trying to recall the movement of a shot from handling the filmstrip might be considered one such strategy for displacement. The rule Beavers established for his next film, *Palinode*, is a general rule for repression: "Don't let yourself know what this film is about, while you are making it."[15]

Beavers did not know the cities of Zurich or Berlin, or more significantly the German language, when he made *The Count of Days*, *Palinode*, and *Diminished Frame*. All three reflect his alienation from his working environment. He tried to work through Freud's case history of the Rat Man, with a German text and a dictionary, seizing fragmentary images without being able to follow the argument. The repeated references to Sadkowski's book, on the screen and on the soundtrack, place at the core of the film an obsessive and sometimes sublimated relationship of the author to his text. When we see the older man reading aloud, he is clearly an anxious figure; his relationship to the young woman to whom he reads suggests erotic longing. In the recorded

---

15. Jeffrey Stout pointed out to me that this extraordinary interdiction corresponds to Emerson's famous assertion in "Self-Reliance": "I shun father and mother and wife and brother, when my genius calls me. I would write on the lintels of the door-post, *Whim*. I hope it is somewhat better than whim at last, but we cannot spend the day in explanation." [Emerson, *Essays and Lectures*, p. 262.] Stout wrote to me July 26, 2007, "Emerson is saying that when he is writing, he doesn't yet know what he is doing, though he hopes it will be more than whim at last."

passages there are plays on prefix variations, a tone of irony, and references to existential alienation and loneliness. The coda from the *Early Monthly Segments* establishes an analogy between the book and the film. Film strips hanging vertically fill the screen, intercut with the pages of the book. The final, repeated word audible on the soundtrack—*suchen* (to choose)—might describe the action of the filmmaker confronting his dismembered shots.

Beavers followed the segment of the editing of *The Count of Days* in *My Hand Outstretched* with a diary-like return to his domestic life: a visit from his friend, the filmmaker Tom Chomont, and Markopoulos sunbathing in Locarno. The interlude terminates with Markopoulos sleeping intercut with a quotation of the opening montage from his *Lysis* (1948). Since this is the only direct quotation of another film in the corpus of Beavers's cinema, it deserves particular attention. The brief passage comes from the opening of the second film of Markopoulos's youthful trilogy: He composed an auto-biographical cascade of images—an embroidered pillow (possibly from his baptism), a still life of oranges, a childhood photograph, a detail from a youthful painting—editing them in the camera. Beavers weaves this brilliant exemplum of Markopoulos's confidence in the expressive power of images, drawn from personal, even hermetic, sources, into the shot of the mature filmmaker asleep, as if the film he had made twenty years earlier, itself recapit-ulating the first twenty years of his life, were now a dream. Situated between *The Count of Days* and *Palinode*, it becomes the model for Beavers's artistic discipline and perhaps even a spur to issue a "palinode" to some earlier, less confidently personal work.

A palinode is a poem in which the author retracts something said in a pre-vious poem. It is not at all certain what Beavers is taking back with this film. When I asked him, he wrote back: "I do not know whether I can help you with explaining the title *Palinode*. I may have intended it as a song of regret, the atmosphere of life unlived in the repetitions of the singer's phrases and breath. I find it difficult to reach these films now."[16]

I believe the film is turning against the Freudian allegory and the "cruelty" of *The Count of Days*, but more significantly, Beavers seems to have felt the need to reorient his filmmaking practice by locating more profound sources for his images and by putting his confidence in their power. Speaking of Ma-tisse, Leo Steinberg saw the first maturation of his art at the point when his excitement at "what he could do with painting" changed to the recognition of "what painting could do." Beavers may have had a similar understanding of his vocation and his medium at that time, although the decisive transition oc-curred two years, and two films, later with the making of *From the Notebook*

16. Robert Beavers, e-mail to P. Adams Sitney, February 14, 2005.

Of... At a seminar at Princeton University, following a screening of *Palinode*, he spoke of his fascination with "the seriousness of the image" and its "philosophical majesty," adding that he made an "ethical decision" when he began it: "I can only live to make that film."[17] That is to say, he could not continue to do several things at once, a dispersed focus he compared to the sexual energy of an adolescent. At twenty, then, he rededicated himself to his art by putting his confidence in the images and rhythms dictated by his intuition.

His few short published texts do not so much illuminate his view of the cinematic image as indicate the importance he gives to a dialectical approach to images grounded in poetics: "The spectator's power of perception, liberated by this order of the sense and not by dramatic empathy, begins to learn what composes film and its harmonies.... I have emphasized harmony because one sees in Film not just an image but the unity of image and its interval while simultaneously hearing the sound and its interval."[18]

In *Palinode*, the camera studies a middle-aged male singer (baritone Derek Olson) singing, eating, window shopping, meeting a young girl who seems to have been awaiting him. Just as Ensor had been a latent source for *Plan of Brussels*, the paintings of Balthus were part of the genesis of this film. Thirty years later it still remains astonishingly original and mysterious; elements suggestive of Fritz Lang's *M* seem translated from criminal psychopathology to aestheticism. Lang had been one of the first filmmakers to interest Beavers, although it was his silent films that caught his attention, especially for the sensitivity with which Lang cast physical types. The film is both a portrait of a singer and of Zurich, where he lives. It opens by intercutting fading views of street traffic with a shot of his face as he sings. This shot is delimited by the first of many custom-made circular masks, ranging from a simple iris blackening out all but the round center of the frame to bulls-eye masks of concentric circles, at times tinted by filter strips of alternating colors; there is even a circular mask surrounded by single frames of film. The respiratory rhythm of the film emanates from shifting focus, fading in and out, and the coordination of masks and montage, while on the soundtrack we hear the subject singing scales and taking breaths. Twice there are fragments of Wladimir Vogel's oratorio *Wagadus Untergang durch die Eitelkeit* (Wagadu's Downfall from Vanity): The first is a melancholy orchestral line and the second ends the film:

Das Feldhunn sang: Hört das Dausi! Hört meine Taten!
Das Feldhunn sang von seinem Kampf mit der Schlange.

17. Robert Beavers (seminar, Princeton University, Spring 2000).
18. Beavers, "Hautprobe for a Spectator."

Das Feldhunn sang:
All Geschöpfe müssen sterben,
werden bergraben und vermordern.
Auch ich werde sterben,
werden begraben und werde vermodern.
[The wild chicken sings: Hear the Dausi! Hear my deeds!
The wild chicken sings of his fight with the snake.
The wild chicken sings:
Every creature must die,
Be buried and turn to dust.
Even I will die,
Be buried, and turn to dust.][19]

Beavers gives us a crucial clue to the film when he describes it as "the atmosphere of life unlived in the repetitions of the singer's phrases and breath."[20] The film opens with the sound of scales in the singer's bass voice and concludes with a soprano and an alto singing of death and obliteration in Vogel's citation of the anthropologist Leo Frobenius's evocation of the lost epic of the Dausi tribe (an influence on both Ezra Pound and Robert Duncan). Out of the repetitions of breath and scales emerges the articulation of song, individual fatality, tribal memory, and the downfall of civilizations through vanity.

Beavers's circular masks and his cinematic rhythms point to a dynamics expressed by Emerson in "Circles":

The life of a man is a self-evolving circle, which, from a ring imperceptibly small, rushes on all sides outwards to new and larger circles, and that without end. The extent to which this generation of circles, wheel without wheel, will go, depends on the force or truth of the individual soul. For it is the inert effort of each thought, having formed itself into a circular wave of circumference,—as, for instance, an empire, rules of an art, a local usage, a religious rite,—to heap itself on that ridge, and to solidify and hem in the life.... But the heart refuses to be imprisoned: in its first and narrowest pulses, it already tends outward with a vast force, and to immense and innumerable expansions.[21]

If the subject of his film has made a religious rite of the rules of an art to solidify them in an "unlived" life, the filmmaker refuses to be imprisoned and,

---

19. Wladimir Vogel, *Wagadus Untergang durch die Eitelkeit* (Zurich: Migros-Genossenschafts-Bund, 1996), MGB CD 1638, p. 68.
20. Robert Beavers, e-mail to P. Adams Sitney, February 14, 2005.
21. Emerson, *Essays and Lectures*, pp. 404–05.

by making *Palinode*, forces an expansion of his vision. Beavers attempted to capture the atmosphere peculiar to Zurich. Stefan Sadkowski, the writer who appears in *The Count of Days*, was a refugee who could not leave Switzerland for fear that he would not be able to reenter the country. Similarly, Wladimir Vogel was living in Zurich when Beavers made the film. He was a composer of German-Russian descent, who had been born in Moscow, wrote his oratorio in Berlin, and had lived in Switzerland as an alien for twenty-one years (1933–54) before obtaining citizenship.

By the time Beavers made *Palinode*, it was evident that the spirit of place had a significant role in his films. The earlier parts of the film cycle had been made in Hydra, Brussels, and Zurich. The remaining two would be made in Berlin and Hydra (again), and London. His distillation of the genius loci in the rhythms of his editing and the timbre of his images and sounds is most overt in *Diminished Frame* (1970), as he described its genesis to Tony Pipolo:

I drew out of each city in which I lived a particular film... *Diminished Frame*... was made when I was in West Berlin on a stipendium. For that film I superimposed simple sounds to suggest crowds: fire, droning bees, horses, and "Sieg Heil!"... In black and white, I filmed the historical sites in Berlin which interested me; and then in color I filmed myself with the filters that I was using at the time, showing how I placed them between the aperture and the lens. It is another example of making an unexpected use of an element of the camera.... On one level, the film simply grew out of the experience of living there for a few months, and when I encountered a description of crowds as being like flames, suggesting that they follow a natural law of some sort, I tried to suggest that.

...There is in *Diminished Frame* a balance between the sense of time seen in the views of Berlin, in the old buildings, the streets, and so forth (filmed in black and white as I did later the architecture in Ruskin) and then the tense in which I filmed myself in color and is shown in the present (how the color was being created). It is the space of the city and of the filmmaker. On my own, I discovered the points which I wanted to film in Berlin; for example the side of the building which had been made bare by tearing down the next building and how the imprint had somehow left an enormous Maltese-like cross there. I was trying to create a space in which something could be revealed in the process of the filming and I pursued an intuitive pattern as I chose the locations and the moments of filming. In other words, there was improvisation within chosen limits. The result contemplates the stillness of Aftermath and a few moments of ordinary existence like the bicyclists or the young mother taking the groceries out of her car. Of course, there were other conscious choices; no one films the Reichstag or the SS headquarters without knowing that they are doing it. Perhaps the result was to suggest this gamut, and it is certainly not to be found solely in one place or one history.[22]

Diminished Frame is the starkest work in Beavers's oeuvre. Even what he calls "a few moments of ordinary existence" appear grim in the harsh winter light of Berlin. The massive, somber buildings to which he returns again and again give these glimpses of daily life a feeling of regimentation and somberness. The insulated touring costumes of the three bicyclists, the fur coat of an elderly woman on a street corner, and the old man slowly walking past the window of an empty restaurant evoke the alienating city's chilliness and stasis, which Beavers calls "the stillness of the Aftermath." Even the shot of the woman loading groceries into her car is weighted by a slow pace of another passerby, all bundled up.

The mixing of color images of filters, and of the filmmaker applying them, with the black-and-white cityscape is masterful; the matching rectangular masks often at the center of both orders of imagery suggest that the filmmaker finds or founds a diminished frame within the frame of the conventional aperture. The two orders are so rhythmically attuned that it seems at times as if the color were superimposed on the black and white or as if one mode were dissolving into the other, although there are only hard cuts between them. The dominantly autumnal colors—yellows, browns, ochres—create a melancholy aura for the images of the filmmaker at work, corresponding to the grim evocation of Berlin.

The overlapping of sounds contributes to the interpenetration of two orders of photography. Of these sounds, the archival citation of crowds shouting "Sieg Heil!" is startling and unique in Beavers's entire corpus. Whereas the sound of horses' hooves points to the modern transformation of a city of wide boulevards planned and built before the advent of automobiles, and the swarming sounds of bees naturalize the intimations of regimentation and collective behavior of its citizens, the imaginary echo of the public adulation of Hitler is shocking in its historical specificity and lack of ambiguity. Its highly rhetorical evocation of sinister mass enthusiasm highlights the *stillness* of the Aftermath, in the sparsely populated, silent present. Beavers probably did not know that Stan Brakhage too had speculated on the "natural" shapes of mobs and crowds when he made *23rd Psalm Branch* (1967), intercutting newsreels of political rallies and street demonstrations during the Second World War with images of his daily life during the Vietnam War, including visits he made to

---

22. Pipolo, "Interview with Robert Beavers," pp. 13, 22–23.

Berlin and Vienna. Similarly, Ernie Gehr did not know of *Diminished Frame* when he made his film of haunted Berlin, *Signal—Germany on the Air* (1985).

In contrast to the three psychodramas, *Plan of Brussels*, *The Count of Days*, and *Palinode*, where the filmmaker had counterpointed fragmentary narratives with the distancing gestures of filtering and masking, *Diminished Frame* decisively emptied out the narrative elements and the rudimentary acting or modeling of Beavers's apprentice filmmaking; it figuratively diminished the frame in which he had been working by focusing the film on the tensions between color and black and white, the projective inventions of the filmmaker and the chilly monumentality of the city, the poetic present and the stillness of the Aftermath. It was therefore his purest lyric expression since *Winged Dialogue*. He would not return again to the psychodramatic mode in the rest of *My Hand Outstretched to the Wingless Distance*. Instead, he followed this winter reduction and chastening of his art with a return to the summer lushness of Hydra, where *Winged Dialogue* had been filmed, to make a very ambitious film about both the erotic power of cinema and the fragility of its reception. The monthly segments shown following *Diminished Frame* emphasize both the pleasures of rejoining Markopoulos and their return to a Mediterranean climate. The climate change is a thematic element in the opposition of the final pairing of the cycle. Beavers seems to have set himself the task of articulating the differences between the qualities of light in Berlin and the Aegean. In fact, at the Whitney screening of the cycle, he connected the quality of light in the final film, *Still Light* (1970), with its soundtrack, which he wanted to be "atmospheric," not to "overwhelm or compete with the image." By implication, that was what the sound, especially the cheering of Hitler, had done in *Diminished Frame*. He had observed in Greece, how "a very distant sound appears quite near." The sounds he used were those of waves, dogs barking, goat bells, a braying donkey, and chirping crickets. He wrote:

> In... *STILL LIGHT*, I place a single figure at the center of the film. His face frames the play of light and color that was equally my subject. I was attracted by the clarity of distant details in the landscape and surrounded his face with these corners of the island Hydra. Within the stillness there is a repeated focus movement between the filtered colors and points of the face and landscape. Following these scenes, I turn back to show my editing process and then to project images from the first Greek scenes into a new context, that of a spectator—in this case, a critic in his living room commenting on Film.[23]

23. Robert Beavers, notes for Walter Reade Theater Program, May 6, 2001, http://www.filmlinc.com/wrt/programs/recur/image/5–2001/beavers.htm#program.

It was filmed in two parts—the first half on the island of Hydra: it has a simple outdoor ambience which is slightly modified in size by adding and taking away echo. The second half was filmed in the apartment of the critic Nigel Gosling. I recorded a kind of cocktail of improvised statements that he made while seeing the first half of the film projected. The filming was directed toward the corners of the room and we see segments of the projection in one of the corners as he speaks and moves around. I kept some of these statements in the re-editing and placed them different... But I was a bit kinder in the second [version].[24]

Still Light is the distillation of Beavers's experience with actors in the first stage of his career. He seems to have recognized that the vibrancy evident in his images of Markopoulos and himself (sometimes recorded with Markopoulos's assistance) in *Winged Dialogue* and *Early Monthly Segments* did not extend to his rendering of the actors he filmed in *Plan of Brussels*, *The Count of Days*, and *Palinode*. *Still Light* takes up the challenge of capturing and holding the nuances of posing for the film camera as the actor and filmmaker perceive momentary changes in their mutual recognition and their forms of self-awareness. Clearly Beavers was responding to what he learned from watching Markopoulos shoot many of his film portraits, in his *Galaxie* and the unreleased parts of *Eniaios*. His influence is particularly strong in the second half of the film when Beavers films Nigel Gosling in his London apartment; for, like Markopoulos, he makes the objects of Gosling's environment metonymies for his personality. However, the ironic distance he keeps from Gosling is greater, just as the apperception in the first half of the film is more intense, than Markopoulos offers in his portraiture. In his attention to the self-awareness of his actor Beavers is closer to Warhol's silent film portraits, but unlike Warhol he does not elicit the model's self-consciousness by withdrawing himself. Instead, *Still Light* sets the extremely ambitious project of revealing (in the first part) the mutual apperceptiveness of the model and filmmaker and (in the second part) the tendency of the critical spectator to reduce the projected film to the status of an object in his environment by idly speculating on the limitations of all filmic images. Gosling muses:

A film image is somehow a very artificial and pre-prepared thing... which is not at all a natural way of taking in an image. I find this effects my whole attitude to the images as they come up....I would like to see a film presented in full daylight—full sunlight—I know

24. Pipolo, "Interview with Robert Beavers," p. 23.

this is impossible but it would be interesting to see.... Film happens somewhere between the projector, the screen, and me.

If the style of Markopoulos's portraits influenced the portrait of Gosling in the second half of the film, the conception of his early film *Charmides* (1948) may have played a role in the ambition of the first part. Markopoulos took the title of Plato's dialogue for his film because the youth, Charmides, startles Socrates with his beauty. Beavers, too, takes male beauty as the starting point of his film.

Beavers's essay "His Image—the Nature of a Filmmaker" lays out the dynamics of the apperceptive exchange:

"Actor" and filmmaker face each other in a relation that is the source for how a figure is presented in the film.... Each gesture of self-assertion or denial is transformed and becomes part of the vital space of the film frame.

Rather than beginning with a character or presenting a predetermined psychology, the filmmaker finds the reality of form in the physical expression of the features of a particular face, in the harmony of light resting upon and within this face....

To recognize the outline of a person's nature—*his image*—is not a common experience. It happens at that moment when habits of seeing open towards a sudden self-awareness, when the filmmaker registers the other's face opposite him.... The face carries a double sense, first as a direct element within the film frame and second as a performance. Only when both are present will the face be like a voice containing its own lyric within the film as a whole.

Because of this symmetry the face is both meaning and mask. One looks upon the actor's face as much as into it.... A face sometimes takes on the ambiguity of a pattern, or at other moments possesses the subjectivity that turns back upon itself to *see* its own outline.[25]

In this essay he also seems to be alluding to the title *Still Light* when he asserts that the eye movements of both the actor and the filmmaker "establish a stillness at certain moments." Within the stillness that Beavers establishes, he explores the phenomena of proximity to his model and distance to the visible and auditory landscape. As the camera stares at the full face and the profiles of the young man before it, we can glimpse behind him a town square, a street, the sea, a rocky hill, trees, donkeys, and meal sacks. At times these settings

---

25. Robert Beavers, "His Image—the Nature of the Filmmaker," in *The Searching Measure*.

attract the attention of the panning camera, but for the most part, the inter-play of shifting focus and filters dramatizes the intimate space between the camera and the actor.

After exhibiting a seventy-minute-long print in the 1970s—there is a copy of it in the collection of Anthology Film Archives—Beavers cut the film down to twenty-five minutes. For the presentation of *My Hand Outstretched*, he inserted the last of the *Early Monthly Segments* between the two parts of the film, so that as the rhythm of color filter changes is increasing, Beavers suddenly cuts from Hydra to his work table in arcing movements back and forth. The table is covered with rolled-up film shots, a plane of circles. He makes a splice and, as he does so, an insert flashes the model's face very near to the camera.

The intervention affirms the exploration of proximity as a function of the filmmaker's handcraft. At the same time it makes of the second part of *Still Light* a virtually autonomous film, almost a parodic satyr play to terminate the first cycle. Nigel Gosling, as the representative of the Critic, sits in his London apartment, looking at the paintings on his walls, flipping through a book, and smoking a cigarette before the electric space heater, pathetically placed in his fireplace. With the film of Hydra projected against the corner of the wall, as if it were the spine of a volume, it rhymes with the book in his hand. The sometimes empty white frame suggests a blank page. The proxim-ity of the paintings, too, indicates the referential blinders that inhibit the Critic's comprehension of the Filmmaker's illuminations.

CHAPTER 7

Beavers's Second Cycle: The Past in the Present—the Present in the Past

After completing *Still Light*, Robert Beavers began to feel that the discipline of producing the *Early Monthly Segments* was becoming a hindrance. The bifurcation of his creative energies into making longer architectonic films and brief personal fragments was "keeping [him] from developing the next form," as he expressed it at the Whitney Museum premiere of *My Hand Outstretched*. He had already given an intimation of his impulse to fuse the two directions of his work in *Diminished Frame*, the only film he completed after *Plan of Brussels* for which there is not a segment depicting some aspect of its production. Then, in 1970, he stopped shooting the segments altogether.

Consequently, he developed the next form with spectacular success, when at twenty-two years old he achieved a remarkable level of artistic maturity with the completion of *From the Notebook Of...* By starting the second cycle of *My Hand Outstretched to the Winged Distance and Sightless Measure* with it, he acknowledged its importance in his oeuvre. More than any other single film, it established his reputation as one of the preeminent avant-garde filmmakers of his generation, at least to the few critics and curators who were able to see his work in the early 1970s. The subsequent three films of the cycle—*The*

Painting, Work Done, and *Ruskin*—confirmed the prescience of that early recognition.

Sometime before making *From the Notebook Of...* the filmmaker read Paul Valéry's *Introduction to the Method of Leonardo Da Vinci* (1895), a meditation on thought and phenomena the French poet published when he was only twenty-four. In this chapter I make much of this encounter of the very young poet and the even younger filmmaker across a gap of eighty years, although I do not wish to suggest that Valéry's essay was a more decisive influence on Beavers than any of the other works I mentioned in the previous chapter or those discussed here. Yet Valéry's little book conveniently brings together several of the themes I wish to explore in my reading of the middle cycle. Beavers has always read widely and urbanely; all of his films reflect his intense study of poetry, music, paintings, and architecture. Much of the core of Valéry's book might even be culled from Emerson's *Nature*, the touchstone of much of this book; for the Sage of Concord wrote "man is analogist," and elaborated:

A leaf, a sunbeam, a landscape, the ocean make an analogous impression on the mind.... [The poet] unfixes the land and the sea, makes them revolve around the axis of his primary thought, and disposes them anew. Possessed himself by a heroic passion, he uses matter as symbols of it. The sensual man conforms thoughts to things; the poet conforms things to his thoughts.[1]

For Valéry, Leonardo was a mere pretext, as he acknowledged at the start of the work, for an exposition of the workings of his own mind: "Remembering that [Leonardo] was a thinker, we are able to discover in his works ideas which really originate in ourselves: we can re-create his thought in the image of our own."[2] Perhaps neither Valéry nor Beavers would have known how close this comes to Emerson's claim at the start of "Self-Reliance": "In every work of genius we recognize our own rejected thoughts: they come back to us with a certain alienated majesty."[3]

Certainly his reading of Valéry's essay put the filmmaker on a path leading to the examination of the complex relationship between his ideas for films and the results of his practice. Consequently, *From the Notebook Of...* centers itself on the filmmaking process and integrates the representation of the city—here Florence—into that process. Every moment of the film reflects the interde-

1. Ralph Waldo Emerson, *Essays and Lectures* (New York: Library of America, 1983), pp. 47, 50, 65.
2. Paul Valéry, *Introduction to the Method of Leonardo Da Vinci*, trans. Thomas McGreevy (London: John Rodker, 1929), p. 31.
3. Emerson, *Essays and Lectures*, p. 41.

pendence of the filmmaker, his tools, the historic environment of Florence, and the compound model of Leonardo-Valéry.

What Valéry calls Leonardo's method emanates from the poet's conception of the nature of thought before and beyond language. He is brutally critical of observers who name everything they see or those who trust in the stability of words to convey fixed meanings:

> The majority of people see with the intellect much more frequently than with the eyes.... When they move they miss the movement of the rows of windows, the transformation of surfaces continually changing their aspect—for the concept does not change. They see through a dictionary rather than through the retinae.... [4]

Valéry's essay is an examination of the aesthetics of phenomena, of things and mental images first of all, and works of art secondarily. In marginal notes he added to the text thirty-six years later, the poet observed that artists were useful because "they preserve the subtlety and instability of sensory impressions." [5] Starting from a concentration on familiar objects, the analytical intelligence moves without the prejudice of names, or habits of conceptualization, to a new knowledge of regularity within a welter of fluctuations, prompting an efflorescence of metaphor and analogy. For him, the dramatic imagination entailed the ability to identify with individual objects. But beyond that identification, Valéry described a superior process of abstraction and expansion that he calls construction: It permits a mode of invention, common to both the arts and science, in which an imaginative freedom in combining and substituting objects or concepts generates unanticipated interplays of self and world, particular and universal.

Furthermore, in examining the nature of thought Valéry sought a universal principle of analogy, more basic than language:

> The actors in this drama are mental images, and it is easy to understand if the peculiarities of these images be eliminated, and if only their succession, frequency, periodicity, their diverse capacities for association, and, finally, their duration, be studied, one is tempted to find analogies in what is called the material world, to compare them with scientific analyses, to give them an environment, a continuity, properties of displacement, of speed, then mass and energy. [6]

---

4. Paul Valéry, *Leonardo Poe Mallarmé*, trans. Malcolm Cowley and James R. Lawler, Bollingen Series XLV, no. 8 (Princeton, NJ: Princeton University Press, 1972), p. 259.
5. Ibid., p. 19.
6. Valéry, *Introduction*, p. 36.

At times he calls the mode of analogy "metaphor." More consistently he refers to construction as the conscious manipulation of mental images. Construction recognizes the ubiquity of substitution—of one medium for another, one image for another, one thing for another. The great artist or great thinker allows himself the freedom to make radical substitutions: He puts himself to the task of figuring out the invisible wholes of which he has been given the parts. He divines the planes cut by a bird in flight, followed by a stone that has been thrown, the surfaces defined by our gestures, and the extraordinary rents, the fluid arabesques, the formless chambers, created in an all-embracing network from the scratching noise of humming insects, the bending of trees, wheels, the human smile, the tides. Sometimes traces of things he imagined may appear in the sands, on the waters; sometimes his own retina itself may later on compare the form of his movement with some object.[7]

Beavers provided the New York Film Festival with the following notes on his own method when *From the Notebook Of...* was screened in the 1999 Views from the Avant-Garde program:

I have returned several times to the question of how to show the "reverse side" of an object in film. How to give the full sense of this as it is related to other facets of prismatic space in film. It retains a fascination for me whether it is the two sides of a hand or the turning of a page or the dialogue between two figures.

When *From the Notebook Of...* was filmed in Florence in 1971, I had already made several films with colored filters and moving mattes. Each film was formed by the place in which I then lived—either Greece or Brussels, Zurich or Berlin. The initial choice in Florence was more complex because the filming locations were selected by drawing upon certain details from Leonardo Da Vinci's life—the little that is known to be related to the city—and from other comments in his notebooks. The very first scene of doves being set free from a shop near the Bargello is inspired by the mention of such a scene in the Vasari biography. It is then suddenly extended into the present (of 1971) by one of my own handwritten notes, so that the flight of the dove is interwoven with the turning of the page (or matte) then juxtaposed to a view of my opening a window onto the Florentine rooftops.

From the first moment, the filmmaker is present as an active observer. This is usually shown in clusters of quick camera movements with my profile framing the view. A natural pace develops between

7. Valéry, Ibid., pp. 43–44.

the searching-on-location and the central scenes of my writing at the table. The notebook is given filmic form and holds a quantity of visual elements in ever-changing relation.

Finding the present in the past: I was stimulated by Leonardo's precepts or his observations on disegno and chiaroscuro. As a result, I filmed certain qualities of shadows and their movement. There was time to observe the placid water under the Santa Trinita bridge or to compare the Arno at a more turbulent point with waves of blonde hair. Inspired by the freedom and range of this autodidact, I attempted to translate a few isolated elements of his vision into film. It reached the point where I could look into the film camera as a camera obscura and place pure colors there.

Finding the past in the present: Because this was a first (extended) encounter with the city, vestiges of the early Florence came to life as I glimpsed them. I saw the window, painted in perspective on the via Maggio, or the ideal proportions of Alberti's facades, and each gained a place in the film. The window, with its painted black recesses, suggested new uses for my matte-forms, and it extended further to that other window in my room, seen at night. All suggest searching and the incandescence of thought.

These layers of reference are sometimes in synch and more often simply overlap. A space appears between the written notes, which are remnants of my earlier intentions, and the actual filming, developing in its own direction. The full gamut of these qualities allows for productive accidents and later intuitions. The measured rhythm of reading—or the glimpse of a few words—is woven into all of the other movements. One passes from the apparent stillness of the notes to actively see the movement in the editing. Each new image and sound changes the meaning of a note as it appears and reappears in the turning of the "matte-page."

Dividing the frame in half, the matte turns from one side to the other and this repetition creates a strong suggestion of perspective, almost a sense of the image turning to its reverse side in a few prismatic moments, when the sound also encourages this impression.[8]

As this extended note indicates, in *From the Notebook Of . . .* the filmmaker continually returns to images of his handwritten notes and of his matte box, exploring the ways in which color filters alter the light on the whole screen or

8. Robert Beavers, "Program Three: '*Winged Distance / Sightless Measure*'—Three Films by Robert Beavers," Filmlinc.com, http://www.filmlinc.com/archive/nyff/avantgarde99.htm.

parts of it. The substitution of filters and mattes gives the film its dominant vivace rhythm, accented by abrupt camera movements, sweeping over sites in Florence mentioned in Leonardo's notebooks. The film makes explicit how thoroughly the images of Florence have been mediated by the filmmaker's readings, writings, materials, and craft.

He wrote in "La Terra Nuova": "The act of filming should be a source of thought and discovery." And in "Editing and the Unseen": "The many hours of patient editing, this listening to the image, waiting for it to speak and reveal its pattern. Often unexpected, it is recognized in its rightness.... *I memorize the image and movement while holding the film original in hand; the memorizing gains weight and becomes a source for the editing. To view the film on an editing table would only distract me from this process and create the illusion that editing was done in the viewing.*"[9] Here we can hear Markopoulos's intuitive self-confidence chastely refined with a Valéryan inflection into a principle of cinematic poetics: filmmaking requires special attention to the acts of thought and discovery occurring while attending the conditions under which short strips of film are imprinted with colored light and images of places; and then it demands concentrated and patient openness to new orders of assembly, as the rhythms of the pieces of film gradually assert themselves in editing. In *From the Notebook Of...*, for the first time, Beavers put this double process at the center of a film. At sixty-five minutes, in its first version, it was the longest film of his career so far. Reediting it for *My Hand Outstretched*, he trimmed it to forty-eight minutes.

The film opens with the sound of bird wings beating air for a moment before an image appears. Then, unusually for Beavers, a series of gestural camera movements locates a cage of doves in front of the medieval tower of Florence's Bargello. Later in the film, the camera tends to pivot on the tripod head, rather than sustaining this opening flourish, although there will be a similar dance of jagged camera movements when the filmmaker surveys the red tile rooftops from his pension's window. For forty seconds the filmmaker intersperses some ten abrupt sweeps of the camera with closeups of the birds and a matte swinging back and forth to bisect the rectangle of the screen. He had constructed a set of masks that pivot from a hinge at the midpoint; by turning a mask he closes off alternately the left and right halves of the image. One mask is black, another white, and a third white on one side and black on the other. Generally the pivoting of the mask is synchronized to a change of image in the unmasked portion of the frame. In effect, it suggests a hand flipping the pages of a book. The dominant rhythm of the film derives from the recurring variations on this pivoting.

9. Robert Beavers, "Editing and the Unseen," *The Searching Measure* (Berkeley: Berkeley Art Museum and Pacific Film Archive, 2004), pages unnumbered.

One of the moving shots follows the flight of a released bird across the Piazza San Firenze. As the film progresses, elements from this scene, including the previously unseen release of the bird, will be woven into the montage. In the fluid transition from the jolting movements of the opening shots to the fixed camera positions of the images that follow, Beavers extends the chain of analogies that began with an association of the bird's wings and the matte baffles to the opening of the window shutters of a room where we will see the filmmaker working with colored filter strips and jotting down notes and drawing diagrams about this and other films. In these interior scenes, the written notes and diagrams become part of the imagery and rhythm of the film. In one of them we read:

> 1.9.70 A relation of camera angle to object to projection angle: equate the camera, the room, and projector.
> A similar principle of analogy (or "equality") is at the heart of Valéry's meditation on Leonardo:
> For, in reality, analogy is only the faculty of varying the images, of combining them, of making part of one coexist with part of another and perceiving, voluntarily or otherwise, the similarities in their construction...
> Consciousness of the thoughts that one has, to the extent that they are thoughts, is awareness of [an] equality or homogeneity: the feeling that all combinations of the kind are legitimate, natural, and that the method consists in exciting them, in seeing them with precision, in searching for their implications.[10]

Likewise, the method of *From the Notebook Of...* consists of combining and associating images—bird wings/pivoting mattes/window shutters/the mechanism of the camera (which Beavers filmed open, running without film so we can see into the flickering of the shutter and the mechanism of the filters)—and "searching for their implications" by recombining them in a steady rhythmic elaboration. At one point he rhymes the dome of Brunelleschi's Santo Spirito Church (seen from the street) with the work of an artisan carving a hemisphere from wood, perhaps as a mold for a hat. At another moment, the edge of the mold matches an arch in the colonnade of the church's cloister.

The release of the bird was an allusion to an incident mentioned by Vasari in his "Life of Leonardo":

> [H]e took special pleasure in horses as he did in all other animals, which he treated with the greatest love and patience. For example,

---

10. Valéry, *Introduction*, pp. 36, 38.

when passing by places where birds were being sold, he would often take them out of their cages with his own hands, and after paying the seller the price that was asked of him, he would set them free in the air, restoring to them the liberty they had lost.[11]

This passage might also gloss the shots of a horse scattered through the film.

In addition to the Santo Spirito, we can see in the film the Ponte Vec-chio, the Campanile of the Badia, and Alberti's facades for the Church of Santa Maria Novella and the Palazzo Rucellai. Unlike the earlier generation of American avant-garde filmmakers, Anger, Menken,[12] and Brakhage, who had preceded him in filming European architectural monuments, Beavers did not treat the historical environment ironically, as if it were the scenography for his psychodrama. Instead, his pursuit of analogy in the rhythmic substitu-tion of one image for another sublimates the psychodrama by creating an air of both apperceptive detachment and eroticized manipulation. The recurring stylistic refinements emphasize the mediations of things and their shadows in figuratively constructing "the filmmaker's mind."

To inscribe his own image in the film, at times the filmmaker even leans into the camera composition so that we see his face, out of focus or in shadow, at the edge of the scene. This gives the shot a subjective inflection while maintaining the crystalline imperturbability of the image, designating the framed world as the object of his gaze while transcending his perspective. In his own terms, he moves continually between the first and third person in this film.[13]

Valéry yet again: "He plays with things, he grows bolder, he translates all his feelings into this universal language, translates clearly."[14]

From the moment Beavers enters the film, he portrays himself playing with things. He adjusts the window shutter to a crack and rocks his upper body back and forth as a thin bar of light moves across him (and across his throat in close-up). In the first five minutes he returns again and again to this scene. Valéry had criticized those blinded to what is before their eyes who "miss the movement of the rows of windows, the transformation of surfaces continually changing their aspect" as they move. Here, in contrast, the film-

---

11. Giorgio Vasari, *The Lives of the Artists*, trans. Julia Conaway Bondanella and Peter Bondanella (Oxford: Oxford University Press, 1991), p. 286.

12. There is an uncanny similarity between the opening of *Arabesque for Kenneth Anger* and *From the Notebook Of...* that seems to be purely coincidental: Both show a symbolic dove amid a flurry of camera movements in a monumental setting; both were made with a significant unseen associate, although in the case of Beavers's film Markopoulos appears in the final mirror image.

13. Robert Beavers, Whitney Museum, October 30, 2005.

14. Valéry, *Introduction*, p. 51.

maker seems to be studying the continually changing aspects induced by his rocking motion, but he does not give us a countershot of what he sees. This is characteristic of his style and his aesthetics. In contrast to Brakhage, he will not attempt to mimic subjective vision. The vision of the camera and that of the filmmaker are autonomous, but linked by analogy. The analogical method depends upon the recognition that both the world and the filmmaker are transformed into "perfect...suspended" images within the film, in the phrase of one of the notes we see during the rocking sequence:

> 12.12.70 While in Hallenbad sitting at one end of the pool and gazing in front of myself after some moments the place became an image, the same but perfect—the image suspended in a great space.

Dante, troping the ad hoc epiphany of *Paradiso* of the *Commedia*, calls the pilgrim's response to what he sees "the opposite error" of Narcissus, when he turns his head assuming the image before him is merely the reflection of a reality behind him. Beavers's Narcissus in Hallenbad contemplates a "perfect...image" without theologizing or devaluing the image for its source. I understand the fascination with "the 'reverse side'" of objects, mentioned at the start of the filmmaker's program note, to be a transformation of the specular drama of the Narcissus myth, which Beavers seems to have embraced in 1971 as a confirmation of his artistic election, although the threatening, magical consequences of this assumption into a "perfect...image" does not manifest itself until the revision of his subsequent film, *The Painting*. He spoke at the Whitney premiere of *My Hand Outstretched* of a revelation of totalizing visuality that engendered *From the Notebook Of...*: "In Florence I understood the power of the image to contain all. Not all cultures have that."[15]

It is significant that the note's poolside epiphany occurs in a written text rather than in a recorded or enacted event. The incorporation of production notes was the decisive innovation that gave the film its startling richness. The handwritten notes demand a concentrated time of reading in counterpoint to the rhythms of the montage. They open the film up to the drama of its genesis, while inviting the viewers to imagine scenes not filmed and to compare those filmed to the verbal sketches. This play between text and image differs strikingly from the nearly contemporary explorations of Hollis Frampton in *Hapax Legomena*, because Beavers abjures the irony Frampton cultivates; instead, his texts expand the representation of thought around which the film circles.

---

15. Beavers, Whitney Museum.

Near the end of this initial sequence of texts we read the germ of the matrix scene itself:

15.3.71 Close the window shutters to a crack; film my reflection in mirror as my head moves in front of the narrow light. It will be first on one side then the other, and outline of light instead of shade.

We can see a mirror to the side of the filmmaker in some of the rocking shots, but he does not shoot directly into it, although he concentrates on his reflection elsewhere in *From the Notebook Of...*, most significantly to end the film with a double portrait of Markopoulos and himself, as if by including his mentor and lover in the mirror image he might resolve the narcissistic psychodrama encrypted in the film. As he plays with the window shutter, Beavers allows us to see his profile in the mirror; it is the most explicit representation of "the 'reverse side' of an object" in the film.

He cuts his rocking motion in time to the turning of the matte on its pivot. The sound of pages turning bolsters the metaphor of the matte book, while sounds of birds flapping their wings and the camera clicking enlarge the analogical spectrum. In the midst of these associations, a note held on the screen longer than most offers yet another simile:

22.7.69 The shutter in the camera is like the wings of an insect, both create movement, one in space, the other in the eye. Film doesn't create the "illusion" of movement; it is movement.

From the scene of rocking in the light, the filmmaker turns to the relationship of objects to their shadows. He manipulates a lens and a matte box as if responding to a note he had previously filmed:

3.1.70 With an object and its shadow; as the object moves closer to the surface of the shadow the shadow becomes more clearly defined. When the objects move back toward the light and away from the shadow, the shadow is less in focus. A series of shots which begin with soft shadow, not showing the object; then the object moves toward the shadow, hardening it, and into frame. The light should be behind and to one side of the object.

The examination of shadows then expands to incorporate color filters and his notes on them as well, for example:

14.1.70 Film at close range the colors as to remove them from their objects.

As the film passes through the camera and the projector, it generates a movement of "perfect," "suspended" images analogically crossing "between things whose laws of continuity escape us" (Valéry's phrase).[16] The rhythmic propulsion of that movement sustains the film, gradually widening its range of reference to incorporate the portraits of a child with a nearly Vincian smile and two young men, one of them posing nude. In the passage in which Valéry writes that his Leonardo "plays with things," he also imagines: "He adores the body, man's body and woman's, the human body which measures itself against all things."[17] Up to this point, the filmmaker had handled his tools with a meticulous and sensuous tactility that gave the film an erotic atmosphere: It culminates in the introduction of the male nude. The closeups of the arms, thigh, and penis of Beavers's model, and of the face and eyes of the other young man, intimate that another domain of association and stimulus to identification at stake in *From the Notebook Of...* might be Leonardo's surmised homosexuality. Sigmund Freud's most elaborate examination of the artistic imagination, *Leonardo Da Vinci and a Memory of His Childhood* (1910), is also the locus of his etiology of homosexuality. Although it is a particularly controversial work, even within the Freudian corpus, and has been frequently criticized for factual errors about Leonardo's life and writings, it led decisively to the recognition of the artist's homosexuality, although Beavers himself found it "confusing and unconvincing."[18] In a survey of the analytical and critical literature on the book, Bradley I. Collins wrote, "Indeed, homosexuality was so widespread in Florence that homosexually inclined men were referred to in Germany as *Florenzer*."[19]

Near the conclusion of the film, Beavers repeats several times the enigmatic note: "18.11.70 Raising the limbs in a phallic oath." When I wrote him to clarify this, he answered:

> I had purchased a book...about certain phallic objects and rites in ancient time...like oil lamps, etc....I found this tradition of swearing an oath by the phallus mentioned in it. In my note I was intending to show the power of the phallus though the entire body, perhaps by showing the arms raised or in some other way. It was never realized and is in the film only as a note. I can not say more about the significance of this in the film. There are a number of notes that are not directly realized in the film. In re-reading my filming notes I have seen

16. Valéry, *Introduction*, p. 37.
17. Ibid., p. 51.
18. Robert Beavers, e-mail letter to author, March 2, 2005.
19. Bradley Collins, *Leonardo, Psychoanalysis and Art History: A Critical Study of Psychobiographical Approaches to Leonardo Da Vinci* (Evanston, IL: Northwestern University Press, 1997), p. 208, n. 39.

how distant some of them are from my actual filming and then other notes still have a life in them and could continue to inspire future films.[20]

Under the pressure of this note, some of the images following it come to evoke phallic authority: the arm and fist of the nude model, certainly the close-up of his penis, more remotely the upward growth of a plant stem, the dome of the Santo Spirito, the repeated lifting of a filter matte, the cross formed by the window mullions, the crosses of television antennas on the roofs outside the window, and even the inner mechanism of the Bolex camera. In biblical literature (Gen. 24:2, 47:29–31; Deut. 67:29) the phallic oath is sworn by placing a hand under the genitals of an authority. It is a token of fidelity, duty, and submission. In the absence of such authority (unless it is incarnated in the final reflection of Markopoulos seated before Beavers and his camera), the film as a whole constitutes an oath of allegiance to what Beavers calls "the image":

> Sustained by the awakening of emotion united to strength, I reach beyond the life-likeness of the actor and the shadow of performance to the figure gathering the life that is in the light of the image.
>   Where is the strength to be found to gather the images in a pattern that instills life in the editing? From within a solitude of being where the filmmaker endures and accepts moments when a single color is the only sign of feeling in an environment in which all else is opposition. The great reality of color: I respond to it directly in the editing, when one image is set after another in a phrase unified by variations of one tone.[21]

While concentrating on the elegant geometry and surface beauty of his cinematic tools, Beavers brings more elements from the Florentine environment into his film—Alberti's facades and anonymous street scenes, studies of plants, a trompe l'oeil window painted on a wall—until a diminuendo signals the end of the film approaching: He closes his briefcase (presumably containing his mattes and filters), fastens the shuttered window, and stands at a news kiosk, as if to illustrate the paradoxical final note to himself:

26.5.69 To film all my actions having nothing to do with making films.

---

20. Robert Beavers, e-mail letter to author, March 5, 2005.
21. Beavers, "Editing and the Unseen," *The Searching Measure*.

However, the final seconds show Beavers in the act of filming himself and Markopoulos in the mirror. First the camera pans down and then up, interrupted by the flipping of the matte on its pivot, like a blank page bound in a book. In the last shot, Markopoulos turns his head to face the mirror. The sounds of a bird's wings flapping rhyme with the click of a camera shutter. The montage of picture and sound reaffirms the play of analogy among wings, mattes, pages, camera shutters, tripods, and the human head. Without denying the symbolical power of the dove as an icon of inspiration, even divine inspiration, Beavers concludes his film under the sign of a reflection of what Valéry called "attention itself":

> As each *visible thing* is to *what sees it*, at once alien, indispensable and inferior, so the importance of these symbols, however great it may at any given moment seem, lessens on reflection before the mere persistence of attention itself and is transferred to that pure universality, to that unconquerable capacity for generalization which consciousness feels itself to be.[22]

If there is an elusive psychodrama hidden within *From the Notebook Of...*, it is a version of Narcissus, perhaps the core myth of the American avant-garde cinema since Maya Deren and Alexander Hammid's *Meshes of the Afternoon*. Even here, Beavers's intimations of the Narcissus situation is closer to the inflection of Valéry, for whom "Narcisse" is often a shorthand for the disjunctive relationships of sound and image, inner and outer, being and knowledge, and "each *visible thing* is to *what sees it*."[23] The suicidal violence of *Meshes of the Afternoon* has no place in Beavers's celebratory film of artistic incarnation. If anything, the final image of him and Markopoulos posing in the mirror might be seen as a reversal of the end of *Meshes of the Afternoon*, where the woman played by Deren shatters the mirror image of the man (played by Hammid) and kills herself, in a symbolic gesture combining drowning with slitting her throat, by showing a string of seaweed, which might be taken for blood at first sight, on the throat of the suicide. In contrast, Beavers first appears in his film with a line of sunlight crossing his throat. His concluding self-portrait with Markopoulos may be seen as an emblem of "prismatic space in film." The examples he had given in his long note for the New York Film Festival were "the two sides of a hand or the turning of a page or the dialogue between two figures." Here, the interior dialogue of the filmmaker meditating on the

22. Valéry, *Introduction*, p. 16.
23. See Christine Crow, *Paul Valéry and the Poetry of Voice* (Cambridge: Cambridge University Press, 1982), pp. 158–66.

genesis of his work momentarily crystallizes in the reflection of the two film-makers. In this way, the second cycle reaffirms the dialogue that began the first cycle. Symmetrically, the third cycle will commence with an interioriza-tion, literalizing the two male voices in *Sotiros*.

The structure of *The Painting*, the next film in the cycle, is so transparent and elegant that it offers a model for Beavers sense of construction. In it he systematically interrupts long takes of a busy intersection of traffic in the center of Bern, Switzerland, with details from the anonymous Flemish trip-tych *The Martyrdom of St. Hippolytus* (acquired by the Boston Museum of Fine Arts in 1962) and, considerably less frequently, shots of dust particles, a cracked pane of glass, a disk of light, and a torn photograph. Even if *From the Notebook Of...* can be said to articulate a Narcissus myth without the violence of *Meshes of the Afternoon* and its precursor *Le sang d'un poète*, or perhaps more crucially works in their tradition such as Markopoulos's *Swain*, the sequence of the first two films in the second cycle reveals a latent tension and, like Deren and Hammid's film, features the mutilated image of the film-maker: not a shattered mirror image but the ripped photograph.

Beavers composed the long shot of the Theaterplatz in Bern to capture the complexity of the movements of cars, motor scooters, buses, trams, trucks, bi-cycles, and pedestrians. Most of the traffic sweeps into the frame from behind buildings in the far right in an arc moving one way that feeds out the lower right of the unswerving frame. Unseen traffic lights determine the rhythms of its stops and starts. However, two-car trams entering from the same starting point do not sweep the arc but snake across the frame to exit on the left side. Other vehicles, so close we cannot anticipate them, move straight across the extreme foreground, from the left to merge with the arcing vehicles just as they pass out of the camera's purview. Two white arrows on the tarmac give a graphic emphasis to the traffic arcs. In the far background, we can see a straight line of cars passing from left to right. On the right half of the com-position, pedestrians cross on zebra lines horizontally in the middle of the image, although once a man rushes vertically, up from the lower center, to board a bus stopped midframe.

The shots of the triptych painting never offer us a master shot of all three panels. Beavers even carefully withholds the figure of St. Hippolytus for more than four minutes, even though his spread-eagled body dominates the central panel with such exceptional boldness that the art historian Julius Held specu-lated that Hugo van der Goes may have designed the composition although the painter who executed it clearly did not have his genius or skill. In fact, Beavers first inserts a blue-toned detail of buildings in the background of the right-hand panel, focusing in and out. This fragment of fifteenth-century Flemish architecture, tucked at the horizon next to a more impressive castle (which we never see in the film), resonates with the vestiges of Swiss Gothic in the Theaterplatz.

If an analogy of architectural backgrounds is at stake in the introduction of the painting, color appears to be the primary motive for filming the ensuing details of clothing, again from the right panel. A red tunic with a blue waistband rhymes with a pedestrian in a red dress and a red automobile (and later a blue one) we see passing though the Theaterplatz. For several minutes the filmmaker avoids inserting anything from the central panel into the montage. Still from the right panel, we see an arm holding a whip, the rump and tail of a white horse—isolated to reinforce a comparison to the motor vehicles— then the face of a sottish courtier, and eventually a full view of the horse and rider. The horse and rider correspond to a bicyclist in the Bern intersection. Later, as we come to see the other horses in the triptych, there will be matches between a group of three riders and three men on motorscooters amid other linkages of color and figure.

Although we never see it in full view on the screen, the triptych is remarkable for the dynamic integration of the side panels with the central representation. The martyr, naked but for a small loincloth, his arms and legs tethered to four horses about to quarter him, has already been lifted off the ground by the straining animals. The two horses pulling his left limbs are contained in the central panel with him, but the cord from his right leg extends to the horse that dominates the right panel, while the horse in the left panel draws his right arm. The survival of another triptych of the same scene by Dieric Bouts (with side panels by Hugo van der Goes) now in the Sint-Salvatorskathedraal of Bruges testifies to its uniqueness, insofar as Bouts puts the saint on the ground and contains all four horses in the central panel, leaving van der Goes to paint onlookers from the two sides. But the anonymous painter of the Boston triptych uses the folding side panels to perform dramatically a symbolic enactment of the brutal torture every time the panels are opened and extended, as if stretching the martyr's limbs until he is raised from the ground.

One might say that Beavers has discovered a way to transfer this tension to the cinematic montage without representing it directly. By postponing the narrative details that will depict the martyrdom, he tentatively delineates a range of analogies before suddenly concretizing the parallels between the horses straining to yank St. Hippolytus in four directions and the vectors of moving traffic in central Bern. Yet as soon as he shows us the head and stretched arms of the martyr, he introduces the first of three different shots (in three degrees of closeness) of a star-shaped crack in a glass slide. As a metaphor for the soon-to-be-shattered body, the pattern of cracked lines gathers up another image the filmmaker had included in the montage shortly before and which will recur, sometimes in a closer view: a torn photograph of Rober

Beavers himself on the floor of what appears to be the pension chamber where the interiors of *From the Notebook Of...* had been shot. As if to make that identification more secure, he adds an image from the earlier film of himself, rocking in the light of the almost shuttered window.

In contrast to the implicit equation of conflicting lines of traffic, the quartering of the body, the shattered glass, and the torn photograph, the montage also includes the random movement of floating dust particles and a centered disk of light, as well as a version of the pivoting matte familiar from his previous film. The rhythmic interplay of all of these elements regularly suspends the metaphoric violence with observational serenity.

Beavers once again seems to have interiorized Valéry's early meditation on Leonardo where he offers this prescription for looking at a painting:

> I believe... that the surest method of judging a picture is to begin
> by identifying nothing and then to proceed step by step to make the
> series of inductions that is necessitated by the presence at the same
> moment of a number of coloured spots within a given area in order
> to rise from metaphor to metaphor, from supposition to supposition,
> to a knowledge of the subject—sometimes only to a consciousness of
> pleasure—that one has not always had to begin with.[24]

By gradually drifting from right to left as he selects details from the triptych, Beavers's camera simulates a virtual pan of the painting. But the induction of its dramatic coherence does not occur until the midpoint when it reveals the figure of Hippolytus and the mechanism of his martyrdom. In contrast, the unbudging, continuous but interrupted activity of the Theaterplatz displays purposiveness without any dramatic accentuation. Its rhythmic fluctuations reveal the periodicity of an ongoing network of directional tensions, while the torn photograph represents the vestige of a unique dramatic event that has, apparently, just transpired. In this context, the cracked glass functions as both a metaphor for that unspecified event and a link to the other elements t play. Together they suggest that the film arises as the sublimation of a cri- of intense conflicts, perhaps involving the filmmaker's relationship with ·opoulos.

subtle sound montage includes traffic noise, a whip, snatches of music n orchestra tuning up), tearing paper, horses galloping, a creaking a thud (matched to a close-up of cracked glass). The play of syn- ł asynchronous sound reflects the intermingling of temporalities ages.

In *Introduction to the Method of Leonard Da Vinci*, we find what might be an abstract scenario for all the films of Beavers's second cycle:

> Thought consists, during most of the time that we give to it, in wandering amongst themes of which we know, more than anything else, that they are already more or less familiar. Things can therefore be classified according to the facility or difficulty that they offer to our understanding and the diverse resistance to the attempts of our imagination to regard the conditions of their existence and their accidents together.[25]

The next film of the second cycle, *Work Done*, propels the mental construction of Florence outside the filmmaker's workroom, as we know it from *From the Notebook Of...*, calling upon the viewer's imagination to synthesize "the conditions of existence" of a series of images with their "accidents." Thus, the filmmaker's thought fuses simple activities that impressed him in and around the city that "places sight and image-making at its center"—bookbinding, frying blood, felling trees, paving a street with cobblestones—into a lyrical affirmation of the dignity and majesty of images, evoking in its careful depiction of labor the illuminated calendars of the Middle Ages. Beavers described its origins to Tony Pipolo:

> One impulse came from reading [Rilke's] *New Poems*, the way of concentrating on an object. Then how the filming could itself suggest the form of the object that I was filming—to film more carefully and to reach the clearest composition and length for each image. It wasn't edited in the camera, but I tried to have every action realized in relation to the object during the filming. I began with an image of a block of ice, then went to the transformation of the solid element in the next image, which was a river. Then I filmed the cutting of trees, followed by the binding of a book. Each object was seen in itself and the unity was implied. In the first version I did not intercut any of the scenes until the last element, the blood, is introduced. It was as if I were saying that it needed all of these images to represent the ice in the film.[26]

At the start of the film Beavers locates the block of ice in a room with a sign in Italian—"It is strictly forbidden for anyone not connected to the work to enter here"—and three pictures pinned to a wall: a black and white portrait of

25. Ibid., p. 46.
26. Pipolo, "Interview with Robert Beavers," *Millennium Film Journal* no. 32/33 (Fall 1998), p. 11.

a man, perhaps the founder of the business, a card with an image of Jesus, and a color image of a female model, lying down, staring at us. Perhaps the best gloss on this conjunction of found images comes from Beavers's essay "The Senses" in which he seems to be offering his own version of the Emersonian trinity of Dionysus, Eros, and Necessity:

> The necessity that is woven into the film by the filmmaker and the psychic direction of the spectator create at certain moments a congruence fed by eros, history, and temperament… and by the always changing physical world. It is at this distance that the pattern of the film can be seen and heard.[27]

The three pictures on the wall correspond roughly to the triad of temperament, history, and eros. At the same time, the forbidding warning suggests the inscription over the gates of Dante's *Inferno*, while the emblematic images of the film—ice, fire, blood, flesh, paving stones, a mountain, and the felling of a tree and the binding of a book—suggest central moments in all three cantiche. Beavers seems to be reminding us of the power of the visual things and events of Dante's world, still visible in Tuscany, without arranging them according to the theological hierarchy of the *Commedia*. Instead, the same essay proposes the need for eliciting the narrative imagination of the viewer: "The image nourishes how we see. It enlivens all our senses by concentration and praises the instant.[28]

What may appear as mere elements of image and sound in projection can speak to us in the shape of the interval as the pattern of the film rests upon the screen. The spectator builds the narrative like a bridge in the vibrant lightness of attention. The coherence is not imposed nor does it exist as literature to be discarded by a discursive understanding.

In its reedited version, *Work Done* proceeds largely by dyadic scenes. The ice block appears by itself, in several shots, and then intercut with the aspects of the room in which he filmed it. A decisive downward pan introduces a swiftly moving river in a forested location. It is followed by the binding of a book in Latin, filmed with similar camera movements, and then intercut with the river and its environs. As the threads are tightened stitching the signatures of the book, the felling of a tree in the forest replaces the river. Then the montage associates the binding and the tree with blades of grass.

The most enigmatic passage in the film concentrates on the side of a nude male torso. The movement of shadows emphasizes the negative space

---

27. Beavers, "The Senses," *The Searching Measure*.
28. Ibid.

between his arm and the side of his trunk. If the narrative bridgework elicited by the editing connects the ice block to the flowing water of the river and the harvesting of trees with the production of paper, then the creaking sound synchronized as the arm and trunk move into and out of shadow conjures the opening and closing of a window shutter or a door through which the light passes.

The dominant trope of this film is a cinematic version of syllepsis (the rhetorical figure in which a word pointedly changes its sense by changing its object; e.g., "She took her time and his cell phone"). For instance, when a mountain first appears intercut with a street-paving crew, we might create a narrative bridge between the mountain and the paving stones, but when the same mountain appears after a shot of lard about to be liquefied, its snowy peaks rhyme with the portion of cooking fat.

The scene of cooking provides a powerful climax to the film, its sacrificial rite and its scene of communion. First, a primitive mural of a pig, stuck by its own hand and spouting its blood into a pan, serves to identify the vat of thick red liquid from which a cook will draw a ladle and eventually fry a crepe of blood in hot lard. The film ends when he sprinkles grated cheese on it, salts it, rolls it, and places it on a plate. During this process, the most elaborate and extended in the film, Beavers returns to images of the river, the book, the forest, the torso, the mountain, and the paving stones, but not to the ice block, which may have once served to refrigerate the culinary ingredients. Just as the globs of lard and mounds of grated cheese become metaphors for the mountain peaks, the river echoes the blood, and the surface of the paving stones the fried crepe; while other, equally evocative juxtapositions resist more strenuously discursive understanding.

In "Em.blem" Beavers tells us:

The spectator must discover why an image was chosen, and the silence of such a discovery is a moment of release. The filmmaker's work is to make the film and to protect what he does in the serenity of a thought without words.[29]

The tension between narrative articulation and the intimations of thought without words gives *Work Done* its exquisite tact; the illuminations of metaphor or figures of thought Valéry called notions of differentiation constitute carefully timed foils to the more elusive juxtapositions that would tease us into a mode of reception Beavers called attunement.

---

29. Beavers, "Em.blem," *The Searching Measure.*

Each of the four films of the second cycle mark stages in the increasing confidence the filmmaker has in his craft and his ability to master the nuances of suggestion immanent in his images and "attuned" through montage and rhythm. One task of the middle cycle seems to have been to invent modes of mediation to curtail, but not deny, the subjectivity of the filmmaker's imagery. The images are objective and referential; yet he glazes their transparency by stressing a context of cultural artifacts. They are images touched by the filmmaker's reading or viewing of historical art, the past in the present. In turn, they ask to be read in the same context, the present in the past.

Ruskin visits the sights of John Ruskin's work: London, the Alps, and above all Venice, where the camera's attention to masonry and to the interaction of architecture and water mimics the author's descriptive analysis of the "stones" of the city. Alpine landscapes and Venetian architecture had been the chief formative influences on Ruskin's sensibility. The former played a major role in his monumental five-volume work, *Modern Painters* (1843, 1846, 1856, 1860) in which he championed J.W.H. Turner as the preeminent artist of his time; Turner was the subject of the three volumes of *The Stones of Venice* (1851, 1853), which Ruskin wrote as a prophetic warning to contemporary England; for he saw his homeland entering a period of moral decline that would destroy its empire as he believed it had destroyed Venice.

In his interview with Pipolo, the filmmaker makes these remarks about the origins of the film:

> I had been visiting my family in Massachusetts and found the three volumes of *The Stones of Venice*, which a childhood friend had given me some years before... So I read it, and I hoped that I could do something with it in film. Then, in 1973, I went to Venice with Gregory.... I filmed the Venetian locations, sometimes at three different hours of the day, in color and then filmed specific architectural details at the same locations in black and white. At the end of 1974, this was all edited and printed with a soundtrack of fragments read from Ruskin's text. Then, I decided to add a coda, which took almost a year to do; this also involved changing the sound of the original part. So I added the coda, which is composed of simple elements—the moving pages of a book with shadows between the pages intercut with falling snow—and I removed the spoken fragments of text from the main part of the film. The pages seen in the coda are from another work of Ruskin's, *Unto This Last*, which is quite an extraordinary text on political economy. Between the body of the film and the coda, I had also placed the date of Ruskin's death—the 20th of January, 1900, but in the final version of 1992, this has been removed. It is now a simple transition from Venice and the Alps to the pages and

my hand.... Whenever I have used a biographical source for a film, whether it was Leonardo or Ruskin, I have always refrained from any attempt to present the person directly and have tried to find other ways to establish their presence.... My interest in the various maskings stems from the practical possibilities that they possess to attract, to control light in a way that could not be done by any other means that I know. Then, at a later point, I stopped using them because... they seemed a limitation.[30]

The extraordinary grace and beauty of *Ruskin*, the polished perfection of its images, might deflect attention from its allegorical theme of the process of becoming in which a nineteenth-century writer's attention to the concrete particulars of water, stone, weather, and metropolis, mediated as images, can at times be recuperated in Venice insofar as it is an archaeological museum, or in the Alps where weather patterns cyclically recur, while in London the traces of Ruskin's city have been largely erased. Beavers's self-representation as a reader-filmmaker, here unseen (aside from his hand on Ruskin's book), links *Ruskin* to *From the Notebook Of...* to bracket the four films of the early 1970s that make up the second cycle.

Nowhere in Beavers's oeuvre is the architectural organization of a city as central to the exploration of film form as in *Ruskin*. In this context, I quote Valéry's essay on Leonardo, for the last time in this chapter:

> I suggest that one should relate [architecture] to the idea of the city in order to appreciate it more generally, and that to grasp its complex charm one should try to recall the infinity of its aspects—a motionless building is the exception—the pleasure is in changing one's position until the building moves, and in the enjoyment of all the combinations of its varying members—the column turns, the depths recede, the galleries glide—a thousand visions emerge from the building, a thousand harmonies....
>
> The stone exists in space—what we call space is relative to the conception of any building we choose to take; the architectural edifice interprets space and leads us to the hypotheses on the nature of space in a particular manner, for it is at one and the same time an equilibrium of materials related to gravitation, a static visible arrangement, and, in each material, another equilibrium, molecular, and ill-understood.[31]

30. Tony Pipolo, "Interview with Robert Beavers," pp. 12–14.
31. Valéry, *Introduction*, pp. 60–61.

Although camera movement plays no role in Beavers's film, "the pleasure in changing one's position until the building[s] move" has its innovative coefficient in the way the filmmaker turned the lens turret while the camera was photographing a building or a detail. This novel effect makes the entire image move quickly in an arc through the film frame, bordered above or below by the curved shape of the lens turret itself, momentarily masking out the remainder of the frame. If the turret twists to the left, the masking arcs upward while the image within the circle of the lens seems to move downward, or vice versa. Beavers called this phenomenon "the double movement of sight."[32]

A notebook entry from March 8, 1978, elaborates upon it:

The physical self (the body) moves always in the opposite direction to what is seen (image). This is obvious when the body moves and less obvious or imperceptible when it is only the eyes that move. When I look in a mirror and yet see the mirror's outline telescoped as a reflection upon my eyes and moving in the opposite direction to which my head is moving, I am startled. At this instant I grasp the two halves of the movement: that of myself and that of the image.[33]

In one of his *Early Monthly Segments*, the filmmaker first experimented with turning the lens in this way. It became a central factor in the dynamics of *Ruskin*, where he coordinated different speeds of lens movement with shot lengths and montage juxtapositions in the overall rhythmic unfolding of the film. Sometimes he continues to twist the turret until a different lens brings into view closer or more remote images of the same building, landscape, or object. In most cases, he cuts away from the shot just as the rotation is completed.

From early on in the film, the most characteristic montage combination nests a still black-and-white shot of a detail—often with shimmering reflections off the canals—between two color shots of Gothic buildings (the filmmaker rigorously fixes his attention on Venetian Gothic architecture, excluding Renaissance structures in accordance with Ruskin's polemicized preference). Generally, the cut to the black-and-white image occurs right after the turret movement of the first color shot. Then there is a static cut from the black and white to the new color image that, in turn, disappears after a twist of the lens.

As the film progresses, the predominance of this structure diminishes. The black and white elements become more infrequent. Sometimes gorgeous color shots of Alpine landscapes from the Bergell appear between images of

32. Pipolo, "Interview with Robert Beavers," p. 15.
33. Robert Beavers, e-mail to P. Adams Sitney, April 6, 2005.

Venice. In contrast to the scarcely populated shots of Venice and Switzerland, we see the pedestrian and mobile traffic of Portland Place in London,[34] representing for the filmmaker, as it did for Ruskin, the modern metropolis where buses push past Georgian facades. Periodically there appear shots of a book (*The Stones of Venice*), often raised and put down by the filmmaker's hand lying flat upon its cover. In the coda to the film, he will flip through pages of *Unto This Last* (Ruskin's widely influential indictment of modern capitalism for undermining the dignity of manual labor and craft), briskly intercutting its barely legible pages with a field of falling snowflakes.

Pipolo persuasively read the shift from *The Stones of Venice* to *Unto This Last* as a function of the relationship of *Ruskin* to *Work Done*:

> For Beavers, *Work Done*, the film immediately preceding *Ruskin*, represented an important shift from his earlier work, which "emphasized the particular qualities of an individual" to becoming "more aware of qualities which are common and shared and can be presented directly." One way of reading this is to see it as a move away from the isolation often associated with artists—which, in this case, may have real parallels with Beavers' chosen severance from his homeland and the different path he may have taken had he remained—to an embracing of art as another kind of endeavor, one that may be connected to "work done" by others.... [I]t seems reasonable to see a certain parallel here between Beavers' shift and the "two voices" of John Ruskin—or, less schematically phrased, the "different emphases" that each book of the writer reflects. One is the lovingly detailed study of architecture by the artist/critic; the other a sober consideration of how Christian principles should be applied more diligently to the British government's social and economic policies.... [G]iving the last "word" to Ruskin, the social reformer, rather than Ruskin, art critic and historian, is somehow not an unfitting conclusion to a work that also strives to observe first principles—including those of justice and economy—concerning the production, edification, and usefulness of the art work.[35]

The public exhibition of the second cycle of *My Hand Outstretched* confirmed Pipolo's intuitions of an internal cohesion between the two films. The

34. *The Stones of Venice* concluded with a discussion of the then newly constructed neo-Gothic All Saints Church on Margaret Street and Portland Place. It won Ruskin's admiration and filled him with optimism: "It is the first piece of architecture I have seen, built in modern days, which is free from all signs of timidity or incapacity.... The London of the nineteenth century may yet become as Venice without her despotism, and as Florence without her dispeace." All Saints Church does not appear in Beavers's film.

35. Tony Pipolo, "*Ruskin*: A Film by Robert Beavers," *Millennium Film Journal* nos. 23/33 (Fall 1998), p. 69.

whole cycle describes moments in the consciousness of artistic election. If we can tentatively assume a Dantean intertext for *Work Done*, each of the four films measures the filmmaker's sensibilities, and the parameters of cinematic cognition, in the face of a challenging master, central to European—as distinguished from American—traditions. The sequence of films charts the growth of the filmmaker's mind, the enlarging of his powers.

In taking Ruskin as a master in the final film of the cycle, Beavers was repeating the lesson of the young Proust, who ended the preface to his translation of Ruskin's *The Bible of Amiens* with a relevant defense of his discipleship as a means of self-invention:

> Ruskin's thought is not like that of Emerson, for example, which is entirely contained in a book, that is, an abstract thing, a pure sign of itself. The object to which thought such as Ruskin's is applied, and from which it is inseparable, is not immaterial, it is scattered here and there over the surface of the earth. One must seek it where it is, in Pisa, Florence, Venice, the National Gallery, Rouen, Amiens, the mountains of Switzerland. Such thought which has an object other than itself, which has materialized in space, which is no longer infinite and free, but limited and subdued, which is incarnated in bodies of sculptured marble, in snowy mountains, in painted countenances, is perhaps less sublime than pure thought. But it makes the universe more beautiful for us, or at least certain individual parts, certain specifically named parts of the universe, because it touched upon them, and because it introduced us to them by obliging us, if we want to understand it, to love them....
>
> It is the power of genius to make us love a beauty more real than ourselves in those things which in the eyes of others are as particular and perishable as ourselves....
>
> There is no better way of becoming aware of one's feelings than to try to recreate in oneself what a master has felt. In this profound effort it is our thought, together with his, that we bring to light.... Actually the only times when we truly have all our powers of mind are those when we do not believe ourselves to be acting with independence, when we do not arbitrarily choose the goal of our efforts. The subject of the novelist, the vision of the poet, the truth of the philosopher are imposed on them in a manner almost inevitable, exterior, so to speak, to their thought. And it is by subjecting his mind to the expression of this vision and to the approach of this truth that the artist becomes truly himself.[36]

36. Marcel Proust, *On Reading Ruskin*, trans. and ed. Jean Autret, William Burford, and Phillip J. Wolfe (New Haven, CT: Yale University Press, 1987), pp. 58–60.

The contrast Proust makes between Emerson and Ruskin sacrifices a comprehension of the Sage of Concord to portray Ruskin as his own elective master. Nevertheless, Beavers, unlike Proust, regrounds his Emersonian heritage when he "subjects his mind" to Turner. Finding the present in the past and the past in the present becomes his path of self-reliance, the artist becoming most truly himself, in the whole of the second cycle of *My Hand Outstretched*.

CHAPTER 8

Andrew Noren and the Open-Ended Cinematic Sequence

Open-ended serial production is one of the characteristics most often associated with diaristic filmmaking where, in principle, the film and the life of the filmmaker are coextensive. Jonas Mekas referred to his films as diaries, but as a veteran keeper of written diaries, he knew that there was a fundamental difference between filming as an event was unfolding and reflecting on the day's activities in immediate retrospect. Furthermore, he never had recourse to sequential dating as an organizational principle for his films.

In the third edition of *Visionary Film*, I used the term *quotidian lyric* in an attempt to circumvent the metaphor of the diary when writing of films by Mekas, Andrew Noren, and others. There I noted the crucial differences between the conventions of home movies and the aesthetic sophistication of quotidian lyrics:

> While the avant-garde quotidian lyric shares the home movie
> maker's recognition of the importance of place, of family celebrations,
> of capturing the look of people and things against the pressures of

time, it is also particularly receptive [as the home movie is not] to nuances of light intensity and to the articulation of mood through the film-maker's manipulation of the time in which events are represented.... The quotidian lyric oscillates between the extremes of pixilated and time-lapse compression and the dilation of time in extended metonymies of landscape or close-up details.[1]

Andrew Noren began making films in the mid-1960s. The *Film-Makers' Cooperative Catalogue No. 4* of 1967 lists eleven films made in the previous two years. At least seven of them were parts of serial works: *A Change of Heart* (1965);[2] two are episodes of *The New York Miseries* (1966); there are three parts of *The Unclean* (1967). The second part of *The New York Miseries* "(Scenes from Life)" is itself described by the filmmaker as "15 documentaries. 'Each about 2 minutes; each about some common thing; talking, eating, the morning shits, the afternoon fucks with light coming in; listening to music, getting stoned, singing, etc. Some fantastic beggars doing their routines on 14th St. Several portraits of people. All of them shot with live sound. The film will go on forever.'"[3] The film did not go on forever, at least not in that form and with that title. In fact, most of Noren's initial work was destroyed by a fire. Nevertheless, the one film he continues to exhibit, in serial form, *The Adventures of the Exquisite Corpse*, challenges Mekas's *Diaries, Notes, and Sketches* in longevity; between 1968 and 2003 he has produced eight films in the sequence, running close to nine hours in all. By 1971, he had withdrawn his early films. He allowed only *Say Nothing* (1965) of the initial eleven to be distributed. *The Film-makers' Cooperative Catalogue No. 5* introduced a new series with *Kodak Ghost Poems—Part 1, The Adventures of the Exquisite Corpse* (1968), the first film he identified as silent. If my recollections are accurate after more than thirty years, material from *New York Miseries* and *The Unclean* was incorporated in this film, which subsequently went through a number of revisions, including a change of title to *Huge Pupils*.

All the films Noren released since 1970 have been parts of *The Adventures of the Exquisite Corpse*: *Part II: False Pretenses* (1974), *Part III: The Phantom Enthusiast* (1976), *Part IV: Charmed Particles* (1977), *Part V: The Lighted Field* (1987), *Part VI: Imaginary Light* (1995), *Part VII: Time Being* (2001), *Part VIII: Free to Go (interlude)* (2003). The first three parts need restoration; they have

---

1. P. Adams Sitney, *Visionary Film*, 3rd ed. (New York: Oxford University Press, 2002), pp. 425–26.
2. "A Further Adventure" suggests a serial project. It seems to be related to *Eat Me* (1966–67), (*Film-makers' Cooperative Catalogue No. 4* (New York:Film-makers' Cooperative , 1967), p. 119.) Also, the description of the lost portrait of Harry Smith, *The Trouble with Harry* (1967), indicates that it was another thirty-minute, aggressive portrait in the style of *Say Nothing*.
3. *Film-makers' Cooperative Catalogue No. 4*, p.118.

been out of distribution for more than a decade. They are the only 16 mm film sections in color. The last two parts are digital.

The critical literature on *The Adventures of the Exquisite Corpse* shows a remarkable consensus. There one finds enthusiasm for the sensual qualities of Noren's color and his black-and-white photography, acknowledgment of the paradox that the more tactile his imagery becomes, the more his films emphasize the evanescence of bodies, and frequently there are citations of poets as guides to his work. In the last two points, critics have been tutored by a remarkable interview Noren gave Scott MacDonald. Rather than speaking to him, the filmmaker wrote and rewrote eloquent answers to his questions. It is the central, ineluctable text about his work and evolution as an artist.

Bruce Elder, following a lead from the interview, wrote of the relationship between Noren's films and the poetry of Christopher Smart and John Clare. Lindley Hanlon briefly explored the implications of a Louis Zukofsky poem Noren quoted in his notes for *Charmed Particles*. John Pruitt found a parallel in Robert Kelly's "Orpheus" and in Keats's "longing for self-immolation" for what he took to be the awesome and elusive female presence haunting the films.[4]

Looming above these poetic affinities, Walt Whitman informs Noren's cinematic "song of myself," as it does so much of the cinema I discuss in this book. The domination of Whitman, like that of his precursor Emerson, is so pervasive that we have to narrow the focus and ask which works of the expansive and self-contradictory poet are operating here. The persona Noren offers us in *Huge Pupils* evokes the relaxed, sensual bard who describes himself as follows in the first (1855) edition of *Leaves of Grass*:

> I loafe and invite my soul,
> I lean and loafe at my ease...observing a spear of summer grass.
>
> ...
>
> Walt Whitman, an American, one of the roughs, akosmos,
> Disorderly fleshly sensual...eating drinking and breeding,
> No sentimentalist...no stander above men and women...or apart from
>   them...no more modest than immodest.[5]

Huge Pupils is the young Noren's self-portrait and carefully calculated self-presentation to the camera. (He was in his twenties when he made the film.) It begins and ends with him loafing on a Manhattan rooftop. Becoming

4. Bruce Elder, *A Body of Vision: Representations of the Body in Recent Film and Poetry* (Waterloo: Wilfred Laurier University Press, 1998); Lindley Hanlon, "Sensuality in *Charmed Particles: Part IV of The Adventures of the Exquisite Corpse*, a Film by Andrew Noren," *Millennium Film Review* no. 3 (Winter/Spring 1979); John Pruitt, "Andrew Noren's *The Adventures of the Exquisite Corpse*," *The Downtown Review* 2, no. 3 (Fall 1980).
5. Walt Whitman, "Leaves of Grass," *Selected Poems 1855–1892: A New Edition*, ed. Gary Schmidgall (New York: St. Martin's, 1999), pp. 15, 34,

visible as the intense white light is notched down, as if he were born of the congealing of light, the filmmaker appears alone with a large dog. The dog is the first of a series of portraits spread throughout the film. The fact that Noren can be filmed, with a handheld camera, implies he is not actually alone. As if aware of our mediated presence on the roof, he holds his tongue out to the camera so we can see he has taken, apparently, a tab of LSD.

If Whitman's boast "I sound my barbaric yawp over the roofs of the world" does not fit this roof treader, it is not merely because his film is silent; Noren is one of the withdrawn, self-contained progeny of Walt. He has divested himself of the prophetic stance, the homoerotic yearner and the mask of the gregarious companion. Mekas and Brakhage have divided the prophetic mantle between them; Warren Sonbert inherited the homoerotic sociability. Perhaps the most significant divergence, in all their films, from the formal register of *Leaves of Grass* derives from the limitations of the second-person address in cinema. In fact, only Mekas even attempts to invoke it. But Whitman made much of his intimacy with the future reader, whom he brought into the poem with the pronoun *you*. In the sublime finale, he predicted quite accurately his place in the American tradition, always underfoot, always out ahead, anticipating his followers:

> I bequeath myself to the dirt to grow from the grass I love,
> If you want me again look for me under your bootsoles.
>
> You will hardly know who I am or what I mean,
> But I shall be good health to you nevertheless,
> And filter and fiber of your blood.
>
> Failing to fetch me at first keep encouraged,
> Missing me one place search another,
> I stop some where waiting for you.[6]

As I described it in the fifth chapter, Mekas's use of the second person is concentrated in the intertitles. He sometimes addresses individuals or his audience in the voice-over. However, a direct address to the viewer in synchronous sound is awkward and seldom used in cinema. The exceptions underline how problematic it can be. In *Blue Moses* (1962), Brakhage implies that the introduction of the grammatical second person is a paradigm for the deceptions he discerns in all narrative arrangements; his actor attempts to arouse anxieties in the audience by reassuring them that one is never alone

6. Ibid., p. 66.

in a film: There is always the cameraman. When George Landow tells us in *Remedial Reading Comprehension* (1970) that "this is a film about you," he is playing with the discourse of advertising. Herbert Jean deGrasse's hilarious *Film Watchers* (1974) hurls abuse at typical avant-garde film audiences. Joe Gibbons makes the most of the awkwardness inherent in the second-person address in *Confidential, Part II* (1980). Until the viewer realizes that the filmmaker's amorous language is addressed directly to the camera itself, the *you* seems to be an offscreen lover.

The silence of Noren's film, without recourse to intertitles, skirts the problem of grammatical persons by eliminating language altogether. From the start, he even defines the camera-protagonist relationship with a unique variant on the specular model of autobiographical cinema; for as soon as we see Noren filming himself in a mirror, the camera reveals that a young woman, with long blond hair, is holding the mirror for him. Thus the initial I-you alternation, implicit in the act of showing the camera the LSD tab on his tongue, collapses into an interpersonal exchange between the male and female figures who will dominate the film. We can account for the presence of the filmmaker in his own film by assuming she filmed him just as he so often filmed her; the gestures he makes to the camera come to be seen as directed to the woman as she is filming him.

At the same time, this erotic contract evokes the work of Stan Brakhage and the role of his first wife, Jane, as subject and collaborator in the decade preceding *Huge Pupils*. According to Noren:

> Brakhage would descend on New York from the mountains once a
> year, grandiloquent and Promethean, lighting bolts in one hand and
> film cans in the other, talking everyone under the table—what a talker!
> And in general burning the place to the ground. It's impossible to
> overestimate his influence on absolutely everyone: you could run but
> you couldn't hide.[7]

Brakhage's inescapable influence permeates *The Adventures of the Exquisite Corpse*. Noren's fusion of Zeus (the lightning bearer) and his antagonist, Prometheus, reflects the degree of ambivalence explicit in the emphasis by the taciturn Noren on the talk of this overwhelming figure. The younger filmmaker's identification with the Promethean victim of Zeus's power is clearest in the opening of *False Pretenses*, the second section of *The Adventures of the Exquisite Corpse*, where he appropriated images from a Hollywood film of a lightning storm and a prisoner on his way to his execution.

Noren owes a significant debt to Kenneth Anger's films as well. The direct stare of his camera resembles Anger's concentration on people and objects, rather than Brakhage's representation of eye movements. Like Anger, Noren extends his engagement with sexual acts to an overriding eroticizing of everything the camera sees. This is particularly clear in their shared fascination with acts of dressing and putting on jewels.

Huge Pupils seems to be divided in sections, each three or four minutes long, as if vestigially recalling the shape of *New York Miseries*; sometimes there are stylistic variations between sections. One such shift occurs when the rooftop preamble moves to autumnal images of Noren walking in a park. Here he uses superimpositions, rhythmic flashes of light, and some swiftly cut short zoom movements. Referring to the stop-motion photography with which he made a portrait of Ernie Gehr, later in the film, he told MacDonald: "I was interested in using single framing to convey kinetic energy. If it's done right, it can evoke high energy states of mind."[8] A narrative reading of the first two segments of *Huge Pupils* might see the filmic rhetoric of the park sequence as an evocation of the kinetic energy of the LSD experience initiated on the roof.

Noren's contemporaries were particularly interested in representing psychedelic and sexual experiences in cinema. Around 1966 John Cavanaugh, a part-time employee of the New York Film-makers' Cooperative, shortly before Noren went to work there, shot *Acid Man*, inspired by his own LSD experiences. It was an 8 mm film that tried to capture "states of high energy in the mind" with short, truncated zoom movements, dramatically shifting colors and trembling foliage, all radically slowed down by projection at six frames per second. Cavanaugh filmed a young man with light rhythmically passing over his face. Then he superimposed a blue tinted image of the same man, apparently on drugs, laughing and howling.

Cavanaugh had dropped out of high school to work as a messenger at the Film-makers' Cooperative. On a trip to Italy as the guest of the Pesaro Film Festival, he was arrested and spent some months in an Italian jail for drug possession. Eventually released and deported—he was still a teenager—he spent years in a New York mental hospital. His film is now lost. Noren's description of poets Christopher Smart and John Clare would have been true of Cavanaugh: "both were mad as March hares, but they both got the full lethal high-voltage jolt of life straight, without protection or defense, the undiluted juice right from the source."[9]

8. Ibid., p. 190.
9. Ibid.

Noren himself had little in common with the psychotic, uneducated Cavanaugh, even though *Huge Pupils* shares techniques and, superficially, themes with *Acid Man*. He was fascinated with artistic derangement, and alludes to it late in the film by filming a picture of Antonin Artaud. But *Huge Pupils* eschews the expressionism Cavanaugh sought. Instead, Noren eloquently described his cinematic aspiration as "Trying to 'record' that light storm of ghostly beauty blowing around me, doomed in the attempt, as we always are."[10] So, in his text for MacDonald, the thought of Smart and Clare leads the filmmaker to reflect on his own aspirations at the time he made *Huge Pupils*:

> Anyway, I was a kid and aspired to such openness, and I had all the things I loved around me in those ghost rooms, now gone. Ghost-woman and ghost-light, and my familiars, ghost-dog and ghost-cat, beauteous apparencies, and I tried to catch them, with my little shadow catcher, to stop their vanishing, but they vanished anyway.[11]

In crossing from the fate of the mad British poets to himself, his tone shifts into an elegiac mode. The destructive force with which he contends is time rather than the "lethal high-voltage jolt of life." In fact, the tension between epiphanous moments and the tempestuous power of time has been the over-arching theme of *The Adventures of the Exquisite Corpse*. That becomes more and more apparent over the more than thirty-year evolution of the film. The opening of *Time Being*, his 2001 work in digital video, synchronizes the sound of a powerful tempest to the very rapid—stop-motion—rush of light and shadows over his lawn and through the rooms of his house, making explicit the sublime metaphor of several of his earlier films: the irresistible storm of time raging through his home.

In *Huge Pupils* the balance remains in favor of the beauteous moment. These distillations of time range from oral and tactile pleasures anticipated or suspended (a steaming cup of orange tea on the floor beside blue slippers, a burning cigarette waiting on the windowsill) to extended sequences (a day or two out of the city to attend a wedding and cavort in the countryside, a trip to Paris). The portraits of friends have a unique temporal dimension; they are extended sequences of direct, intrusive confrontation by the camera. In two of them, he raises the coefficient of self-consciousness by filming couples nude: One pair take a bath together for him; another stand naked on the roof, the man holding a camera, iconographically signaling his status as a filmmaker himself. The shots of the first couple might have come directly from Noren's

10. MacDonald, *A Critical Cinema 2*, p. 187.
11. Ibid., p. 191.

lost series of bath portraits, *The Unclean*. For their portrait, Ken and Flo Jacobs appear not only dressed but wearing novelty store masks of Jack and Jacqueline Kennedy before baring their faces, as if they were forestalling exposure to Noren's camera. Ernie Gehr's portrait inverts the temporality of the others. Here Noren shot the filmmaker sitting at a table with single frames, compressing a stretch of time into a revelation of the kinetic energy roiling in the subject's stasis.

The frank and frequent depiction of sexual acts distinguishes *Huge Pupils* from the quotidian lyrics of other major filmmakers. Early in the film, by pointing the camera down at his own lower body, he records his girlfriend unzipping his fly and caressing his penis. Later, he filmed fellatio and, at the end of the film, vaginal penetration from similar subjective positions. The camera sometimes dwells on the woman's genitals and in one sequence she masturbates, apparently for the scopic pleasure of the filmmaker and, by extension, the viewer. Only once do we see Noren performing a sex act without his eye to the camera: At the end of the masturbation scene he performs cunnilingus.

There is nothing remotely like this sexual candor in the quotidian lyrics of Mekas or Sonbert. One might cull some fleeting, dispersed moments of sexual activity from the vast corpus of Brakhage's cinema. Yet he had recourse to negatives for such images in his early films, such as *Flesh of Morning* (1956) and *Wedlock House: An Intercourse* (1959). Later, superimposition, very fast montage, hand painting, shifting focus, or offscreen action tended to deflect his erotic gaze, even in the *Sexual Meditations* series.[12]

The robust sexuality of *Huge Pupils* is an important dimension of the filmmaker's self-representation as a bodily presence throughout the film. Not since the trance films of the 1940s and 1950s had a filmmaker played so central a role in his own film. But unlike the creators of those films, Noren freely shuttled behind and in front of the camera, vividly documenting the libidinal scenario those films had symbolized. The massive achievement of Brakhage's lyrical films of the late 1950s and early 1960s had been to transfer the quest mode from a drama enacted by the filmmaker or his or her representative to the crisis film of a generally unseen protagonist behind the camera and directing the montage. Noren not only reintroduced the filmmaker's presence in the imagery of his film (without reinstating the drama), he reversed the quest status: Whereas the trance films charted unsatisfied desire, Noren called *Huge Pupils* "news of what I took to be heaven."[13] *News* is a crucial term here. The

---

12. *Lovemaking* (1968) is an exception. It is a four-part film depicting first a heterosexual couple, then dogs, then two men having sex, and finally a group of little children running around naked. Brakhage removed the film from distribution.

13. MacDonald, *A Critical Cinema 2*, p. 187.

newsreels of his childhood were a vital inspiration to Noren's early style of cinematography:

> a window on the way things were in the Big World, which I was dying to get to. It was thrilling actuality, glares and flashes of "reality," what people really did. And I loved the style—simple, straightforward, direct—and the basic idea of "witness": eyes and ears of the world you might say, Buddhalike, nonjudgmental eye on suffering and on joy.[14]

Although the "news" of *Huge Pupils* was of what the filmmaker "took to be heaven," there is a countercurrent in the film that all of its commentators note. John Pruitt writes:

> The more vividly Noren immerses us in his intensely sensual world, the more we as spectators recognize a bizarre and disturbing absence. Though, for example, we see lovemaking on the screen, it all seems strange to us because the images don't carry the actual feeling of sensual arousement which gives sex its meaning. It is ultimately ethereal, bodiless sex, a contradiction in terms.... With that inherent contradiction, *Huge Pupils* achieves a tremendous tension.[15]

Astutely, R. Bruce Elder suggests that the filmmaker induces a "scanning" effect, due to both the unusual intensity of the film's colors and its temporality, which he characterizes as an open form lacking "teleological focus and eschewing hierarchization in local areas." The consequence of this shift of viewing perspective is "rendering bodies discorporate. Thus, for all their explicitness, Noren's films are not really carnal films, for the nudes that we see are more appearance than substance, more spirit than body."[16]

In using the term *scanning*, Elder invokes the work of Anton Ehrenzweig, whom I discuss later in relation to Brakhage's use of uncentered vision. Ehrenzweig distinguished between "cotensive" and "intensive" vision, a relaxed scanning of the visual field with equal sensitivity to peripheral and central stimuli and a focused scrutiny of the center of attention. Elder offers a temporal interpretation of this spatial distinction. The events, not the sights, of *Huge Pupils* are divested of "teleological focus" and local "hierachization." Nothing could be further from Brakhage's way of "mak[ing] the visible a little hard to see" (in Wallace Stevens's phrase) through the mimesis of eye movements and

---

14. Ibid., p. 180.
15. Pruitt, "Andrew Noren's *The Adventures of the Exquisite Corpse*," p. 19.
16. Bruce Elder, *A Body of Vision*, p. 326.

phosphene activity than Noren's intensive gaze. He probes with his camera as if it could touch the things of the world and affirm their presence by coming closer to them, or by bringing them closer to the camera, as he does the LSD tab or, later, turquoise jewelry.

I believe it is the centrality of the subjective camera position within the "simple, straightforward, direct" or newsreel style that makes the dialectic of presence and absence so powerful in *Huge Pupils*. So that while we see, for example, the woman shot from above, unzipping the fly and caressing the penis, we have a mental picture of the now familiar filmmaker looking down at her with the camera to his eye. There was even a shot, in an earlier version of *Kodak Ghost Poems*, of Noren filming into a mirror reflecting himself and a woman in flagrante delicto. "When are we not acting?" is his rhetorical question for an actress in *Say Nothing*. The question applies to his own persona in *Huge Pupils*: "[I] was...fascinated with the idea of identity or personality being a series of masks—a young man fascination—and I was curious to see if it were possible to set up a mask-removal procedure, and finally discover the 'real' person behind all the smoke and mirrors that constitute the 'official' personality."[17]

The play of presence and absence in *Huge Pupils*, in the tropes of tactility, conjures both the "ghost" of the young Noren captured on the celluloid traces and the "ghost of the filmmaker" standing apart from his imagery, the unattainable "'real' person behind all the smoke and mirrors." Whitman, yet again, trumps this ironic stance toward "the real Me":

Apart from the pulling and hauling stands what I am,
Stands amused, complacent, compassioning, idle, unitary,
Looks down, is erect, bends an arm on a impalpable certain rest,
Looks with its sidecurved head curious what will come next,
Both in and out of the game, and watching and wondering at it.[18]

The end of the film reverses the opening. Where the portrait of the filmmaker had appeared as the white light ratcheted down to make him visible, the conclusion shows him in an increase of light, his long hair blowing in the wind. That, of course, is the conventional iconography of poetic election, Apollo's capillary gift of inspiration.

On October 19, 1971, Noren presented a second part of *Kodak Ghost Poems* at a Cineprobe screening at the Museum of Modern Art. That film eventually became *False Pretenses*. The third section, *The Phantom Enthusiast*, was

17. MacDonald, *A Critical Cinema 2*, p. 183.
18. Whitman, *Selected Poems 1855–1892: A New Edition*, p. 17.

screened at the same venue February 9, 1976. After five parts of the film had
been completed, Noren revealed the overall schema to MacDonald:

> In general, *The Adventures of the Exquisite Corpse* is a reworking of
> the world's oldest story, "the fool's progress," how the fool became
> wise.... [T]he young fool leaves home to set off down the road of the
> world, hoping to find the great treasure that is hidden behind the veil
> of the world's illusions, behind the screen of the movie of the world,
> as it were. After many dangers and hardships, and in the exercise of
> strength and cunning, the fool tears away the veil and discovers that
> what is behind it is "nothing."...
> Another narrative aspect of the film is about the famous journey
> to the "other world." In my program notes when I released the film,
> I identified the "other world" as being "this world," which I hope is
> self-explanatory. And yet another narrative level is that of the entire
> film as after-death hallucination, in the tradition of Sunset Boulevard
> [1950] and a great novel of Flan O'Brien, The Third Policeman.[19]

His notes for his 1987 Cineprobe at the Museum of Modern Art repeat
and elaborate that scenario:

> "The Exquisite Corpse" is a kind of cinematic alchemy, the goal of
> which is the recognition and revelation of the "ordinary" as being, in
> fact, extraordinary and magical, for anyone to see if they have eyes for
> it. It is also a re-telling of the world's oldest story, that of the "Fool's
> progress" through the world of appearance and illusion. Starting from
> nothing/darkness, becoming something/light, ending again in dark-
> ness, moving from the small to the large, the particular to the whole
> and back again. In the end, the finished work will incorporate my
> entire life; it will end at the last moment I am able to register light on
> the ghostly flesh of film, bringing the circle to a close.[20]

Deprived of the opportunity of reexamining the second and third parts,
I turn to the evidence of their critical reception to gauge the crisis suggested
by the title *False Pretenses* and the hyperbole of the death row metaphor that
opens it, although two critics, Gail Cahmi and R. Bruce Elder, differ from a
third, John Pruitt, in locating the onset of the crisis in the third rather than
the second part.

19. MacDonald, *A Critical Cinema 2*, p. 201.
20. Andrew Noren, Cineprobe Program Notes, Museum of Modern Art, New York, 1987.

This much we can extrapolate from Noren's interview with MacDonald, who was also unable to resee those elements of the series:

> [Carnality] is the most important part of the "trick" that life is: it's the lure, the bait. What animal can resist orgasmic pleasure? We don't learn until later that the other part of the trick is more sinister and ominous, at least as far as our cheerful and bright-eyed "personal identity" is concerned.... The bad news is revealed in stages, broken to us gently. The trick has fatal consequences.[21]

The gentle revelation of this bad news in stages makes it difficult to pinpoint the negative turn in the film. Noren's version of the Emersonian trinity—Eros, Dionysus, and Ananke—embraces the bond between Dionysus and Apollo. In his terms, the triune forces would be "carnality," the pair "illusion and light"[22] and "nothing." An enthusiast is, etymologically, one filled with the force of a god or gods. Insofar as Noren can call himself, or call the cinema, "the phantom enthusiast," these are the gods suffusing and battling within him or it.

Camhi notes the onset of a major crisis: "*The Phantom Enthusiast* reveals to us that certain darkenings have taken hold. This work was made during what the artist has referred to as 'a time of crisis.'"[23] Jonas Mekas expressed disappointment in his Movie Journal in *The Soho Weekly News*: "A few of us who found Part 1 of 'Kodak Ghost Poems' ecstatically beautiful in its uninhibited sensuousness, will find Part 3 a relative letdown."[24] Elder, however, does not pass judgment on the films:

> If *False Pretenses* has a joyous tone, the next film in the series, *The Phantom Enthusiast*, is much darker.... The evolution of *The Adventures of the Exquisite Corpse* suggests the necessity of detaching oneself from sensuous involvement with things; the visual correlative of this progression is the increasingly distanced and ever more austere quality that Noren's imagery assumes as the series proceeds.[25]

21. MacDonald, *A Critical Cinema 2*, p. 189.
22. A program note from London, 1973,(Noren files, Anthology Film Archives), subtitled "Provisional Ravings—I" is an ode to the sun: "The cinema of Heaven, vast galactic Sun machines flashing shadow images onto our retina-screens and thus to our dreams and imaginations—non-stop screenings at the mystery theater, price of admissions our ectoplasmic vanishing flesh...The title of this lavish spectacle—'Pure Being.'...'Seeing' as access to the light, and light as the literal substance of matter, of the very eye that 'sees'— light as the hallucinary 'thought' of the golden brain of the Sun...Ghostly projector, ghostly film, the projectionist equally ghostly; an audience of ghosts, dreaming ghostly dreams, fluttering in the wind of the light."
23. Gail Cahmi, "The Films of Andrew Noren," *Film Culture* nos. 70–71 (1983), p. 108.
24. Jonas Mekas, Movie Journal, *Soho Weekly News*, April 15, 1976.
25. Elder, *A Body of Vision*, pp. 340–41.

Finally, John Pruitt astutely reads the filmmaker's self-revelation in the second film of the series:

> Noren displays a subtle morbidity, a longing for self-immolation.... [W]henever our personal filmmaker is caught alone before the camera, there is always the deliberately slow gait, the dangling cigarette, the pensive facial expression, and the boots, the jade jewelry. One guesses that... Noren feels uneasy about having his formal portrait taken. Not wanting to be caught, he takes up the mask of a poseur; he clutches a role. As a consequence, as a metaphor, Noren's own real subject, himself; remains elusive as well. In the beginning of *The Phantom Enthusiast*, Noren is a mere shadow and ultimately he remains so throughout all of his films.[26]

This analysis too echoes Whitman's explicit and paradoxically triumphant acknowledgment of self-defeat in "As I Ebb'd with the Ocean of Life":

O baffled, balked,
Bent to the very earth, here preceding what follows,
Oppressed with myself that I have dared to open my mouth,
Aware now, that, amid all the blab whose echoes recoil upon me, I have not
    once had the least idea who or what I am
But that before all my insolent poems the real ME stands untouched,
    untold, altogether unreached
Withdrawn far, mocking me with mock-congratulatory signs and bows,
With peals of distant ironical laughter at every word I have written or shall
    write,
Striking me with insults till I fall helpless upon the sand.

O I perceive I have not really understood anything – not single object – and
    that no man ever can,

I perceive Nature here, in sight of the sea, is taking advantage of me, to dart
    upon me and sting me,
Because I was assuming too much,
And because I have dared to open my mouth to sing at all.[27]

26. Pruitt, "Andrew Noren's *The Adventures of the Exquisite Corpse*," pp. 19–20.
27. Whitman, "As I Ebb'd with the Ocean of Life," *Selected Poems 1855–1892: A New Edition*, p. 196.

The artificially sudden leap from *Huge Pupils* of 1968 to *Charmed Particles* in 1979, caused by the unavailability of the two intervening films, dramatizes the shift from the "simple, straightforward, direct" representation of the film-maker in his world and reacting to it, to a vision of an environment consti-tuted essentially by light. From this moment through to the new century the very titles shift from allusions to the status of the filmmaker—the god-possessed ghost with dilated pupils making his work on false pretenses, or perhaps called a diarist on false pretenses—to descriptions of the categories and elements in the world he encounters or reveals: *Charmed Particles, The Lighted Field, Imaginary Light, Time Being*.

Noren effects this metaphysical transformation with a range of stylistic choices: black-and-white cinematography, the predominance of pixilation, and a more circumscribed set of locations. Above all, the observation of sur-faces as fields reflecting light and shadows results in the reduction of objects and even the human body to the condition of such surfaces. The filmmaker no longer holds things up to the camera as if to make them more tangible. For instance, he abjures the gestural power of filming sexual organs and sexual acts.

In a sense, the fourth part makes a new beginning. Noren reestablishes his relationship to cinema on an even more fundamental, elemental basis. The paring down of his formal vocabulary and the concentration on fewer subjects indicates a corresponding shift in the filmmaker's worldview. Having distinguished himself and earned the admiration of veteran filmmakers for the candor of his depiction of his robust sexuality, he implicitly repudiated that success. Thus, he begins all over again, even more firmly in possession of his axis, to paraphrase Emerson. One woman (Rise Hall) replaces the se-rial lovers of the earlier films (especially marked in their earliest versions); a ubiquitous mesh of shadows discreetly obscures her occasional nudity; a carefully orchestrated kiss replaces the explicit sexual acts; he films from his urban apartment and what seems to be a country house (apparently filmed primarily in the summer); gone are the portraits of friends and the experi-ences of travel.

This new beginning with its concentration on the domestic life, and the celebration of a central female presence within it, reaffirms incidentally Bra-khage's influence, although no single work dominates the complex legacy *Charmed Particles* inherits. The shadow protagonist may ultimately derive from *Anticipation of the Night*; the very structure of that film's interlocking episodes of the filmmaker's encounters with everyday sights treated as mys-teries, symbolic quests, and affective wonders constitutes a model for Noren's film that is nearly twice as long: it runs seventy-eight minutes at eighteen frames per second. Both films indicate that the filmmaker is in a particular place for an extended period of investigation or contemplation of the objects of his environment, and then he projects a different place and other objects of attention. Brakhage himself mined *Anticipation of the Night* for dozens of shorter lyrical films. For instance, *Hymn to Her* (1974) portrays Jane in her greenhouse, drawing upon the sensual exploration of plant forms in the 1958 film. The superabundance of vegetation in Noren's film, both in the apartment and outdoors, similarly represents Rise as a Demeter or Flora figure. In *Pasht* (1965), Brakhage orchestrated a hot spot of light moving irregularly all over the screen to give his five-minute color film its rhythmic dynamics. Similarly, Noren's use of high-contrast black and white gives virtually every frame of *Charmed Particles* hot spots of white light.

The pixilation with which most of the film is recorded makes these spots flicker about the screen like a flame. The tempo of the film occasionally plays these dynamic, rapid fluctuations against more static shots. This pixilation is even more persistent than that in Mekas's films, where the rapid changes emphasize ellipses in the implicit continuity of the filmmaker's experience of the world. The multiplicity of his subjects and social encounters point back to Mekas's sensibility and personality. In contrast, Noren's pixilation emphasizes the metamorphic nature of the very universe he films, where light and matter coalesce. Thus he took his title from quantum physics where some particles show persistent longevity. He has interpreted the title rather freely as "the point at which energy becomes matter, intangible 'nothing' becomes 'something.'"[28] "Charmed particles" describes as well the magical behavior of grains of photographic emulsion that can manifest the illusion of matter and project their dissolution.

The technique of *Charmed Particles* sensualizes the filmic surface as if it too were flesh. The pulsing rhythms of the film and its often ambiguous images further suggest a sexual dynamic. It is as if Noren were claiming a sexuality for the very materials and temporality of cinema. In describing how he made the film, Noren told Scott MacDonald that his small New York apartment was like a camera:

> *Charmed Particles*...was totally improvised, starting with the very
> first image that appears in the finished film and continuing on from
> there. It was shot over a period of several years and the operating rule
> was that I would shoot every day, if at all possible and if the light was
> good, working with light and shadow and whatever was around me,
> not knowing in advance what I would be shooting, trusting that in the
> end everything would cohere and come to meaning. Rise and I were
> living at that time in a tiny apartment on West Tenth Street, so small
> it was like living in a camera, although it got splendid light, and I took

28. MacDonald, *A Critical Cinema 2*, p. 193.

the basic elements of our life there and worked to see what improvisation and variations were possible, to see if I could charm the disparate elements into form.

At its best, this is done in a special state of mind. It's not a trance state, and certainly not the talking of angelic dictation as Rilke meant it. I think of it as a state of "health," where thought and feeling are one and the same. The response to light: the process of seeing and feeling and thinking about it, and "capturing" it, is harmonious and simple and direct, without doubt or hesitation. In this condition I know exactly what to do and how to do it, no questions.... In editing, I gather material shot over a period of time and assemble it more or less in the order in which it was shot, chronologically, and then I study it until I begin to see how things belong together, what connections to make.... There is only one "right" way for it to go. It's very much as though the film were already "made" in a part of my mind, and the working process is simply letting it reveal itself. This is a very painstaking process. It's frustrating and extremely exhilarating at the same time, and it's very hard work.[29]

To shoot every day and to study the fortuitous connections created thereby is to turn the surrealists' exquisite corpse into a temporal figure. The very hard work of constructing the film would entail the discipline and courage to allow the film priority in determining how the domestic life is to be represented rather than making the film reflect the filmmaker's memory or perception of his and Rise's life together.

In making a new beginning, Noren also calls upon his own earlier achievements. The recurring images of sheets flapping on a clothesline and other fabrics stirred by breezes reminds us of his early film *The Wind Variations* (1969), eighteen minutes of patterns made by air moving window curtains. By bracketing the film with matching shots—a closeup of a woman's eye at the beginning, the filmmaker's eye at the end, examining a strip of 16 mm film—he may be alluding to the mirror shots of himself and the woman near the start of *Huge Pupils*, and to the title of that film.

The framing trope of the eyes—the woman's directly observing the light, the man's mediated by the shadow of the filmstrip—underlines the emphasis on vision, while the mirror play would figure the realm of representation. But the self-portraiture of *Huge Pupils* is nearly abolished in *Charmed Particles*, where we seldom get a direct view of the filmmaker. The elaborately orchestrated kiss, with its version of shot-countershot, is the major exception. There is a second bracketing gesture within the film: Within the first five

29. Ibid., pp. 193–95.

minutes a black screen becomes the opening of a door onto pure white light. We see Noren for the first time at the top of a staircase in one of the rare fixed camera shots. As he opens the door onto the roof, the incoming light projects his massive shadow onto the stairwell wall. If the film can be said to begin with the woman's eye followed by what she sees (the vibrant life of plants and their commingling with light), then Noren correspondingly enters his film as the figure who opens the interior to the light of the sky. Significantly, this fixed shot reappears late in the film and announces its finale when Noren ascends the stairs to close the door, rendering the frame black.

The film moves through spring and summer to winter as if they were states of mind, but it does not adhere to a seasonal structure. Instead, it seems to dwell upon repetitive daily acts—washing dishes, drying clothes, sweeping, reading the newspaper, drinking coffee or tea, and above all Rise rocking in a chair or hammock as if it were the very emblem of the ecstasy of repetition (and the correlative of the daily commitment to film). In filming these repetitive events Noren pushes them, sometimes even seems to break them open, to capture the traceries of light and energy that constitute their charm, not only as the term is adopted by physics but in its etymological roots to Latin *carmen*, song, poem, incantation, spell.

The worldview that molds the vision of *The Adventures of the Exquisite Corpse* is Lucretian. Of the American avant-garde filmmakers, Noren shares this affinity with Frampton, who as I mentioned in chapter 5 makes at least one direct allusion to Lucretius in his essays. The major Roman poets have remained powerful models for the varieties of European and American poetry, and several of the filmmakers I discuss in this book are in different ways heirs of those traditions. Lucretius devoted his life work to an epic elaboration of the atomic theories and moral reflections of his philosophical master, Epicurus, making poetry of the speculative observation of nature and from an anthropological scrutiny of human behavior. Noren is at his most Lucretian when offering an analysis of matter as organized energy or speaking of the psychic trickery of the erotic impulse. The epicurean withdrawal from the world of society to the cultivation of one's garden and the moderate enjoyment of the pleasures of the senses clearly finds its echo in the black-and-white parts of Noren's film.

A fundamental difference between the quotidian lyrics of Noren and those of Mekas might even be understood as a difference of Lucretian and Virgilian sensibilities. Virgil extolled the music of shepherds in his *Bucolics* and the routines and techniques of farmers in his *Georgics*, but his epic masterpiece, *The Aeneid*, narrates the fate of the exile from Troy destined to found the Roman Empire at enormous personal cost. Mekas's cinematic persona as a melancholy but indomitable exile from the agrarian simplicity of his childhood is distinctly Virgilian. When he calls the composite portrait of his friends, predominantly filmmakers and other artists, *The Birth of a Nation* (1997), he invokes that problematic hyperbole with Virgilian irony.

A third poetic tradition ultimately emanates from Rome: the urbane verbal and phantasmagoric wizardry of Ovid's *Metamorphoses*. Ovid retold the inherited myths of Greece and Rome, vividly describing the physical sensations and astonishments of bodily transformation. His hyperbolical scenarios of metamorphosis indirectly attest to the range and qualities of human sensations and emotions. His ironic relationship to traditional religious and cultic ideas and his collapsing of material metamorphoses and poetic processes inspired Renaissance and modern poets. The earliest theoreticians of the cinema—Lukacs, D'Annunzio, Papini—recognized the Ovidian propensities of creating magical imagery by stopping and restarting the camera after details of the scene have been altered. Maya Deren, Ian Hugo, Harry Smith, and Robert Breer have demonstrated the range of Ovidian sensibilities within the American avant-garde cinema.

Debts to the tradition of Ovid merge with those to Lucretius in the fifth part of *The Adventures of the Exquisite Corpse: The Lighted Field*, another black-and-white film dominated by pixilation. This film, corresponding to *False Pretenses* as *Charmed Particles* had to *Huge Pupils*, introduces archival footage as a bracketing device. It is surprising that Noren does not use found footage more often, since he has earned his living for many years finding film clips for news services and commercial films. Yet one way of reading *The Lighted Field* would be as a commentary on that aspect of his life, touching upon how his work as an archivist affected his private life and how he had come to see all cinematic artifacts as fictions. His metaphor for the conjunction of these ideas is the dream.

He wrote to MacDonald:

What you see on the evening news, compared to the raw material, is a very carefully constructed entertainment, disguised as reportage.... The raw material is the real thing, and it is frequently horrifying.... Working with this kind of material on a daily basis can have a profound effect upon a person.[30]

Further, elaborating an idea of the ubiquity of narrative that closely corresponds to Frampton's "A Pentagram for Conjuring the Narrative," he exposed the theoretical foundations of this section of his ongoing film cycle:

Whatever else it is, *The Lighted Field* is a narrative, a carefully constructed one, the telling of a tale. Of course, every film is a narrative,

---

30. Ibid., pp. 199–200 (ellipsis mine).

isn't it, whatever other pretenses it might have, simply by virtue of the fact that one frame must follow another in time. Our minds are such that we are obliged to make a story out of everything we experience, obliged to frame things to make them comprehensible. We are constantly telling ourselves stories that allegedly interpret the play of light and shadow on the retina screen, and the play of imaginary light in the screen of the "mind," or "the lighted field," if you will.... "story" is the absolute basic essential of thinking. Our minds consist of a "teller" and a "listener."...

And our "story" of consciousness is dream by definition. We live a dream of waking, we dream that we're "awake," imagining past and future, telling ourselves elaborate stories about both....

We invented cinema deliberately as a device to allow us to dream while waking, and to give us access to areas of the mind that were previously only available in sleep.[31]

Preceding the archival clips in *The Lighted Field*, Noren has placed an image of himself asleep near the beginning of the film amid images of light on water as if to indicate a primal moment, an oceanic medium of light from which dreams come. Then, echoing Brakhage's autobiographical signposts in *Scenes from Under Childhood* and *Sincerity*, he presents a still photograph of himself as a child beside his mother. His handheld camera gesture emphasizes and isolates the child. Although the filmmaker rejects Freudian dream interpretation as "incredibly cynical," the film locates the dream screen within the force field of fusion and separation of mother and child. Furthermore, the question of parenthood will be one of the most haunting and elusive aspects of the whole film, as the filmmaker imagines the past and future, telling himself elaborate stories about each.

Bruce Elder's meticulous description of the film's photographic style and tonal range concludes that "represented objects in *The Lighted Field* maintain their distinctiveness, their particularity, their objecthood; thus, the film establishes a more complex balance between the beings of the particular objects represented and the being of light—and between particular objects and the Being which light's ontological status approximates."[32] He argues that the aim of formal transfiguration requires a greater stability of objects than Noren presented in the previous episode of his cycle. In stressing what I have called the Ovidian aspect of the film, Elder bypasses the filmmaker's claims about narrative.

31. Ibid., pp. 200–210 (ellipses mine).
32. Elder, *A Body of Vision*, pp. 347–48.

However, John Pruitt, in his extraordinary essay "Metamorphosis: Andrew Noren's *The Lighted Field*," takes up what he calls "an explicit dare to interpret his imagery" implied in Noren's film:

Noren's idiosyncratic view [holds] that cinema embodies a transformative process, that is to say, the capturing of a person's image on film is not unlike a rite of "death and transfiguration."...At the heart of cinema, in fact, lies a radical disjunctiveness implanted in the stuttering, stop-start action of the shutter. Hence Noren's dependency on stop-action photography....Noren has forcefully expressed to the viewer that a lens is an instrument of vision containing such intensity that it "burns" i.e. "transforms" the objects placed before it....The field of Noren's title might mean "field of vision,"...but once confronted with the final section of Noren's film we see a poetic evocation of "Elysian Fields"—the mythical, pastoral paradise that heroes passed over to after death.[33]

He reads the sleeping figure thus:

Significantly, we never see [the sleeping figure of the filmmaker] wake up, and the stillness of sleep or perhaps a pre-figuring of death (the series title suggests the protagonist is an "exquisite corpse" after all) thus hangs over the rest of the film.[34]

The found images of a man first encased in a block of ice and later released registers, for him, another variation on that theme:

Noren's incisive comment on the double-stage of cinematic process, whereby the moving, vital world must be initially "frozen"—made lifeless—before it can move again with a newly charged energy *not* of its own making (why a corpse can go on an adventure in the first place), should by this time be obvious.[35]

Actually, very little is obvious in this subtly evocative film. Granted, the oneiric framework is clearly articulated. But right from the start, the photograph, an icon in this genre of the elusiveness of autobiographical temporality,

33. John Pruitt, "Metamorphoses: Andrew Noren's *The Lighted Field*," First Light, ed. Robert Haller (New York: Anthology Film Archives, 1998) pp. 55–58. A revised version of this essay was published in *CineMatrix*, 1, No. 2, Winter 1999 (Anandale-on-Hudson, NY), pp. 5–8.
34. Ibid., p. 54.
35. Ibid. p. 55.

sets in motion a thread that is never obviously developed. Its relationship to the found footage montage that shortly follows is very ambiguous.

We see the process and the results of X-ray cinematography: a female skeleton putting lipstick where we see no lips, combing her invisible hair, washing her fleshless face, talking on the telephone, yawning, and talking to another skeleton—actually, talking at the same time as the other talks back. Are these the essential acts of our cosmetic, chattering, bored vanity? Does this living skeleton stand in for the mother of the photograph? Does it figure her actual or perhaps imagined death?

Imagined death is not far away. We see men on a scaffold fix a noose and drop a body, an echo of *False Pretenses*. But the splash it makes hitting water turns out, instantly, to be the slow-motion, reversed image of two dogs, surging back up to a perch high above the river into which they had fallen. Much later, their fall, in forward motion, will be one of the signals that the film is moving to its conclusion. Although the dogs are German shepherds, not the Great Danes of *Huge Pupils*, these resurrected emblems of fidelity naturally recall the earlier dogs Noren bathed in one version of the first episode.

In the found footage we see a woman holding the telephone to the ear of a dog, a giant spherical mirror burning a plank of wood, a laser beam focused on an eye, and finally the man entering the ice block. Pruitt reads the fiery mirror as a metaphor for the lens that "'burns' or 'transforms' the objects placed before it."

Here is Noren yet once more from his written interview with MacDonald, delineating something of the film's plot:

> I found [the newsreel images] very resonant and beautiful in themselves, and so I employed them, as though they were actors under my direction, frequently portraying me or acting as stand-ins for me....

> Anyway, in *The Lighted Field* "dream of story" and "story of dream" are closely interwoven as themes. It is also a ghost story in a sense. It was calculated in a way to be posthumous work, a tale told from the grave, and of course, in time it will become exactly that....

> There is a straightforward "documentary" level on which it's "about" being at home, going to work, and being at home again.... It's a tale of a dreamer, who dreams what you, the viewer and also a dreamer, "see," and is what he sees and what you see.[36]

The central rhythm, home-work-home, is indeed an obvious dimension of the film, but even that is not quite so straightforward insofar as the location

---

36. MacDonald, *A Critical Cinema 2*, p. 199, 200–201, p. 202.

of home shifts in the later part of the film from an urban upper-story brick apartment to a suburban house with a garden. The first set of "home" images follows the montage of the found footage. By and large they are familiar to viewers of *Charmed Particles*: Rise hanging curtains, leading to another poem of "wind variations"; the light glinting off glassware; winter and spring out of an apartment window; the filmmaker's self-portrait.

"Work," then, would mean mostly traveling to and from the stock footage archive in the subsequent cataract of images of elevated trains shooting through zones of light and shade, the reflections on vehicles and in windows on the urban streets. Brakhage's *Wonder Ring* may be a direct ancestor of the elegant train sequence; the apparently translucent cars share a core of visionary insight with Gehr's *Still*—Noren and Gehr worked together at the Filmmaker's Cooperative; in front of that office the latter shot *Still*—and the pace and pleasure the filmmaker derives from pixilating the city marks his affinity to Menken's much more whimsical *Go!Go!Go!* In the middle of this song of the city, we glimpse Noren's workbench with 35 mm filmstrips and a splicer. Strollers on a tree-lined street represent the return home from work at the newsreel archive.

The last third of the film, the second home sequence with its two locations, poses some problems of analysis; its narrative is teasingly ambiguous. A portrait of Rise and play with the family cat, including opening and closing a drawer with the cat inside, leads to shots of Rise dressing a young girl, perhaps three or four years old, and feeding birds with her out of the apartment window. Then, after a moment of Noren and Rise kissing, we see a boy about ten years old, goofing with a safety razor and playing with paper money. A few minutes later we see him again, picking vegetables with Rise in the garden of the suburban home. When she whispers in his ear, the found footage of the man in ice comes back, as if his release were the secret she has shared with the boy.

When John Pruitt consulted Noren about the details of his essay, the filmmaker advised him to refer to the woman and boy as "his wife and child." But Noren and Rise do not have children, and there seem to be two children in the film.[37] Are we to understand their appearance in the film as "actors under...direction"? Imaginative figures of the past and future? Rather than offer Pruitt an anecdotal account of the imagery—say, the visit of perhaps a niece and nephew—Noren encouraged the critic to read *The Lighted Field* as a fictive construction: the family of the shadow protagonist. We might conclude from this and from the filmmaker's remarks to MacDonald that

---

37. Bruce Elder apparently noticed a discrepancy between the biography of the filmmaker and the fiction of the film when he described the scene as "a woman (presumably a mother) whispering intimately in a boy's (presumably her son's) ear. Elder, *A Body of Vision*, p. 345.

within the evolving structure of *The Adventures of the Exquisite Corpse* this episode focuses on the nature and necessity of fiction.

In the interval between the two appearances of the boy, the filmmaker carefully transits from a graveyard scene in which he, or more precisely the shadow of the cameraman, seems to search out a grave. The moment he pauses at one marker, the scene cuts to Rise planting a garden, stalked by the same shadow. The symbolical equation of graveyard and garden supports the other tropes of resurrection and regeneration in the film. But would that be the kind of "story" the filmmaker meant in his discussion of the film? Or are we to look for a more specific narrative, say, one of an inheritance that supported the move from the city; or following, instead, the thread of the children, a narrative of tragic loss?

Noren's editing puts into play a series of symbolical equations, simultaneously encouraging and frustrating narrative development. The most blatant, and commented upon, is the substitution of the dogs for the hanged man. Without ceasing to be icons of fidelity or guides to the netherworld these dogs embody the principle of metamorphosis in this film. In the condensations and displacements of the dream work structuring this film, animals play a central role. Other clips involving dogs underline their uncanny presence here: the woman holding a telephone to a dog's ear and, just before the dogs leap into the river, a shot of a young man hugging a dog in bed. The dogs facilitate the transitions between the mundane and the magical, the present and the past, death and life.

Looking at the sequence following the emergence of the stuntman from the ice, we see a dynamic pixilated movement through the pointillism of grains of light and shadow in the yards surrounding the suburban house, a prelude to the spectacular finale of the film. It is as if the freeing of the man from the ice block signaled an imaginative rebirth of the shadowy filmmaker. The subsequent return of the dogs negates the nightmare of death by hanging. They usher in a new and conclusive set of found shots: an old man reads with birds and a squirrel perched on him; the squirrel eats nuts from his mouth; when he plays a flute, the bird sits on the instrument and the squirrel sports with it. A condensation of Orpheus, Dionysus, and Francis of Assisi, this droll figure celebrates the regeneration of the filmmaker's vocation after eight years without a finished work.

The last ten minutes of the film show the movements of the filmmaker moving though the new house and yards, and when the camera is still, the stop-motion reveals the passage of light in this new arena of vision. The final image of the film is the shadow of a massive tree from which what appears to be the shadow of the filmmaker's arm emerges, either pointing toward the camera or gesturing in triumph. The imaginary fusion of filmmaker and tree into one being hyperbolizes Noren's persistent attraction to vegetation. It is as if the photosynthesis sustaining plant life energized as well the filmmaker's drives. Pruitt brilliantly reads this image as an analog to the opening lines Ezra Pound's poem, "The Tree": "I have stood still and was a tree amid the wood / Knowing the truth of things unseen before."[38] He sees the apparent hand gesture "mimicking the pressing of the camera's shutter button."

Noren insisted to MacDonald that he did not make that gesture, but that he captured the shadow of a movement by the branches of the tree he was filming. It is an astonishing, almost incredible claim: It seems so like the flexing of an elbow and the configuration of a fist that everyone who has published on the film took it to be the filmmaker's shadow. For Elder it was "a chilling evocation of triumph"; Pruitt saw it mimicking the raising of a finger to press the button of the camera; MacDonald called it the play of flexing a muscle.[39] Like the archival footage, this shadow play was something of a found object even though Noren filmed it. It is an ambiguous image in which the field of light, the pictorial air itself, announces the film has come to its end.

Near the conclusion of *The Lighted Field* there are two images of a book and a cup on a table, the second closer than the first: The pages of the book flutter in the synthetic atmosphere of pixilation. This is the last and most potent manifestation of the objecthood of things that captivated Elder. The cup and the book are instruments of metamorphosis insofar as they are the vessels of his bodily and spiritual nourishment and pleasure. As much as the ubiquitous shadow, they stand in for all his interrelations with the world of *The Lighted Field*.

After another eight years, Noren released the next film of the sequence, *Imaginary Light*. In it, objects lose their referential status. They are virtually engulfed in the perpetual movement of light. In fact, aside from the shadow of the filmmaker, there are no human forms in the film. Sometimes the cat appears and instantly vanishes in the steady rush of pixilation. The film itself has a more rigorously outlined structure than any other part of *The Adventures of the Exquisite Corpse*: it has five clearly delineated movements. The first, a one-minute prelude in which the camera rushes forward along a path in a wooded park with dazzling pools of white sunlight on the ground and the outlines of black foliage above the patch, is matched by similar shots, upside down but not running backward, constituting the final section, also approximately a minute long. Only in these handheld shots do we sense the somatic presence of the filmmaker. The second section consists of rhythmically subtle waves of single-frame photography outside the house we recognize from the end

---

38. John Pruitt, "Metamorphoses: Andrew Noren's *The Lighted Field*," p. 58. "The Tree" is the opening poem of Pound's *Personae* (New York: Boni & Liveright, 1926), p. 3.
39. Elder, *A Body of Vision*, p. 345; Pruitt, "Metamorphoses: Andrew Noren's *The Lighted Field*," p. 58; MacDonald, *A Critical Cinema 2*, p. 204.

of *The Lighted Field*. As the sun moves, the shadows sweep alternately away and toward us, to the left and the right, as the filmmaker alternates between forward and upside-down-backward shots for about ten minutes. Then the middle movement of the film shows the passages of light through the interior of the house. For the most part, the dynamics that seemed to move forward and backward outside now shift between movements to the left and right as the filmmaker follows the ebb and flow of light in different rooms for about seven minutes. The longest and most abstract section of the film is the fourth, which concentrates on light reflected off flowing water. MacDonald identifies the source as a stream near Noren's house, but Elder calls it a birdbath. There is a concrete birdbath on the property, visible in several passages from the second section. But if there are actually images recorded from it, they are less prevalent than those of the stream, whose contours and shoreline foliage are often visible. This fourteen-minute section has a hypnotic, throbbing rhythm induced by f-stop changes every frame, which seem to run in three-second cycles from brightest to a black frame. Although the camera appears to be fixed on a tripod for all but the opening and closing minutes, the stop-motion never seems mechanical but rather the subtly shimmering work of single-frame exposures in response to the minute nuances of shifting shadows.

The dialectic of presence and absence is one of the distinguishing themes of Noren's work. It unites the paradoxical effect of his boldest synecdoche in *Huge Pupils*, representing himself by filming his genitals in sexual acts, to the persistent irony of the black-and-white films, the filmmaker as shadow. If, in the former case, the sight of the body of the filmmaker in sexual acts renders the image ephemeral by its inability to convey the obviously tactile experience, the recurring shadow of the filmmaker in the later work, concentrated in the second part of *Imaginary Light*, acknowledges that his body is projecting a phantom presence into the field that it films, only by blocking the sunlight that makes the imagery of the whole film visible.

The regular manipulation of the f-stops in the reflections off the water calls to mind the work of Ernie Gehr, especially his *Serene Velocity*. A brief digression on how much Noren and Gehr have in common will help me articulate the fundamental differences between their works. They came to New York at approximately the same time in the 1960s and encountered the avant-garde cinema through the screenings of the Filmmakers' Cinematheque. They were influenced largely by the same filmmakers. Brakhage's films and Ken Jacobs's passionate articulation of the complexities of filmic illusionism were central to their formations. They worked side by side at the Film-makers' Cooperative. They both participated in Richard Foreman's Ontological-Hysteric Theater. In *Huge Pupils* there is a portrait of Gehr as a visionary, shot in fast motion with short zooming movements; and Gehr returned the compliment with *Reverberation* (1969), which portrays Noren and Margaret Lamarre, with whom he lived at the time. They both took teaching positions; they were even both on the faculty of Bard College, but at different times. Gehr continues to earn his living teaching, but Noren quickly left academia to become an archivist and consultant in stock footage. They even started to replace celluloid filmmaking with digital video at the same time.

They share so much of the history of their métier that the distinctions between their works are instructive. Gehr has concentrated his attention on public spaces: an institutional corridor, the sites of a Gestapo headquarters and an immigrant flea market in Berlin, the streets of New York, and an exterior elevator on the side of a San Francisco hotel. Even the portrait of Noren and Lamarre represents them against the backdrop of monumental stonework: It was filmed on a New York street in the financial district.

Noren prefers to film at home; he almost always includes images of himself or his shadow in his films. Gehr never does; his subjects are rigorously impersonal with the exception of *For Daniel*, the portrait of his infant son. Above all, Gehr invests each of his films with a formal autonomy; one is composed of superimpositions of cars on a street, another of zoom movements and f-stop variations in a corridor, yet another a slowed-down strip of film depicting a cable car ride from the early twentieth century. He never combines such different strategies in one film. Noren's quotidian lyrics derive their internal dynamics from the alternation of stylistic gestures. Even the rigorously organized *Imaginary Light* shifts between moving camera and static stop-motion passages and reserves the Gehr-like cycling of single-frame f-stop variations for the tour de force crescendo of water reflections.

Both Gehr and Noren are proud of their ability to create their most impressive effects in the camera without recourse to optical printing. The virtuoso processes of their filmmaking fulfill Emerson's invocation of the fundamental aesthetic experience in America: that through "certain mechanical changes...the most wonted objects...are unrealized at once, or, at least, wholly detached from all relation to the observer, and seen as apparent, not substantial beings."[40] It may be objected that I have been claiming this for all the filmmakers in this book. Yet within that spectrum Noren and Gehr place a particularly strong emphasis on the evocation of apparent, not substantial entities, which Noren calls ghosts and phantoms and Gehr, writing of his portrait of Noren and Lamarre, identifies as "images...offered up and simultaneously swept away by conflicting energies."[41]

40. Ralph Waldo Emerson, *Essays and Lectures* (New York: Library of America, 1983), pp. 33–34.
41. Ernie Gehr, "Program Notes by Ernie Gehr for a Film Showing at the Museum of Modern Art," *Film Culture* nos. 53–55 (Spring 1972), p. 36, reprinted in *The Avant-Garde Film: A Reader of Theory and Criticism* (New York: Anthology Film Archives, 1987).

Emerson's brilliant speculations have been prophetic. The mechanical means became an art instrument. In learning to work with this instrument, or in coming to attend to the implications of its mechanical means, many of the filmmakers of the American avant-garde cinema have discovered automatisms[42] through which "a small alteration in our local position" or other simple "mechanical means" open the possibility of generating whole films or, within films compounded of several automatisms, of revealing a "pictorial air" by which we are "strangely affected."

The magnificent trajectory of Gehr's career has been the ability to discover, one after the other, small alterations of the mechanisms rich enough to sustain whole films. He has been extremely reluctant to make two films the same way. The same might be said of Michael Snow, who foregrounds his mechanical means—zoom, pan, dolly, and so on—and lavishly explores their variations, or the Austrian Peter Kubelka, who made seven films, each using a different formal strategy for maximal formal compression. Noren, on the other hand, has an expanding repertoire of automatisms that he tends to combine in fresh ways in each part of his serial film.

This is particularly apparent in *Time Being* (2001), Noren's first digital film, whose color and black-and-white sections have more than twenty distinct automatisms. Some reflect and amplify earlier parts of *The Adventures of the Exquisite Corpse*: a black-and-white curtain blowing in the wind; single-frame stop-motion movements of light outside and inside his house, this time in color; passages that might be quoted directly from *The Lighted Field* and *Imaginary Light*; there is even a long section in very soft focus in which globules of colored light press and intermingle, suggesting that the camera was turned on sexual intercourse, creating an abstraction of the imagery so striking in the early *Huge Pupils*. That we are watching people at all is a deduction: The human figure is almost as radically eliminated from *Time Being* as from *Imaginary Light*. In the whole episode we rarely glimpse the filmmaker's shadow; at times fluctuations of the light suggest that Rise may be passing between a window and the camera. Instead, the work is infused with an enthusiasm for the new tools, the digital apparatus and the ways it coincides with film and diverges from it.

---

42. See Stanley Cavell, *The World Viewed*. (New York: Viking, 1974). Cavell's apology for American feature films entails an argument that all cinema is a "succession of automatic world projections" that distinguishes film from the automatisms modernist painters have found to sustain their works. I have found his discussion of modernist automatisms exceptionally fruitful even though I cannot subscribe to his arguments for how cinema escapes the fate of modernism.

CHAPTER 9

Ernie Gehr and the Axis of Primary Thought

Ernie Gehr presents each of his 16 mm films, digital films, and installations as an autonomous monad. He never organized his films into series, although, when I inquired, he mentioned attempts to group some of his works. "Ultimately," he wrote, "all the works may be seen as fragments of a larger and oblique autobiography of sorts (very funny)."[1] The parenthesis acknowledges his resistance to the autobiographical mode.

1. In an e-mail of January 28, 2006, Gehr wrote: "Series....The four recent NYC pieces on video (Essex Street through Green Street) can be seen as either four related works or as a single piece. They can also be considered as part of a larger work on NYC. *Untitled—Part One* (the Brighton Beach film) was originally going to be the first of a 2 or perhaps even a 3 part work. Technical problems with the second part and subsequently going to Berlin ('82) and Chicago ('83 & '84) shifted my priorities elsewhere. Yet in a way, some subsequent work closely relates to it (*Signal, This Side of Paradise, Passage, The Collector,* even *Side/Walk/Shuttle*). Ultimately, all the works may be seen as fragments of a larger and oblique autobiography of sorts (very funny)." *For Daniel* (1996), his portrait of his infant son, is the most conspicuous exception to his autobiographical reticence. *Signal—Germany on the Air* (1982–85) obliquely refers to his family's experience in prewar Germany; even more obliquely *Untitled—Part One* (1981), *This Side of Paradise* (1991), *Passage* (1991–2003), and *The Collector* (2003) allude to the same experience. *Side/Walk/Shuttle* (1991) reflects the filmmaker's sense of displacement and homelessness.

Gehr rarely even provides information about his background and education. When Scott MacDonald asked him about this reticence, he said: "For some of my work, you do not need to know much about my personal or family life. In fact, it can even get in the way of the work. With some work, especially some of my later work, some personal information may be useful—at least in order to understand where the work may be coming from. But my personal history is something I am not ready to talk about."[2] Profoundly discomfited by the psychological representations and emotional manipulations of narrative films, he told MacDonald of his interest in "neutralizing the primary focus in cinema: the human figure."[3] Although he has gradually become more forthcoming about his working processes and his inspirations in his public appearances over nearly forty years, he has consistently worked to keep his persona, as filmmaker, out of the films. Since the serial structures I have been discussing in this book highlight the filmmaker's persona, in this chapter I address what Gehr ironically called his "oblique autobiography" and the strategies he created to complicate that attempt.

From various sources I have been able to piece together the following: He was born in 1943 while his German-Jewish family was in a circuitous process of immigrating to the United States. He grew up in Wisconsin, where he briefly attended the university with an interest in drama. His subsequent military service was traumatic for him, even though he managed to get the status of a medic in a West Coast hospital. After the army he looked for work in a few cities without finding anything satisfactory. It was during a stay in New York that he wandered into a screening at the Filmmakers' Cinematheque. As he tells the story, he literally came in out of the rain. In the mid-1960s the Filmmakers' Cinematheque occupied the basement theater in an unlikely building with entrances on Forty-first and Forty-second Street in midtown Manhattan. Gehr stepped into the doorway to avoid a downpour and decided to wait out the storm in a movie. As far as he can recall, it was one of Brakhage's early masterpieces, either *Anticipation of the Night* or *Dog Star Man*.

This fortuitous accident turned out to be a decisive event for Gehr, although he did not realize it then. Not only would Brakhage's work remain an inspiration to him, it represents the kind of avant-garde cinema to which his future films would be an antitype. The volcanic subjectivity of Brakhage's art has no counterpart in Gehr's films, which systematically suppress the psychology of the filmmaker.

2. Scott MacDonald, *A Critical Cinema 5: Interviews with Independent Filmmakers* (Berkeley: University of California Press, 2006), p. 389.
3. Ibid., p. 367.

He told Jonas Mekas:

Before I made *Wait*, I made some 8mm films[;] they were, in a way, in the tradition of the Underground film, essentially Stan Brakhage's work after *Anticipation of the Night*. But I found that I couldn't work that way. I realize this in the midst of shooting a scene for a film. I actually stopped. I couldn't go on. It wasn't clear to me at the time why. I had mixed feelings about what movies did in general but the thing that did it, that stopped me[,] was actually facing the camera on the tripod, standing there, and really being puzzled by what it had to do with what I was trying to do.[4]

Seeing films during his childhood and youth played a less obvious role in Gehr's cinematic formation than that of many other avant-garde filmmakers, if we can trust his reluctant account. He remembers the incidental associations of the film situation more intensely than the films themselves. That there would be bright daylight outside the movie theater after a Saturday matinee in the dark particularly struck him. He would study the light beam of the projector as it moved through smoke. There was a disappointment when someone shining a flashlight behind the screen accidentally revealed that the horses and stagecoaches were not actually there. More significantly, he stopped seeing films entirely during his adolescence because he could not bear the emotional manipulation to which they subjected him.

After his fortuitous encounter with Brakhage's films that rainy evening on Forty-second Street, Gehr sought out more screenings of avant-garde films. At one of these he met Ken Jacobs, who was then one of the directors of the Millennium Film Workshop, newly created to provide access to equipment for poor filmmakers. Jacobs saw in Gehr a version of his own uncertainties and anxieties after he had been discharged from the Coast Guard. With his encouragement, Gehr decided to borrow an 8 mm camera from the Millennium. When none were available, he took a light meter instead and wandered about the city studying the variations in luminosity. It would be hard to find a more fitting image for the scene of Gehr's incarnation as a filmmaker than the picture he hesitantly paints of himself calculating light readings at various city sites without a specific film in mind.

He was soon making his own films. Between 1968 and 1970 he released eight. They established his reputation on a level with the most acclaimed filmmakers of his generation: George Landow, Paul Sharits, and Hollis

---

4. Jonas Mekas, "Ernie Gehr Interviewed by Jonas Mekas, March 24, 1971," *Film Culture* nos. 53–55 (Spring 1972), p. 30.

Frampton to cite three. His contemporaries Andrew Noren, Robert Beavers, and Warren Sonbert were much slower to gain recognition. In fact, one critic said to me, "I never saw a filmmaker move so fast up the avant-garde ladder." However, Landow, Sharits, and Frampton were much more fortunate in finding opportunities to teach film. For years Gehr worked for the Film-makers' Cooperative or eked out a living from adjunct teaching jobs, sometimes replacing his friends on their sabbaticals until he found a permanent position at the San Francisco Art Institute in 1986.

Although he might seem, at first, to be the least Emersonian of the major American avant-garde filmmakers, his cinema constitutes the purest enactment of Emerson's recommendation for the attainment of "a pictorial air." *Side/Walk/Shuttle* (1991) may be the most spectacular example of the inventive reformulation of the world from a moving platform; *Eureka* turns to the origins of cinema to affirm the power of the moving camera. On a more muted scale, *Untitled* (1977) subtly unfolds spatial planes by "a mechanical change"—a continual small alteration of the focal plane of a lens. The throbbing zoom movements of *Serene Velocity* (1970) "strangely affect us" even though they are virtual, growing out of the manipulation of light intensities in Gehr's first films.

Gehr is also the master of the converse stratagem: holding the camera still to intensify the movement within the frame. Rather than negating the dynamic of the moving perspective, such a concentration of attention, often accompanied by a retardation of movement, brings into focus the fundamental ground that gives the moving camera its charge. Emerson, yet again, in his essay "Art," declares:

> The virtue of art lies in detachment, in sequestering one object from the variety.... It is the habit of certain minds to give an all-excluding fullness to the object, the thought, the word, they alight upon, and to make that for the time the deputy of the world.... The best pictures are rude draughts of a few of the miraculous dots and lines and dyes which make up the ever-changing "landscape with figures" amidst which we dwell.... [A]s I see many pictures and higher genius in the art, I see the boundless opulence of the pencil, the indifferency in which the artist stands free to choose out of the possible forms.[5]

The Emersonian indifference with which Gehr stands free to choose his possible forms is often extraordinary. His *Reverberation* detaches a few static shots of a posed portrait to expand them for twenty-three minutes.

5. Ralph Waldo Emerson, *Essays and Lectures* (New York: Library of America, 1983), pp. 432–34.

Still (1969–71) uses the flow of traffic on one New York street to manifest the boundless opulence of the camera over fifty-five minutes. *Signal—Germany on the Air* sequesters a few locations in Berlin as the deputies of a world depleted of spirit. *Shift* (1972–74) gives vehicular movements an all-including fullness in a nine-minute ode to the sounds and glimpses of the city street, seen from high above. Looking down again, but from a much lower perch, Gehr alights upon the sad gestural music of aging Jews in *Untitled—Part One* (1981), once more making them the deputies of a nearly lost world. In *Field, History* (1970), *Untitled*, and *Mirage* (1981), the miraculous dots, lines, and dyes constitute the discernable matter of the films.

Gehr:

A still has to do with a particular intensity of light, an image, a composition frozen in time and space.

A shot has to do with a variable intensity of light, and internal balance of time dependent upon an intermittent movement and a movement within a given space dependent upon persistence of vision . . .

A still as related to film is concerned with using and losing an image of something through time and space. In representational films sometimes the image affirms its own presence as image, graphic entity, but most often it serves as a vehicle to a photo-recorded event. Traditional and established avant-garde film teaches film to be an image, a representing. But film is a real thing and as a real thing it is not imitation. It does not reflect on life, it embodies the life of the mind. It is not a vehicle for ideas or portrays of emotion outside of its own existence as emoted idea.[6]

Peter Kubelka, the Austrian filmmaker, had come to the United States in 1966. Just as Gehr was beginning to make films, Kubelka was formulating a radical theoretical position in a series of public lectures at a number of American universities and film centers. I believe Gehr had developed his basic view of cinema before he first heard Kubelka. Nevertheless, their starting points are very similar. Central to Kubelka's concept of metrical film was the notion of the arbitrariness of the image. For him, cinema is, first of all, a frame-to-frame articulation: The "weakest" possibility would be the repetition of a frame as in a frozen still image; the "strongest" would be a shift from pure white to pure black. The metrics of cinema emerge from the pacing of these strong and

6. Ernie Gehr, "Program Notes by Ernie Gehr for a Film Showing at the Museum of Modern Art," *Film Culture* nos. 53–55 (Spring 1972), pp. 36–37.

weak articulations in counterpoint to corresponding sound combinations, which he called synch events.

Gehr's text is an alternative, I want to say Emersonian, version of the arbitrariness of the image; for it is predicated on a fundamental dualism between an illusory moment of stability ("a still") and a spectacle ("the image…dependent upon persistence of vision"). With his definition of the shot he decisively veers from the claims of Kubelka, who would stress the qualitative differences between frames. Gehr's turn entails the acknowledgment that the image is fundamentally a fluttering variation of light intensities, driven by the shutter mechanism and the inescapable substitution of frames.

Whereas Kubelka preached the maximal condensation of strong articulations in the shortest possible time, Gehr suggests that the filmmaker should respect the immanent temporality of the film projector, the perpetually shifting grains of emulsion, and above all the ineluctable variations in both recorded and projected light. Actually, "emoted idea," the embodiment "of the life of the mind," "images…offered up and simultaneously swept away" refers to the movement, or what Emerson called the dualism, between perception and apperception, which lies at the heart of what Gehr calls "established avant-garde film":

Gehr:

When I began to make films I believed pictures of things must go into films if anything was to mean anything. This is what almost anybody who had done anything worthwhile with film has done and is still doing but this again has to do with everything a still is—a re-presenting. And when I actually began filming I found this small difficulty: neither film, filming nor projecting had anything to do with emotions, objects, beings, or ideas. I began to think about this and what film really is and how we see and feel and experience film.[7]

"This small difficulty": litotes for a massive misconception that the subject matter of cinema should be "emotions, objects, beings, or ideas." Behind Gehr's irony, the doctrine of the arbitrariness of the image serves as a defense against his anxiety about melodramatic or intellectual manipulations in film. Yet having banished melodrama and the theater of ideas from the manifest content of his films, he reintroduces ideation and affect ("see…feel…experience") and a category of objects ("film") as central to his work. His adolescent rejection of commercial films reveals a fascination that drives his desire to

7. Ibid., p. 37.

create a cinema in which action, agent, and medium are inextricably fused, where the sequestering of the emoted idea of the filmic material holds out the promise of serene detachment.

The program notes culminate in brief comments on six films that chart an elliptical narrative of the filmmaker's growth as an artist. In that schema, his work progresses from emphasis on the still frame to a scrutiny of the conditions of movement in the shot. Then he anatomizes the illusions of movement and virtual space and finally devotes a film to the status of the image. Thus *Morning* and *Wait* (1968) were his attempts "to break down the essential contradictions still and shot by enormously enlarging the still frame," and *Reverberation* grew out of a desire to turn a portrait (of filmmaker Andrew Noren) "into a presentation of the physical movement of film itself." Here the image seems to be primarily the occasion of its dramatic abolition; the slowing down and rephotographing of the original material succeeds in "stranding the photo-memory of persons/ objects/ their relationships in a cinematic force field wherein images are offered up and simultaneously swept away by conflicting energies."[8]

The next film in the sequence, *History*, is crucial to the development implied in the text. The film was shot without a lens, by exposing film to a black cloth with a minimal light source. Although it originally had a long monologue by Ken Kelman as a soundtrack, the final thirty-two-minute version is silent. In black and white, we see roiling patterns of grain. Gehr told Mekas: "I assume I always wanted to see a film like *History*. A film in which I could really look at film in its most fundamental state...where a direct meeting of film, seeing, and consciousness was possible."[9] His program notes on *History* stress apperception and even introduce a primal cosmology:

> The whole process of seeing something in seeing.... History. Film in
> its primordial state in which patterns of light and darkness—planes—
> are still undivided. Like the natural order of the universe, an unbro-
> ken flow in which movement and distribution of tension is infinitely
> subtle, in which a fine organization seems impossible.[10]

So, in this plan *History* offers us the shot in its purest form; the undoing of repeated grain patterns, the frustration of any "fine organization" forming an image, undermines the moment of the still. Uncharacteristically mythopoeic, Gehr is never closer to Brakhage than when he compares the filmic ground

8. Ibid.
9. Mekas, "Ernie Gehr Interviewed by Jonas Mekas," p. 34.
10. Gehr, "Program Notes," p. 37.

to "the natural order of the universe" and plays on the conceit of recovering a moment before the God of Genesis divided light from darkness.

The prolific output of initial films climaxed with the tour de force *Serene Velocity*, which is still his most widely discussed film. For the first and I think only time, he utilized a systematic plan Kubelka would call metric. Filming in a corridor of Harpur College in Binghamton, New York, he set his camera on a tripod and shot one frame at a time. He selected four different exposures, alternating them with every frame in cycles of four. Each cycle would last a quarter of a second at the preferred projection speed of sixteen frames per second. At the completion of every four-frame cycle, he changed the zoom lens setting: at first minimally from the middle range of the lens, so that the orthogonals of the corridor shimmer. Then he gradually extends the zoom differential until, after more than twenty minutes, the farthest view slams again and again against the closest.

Gilberto Perez writes:

As Gehr himself has observed, there are five movies going on at once in *Serene Velocity*: we can watch the fluorescent lights and the red exit signs on the ceiling, or watch the reflections on the floor, or watch either of the two walls and the new objects, doors, water fountains, hanging ashtrays, coming into view from the sides as the focal length changes—coming into view only to be abruptly yanked back, and come in again the next moment, or we can focus on the center, the sets of double doors halfway down the corridor and all the way at the far end.[11]

At the end of the film through the opaque windows of the double doors, we glimpse a brightening light. A corridor in the State University of New York at Binghamton is an unlikely vantage point to view the dawn. Of course, Gehr did not plan to film all night long and into the morning. But when that happened he took advantage of it. It was among the felicitous events that make *Serene Velocity* such a success.

A stretch of New York's Lexington Avenue in the thirties is almost as unlikely a spot to hail the coming of spring. Nevertheless, between the fourth and fifth sections of Gehr's next film, the eight-part, fifty-five-minute *Still*, just as the previously silent work begins to emit sound, a tree that had been barren at the edge of the unbudging frame in earlier sections has blossomed with leaves. Only in the final section do we see another tree, to the right, also in bloom. Until then it had been obscured by shadow.

---

11. Gilberto Perez, "Ghosts of the City: The Films of Ernie Gehr," *Yale Review* 87, no. 4 (October 1999), p. 179.

Still is a film of superimpositions. Gehr fixed his camera on a tripod, shot, rewound the film, and shot again, sometimes with several layers. Since the background was always the same—the facades of apartment buildings with stores at street level, most prominently a luncheonette—they appear solid in the final film, while cars and people passing by are translucent in varying degrees. So, in *Still* we watch the movement of shadows from section to section, gauge the differing intensities of light, and observe the gradations between walking shades, light-pierced men, and nearly solid beings. But surely the most attractive and exciting phenomenon in this film is the interlacing of depth.

In the fifth section this becomes spectacular. The differential between parked cars and flowing traffic establishes the principle of this mesh. Superimposition has layered two sets of parked cars on each side of the street. When a large vehicle, a truck or a bus, passes it naturally blocks out one set—the cars parked on the far side of the street, since contrary to the persuasive illusion of this film, the camera cannot see through solid forms. As the truck or bus moves through, then, one set of parked cars gets covered over just as the other seems to pop forward through the moving vehicle. By superimposing different layers of traffic, Gehr has orchestrated a dazzling interplay of imaginary cars vying with one another to pop forward in that shallow street theater.

In 1977, Richard Foreman wrote a panegyric of the film in *Film Culture*:

> Ernie Gehr's films—high art (be sure of that)—plunge us very directly into...intimations of paradise, perfection, beauty: his new film *Still* seems to me perhaps his most mysterious (a very profound film in which the elegance and intelligence and yearning come from the artist—Gehr, and the profundity comes from the secret depth of the world itself which Gehr, as master-craftsman, has the good sense, courage and purity of spirit to allow to manifest itself within the cannily plotted matrix of his structure)....
>
> *Still* is, for me, the first truly Proustian film in which I see mood and atmosphere seem to become slowly crystallized on particular objects—as if the whole framed scene and its mood slowly coagulates into—for instance—the mysterious recesses of the lush foliage of the tree across the street which the breeze slowly stirs.[12]

Foreman's phrase "the cannily plotted matrix of his structure" points toward Gehr's capturing and unveiling what Emerson called "the perception of real affinities between events" and Foreman himself identifies as "the secret

---

12. Richard Foreman, "On Ernie Gehr's Film 'Still,'" *Film Culture* nos. 63–64 (1976), pp. 29, 30.

depth of the world." *Still* becomes a "cannily plotted matrix" for revealing the mystery and meaning of the spectacle of the street, just as *Serene Velocity* had cannily contrived the sunrise to manifest itself as its conclusion, turning the film into an aubade. These mysteries are all the more profound and elusive because they are so mundane. They are revealed by what Emerson called mechanical means:

> In these cases, by mechanical means, is suggested the difference between the observer and the spectacle,—between man and nature. Hence arises a pleasure mixed with awe; I may say, a low degree of the sublime is felt from the fact, probably, that man is hereby apprized, that, whilst the world is a spectacle, something in himself is stable.…
>
> The perception of real affinities between events (that is to say, of ideal affinities, for those only are real,) enables the poet thus to make free with the most imposing forms and phenomena of the world, and to assert the predominance of the soul.[13]

Although the terms *ideal* and *soul* (*nature* and *spirit* in other central passages of Emerson) might seem inappropriate to Gehr's enterprise and his way of talking about it (if not Foreman's), his evocations of light and energy, mind and consciousness, account for the oscillation Emerson posits. Gehr's prolonged meditation on the film stock and its grain, on the camera and projector, with its intermittent shutter and rectangular framing mask, form the ground of his small alternations to produce a low degree of the sublime. The effect of the intense foregrounding of the mechanical principle, say, the zoom lens or in-camera superimposition, is both "an all-excluding fullness of the object" and a "dualism." When Mekas asked him for his "thoughts, considerations, aspects of film that went into making *Serene Velocity*," Gehr framed that dualism as "the spatial and temporal relationship between the spectator and the image on the screen. The source of power and the kind of energy beamed through space from the projector to the screen and from the screen to the mind. The projector's single beam of light. Stillness and stimulation around which consciousness oscillates as well as film."[14]

Perez has analyzed how the final section of *Still*, the only one without superimpositions, strangely affects us:

> The sense of unreality is a familiar enough experience of city life, but it is curious that in *Still* it should be felt most keenly when representation gets to be most realistic. Surely this is the return of

---

13 Emerson, *Essays and Lectures*, pp. 34, 36.
14. Jonas Mekas, "Ernie Gehr Interviewed by Jonas Mekas," p. 29.

the repressed that for Freud characterized the uncanny—which, significantly, in German is the unhomely. The street was home, the street was happy, when it was able to accommodate its ghosts, when they were interwoven into the fabric of its daily existence.[15]

When Foreman writes of the projection of a mood upon objects, and Perez of the return of the repressed, they are coming to terms with the pervasive dualism, the "emoted idea," in Gehr's cinema. The more insistently the film seems to concentrate on objects or on repeated or prolonged mechanisms, the more it apprises us of the unseen consciousness behind the mechanism, absorbed in the objects.

After citing Michael Snow's hyperbole for *History*: "At last, the first film!," Gehr's program notes, to which I keep returning, posit the subject of *Serene Velocity* as the "optical and psychological" conditions for persistence of vision. The final note, on *Still*, should be quoted in full:

A pictorial orientation of a surface of light populated by opaque, semi-opaque and transparent shadows (light apparitions). Our experience of the film plane filtered (colored and pulled on) by the film image is determined by inner human conditioning and development of perception.[16]

Such inner conditioning and the education of the senses—if they are not the same thing—are the lords of our experience of the film image. Following upon the sentences about the subject of *Serene Velocity*, this statement implies that *Still* makes thematic the pictorial orientation of the light projected on the screen; it is about how the ghosts of things tint and tease our perception of the screen with our knowledge and expectations of the world of automobiles, trees, and luncheonettes.

In 1972 Gehr began a serial film for which he shot perhaps twenty-five reels of continuous three-minute takes. The then current vogue for films by artists—meaning sculptors or painters associated with major galleries—contributed to his discouragement in this project, especially when he found himself cited as part of a minimalist movement. He felt, rightly, that superficial stylistic features of his work were being misconstrued as its essence.[17] Only one reel of this aborted project has been released: *Untitled* is an astonishing film. As it begins, the focus is very soft and the tone pastel. Initially it gave

15. Perez, "Ghosts of the City," p. 187.
16. Gehr, "Program Notes," p. 38.
17. My own lack of attention to his films in my writing and curatorial activities of that time also contributed to his distress.

me the impression of an overgrown field, spotted with flowers, but as the focus changed—and it does so very slowly and continuously—I took it for a pond with water lilies before, at the arbitrary point we call sharp focus, I saw distinctly a brick wall with snow falling in front of it. It is a miracle of simplicity and perfection.

In 1974 Gehr received a moral and intellectual boost when he was invited to Europe for the first time. Annette Michelson had organized New Forms in Film, a program of recent American avant-garde films for Montreux, Switzerland. The idea of visiting European museums thrilled the filmmaker, but when he reached Switzerland, he found himself unexpectedly entranced by the very look of the cities, so much so that he could not devote himself to the museums as he had planned. At the festival, Michelson showed a film of archival interest, a single take of a San Francisco trolley ride, shot in the early 1900s. Ruth Perlmutter, formerly a graduate student of Michelson's, had given her a print of the film, originally shot by one of her distant relatives. She gave a print to Gehr as well when he requested it. In his mind, the images of San Francisco before the 1906 fire were collapsed upon his first impression of Europe. Out of that experience and with that footage he made *Eureka* but did not release the film until 1979.

Gehr had said, furthermore, that the archival film reminded him of his first impressions of San Francisco after being discharged from the army. Those same impressions were refracted through the civil nostalgia of European cities. (It is a strange and fortunate accident that one of his first impressions of Europe would be of Swiss cities, which more than many others preserve aspects of Europe untouched by the wars of the twentieth century.) Gehr removed the panoramic turnaround of the trolley after it arrived in the station and reprinted the film holding every frame of the original between four and eight times longer. In these gestures of retardation he found his tempo, infusing the old footage with shifting planes of grain, challenging the illusion of movement, and making film history and the archives of urban geography ostensible subjects of the film; in fact, he called it *Geography* the first time he showed it in public.

Seeing it at the slower pace, we become all the more aware of moving vehicles; for the scene not only shows other trolleys amid rushing pedestrians, themselves almost halted in their leaps by the reprinting, but bicycles, early automobiles, landaus, and horse-drawn trucks. J. Hoberman was the first of several commentators to observe that the long camera movement nearly ends on the plaque of the Ferry building, "erected 1896."[18] Since the Lumière brothers presented the first film show in December 1895, *Eureka*

18. J. Hoberman, "Ernie Gehr's *Geography*," *Millennium Film Journal* no. 3, (Winter/Spring 1979), p. 114.

culminates in an acknowledgment of the birthdate of the art, or in Bart Testa's formulation, "the first year a film camera could have taken the trolley through San Francisco."[19]

Gehr implicitly encourages such free ranging of the eye and mind by taking the title of his film from a horse-drawn truck that appears near the end. "Eureka, California" can be read on its side. The town is named with the first person perfect active of a Greek verb: It means "I have found," to which we customarily affix "it." I assume the fathers of the town found gold; for since the biography of Archimedes was first recounted, that innocent verb has borne an implicit exclamation mark. So Hoberman, Testa, and others have critically exclaimed that they have found within the film a monument to the erection of the cinématographe. We presume Gehr too found this, and found it meaningful.

Myrel Glick's lucid 1980 article on the film may be taken as corroborating evidence; she is Gehr's wife and was his companion throughout the making of the film. In addition to exclaiming "What a coincidence that the plaque should read 'Erected 1896' so close to the first public projection of films by the Lumière brothers in 1895," she offers a reading of a young boy who repeatedly intrudes on the image as if running to get into the film and an old man, whose beard blows in the wind, at the very end:

> The young boy and the old man embody some of Gehr's concerns
> in *Eureka*. The boy is analogous to the original film: shot in length,
> having a somewhat quick/hurried pace, fairly new and in good condition with little surface wear and tear. While the old man, like the film
> Gehr has subsequently created is more complex, greater in length, and
> reveals its age through its restrained pace and chemical/physical deterioration in time.[20]

Hoberman even imagined an identity for the old man: "like an apparition of Muybridge (d. 1904)."

It would seem that something about the film encourages such speculation. In one wonderful passage, the cloth flap over the back of a car, which seems permanently crinkled because of the eightfold repetition of each frame, is parted and a boy, resembling a figure emerging from the curtain in an intimate theater, or at the frame of a Renaissance painting, stares curiously into the camera (which must have been fixed to the front of the oncoming trolley). It is not long after that the name Nathan Hale appears on a wall, apparently

19. Bart Testa, *Back and Forth: Early Cinema and the Avant-Garde* (Ontario: Art Gallery of Ontario, 1992), p. 17.
20. Myrel Glick, "'Eureka' by Ernie Gehr," *Film Culture* no. 70–71 (1980), p. 118.

advertising something now forgotten. But in the accident of association that the retardation underscores, the name itself alludes to that other adolescent boy, our Revolutionary spy, who was hanged for what he saw and heroically conveyed. More onomastic magic: Hale's tours were travel films, often shot from moving trains and projected for audiences sitting in a simulated train car. Bart Testa has shown that the footage Gehr used preceded the first Hale's tour by at least a year but, he adds, "This detail of provenance matters much less once we recall that many kinds of urban views and films shot from all manner of mechanical conveyances were commonplace from the first phases of film production."[21]

In his 1969 masterpiece, *Tom, Tom, the Piper's Son*, Ken Jacobs made a new film by analyzing and expanding a 1905 movie. He had signaled the discovery of significant details by isolating and repeating zones within the frames of the original film. One might well consider it the greatest lecture in the criticism of the primitive cinema ever delivered. Furthermore, the object of his attention upholds the investment of Jacobs's rhythmic pedagogy: a film attributed to Billy Bitzer, with sets inspired by Hogarth's etchings. By contrast, the original San Francisco trolley film did not come with authorial pedigrees; nor does Gehr let us know what attracted his attention by focusing and repeating details of the film; rather, he evenly applies the one-to-eight ratio of retardation over the whole strip. So the demon of chance seems to be cramming the film with allusions—1896, Nathan Hale, youth and age, Muybridge, Eureka. That must be a crucial point: Cinema is an art where things are found, where meaning grows. The film that initially reproduced the motion of a trolley through San Francisco became the film that reproduced a lost San Francisco after the fire of 1906.

Eureka is Gehr's prolonged shout about cinema itself: "I have found it!" He found the footage. He found the title in the footage. He found the simple and effective means of reducing it to grain and near stasis while elevating it to the dallying stresses of song. But most effectively and movingly, when Gehr shouts "eureka," he celebrates that he found his métier, his art, the ground in which his deeply repressed passions and his hard-won moments of serenity find form and meaning. In the light of his work after 1980, we can also hear in that cry that he found a way out of the impasse of the late 1970s, and new directions for his cinema.

While house sitting for Richard Foreman and Kate Manheim's loft in downtown Manhattan, Gehr shot footage of street traffic through the sixth floor window, sometimes hand cranking his camera to create reverse motion and a passage in which the frame is deliberately misregistered: the lowest

21. Testa, *Back and Forth*, p. 15.

quarter of the frame appears on top. In constructing this marvelous film, *Shift*, from this material, he edited as he never had before, with both synchronous and asynchronous sounds.

J. Hoberman succinctly described the film:

> The spastic ballet mécanique is accompanied by a sparse score of traffic noises, obviously culled from a record of sound effects. Not only is the action but Gehr's deliberate camera movements are synched to the music of honking horns, screeching brakes, and grinding gears. The eight-minute film is structured as a series of obliquely comic blackout sketches: Trucks run over their shadows; cars unexpectedly reverse direction or start up and go nowhere. The general acceleration of the last third is signaled by the sound of an offscreen crash. Here, Gehr throws the film registration out of alignment so that parts of two frames are visible at once and the traffic becomes an ecstatic blur of opposing diagonals.[22]

The bold white lines dividing the asphalt into two, sometimes three, lanes provide a strong graphic orientation to the image; dominating nearly every shot, they anchor the rhythm as if with a visual ostinato. Sometimes Gehr will hold the camera on the street lines for several seconds before the traffic enters, or after it leaves; more rarely, there are short shots without any traffic at all. The first element to impress us in every shot, then, is the angle of the white parallel lines within the frame (unless a stopped truck blocks them for a moment). They are rarely horizontal, and only at the very end is one truly vertical. Generally they are pitched at thirty, forty, or fifty degrees, right or left. Often he clusters shots together in which the angle alters less than ten degrees from shot to shot to wrest exquisite modulations from these shifts.

Brief passages of blackness divide *Shift* into about a dozen montage phrases or stanzas. Beginning with an introduction of elements—the angled street, the stopping and starting of vehicles, forward and reverse motion, some upside-down shots—the film offers a witty series of variations and climaxes with a glissando of movement across the misregistered frame line, then quickly ends on a double diminuendo: The camera follows a vertical white line straight upward to a hitherto unseen truck, and then a vehicle gradually blots out the final white diagonal. Although many of the images are silent, Gehr has carefully selected an array of street sounds from the effects record: motors starting, choking, and purring or grinding gears and squealing brakes underscore

22. J. Hoberman, "Ernie Gehr: A Walker in the City," in *Ernie Gehr: The 1995 Adaline Kent Award Exhibition [Brother, Can You Spare Some Time]* (San Francisco: San Francisco Art Institute, 1995), p. xiv.

the initiations, continuities, and hesitations of movement; a siren, horns, and a door slamming counterpoint those with punctual sounds of closure and interruption.

The long pauses, the emphasis on stopping and starting (for an unseen traffic light), elegant arcs as police cars or trucks transgress the lane dividers, impart a lento rhythm to most of the film. One exquisite moment is beautifully repeated in reverse: The camera suddenly readjusts leftward from a parked car to the curb-break abutting it. Four stanzas later, an apparently identical shot budges from its hold on the curb-break back to the car. Between those moments, we had seen the car move backward out of the parking space, realizing that Gehr must have been filming the empty spot when it slowly pulled in. With such minute mechanical changes he has been able "to turn the street into a puppet show," in Emerson's happy expression.

The lento pacing gives way at once to the presto of the climax. First with the beep of a horn, then a second later with the sound of a collision and broken glass, the frame line appears across the upper quarter of the image. It is as if the filmmaker had crashed through the filmic frame itself, jumped the frame line. Perhaps he is even informing us that this dazzling shift in the film is the result of an accident, as frequently occurs when a sprocket slips in the camera (here because he was shooting with the hand-cranking mechanism, designed to rewind film for superimposition, not to photograph in this way). Capitalization upon accidents is one of the central assets of Gehr's poetics, the fruit of the "cannily plotted matrix of his structure[s]."

Usually when this sort of misregistration occurs there would be a distinctive difference between the top quarter of the frame and the rest. But because of the continuity of the diagonal lane dividers, the white lines perfectly cross the frame line. Furthermore, the swiftly moving traffic photographed this way reinforces the illusion of continuity. Therefore, the inevitable flashes and variations of this registration shed their mechanical quality; instead they syncopate and counterpoint the rush of traffic. It is characteristic of Gehr's genius that this effect emerges from the brilliantly simple realization that an oblique angle of movement will remain congruent across the misregistration of the frame. Equally characteristic is the craftsmanship with which he meticulously interspersed short shots of movements without the overhanging frame line, including a delicious synchronized moment of a teamster slamming his cab door: They bleed upward into downward trajectories or flip the flow along one diagonal to its complement.

Like that of *Eureka*, the title of *Shift* refers incidentally to the filmmaker's relationship to the film. By turning to editing and to synchronous sound, Gehr is shifting his orientation. "Shift" derives from Old English *sciftan*, to arrange. Editing is shifting materials in the sense of arranging them. The imperfect pun "Gehr shift" also shadows the title, appropriately for the filmmaker's wittiest film, the one where his sense of humor is most manifest. Even the climactic change of tempi within the film can be called a gear shift, or a slipping of gears.

But "shift" can also mean a dodge, evasion, artifice, trick. What does the film evade with its artifice? Most immediately, the noise, the shock of the street. Gehr is hypersensitive to ambient noise; he has said that quiet is an essential condition for his work. This may beg the further question, why? What does the invasion of unexpected sounds represent for him? This unusually private filmmaker offers us little with which to speculate. But his comments on a later film may help us understand his aesthetic displacements. At a retrospective of his films at the American Museum of the Moving Image in 1999, Gehr spoke of his *Rear Window* (1986–91) as "a very emotional" film made, significantly, in "tears and anger" subsequent to his father's death shortly after he had returned from a fellowship in Berlin and the making of *Signal—Germany on the Air*. The film studies a Brooklyn yard: laundry drying with rhythmic fluctuations of light and dark and the strong verticals of window bars coming into focus in different places on the screen. In a note he says, "I cupped one of my hands in front of the camera to make tactile light, color, and image."[23] Aided by such autobiographical hints, we can see mourning in operation in the film. As the season shifts from winter to spring, and red, white, and blue clothes appear on the line, there is even an allegory of his family's decisive emigration and his own recent return from Germany. The repeated modulations of the colors of the film to whiteness suggest an imaginary equation between the laundry and the screen, where the work of mourning becomes a form of cinematic drying, by exposure to the light. Similarly, the effort to master the traumatic irruptions of noise and chaos manifestly dominates *Shift*, whatever the drive that deeply animates the film. In the middle of it we might read the only really legible truck panel: Fox Piano Movers. Invisible, then, in the transits of the street, there might be a musical instrument in motion. Even the shadow of the lamppost in this cinematic stanza comes to look like a curved quarter note. Gehr's major shift is to find music in noise and to make of random street traffic a cinematic sonata. One might say the sole bicyclist at the end of this stanza emerging from the shadow of a truck—and from his own shadow beside that of the lamppost—is an emblem of the filmmaker negotiating his way in the field of danger, against the traffic. The bicycle and its rider, as Hugh Kenner observed of Beckett's cyclists, is a modern centaur. In this film it is the sole vehicle powered by a man, an oxymoron; like an avant-garde film. "Pianoforte" is another

23. Ernie Gehr, "Notes on Recent Films," *Films of Ernie Gehr* (San Francisco: San Francisco Cinematheque, 1993), p. 20.

oxymoron: soft-loud, an instrument spanning the range of intensities, which we habitually reduce to its first element, "piano."

The exfoliation and exploration of intensities of contradiction occupy the center of Gehr's art. Emerson, in the passage to which I keep returning, tells us, "Certain mechanical changes, a small alteration in our local position, apprizes us of a dualism." The young Emerson identified that dualism as nature and spirit. Gehr's oxymorons are expressions of a similar dualism, but he would not invoke Emerson's terms. Yet the transformation of the visible world into "a spectacle, [while] something in himself is stable" does characterize Gehr's entire cinema. More than any other filmmaker I discuss in this book, he has created forms that seek, in Emerson's elaboration in "The Poet," the "manifold meaning, of every sensuous fact." He orchestrates the transition from sensuous fact to manifold meaning through one of the following means, but rarely more than one in a given film: superimposition, rephotography, slowed and reversed motion, rack focusing, swish panning, abstractive lenses, and even merely by isolating gestures at oblique angles. By these mechanical means he has pushed his filmed subjects into the realm of spirit—ghosts, eidolons, melancholy traces—more quickly and more consistently than any of his peers. In doing so, he has gone farther than any other filmmaker in exploring the implications of Emerson's scenario, although he probably never even read *Nature*, and he surely did not follow its prompts deliberately. Nevertheless, as if responding to Emerson literally, he made the digital works *Glider* (2001) "in a camera obscura," and *Crystal Palace* (2002) seemingly "by seeing a face of country...in the rapid movement of the railroad car!" even if the frozen, snow-glazed countryside he filmed from an automobile cannot be called familiar. He does not quite "turn the eyes upside down, by looking at the landscape through [his] legs," to achieve the "pictorial air" of *Shift*, but he does often turn the camera upside down to render a comparable effect in that film and much more spectacularly in *Side/Walk/Shuttle* (1991).

More than any other film Gehr had made before it, *Side/Walk/Shuttle* "apprizes us of a dualism" between "nature...afloat" and "the axis of his primary thought."[24] We see a continually moving cityscape and intuit the unseen subject moving up and down in it. Gehr made the entire film at the Fairmont

---

24. Again I am drawing upon Emerson's *Nature*, from sentences framing the paragraph I have cited repeatedly: "The first effort of thought tends to relax this despotism of the senses, which binds us to nature as if we were a part of it, and shows us nature aloof, and, as it were, afloat.... By a few strokes [the poet] delineates, as on air, the sun, the mountain, the camp, the city, the hero, the maiden, not different from what we know them, but only lifted from the ground and afloat before the eye. He unfixes the land and the sea, makes them revolve around the axis of his primary thought, and disposes them anew" (*Essays and Lectures*, pp. 33–34).

Hotel on San Francisco's Nob Hill by shooting from the windows of a three-sided exterior elevator that shuttles clients between a rooftop plaza and a penthouse restaurant. For forty-one minutes, in some twenty-five long takes, shots of ascent and descent alternate forward and backward movement, right-side-up and upside-down orientation. But the film gives no visible signs of the restaurant or of other passengers, nor even that the camera is ascending and descending the side of a hotel; there are no visual cues that it has been filmed from within a glass enclosure; experience and reason compel us to read the steady, breathtaking movements as vehicular.

Gehr's "mechanical means" situate the dualism of his film between the coordinates of bodily orientation and motorized movement. Divested of proprioceptive information about gravity and distance and vestibular sensitivity to the spatiality of sound, *Side/Walk/Shuttle*'s cinematic subject must rely on the visual field for location and position. The soundtrack, with its long stretches of silence, offers a montage of associations rather than directional guidelines. The top and bottom, and right and left, of the screen do not underwrite the corporeal coordinates of a viewer, who can nevertheless rapidly adjust to Gehr's systematic disorientations. Sometimes the filmmaker composed his shots so inventively we momentarily lose track of the direction, but even when the direction is clear it is easy to get so caught up in the wonder of the film that one loses awareness of its horizontal and vertical reversals.

In fact, the filmmaker seems to be taking the viewer's adjustments into account because he subtly subverts the very system he sets up in order to sustain and even increase the viewer's astonishment by repeatedly introducing new degrees of displacement. The simplest instance of this underlines the film's finale: After following twelve descents of the elevator with twelve ascents, he ends the film with a spectacular upside-down ascent image (shot 25), culminating in a vision of the skyscrapers as stalactites. This exceptional ascent, when we have been accustomed to expect a descent, gives an added and conclusive boost to the dazzling shot.

A more complex design operates in the sequence of twelve descents. Regularly, Gehr held the camera upside down for these shots, so that we soon expect to float up screen from the roofs toward the street in every other shot. Only the sixth and seventh descents (shots 11 and 13) break this pattern by moving sideways from left to right as the elevator transports the filmmaker in the direction of the street. Conversely, the ascents generally move from screen bottom to top. However, in the sixth of these (shot 12), Gehr gives us the first of three upside-down ascents in between the two sideways descents. These startling variations at the center of the film sustain the amazement of the spectacle of the floating and plunging camera eye while retaining the rhythm of alternations.

Furthermore, five times in the film the people and vehicles on the street, or vessels in the distant bay, move backward (shots 9, 10, 18, 19, 24). The reverse motion is not immediately apparent in most of these shots because the camera never comes closer than five stories to the moving figures.[25] Thinking about how these shots were filmed induces an intellectual vertigo to complement the antigravitational illusions: If the shot looks both upside down and backward, it means it was filmed with the camera right side up and spliced into the film in reverse. That, in turn, suggests that the two ascending shots (shots 10 and 19) in which the motion is reversed are probably simple descending shots spliced in reverse. Thus, even the relationship between the direction of the camera and the imaginary subject producing it can be in doubt.

Rhetorically, the title is unlike any other Gehr has given his films. The slashes graphically represent the titled vertical path of the camera and emphasize the tmesis and zeugma of "sidewalk," "shuttle walk," and "side shuttle." The title is also a metalepsis of a suggested but unstated metaphor that would substitute *space* for *side*, conjuring both a space shuttle and a space walk. Scott MacDonald perceptively alluded to Kubrick's *2001: A Space Odyssey* in his discussion of Gehr's film.[26] The film evokes the etymology of the three words: *Side* is cognate with *sow* and meant something long and pendulous before it came to assume the range of meanings current in English—a surface, the right or left part of the human body, the space next to someone; *walk* comes from an Old English word meaning to roll, and distantly reflects the Sanskrit verb *vayati* (he, she, it hops, jumps); a *shuttle* was a weaving device to ferry the woof of thread back and forth between the warp. It became a metaphor for all back-and-forth movement. Originally it derived from Old English *scytel* (dart) with roots linking it to the "shoot" family. The title directs us to the elevator on the side of the Fairmont Hotel shuttling customers from a rooftop level to the unseen Fairmont Crown restaurant on the twenty-fourth floor and back. More significantly, it points to the lateral orientation of our bodies and the ways in which we account for space from that orientation; it contrasts the eccentric (rolling, hopping) self-propulsion through space of walking with the straight darting shot of a shuttle. The metaphors of the space shuttle and the space walk remind us that the film operates within a gravitational field in which traction, friction, and the position of the body play crucial roles in our sense of place.

At his retrospective screening at the Museum of the Moving Image in 1999, Gehr eloquently described the film as "a horizontal pan of San Francisco

25. The elevator starts at the seventh floor of the hotel above the corner of Powell and Sacramento Streets. Powell Street itself rises two stories along the length of the hotel to the corner of California Street.
26. Scott MacDonald, *The Garden in the Machine: A Field Guide to Independent Films about Place* (Berkeley: University of California Press, 2001).

broken up into a series of closeups, each a vertical panorama." He admitted that he was enthralled by the way an upside-down image seemed to be right side up in one part of the frame and that the movement of the camera seemed suspended, always taking off and just about to land but never quite landing, as if it were a rocket ship (shuttle) leaving earth, making the broken sweep of the city a metaphor for a panorama of the globe. In calling attention to the panoramic sweep of the twenty-five shots, the filmmaker was acknowledging the frequently cited relationship of his film to Eadweard Muybridge's 1877 and 1878 panoramas photographed from nearly the same spot on Nob Hill. Muybridge was not the first panoramist to choose that location as his vantage point. The earliest dates from 1858.[27] Gehr's twenty-five shots drift from west to east along Powell Street, although there is not a precise correlation of overlapping perspectives, such as can be found in Muybridge's 360 degree construction. The oblique allusion to Muybridge entails both recognition of his protocinematic achievements and his impressive record of San Francisco. As Gehr alters his camera angles in the eastward direction, he often assembles sets of shots in which the distinctive features of a building give cohesion to two or more sequential shots. The most spectacular of these conjoinings is the fulcrum of the film: Shot 17 shows an upside-down ascent across a seemingly horizontal building moving into right corner of the screen. The camera movement keeps the image in place until it suddenly reverses itself (with a flash frame and a jump cut) into an ascent (shot 18), which moves from the top of the building to the bay at the horizon: Eventually, from the wake of a boat in the bay we read this shot as backward. (It is accompanied by the sound of birds and airplanes, accentuating the analogies to flight.)

The soundtrack of *Side/Walk/Shuttle* begins forty seconds before the first image. German dominates in the mix of its barely decipherable voices, perhaps obliquely representing the sound within the implied elevator. After the initial shot, the film goes silent for the next four. When the sound resumes (shot 6), we hear the noises of an American delicatessen (recorded at Grand Central Station). The sound of footsteps, traffic, distant bells, and singing in shot 7 (and several subsequent shots, recorded in Geneva) suggest the life of the street outside the confines of the elevator. By the middle of the film (shot 12), we can identify Italian speech and Veneto dialect (from Venice). The barking of a dog or the songs of birds (from Geneva, shots 13, 14, 16, and 18) enlarge the domain of the film to include unseen fauna. There is a hint of synchronization when wind, birds, or airplanes can be heard later in the film

27. See David Harris, with Eric Sandweiss, *Eadweard Muybridge and the Photographic Panorama of San Francisco, 1850–1880* (Montreal: Centre Canadien d'Architecture/ Canadian Center for Architecture, 1993).

(shots 14, 16, and 18) as we reach the upper limits of the elevator. Near the end of the film there are passages of sound recorded in London and Berlin.[28]

We can take the opening five shots as an introduction to the principles of the film. Only the first of these has sound. As I pointed out, that sound alone can be heard as indicative of the auditory environment of the elevator. When the sound returns in the sixth shot we move into the poem of the street: The sound of footsteps, the noises of the delicatessen, and the visibility of pedestrian and vehicular movements focus attention on the life of Powell Street in shots 6–11. From this point the center of attention shifts to the tall buildings surrounding the Fairmont Hotel. For the first time in the film, Gehr emphasizes both the verticality of the buildings (shot 14) and the illusion of horizontality the camera can bestow upon them (shots 12 and 16). With the emergence of Italian voices in this section, we seem to be joyriding on the Tower of Babel. Following the matched jump cut of shots 17 and 18, a double movement on a single building, the earlier verticality is reversed when a building comes straight down from the top of the screen as the upside-down camera descends in shot 19. The floating subject projects a floating world in this section of the film (shots 17–20). In the last five shots, *Side/Walk/Shuttle* becomes a cosmological poem or, in the filmmaker's expression, a "panorama of the globe."

In Emerson's terms, Gehr ultimately achieves his cosmological poem when he "unfixes the land and the sea, makes them revolve around his primary thought, and disposes them anew." Emerson suggests that primary thought entails the sublime feeling that "something in himself is stable." In turning the phrase toward Gehr's film, I understand his primary thought to be itself a reflex of the awe or sublimity engendered by the aesthetic power he discovered in his ability to transform the filmed elevator rides into a visionary cityscape. However, the exhilaration of the vehicular movement and the deracination of skyscrapers reflect the filmmaker's ambivalence about living in the California city. He told Scott MacDonald: "For a long time I thought of New York as my 'home,' but due to economics, I moved to San Francisco in 1988. It's a beautiful city, but I found it difficult to ground myself there. That difficulty was what prompted the making of the film."[29] The principal economic motivation for his translation from New York was a permanent teaching position at the San Francisco Art Institute. Gehr was renting an apartment on Russian Hill (the affluent neighborhood near Nob Hill where the SFAI is located) when he was making *Side/Walk/Shuttle*.

---

28. MacDonald, *A Critical Cinema 5*, pp. 396–97. MacDonald generously shared the results of his research with me before the publication of his interview with Gehr.
29. Ibid., p. 396.

The hotel refused permission for the filmmaker to shoot from the elevator. He did it surreptitiously and was repeatedly told to cease. The very atmosphere of the expensive Fairmont Hotel and the prohibition against filming must have contributed to the alienation embedded in the film's primary thought. Yet economics and intimidation may not have been as crucial to the genesis and tone of the film as his difficulty grounding himself in the new city. Groundlessness is as central to Gehr's cinematic oeuvre as the allegory of the displaced person is to Mekas's or the loss of home to Brakhage in his *Visions in Meditation* series.

CHAPTER 10

Warren Sonbert's Movements in a Concerto

Despite Warren Sonbert's consistent denial of the suggestion that he made diary films, it remains a commonplace in the critical literature to discuss his work as such. In fact, it is parallel to the argument that the differences among the ten films of his maturity are nearly undetectable. For instance, John Gartenberg, the curator of the memorial retrospective of Sonbert's work, began his catalog essay with an effort to correct this tendency: "Warren Sonbert (1948–1995) has typically been regarded as an avant-garde 'diarist filmmaker,' yet a look at his creative output as a whole suggests that this is an oversimplification."[1] Philip Lopate, in turn, wrote:

> Recently, Paul Arthur in *Film Comment* made a strong case for
> Sonbert's artistic variety, pointing out not only the different thematic
> emphases of each film, but shifts in technique from movie to movie.
> Arthur warns of the mistake many viewers make when they "conclude

---

1. John Gartenberg, "Friendly Witnesses: The Worlds of Warren Sonbert," Solomon Guggenheim Museum, New York, 1999. Available at http://www.artistswithaids.org/artery/centerpieces/centerpieces_sonbertintro.html.

that Sonbert's films are more or less the same in tone and ideas." And yet I must admit that sometimes it seemed to me he was making the same film over and over. He had perfected a form which suited him, and which yielded quality results, even though it did not quite express the full brio and range of the man.[2]

For Sonbert, the term *diary film* implied there was no editing after the film came out of the camera. Perhaps more fundamental to his rejection of this label was his fierce resistance to the confessional mode. He rarely even appears before the camera in his own films. We can spot him in *The Bad and the Beautiful* (1967) as one of a party of picnickers at an elegant estate. But in this film about couples, he denies us any glimpse of his own domestic life or his amours. As if presaging his vehicular obsession, he rides a bicycle. Later, in *Divided Loyalties* (1978) he steers a motorboat, and in *Short Fuse* (1991) we see him riding a train.

The films oscillate between affectionate glimpses of the lives of friends and blatantly banal icons of shared spectatorship—fireworks, circus, magnets of tourism. The selfhood at the center of this quasi-autobiographical oeuvre rejects the model of Rousseau, who wrote that his *Confessions* would record a radically unique individual. The narrator of *Carriage Trade* (1972) and all of Sonbert's subsequent films poses as a typical, representative man (the Augustinian premise allegorized by Emerson), or one whose uniqueness is reflected in the tone he distills from his typical, representative experiences.

Sonbert's works are not diaries or quotidian lyrics but crisis films in the mode Brakhage perfected. Making *Carriage Trade*, he found the automatism that allowed him the complexity and subtlety of nuance he had been seeking for six years, and he stuck to it until the end of his short life. Viewers who knew Sonbert's first films might have got the impression that he was continually remaking the same film when they saw *Carriage Trade* because he incorporated excerpts from his earlier films in it, as he had in an earlier draft, released as *Tuxedo Theater* (1968). In his subsequent films he often returned to an archive of materials he had filmed to cull an image so similar to one he had used previously that even the most attentive viewer could hardly be expected to notice the difference after an interval of years between films. Compounding the impression of repetition, he apparently reedited excerpts from his earlier films to make *Friendly Witness* (1989), this time synchronizing the passages to popular songs, to make his first sound

2. Philip Lopate, "Warren Sonbert," in Edmund White, ed. *Loss Within Loss: Artists in the Age of AIDS* (Madison: University of Wisconsin Press, 2002); also available at http://www.artistswithaids.org/artery/centerpieces/centerpieces_sonbert1.html. See Paul Arthur, "Dancing on the Precipice: The Films of Warren Sonbert," *Film Comment* 35, no. 2 (March/April 1999).

film in twenty years. So Paul Arthur's discrimination of Sonbert's different themes and styles was evidence of his connoisseurship, filling a gap in the critical literature.

Sonbert himself actually encouraged the notion that his work was taking the form of a serial project after he had completed *Rude Awakening* (1976) and *Divided Loyalties* by discussing the three films in terms of a concerto form:

> I indeed regard the works in a Mozartian key scheme: *Carriage Trade* being E-flat Major, broad, epic, leisurely, maestoso; *Rude Awakening* in D minor, brooding, cynical, fatalistic, dancing on the precipice; *Divided Loyalties* in C Major, agile, dynamic, spry, with a hint of turbulence (and even this scheme of keys can be seen as a classical instrumental concerto: first movement [*Carriage Trade*] setting the scene and longest in time and investigation; the second movement [*Rude Awakening*] a dark melancholy adagio; the third [*Divided Loyalties*] a breezy rondo to clear if not quite dispel the heavy air, gracious, with a let's-get-on-with-life feeling, a caper to what has gone before.)[3]

The generic and stylistic changes in his films after *Divided Loyalties* were no more pronounced than within the "concerto." No wonder many of his admirers continued to think of his oeuvre as a serial work. In this chapter I concentrate on the three films of the concerto and the one that followed them, *Noblesse Oblige* (1981).

Although the references the filmmaker often made to literature centered on the nineteenth-century novel—Balzac, James, Tolstoy, and Dickens (from whose *Our Mutual Friend* he took his title *The Cup and the Lip*, 1986)—I take Emerson and Whitman, yet again, to have created the prototype of his films. The passage from *Nature* I cite so often could be the floor plan for *Carriage Trade*, the film in which he forges the automatism that became the ground of all of his subsequent films: a fusion of rapid rhythms, cross-cutting, euphuism, and subtle wit. This automatism was so powerful and generative that the filmmaker created all of his subsequent work with it over the last twenty-four years of his life. Shooting from and within airplanes, merry-go-rounds and other amusement rides, cabs, buses, boats and ships, trolleys, elevated subways, fast trains, from observation cars, helicopters, escalators, automobiles including a convertible, occasionally turning the camera upside down in "unrealizing" the spectacle of "apparent beings,"

---

3. Warren Sonbert, "Lecture, San Francisco Art Institute, August 1979," *Film Culture* 70–71 (1983), p. 72.

he fused the Emersonian litany of familiar sights with his version of Whitman's great catalogs, the dilation of the spirit that widens to engulf what it sees and hears. He followed the movements of camel riders, skaters, gondoliers, bicyclists, equestrians, rickshaws, kites, ferries, amusement jumpers, men swimming and floating in rapids, trapeze artists, and people swaying in a wide range of prayers. Readers of Whitman's early "Poem of Salutation," later called "Salut au Monde," will recognize the heaping of geographical details characteristic of Sonbert's mature cinema:

What widens within you, Walt Whitman? ...

Who are the infants? some playing, some slumbering?
Who are the girls? Who are the married women?
Who are the three old men going slowly with their arms about each others'
    necks?
What rivers are these? What forests and fruits are these? ...

I see where the Seine flows, and where the Loire, the Rhone, and the
    Guadalquivir flow,
I see the windings of the Volga, the Dneiper, the Oder,
I see the Tuscan going down the Arno, and the Venetian along the Po,
I see the Greek seaman sailing out of Egina bay....

I see the picturesque crowds at the fairs of Khiva, and those of Herat,
I see Teheran, I see Muscat and Medina, and the intervening sands—I see
    the caravans toiling onward;
I see Egypt and the Egyptians, I see the pyramids and obelisks...[4]

The dazzling mélange of locations in *Carriage Trade*—India, France, Egypt, Morocco, Turkey, Greece, Iran, England, and the familiar New York and San Francisco—suggests that Sonbert made the voyages Whitman imagined. The love of opera, window shopping, and of the physical companionship of men are affinities he shared with the poet of "Song of Myself" and made the core of his films:

I hear the chorus...it is a grand-opera...this indeed is music![26]
Looking in at the shop-windows in Broadway the whole forenoon....
    pressing the flesh of my nose to the thick plate-glass,

4. Whitman, "Poem of Salutation," *Selected Poems 1855–1892: A New Edition*, ed. Gary Schmidgall (New York: St. Martin's, 1999), pp. 121, 124–25, 132.

Wandering the same afternoon with my face turned up to the clouds;
My right and left arms round the sides of two friends and I in the middle;
Coming home with the bearded and dark-cheeked bush-boy...

Voyaging to every port to dicker and adventure;
Hurrying with the modern crowd, as eager and fickle as any...[5]

If the analog of toponymic poetry is the visible monument, unmistakable symbolic or iconographic index of a specific place, then the images of the Eiffel Tower, the Sphinx, the Taj Mahal, Golden Gate Bridge, bathers in the Ganges, Brooklyn Bridge, the Parthenon, and so forth anchor *Carriage Trade* in the familiar rhetoric of world travel. In a typically witty gesture, early in the film, Sonbert shows an Arab perusing a postcard stand, to acknowledge that the filmmaker is conscious of the banality of these monumental and inescapable images. "Puns, visual metaphors, points about clichés of language, even extending to the titles themselves,"[6] were at the center of his work.

Nathaniel Dorsky drolly teased the filmmaker that he should call his film *Mondo Sonbert*, alluding to the successes in the late 1960s of *Mondo Cane* and its derivates such as *Mondo Topless*.[7] Sonbert's quest romance is neither as focused nor as dominated by a mood of despair as the enormously influential, inescapable crisis lyric, Brakhage's *Anticipation of the Night*, which culminates in suicide. The elusive protagonist of *Carriage Trade* insists on keeping open his options, including that of disappearing from the film. The whole film is more fluid than shaped; it seems to be crystallizing as we watch it, as if the filmmaker were as helpless as the viewer to predict where it is going. Still, the filmmaker's ability to convey his own excitement over what can be achieved by editing sustains the momentum of the film, by sharing his discovery of associations and antithesis latent in material he recorded in places far from each other, over six years.

For approximately one hour *Carriage Trade* circles around its recurring motifs in a paratactic ramble, with few shifts in tone or pacing to convey a sense of ground covered or to anticipate a terminus approaching. Four minutes into the film, a sequence encourages us to abandon ourselves to the flow of imagery and kinesis: A goose is carried from the center of the screen leftward by the current of the stream on which it sits; a man floats in the same direction along a swift river; from inside an airplane, Sonbert films the propeller on a wing during takeoff, again rushing leftward; and that movement is

5. Whitman, "Leaves of Grass," *Selected Poems 1855–1892*, pp. 37, 44.

6. David Ehrenstein, "Interview with Warren Sonbert," *Film Culture* 70–71 (1983), p. 186.

7. Telephone interview with Nathaniel Dorsky, July 31, 2000. Dorsky was an invaluable source of information about the genesis of *Carriage Trade* and about figures who appear in other Sonbert films.

continued in a pan of vegetation and red flowers. But then, as if to announce that our ride will not be untroubled, he cuts to a winter scene in New York: A woman in a fur coat stands before a car, rocking back and forth to extricate itself from snow.

Carriage Trade hits its stride after about ten minutes, when the mood of setting out and the thrill of new, exotic locations wears off, so that Sonbert is able to drop into the film passages from his two most ambitious earlier films, *The Bad and the Beautiful* and *The Tenth Legion* (1967). The personal travelogue put a new perspective on the now-fragmented images of the couples from the former and the company of friends in the latter. The relentlessly mobile filmmaker is their intimate yet he is not quite one of them. He returns to them again and again while engaged in a perpetual quest. There is a play between the relaxation and poignant tension in Sonbert's images of his friends. The comfort of some of them with each other and with the presence of the filmmaker contrasts with transparent failures to sham naturalness: The studied manner of an older woman with a younger man painfully reveals her desperation to sustain an illusion for the camera as if her romantic relationship depended upon it.

In *Carriage Trade* Sonbert had found the form that gave new meaning to his earlier work and defined his vocation. At one point he joins images of filmmakers Dorsky and Jerome Hiler ice skating to Indians worshiping at a shrine and a couple from his earlier films; later, he intercuts young women rushing around town with shots of a graveyard—there are many in the film—and then follows a wedding with a young man entering a classroom (again from his earlier work). He seems to be acknowledging that although exhilaration, prayer, and affection are at the center of this film, he finds the occasion to remind himself of his mortality, and that making this film is still a work of instruction and optimistic initiation. The structure of the film itself is an exploration of what the filmmaker called "maintaining one's options":

> One of the liberating aspects of being gay is that it gives one a unique, delirious, and broad perspective on the world. The gay aesthetic centers on choice, on maintaining one's options. Cinematically this leads to an embrace of the mise-en-scene and an eschewal of didactic presentation. Rather than hit one over the head with propagandistic editing, the aesthetic I have in mind leaves the viewer with the enviable task of putting the pieces together, as the camera tracks, glides, pans, and cranes its way through the narrative.[8]

---

8. Warren Sonbert, "Reel Companions: Contemporary Gay Cinema," *Tikkun* 5, no. 5 (1990), p. 89.

He terminates the film with images of ascent. The camera peers from a roof or bridge straight down at a Venetian canal, locates a rooftop, then an outdoor spiral staircase, finally a Moorish door in mottled light. How do we put these pieces together? Stages of grace? Visionary, purgatorial ascent? In any case, it corresponds to the opening of Emerson's "Experience":

> Where do we find ourselves? In a series of which we do not know the extremes, and believe that it has none. We wake and find ourselves on a stair; there are stairs below us, which we seem to have ascended; there are stairs above us, many a one, which go upward and out of sight. But the Genius which, according to the old belief, stands at the door by which we enter, and gives us the lethe to drink, that we may tell no tales, mixed the cup too strongly, and we cannot shake off the lethargy now at noonday. Sleep lingers all our lifetime about our eyes, as night hovers all day in the boughs of the fir-tree. All things swim and glitter. Our life is not so much threatened as our perception. Ghostlike we glide through nature, and should not know our place again.[9]

Carriage Trade introduced a reign of silence that lasted seventeen years, bolstered by a polemical assertion: "To have a sound track is not taking film seriously."[10] Sound, he repeatedly claimed in the manner of Brakhage, was redundant and undermined the fundamental musicality of film itself. In his first films, Sonbert had invariably followed the then recent innovation of Kenneth Anger and Bruce Conner of using popular songs for his soundtracks. The silence of the montage of *Carriage Trade* abets every new shot in threatening to alter the context of some of those that preceded it. The resulting effect of concentrating pressure on the individual shot at the expense of larger units of organization is to immerse the viewer in a maze of seductive images, continually suggesting different lines of association or narrative, which are so frequently superseded that the play of distraction and renewed attention seems to be crucial to the film's aesthetic. Perhaps this may be what Sonbert meant when he told David Ehrenstein that his films' "poetry" resists "dehumanizing entertainment":

> [I]t's a split between shaking people up and making them feel *central*. It's definitely a criminal act—going against the grain.... It's taking people to different places. It's not patting them on the back. If you

9. Ralph Waldo Emerson, *Essays and Lectures* (New York: Library of America, 1983), p. 47. I am grateful to Jeffrey Stout for pointing out this reference.
10. Sonbert, "Lecture, San Francisco Art Institute," p. 166. Twenty years rather than seventeen if we take into consideration *Tuxedo Theater* (1968), an early version of *Carriage Trade*.

have a work and no one boos it, there's something wrong. I just follow my own needs and wants and desires. Do I sound megalomaniacal? ... Well, I am. I think all artists have to be solipsistic.[11]

As the solipsistic center of his film, he evokes the Whitmanian "I" obliquely. He has described the individual shot as a piece of evidence subjected to the arguments and counterarguments of montage. So he would have the figure of the cinematic author emerge from the connotative play of the images, as the implied mediator of the evidence. His addiction to creating tension between the often banal images and the ironies of their contextualization, counterpointed by the fluctuating indices of the presence of the filmmaker and his reabsorption into the material, make Sonbert a genuinely difficult filmmaker; his refusal to coach the viewer in assigning values to what he shows us exacerbates the difficulty. The neutrality of tone, the studied casualness of the dandy's gaze, and the ironical fermatura that finds beauty almost everywhere the camera points, put Sonbert in the company of those of Whitman's late modern descendants whose principal avatar is John Ashbery.

In fact, at an early turning point of his career, when he was on the verge of abandoning the long take and in-camera composition for elaborate editing, Sonbert was spending many evenings with Dorsky and Hiler—the three came to know each other by way of Gregory Markopoulos's mentoring—looking at each other's footage and discussing what an abstract film form would look like, one not based on mythology as Markopoulos's oblique narratives were, or grounded as the psychological and visionary experience of a selfhood, as Brakhage's were, or celebrations of a place, as Menken's often were. Dorsky's reading of Ashbery's *The Tennis Court Oath* and especially *Rivers and Mountains* fueled these shared imaginings of "synapses that would give you hits shot for shot, as Ashbery's poems did word for word; in which narrative would disappear in the palm of your hand; so that each move was completely open but resonant of the situation... and the film would end when it starts to hurt itself."[12] Dorsky claims that the camera rolls Hiler showed him and Sonbert during those sessions represented the origin of such a cinematic form, "the mind selflessly organizing the material" of normal seeing— parades, circuses, fireworks, train rides, stained glass windows, upside-down boats. The experience of those discussions and the influence of Hiler's still unreleased films may have been crucial to Sonbert's maturing as an artist. However, the continuing inaccessibility of Hiler's work blocks the serious consideration of the historical value of this matter.

11. Ehrenstein, "Interview with Warren Sonbert," p. 196.
12. Dorsky, telephone interview, July 31, 2000. Dorsky's formulations, of course, were made more than thirty years after the events.

As soon as he started to make films, as a student at New York University, Sonbert was attracted by the work and company of Gregory Markopoulos, whose circle included some of the young poets around Andy Warhol's Factory. Although his camera work perpetuates Markopoulos's aesthetic, his stance toward what he shoots owes more to Warhol's ironic distancing. He was infused at the same moment with enthusiasm for the acclaimed auteurs of the Hollywood cinema, especially Hitchcock, Sirk, and Minnelli, from whom he filched the title *The Bad and the Beautiful* for his portrait gallery of couples. His initial student work, *Amphetamine* (1966, coauthored by Wendy Appel), his only black-and-white film, revealed his youthful affinities to both Hollywood narratives and the avant-garde cinema by including errors of focus and fluttering camera work, apparently in an economy to salvage everything shot: One young man injects the drug in the company of another—we never learn how they met or if the companion is a fantasy figure; they kiss, make love, and part. The narrative is so elliptical that it seems that from the start Sonbert had no patience or taste for the syntax of storytelling: Instead, he rushes to a striking rendering of the discomfort of the neophyte in his use of the syringe and to the postcoital drowsiness of one lover in contrast to the affection of the other. If the affinity of *Amphetamine* to the trance films of Deren, Markopoulos, and, above all, Kenneth Anger's *Fireworks* (1947) is conscious, the filmmaker has nevertheless ignored the inherited tropes that would indicate that the lover may be imaginary.

The fusion of narrative elements and avant-garde gestures is more pronounced in Sonbert's next film. *Where Did Our Love Go?* (1966) strings together a number of scenes in which one or more of a group of his friends appear: He dynamically pans the camera around a crowded opening of a show of Tom Wesselman's flamboyant Pop Art nudes; shows what a young man encounters in a visit to a loft; follows a couple in a nonstop stroll through the permanent collection of the Museum of Modern Art; goes to films at an art cinema (there are glimpses of *Contempt* and *North by Northwest* filmed off the screen) and on Forty-second Street; and attends a live music performance. Brakhage's *Desistfilm* might have been the prototype of this evocation of a collective saturnalia; its dynamic handheld camera seems at times anchored as the point of view of one or another of the young men and women in the film; at times it seems to introduce a new, invisible protagonist to the loosely assembled youth coterie. The film includes light flares and even may have been built of episodes largely composed in the camera. But even at the start of his career, Sonbert claims for himself a much more cosmopolitan persona than the isolato of Brakhage's early work. He is the dandy, the urbane observer rather than an eager participant.

By cutting directly from the cruise through the Museum of Modern Art to a merry-go-round ride, he introduced a metaphor that would recur with numerous variations throughout his career. This is not merely a comment on the childish superficiality of his protagonists' relationship to the great art they scurry past, perhaps in a coy mating rite, or merely an assertion of the continuity of a child's robust imagination and kinetic exhilaration in aesthetic creation, but a premature effort to put both of these ideas, at least, in play. "No image or icon has a simplistic easily solvable frame of reference," he later wrote in undated notes for his students to study Sirk's films:

> The fetid taste of intrinsic imperfection, of behavioral mistakes endlessly repeated from generation to generation, find expression in the staggeringly demonic visual motifs recurring throughout Sirk's films of the merry-go-round, the amusement park ride, the circular treadmill, the vehicle that really goes nowhere, insulated hopeless activity, the Western frame of mind, people struggling to get outside cages of their own building yet encased by their own unique palpable qualities. Mirrors and surfaces as distancing agents (revealing yet qualifying and placing.) A flight of stairs—stages of grace? No image or icon has a simplistic easily solvable frame of reference. An immediate appreciative laugh shouldn't obscure the double puns & and triple meanings to be found in Sirk's "outrageous" moments. A lot of them happen in "Written on the Wind", probably Sirk's richest work. One will suffice. Bob Stack after being told by his doctor he's impotent immediately comes upon a young boy jiggling furiously atop a stationary (natch) penny machine rocking horse (like Berg's "Wozzeck"). He's straddled around an enormous horse's head with a gleeful cinematic smile (this in 1956 remember) totally oblivious to Stack's woes. How many ironic meanings can you count? Here's the son Stack will never have, performing a function Stack isn't up to, on a machine that isn't going anywhere, but enjoying himself nevertheless.[13,14]

The filmmaker wants his viewers to read his images as he reads Sirk's, multiplying ironic meanings. Yet he wants them to issue forth from his film without the ligature the character and story of Bob Stack give the viewer of Sirk's melodrama.

In the 1979 lecture at the San Francisco Art Institute in which he introduced the analogy of a three-movement concerto to describe the cumulative effect

---

13. As Jeffery Stout noticed, this passage corresponds to the Emersonian image from "Experience" cited earlier in this chapter.
14. Warren Sonbert, notes on Sirk's films (Sonbert files, Anthology Film Archives).

of *Carriage Trade*, *Rude Awakening*, and *Divided Loyalties*, he also provided useful guides to the differences among his films:

> *Carriage Trade*... is about travel, transportation, anthropological investigation: four continents, four organized religions, customs; about time with its 6sixyears in the making and cast of thousands; about how the same people age and grow and even change apartments over six years. *Rude Awakening* is about Western civilization and its work; activity ethic and the viability of performing functions and activities. *Divided Loyalties* ... is more about art vs. industry and their various crossovers.... *Noblesse Oblige* is about journalism, reportage, news events that you might see on the six o'clock report, how the news is created, how it might effect our lives, and journalists' responsibilities.[15]

Taken individually, the shots of *Rude Awakening* and *Divided Loyalties* seem of a piece with those of *Carriage Trade*: lots of vehicular movement, dancers, fireworks, circuses, parades, animals. (*Noblesse Oblige*, on the other hand, distinguishes itself from its predecessors by incorporating into a similar matrix dramatic images of demonstrations and riots after the Moscone-Milk murders.) In *Rude Awakening*, Sonbert disperses events throughout the thirty-eight-minute film: a basketball game, several shows from what appears to be a Renaissance fair, a Hispanic dance perhaps at a street fair, the Smile beauty contest, and a solo male dancer (Douglas Dunn) and a solo ballerina rehearsing in separate spaces. There are brief a-b-a-b alterations of parallel montage. Several times the rhythm speeds up to suggest dissonance and disorientation in the flow and argument of the film. Above all, many of the images and editing structures suggest mild frustration or lack of coordination.

The very first shot, an archer shooting an arrow offscreen, creates the expectation of a subsequent image of the arrow reaching, or missing, its goal, but it never appears. A dog tries to fetch a board that is too large for it to maneuver; a couple (perhaps Sonbert's parents) hesitate as they walk the gangplank to a cruise ship, back up, then proceed, as if adjusting their pace to the camera; a logger cuts a tree disproportionately small for the scale of his chainsaw; acts of sport—volleyball, frisbee, a punching bag, golf—are awkwardly placed, or slightly ungraceful, or unsatisfying in the limited abilities of players to catch, return, or putt.

The final image presents a child in a sandbox, through light flares on the emulsion, throwing or pouring handfuls of sand. The ambiguous play of

15. Sonbert, "Lecture, San Francisco Art Institute," pp. 161.

frustration, pleasure, and bewilderment conveyed by the gesture suitably caps the whole film even though nothing has prepared us to expect that to be the last shot. At one point Sonbert recalls the rhythmic grotesquery of Bruce Conner's *A Movie*, when shots of an accident and the removal of a victim on a stretcher lead to images of wrecking a building and a bizarre perpendicular vehicle in a soapbox derby.

Circular rides that go nowhere seem even more prominent and portentous here than in the previous film. Jerome Hiler's clowning is more exaggerated than in other Sonbert films; he even gestures to cover the lens with his hand. Several young women are self-consciously posed or oddly photographed. A nude stands alone in a room recalling the model in Courbet's *Atelier* as Sonbert sweeps past to glimpse the city through her window; perhaps the same woman takes a bath for him à la Degas; another reenacts a shot of Kim Novak in *Vertigo* under the Golden Gate Bridge. A woman drinking beer on a stoop, another who cannot stop laughing as Sonbert's camera dogs her on the street, and even a sunbather avoiding glare on the beach at Venice, California, cumulatively confirm Philip Lopate's observation that "after awhile one experiences the accumulated sadness behind all the joy and motion, and the title, *Rude Awakening*, becomes more fitting and darker in its double-edge irony."[16]

If a rude awakening is a robust shock of self-recognition, the principal subject must be the filmmaker himself. In thus titling his film he acknowledges some previously unconscious aspect of his work, probably an aspect of *Carriage Trade*. What would that be? The infectious exuberance of that film had celebrated both what the filmmaker realized he could achieve and what montage itself could do, "comparing different places, different people, different pastimes in different parts of the world, four seasons, four elements—really broad concerns."[17] However, "*Rude Awakening* continued along that line with things not working out, things not materializing, people having certain expectations, plans, input, and those dissolving."[18] From this I surmise that Sonbert was not only disappointed by the reception of *Carriage Trade*, the failure by both the small community of the American avant-garde cinema and the larger film world to appreciate the scale and depth of his achievement, but was rudely awakened to something dark and beyond his control in his work, perhaps in filmmaking itself:

> The people in my films aren't really basking in the sun on the beach, they're actually out there doing something. We watch ten seconds

---

16. Philip Lopate, "The Films of Warren Sonbert," *Film Culture 70–71* (1983), p. 181.
17. Ehrenstein, "Interview with Warren Sonbert," p. 193.
18. Ibid.

of what people do all their lives—construction men or people in a bookstore. It tends to qualify the importance—or what Sartre might call "bad faith"—of people throwing themselves behind their own works. In a sense, it's a cruel touch of just showing glimpses of what people feel is very important.[19]

The film suggests that the filmmaker was rudely awakened to his own "bad faith" and cruelty. The unfashionable reference to Sartre is revealing. Brakhage's lucubrations a few years earlier around the term *sincerity* and its implications for personal filmmaking might also have had their origins in the second chapter of *Being and Nothingness*, where Sartre identified bad faith as the problematic of sincerity:

> [T]he essential structure of sincerity does not differ from that of bad faith since the sincere man constitutes himself as what he is in order not to be it. This explains the truth recognized by all that one can fall into bad faith by being sincere.... Bad faith is possible only because sincerity is conscious of missing its goal inevitably, due to its very nature.[20]

Sonbert must have in mind the same chapter in which Sartre insists a café waiter "plays at being a waiter in a café" in flight from his freedom. The glimpses *Rude Awakening* shows us of people at work and play are revelations of their bad faith, their self-deception in the face of freedom. It is not far to the recognition that the filmmaker too throws himself behind his work in another act of bad faith. Sartre said, "The goal of bad faith is to put oneself out of reach; it is an escape."

Early in the film there is a fascinating sequence: Sonbert intercuts a shot of a model's mannerist turns in an outdoor fashion show with a tank truck on the road; from the car behind we read the warning: flammable. He follows the return shot of the model with a montage of fireworks superimposed over the image of a bridge, then a dragon dance from Chinese New Year and, after the briefest images of fingers (perhaps picking something from hair), a juggler with two flaming torches. The filmmaker is playing with fire, admitting the proximity to a more dangerous, explosive combustion: the assignment of meaning itself is perilous, pyrotechnical.

19. Ibid.

20. Jean Paul Sartre, *Being and Nothingness*, trans. Hazel Barnes (New York: Philosophical Library, 1956), pp. 65, 66. Brakhage filmed on commission an episode from Sartre's novel *Nausea*, which he used to make his film *Black Vision* (1965).

This sequence leads immediately to the Courbet-like female nude posed in the center of an apartment or studio. Her head is turned away from us toward a window on the back wall. The handheld camera pushes past her, almost as if she were an obstacle, to view the complex of high-rise apartments visible from the window. A still shot of trees reflected in water follows. In Courbet's great allegory of painting, the artist sits in his studio before an easel on which there rests a landscape that he is completing as the nude model and a room full of celebrities from the world of poetry, politics, and art look on. Sonbert follows Courbet in using the nude as a decoy; she heightens the intensity of his unveiling of the urban site and its uncanny reflection. Lopate wrote of this film: "The connection between shots, even without a story-line, has an intuitive rightness that feels mysteriously syllogistic, though the fun is in knowing that much of this meaning may be audience projection while some may have been the film-maker's intention."[21] Far from fun, Sartre contends that bad faith is an escape from anguish.[22]

Fun or not, Sonbert withholds any evidence to confirm that we have caught his allusion. But whether or not Courbet's masterpiece mediates the conceptual schema here, we can say with confidence that the pose of the woman in the center of the room claims her as an artist's model, one who makes visible female anatomy just as the fashion model a minute before had displayed, or made visible, the stylish elegance of the clothes she wore. Furthermore, the camera does not pause to contemplate her form but seeks to share the object of her gaze. And yet it is not the modernist urban cityscape that is at stake so much as the very proximity and optical accessibility of the artist's studio to the icons of the metropolis. The filmmaker trumps that proximity by the instantaneous substitution of the sylvan image, itself a specularity that might remind us of the fuzzy reflection of the road and trees in the metallic surface of the ominous tank truck still fresh in our optical memories.

Finally, if all this seems an inane whir of ideas and associations whipped together, we need only recall a minute farther back to the shots before the fashion show to find the frenetic vertigo of a mad teacup ride (perhaps from Disneyland) into which the filmmaker edited split-second blurs of shots "ruined" by the loss of a loop in the camera threading so that images of an orchestra, cats, and traffic jump and bleed vertically. There he implicitly announced that his *Rude Awakening* will be a kinetomanic tea party of perspectival ambiguities and puzzling shocks.

---

21. Lopate, "The Films of Warren Sonbert," p. 181.
22. Arthur C. Danto illuminates this hermeneutic *angoisse* ("Anguish is the recognition that things have the meanings we give them, that the system of meanings through which we define our situation from moment to moment are assigned to the world through us, and that we cannot then derive them from the way the world is") in *Jean-Paul Sartre* (New York: Viking Press, 1975), p. 75.

Bad faith is not lying to others but a form of willing self-deception. There remains in bad faith a transcendental, if evanescent, recognition of the truth it conceals. Part of my consciousness realizes that I am in bad faith. Whitman had given sublime voice to a version of this problematic in his sea chant "As I Ebbed with the Ebb of the Ocean of Life."[23] Not even Brakhage attempted so radical a formulation of orphic bad faith. Despite his confession of solipsism, Sonbert is a gentler egoist than Brakhage; he is a Whitmanian of the school of Ashbery, as I have already suggested and as Lopate had before me. He can treat self-absorption comically as an academic discipline. In one of the wittiest shots in *Rude Awakening*, he depicts his filmmaking class at Bard College, filming outdoors: Each student is absorbed in capturing with a handheld camera a different detail of the landscape as Sonbert weaves among them. These apprentice solipsists, crowded so close together, carefully exclude each other from their shots.

I believe Sonbert thoroughly understood bad faith as a relevant description of his situation as a man and an artist. More than any other avant-garde filmmaker, he loved film festivals (and their parties) and touring with his latest work. He knew that he sometimes alienated his hosts and supporters by demanding repeated invitations to accommodate a schedule of operas he wished to attend, exacerbating the situation by demanding immediate payment for his shows. Like Sartre's café waiter, "he [was] playing, amusing himself." By contrast, his theory of montage, insofar as he expressed it fragmentarily, was a quest for good faith through the exercise of interpretive freedom. When Sartre wrote, "A person can live in bad faith, which does not mean that he does not have abrupt awakenings [*brusques réveils*] to cynicism or to good faith, but which implies a constant and particular style of life,"[24] Sonbert seems to have found "rude awakenings" a more colloquial translation for *brusques réveils*.

Of Sartre's three examples of bad faith—the woman on a first date, the café waiter, and the guilty homosexual, the last could not have escaped Sonbert's attention.[25] Again playing with fire, when he responded to the survey of *Spiral* on the relationship of avant-garde cinema to politics with an essay beginning, "Now it is quite possible to hide behind being a Gayist, a Feminist or a Marxist and still be a lousy artist," he extended the concept of bad faith to homosexual identity politics. "Art is Politics," he contended, "only in the sense of expanding horizons, broadening sensibilities, undermining the

23. Walt Whitman, "As I Ebbed with the Ebb of the Ocean of Life," as quoted in Chapter 8 of this book, p.182.
24. Sartre, *Being and Nothingness*, p. 50.
25. The attribution of guilt and the description of homosexual acts as "misdeeds" from which the "pederast tries to disassociate himself" would surely be labeled homophobic today.

codes, being presented with multiple, often conflicting, points of view and the breakdown of that statement, and then following that qualification with yet another objectivity."[26]

I take the title of his next film, *Divided Loyalties*, to refer foremost to the complexities of his artistic vocation and his commitment to the gay community. He told Ehrenstein: "*Divided Loyalties* is about Art and industry and contemporary lifestyles like Gays in San Francisco, and I think all these things come in for a lot of criticism and a lot of almost scathing mischievous sly treatment." Then, illustrating his point with textual details, he referred to a sequence in which a gathering of gay men, many of them bare chested, is followed by shots of a graveyard, sitting ducks, and the shearing of a sheep: "It's people being exploited and not really knowing it. It's both embracing everything and being unbelievably critical at the same time."[27] Even more than his other films, *Divided Loyalties* is about ambivalence. The filmmaker, seen at the helm of a motorboat, tries to navigate a course through the commercial and social facades of the opera, the circus, and the museum. He repeatedly takes recourse to an elevated view: Sonbert himself, or a stand-in, peers down at a city street through binoculars from a high-rise balcony.

The film opens with opera subscribers arriving in evening dress and ends with an art auction. Before it is a quarter over, an escalator shot of a department store rhymes with a similar view of a museum. The first of two accelerated moments uses Sonbert's typical whirling rides as part of an evocation of the excitement of arrivals—even the Statue of Liberty makes an appearance. In this scene, one of the stand-ins for the filmmaker rolls down a hill with his camera, showing us, in the revelatory rhetoric of Vertov's *The Man with the Movie Camera*, how the frenzy of the shot was recorded. This montage (and a strange vision of a field of pumpkins) introduces the gathering of mostly topless men at a Castro Street fair in San Francisco's gay hub.

The second extended roller coaster ride is more ominous. After an allusion to Hitchcock's *Marnie*, where a woman floating in a pool recalls Marnie's shipboard attempt at suicide on her wedding night, the chaotic crescendo of wild rides leads to a doctor rushing to an emergency. But that is soon supplanted by the curtain call at the opera. Sonbert was an enthusiast as well as a professional critic of opera; he arranged his nearly annual, international film tours to correspond with the operas he wanted to attend. Lopate identified the diva of this curtain call as Tatiana Troyannos, Sonbert's favorite at the time. But there is even ambivalence in his incorporation of her image into his film. If he is taking his own premature bow through her, these are

26. Warren Sonbert, "Point of View," *Spiral* no. 1 (October 1984), p. 4.
27. Ehrenstein, "Interview with Warren Sonbert," pp. 193–94.

"mock congratulatory signs and bows" insofar as the identification is both understated and ironical.

Divided Loyalties projects and examines acts of identification. The opening shots obliquely anticipate the primary arenas and modes in which these acts will occur: A woman carrying evening clothes will be given a context when we see the opera crowd; a bird in flight suggests both the kinetic and aerial perspective, first illustrated by an impressive overview of the freeway and its exit ramps; shirtless poet Gerard Malanga, playing football, mediates the game the filmmaker plays with many shirtless gay men who will later appear. In this film, Sonbert will be one of the opera crowd, perhaps with the intense identification with the diva Wayne Kostenbaum describes in *The Queen's Throat* as a characteristic of gay culture. More problematically, he will even identify with the men publicly exhibiting their affection for each other, "the Castro Street clones" as he labeled them for Lopate. Then, recoiling against these identifications, he assumes identity with the solitary bird, as Whitman did in "A Word Out of the Sea."

Throughout the film he weaves variations on hand movements and social embraces. "Touch" football is one example. An early riff runs together piano playing, card playing, a priest shaking hands with parishioners, and girls stroking a cat. A little later the gestures of a Santa Claus almost seem to be seducing a young boy. Then we see a palm reader and some emphatic hand rhetoric during a press conference at the Theater Club of New York. Although he never actually shows a film editor clipping and fastening shots, he suggests it with such accumulations and with the many kisses filmed as distinctly social greetings, an exchange of signs more than sexual acts: They point to the montagist's work, bringing two images into momentary contact.

In his lecture at the San Francisco Art Institute (August 1979), he was particularly hard on himself. Elucidating a sequence in which an apparently stoned young man listens to rock bands while another is dazed by an automobile accident, he comments:

> [T]here is somehow a link, a chain, by the very act of editing, of putting shots/images next to one another, that says our pleasure is somehow at the expense of another's suffering.
>
> This is emphasized by the next image after the dazed bleeding man— which is a close-up of a Cézanne painting being cleaned. The image of art naturally refers back to the artist-film-maker, saying that art is both objective and merciless, the film-making being both callous and opportunistic, sharing in the guilt, taking advantage just as much as the audience of other people's misfortune to build his argument. There is a coolness, and objectivity that seems almost cruel and ruthless, to follow this image of human suffering by an image of, very specifically, art

going about its own business, as oblivious as the drugged young man and the audience wanting to be entertained.... The metaphor would then allude (without lessening the guilt shared among the drugged young man, the cinema audience, and the artsy film-maker) to the young man's closed eyes, but would focus on the process of reopening, of lifting veils of obscurence...

This is followed by a shot of a photographer (again, a stand-in for the film-maker)..., looking for something to film, shoot, contain within the lying objectivity of still photography in which just an instant is recorded. This image is a criticism of a whole art form, the fact that nothing has a valid reality outside the whole chain of images, which is what cinema is; so this image of non-artist (funny enough in itself) becomes just another underlining of the responsibility of the artist and view.[28]

He accurately described the mood of the film when he called it "breezy," "gracious," "agile, dynamic, spry with a hint of turbulence." In the end, the anguish of representing his often conflicting points of view on the gay community gives way to his growing confidence as a filmmaker. This confidence is compounded by an obscure allusion at the film's climax, after we have seen him piloting a boat, and a montage of views from the vessel moving through water: Familiar friends Dorsky and Hiler, who by this point in the film have become both the filmmaker's icon of the gay couple and his fellow filmmakers, are joined by an older man. Locking arms to pose for the camera, the irrepressible Hiler does a chorus line kick. The third man, it turns out, is the choreographer Jerome Robbins, Sonbert's lover at that time. The signature moment, then, is an outing of two couples, with the "guilty, artsy" filmmaker himself completing the foursome, while hiding behind the camera.

Noblesse Oblige is the companion piece to *Divided Loyalties*. The riots following the acquittal of Dan White for the homophobic murder of Harvey Milk and San Francisco Mayor George Moscone form one epicenter of this intense lyric, its danse macabre. The other is an epithalamium, ostensibly recording the wedding of a heterosexual couple but, I believe, indirectly celebrating the filmmaker's relationship with designer Ray Larsen, with whom he was to live until Larsen's death from AIDS complications in 1992.

There are at least three shots of Larsen in the film: The first shows him at his drafting table, drawing a straight line that becomes the sleek grid of the glass facade of an office building; one of him with Dorsky in a garden; another of him climbing a ladder up a tree. Elsewhere in the film, wedding

28. Sonbert, "Lecture, San Franciso Art Institute," p. 175.

and *Totendanz* conjoin for a moment in *Noblesse Oblige* with a shot in which a bride dances with figures in skeleton costumes.

Who are the nobility of the title? And what are their obligations? One the one hand, I presume they are homosexuals; their responsibilities include mutual self-defense and what the filmmaker had called the gay aesthetic of choice, "maintaining one's options." On the other hand, the nobility in the title are artists who are obliged to reveal the truth in all its complexity; for at the center of the film is a critique of news reportage, both written and televised. In his classroom notes on Sirk, Sonbert had written:

> Sirk, the uprooted emigré, sees the world and the subjects he under-
> takes with an anguished objectivity; observing, absorbing and re-
> flecting his material. Like Ozu, Sirk takes on the least facile task of
> presenting the present; what is accepted by custom, mores and stan-
> dards taken for granted, caste rules and stratifications, and qualifies
> them by his treatment and eye-of-God attitudes.[29]

More archly, he writes: "After you see [*There's Always Tomorrow*] you'll be glad you're not straight." Sirk himself shows up as the icon of artistic nobility at the end of the film: He is having coffee with Dorsky, Hiler, and by implication Sonbert.

Jon Gartenberg claimed the film was patterned after *Tarnished Angels*. Its protagonist of the film is a reporter (played by the gay icon Rock Hudson) for a New Orleans newspaper. (Mardi Gras pageantry and shots of newspaper offices are common to both Sirk's and Sonbert's films.) The trapeze artist stripping down to her underwear while swinging suspended by her hair in *Noblesse Oblige* echoes Dorothy Malone as the stunt-performing wife of the pilot the reporter has come to write about; her dramatic parachute act gives Sirk the excuse for several shots of her panties. He preceded Sonbert in the juxtaposition of carnival rides and flying feats.[30] There are images from *Tarnished Angels* on a bank of monitors in Sonbert's homage and a great deal of airplane imagery, including shots of stunt flying; there is even a little girl in an angel costume, untarnished. Doubtless, Sonbert believed the films of Sirk (as well as Hitchcock and Welles, who are part of the film's subtext) had access

29. Warren Sonbert, notes on Sirk's films.
30. But the erotic triangle of this screen adaptation of Faulkner's *Pylon* seems as remote from the core of *Noblesse Oblige* as do references to Hitchcock's *Topaz* Paul Arthur reported (cued by the filmmaker). See Jon Gartenburg, *Friendly Witnesses: The Worlds of Warren Sonbert*, catalog of the Solomon R. Guggenheim Museum Retrospective, April 21–May 8, 1999, New York; and Arthur, "Dancing on the Precipice," p. 58. There may be an erotic triangle obscurely inscribed in the film. In a prominent moment, a mustached man walks on the street in New York, tossing and catching a stick, which leads into the first shot of a stunt airplane. Dorsky identified this man as Sonbert's New York lover at the time of his liaison with Larsen.

to truth that escapes newspaper and television reporters. He describes them as severe moralists. For Sirk "the value of the community, of the family, of Church and State are seen as detrimental to the freedom of mind of the individual"; of Hitchcock, he wrote: "By having disturbed individuals for heroes, casting these parts with attractive and established stars and by deliberately using this technique [subjective realism] for identification, Hitchcock's scorn for the false values of his audience cannot be more clearly exemplified."[31]

Sirk's melodrama might have inspired the shots of circus performers failing to catch each other on the trampoline—perhaps taken at a rehearsal—and Hitchcock's *Topaz* may have encouraged Sonbert to include so many shots of Washington and its monuments in the film, and perhaps was even meant to suggest that the murders of Milk and Moscone could be part of a larger conspiracy.

Sonbert generally buffered his montage effects by intercalating a neutral shot between two dominant images. In this way he tended to separate cause and effect, distance metaphors, and suspend antitheses. He sometimes called them bridge shots or used culinary metaphors—after-dinner sherbets, palate cleansers, mints. This montage technique is as crucial to his style as Markopoulos's single-frame innovation had been to his. At the time Sonbert met Markopoulos, the older filmmaker had invented a new editing technique and had been writing short theoretical articles elaborating on its implications. In this technique, Markopoulos would anticipate a new shot with single-frame evocations and then insert single-frame echoes of the previous shot after the transition. The ephebe, ever conscious of the career dynamics of his metier, could not have missed the importance of this stylistic signature at the turning point of his mentor's lifework.

Frequently Sonbert's neutral intersepta were shots of actual bridges, often filmed from a moving vehicle. The spectacular opening of *Noblesse Oblige* exploits this literalization. First the shadow of an airplane descends for a landing in a witty reprise of a commonplace in American avant-garde cinema: here the shadow protagonists of *Meshes of the Afternoon* and *Anticipation of the Night* cede place to Sonbert, metonymically represented as the shadow of a jet. A glimpse of the elegant opera set, followed by fireworks, seems to place us in familiar territory. But then several shots of a crowd soberly observing something offscreen, without the typical buffers, suggest a new direction. (Eventually we conclude that they are keeping a vigil for the Moscone and Milk murders.) In a Vertovian trope, the filmmaker tentatively suggests they

---

31. Warren Sonbert, "Alfred Hitchcock: Master of Morality," *Film Culture* no. 41 (Summer 1966), pp. 36–37.

are looking at an industrial bridge, a static shot, for a few seconds. Then suddenly the bridge explodes, purposely demolished.

The staged shock of this constructed event reverberates through the film in several registers. Sonbert suggests with this that he is no longer only an artist taking his camera everywhere he goes, but one going to places where he knows there will be significant action; for without doubt the carefully composed shot of the collapsing bridge was no accident of inspired timing. Nor would the subsequent images of rioting following the acquittal of White be within the accustomed range of his filmmaking practice. Instead, much of the film is devoted to the imagery we might expect to see on television: a candlelight march, riot police marching and confronting protesters, news commentators talking into their microphones. There are some images that would have one sense on television but quite another in earlier Sonbert films: a marathon, a rodeo, a ticker tape parade, the Mardi Gras, and a wedding, which, like the events following the assassinations, were dispersed throughout the film.

The explosion of the bridge also announced the partial abandonment, for this urgent film at least, of the palate-cleansing intermediates. More than any of his previous films, *Noblesse Oblige* embraces Dionysian enthusiasm. Dionysus himself appears, in his traditional image as a handsome young man with a leopard, in the guise of a circus act. Sonbert allows him seven unbuffered shots, one even hinting at sexual congress with the beast. In detonating the bridgework, Sonbert risks losing his usual Apollonian distance, the freedom of mind, central to his theory of editing. Dangerous conjunctions become possible once the bridge shots are exploded but, more to the point, the reduction of the intersepta—nevertheless, they still play a major role in this film—allows the filmmaker to change the pace and exploit readjusted expectations. He knew, of course, that Nietzsche had postulated the marriage of Apollo and Dionysus as the birth of tragedy (and opera). He suggests in turn that the antithesis of tragedy is journalism, daily or nightly news.

In *Divided Loyalties*, Sonbert had set up a reproduction of a scene from the classic "newspaper film" *Citizen Kane*: His friends Jeff Scher and Susanne Fedak breakfast in an affluent house, dressed to recall the scenes of Kane and his wife breakfasting in which Welles signals the alienation of their marriage. He edited it together with the first appearance of the Castro Street festival and the buffer shot of a cemetery:

> [A]ll is vanity, almost of a biblical oppression, and lest anyone think this is rabidly anti-gay (which it is), this is followed by an affluent heterosexual couple..., a *Citizen Kane* quote, the pettiness of their supposed just-completed argument qualified by the gravestones image (why squabble when death is just around the corner)....So both straights and gays come into criticism and are linked to death and

dissolution: though one would never cut from one to the other, it is clear enough they are linked by the more neutral yet charged images of the cemetery.[32]

Kane, the yellow journalist, brags that he manufactures news and that his readers will think what he tells them to think. The protagonist of *Tarnished Angels* loses his job because he insists on sticking to the stunt flyers with whom he is passionately obsessed, rather than covering the visit of a politician. Sonbert throws in his lot with the cinematic nobility, with Sirk, Welles, and Hitchcock (whose *Topaz* fantasizes an unreported, secret truth behind the Cuban missile crisis) when he suggests that the truth of Gayist politics and of marriage requires (oblige) a tragic vision that is never news.

In 1983 he gave the Whitney Museum of American Art the following artist's statement:

> These films are accumulations of evidence. The images must be read: not only what narrative connotations are given off by the representational imagery as regards both language and figure-engaged activity, but also the constructive signposts of point-of-view, exposure, composition, color, directional pulls and the textural overlay. But in film the solo image is akin to an isolated chord; the kinetic thrust emerges with montage. That process expands, deflates, contradicts, reinforces or qualifies. It is this specific and directed placement that provides film with both its structure and its freedom.
>
> Film can do flips, is acrobatic. A highly charged shot, though still potentially balanced by a multitude of suggestibles, may in turn, by replacement by a more neutral image, shift into objectivity the initial heightened response. This play with expectations, both frustrated and enhanced, constitutes a reason to look at the screen. The variables of an image, its visual qualities being punctuation, swell to a series of statements, whose provocative strains demand a measured vigilance of the viewer, when editing can either underline, comment upon or upset the fluctuating contiguities. This is not to say that the possible pleasure produced refuses rigor, but rather the cerebral sleight-of-hand implies control.[33]

32. Sonbert, "Lecture, San Francisco Art Institute," p. 173. Scher and Fedak appear on the street in *Noblesse Oblige* (as they do in many Sonbert films; they are the heterosexual counterpart of Dorsky and Hiler in his private mythology) with a *Citizen Kane* reference.

33. Warren Sonbert, "Artist's Statement," New American Filmmakers Series 10, Oct 11–23, 1983, Whitney Museum of American Art, [one two-sided sheet of notes].

The clause "a highly charged shot…may…shift into objectivity" may provide us with a key to Sonbert's problematic representation of selfhood in his films. If a shot may shift into objectivity, it may also emanate its subjective connotation. In Brakhage's work, such "suggestibles" are ubiquitous and ineluctable. Even though, for Sonbert, Brakhage was the equivalent of Emerson's orphic poet, a liberating god—he called him "the great hero of film history…who 'liberated' film"[34]—he did not concede to him the inescapably subjective status of all cinematic images. One way that montage may shift into the domain of objectivity would be to trope the omniscient fictive world of narrative cinema, where Hitchcock and, above all, Sirk are his primary exemplars.

The achievement of Sonbert's art is to keep fast to the area where several potentials remain in effect, the zone in which the filmmaker's apperception of his rhetorical options (cerebral sleight of hand) takes account of the viewer's play of expectations. He bifurcated his sensibility into that of the magician and his audience. Sonbert astutely recognized the role of language in this process. The didactic analysis he made of the passage following the image of "the dazed bleeding man" nearly construed the image sequence as a rebus. At that theoretical juncture, he was at his farthest from Brakhage, who strove to disengage and transcend the naming process through photographic, kinetic, and editing strategies. His hypothetical abolition of linguistic mediation excluded any consideration of the expectations of an imagined viewer.

34. Sonbert, "Lecture, San Franciso Art Institute," p. 161.

CHAPTER II

Brakhage and the Tales of the Tribes

I ntroducing Andrei Tarkovsky to an audience at the Telluride
Film Festival in 1985, Stan Brakhage declared:

> I personally think that the three greatest tasks for film in the
> 20th century are 1) To make the epic, that is, to tell the tales of
> the tribes of the world. 2) To keep it personal, because only in the
> eccentricities of our personal lives do we have any chance at the
> truth. 3) To do the dream work, that is to illuminate the borders
> of the unconscious.[1]

Although he praised Tarkovsky as "the greatest living narrative film maker"
and the only one who "does all these three things equally in every film he
makes," Brakhage seems to have been acclaiming Tarkovsky for independently replicating his own agenda, most obviously in the requirements for
personal filmmaking and explorations of "the dream work." In the more than

---

1. Stan Brakhage, "Brakhage Pans Telluride Gold," *Rolling Stock* 6 (1983), p. 11.

two decades since he made that introduction, Brakhage accelerated his own version of affirming the tales of the tribe: Pueblo Indians, Dante, Marlowe, Goethe, Novalis, Stephen Foster, D. H. Lawrence, Rilke, Mann, and Stein have been evoked in the titles and themes of various films.

An even more revelatory catachresis of the words *telling* and *tales*—implicitly acknowledged by Brakhage's use of quotation marks—appeared in a theoretical text of 1993:

> Some ur-consciousness also then must be inferred—each cell both shaper and carrier of every spark struck from and through it, affected by each impulse-backlash and in synaptical montage with each previous and following impulse: the whole organism feeding its varieties-of-fire into this interplay between brain and eye, as finally each cell of the foetal body can be intuited to be "telling" its "story" interactive with every other cell's story throughout the developing body, over-ridden by some entirety of rhythming light (as every individual heart-cell is conjoined to the dominating beat of each heart-part's over-riding beat) in the conglomerate rhythm of the whole heat-light of any given organ...of which each cell is a radical part compromised by every other cell's variable interaction, all contributory to the organic "tales" of these cells in concert.[2]

Through an ironic loop in the history of avant-garde film theory, here Brakhage offers, in 1993, a physiological phantasmagoria in justification of what Hollis Frampton facetiously called Brakhage's theorem (1972)—that all films are narrative. More narrowly conceived, the biblical and classical tales of the tribes have been elliptically retold in Brakhage's films, off and on, since the 1950s: Oedipus (*The Way to Shadow Garden,* 1954), the descent to the underworld (*The Dead, Dante's Styx,* 1975), the Sinai theophany (*Blue Moses*), apocalypse (*Oh Life, A Woe Story, The A Test News,* 1963), Genesis (*Creation,* 1979), the Fall (*The Machine of Eden, The Animals of Eden and After*), the vision of Isaiah (*The Peaceable Kingdom,* 1971), the afterlife and Orpheus (*Dante Quartet*), and Plato's allegory of the cave (*Visions in Meditation #3,* 1987).

Creation is the purest and most powerful example of the many films of vehicular motion in the Brakhage corpus. In it he recorded a visit to Alaskan glaciers during the period he was completing the *Sincerity/Duplicity* series. The proximate inspiration for the sublime vision of a world of massive ice and scarred rock was the art of the nineteenth-century American landscape

---

2. Stan Brakhage, "Time...on dit," *Musicworks* 55 (Spring 1993, Toronto), p. 56.

painter Frederic Edwin Church, whose works the filmmaker had been studying for more than a decade. Behind Church's paintings of icebergs lay a rich
pictorial and literary tradition highlighted by Caspar David Friedrich's Arctic
scenes and the Antarctic fantasy of Poe, in his conclusion to *The Narrative of
A. Gordon Pym.*

David Huntington called upon Church's writings to supply the spiritual
context of his art:

> The artist, we read in *The Crayon* in 1857, should restore things "to
> what they were at Creation." Or, on another page of the same journal,
> he should paint "the image of the World redeemed."...The Ameri-
> can created a natural God. Church used the method of a Raphael
> or a Poussin to invent the perfect Creation....To borrow a line of
> Emerson's quoted in praise of [*The Heart of the Andes*], it was "a fairer
> creation than we know."[3]

The conclusion of Brakhage's film seeks some of the restorative energy
Huntington associates with Church. Gerald Carr's paraphrase of the kind of
allegorical interpretation of the 1861 masterpiece *The Icebergs* Church and his
contemporaries encouraged could almost describe *Creation*:

> Under the genial influences of late afternoon light and summer
> winds and currents, a marvel of nature's poetry unfolds before our
> eyes....What had in "dull atmosphere" been "dead white,—ghastly
> and spiritless" (Church's own words) the sun kindles with evanescent
> hues and tints, the most limpid, tender and pure. Angles of crag and
> scarp flash and sparkle. Surfaces of satin and velvet "flicker and fade."
> Transfigured, the elements "glow and quiver." Born of the realm of
> eternal winter, "a miracle of beauty" proclaims "the moving pres-
> ence of the Lord." In this moment of transcendence spirit and matter
> are regenerated as one. For the spectator of 1861, The Icebergs was a
> promise of Nature's and Man's immortality.[4]

However, in 1979 Brakhage would probably have treated with irony
the Judeo-Christian theology underpinning this passage: For him the natural phenomenon was primary; the Judeo-Christian God was a trope to

---

3. David C. Huntington, *The Landscapes of Frederic Edwin Church* (New York: George Braziller, 1966),
pp. 51–52.
4. Gerald L. Carr, *Frederic Edwin Church: The Icebergs* (Dallas: Dallas Museum of Fine Arts, 1980), p. 18.

domesticate and ventriloquize the natural sublime.[5] So the phrasing of imagery in *Creation* mimics a skewed version of the opening chapter of Genesis, from which he derives his title. Sweeping over a surface of dramatic lights and darks like the divine wind, camera shortly discovers water. A few minutes later in a brilliant and dramatic coup, Brakhage suggests the division of the waters into upper and lower, heaven and earth, by flipping the filmstrip over, so that icebergs seem to hang down from a fluid sky. Thus by boldly reversing top and bottom, as well as forward and backward motion, Brakhage presents the gorgeous illusions of airborne icebergs flowing backward as indeed illusionary. As in *Blue Moses* and in the biblical allusions in *Metaphors on Vision*, he draws attention to the trope—above for below, forward for backward—in order to qualify its representational force and in so doing evacuates the religious and moral intimidation driving the sublime invention of the priestly cosmologist of Genesis.

But in the balance between the filmmaker as a skeptic and critic of referential authority and the filmmaker as the Emersonian celebrant of newfound vision and inventive vitality, Brakhage comes down strongly on the visionary side. As early as 1960, in a scenario quoted in *Metaphors on Vision*, he had remarked on Novalis's visionary postulation of a heavenly river: "'Where is the stream?' cried he, with tears, 'Seest thou not its blue waves above us?' He looked up, and lo! the blue stream was flowing gently over their heads." In that early grant proposal, for the idealized "dailiness film," he promised to reconcile Novalis's "mystic" vision with Eddington's description of the dynamism of atomic physics; it was to be made "taking no image for granted," so that the filmmaker could set forth his cyclic theory of nature and imagination: "A walk with our child can transform forests into the fairylands which they originally inspired." Here each creative act is a recovery of an earlier, original, trope. Thus the opening narrative of Genesis would be a reorganization of a number of spontaneous perceptual figurations, primal myths of nature, powerfully rearrayed in a dramatic sequence to persuade hearers that the narrator is aligned with an awesome power. As he retells the tales of the tribes of the world, Brakhage exposes the religious rhetoric and recovers the original inspiration behind it. In that sense his somewhat playful repetition of Genesis is his own "*Creation*."

---

5. Brakhage's public statement on his belief in God ("Having Declared a Belief in God," *Telling Time: Essays of a Visionary Filmmaker* (Kingston, N.Y.: Documentext, 2003), pp. 135–36; originally published in *Musicworks* 63, Fall 1995) and his subsequent claim that he had always remained a Christian does not alter the fact that he was a penetrating critic of the rhetoric of religious revelation in *Metaphors on Vision*, *Dog Star Man*, *Blue Moses*, *The Animals of Eden and After*, *Creation*, and *Christ Mass Sex Dance*. His reading of Spinoza in the early 1960s profoundly shaped his view of political theology.

The organization of material in *Creation* unmistakably follows the basic biblical scenario although even before the division of the waters, Brakhage introduces images of vegetation, as masses of fog rise from pine-covered mountains. The rhythmic intercutting of forward and flipped movement through the glaciers incorporates shifts of lighting suggestive of day and night. Later the water is alive with living creatures—seals—and only then do birds fly under the vault of heaven. But subsequently the most startling shots in the film appear: two glimpses of Jane Brakhage—her face, then her hands, perhaps the only stilled images in the whole film. A little later, a man, perhaps a fisherman, briefly appears, the only other human in *Creation*, as if the formula were "female and male created He them."

Formally and psychologically, the two shots of Jane are not integrated into the rhythmic fabric of the film; they bring us up short by surprise, for the intentional structure of the camera movements and the boat's movement had tacitly implied that the filmmaker was alone. By contrast, from its beginning Menken's *Excursion* stressed that she was with companions amid a jostling crowd, the heirs of Whitman's ferryboat passengers. And the gliding camera of *Ai-Ye* posits Hugo guided and navigated by natives through the Mexican swamps. But Brakhage pretends to be so utterly alone in the Alaskan bay that his persona imperceptibly emerges from an embodiment of the divine wind itself. Wordsworth famously startles his readers when he discloses after 115 lines of "Tintern Abbey" that his sister, Dorothy, has been with him the whole time. Nothing could have been further from Brakhage's mind when he edited *Creation* than Wordsworth's abrupt shift from the egotistical sublime to the tutelage of Dorothy's "flashing eyes." Nevertheless, his film re-enacts Wordsworth's uneasy shift from solitude to companionship.

Similarly, Brakhage surprises us when he reveals, in *Metaphors on Vision*, that Marie Menken and Kenneth Anger had accompanied him into Père Lachaise cemetery when he filmed *The Dead*. There is a brief image of Anger at the beginning of the film but none of Menken. (Of course, she played the same game with Anger herself, pretending to be alone in the Alhambra and indirectly acknowledging his companionship in the dedicatory title *Arabesque for Kenneth Anger*.) But even more interesting is the silent and unseen accompaniment of Marilyn Jull during their courtship as Brakhage filmed *Faust IV* and *Visions in Meditation*, as we shall see.

To comprehend the moment Jane enters *Creation*, we must consider just what Brakhage did to make the film. Obviously he visited Alaska with his wife; they took a boat ride as tourists, probably with other tourists framed out of the film. Brakhage was at great pains to eliminate almost all traces of other people or signs of civilization in filming the landscape, which probably reminded him of Church's Labrador. The two shots of Jane could have been taken anywhere, perhaps even indoors. In fashioning the material he brought back to his editing room, the filmmaker gave precedence to the smooth movement through water that the shots from the boat gave him; he supercharged some of these shots with visionary power and wit by running the film upside down and backward. He fleshed out this firm skeleton by a slow transformation of the landscape: The starkest images appear early, the vegetation and shafts of sunlight near the end.

Sometime in this formative process, perhaps from the start, he realized that he could order the seventeen-and-a-half-minute film with allusions to the priestly narrative of creation that opens Genesis, ending in a suggestion of the Jahwist's Eden that occurs in the second chapter. Thereby Jane enters the film: as the first human figure, the female, wife, friend, or dedicatee, but not touching the being of the fictive isolato behind the moving camera, and not as the Eve-like presence she had been in his earlier films.

There is a theoretical and historical dimension, as well as a practical one, to this kind of self-representation. For Emerson, "The American Scholar" is the American artist: "The poet, in utter solitude remembering his spontaneous thoughts and recording them, is found to have recorded that which men in crowded cities find true of them also.... [T]he better part of any man feels, This is my music; this is myself."[6] The invention of solitude is a crux for Brakhage's cinema. In 1963 he concluded the introduction to *Metaphors on Vision*, an interview, with a variant on Emerson's conjunction of solitude and universality that swerves into a connubial mystical union:

> I would say I grew very quickly as an artist once I got rid of drama as prime source of inspiration. I began to feel that all history, all life, all that I would have as material with which to work, would have to come from the inside of me out rather than as some form imposed from the outside in. I had the concept of everything radiating out of me, and that the more personal or egocentric I would become, the deeper I would reach and the more I could touch those universal concerns which would involve all man. What seems to have happened since marriage is that I no longer sense ego as the greatest source for what can touch on the universal. I now feel that there is some concrete center where love from one person to another meets; and that the more total view arises from there.... Where I take action strongest and most immediately is in reaching through the power of all that love toward my wife, (and she toward me) and somewhere where those actions meet and cross, and bring forth children and films and inspire

---

6. Ralph Waldo Emerson, *Essays and Lectures* (New York: Library of America, 1983), p. 64–65.

concerns with plants and rocks and all sights seen, a new center, composed of action, is made.[7]

In nuce this testament even prophesies the outline of the first three parts of *Sincerity*: the egocentric election as filmmaker, the connubial dialogue as geographical movement, and the finding and founding of a new center. However, Emerson's election is radically self-reliant; in the eponymous essay he tropes the severe demands of Elijah and Jesus: "I shun father and mother and wife and brother when my genius calls me." When Brakhage follows suit it is with intense resistance and in pain, in large part because he so fiercely willed "by Brakhage" to mean " 'by way of Stan and Jane and the children Brakhage' because all the discoveries which used to pass only thru the instrument of myself are coming to pass thru the sensibilities of those I love." So to acknowledge his creative solitude is to confess duplicities; it may even be to recognize in the alternation of sincerities and duplicities the systaltic rhythm that founds "the music of myself" and motivates the assembling of ever larger and more complex series of films.

Throughout the 1970s Brakhage periodically sought solitude to find "the music of myself" in the landscapes of high Romanticism: the enchanted forest of *The Wold Shadow* (1972), fields of luminosity revealed in intense absorption with the glass ashtray of *The Text of Light* (1974), or the stark wilderness of *Desert* (1976). But in *Creation* the brief images of Jane break the illusion of solitude without pushing the film toward the exploration of being-with-others that voyeuristically drives the Pittsburgh Trilogy of 1971 (*eyes* with the police, *Deus Ex* with a surgical team in an operating room, and *The Act of Seeing with One's Own Eyes* with a coroner performing an autopsy) or the explicitly scopophilic *Sexual Meditations* of 1970–72.

The shots of Jane are so still and separated from the Alaskan environs that they check the dilation set in motion by the frisson of isolation in the landscape, and heightened by the camera motion and rhythmic editing, before it is even clear that another order of disturbance is embedded in the composition of the two shots: Jane is absorbed by something unseen offscreen; for an instant Brakhage shows us her hands, still in her lap, the left hand curled and empty. This is unique among the hundreds of portraits he filmed of his first wife. Repeatedly he had shown her either addressing the camera with love, anger, or embarrassment, or engaged with her children or animals, or silently absorbed (but with the object of her concentration represented in the frame or through editing). Of course we may conclude that the passing landscape

7. Stan Brakhage, *Metaphors on Vision* (New York: *Film Culture* no. 30, 1963), pages unnumbered.

enthralls Jane too in these brief shots, but the film refuses to make that explicit
and in that reticence underscores her separation from the filmmaker.

The disturbance of the genre—of the solitary filmmaker overwhelmed
by awesome nature—may be the point, or part of the point, of *Creation*. It
reflects the crisis of *Sincerity IV* and *V* in a sublime rhetoric; that is to say, the
film sublimates the failure or decay of the "new center, composed of action"
heralded sixteen years earlier. Like his model, Frederic Church, who painted
his Edenic visions of Jamaica immediately following the tragic loss of two
of his children to diphtheria, Brakhage achieves an optimistic resolution to
his examination of the bleak Arctic bay in the last five minutes of the film by
contrasting the surging waters and the flinty crags with a vision of verdant
northern woodlands and sunlight piercing vaults of leaves. In this personal
and dreamlike retelling of a tale of the tribes of the world, he enacts a spiritual
renovation through an homage to one of his artistic heroes in a crisis film
that surprisingly parallels the evolving form of his visual autobiography, the
Sincerity films.

The crisis deepened; the marriage ended. Through the last six years of that
crisis, Brakhage painted and edited off and on the four-part, eight-minute
film that would become *The Dante Quartet* in 1987. If *Creation* brought the
filmmaker's meditations on Genesis and Frederic Church together, *The Dante
Quartet* drew upon his readings of the *Commedia*, Blake's *The Marriage of
Heaven and Hell*, Rilke's *Sonnets to Orpheus*, and Parker Tyler's *The Divine
Comedy of Pavel Tchelitchew*, as well as Robert Rauschenberg's illustrations
to the *Inferno*. He would have seen *A Modern Inferno*, the six-page series of
collage drawings Rauschenberg did for *Life* (December 17, 1965) before he
had access to John Chamberlain's copy of the limited edition of the thirty-
four illustrations, one for each canto, the artist had made between 1959 and
1960. The fusion of transfer photographs, watercolor, gouache, and pencil
that Rauschenberg first used in this series bore superficial resemblances to the
mixture of painting, staining, and scratching over previously photographed
images Brakhage had employed independently in *Dog Star Man: Prelude*
(1961) and *Thigh Line Lyre Triangular* (1961). The study of Rauschenberg's
drawings encouraged his elaboration of the technique in *The Horseman, the
Woman, and the Moth* (1968) and in subsequent films partially or wholly
hand painted.

Brakhage's Dante is a poet of visionary and visual discriminations, rather
than the social prophet of cosmic justice and redemption, and his homage
to him is a series of hand-painted films inspired by hypnogogic vision. By
making a quartet of the three cantiche of the *Commedia*, from the start he
dramatically rejects the triadic, trinitarian, infrastructure of the epic in *terza
rima*. Tyler's 1967 biography of Tchelitchew, actually an allegory of artistic
life, had tutored the filmmaker to read Dante's poem as a ritual of terrestrial

life, while triggering an obsessive worry that no modern artist can complete a *Paradiso*; for he compared Tyler's discussion of his subject's death before he could finish the third of his major paintings with Ezra Pound's fragmentary final Cantos.[8]

Brakhage to Ganguly:

> The four parts are *Hell Itself*, *Hell Spit Flexion*, *Purgation*, and *existence is song*, and they appear in that order.... I made *Hell Itself* during the breakup with Jane and the collapse of my whole life, so I got to know quite well the streaming of the hypnogogic process that's hellish. Now the body can not only feed back its sense of being in hell but also its getting out of hell, and *Hell Spit Flexion* shows the way out—it's there as a crowbar to lift one out of hell toward the transformatory state—purgatory. And finally there's a fourth state that's fleeting. I've called this last part *existence is song* quoting Rilke, because I don't want to presume upon the after-life and call it "Heaven". So what I tried to do in the quartet was to bring down to earth Dante's vision, inspired by what's on either side of one's nose and right before the eyes: a movie that reflects the nervous system's basic sense of being.[9]

Painting the first and fourth parts on the broad expanse of IMAX film stock, *Hell Spit Flexion* (1981) in 35 mm, and *Purgation* over bits of a 70 mm CinemaScope print of Billy Wilder's *Irma la Douce*, Brakhage fueled his painstaking labor with fantasies of seeing his Dante series projected on an immense screen—the type used at the National Space Museum or at World Trade Expositions. The minimal iconography befits the monumental scale of this conception: broad swirls of color, latticeworks of cracked paint, holes and crevices of white light bore through a throbbing wall of blended hues. Only *Hell Itself* lacks photographic imagery. The optical printing, holding some frames as long as half a second, retards its thick churning motion, then spasmodically accelerates and decelerates it, in three unequally long phrases. It has a creamy white base that engulfs and slowly seems to push across the screen the red-orange-yellow blends and the pure blues and blacks that enter it.

Hell Spit Flexion (separately released in 1983) sits framed in the center of the screen, a film within a film. At first a whirl of camera-generated images prevails—blurs, a pure blue frame as if of the sky, the disc of a solar corona—before a thick layering of ochreous paint shimmering on a black base takes precedence.

---

8. At the end of his life, Brakhage confronted this issue when he made his longest hand-painted film, *Panels for the Walls of Heaven* (2002), as the fourth and final part of his Vancouver Island series.

9. Suranjan Ganguly, "All That Is Light: Brakhage at 60," *Sight and Sound* (London), October 1993, p. 26.

Brakhage's note reveals the source of its rasping rhythm, as if coughing up a phlegm of cosmic fragments:

> My moving-visual response to William Blake's 'The Marriage of Heaven and Hell,' this hand-painted film seems the most rhythmically exact of all my work: it was inspired by memories of an old man coughing in the night of a thin-walled ancient hotel.[10]

Reading Blake's repudiation of religious orthodoxy and the elevation of poetry as prophecy in *The Marriage of Heaven and Hell*, Brakhage would have encountered a powerful formulation of the position implicit in his use of scripture from *Blue Moses* and *Metaphors on Vision* in the early 1960s through *Creation* in 1979:

> The ancient Poets animated all sensible objects with Gods or Geniuses....
> Till a system was formed, which some took advantage of & enslav'd the vulgar by attempting to realize or abstract the mental deities from their objects; thus began Priesthood.
> Choosing forms of worship from poetic tales....
> Have now another plain fact: Any man of mechanical talents may from the writings of Paracelsus or Jacob Behmen, produce ten thousand volumes of equal value with Swedenborg's, and from those of Dante or Shakespear an infinite number.[11]

Inserting the autonomous *Hell Spit Flexion* into the triad may be Brakhage's indirect way of saying he cannot retrace Dante's theological pilgrimage without subscribing to Blake's dialectical identity of the poles. The fiery volcano is not a signpost in hell; the movement from pure paint to complex fusions of paint and photography is not a valuation or a progression, as Brakhage's concentration on hand-painted films in the 1990s witnesses.

A less flamboyant articulation of the superiority of revelation through poetry to religious dogma could be found in Emerson himself. Consider this skimming of points from "The Over-Soul":

> When I watch that flowing river, which, out of regions I see not, pours for a season its streams into me, I see that I am a pensioner; not a

---

10. *Film-makers' Cooperative Catalogue No. 7* (New York: Film-makers' Cooperative, 1989, p. 61.
11. David V. Erdman, ed., *The Poetry and Prose of William Blake* (New York: Doubleday, 1965), pp. 37, 42.

cause, but a surprised spectator of this ethereal water; that I desire and look up, and put myself in the attitude of reception, but from some alien energy the visions come.... From within or from behind, a light shines through upon things, and makes us aware that we are nothing, but the light is all.... Men ask concerning the immortality of the soul, the employments of heaven, the state of the sinner, and so forth. They even dream that Jesus has left replies to precisely these interrogatories. Never a moment did that sublime figure speak in their *patois*.... The moment the doctrine of the immortality is separately taught, man is already fallen.... By the same fire, vital, consecrating, celestial, which burns until it shall dissolve all things into the waves and surges of an ocean of light, we see and know each other, and what spirit each is of.... There is, in all great poets, a wisdom of humanity which is superior to any talents they exercise.... The reliance upon authority measures the decline of religion, the withdrawal of the soul.[12]

Ever subtle, Emerson's writing so possesses the national aesthetic sensibility that it frequently goes unnoted and unacknowledged. The alienated strangeness of Blake's ironic vision seemed to have attracted Brakhage's attention, but concepts liker those as articulated in "The Over-Soul" are so familiar, so thoroughly incorporated in the American artistic psyche, that they evade notice despite the closeness of Emerson's metaphors—fire and oceans of light—to Brakhage's practice.

The base of *Purgation* is clear leader, so that the pure white light of the projector radiates though the gaps, holes, and cracks in the veils of paint and—more dimly—filmed images. All the paint, dominantly red with a strong presence of blue, is mixed with black, heightening the intensity of the white light.

The longest section has nearly twenty fades to blackness articulating its many transitions. It consistently points to and at the same time obscures a nearly eradicated liminal imagery behind the skein of paint and stellar suggestions of white light Brakhage put over the vestiges of *Irma la Douce*. Perhaps the underlying shots are of a Parisian studio seen from outside; for a window or door frame can be discerned. Later a man in sunglasses appears, either looking through a window or as a framed photograph. All that seems to matter is the suggestion of a passage for light and perhaps movement, and a figure whose gaze cannot (yet) bear the light or transit the frame. Giving new meaning—by painting over and scratching marks for light to break through

12. Emerson, *Essays and Lectures*, pp. 385, 387, 393–94, 396, 399.

the Hollywood image—is Brakhage's act of purgation, working through the suspended time between the trauma of his divorce and a renewal.

Parker Tyler, reading deeply into Tchelitchew's painting *Hide and Seek*, interpreted purgatory as the experience of childhood: "Purgatory is the very realm of anticipation. And so is childhood.... [It] can be nothing but expectation; whatever is suffering it is illuminated with hope and a strong feeling for the future; as involved with a sense of Fate and Fortune, further, it is combinatory."[13] Brakhage does not follow Tyler's association of purgatory and childhood, as far as I can see, but "suffering...illuminated with hope and a strong feeling for the future...a sense of Fate and Fortune" could be a gloss on the segment, pointing toward the recessive thresholds in deep space that seem to draw us through the painted atmosphere, an anticipation of the light, to reverse playfully Brakhage's early title.

Blue predominates in the palette of *existence is song*, the climax of the quartet and its most eloquent part. The almost obscured opening image might have descended from *Bells of Atlantis*. One gets a fleeting impression of underwater coral, blue on blue, before the darkened paint, a mixture of blues and reds, fuses that image with an even more fleeting suggestion of the craterous surface of the moon. The ensuing phrase, a wrestling match of blue and red, culminates in a quick, gorgeous series of red volcanic eruptions behind the wall of paint. In the final imageless minute of the film there is more blue paint than anywhere previously. So we can conclude that Brakhage follows the symbolical association, favored by medieval and Renaissance painters, of blue as the heavenly color, even if he might prefer to argue that the findings of his neuro-optical apperception can tell us something about the origins of that symbolism (without contradicting the economic argument that the conspicuous use of very expensive azure pigment gave added value to celestial representations).

Brakhage's earlier efforts at hand painting on film had been tied to his study of closed-eye vision (as in *Dog Star Man* and *Thigh Line Lyre Triangular*). The self-scrutiny of his visual imagination during the 1970s brought with it the more comprehensive formulation of "moving visual thinking," an idea which, according to Bruce Elder,

> is fabulously elusive; it seems, however, to have to do with a transitional form of awareness that exists only fleetingly, and mostly without our being consciously aware of its contents. These are in any case indefinite and without rigid boundaries, for they are the forms of incipient percepts before the mind has labeled them as belonging to a

13. Parker Tyler, *The Divine Comedy of Pavel Tchelitchew* (New York: Fleet, 1967), pp. 119–20.

certain type, and has filled out the details of their shapes.... Brakhage
described "moving visual thinking" as a form of awareness close to
the actual excitement of the nervous system [–]... awareness before it
develops into the visual forms of focused attention.[14]

The hand-painted films that gradually came to dominate his oeuvre in the
1990s are forays into visual ontology, prepared by the "imagnostic" *Roman
Numeral* and *Arabic* series (1979–81). Thus, the trilogy *I Take These Truths, We
Hold These,* and *I...* (all from 1995) are efforts to invoke respectively a visual
field of self-evident a priori truths, a commonality of abstract vision, and the
optical signature peculiar to the filmmaker.

During the formative years of Brakhage's career, probably unknown to
him, Anton Ehrenzweig formulated a theory of creativity that runs parallel
to his own ideas. *The Psycho-analysis of Artistic Vision and Hearing* (1953) argued the importance of nonfocused vision for painters and saw the work of
Cezanne and his successors in modern and abstract art as representing that
vision. Ehrenzweig elaborated on Freud's interpretations of jokes and dreams
in his efforts to enlarge the theories of artistic perception he derived from
gestalt psychologists. In *The Hidden Order of Art* (1967) Ehrenzweig turned
to the psychoanalytic concept of primary process, the oceanic undifferenti-
ated structure of the unconscious in which multiple perspectives and contradictory values coexist timelessly, for theoretical support of the aesthetics of
unfocused vision of what he then called dedifferention. For him the creative
process operates on an alternating rhythm of incorporation and projection
that corresponds to oral and anal phases of infantile development.

The affinities between Brakhage's interpretation of his own work and Ehrenzweig's analysis of art grow more evident in the light of the filmmaker's
description of the *Roman Numeral Series* as films "which explore... that pre-
language, pre-'picture' realm of the mind which provides the physical *grounds*
for image making (imagination)" and the *Arabics* as "formed by the intrinsic
grammar of the most inner (perhaps pre-natal) structure of thought itself."[15]
The dynamics of eye scanning and peripheral vision—foci of Ehrenzweig's
initial investigations—had been central to Brakhage's art since the mid-1950s,
but with the imagnostic films he centered his attention on the arena of dedif-
ferentiated oceanic vision, the subliminal perception of a ground that absorbs
all figures, which Ehrenzweig postulated was the foundation of all fantasies.
Painting on film subsequently provided Brakhage with a means to recontact

14. Bruce Elder, "On Brakhage," in *Stan Brakhage; A Retrospective 1977–1995* (New York: Museum of Modern Art, 1995), unnumbered pages.
15. *Film-makers' Cooperative Catalogue No. 7* , p. 58.

both the oral and anal levels of that fantasy formation. In *The Dante Quartet*, brief glimpses of an erupting volcano and the craters of the moon are what Ehrenzweig called poemagogic images:

> I have coined the term "poemagogic" to describe [the] special function of inducing and describing the ego's creativity.... Poemagogic images, in their enormous variety, reflect the various phases of creativity in a very direct manner, though the central theme of death and rebirth, of trapping and liberations, seems to overshadow the others.[16]

At the climax of Brakhage's quartet, these images mark the exchange between anal and oral expression (to use Ehrenzweig's dichotomy). The note to *Hell Spit Flexion*, invoking a primal scene of expectoration, confirms by (free) association the fantasy complex driving the film: the "old man coughing at night" displaces the mythic idea of Cronus swallowing and regurgitating his divine children; he is confined to Tartarus with Typhon, whose fury produces volcanoes. In his later hand-painted films, the poemagogic images, allegorical of the psychodynamics of creativity, tend to disappear, but nevertheless he vividly reasserted the antithetical juxtaposition of oral pleasure and anal anxiety in the title of *Delicacies of Molten Horror Synapse* (1991).

The story of *The Dante Quartet*, as we glean it from Brakhage's catalog notes and interview statements, is that there is a way out of the spasmic magma of hellish proprioception: an optical reflex, like the rhythmic expectoration of phlegm, transits through a liminal stage of purgation into the realm of song, where the psychic and somatic narrative is sublimated in orphic and Promethean myths: The earth sings in perpetual, volcanic self-creation. Frederic Church once again was among Brakhage's Virgilian guides in this revelation of tellurian ecstasy when he painted the volcanic landscape of Cotopaxi in 1863.

Brakhage takes the titles of his *Paradiso* from Rilke's *Sonnets to Orpheus*, book 1, sonnet 3: "existence is song." The ontological force of the revelation is more evident in the German: Gesang ist Dasein. Brakhage would have noted, of course, that Rilke wrote all twenty-six orphic sonnets of the first book in an inspired trance lasting three days; for he has often spoken of the trance of motor dictation that drives his filmmaking and of the necessity of his obedience to a muse. When Rilke writes "Gesang ist Dasein," he reveals the identity of Being and poetry at the core of his trance: He must make his songs in order to exist; and the subject of his songs is that Being sings.

---

16. Anton Ehrenzweig, *The Hidden Order of Art: A Study in the Psychology of Artistic Imagination* (Berkeley: University of California Press, 1971), pp. 176–77.

Brakhage identified the term *song* as crucial to his sense of his own work. He elaborated on it to Suranjan Ganguly:

Ganguly: Looking back over 40 years of film-making, what matters most now?

That I believe in song. That's what I wanted to do and I did it quite selfishly, out of my own need to come through to a voice that is comparable with song and related to all animal life on earth. I believe in the beauty of the singing of the whale; I am moved deeply at the whole range of song that the wolf makes when the moon appears, or neighborhood dogs make—that they make their song, and this is the wonder of life on earth, and I in great humility wish to join this.[17]

Rilke's artificial, mythologized evocation of Orpheus and Greek divinities may be more conformable for Brakhage than Dante's conviction of the Trinity. In the stanza from which he takes his title for the segment, the addressee is ambiguous: perhaps Apollo or the young, dead dancer to whom the sonnets are dedicated:

> Song, as you teach it, is not desire,
> not suing for something yet in the end attained;
> song is existence. Easy for the god.
> But when do we exist? and when does he
> spend the earth and stars upon our being?[18]

Dante's quest for Beatrice and Orpheus's descent to Eurydice may well have suggested to the filmmaker at this time his loss of his wife (through divorce, not death). Turning to the poets while painstakingly painting film frames for several years during this crisis, Brakhage refound what he had discovered in *23rd Psalm Branch*: the meaning of "song." In the 1966 film he had photographed the pages of Louis Zukofsky's *A:11* beginning "Song, my song, raise grief to music" as the motto for transforming into art his compound agony over the Vietnam War and over the mass protests against it.

Emerson, mourning the death of his young son, wrote in "Experience" of surviving loss:

But the longest love or aversion has a speedy term. The great and crescive self, rooted in absolute nature, supplants all relative existence

17. Ganguly, "All That Is Light," p. 23.
18. Rainer Maria Rilke, *Sonnets to Orpheus*, trans. M. D. Herter Norton (New York: Norton, 1942), p. 21.

and ruins the kingdom of mortal friendship and love. Marriage
(in what is called the spiritual world) is impossible, because of the
inequality between every subject and every object.... All I know is
reception; I am and I have: but I do not get, and when I have fancied
that I had gotten anything, I found I did not. I worship with wonder
the great Fortune.[19]

As Brakhage once implied of Zukofsky, he now indicates, quoting Rilke,
what Emerson affirmed in response to all genuine poetry: "This is my music;
this is myself." In *The Dante Quartet* Brakhage puts the hand-painted film on
a new basis: The colored rhythms become the ground of Being, the matrix
for condensing his intimations of prenatal and postmortem vision and for
making a place for cinema within the music of thanatotopic poetics.

19. Emerson, *Essays and Lectures*, pp. 487–88, 491.

CHAPTER 12

Frampton's *Magellan*

$\mathbf{B}$y the time he completed *Hapax Legomena*, Frampton had achieved the success as a filmmaker that had eluded him in his earlier vocations of poetry and photography. After he accepted a teaching position at the State University of New York at Buffalo in one of the programs most sympathetic to avant-garde cinema in America, he moved from Manhattan to his farm in Eaton, New York, with the photographer Marion Faller and her young son, Will. There he worked on his monumentally ambitious film cycle *Magellan* until his death from cancer in 1984, appropriating the title itself from an earlier photographic project, just as he had transported the title *Hapax Legomena* from a projected volume of poems to the film cycle. As he imagined it, *Magellan* would run thirty-six hours but would be shown over 371 days with special works for the seasonal changes and the filmmaker's birthday.

Although Joyce's *Finnegans Wake* became the acknowledged model for *Magellan*, the prodigious works and theoretical position of Stan Brakhage played a large role in the evolution of the project. In 1971 Brakhage made and released his startling film, *The Act of Seeing with One's Own Eyes*, in which he observed and filmed autopsies in the Pittsburgh coroner's office. Sally Dixon, then the director of the film program at the Carnegie Museum, had arranged this extraordinary privilege. Frampton too took advantage of her ability to gain unusual entry for filmmakers when he shot *Winter Solstice* (1974) in U.S. Steel's Homestead Works. Shortly after Brakhage shot in the coroner's office, Frampton asked Dixon to get him permission to film in the Gross Anatomy Laboratory at the University of Pittsburgh. This parallelism, or competition, with Brakhage is a symptom of a much more serious engagement, which was central to Frampton's maturity as a filmmaker. Of course, both filmmakers were following another lead from Emerson, who outrageously declared in the chapter of *Nature* called "Beauty": "The ancient Greeks called the world [kosmos], beauty....And as the eye is the best composer, so light is the first of painters. There is no object so foul that intense light will not make beautiful. And the stimulus it affords to the sense, and a sort of infinitude which it hath, like space and time, make all matter gay. Even the corpse has its own beauty."[1] Initially, a shared Emersonian heritage, or even the more explicit affiliation with Ezra Pound, did not forge a sympathetic bond between Brakhage and Frampton. Frampton had entered cinema from still photography and from the social milieu of painters and sculptors in New York. In the ambit of that milieu, avant-garde cinema played an insignificant role until 1967 when Michael Snow made *Wavelength*, in which Frampton briefly appears. Frampton had included a portrait of Snow in his first released film, *Manual of Arms* (1966). His public recognition began with *Surface Tension*, a work that assured his place as one of the chief artificers—along with Ken Jacobs, George Landow (aka Owen Land), Joyce Weiland, and Snow—of what I called structural film. Frampton's unique contributions to that mode were his use of language and of systemic matrices.

Brakhage publicly denounced structural film on several occasions. He was theoretically opposed to the overpowering effects of both language and system on the nuances of "moving visual thinking," and he may have felt slighted, fearing that his preeminence was threatened by the attention structural films were attracting. But by 1971 Brakhage and Frampton recognized their grounds of affinity: Both traced a spiritual lineage to Ezra Pound, an intellectual and aesthetic allegiance both maintained after giving up writing poetry. As early as 1964, Frampton responded positively to an interest in Brakhage's films by his fellow Poundian Reno Oldin; he had seen *Mothlight* and *Window Water Baby Moving*: "what of Brakhage I've seen, I admire," he wrote, and he showed a qualified interest in Brakhage's public persona.[2] In the early 1970s, Brakhage became a champion of Frampton's films (to the

---

1. Ralph Waldo Emerson, *Essays and Lectures* (New York: Library of America, 1983), p. 14.
2. Hollis Frampton, "Letters from Framp 1958–1968," *October* 32 (Spring 1985), pp. 49, 51. Correspondence with Reno Oldin, edited with notes by Oldin.

detriment of Snow's) and a personal friend. *Zorns Lemma* and Frampton's theoretical writings were significant influences on Brakhage's *The Riddle of Lumen* (1972), to which I return in chapter 15.

Embracing the *Magellan* project meant entering the terrain of Brakhage's encyclopedic, serial cinema, on an even grander scale than Brakhage was then proposing. If Brakhage thought out loud that *The Book of the Film* might run twenty-four hours, then Frampton declared that *Magellan* would be thirty-six. Even more daunting was Frampton's new openness to Brakhage's cinematic rhetoric. The three "Eisensteinian" parts of *SOLARIUMAGELANI* are variations on Brakhage's silent, intuitive organization of visual material. At the initiation of the *Magellan* project, Frampton not only emulated Brakhage's mode but basked in the light of his approval.

After they quarreled, in the mid-1970s, Frampton was anxious to clarify the distinction between his handling of this material and Brakhage's, but he reaffirmed his admiration for Brakhage's films:

> I feel nothing but sympathy and congratulations for the magnitude of that effort, its relentlessness, its coherence.... By its continuity, by its size, by its enterprise, and by the fertility of the perpetual soil in this culture which is always ready to receive the seed of romantic idealism that is cast upon it from time to time, there will always be a special place for Brakhage's body of work.[3]

Characteristically, Frampton smuggled into his encomium the dig about "romantic idealism" (and another calling the work "predictable"), implying that that accounted for what he imagined to be Brakhage's greater critical reputation.

Frampton:

> Brakhage's camera diction... is like the broad-brush diction of abstract expressionist painting.... He does it for plenty of reasons, but he does it, one would suppose, out of some core conviction that that diction is *the* mediator, that it is *the* discipline of the camera, that it is *the* center of the circle.
>   ...If such a film, for instance as *Autumn Equinox* seems to have the kind of camera diction that a Brakhage film does, it might be worthwhile for me to suggest that perhaps it is not Brakhage's

---

3. Bill Simon, "Talking about *Magellan*: An Interview with Hollis Frampton," *Millennium Film Journal* 7/8/9 (Fall/Winter 1980/1981), p. 21.

diction but the diction of abstract expressionism which is at stake.
...I think it's probably fairly easy to establish or to argue also that
the montage is entirely different, that it subjects the motor diction of
the cinematography to a kind of challenge and contradiction which
Brakhage does not....

There are plenty of differences in the circumstances [of Brakhage's
and Frampton's filming of autopsies]. For all that the autopsy room may
represent a certain kind of liberal taboo—one that Brakhage is extremely
fond of and he has a very good nose for the liberal taboo—it is a film for
which I have a great, great respect. It's also a film that I think of as having a fundamentally didactic strain which is odd to encounter in Brakhage. I think that in watching the film one could recover the standard
method for performing an autopsy.... At the very least, I think that is
not something that could be said of *Magellan at the Gates of Death*...[4]

Thus, Frampton marshaled his formidable intellectual power and linguistic
gifts to deflect a fundamental criticism: The films he made without his ironic
use of words and without his characteristically paradoxical structures lacked
the wit and originality his sympathetic viewers had come to expect. At the
same time, it seemed that the effort to work, at least partially, in Brakhage's
idiom brought about the decline. In 1988 Scott MacDonald concluded: "But,
for all their visual and structural elegance, many of the [*Magellan*] films seem
somehow empty of the personal passion that, deflected or reconstituted, gives
Frampton's best earlier work its power."[5] At the time of his interview with
Simon, Frampton was directly responding to comments I had made on the
first *Magellan* films he released and, especially, Lindley Hanlon's review of
Otherwise Unexplained Fires (1977), in which she observed, "this Brakhage-
looking footage doesn't have the emotional conviction and urgency (shall I say
'sincerity') of the 'real' thing by Brakhage." Wondering, "Is he mocking a style
by replicating that style without conviction on his part?" she speculates that
this might be the "Brakhage chapter in Frampton's metahistory of film...in
which metaphor and subjectivity are exposed and deposed as cinema's primary
illusions."[6] Hanlon's recuperative hypothesis ultimately reflects the weakness
of some of Frampton's early *Magellan* films where, in his effort to come to
terms with Brakhage's achievement, he failed to marshal the intense irony
that had been most exciting and distinctive in his own earlier works.

4. Ibid., pp. 20, 22.
5. MacDonald, *A Critical Cinema*, p. 25. He exempts *Gloria!*, *Less*, and *Straits of Magellan: Drafts and Fragments* from this judgment.
6. Lindley Hanlon, "Arson: A Review of *Otherwise Unexplained Fires* by Hollis Frampton," *Millennium Film Journal* nos. 4/5 (Summer/Fall 1979), pp. 157–159.

Keith Sanborn eventually responded to Hanlon's criticism, asserting that the film was focused on Brakhage's theories and practice:

> What these admirers at the time and other commentators in the interim have failed to note is that what makes *Otherwise Unexplained Fires* all but plausibly by Brakhage is its bracketing, at the beginning and the end, by two halves of a familiar chemistry class experiment where a strip of magnesium is set alight to produce a brilliant and transient illumination. They function as metahistorical quotation marks. As Hollis told me in 1979, this was meant to evoke a particular passage in Brakhage's writing for which I have since sought in vain, though I confess my memory is faulty, my tolerance for Brakhage's excursions into text limited and that Hollis sometimes paraphrased in citation.... With mock-Hegelian modesty, Frampton presents a cut-out Brakhage as one case among the varied and colorful effluvia of film history, of which he, Frampton, is in possession of the general laws.[7]

What are those laws? In the most rigorous examination of modernism in the cinema, "Notes on Composing in Film," Frampton enumerated four primary modes of composition:

> It has been customary to assert, of words interacting with one another, that each word is, as it were, segmented into a dominant part, or denotation, and a subordinate attenuated series of connotations. Some have reasoned that writing consists in joining denotations, in such a way as to suppress connotation; others have been content to let the connotational chips fall where they may; and a third school proposes to fabricate a connotational subtext and let the denotative text take care of itself. But if we examine words, whether as a system of marks ordered upon a surface, or as a system of sounds disturbing the air, we can discover no difference between the manner in which they denote and the manner in which they connote.
>
> It is possible, then, to view the denotation of a word as no more than that particular term in a series of connotations which has, through the vicissitudes of history, won the lexicographical race. In *Finnegans Wake* Joyce, while implicitly accepting the assumption that words are made up of parts, *displaces* the privilege of the denotation, making of the word a swarm of covalent connotations equidistant from a

7. Keith Sanborn, "Hollis Frampton's Algorithmic Aesthetic," lecture presented at conference, Gloria: The Legacy of Hollis Frampton (Princeton University, Princeton, NJ, November 5–6, 2004).

common semantic center. Which such connotations will be identified with the notation [sic], then, is decided in each case not within the cellular word, but through interaction with the organic context.[8]

Frampton again is pellucid on the compulsion to define, in "Film in the House of the Word":

Now we are not perfectly free to make of language an agonist in the theater of desire which is itself defined by the limits of language. Every artistic dialogue that concludes in a decision to ostracize the word is disingenuous to the degree that it succeeds in concealing from itself its fear of the word... and the source of that fear: that language, in every culture, and before it may become an arena of discourse, is, above all, an expanding arena of power, claiming for itself and its wielders all that it can seize, and relinquishing nothing.[9]

In 1979 Frampton released the dedication to the *Magellan* cycle: The film, *Gloria!*, is an exemplary representative of both his use of language and the displacement of denotation by connotation. Four elements structure this short film: At the center is a text, composed with a word-processing program and filmed off the screen of a computer, consisting of sixteen statements about his maternal grandmother; it is bracketed by quotations of two films from the Paper Print Collection of the Library of Congress, *Murphy's Wake* (1903) and *A Wake in Hell's Kitchen* (1903); and there is an auditory quotation of "Lady Bonaparte," an Irish gig. Here Frampton seems to be extending his etymological activities into the film archives, as if the "fossil poetry" Emerson found in all words was to be found in the oldest films as well. Although linguistic distinction between denotation and connotation was not available to Emerson, he wrote of the pervasive power of hints, suggestion, and intimation in *Nature*, "Manners," "Thoughts on Modern Literature," and "Inspiration." In the last of these, he asserted the universal effect of connotation: "every word admits a new use, and hits ulterior meanings." In "Compensation" he even

---

8. Hollis Frampton, *Circles of Confusion: Film, Photography, Video, Texts 1968–1980* (Rochester: Visual Arts Studies Workshop, 1983), p. 121. The problematic distinction between denotation and connotation need not be definitive for the validity of Frampton's point. The classical trivium of grammar, rhetoric, and logic offers an alternative schema for the polarity he foregrounds. Allen S. Weiss argues that Frampton's four modes "not only present a typography of rhetorical types similar to those of classical rhetoric, but they are also assimilable to the Freudian hermeneutic presented in *The Interpretation of Dreams*, which reveals the modes of dreamwork in terms of condensation (substitution), displacement, conditions of representability (a type of constrictive system of rules), and secondary elaboration (augmentation)." See Allen S. Weiss, "*Poetic Justice*: Formations of Subjectivity and Sexual Identity," *Cinema Journal* 28, no. 1 (Fall 1988), p. 58.
9. Ibid., p. 83.

attributed to the principle of polarity in nature a dualism in which "each thing is a half, and suggests another thing to make it whole."[10]

The language of the computer text in *Gloria!* exerts "power" over the sound and visual citations so that their denotations dwindle in significance and an expanding connotative range predominates. The clearest instance in the film of this exercise of power would be the effect of the fifteenth "proposition" on the subsequent musical passage: "That she remembered, to the last, a tune played at her wedding party by two young Irish coalminers who had brought guitar and pipes. She said it sounded like quacking ducks; she thought it was called 'Lady Bonaparte.' [A]" (The bracketed letter encodes the degree of certainty the filmmaker has in the statement; by marking it A he asserts his conviction.) Yet again Emerson described the effect of such connotative power when he wrote in "Thoughts on Modern Literature" that the illumination he gets from poems "is not in their grammatical construction which they give me. If I analyze the sentences, it eludes me, but is the genius and suggestion of the whole."[11]

When, following the sixteenth proposition, the screen goes blank and we hear a pipe and string tune played at length, under such prompting the music sounds humorously like ducks quacking, and more important, the entire musical interlude evokes the wedding, of which we also know from the eleventh proposition "that she was married on Christmas Day, 1909, a few weeks after her 13th birthday [A]." In the further spread of language's power of suggestion—the film clips shown at the beginning of the film and after the music seem to represent the world of that succinctly depicted wedding— the short six-year span between their production and the wedding is inconsequential: in *Gloria!* they become relics of the same era, so that we are not so much seeing a film, or only seeing a film, as reconstructing the atmosphere of seventy-plus years earlier.

Although Frampton had declared, ironically, that narrative was a constitutive element of every film, he shows us that the manifest narrative of *Murphy's Wake* is less interesting than the other resonances—the connotations—he can derive from it. His narrative is actually the story of his grandmother's life as he knows it, and the elliptical story of his own extraordinary childhood, schematically fragmented in the modernist mode. He carefully lets slip that he was mildly autistic while conjuring the image, connotatively, of his grandmother as a figure of magic and vital humor: Her pet pigs suggest Circe of the *Odyssey*; although he does not name the motive for her reading him *The Tempest*, and despite her reproving of his identification with Caliban, he hints she was a benign version of the witch Sycorax; he also makes it clear that he

10. Emerson, *Essays and Lectures*, p. 287.
11. Ibid., p. 1150.

was her one male heir. (The suppression of information about his mother, aside from the fact that she was the first of ten children born when his grandmother was sixteen, is perhaps significant. The joke of his skepticism about the second proposition—"That others belong to the same kinship group and partook of that tie [Y]"—underscores an effort to displace her memory and make his grandmother his mother.)

The propositions are framed by indices of abstract systems: kinship taxonomy and quantified measurement. The joke of the second proposition suggests that there is a spiritual kinship not defined in conventional family nomenclature. The sixteenth proposition "that her last request for a bushel basket full of empty quart measures" is (1) the quaint dementia of a dying eccentric; (2) an oxymoron—"full of empty"—emblematic of the presence in absence conjured by the propositions; (3) a numerological riddle, insofar as there are thirty-two dry quarts in a bushel, suggesting that the sixteen propositions are one half (half full? half empty?) of the request fulfilled; and (4) a suggestion that she was preparing her wake in calling for containers for, presumably, homemade whiskey.[12] The last option is enhanced by the excerpts from the Paper Print Collection, two films that share images of the revival of a corpse by drinking liquor. Of course, the incorporation of the two films of 1903 into Frampton's *Magellan*, an encyclopedic film cycle, emphasizing the calendrical festivities and rites, is an allusion to Joyce's encyclopedic *Finnegans Wake*. Joyce took his title from a nineteenth-century music hall ballad about Tim Finnegan, a mason who "had a sort of tipplin' way,/With the love of liquor he was born." He fell to his death from a ladder, drinking on the job; at his wake a drunken fight ensued: "The liquor scattered over Tim; bedad he revives, see how he rises." Both of the films Frampton found in the Paper Print Collection ultimately derive from the music hall numbers, which included versions of that song. Nowhere in *Gloria!* does Frampton say that Fanny Elizabeth Catlett Cross had "a tipplin' way"; however, in an interview with Bill Simon he helpfully stated, "she was my Irish Grandma with the style of a drunken sailor...there's a lot of loose punning about Irishness in the whole thing....For me, the most important part of English language literary modernism is Irish."[13]

Murphy's Wake, the longer archival film, is an anthropological document of some interest, of which its makers at the American Biograph and Mutoscope

12. Keith Sanborn offered a different reading of the sixteenth proposition in his lecture "Hollis Frampton's Algorithmic Aesthetic": "It is Borgesian in the sense that [the] entire project of constructing meaning is lost in a labyrinth where emptiness encloses emptiness. As a poetic artifact of propositional logic it transforms a terminal speech act into the logically contradictory and poignantly redundant suggestion that death is an empty set consisting entirely of empty sets." Sanborn generously shared his manuscript with me and made suggestions for improving an earlier version of this chapter.

13. Simon, "Talking about *Magellan*," pp. 6–7.

Company were probably not aware. The first tableau shows a fight between two men in which "Murphy" dies. Such fights were frequently staged, often with violent results, at Celtic wakes, which included, as well, riddle games and ithyphallic pantomimes. In addition to being one of the dedications of the *Magellan* cycle, *Gloria!* is also its wake, with intimations of the pagan heritage of such rites. Frampton told Simon: "I have gone through the paper print collection of the Library of Congress like Levi-Strauss went thorough the distant cultures of South America, desperately seeking primitive film."[14] It could hardly have escaped him that it is more than an archive of cinematic relics; the Paper Print Collection is itself a miracle of resurrection. American copyright law required that a photograph be deposited of every frame of every film legally protected. Sixty years after most of the films disappeared, the Library of Congress recreated the films by animating the copyright stills a frame at a time.

In *Cadenza 1* of *Magellan*, when Frampton wanted to conjure up a central modernist artwork, he used another American Biograph and Mutoscope film, *A Little Piece of String*, to riddle the idea of Marcel Duchamp's most ambitious project: *The Bride Stripped Bare by Her Bachelors, Even.* In the 1902 film, two men encounter a woman outside a dress shop. They both admire her, as one pulls a loose string on her dress until, eventually, she is reduced to her underwear. Similar gags are common among the paper prints: *A Lover's Yarn, Her New Party Gown, The Dressmaker's Accident, Busy Day for Corset Models.* Frampton intercut brief moments of *A Little Piece of String* with short takes of a scene he shot in Puerto Rico of a bride being photographed in a park. He calls attention to his own photography by shooting with a handheld telephoto lens to exaggerate the effect of his body tension, as he had done in *Hapax Legomena: Special Effects*. As the opening gambit of the *Magellan* cycle, *Cadenza 1* proposes to supplant Duchamp's critical allegory of painting as aggressive voyeurism, transparent to itself, with another allegory in which the accumulation of photographic records would be the aim of sacred and secular rituals.

At another point, necessarily later in the cycle, perhaps even at several points, Frampton photographically strips the bride bare, even. *Ingenium Nobis Ipsa Puella Fecit* concentrates on a naked young woman performing elementary gestures, such as sitting, bouncing a ball, turning, and so on; her motion is often retarded or frozen, so that the ghost of Eadweard Muybridge joins Frampton as one of her bachelors. The filmmaker indicated that this sixty-seven-minute film, whose title could be translated "The Girl Herself Gave Us the Idea," or "The Girl Herself Did the Trick for Us," might be

14. Ibid., p. 25.

dispersed throughout the cycle. He foretold the same scattered future for the other lengthy parts of the cycle he had released: *Straits of Magellan: Drafts and Fragments*, and the two-part *Magellan: At the Gates of Death*.

Even the released films from the cycle were subject to change. The first *Magellan* films he completed, *SOLARIUMAGELANI*, were to be celebrations of the four seasonal changes. At first he gave the title *Vernal Equinox* to *Ingenium Nobis Ipsa Puella Fecit* but later he separated the film from the other three and announced that he had replaced it with a new (unreleased) celebration of spring that some might judge pornographic.

As set forth in his modernist polemic, "Notes on Composing in Film," the second mode of composition is constriction of the tradition to a single author. Frampton cites the example of Joyce's isolation of Flaubert as the conduit of the fictional tradition. Here he rhetorically exaggerates the role Flaubert played for Joyce, whose range of traditional sources was as wide as Frampton's. Similarly, at times the filmmaker tried to make his major Soviet precursors the constricted focus of his tradition, in a characteristically oblique way: *Winter Solstice*, *Autumn Equinox*, and *Summer Solstice* are examinations of topoi associated with Sergei Eisenstein. The winter film, shot in a steel mill, and the autumn festival, made in a slaughterhouse, elaborate on two crucial sites of imagery in Eisenstein's *Strike*; the cows of his summer film are imaginary descendants of the stud bull of the Soviet filmmaker's *The Old and the New*.

Furthermore, in its playful allusion to Dziga Vertov, *Apparatus Sum* (1972), the earliest completed segment of *Magellan*, illustrates the agonistic relationship to film history we might expect from the whole of *Magellan*, if it were completed according to plan. Frampton examines a corpse by slowly gliding around its dissected body with a continually moving camera, for the most part compounding the image with superimposition, until he presents the corpse as if with "eyes upside down." At first the skull alone slowly rises into the frame with the hieratic dignity of a Mayan mask. When the camera dramatically travels to the severed esophagus, we suddenly see the full horror of the object before us. The Latin title literally means, "I am thoroughly prepared," as if the filmmaker were announcing, brashly, his accommodation to his own mortality. However, the viewer, of course, is utterly unprepared for the disclosure: That is the point of the slow movement from the strange head to the dissected throat. A mordant reading of the title would have the corpse speak, declaring his readiness for the anatomy class or the medical examiner.

Frampton would have seen Val Telberg's translations of excerpts from Dziga Vertov's polemical and theoretical writings in *Film Culture*:

> I am eye. I have created a man more perfect than Adam; I created thousands of different people in accordance with previously prepared plans and charts...

I, a machine, am showing you the world the likes of which only
I can see.

This is I, apparatus, maneuvering in the chaos of movements,
recording one movement after another in the most complex
combinations.[15]

Speaking of Eisenstein's influence on the *SOLARIUMAGELANI*, Frampton told Simon "nothing tickles me pinker than to take a suggestion literally and seek the consequences of the working out of a literal reading in detail."[16] *Apparatus Sum* undoes the utopian rhetoric of Vertov's new Adam by taking literally the assembly of body parts. In its much-expanded version, *Magellan: At the Gates of Death* (1976), there is an exhaustive inventory of severed body parts in an anatomy laboratory.

To some extent, Frampton's anachronistic conversation in images with the masters of Soviet cinematic modernism masks his more troubled relationship with Stan Brakhage. It is precisely those films that are closest to Brakhage's visual rhetoric that seem to impel Frampton to speak of the Soviets. The epic scale of *Magellan* and its cyclic theme of birth and death took the filmmaker into mythopoeic domains he resisted, as he indicated with self-irony to Deke Dusinbere and Ian Christie: "Within those thirty-six hours there are a series of...categories....Those categories are 'Straits' and 'Clouds' [of Magellan], and there's a section which corresponds to a 'Birth of Magellan' (itself comprised of subsections), and there's another which relates to adolescence. Then there's a 'Death' and even, heaven help us, a 'Resurrection.'"[17] It is as if he can hear himself describing his plan as a version of *Dog Star Man* when he speaks of resurrection.

So much of the structure of *Magellan* was tentative when Frampton died in 1984 that it is impossible to determine the interrelationship of pieces in the grand cycle. As if intimating this situation, he spoke of the examination of released parts of the work in progress as the archaeology of a midden heap:

I would rather, for this occasion, approach this thing I am making, which is a cycle I have called *Magellan*, as a kind of archeological enterprise, as a sort of new stone-age kitchen midden....This suits me because it maintains the images in a spectrum of the problematic rather than in that of a kind of religion, a dogmatic. One does not,

15. Dziga Vertov, "The Writings of Dziga Vertov," trans. Val Telberg, *Film Culture* no. 25 (Summer 1962), p. 53.

16. Simon, "Talking about *Magellan*," p. 16 (emphasis mine).

17. Deke Dusinbere and Ian Christie, "Episodes from a Lost History of Movie Serialism: Interview with Hollis Frampton," *Film Studies* 4 (Summer 2004), pp. 105–6.

unless one is enormously privileged, come into the world in a state of
perfect alienation.... It is a great luxury to be *totally* alienated, to be
totally outside your culture. All the film we know about is involved
in the culture; all the film we know about and, in my case deeply
care about, is massively involved in a criticism, and attack upon, an
attempt to understand the world that we live in, which of course is
made up largely of images that come from that culture.[18]

Frampton's ironic idealization of alienation here echoes Emerson's observation in "Self-Reliance" that "in every work of genius we recognize our own
rejected thoughts; they come back to us with a certain alienated majesty." He
seems to be saying that Emersonian self-reliance is an impossible quest for the
state of perfect alienation. Yet he invokes the very cultural criticism Emerson
extolled in "Life and Letters in New England" as the contribution of his age
and the strength of his mentors. Even when he questions the Emersonian
optimism of his fellow filmmakers of the American avant-garde, he cannot
escape the Emersonian basis of his declaration of autonomy.

His approach to his work in progress shares the terms of his description
of the Paper Print Collection where he failed to find the "primitive" cinema
he sought "desperately," "because all film assumes from the moment it comes
into the world, as the child does, that it has a complete grasp of the universe.
Later on one revises that, but it is not rejected."[19] In Frampton's work, serialism was one of several means of revising, or dramatizing the revision of, our
illusion of maintaining "a complete grasp of the universe."

18. Hollis Frampton, lecture at the Carpenter Art Center, Harvard University, December 1979 (transcript,
Anthology Film Archives, New York).
19. Simon, "Talking about *Magellan*," p. 25.

CHAPTER 13

Abigail Child: Textual Self-Reliance

I read somewhere that Olson once said that in Billy
Budd, *"the stutter is the plot."... It's the stutter in
American literature that interests me. I hear the stutter as
a sounding of uncertainty. What is silenced or not quite
silenced. All the broken dreams... History has happened.
The narrator is disobedient. A return is necessary, a
way for women to go. Because we are in the stutter.
We were expelled from the Garden of the Mythology of
the American Frontier. The drama's done. We are the
wilderness. We have come on to the stage stammering.*
—Susan Howe, *The Birth-mark*

Coming to avant-garde cinema at the time Warren Sonbert
reached his maturity, Abigail Child shared his commitment
to montage and his affiliation with the so-called language poets. Yet her route
to these affinities was significantly different and that difference had important
consequences. Child first realized filmmaking was her vocation when she
was editing documentary films. Her later embrace of the avant-garde cinema
coincided with a crisis that included a self-directed reeducation as a poet and
a divorce from Jon Child, with whom she made her first two films, *Except the
People* (1970) and *Game* (1972). Later still, the transformation of her poetics,
verbal and cinematic, occurred through her affiliation with the language poets.
The seven-part serial film she made between 1981 and 1989, *Is This What You
Were Born For?*, is the strongest manifestation in film of the poetic sensibility of
language poetry and one of its most impressive achievements. With those poets
she shares a thoroughly Emersonian rejection of Emerson and his tradition.[1]

1. See Kevin McGuirk, "'Rough Trades': Charles Bernstein and the Currency of Poetry," *Canadian Review
of American Studies* 27, no. 3 (1997). McGuirk reads Bernstein's assertion "Poetry is aversion to conformity
in the pursuit of new forms" as "Emerson with text rather than self as ground: textual self-reliance." His
phrase is so apt to Child's work I have snatched it for the subtitle of this chapter.

In the mid-1960s at Harvard University Child had been introduced to the work of Stan Brakhage, Len Lye, and Arthur Lipsett in the classroom of the animator Derek Lamb. But it was Robert Gardner and the documentary filmmakers at MIT who influenced her early films, made while she was a graduate student at Yale's School of Art. At that time she imagined she would make anthropological films in Latin America, drawing upon her earlier field experience in New Mexico and Chiapas.

Encounters in New Haven with the Living Theater and subsequently the inclusion of her first films in programs at the Whitney Museum and the Flaherty Film Festival sparked an interest in avant-garde art and performance. She attended seminal works of Richard Foreman, Nam June Paik, Laurie Anderson, and centrally Robert Wilson, in whose *Life and Times of Joseph Stalin* she performed. Fatefully, she took a summer workshop in optical printing at Hampshire College in 1975 taught by the avant-garde filmmaker Jon Rubin. Breer, Hutton, and Landow were among the visiting faculty.

This was the period when she began to read and write poetry seriously: The work of Louis Zukofsky particularly inspired her; Charles Olson and Susan Howe engaged her enthusiasm. A romantic relationship with Andrew Noren accelerated her introduction to poetry readings as well as avant-garde films. Eventually Child would become the central representative of her generation in the intricate and intimate relationship between poetry and cinema in the American avant-garde.

That relationship had been crucial to the evolution of the avant-garde cinema since the 1920s when the surrealists saw cinema as an extension of poetry. Since it was made in 1930, Jean Cocteau's *Le sang d'un poète* had been the most influential European film for young avant-garde filmmakers in America. Maya Deren wrote a master's thesis on symbolist poetry before she made her first films, and she had somewhat tentatively written poetry herself. Willard Maas and James Broughton were the chief poet-filmmakers of Deren's generation. Broughton, in fact, had a distinguished career as a poet before taking up cinema; he never ceased writing and publishing during his long, intermittent periods of filmmaking. Jonas Mekas, in the next generation, was an important poet in Lithuanian before he made his first film. He has continued to publish in his first language.

Brakhage had asserted a place for himself in American poetic history by association. Although Stan VanDerBeek was the only future filmmaker to attend Black Mountain College, as far as I know, Brakhage, who did not, claimed the mantle of his mentors and friends, Olson, Duncan, and Creeley—the primary Black Mountain poets—among the filmmakers. He acknowledged as masters Ezra Pound (in common with Olson and Duncan) and Gertrude Stein (via Duncan). His correspondence with poets Michael McClure and Robert Kelly figures prominently in his theoretical writings on cinema.

Later Hollis Frampton would assert an alternative to that poetic heritage. Having come to cinema some fifteen years later than Brakhage, by way of art photography among generational peers who were largely sculptors and painters, he alone had been a genuine acolyte of Pound's, a junior member of the faithful who gathered in Pound's cell at St. Elizabeth's Hospital in Washington. He remained an orthodox Poundian, without much interest in the work of Stein or Olson; not poets but Marcel Duchamp, Buckminster Fuller, and Jorge Luis Borges complemented the influence of Pound on his thought. He became the leading theoretician of the generation of filmmakers, such as Michael Snow, Ken Jacobs, Paul Sharits, and Ernie Gehr, who looked to the visual arts rather than poetry for models; with the ascendancy of his position as a theorist, poetry declined as the primary analogy to avant-garde cinema. Poets and poetry play almost no role in his book, *Circles of Confusion*.

So the relationship of the avant-garde cinema to poetry was no longer a vital matter in 1976, when Child left New York for a course in poetry at the Naropa Institute in Boulder, Colorado. (She had no contact with Brakhage then; he was wary of Naropa at that time.) From there she moved to San Francisco with people she had met in Boulder. She joined a reading group with the poet Ron Silliman and experienced an intense intellectual exhilaration discovering the critical and theoretical work of Barthes, Benjamin, and Jameson in that company.

Through Silliman she met Barrett Watten, who published her work in *This*. She also formed an enduring friendship with Charles Bernstein, poet and coeditor of $L = A = N = G = U = A = G = E$, where some of her writing on films and poets appeared. These poets were challenging the "natural" priorities of speech and reference. Claiming Stein, Zukofsky, Cage, Olson, Mac Low, and Ashbery (for *The Tennis Court Oath* rather than his later work) as their precursors, they insisted on the grounds of historical and political urgency that they "should turn their attention to the origin of [the writer's and their audience's] displacement, the constituting mechanism of 'private life,' language itself." For them "style has an ethical rather than an aesthetic basis."[2]

Child's allegiance to the poetics and politics of the language poets came with a price. She ran counter to the prevailing feminist aesthetic within the American avant-garde cinema at the very moment when it became the dynamic center of attention. Her fast editing, lyrical density, and hermetic obscurity were associated with the work and polemics of Brakhage and Kubelka, then regarded as the most conservative of the "patriarchs" in the field. Many of the most prominent feminist filmmakers considered that by making ambitious

2. Ron Silliman, Barrett Watten, et al., "for CHANGE," in *In the American Tree*, ed. Ron Silliman (Orano: National Poetry Foundation, University of Maine Press, 1986), pp. 484, 486.

feature-length narrative films, with long sequence shots and synchronous sound infused with theoretical rhetoric, they had launched a direct attack on the aesthetics of the patriarchs of the avant-garde cinema.

Warren Sonbert's relationship to some of the poets close to Child grew more from his gregarious social presence within artistic circles in San Francisco and New York than from his approach to filmmaking or his poetics of cinema, which might be assimilated to their programs by analogy but only tangentially met their concerns. His lecture at the San Francisco Art Institute, which I have quoted extensively, first appeared as "Film Syntax" in *Hills*, a journal featuring the language poets, edited by poet Bob Pereleman.[3] However, in the introduction to the crucial language poetry anthology, *In the American Tree*, the only affiliated filmmakers mentioned are Abigail Child and Henry Hills.[4]

Whereas Sonbert came to his editing style through encounters with the films of Gregory Markopoulos, Stan Brakhage, and Bruce Conner, Child owed a debt to the structural cinema of the late 1960s and the 1970s, especially to the work of Hollis Frampton, and to its precursors, Robert Breer and Peter Kubelka. Sonbert sought to infuse what he learned from his study of Hollywood auteurs in his "world melodies"; Child had little use for Hollywood, but her early work as a political documentary filmmaker informs her major sequence, *Is This What You Were Born For?*

In an interview with Charles Bernstein, Child said:

> I'm very surprised how some writers will go, and go again and again, to Hollywood movies, even as they disparage, and sometimes vehemently, narrative in writing or poetry. I love movies. I like seeing Hollywood or independent or foreign features, but if that were my only diet in films, it wouldn't be enough. This tolerance, avidness, for the commercial entertainment seems to me only a measure of how large Hollywood's monopoly has become, in people's consciences and imaginations, and how large in culture it is and how it's your kind of hot dog and you don't even see the forces behind your desire and that "blindness" gives these monopolies the freedom to shape and change and distort everybody's minds. I want my work to challenge these assumptions, upset the torque of culture, at least enlarge the field.[5]

---

3. Warren Sonbert, "Film Syntax," *Hills* 6/7 (Spring 1980), pp. 120–38. In the question and answer session, omitted from the *Film Culture* reprinting, the poets Barrett Watten, Ron Silliman, Lyn Hejinian, and Bob Perelman make interventions.

4. Ron Silliman, "Language, Realism, Poetry," in *In the American Tree*. Hills's films *Plagiarism* (1981), *Radio Adios* (1982), and *Money* (1985) feature several of the $L = A = N = G = U = A = G = E$ poets.

5. Abigail Child, *This Is Called Moving: A Critical Poetics of Film* (Tuscaloosa: University of Alabama Press, 2005), pp. 187–88.

Ernie Gehr: *Shift*

Still courtesy
of Ernie Gehr

Warren Sonbert: *Noblesse Oblige*

Stills courtesy
of Jon Gartenberg
and Fred Camper
(www.fredcamper.com)

Stills courtesy
of Jon Gartenberg
and Fred Camper
(www.fredcamper.com)

Stan Brakhage: *Creation*

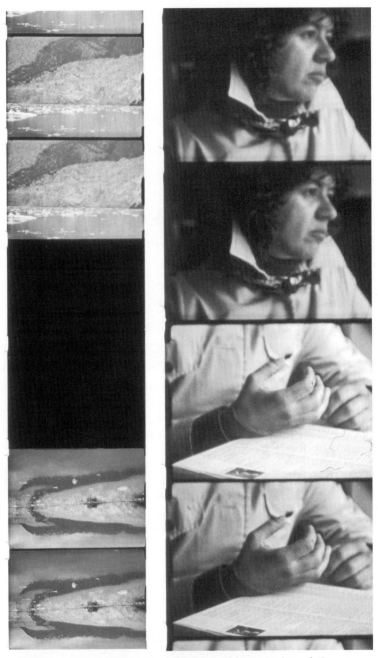

Stills courtesy of the estate of Stan Brakhage and Fred Camper
(www.fredcamper.com)

Stan Brakhage: *The Dante Quartet*

Hell Itself

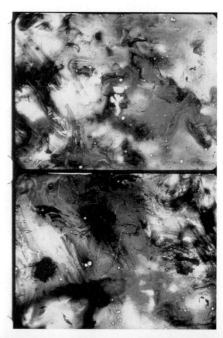

Purgation

existence is song

Stills courtesy of the estate of Stan Brakhage and Fred Camper
(www.fredcamper.com)

Hollis Frampton: *Magellan*

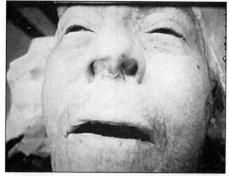

The revelation
of the corpse in
Apparatus Sum

Gloria!, [*Wake in Hell's Kitchen*]

Gloria!, [*Murphy's Wake*]

Stills courtesy of
Anthology Film
Archives

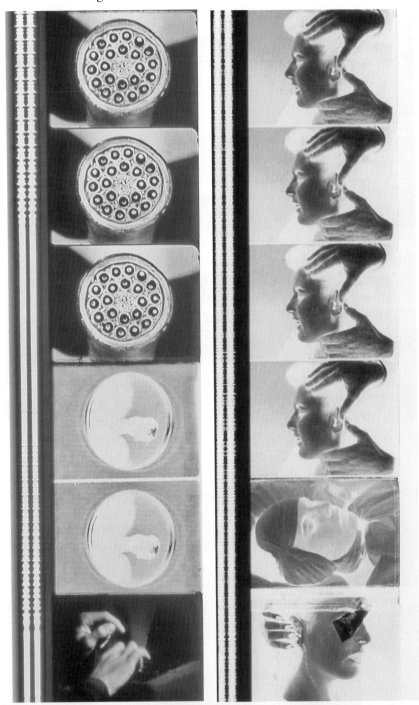

Prefaces
Stills courtesy of Abigail Child. Filmstrips made by Arunas Kulikaukas

Abigail Child: *Is This What You Were Born For?*

Mayhem

Perils
Stills courtesy of Abigail Child

Mutiny   *Covert Action*

Covert Action
Stills courtesy of Abigail Child

Su Friedrich: *Gently Down the Stream*

Stills courtesy of Su Friedrich

Su Friedrich: *Gently Down the Stream*

Stills courtesy of Su Friedrich

Su Friedrich: *Sink or Swim*

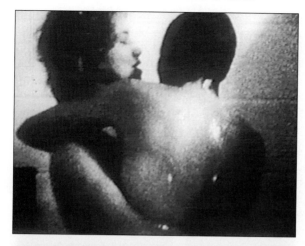

"Kinship"

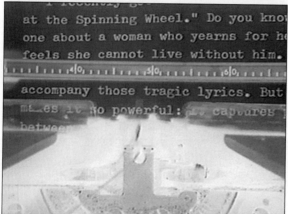

"Ghosts"

"Bigamy"

Stills courtesy of Su Friedrich and Fred Camper
(www.fredcamper.com)

Robert Beavers: *My Hand Outstretched to the Winged Distance*
and Sightless Measure: Cycle Three

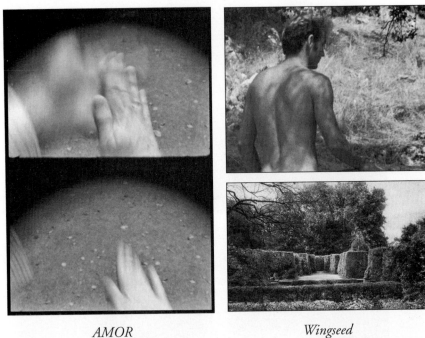

AMOR

Wingseed

Sotiros

The Hedge Theater

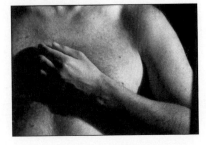

The Ground

Stan Brakhage:
Visions in Meditation #1

Two strips of sequential images
Filmstrips courtesy of the Estate of Stan Brakhage and Arunas Kulikauskas

Stan Brakhage: *Visions in Meditation*

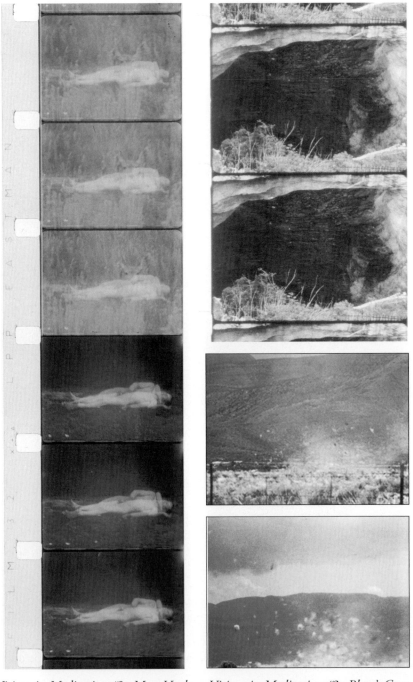

Visions in Meditation #2: Mesa Verde   *Visions in Meditation #3: Plato's Cave*

Stills courtesy of the estate of Stan Brakhage and Fred Camper
(www.fredcamper.com)

Jonas Mekas: *As I Moved Ahead Occasionally I Saw Brief Glimpses of Beauty*

Jonas Mekas and Hollis Melton

Jonas Mekas

Sebastian Mekas

Stills made by Arunas Kulikauskas, reprinted courtesy of Jonas Mekas

Larry Jordan: *Sophie's Place*

The balloon with eyes turns upside down at the end of the film.
Filmstrips made by Arunas Kulikaukas. Stills courtesy of Jonas Mekas

Other avant-garde filmmakers before Child had expressed chagrin over the apparent contradiction in values shown by fellow artists who were enthusiastic about mainstream films and uninterested in or even disparaging of more demanding work, while polemically rejecting conventional forms in the media they practiced. Here she implies that even among the poets who rejected the transparency effects in the writings of most of their contemporaries, some preferred to see Hollywood films. Bernstein himself was thoroughly familiar with the native avant-garde cinema. He had addressed the contradiction Child observed in "Frames of Reference":

> It may seem odd that what I find so compelling in film is what, in writing, I am most prone to distrust: the disappearance of the word / the appearance of the world; that is, writing in which the words are made as transparent as possible to allow a sensation of wordless images to be conjured up by them. But there is no easy analogy between writing or poetry that brings the conditions of language into audibility, and film that brings the apparatus of cinema into visibility.
>
> Stan Brakhage, for example, relies, in part, on the metaphor of the eye, and on film disclosing what the eye sees; although he breaks with the conventional patterns of representing the eye = camera equation.... Brakhage like other film artists as different from him as Ernie Gehr, has not abandoned the transparency effect but re-envisioned it.[6]

Bernstein's criticism of Brakhage reflects the growing discomfort with the Emersonian exaltation of vision and visibility in the poetics and film theory of the late 1970s and the 1980s. Film became for Bernstein the locus of fascination with the seduction—he calls it *imagabsorption*—of voyeurism and the frisson of fear accompanying the detachment from the world turned into a spectacle. He found films as radical as Snow's *The Central Region* and as conventional as *Mad Max* offering versions of this experience worthy of his attention. Furthermore, he cited acts of resistance to the transparency effect in the works of Kubelka, Lye, Godard, and even Ross's *Pennies from Heaven*. (The British avant-garde cinema, which he does not mention, had brought this issue into polemical focus and practice before it began to absorb the attention of Americans.) His meditation on cinema may be called an attempt to "see the forces behind [this] desire," as Child described the aim of her work.

Bernstein's essays are particularly interesting in this respect because he grounds the problematic of cinema's vision and voyeurism in the debate about

---

6. Charles Bernstein, *Content's Dream: Essays 1975–1984* (Los Angeles: Sun and Moon Press, 1984), pp. 94–95. "Frames of Reference" was delivered as a lecture at the Collective for Living Cinema, March 1982, as part of Image Talks, a series curated by Child.

the visualizing power of language. In "Words and Pictures," he went to the heart of the poetics of optics espoused by Brakhage when he critically argued that, in spite of its claim to dispense with metaphysics, Louis Zukofsky's "theory of sight [in his *Bottom: On Shakespeare*, a touchstone work for Brakhage] is purely metaphysical and naively neopositivist at that," even though Zukofsky's poems "present some of the most realized alternatives to the poetry of sight in modern American writing."[7]

Even though Child shares with Bernstein many political and aesthetic allegiances, including the debt to Zukofsky's "alternatives to the poetry of sight," the visuality of film presented no serious problems for her. Her education at the margins of language poetry simply made her more sensitive to the "materiality" of cinema. The antivisual bias of the more theoretical British filmmakers—Peter Gidal, Laura Mulvey, Anthony McCall—neither seduced nor challenged her as it did Yvonne Rainer, who became a crucial influence on the generation of women making avant-garde films in the late 1970s. Indebted to Godard and even Bergman, in his work from the mid-1960s on, Rainer was untouched by the generally overwhelming influence of Brakhage. Child, however, engaged the rhetorics of Menken, Brakhage, and Breer in her silent films of 1977–79 as she reeducated herself as an avant-garde filmmaker.

Although Hollis Frampton did not participate in the Hampshire College summer session the year Child attended, several of his films were shown. They made a powerful impression on her. His ironical stance, especially in relation to his contemporaries and to film history, corresponded to her emerging sense of the poetics of cinema. From his serial work, *Hapax Legomena*, especially the fugal spat of sexual jealousy in *Critical Mass*, she took the liberating permission to let language play a major role in her own serial project, *Is This What You Were Born For?* In five of the seven parts, she adapted the poetics of Silliman, Watten, and Bernstein to the creation of multivoiced collage poems on the soundtrack. (Only *Both* is silent; *Perils* credits "sound improvisations by Charles Noyes and Christian Marclay.") The auditory determination to range the units from the monosyllabic word to the short sentence extends by analogy to the split-second, fractive cutting of the images.

The inventiveness of its sound possibilities, the scale and sustained success of the serial project spanning the 1980s, and the fusion of auditory and kinetic ideas mark *Is This What You Were Born For?* as one of the most important and original sequences of the American avant-garde cinema. Like most of the filmmakers of the 1970s, Child was tutored in the subtleties of frame-by-frame sound-picture juxtapositions by Peter Kubelka's *Unsere Afrikareise*, and perhaps by Kubelka's theoretical elaboration of the principles of his practice

7. Ibid., pp. 149, 151.

in his remarkably successful public lectures of that decade. The abrasive music of her disjunctions was anticipated by the Super-8 mm magnetic sound films of her friend Saul Levine in the late 1970s.

Is This What You Were Born For? is a Menippean satire. The Menippea is a composite genre, often combining essays, narratives, parodies, minimalist structures, and lyrics in an ironic dialogue of ideas. Most of the ambitious epic structures of the avant-garde cinema in the 1970s and 1980s were versions of that genre. Child has repeatedly acknowledged her debts to the Menippean satires of Frampton and Snow: *Hapax Legomena* and *Rameau's Nephew*. The latter is an encyclopedic examination of sound-picture variations. Child too sought to sample an exhaustive array of sound options for her series, but she condensed them into tiny "synch events," in the phrase of Peter Kubelka.

All of Rainer's films, many of Landow's, and most of Benning's are Menippean satires, a mode that derives from the Alexandrian Greek tradition and can be found in the American avant-garde cinema as early as the 1940s in the films of Sidney Peterson. Even Brakhage was making a Menippean satire, his *Faust* series, during the years Child was composing *Is This What You Were Born For?* Not since *Dog Star Man*, with its links to the mythopoetic themes and aesthetic principles of the Black Mountain poets, had a film, or rather a filmic sequence, been as distinguished by an affinity to contemporary poets as Child's serial film was to the language poet group. Not just its disruption of syntax on the soundtrack but its insistence on the political nature of syntactical dissonance, on the visual as well as the auditory level, recalled their program.

In fact, the plan of the sequence suggests at times a parody of *Dog Star Man*, to whose prelude Child responded with her *Prefaces*. The antithesis is most direct between Brakhage's *Part Two* and *Part Three* and *Both* (1988), the third part of Child's serial—it had been in the second position before she made the final arrangement. The only silent film in *Is This What You Were Born For?*, it shows two female bodies where Brakhage had mythologized an Edenic male and female (*Dog Star Man: Part Three*); instead of the lactating breasts of *Dog Star Man: Part Two*, Child shows one figure cleaning and scraping her nipples. In the first version of *Both*, a second part showed a beating heart. *Dog Star Man: Part Three* superimposes a reel of male images, a reel of female images, and a beating heart with its rhythms emphasized by hand painting on the celluloid.

In *Metaphors on Vision*, Brakhage had described the making of *Prelude: Dog Star Man*. First, he edited a thirty-minute reel, putting shots together by chance to get new perspectives on the welter of material he had shot. Then he crafted a parallel thirty-minute reel in response to the images on the first, changing the chance roll when he did not find an inspired correspondence.

The finished film was a superimposition of both rolls, but in *The Art of Vision*, which cycles all the permutations of *Dog Star Man*, he showed the two reels and the composite in seratim.

In her brilliant essay "Notes on Sincerity and Irony" in David James's collection, *Stan Brakhage: Filmmaker*, Child speculates that had she first seen *The Art of Vision* rather than *Dog Star Man*, she might have come to appreciate Brakhage's achievement much earlier:

> There is a heroic sincerity in Brakhage's work that I distrust, a reliance on unitary consciousness, purity, wholeness, that takes me away from his work. I would posit a more useful way to look at his films, both his camera work and montage, is as a series of "re-descriptions," the word Richard Rorty uses in *Contingency, Irony, and Solidarity*. For Rorty, ironists are always aware "that the terms in which they describe themselves are always subject to change always aware of the contingency and fragility of their final vocabularies and those of themselves."[8]

Here she implies that she sees herself as an ironist. She elaborated on her reaction to *Dog Star Man* in a letter to me:

> Since Brakhage was incredibly useful to me for the materiality of his research, for his inclusion of the quotidian as subject (already classic material for verbal poets at this point in the century), and for his masterly display of rhythm (though on occasion solipsistic and indulgent), I both agreed with Charles [Bernstein] and R[on Silliman]'s critique in large part yet appreciated B's brilliance. Not being the son, I didn't need to kill the father—perhaps? I never loved *The Prelude* [sic] in fact—a bit of film that has always seemed kitsch to me in its parading of selfness up and down that snowy hill with axe—I much prefer *Art of Vision*, say, the unspooling of same efforts.... It seems there are two, at least two surely, multiples more surely, factors or levels of consideration in filmmaking. What are the materials? and in what order? are basic decisions—even if order becomes so-called "realtime"—since then you have decided on a simulated chronology. Frampton opens out both questions considerably and his freedom and research into/ with image as representation as a system of semiotics, even a failed, erased, translated, mistaken system paralleled my own curiosities. (August 23, 2000)

8. Abigail Child, "Notes on Sincerity and Irony," in *Stan Brakhage: Filmmaker*, ed. David E. James (Philadelphia: Temple University Press, 2005), pp. 197–98.

Although Child did not use chance operations in the construction of *Prefaces*, as far as I know, the fractile, allusive, polysemous poetry of the soundtrack resembles the works of a poetic tradition—John Cage, Jackson Mac Low—that did rely on chance. A typical passage from the transcript of her film would be: "exaggerate/ *sort of like the light popping off the head/* then the sky working in/ we I we/ using pure metal/ within your own power/ to come,/ to interact/ light screen/ in the thick/ another flash." Edited musical notes, fragments of song, and elongated syllables compose at least as much of the soundtrack as the words in the transcription, and not all of them are distinguishable even on repeated viewings. In the twenty-five seconds this passage takes up, there may be fifty shots from at least ten different sources. A boy swinging a baseball bat rhymes with a ritual dance and a boxing match; barely discernible forms in red and yellow clash against fragments of police breaking up a demonstration. A brief light-struck flare synchronized to the phrase "light screen" is the only overt fusion of text and image in this sample section, which I have randomly selected. Its density and connotative range are comparable to that of *Prelude: Dog Star Man*, although it uses tangents of sound and picture where Brakhage had quickened the semantic field with superimposition.

A suggestion of dialogue on the soundtrack points back to one of its sources: a recorded conversation between the filmmaker and Hannah Weiner as they walked in New York. Weiner was a poet, video maker, and performance artist who drew upon her psychotic (and psychic) episodes for her visionary art. She saw words everywhere, especially on her own forehead. She was taken up by the language poets; Bernstein introduced her to Child. Although she participates as a voice on the soundtrack, the film does not show the influence of her writing. Rather, along with most of the other parts of *Is This What You Were Born For?*, it conforms to some of the shared aesthetic principles of the language poets.

The voices of Weiner and Child are part of a rapidly changing moil of sounds including snippets of song in English and German, narration from a medical or anthropological documentary, typing, movie music, the buzz of sprocket holes, and a sudden silence. In "Preface for *Prefaces*," Child suggests that sound constitutes the Mallarméan backdrop to the cascade of images:

> You could say sound plays the part of the page, the way its field excites the eye turning the meanings the word sounds make (polyphonic) or that it is modeled after the mind's divergent attention (jumpy overlaps) or perhaps that the relation of sound to image is prepositional, is a repositioning. . . .

The motives are set in motion from a more tentative dream of a landscape of vortices, constant corners, contrast switching and the concrete simultaneity of every day.

...I wanted to use found images as a resource, a dictionary, to deacculturate our "image bank"—to break the bank image in fact, to redistribute.[9]

She even cites Mallarmé: "The paper intervenes every time an image on its own, ceases or retires within the page, accepting the succession of the others," from the preface to *Un Coup de Dés*. Poetic diction, ellipsis, and hysteron proteron come to dominate her prose when she writes in conclusion:

The structure is density, a tessellation. More than any "once" even to see it. The desire for—maneuverability (to meet every day), and sense, the base of position in principle.

The character of the material analyzes the mind.[10]

Tessellation, from *tessera*, means a mosaic. To read the next sentence we might add "you must watch an image" to "more than any 'once' to even see it." Finally, the subject and object of the last sentence seem to be reversed; it would be more legible as "the mind analyzes the character of the material." At stake in this final reversal is the shared aspiration of the language poets to overcome romantic subjectivity, by making language the subject—what Barrett Watten calls "total syntax"—of the poem, so that selfhood (and mind) are unmasked as its epiphenomena. Yet this powerful and productive myth actually reinstates the romantic longing for self-transcendence that it pretends to despise.

Even the title, *Prefaces*, in eccentrically asserting the plural, denies a singular, coherent, univocal form to the film. It suggests a multiplicity of starts, tentative efforts to situate the serial film to follow, or it points to a genre instead of naming a particular instance. But there is nothing tentative or unsure about the film itself: a meticulously crafted storm of rapid images and sounds, so insistent in its relentless shifting between black and white and color, positive and negative, that it puts up a barrier to broad internal modulations; we never feel with assurance that one section of it has ended and another begun. I understand that aggressive rhythm to be an effort to defeat the emergence of a subjective stance, to insist that the film rather than the filmmaker is talking. Such speed and fragmentation eventually force us

9. Child, *This Is Called Moving*, pp. 197–99.
10. Ibid., p. 199.

to recalibrate our expectations of modulation (as do some of Robert Breer's films) so that microrhythmic differences suggest the articulation of possible divisions in the film.

The film begins in black with dramatic music introducing the image of a waterfall, as if setting the site for the film to follow. Even the sudden shift to sentimental, lyrical movie music does not disorient us as much as the cascade of images and sounds that follow. All through the film anthropological, scientific, medical, and industrial imagery indicate a melange of evenly dispersed documentary quotations. Of the sound, Child wrote: "with *Prefaces* I begin to create chordal relations...where the sound does not *complete* the image but is an addition to it, to *change* the reading of the image. One of the things that interested me was dissonance—in the sense of how far I could go to have images not match up, yet exist together. This process began to create what I saw as a corner of a building—*corners* of linkages (torsions), rather than surface."[11] She quickly jumps among orchestral music, art, and popular song snippets, in English and German, disjointed phrases in many voices, some with distinctive New York or African American inflections, others with the unctuous fluidity of professional narrators.

The graphic alignment of a petri dish, a rearview mirror, and the cross-section of a cable lends some emphasis to the circular form early on. A minute or so later, a brief instance of synchronous sound gives unusual prominence to a shot of fingers typing. Midway there is a pause: The image of a white colonial doctor tending a sick African goes black for a moment as we hear the longest unbroken speech of the film: "some of them even cured of their disease but unfortunately, there is no room for all of them." In the second half, fantastic images from *Willie Wonka and the Chocolate Factory*, most memorably boxing gloves on pistons, weave into and out of a rhyming montage of fluids—funneled water, flowing chocolate, and smelted iron. As the film nears its unanticipated conclusion, we often see a nexus of recurring shots: a young man swinging a baseball bat, the shadow of a flying biplane, and a man jostled by police at a political demonstration. No sooner do images and sounds call attention to themselves or montage fusions seem about to elaborate new subdivisions of the film than the power of the matrix quickly reasserts itself, frustrating segmentation.

For the sake of "those moments full of opposition to public expectation... [t]o upset the Model within us," Child situates *Prefaces* in "an other previously erased space."[12] The opening black-and-white waterfall falsely suggests a small-town setting, with contradictory musical cues, indicating a melodrama

---

11. Abigail Child, "Sound Talk," *Dialogues*, (Sarah Lawrence College) 1994, unnumbered pages. Mss of *This Is Called Moving*, p. 133, omitted from published book.
12. Child, *This Is Called Moving*, p. 134.

or a romance; but that is a foil to the urban rhythms of most of the series (the "vacation" home movies of *Covert Action* is the exception). Although Vertov holds a privileged place in Child's book, the city she evokes is a teeming metropolis like that of Ruttmann's *Berlin, Eine Sinfonie der Grossstadt*, the city of Georg Simmel's "The Metropolis and Modern Life," where the sensibility must parry and master the aggressive barrage of stimuli in order to survive:

> In *Prefaces*...the body as worker...is very embedded in machinery in a troublesome way...I...use images—mountains of sawdust, machines purring liquids, surgical procedures—that communicate this sense that the body is being pulverized. But at the end, to counter the technology and force, I use shots of dancers and children skipping, part of a Billie Holliday song. It's a way to present the alternative power of the human body to reject this pulverization, or...at least dance with it. *Prefaces* is a fast, vividly colored world—I'm trying to raise with energy and rhythm a certain sense of the human will to persist....
>
> One thing I discovered in making *Prefaces* is that we blind ourselves to survive in an urban environment. I want to be fully conscious, which necessarily means to stay alert...The question, then, is can I make myself eye-open?...The challenge is to be open in an uncontrollable environment.[13]

Not only the city, but the film image itself might be considered an uncontrollable environment: It automatically and immediately offers a multiplicity of meanings. The short essay "Cross Referencing the Units of Sight and Sound/Film and Language" insists on the limits of the analogy of film to language:

> APART FROM THE ATTENDANT INEQUALITIES IN THE MODE OF PERCEPTION, FILM IS LESS CODIFIED THAN LANGUAGE...THE FILM FRAME REMAINS AN OPEN VARIABLE. IT CAN CARRY A MULTIPLE OF COMPLEX MEANINGS WHICH CAN BE REGISTERED, IF NOT READ, AT A GLANCE. PERHAPS OH or AHAH or OUR EXPLETIVES ARE COMPARABLE.

Film, I am suggesting is more a language inventing machine than a language (this, once the narrative stranglehold is dropped). It is not about something: image codified for social use. Inherently mechanical and optical, film (like the instruments of science) provides us with insight (in site) proof of new thought and conceptualization.[14]

The stance Child takes to generate new thought and conceptualization might be called mutiny; for that is what she titled the second film of *Is This What You Were Born For?* From the Indo-European root *mew, *mutiny* is cognate with *motion, motive, emotion, moment, momentum,* and *mob.* The film ends with a figura etymologica, the expression "this is called motion," which becomes the title of her collected writings on film. So, she intimates, to make films seriously, responsibly, is to instigate a mutiny. Although *music* and *mute* derive from different roots, they are drawn into the commotion of the film by homophony.

Len Lye, one of Child's heroes, once accepted a commission to reedit a conventional documentary on the assembly of a Chrysler sedan. By radically reducing the film to a minute, in thousands of jump cuts, he created *Rhythm* (1957), an aptly titled work, for it affirms the priority of the twenty-four-beats-per-second pulse of cinema over the industrial pace of the assembly line. *Mutiny* appears to be a parallel reduction of conventional documentaries: three performance artists—Shelley Hirsh, a singer who makes trilling sounds and does other vocal gymnastics; Sally Silvers, a dancer performing in a working office; and Polly Bradfield, a violinist playing an amplified, often screeching instrument with both a bow and a toothbrush on a busy street—dominate the montage of women, talking, working, and exercising. One would not know that some of the other interview fragments come from a documentary Child made in the 1970s on prostitutes and pimps, if she had not made the point in her book. The tacit incorporation of this material into her film is, as Jeffrey Stout reminds me, a thoroughly Whitmanian gesture.

Child's mutiny against the documentary genre exceeds Lye's: We cannot even discern the subject of the original film or films. Even though women predominate, there are glimpses of a middle-aged man dancing on a stage, a male rock band, and filmmaker Henry Hills dancing or leaping in his studio. The soundtrack enacts an even more fundamental subversion of the generic conventions. Split-second images are sufficient to show that Child had interviewed some black women and that she shot two Hispanic women angry about an undisclosed event occurring on the street (from her 1975 documentary *Savage Streets*), but her radical fragmentation of synchronous speech drives all the imagery in the direction of the performance art. She extenuates this tendency by manipulating the speed (and therefore pitch) of sound

14. Ibid., p. 89.

within many of the fragments, turning the interviews and protests into a theater of gesture. She wrote:

> There is a whole section of *Mutiny* featuring high school girls, full of telling gestures, interrupted speech. They are talking about intense emotional experiences, and they are embarrassed to speak in front of the camera....I felt their gestures spoke worlds, if not words, and their speech was foregrounded by the machine between us. All those blurps and bleeps of the camera in *Mutiny*. It's about constraint and repression, or rather it uses the bunched gestures as a vocabulary for a musical composition in film. The question is how to let us speak, be present without falling into romantic personae, or other "assumed" poses....
>
> I think I was always composing, as early as *Prefaces*, influenced by John Cage, his taped collages—I loved his *Variations*. When I was filming the high school scenes in *Mutiny*, I was struck by how noisy everything was. The toilet paper roll in the bathroom even sang a little song when you pulled it! It was a sort of revenge that I could make a music out of this noise.[15]

While the editing rhymes the dancers, the gymnasts, the interview subjects, and the rock musicians in pairs or continuous strings, the sound plays with repetitions of a word from different situations. Take the following auditory run over seventeen seconds: "What's that one? *Dormer*/ Are you? But/ But/ What?/ No buts oh/ You know like/ at that point/ maybe the earthquake was coming." This comes late in the film, so all the imagery of almost thirty shots is familiar. A gym coach asks, "What's that one?" The singer, clearly in a different place, seems to answer with the French infinitive *dormer*. "Are you?" sounds over the close-ups of Hispanic women, but the speaker is not identified; then a black woman, addressing the camera "perhaps, but" introduces a string anchored in a shot of two women, late teens, one blonde and one dark, sitting at a table. The blonde says, "but...but," and her companion responds, "No buts." Child interrupts the blonde with a shot of figures in a swimming pool; then she inserts a swimmer asking "What?" before the dark-haired woman terminates the series with "No buts."

The riff on "but" sets up the nonverbal flourish that follows: two extended notes of the singer frame three shots—of a dancing man, a single guitar note from a 1950s rock and roll film, and the dancer in the office. The second snippet of song is an electronically modified quaver an octave above the

---

15. Ibid., pp. 221, 224. The high school scenes were shot for her documentary *Between Times* (1976).

first. Finally, one of the longest speeches of the film begins before we see the speaker; we hear "at that point," and then we see a woman standing before a wall of photographs, who continues, "maybe the earthquake was coming." Some five minutes earlier, at the very beginning of the film, Child had shown the same woman, beautifully interrupting her simile ("that my mind...goes like this") by synchronizing the sound of the toothbrush on the violin over her hand gestures. Only repeated viewings, and an intimate familiarity with the film, would permit us to link the screeching of the mind with the imminence of an earthquake.

Following the poetic calculus of Louis Zukofsky—lower limit speech, upper limit music—the voices and sounds of *Mutiny* continually glide between language and pure sound to create a choral effect. Nouns echo their participle or adjectival forms: "remember/ remembering/ remember..." or "it's my love, the peace/ peaceful/ a beautiful but maybe embarrassing/ beauty/ Beauty..." A penultimate string puns on *I* and *eye*: "I/ eye/ eyes/ momentum/ desire/ I mean,/ so,/ this is called/ moving." Child has compressed the discursive documentary into an avant-garde musical or opera: moving as mutiny. Marjorie Keller wrote of it:

> Her training and skill have been given over to an enterprise that is
> wholly her own and the sense of empowerment she enjoys is conveyed
> in the images and energetic editing structures she uses. The women
> in the film are multidimensional. They dance, they fight, they sing,
> they yell. They are one, and it is their activity that energizes the film.
> Toward the end, in a line that comes as close as any to a theoretical
> summary, a voice speaks of all that has gone before in the film: "So
> this is called moving." Read with its broadest interpretive possibilities,
> the line is descriptive of the film's action and carries a critique of con-
> ventional notions of drama. For Child, the women we have seen in the
> bits and pieces permitted to us, are moving. They move us, or ought
> to, by their struggle to find their own place in the world. This struggle,
> I suspect, is Child's as well.[16]

The third and fourth elements of the series are the only films without speech. *Both* is silent; *Perils* has a music track for which a percussionist (Charles Noyes) and a turntablist (Christian Marclay) are credited. In one early schema, *Both* was the second part and *Perils* the fifth. The reorganization gives more prominence to *Mutiny* and separates *Perils* from its longer and more complex companion film, *Mayhem* (1987), in which most of the same

16. Marjorie Keller, "*Is This What You Were Born For?*" XDREAM 1, no. 1 (Autumn 1986), p. 4.

actors appear, again in high-contrast black and white. Formerly coming right after *Prefaces*, *Both* seemed a covert dedication, a declaration of erotic love. It is the only film in the sequence without the mediation of artifices and masks, but even so, insofar as it records an act of grooming and the presentation of naked bodies to the camera, it is in keeping with the investigation of the relationship between voyeurism and exhibitionism that so dominates these films that it could be the referent for *this* in the title, *Is This What You Were Born For?*

Freud, in his *Three Contributions to the Theory of Sex*, links voyeurism and exhibitionism as an instinctual pair:

> The partial impulses which usually appear in contrasting pairs play a very prominent role in the symptom-formations of psychoneuroses. We have learned to know them as carriers of new sexual aims, such as a mania for looking, exhibitionism, and the actively and passively formed impulses of cruelty. The contribution of the last is indispensable for the understanding of the morbid nature of the symptoms; it almost regularly controls some portion of the social behavior of the patient.... He who in the unconscious is an exhibitionist is at the same time a voyeur, he who suffers from sadistic feelings as a result of repression will also show another reinforcement of the symptoms from the source of masochistic tendencies.[17]

The issue of cruelty, active and passive, emerges in *Perils* and reaches its culmination late in *Mayhem*. In the *Canyon Cinema Film/Video Catalogue No. 7*, Child wrote of the former:

> An homage to silent films: the clash of ambiguous innocence and unsophisticated villainy. Seduction, revenge, jealousy, combat. The isolation and dramatization of emotions through the isolation (camera) and dramatization (editing) of gestures. I had long conceived of a film composed only of reaction shots in which all causality was erased. What would be left would be resonant of voluptuous suggestions of history and the human face. *Perils* is a first translation of these ideas.[18]

In her book, she glosses the concept of translation thus: "For *Perils*, I didn't work with a script. It was more a translation. I took still photos from strongmen movies of the 1930's and had performers strike poses, moving from point

---

17. Sigmund Freud, *Three Contributions to the Theory of Sex*, in *The Basic Writings of Sigmund Freud*, trans. and ed., with an introduction by A. A. Brill (New York: Random House, 1938), pp. 575–56.
18. *Canyon Cinema Film/Video Catalogue No. 7* (San Francisco: Canyon Cinema, 1992), p. 81.

A to B to C back to A then to D."[19] The title looks back to the melodramatic serials of the early American cinema, to *The Perils of Pauline*, but the film's flagrant disavowal of danger in its posed moments of violent conflict and romance suggests that more serious perils lie in the illusions of narrative film and in the social effects of those films. The etymology of peril points to danger or trial, as in the related experiment and experience.

The film is a farce, resembling Broughton's *Mother's Day* (1948) more than any Hollywood narrative. The two men and two women in it are always posing. They seem just as affected in their raucous laughter over their own antics as in the charades of passion they pretend to be filming; for there is a minuscule movie camera, on spindly tripod legs, in some of the shots.

Intertitles divide the film into three parts: *1.*, *2.*, and *earlier*. Before the first, each of the four actors are introduced with close-ups. Dressed to recall stage thugs from the first decade of the twentieth century, they casually walk into the frame and assume melodramatic poses of tough-guy romance or a fist-fight. The second section includes the rudiments of reaction shots, often with all four characters in both the initial action and the collective reaction to it.

A final title, "to be continued." leads to the home movie collage, *Covert Action* (1984), the next film in the sequence, and beyond that to *Mayhem*, where the same figures appear in film noir parodies. The hyperboles of "seduction, revenge, jealousy, combat" in *Perils* guide our scrutiny of the latent tensions Child's editing and soundtrack seek to uncover in the anonymous home movie footage (probably from the 1930s):

> *Covert Action* was the first in a series [it was made before *Perils*] that began to look at narrative structures, the way of making up a story and filling in the gaps. The beginning of narrative *is* speculative fiction. As an indictment of patriarchal authority, *Covert Action* operates in the field of speculation, what we *don't* know. When I saw the raw footage, it seemed to be an account of two brothers who on successive weekends or successive years, I never knew, take out two different women. I could never make that totally clear to the audience. It was like an attempt to order a family history that had a peculiar, hidden secret. [20]

Covert Action excavates repressed vestiges of seduction, revenge, jealousy, and combat, the explicit issues of *Perils*, latent in the body language of home movie images of displays of affection and the celebration of vacation fun. The footage she reworked was "both familiar and awful in the way women

19. Child, *This Is Called Moving*, p. 225.
20. Ibid., p. 217.

performed for the camera."[21] Here what she calls the "spiral structure" she initiated in *Perils* is even more apparent. There is a prefatory image: a policeman
and a man escorting a woman against a high wind. Their solicitous manner,
but not her body shape, suggests she might be pregnant. Then there are two
unequal numbered parts. In the first, a series of women briefly appear—the
cast of characters. The second may actually stand for a series of nine parts
and an epilogue, as I elaborate later. In expanding cycles, we see a montage
of rapidly edited scenes of two men vacationing with a number of women.
Often they have filmed themselves kissing the women. Often the women
are in pairs, hopping across a stream, giving each other piggyback rides, one
pushing another in a wheelbarrow; as the cycles progress, we see these activities more fully developed, intercut with each other. The men too are rather
clownish. A clip of a bathing beauty contest orchestrated by a male harlequin
is emblematic of the critique of sexism throughout the film. The film ends
with the uprooting of a full-grown tree, an epilogue in which, Child glosses,
"I'm saying enough of this congealment; enough of those embraces, those
gestures, those postures to the camera, the 'front.' It blows the lid off *Covert
Action.*—what is hidden to the world."[22]

A dialogue between the language poets Steve Benson and Carla Harry-
man offers a tangential commentary on the images, reminiscent of the brilliant dialogue between Vito Acconci and Amy Taubin in Yvonne Rainer's
Journeys from Berlin/1971 (1980). But whereas Rainer elaborated a leisurely
offscreen conversation between art-world stereotypes, Child has fragmented
her soundtrack, mixing into the speech of the poets bits of music, song, and
other voices that push the foregrounded conversation to the limits of comprehension, which she called "a fragmentary music of memory and rupture."[23]
The soundtrack warns us from its very opening that a desire to vacate "our
obsessions" guides the film. The male voice claims, "We don't want obsessions. What we want is to be halted in our tracks. Don't you agree?" The
female voice dissents: "No. They keep us going."

Between "halted in our tracks" and "keep us going," the stuttering movement of the film issues in a variety of enigmatic intertitles. Sometimes they
imitate the labels of home movies: "Five Years Later," "Southern California
1937," or "A Beauty Contest Among Friends," or they give the names of those
friends. At the other extreme we find the direct intervention of the filmmaker: Near the end of the film she confesses, "My goal is to disarm my
movie." Between these poles she inserts social criticism ("In this society flesh
is gummed with sentiment"), a free-floating, not even dangling, participle

21. Ibid.
22. Ibid., pp. 217–18.
23. Ibid., p. 130.

("ending with a rupture of the hypothesis"), and several teasing fragments of an occulted narrative: "The whole lumpish question of B's past." "He had to be eliminated...She had to be bitten," "It seems strange to me now," and "talking at cross purposes." Although the last of these could describe the relationship of image to sound, the others suggest that Child would disarm her movie by introducing red herrings. We might wonder, who is B? A Beatrice and a Babs are among the friends named in the beauty contest, but such tenuous connections only reveal the false security of proper nouns in the enigma of this unexceptional footage.

B could just as well be one of the principal males in the film. Since the title immediately precedes the number "2." the rest of the film might be seen as an evocation of the whole lumpish question of B's past, the functional equivalent to placing the title "earlier" in the middle of *Perils*. That is, if there are just two parts. There is no intertitle for "3." But there is a "Scene Four," immediately followed by "Historically,"; even after that, the Academy leader numbers for 5, 6, and 9 appear as if marking subsequent divisions of the film. However, I have not been able to discern discrete principles animating these segments, beyond the tendency to expand in later sections material presented initially. It seems that Child may be deliberately introducing, and frustrating, the principle of articulation by subdivision, as Gertrude Stein often did.

Do we always give up too soon trying to understand how the parts function and thus confirm the intertitle "ending with a rupture of the hypothesis"? One effect of such ruptures is to shift attention from the messages of the intertitles to the nature and functions of intertitles as such. Similarly, the editing of exhibitionistic kisses—perhaps the dominant gesture of the film—with self-conscious posturing and playing, while precluding a narrative engagement with the events depicted, dissects the sociology of body language, particularly as coded by gender, in home movies.

Just as the voices of the intertitles shift and come loose, the spoken language of dialogue and collage does not seem to originate with the characters in the film, or reflect their subsequent thoughts, but for the most part point to the exterior, commenting position, as when we hear the male say, "Their bodies were completely automatically political" in conjunction with "In this society, flesh is gummed with sentiment." Yet a pronoun difference sometime later aligns the woman's voice to one of the figures in the film: "I felt that I was in a kind of improbable body in this particular photograph." Then, when she says, "I was really trying to communicate something to you...but it definitely feels like...this isn't like the point," a rapid succession of kisses halt, one after the other, as if exhibitionistic, amorous vacationers were responding suddenly to the intensity of her insistence that "this isn't...the point."

What, then, is the point? There is a covert interaction between images and words and across phrases and images dispersed throughout the film. The point is that such covert action requires constant scrutiny but hides no key, ends with a rupture of every hypothesis. So even if we connect "ending with a rupture of the hypothesis" with the previous intertitles "Scene Four, Historically," we still do not know what hypothesis is at stake. It might or might not be the even earlier proposition about flesh and sentiment. While the word *hypothesis* can be seen on the screen, the phrase "of symbiosis about them" is fresh in our ears. Both words of Greek derivation give a charge to the next shot, of a woman holding a flame under an object, perhaps from a scientific film—one of a few examples of foreign material artfully smuggled into the home movies. Even the penultimate intertitles, "Yes but" followed by "No" forty-five seconds later, neither quite affirm nor negate but gesture at cross-purposes.

Within the covert actions embedded in the film there are insidious connections between leisure, voyeurism, exhibitionism, and imperialism. Not only do the women mouth Inuit speech, but a hula dance takes a prominent place in the middle of this film, incorporating, as the United States did between the time the images were shot and Child reedited them, the outer reaches of our territorial empire, Alaska and Hawaii. The hula sequences especially underline the imperial pressure to make erotic exhibitions the objects of vacationers' pleasure.

Although the pronominal adjective in "my goal is to disarm my movie" apparently makes lucid sense, pointing to the filmmaker herself—like Brakhage scratching "I can't go on" while editing the horrors of his *23rd Psalm Branch*—the pronoun of "It seems strange to me now" might reflect the language of the home movie subjects. They look like urban middle-class Americans of the generation of Child's parents, on vacation in the Catskills or Poconos in the 1930s or 1940s. (It is difficult to imagine any of them saying "flesh is gummed with sentiment.") In the expression, "It seems strange to me now," whatever "it" is, the speaker once took it as normal, but now—whenever that is, perhaps even when reseeing the old home movies, it has become strange. Such "making strange," following the formula of the Russian formalists whom the language poets studied, is the burden of Child's reediting, through repetition, parallel montage, and asynchronous sound.

Mayhem explores the third of Freud's scopic triad, cruelty, as a function of the drive to see and be seen. The word *mayhem* comes into English from Norman French *maihem*, "injury." It is directly related to *maim*, from a root *mai- of words for cutting and biting. There is mayhem, in this as in most of the films in the sequence—wildness, violent impacting of imagery directly emerging from the cutting of the film. But there is also theatrical violence, the staging of pain and cruelty, as in *Perils*.

Child lists the Marquis de Sade's novel *Justine* as one of its sources and she acknowledges the importance of Roland Barthes's book *Sade, Fourier, Loyola* for her. Barthes read de Sade's project as the invention of a language: Its elementary unit is the posture; postures combine "grammatically" to form operations; static operations generate figures; diachronically they compose episodes. He argued that it is crucial to the Sadean system that all bodies are interchangeable in postures and operations; there are no active and passive characters. This systemic exchange eliminates the category of the self. The power of speech alone confers mastery: "*Imagination* is the Sadian word for *language*."[24]

In *Mayhem* the postures replicate the iconography of film noir. The details suggest the elements of the genre: a pistol, telephone, alarm clock, a grimy stairwell and an elegant spiral staircase, a nightclub, a dark office with file cabinets, chains, smoke rings, a lone car at night. The characters are stereotypes: femme fatale, street thugs, police detectives, gang moll, victim. Rich black-and-white compositions in depth, barred lighting, tilted angles, slow, expressive dissolves exemplify the formal strategies of film noir. Above all, the mélange of musical cues dominates the soundtrack; the fragments of speech are minimal but evocative: "It's ridiculous. I mean to believe someone would have committed such a deed"; "Why did you call the police?" The "figures" include an interrogation, stalking, a chase, and sexual acts. These are blatantly simulated; the infliction of pain is theatrical. But in contrast to the posturing of sex, Child has worked "episodes" into the final minutes of the film from an old Japanese specimen of pornography. A masked jewel thief happens upon a lesbian seduction. The sight of the women performing cunnilingus fascinates him, but they catch him masturbating and force him at gunpoint to satisfy them *a tergo* and orally, before they mount each other.

The relationship of film viewing to the sexual imagination is the subject of the film. Child suggests, following Barthes, that the sexual imagination is a language. She had said explicitly that its charge derives from its temporality: "I discovered that it wasn't the violence in noir that was erotic. For me the thrill lay in the anticipation and the suspense.... The interest lies in opening up what is seamless; uncovering the hidden."[25]

When the curtain of *Mayhem* rises on the found object, the Japanese pornographic film, with its fantasy of female domination, the filmmaker makes mayhem of the generic law of film noir that requires the dominating female be punished in the end for her transgression; but pornography, itself transgressive, refuses to submit to that moral closure. The sexual exploitation of the thief, instead, excites a final lesbian embrace, which Child has comically orchestrated to exuberant Mexican music.

---

24. Roland Barthes, *Sade, Fourier, Loyola* (Baltimore: Johns Hopkins University Press, 1997), pp. 35–36.
25. Child, *This Is Called Moving*, pp. 216, 219.

In a passage eliminated from the published text of *This Is Called Moving*, Child described the aim of *Mercy*, the finale to the series:

> In *Mercy*…almost all the source material…comes from educational films and science films. Here I'm subverting the original meaning. I'm looking at the material to reveal its essence, what's hidden from us in the form it was originally, whether scientific, "objective," or advertising—forms you're not supposed to question, or footage that's kinkily beautiful, looks playful but is documenting something very different, the unnamed ideology at the heart of American culture. In that sense *Mercy* is an archeology of the document, forcing the image to "give up" its history.…As a filmmaker, as an editor, I'm trying to dislodge, unearth and subvert the image, exploring the limits of representation, asking how I can bring forward the contradictions in the image, its partialities, its beauty, or as the case may be, its horror.[26]

Mercy (the last segment to be made, as well as the concluding work, 1989) returns us to the rhetoric of *Prefaces*. It is a masterful collage of found footage and some choreographed actions, a critique of masculinity, colonialism, and consumerism, especially of snapshot photography as the manufacture of keepsakes. The title might as well be *No Mercy*, for we hear the cry "No" just as the title card appears.

Mercilessly, the filmmaker gives a double emphasis to a shot of a young soldier embracing his mother in the later part of the film: It is immediately repeated and it alone has its original soundtrack intact: "How does it feel to see your son become a man? You're as proud as he is." Apparently, this comes from an army promotional film. A close-up of a woman taking a snapshot—we hear "Was even worth a thousand words"—introduces this blatantly hyperbolic rite of passage. Is this what you were born for? To provide sons for the military? To inflate and memorialize the moment he "becomes a man"?

A dead body near the opening of the film established its somber tone, sustained a little later by detonations and a diver wrestling a shark. A woman dancing on the street, in a dump, among mannequins, and in a classroom brings one line of development directly from *Mutiny* into *Mercy*. Her stylized gestures rhyme and contrast with male wrestlers and a rodeo cowboy right after we see the soldier. At another point they bind a kinetic riff in the manner

26. Abigail Child, "Speaking of Found Footage," *Recycled Images: The Art and Politics of Found Footage Films*, ed. William C. Wees (New York: Anthology Film Archives, 1993), pp. 73–74.

of Sonbert—diver—dancer—wrestlers—children jumping—a parade—fair rides. The recurrence of laboratory experiments and medical examinations throughout the film, almost to the end, contributes to a rather threatening mood, despite the grotesque comedy of some of the experiments and flights of montage choreography in which the disparate elements of the found footage suddenly turn into quadrilles.

Bruce Conner is the master of transforming ironies and absurdities into haunting dream collages. Child's debt to him is most apparent when she ends the film with several shots from a moving camera floating through a tropical swamp surrounded by cypress trees. The scene is reminiscent of Ian Hugo's *Ai-Ye*, which Child may not have known. Her images, probably drawn from a travelogue, lack the richness and splendor of Hugo's; like the shots of a diver exploring a sunken boat that end Conner's *A Movie*, their beauty shimmers, especially in their isolation from their original context. But even here she insists on undercutting her own facility with a visual stutter; so she interrupts these languid, often sensuous shots with images in black and white of men and women kissing. I take this conclusion to be a critique of what she called "romantic invention" in her catalog note for the film: "*Mercy*, the last in the series, is encyclopedic ephemera, exploring public visions of technological and romantic invention, dissecting the game mass media plays with our private perceptions."[27]

Child seems to be in constant anxiety about the seductions of craft. She never permits herself the sustained effects of her exemplars, Connor, Kubelka, Frampton, Sonbert, Vertov (the opening and later recurring shot of a woman with headphones quotes the start of his *Enthusiasm*). In an essay devoted, in part, to Conner, she defines her collage: "through the breakdown and establishment of so-called inappropriate/neglected/denuded connections, through the scattering friction of obsessive repeating, we relocate and reimagine the world."[28]

In the case history of the Rat Man, Freud links obsessive behavior to ambivalence. Ambivalence, of course, is at the heart of *Mercy*—"No" mercy, "Nein...yes"—and it structures her statement about the film: "kinkily beautiful...contradictions in the image." It is central to the aesthetic of the entire sequence: *Mercy* ends, just as *Mayhem* did, with expressions of primal ambivalence. *Mercy*: "Nein. Nein. Nein. Yes yes yes. Nein. Oh—oh, yes." *Mayhem*: "No. No. Ah ah just. Yes yes."

Although Child's project is grounded in a repudiation of the authority of the selfhood in filmmaking, she has nevertheless made in *Is This What You*

---

27. *Canyon Cinema Film/Video Catalogue No. 7*, p. 81.
28. Child, *This Is Called Moving*, p. 131. In the manuscript draft the final phrase had been "we re-imagine the human mind."

Were Born For? a major crisis lyric in the tradition of Brakhage and Frampton. Freud's discussion of ambivalence in *The Ego and the Id* provides an interpretive context for the sequence:

> Closer study usually discloses the more complete Oedipus complex, which is twofold, positive and negative, and is due to the bisexuality originally present in children: that is to say, a boy has not merely an ambivalent attitude towards his father and an affectionate object-relation towards his mother, but at the same time he also behaves like a girl and displays an affectionate feminine attitude to his father and a corresponding jealousy and hostility towards his mother.... It may even be that the ambivalence displayed in relation to his parents should be attributed entirely to bisexuality...[29]

Child has condensed the struggle for self-definition as a filmmaker, engaging and challenging the mode of Brakhage and Frampton, with a drama of sexual orientation. The final arrangement of the elements of *Is This What You Were Born For?* sets up an intricate pattern of associations and counterbalances. *Prefaces* and *Mercy* frame the five central chapters. *Mutiny*, as a catalog of women's aesthetic expressions, presents an alternative to the satyr play of *Mayhem*'s parodies and ironies. The women's bodies of *Both* calmly contrast with the heterosexual confusions and jovial delusions of *Covert Action*. *Perils*, in the middle like James Broughton's *Mother's Day*, which it resembles, allegorizes the power of archaic forms. In it adults play as ferocious children, while the filmmaker reimagines the origins of cinema.

In this schema, *Covert Action* represents the pivotal mystery of parental sexuality. It is bracketed by the grown-up child's play of *Perils* and *Mayhem*; the two parts enact, in different ways, the truth of *Covert Action*—rounds of seduction, jealousy, and revenge; economies of voyeurism, exhibitionism, and sadism. Child's critical scrutiny and dissection of the duplicitous smiling face the home movies had painted over the primal scene had ended with a radical deracination. *Mercy* terminates with the gestation of new roots: In fast motion a tangle of fibrillae emerge in a transparent medium. The women's bodies of *Both* complement the lesbian images of *Mayhem*, while the final back-to-front embrace of the pornographic quotation rhymes with the piggybacking women of *Covert Action*. Ambivalence structures the complex threads of association among these images.

---

29. Sigmund Freud, *The Ego and the Id*, trans. Joan Riviere (London: Hogarth Press, 1927), p. 33.

Although the American avant-garde cinema had candidly depicted male homosexuality since the 1940s, lesbianism remained a covert subject until the 1970s. Barbara Hammer's prolific and pioneering work dominates the initial, celebratory phase of lesbian avant-garde cinema. Child's serial project represents, in this respect, the most sophisticated filmic expression of the dialectical intricacies of theoretically inflected lesbian feminism. The play between "veil and confession" that Judith Butler finds operating in "the lesbian phallus" characterizes the mediations of Child's stuttering revelations.[30]

30. Judith Butler, *Bodies That Matter: On the Discursive Limits of "Sex"* (New York: Routledge, 1993), p. 88.

CHAPTER 14

Su Friedrich: "Giving Birth to Myself"

The filmmaking career of Su Friedrich, Abigail Child's contemporary, had a remarkable start. After a brief self-apprenticeship to the medium during which she made four short films in three years, she found her own powerful voice with *Gently Down the Stream* (1981), a film that immediately commanded attention. A second short film, *But No One* (1982), explored the same material. But two years later, she surged to the forefront of her generation of avant-garde filmmakers with a fifty-five-minute portrait of her mother, *The Ties That Bind* (1984). She followed that in 1987 with a forty-two-minute narrative film. Thus she demonstrated her originality in lyrical, documentary, and narrative modes in her first decade of filmmaking. Her subsequent work has moved through those genres, often mixing them. The first narrative film, *Damned If You Don't* (1987) also concretized her reputation as one of the important new voices of lesbian cinema, an aspect of her work that has been prominent in her films since then.

She had the good fortune, rare among her generation, to become an avant-garde filmmaker without wanting to. After graduating with a degree in art history from Oberlin College where she taught herself still photography, she traveled in Africa taking photographs. Subsequently, she worked in New York as a graphic designer and volunteered her time to *Heresies*, a radical feminist journal. When she sought equipment to make her first films and venues to show them, she came in contact with her contemporaries who, unlike her, had often studied avant-garde filmmaking and its history in the classrooms of such charismatic filmmakers as Hollis Frampton, Ken Jacobs, Peter Kubelka, Paul Sharits, and Stan Brakhage. They were the first generation of avant-garde filmmakers trained in universities and art schools. Many of them venerated their teachers and subscribed to their aesthetic principles. It was often painfully obvious in a program of new works which filmmakers had studied at SUNY Binghamton (with Ken Jacobs, Larry Gottheim, Saul Levine, Dan Barnett, and Ernie Gehr), who had come from SUNY Buffalo (where Hollis Frampton, Paul Sharits, and Tony Conrad taught), or from Antioch College (where Conrad had succeeded Sharits before he too went to Buffalo), the San Francisco Art Institute (whose large faculty then included Larry Jordan, Janis Crystal Lipzin, James Broughton, and George Kuchar), or Bard College (where Adolfas Mekas ran the program in which many filmmakers briefly taught: Bruce Baillie, Andrew Noren, Ernie Gehr, Barry Gerson, Storm De Hirsch). Later the Massachusetts College of Art became a center for avant-garde cinema (with Saul Levine, Mark LaPore, Erika Beckman, Abigail Child, and Dan Barnett on its faculty).

Friedrich had not seen avant-garde cinema before she started to make her own films. European art films—Fassbinder, Buñuel—inspired her. She encountered the work of the major avant-garde filmmakers unsystematically. Rather than seeking their approval or benediction, she maintained a vigorous skepticism, bordering on hostility, toward even the filmmakers from whom she learned the most: Stan Brakhage and Hollis Frampton. During the time Friedrich was teaching herself to make films, Brakhage's work had been singled out for criticism by feminists and by the Left: His emphasis on individualism, the nuclear family, and poetic election made him politically suspect. Furthermore, his public rejections of collective action, propaganda, and semiological theory exacerbated his vulnerability as the influence of theoretically minded avant-garde filmmakers from Great Britain began to exert an influence in America. Frampton, who had painfully experienced the political consequences of his adolescent championing of Ezra Pound's poetry and polemics, warily and successfully negotiated his way in the same political minefield.

In contrast to Friedrich's career, that of Leslie Thornton might illustrate the experience of a filmmaker with a cinematic education. I cite her because she was closely associated with Friedrich in the 1980s: They shared an editing studio and often traveled together to show their films. Thornton had studied at SUNY Buffalo with Sharits and Frampton and did graduate work in filmmaking at MIT. Although she started to make films in 1975, three years before Friedrich, and worked prolifically, she did not find her own distinctive voice (and with it a degree of recognition) until 1985 when she made *Adynata*. Yet very few of the school-trained avant-garde filmmakers ever achieved Thornton's breakthrough. (Only Peter Hutton, as far as I know, moved more quickly than Thornton from the classroom to prominence as an avant-garde filmmaker. The film he made at the San Francisco Art Institute, *July '71 in San Francisco, Living at Beach Street, Working at Canyon Cinema, Swimming in the Valley of the Moon*, 1971, immediately launched his career.)

Friedrich's earliest films, *Hot Water* (1978), *Cool Hands, Warm Heart* (1979), *Scar Tissue* (1980), and *I Suggest Mine* (1980), instantiated both her commitment to an explicitly feminist cinema and her hesitation to operate in a personal mode. Speaking of the third film, she told Scott MacDonald: "I thought I should try to do something very personal, entirely about me. I failed miserably."[1] Her maturity as a filmmaker began in 1981 when she turned to her dream journals for material. The confluence of several factors made her *Gently Down the Stream* a remarkably successful film. In the first place, by concentrating on her dreams, she unwittingly aligned her film to the central tradition of the American avant-garde cinema and especially to the heritage of Maya Deren, who had attained iconic status with the upsurge of feminism at that time. By adhering to the textual evidence of her dream journal, Friedrich stressed the mediation of language in the consciousness of dreams as no filmmaker had done before her. Furthermore, at that very moment the function of language in the relationship of the unconscious and conscious mind was becoming a central concern of film theory. The film's almost incidental acknowledgment of lesbian desire fused the filmmaker's feminism to her use of film as an instrument of self-examination.

Gently Down the Stream combines aspects of Frampton's work and Brakhage's without becoming derivative of either. The priority of language in the film reflects the influence of Frampton, then at its apex. Yet she adapted Brakhage's technique of scratching words directly onto the emulsion in order to give her journal entries the dynamics of single frame changes. In so doing, she actually preceded by seven years Brakhage's own commitment to that method of dynamizing texts in *I...Dreaming* (1988) and a number of later films; since 1958 he had made his titles that way, and in *23rd Psalm Branch* he had scratched some words on the 8 mm filmstrip. Evidently Friedrich saw the potential for organizing a whole film around scratched texts before Brakhage himself realized it. Of course, he knew that Larry Jordan had pioneered and elaborated the strategy in his prescient *Man Is in Pain* (1953), but

1. Scott MacDonald, *A Critical Cinema 2: Interviews with Independent Filmmakers* (Berkeley: University of California Press, 1992), p. 290.

Friedrich certainly did not. In her manipulation of the scratched text and the photographic images, she used the optical printer available to her at the Millennium Film Workshop as an instrument of rhythmic invention. Again, the interplay of single-frame inscription and optical freezing and looping would not become an integral part of Brakhage's working methods until the 1990s when Phil Solomon (a contemporary of Friedrich's, himself formerly a student of Ken Jacobs at SUNY Binghamton) accepted a teaching position in the same department as Brakhage in the University of Colorado and put his remarkable mastery of the optical printer at Brakhage's disposal. Brakhage insisted the resulting films were collaborations.[2]

Friedrich talked to MacDonald about *Gently Down the Stream*:

> If people see the film without knowing it's made from dreams, they do tend to get very anxious. But if they recognize that the texts are dreams, they tend to accept the film.... I asked my current lover, who was a man, and a former lover, who was a woman, and one male friend and one female friend (both of whom are gay) to read all the dreams [ninety-four from her journals] and tell me which ones they liked.... I didn't really use that as the basis for making a final decision about which to use but it did help me to think about the dreams. Finally, I chose to do the dreams about women with moving scratched words and the dreams about men with optically printed freeze-framed scratched words. I did about forty dreams, some with images, some without.... [T]he timing is important. I started out with each dream on an index card, and kept whittling down the phrasing until it was really succinct. Then I started breaking it up into lines to see how it should be phrased in the film. I heard the rhythm of each dream very clearly in my mind before I started scratching...if something wasn't right, I'd cut out a few frames or add a few frames.[3]

When MacDonald asked her if she read much poetry, she answered, "I read Walt Whitman one summer—almost nothing but him. The only other poets I've read closely are Sappho and Anna Ahkmatova."[4] However, *Seeing Red* (2005) gives evidence of the centrality of poetry in her formation. The film is

---

2. Solomon is another instance of a schooled filmmaker (SUNY Binghamton, Massachusetts College of Art) whose critical reputation crystallized very slowly. After more than twenty years of making films, he began to achieve some prominence in the mid-1990s.

3. MacDonald, *A Critical Cinema 2*, pp. 291–92.

4. Ibid., p. 290.

a confessional monologue, which she calls a diary. At one point the filmmaker quotes two lines of Emily Dickinson:

> To make a prairie, it takes a clover, a bee and a reverie
> The reverie alone will do if bees are few.

And later she reads us Whitman's "O Me, O Life!" from a volume she has had for thirty years. In both instances she invokes the poets to demonstrate the "scary" persistence of the anxieties of her youth as she enters her fifties.

The anxieties evinced in the texts of *Gently Down the Stream* might be deduced as dream records from the elliptical transitions and the fantastic images evoked, or from the title of the film, if the viewer calls to mind the next phrase of the lullaby: "Life is but a dream." Yet where one dream ends and the next begins is ambiguous. In the published transcription, the division into thirteen dreams is much clearer than in the film itself. Moreover, the alternation of moving and frozen titles is less systemic than the filmmaker indicated to MacDonald. The play between male and female themes, reflecting the filmmaker's bisexuality during the period of the film's genesis, would seem to owe something to Frampton's playful use of set theory in the organization of *Zorns Lemma*. Of the thirteen dreams that make up the film, only four have frozen-frame writing. The ninth dream clearly refers to a man: "Building a model/ house for/ some man/ Do it/ without/ getting paid/ Do it/ wrong." In the fourth, the change of style emphasizes the direct speech of a woman: "A woman sits on a stage/ hunched over in the corner/ She calls up a friend from/ the audience/ asking her/ Come and make love to me/ She does/ I can't watch." All the words move except "Come and make love to me." Similarly, there is an alternation between dancing and still words in the sixth dream. First we see the moving words: "Woman on the bed shivers." Then the still letters read: "I wake her/ She is angry/ Smears spermicidal jelly/ on my lips." The dream concludes with the word "No!" in motion, growing larger and larger.

Even the first dream, registered with frozen letters, turns out to be an encounter with a woman, although the designation "old friend" is at first ambiguous: "Wander through large quiet rooms/ An old friend says What/ are you doing here?/ I say The weavers/ worked as slaves to make these rugs/ Think/ She shouts Why/ do you come here/ and SPOIL everything?/ This pure/ civilization."

It would seem, then, that despite the systematization of moving and frozen words Friedrich mentioned to MacDonald, the alternation has a purely rhythmical function. The still words at first serve as a foil to set up the dynamics of the trembling text of the second dream: "Walk into church/ My mother trembles/ trances/ reciting a prayer about orgasm/ I start to weep."

Furthermore, although the first dream indicates guilt about the abrasive manner of the dreamer's "politically correct" comments, the imagery surrounding the exfoliation of the words is of votive statuary, as if proleptically announcing the ecclesial location of the second (and the seventh) dream. In fact, the imagery of the whole film moves through three sites: a church (here metonymically represented only by religious statues); subsequently a spa where we see one woman on a rowing machine, another stepping into a pool, and a third swimming; and finally we see first surf and then the open sea with sea mammals, perhaps porpoises, viewed on a whale-watching trip. These images sometimes have tangential connections to the texts. For instance, the third dream text ("In the water near a raft/ I see a woman/ swimming and diving/ in a wet suit/ See her pubic hair") shares an erotic fascination with the rower and swimmer, but there are no shots of a raft, diving, or pubic hair in the film. More obliquely, when we read the fourth dream ("A woman sits on a stage...") the posture of the rower seems hunched, and her apparatus a stage on which she sits before the camera. The editing juxtaposes the backstroke of the swimmer to the text of the seventh dream ("Walk into church/ Look in a cage/ A bloody furry arm is torn/ from the body of an animal/ Did it rip its own arm off?"), fixing our attention on the arm of the swimmer amid fantasies of imprisonment and self-destructive violence. Insofar as the montage of word and image links the dream of dismemberment to the erotically charged swimmer, the images function as free associations to the materials of the dream.

In rebellion against her Roman Catholic upbringing, Friedrich typically identifies the church as a site of sexual repression and imprisonment, as when her mother comically prays for orgasm. In that dreamworld, the church would encourage the autocastration of its captives. Friedrich's first long dramatic film, *Damned If You Don't*, triumphantly depicts the liberation of a nun into a satisfying lesbian relationship.

The return to the site of the church in the seventh dream vividly invokes an image of castration in picturing the vulva in menses ("bloody furry"). When we recall that Buñuel was one of her tutelary filmmakers, we can see how the image of the severed hand in *Un chien andalou* predicts the animal's dismembered arm. Both encode a punishment for masturbation, which Friedrich's dreamer believes might be self-inflicted. If the five women singing "wahrheit" in the twelfth dream stand for the five fingers of a hand, the blindness the dreamer spells out would be the folkloric result of onanism. In the church dream, the votive animal is a rebus for the harsh saying of Jesus: "If thy right hand offend thee, cut it off" (Matthew 5:30).

The connection of religious devotion to sexuality is more obliquely encoded in the first moving image of a strip of film on which we see the face of a female saint, or perhaps the Virgin Mary, fluttering up and down, misregistered in the optical printer. While it manifestly asserts the ad hoc nature of the filmic image, it connotes too the iconography of female ecstasy, most familiar from Bernini's *Saint Teresa*, as the sublimation of sexual satisfaction. The irony of the montage pits the repression of sexuality in the church against the narcissistic theater of the health spa, as if it were itself a church, requiring daily devotions, teasingly offering a grail of glimpsed pubic hair. But at the same time it suggests that labor at the optical printer, and even filmmaking itself, might be a form of devotion.[5]

Gently Down the Stream is one of the great films of poetic incarnation. The first lines of the eleventh dream could be a motto for the whole film: "I lie in a gutter/ giving birth to myself." It is always as much about becoming a mature filmmaker as it is a quest-romance of erotic self-discovery. If Friedrich's dreams constitute a psychological autobiography, their reassembly within the work, juxtaposed at times to the imagery of her first film, *Hot Water*, inflects the personal meaning of the oneiric allusions as aspects of her cinematic vocation. Therefore, another facet of the "church" the filmmaker walks into is the cultic sanctuary of the avant-garde cinema itself. In his seminal book, *The Three Faces of the Film*, Parker Tyler divided his chapters into three categories, "The Art, the Dream, and the Cult." Friedrich's film characteristically acknowledges all three.

There has always been a cultic dimension to the avant-garde cinema and its audience. Friedrich herself told me in the early 1980s that she was particularly sustained by showing her films to friends and by seeing their films. This candor struck me as particularly revealing of the avant-garde film community of the period. I frequently alluded to her position in lectures then, exploring the notion of a cinema of friendship. When the audience is expanding and vigorous, as it was in the 1960s and early 1970s, and seems to be once again in the early years of 2000, the public screening locations become the sanctuaries of the cult of avant-garde cinema. In more difficult times, filmmakers have gathered together in small informal groups or sent each other prints of their films. (The current widespread use of videotapes and DVDs may alter that phenomenon.)

In *Gently Down the Stream*, the prevalence of primal scene fantasies makes the transition from private to public arenas fluid. The emblematic dream is the fourth, in which a performer calls a woman up from the audience to have sex with her. The dreamer says, "I can't watch," but the enlarged, frantic titles "MOANS, ROARS, HOWLS" indicates that she cannot shut out the fascinating and terrifying experience. Of this portion of the film, Friedrich said to MacDonald: "Every time I show the film and I'm in the audience, I think about how some-

5. For an elaboration of this idea, see Nathaniel Dorsky, *Devotional Cinema* (San Francisco: tuumba, 2003).

body in the audience feels. As a filmmaker, I'm doing just what the woman in the dream is doing. I think there's something about making a work that has to do with wanting to please people, to make love with the audience. This dream is a bald statement of a desire that I think is part of a lot of films."[6] She does not see, or acknowledge, the concurrent aggression, so typical of primal scene representations, to force the audience to experience what they cannot bear to see.

Gently Down the Stream elicits our erotic imaginings with its elliptical narratives and the ambiguous associations among the dreams. Consider the sixth dream, in which the awakened sleeper might be angry at the dreaming narrator for her bisexuality, punishing her by acting out her own pain at discovering the evidence of the betrayer. However, the dream logic does not foreclose alternative scenarios: The awakened woman could be heterosexual herself, the covert referent of the dream simile "like being in love with/ a straight woman," and the taste of spermicide would then be the displaced consequence of making love to her.

Behind these fantasies looms the archaic image of the punishing mother taking revenge for her own frustrated and sublimated orgasm on the daughter for her sexual awakening. Regressing even farther, her punishment may be the negative consequence of the pleasure of bed-wetting. For Freud tells us in *The Interpretation of Dreams*: "People who dream often, and with great enjoyment, of *swimming*, cleaving the waves, etc. have usually been bed-wetters, and they now repeat in the dream a pleasure which they have long since learned to forgo."[7] In fact, the title of Friedrich's first film, *Hot Water*, the very source of the swimming images here, could be read as an allusion to nocturnal urination with its pun on "trouble," a situation inviting punishment.

From the exhibitionistic sex and the smearing of spermicidal jelly the dream sequences turn more violent: the bloody limb of the beast ripped off in church, the dreamer making a second vagina and suffering the anxiety of not knowing "which/ is the original?," the ambivalence of masturbating with the inflated skin of a cartoon man, ending in the most painful and witty line of the film: "It's like being in love with/ a straight woman"; giving birth to dying fetuses in a gutter, and culminating in the frightening aggression of the leopard eating two hummingbirds. There we find a savage identification of the dreamer with the leopard, the symbolical beast of Dionysus. The shots of porpoises, from a whale-watching boat, reinforce this allusion: they

---

6. MacDonald, *A Critical Cinema 2*, p. 291.
7. Sigmund Freud, *The Interpretation of Dreams* ["The Dream-Work"], in *The Basic Writings of Sigmund Freud*, trans. and ed. A. A. Brill (New York: Modern Library, 1938), pp. 390–91.

too are the cultic animals of Apollo, Dionysus's brother god; together they are the patrons of poetry, the theater, and prophecy. That there are two blue hummingbirds must mean they are linked to the two dark green fetuses of the eleventh dream. Eating the hummingbirds and feeling their feathers "humming/ on my/ tongue" gives an aggressive and triumphant cast to the cunnilingus it symbolically depicts.

If we see the leopard as the symbol of Dionysus, the five final dreams would seem to dwell on the magic of art or creation: The dreamer makes a second vagina; she builds a house, a common dream symbol for the body; she draws a man; she gives birth to herself. That she builds the house "wrong" in the eyes of the male authority, and does it without pay, may refer to the thankless genre of her filmmaking, the construction of exquisite corpses. Rather than submit to the rewards of the man who would pay for the normative house, she draws a man in the subsequent dream and, like a Pygmalion in reverse gender, makes love to her creation. From the two vaginas she then gives birth to twins, herself and a double. But these dreams of creative power are filled with anxiety and guilt. The creation of the second vagina, a defense of her bisexuality and a guarantee of her femininity, makes her anxious about her sexual nature as well as her artistic originality; twice she asks, "Which is the original?" In the birth scene she must breathe to sustain her children, but the double begins to "crumble up" in her hands.

The penultimate dream invokes the power of language and song: "Five women sing in a cappella/ funny harmony/ they spell the word truth/ in German/ I spell B-L-I-N-D-N-E-S-S/ A man says/ Their Song is A Very Clever Pun/ I say I can't agree/ I don't know German." The punishment of blindness for truth is the story of Oedipus. Since Friedrich's mother emigrated from Germany to America as a war bride, the language she claims not to know is her mother's *muttersprache*. In the finale of the film, "mutter" appears between "flutter" and "utter" on the tongue of the leopard-filmmaker.

The summer that Friedrich devoted to Whitman she would have seen that his greatest poems of poetic incarnation occur at the seaside—"As I Ebbed with the Ocean of Life" and "Out of the Cradle Endlessly Rocking"—where the sea itself was his "savage old mother incessantly crying." Like Whitman, Friedrich must wrest the power of speech, overcome the silencing of the angry mother who haunts the film and would prevent the poet giving utterance to herself by smearing spermicide on her lips.

The mother's voice is fulcrum of *The Ties That Bind*, Friedrich's next film, her first with sound. The hand-scratched titles of *Gently Down the Stream* had been a brilliant ploy to forestall the problem of sound, but she could no longer sustain her project without it. She admitted to MacDonald: "I [felt] very intimate with that device [scratched texts], but I also [felt] that I might not be able to use it much longer....I was really scared about editing sound and picture. It was completely unknown territory for me."[8] In fact, one of the vital powers of the feminist avant-garde cinema of the 1980s was its exploration of sound montage. The work of Yvonne Rainer was central to this moment; her *Journeys from Berlin/1971* provided a model for the Menippean satire that was the dominant genre of ambitious films at that time. It brought into ironical collision personal history, world politics, film theory, and psychoanalysis. Rainer's success in this genre and her influence may have been a factor in Friedrich's avoidance of Menippea (although there are traces of it in her two feature-length dramatic films *Damned if You Don't* and *Hide and Seek*, 1996).

The Ties That Bind is a palinode to *Gently Down the Stream* and a prologue to *Sink or Swim* (1990), her abecedarium of childhood distress. It begins with a series of images reflecting the dreams of the earlier film but quickly replaces the threatening archaic mother with a rather sympathetic portrait of Lore Bucher Friedrich. She is intimately connected with the sea, or rather Lake Michigan, where we frequently see her swimming. It both beckons her to death and sustains her life; two scratched titles read: "Sometimes she says/ One day I might swim out so far that I wouldn't make it back to shore," and "At other times she says/ Having the lake near me has saved my life." We see the filmmaker building a model house (but not "for some man" this time); five girls are playing on a beach. Of course, they do not spell out "the word truth in German," but the oppositions of truth and blindness, German and American, mother and daughter bind this film as tightly as they do the dream diary. If *Gently Down the Stream* can be called a film of the unconscious, *The Ties That Bind* continually shows the work of the superego.

In this first sound film, the mother's voice, in a sustained interview, is virtually all we hear. The daughter speaks twice: once to offer the date when Roosevelt learned of the death camps for Jews, and once, very briefly, when her mother scolds her for recording her playing an Austrian folk tune haltingly on the piano. The filmmaker inserts her questions by scratching them, silently, onto the image track, to which she adds, occasionally, brief asides and quotations of her mother. Yet there are no synchronized images of Lore Bucher speaking in the film's fifty-four minutes. When Friedrich films her at home, she is talking on the telephone, serving and eating breakfast, or playing the piano, but even here the visual style shows the influence of Stan Brakhage's *15 Song Traits*, with more attention to hands, feet, and torso than to the face. In counterpoint to the single voice of the interview, the filmmaker has fashioned an intricate montage of Super-8 mm material blown up to 16 mm (a visit to Germany, a few home movies), images of the mother swimming, shots

8. MacDonald, *A Critical Cinema 2*, pp. 293, 295.

from television, fragments of World War II documentaries, and the filmmaker herself constructing, crushing, then burning a model Bavarian house. She also uses headlines that appeared in the *New York Post* while the film was being made and shots of political demonstrations in which she participated to contrast her times and her political life to that of her mother's stories.

Unstated, but clearly evident in the film, is the compulsion to call her mother to account for her German childhood and youth during the Third Reich and to test the strength of her own political convictions against the backdrop of her mother's narrative. The filmmaker seems to share the dominant myth in America of Nazi Germany: that the population nearly universally acquiesced to the ideology of the Hitler regime and knew of the extermination of the Jews. Lore Bucher Friedrich speaks with apparent frankness on both issues, consistently representing herself as a victim of history. Hers was an anti-Nazi family. She was punished in school for her friendship with two Jewish girls, humiliated for insisting on the greeting "Gruss Gott" rather than "Heil Hitler," and for parading out of uniform. Yet she admits she would not risk her life as the members of the White Rose underground did (there is an homage to five White Rose "martyrs" in the film). She fiercely contends that she knew of concentration camps but not of extermination, countering by citing an article she clipped which asserts that not only the German leadership but the Allied chiefs, the Pope, and even the leaders of Switzerland and Sweden knew of the death camps and did nothing. Even while asserting her ignorance she admits a shame for being German, only to claim its unfairness:

> I felt ashamed being a German. Embarrassed. And to this day and
> always will, no matter what. Because I hear it, I get it from right and
> left. It is a persecution to the end of my life and I don't deserve it.
> But that's the way it is.

It is when her mother says that she knew only of Dachau and that it was not a death camp until the very end of the war that the filmmaker carves her longest and most passionate intervention on the celluloid, amid shots she took herself on a visit to Dachau: "NO. From 1933–1945, 30,000 people were either shot, killed in medical experiments or worked to death. And after I blame the Germans OR WISH THAT MY MOTHER COULD HAVE DONE SOMETHING ANYTHING I ask myself what I would have done AND WHY THE AMERICANS DIDN'T BOMB THE RAIL LINES TO THE CAMPS They were begged to do it."

Here at the heart of the film Friedrich struggles with her own political ineffectualness as well as her mother's. Yet despite the efforts of her montage to align the American militarism of the early Reagan government—through newspaper headlines, a letter from the Weisenthal Center about the rise of anti-Semitism fueled by American Nazis, and images of the demonstrations in which she participated—with the events her mother described, Lore Bucher Friedrich's narrative overwhelms the film. Her daughter's political protests seem trivial against that historical backdrop. The very fact that Friedrich was permitted to film women in passive resistance being carried to police vans undermines any comparison to the White Rose. Of course, the filmmaker is aware of this problem and attempts to work with it. In MacDonald's interview, she says:

> The temptation was to have this strong sound carry the image, but I was afraid of the image getting lost. I started with a forty-five second bit (when she says she feels so horrible that she's a German) and inched my way along from there, going to a two-minute section, then to a five-minute section, and finally I could work on a ten minute section comfortably.[9]
>
> Before I made *The Ties That Bind* I had such bad feelings about being German, being the daughter of a German; and my father is half German too. I don't think I really trusted the material I had. When I was working on the film, I told myself to stop worrying, to stop thinking I shouldn't be doing it, to stop disbelieving her, to trust her.... It was strange to suddenly be thinking of my mother in this respectful way, to really be admiring her for what she did, for surviving. I had never thought of *her*.[10]

The film succeeds in conveying the impression of intimacy, as if the filmmaker had not heard all her mother's stories before. It also reflects the process of its construction as Friedrich described it: Its dialogue is between "strong sound" and image. The mother's voice defeats the attempts to distrust her and wrests a confession of admiration in the final title, printed, not hand scratched: "In 1980 (after raising three children alone) she bought herself a piano and began to practice the scales." Her aspirations to a professional education, as a physician, horticulturist, or musician, had been thwarted when she was a high school student by the death of her father, who is the central focus of her affections in her narrative. Throughout the film the piano is the constant symbol of her hopes, resistance, and survival:

> I had taken up piano again. My teacher was Mrs. Pongratz.
> Mrs. Pongratz was a Party member. She was the only piano teacher

9. Ibid., p. 295.
10. Ibid., pp. 294–95.

in our neighborhood, right? She also played in our cathedral, she was
very well known, and I felt, "well, to hell with it, all she does is teach
me music." But that was not all she did, because every time she was
talking about how I should join and she was showing me pictures
and I said, "No, I don't want to." Then I stopped and I said I did not
want to have lessons anymore. It must have been half a year that
I had lessons and that was all because I just couldn't STAND her. And
one day when she came, my oldest sister had opened the door and
said, "Here is Frau Pongratz again. She wants to know whether you
would join the Party or the BDM," and I said "No" and I went out
and I threw her down the stairs. I gave her one push. And she grabbed
herself, thank god she didn't hurt herself, but she did fall down.

Her litany of oppression, humiliation, and disastrous timing includes
punishment at school from Nazi teachers, refusal by the executor of her
father's estate to pay for her higher education on the grounds of insufficient
funds (which she did not believe), and the firebombing of Stuttgart while
she was visiting her sister in a hospital there. The incident with the piano
teacher led to her arrest and a period in a forced labor camp from which
she was released only when her mother was dying of cancer. Even after the
fall of Germany, drunken GIs maliciously trashed her home: "I really hated
them. All I could say was, well, if they want to be liberators, then good
night—they are no better than anybody else." This catalog of disasters culminates in the brief account of her marriage, in which the piano played a
symbolical role:

> I have been often very sad that I could not do what I really wanted to
> do. And somehow the meeting of your father was...like a straw.
> I thought, ah, now God is good after all, I couldn't do it then, eventu-
> ally I will do it. Because I started the piano after the war. With ice cold
> fingers and in this old fur coat I would sit there and practice in gloves,
> right? And I remember very clearly talking with your father about it
> and saying, "Someday I can regain what I feel I have lost, because
> I could not go to a university and study." And he said, "Oh don't
> worry about it, you will be able to do this and you will be able to do
> that, you can play the piano and you can go and sing." Of course
> I had no idea just how poor we were going to be!...
> True, I have told him I will do anything...I will do anything. As
> a matter of fact, I have gone as far as saying, "I want to get out of
> Germany and if someday you're tired of me and you don't love me
> anymore, well..." Of course that was always understood not if we had
> a family. And that was one thing which he told me when he came and

said, "Here is my ring. I want a divorce and once you told me that if I don't like you anymore I can leave you." I said, "Paul, that was not meant after 15 years of marriage and what I have gone through with you! That was meant perhaps after one or two years having come to this country." Right? But of course as long as it was convenient for him to interpret it that way, that's what happened.

Just as the death of her father and the subsequent termination of her education loom as the decisive events of Lore Bucher's autobiographical account, for Su Friedrich the divorce of her parents, when she was ten, becomes the fulcrum of her autobiographical films: *The Ties That Bind* ends with it; *Sink or Swim* centers on it; and even *Rules of the Road* (1993) explores its psychic echoes. To MacDonald she admitted: " when I was interviewing my mother for *The Ties That Bind* and she got onto the subject of them getting divorced, it really struck a nerve and I thought it might be something to explore later."[11]

In *Sink or Swim* she found a form adequate to the complexity of the subject. Perhaps the experience of making her first dramatic film, the forty-two-minute *Damned If You Don't* helped to prepare her for this work. There, in accord with the Menippean satires prevalent at that time, she expanded the visualized narrative of a young nun stalked and seduced by a laywoman with voice-over reminiscences by nuns and the reading of an account of a visionary lesbian nun in the Renaissance. Frequently the filmmaker included her own voice coaching and correcting her narrators. The black-and-white images of the anguished nun and the woman cruising her recall the trance film genre of the 1940s and 1950s, but its climax is not a symbolical denouement but a close-up representation of their lovemaking. For *Sink or Swim* she adapted a simple and liberating ploy to relieve the autobiographical anxiety: She hired a young woman to read the texts and she changed the first-person references to "The Girl" or "she."

Hollis Frampton's *Zorns Lemma* and *Hapax Legomena: (nostalgia)* were formative influences on the structure of *Sink or Swim*. The central and longest section of *Zorns Lemma* consists of one-second shots of one-word street signs edited in alphabetical cycles. Using the roman alphabet, with *j* and *i* syncretized as well as *u* and *v*, each cycle lasts twenty-four seconds. Gradually letters are replaced with nonverbal images in inverse frequency to their use as initial letters in English words; so the final letters of the alphabet (*x*, *y*, *z*) are the first to fall out. Friedrich organized her film in twenty-six unequal segments and an epilogue, running from *z* to *a*.

11. Ibid., p. 310.

Initially, following Frampton's model, she thought to have several sections for each letter, or several words in each section. Her working manuscript moves from "Z, zeal, zero, Zeus, zygote" to "ALIMONY, abandonment, absence, abuse, academia, addiction, adoration, adversity, advice, ambivalence, anger, anniversaries, anthropology, anticipation, anxiety, archetypes, argument, arrogance, artifacts, asshole." In this expanded form the principle of free association is transparent. "Ambivalence" in A-catalog is characteristic of the whole film, as the list itself demonstrates. Whereas Frampton used the alphabetical model to filter out personal references (with limited success), Friedrich employs it as a confessional tool in her exploration of the psychodynamics of her relationship to her father. That is even clear in the final titles that largely retain the topic words of her original manuscript. Where she has made a change, I put the original in brackets: Zygote, Y Chromosome, X Chromosome, Witness [Warrior], Virgin [Virginity], Utopia [Umbilical Cord], Temptation, Seduction, Realism [Romance], Quicksand, Pedagogy, Oblivion, Nature, Memory, Memory, Loss, Kinship, Journalism, Insanity, Homework [Help], Ghosts, Flesh [Femininity], Envy, Discovery [Debt], Competition [Context], Bigamy, Athena/ Atalanta/ Aphrodite [Alimony]. In every case, the words are tangential to the visual and verbal material of the episodes.

Like the voice-over reminiscences of *Hapax Legomena: (nostalgia)*, Friedrich's commentaries smuggle an autobiographical narrative into the displaced descriptions. But she is neither as systemic nor as monomorphic as her precursor. The chapter headings allow her to create a poetic sequence of semi-autonomous nodes, functioning like the thirteen dreams of *Gently Down the Stream* but more distinctly divided. As in the dream diary, each section is a monad reformulating images and suggestions dispersed throughout the film. The changing chapter titles announce a new perspective or a variation on what we have already learned or surmised from the previous sections.

Friedrich's episodes range through a variety of styles and materials, sometimes directly related to either the key word or the narrative texts, but more often obliquely alluding to one or both. For instance, the opening montage of microscopy illustrates the title "Zygote" directly by showing sperm inseminating an egg. But it bears a negative relationship to the voice-over story of the birth of Athena directly from Zeus's head. The narrative implies a strong identification of the narrator with Athena and her father with Zeus in early childhood, despite the visual evidence of natural human conception. Scott MacDonald cogently analyzed this opening trope as a comment on cinematic editing and dramatic illusion as much as on biology:

The opening "Zygote" sequence, though only one minute and
43 seconds long, can be read as a witty encapsulation of conventional

film history. The passage of intercutting that leads finally to the climax of fertilization and cell division provides a sly commentary on commercial cinema since D.W. Griffith. What is more central to conventional movie pleasure than a dramatic chase, expressed through intercutting, that leads to the maintenance and confirmation not only of the species, but of conventional definitions of gender and family?[12]

The two silent sections that follow—"Y chromosome" and "X chromosome"—are metaphorical: A hand releases airborne milkweed pods in one and we see the tip of an elephant's trunk and foot in the other. According to the filmmaker, these are visual jokes.[13] There is a feminine quality to the soft milkweed fuzz representing the male Y chromosome and a phallic overtone to the elephant's vagina-like trunk opening, reinforced by its massive leg. However, the rubric "Witness" offers an ambiguous piece of evidence—a home movie showing the filmmaker as a young child playfully tossed in the air by her father. It is accompanied by a nursery rhyme about ambivalence: "When she was good, she was very, very good, and when she was bad she was wicked."

As the film proceeds, both the visual materials and the narrations trace a chronological development from conception and early childhood to maturity while the alphabet is running in reverse. Sometimes the visual theme of one section will continue into the next, even if the texts are not similar. We gradually understand why we are seeing circus performers in "Utopia" when the text reveals that despite the father's forbidding his daughters to eat sugar and his refusal to acquire a television, they were treated by a neighbor every Friday evening to ice cream sundaes and a chance to watch Don Ameche's *Flying Circus Show* on his television. But in the subsequent episode, which continues the circus imagery, "Temptation" alludes to the erotic temptation of seeing muscular female acrobats dressed in skimpy bras and thongs, while the text recounts the myth of Atalanta (the "great athlete and hunter" who proved to the father who abandoned her that "she was as good as a man"). We also learn that after she received a book of mythology from her father on her seventh birthday, the girl "would sit in the closet and read the stories long after being sent to bed," waiting for her father to come home. This is, of course, the point at which the filmmaker explores the childhood indications of her homosexuality, linking them to her adoration of her father and the antinomian pleasures of defying his rules.

---

12. Scott MacDonald, "From Zygote to Global Cinema via Su Friedrich's Films," *Journal of Film and Video* 44, no. 1–2 (Spring–Summer 1992), p. 31.
13. Telephone conversation with filmmaker, August 22, 2003.

When he "caught her" reading in the closet, he asked her to recount her favorite myth. As she told him the story of Atalanta, he fell asleep. Both the narrative and the circus material continue in the next section, appropriately called "Seduction." Here we learn that the father did not stay awake long enough to hear of Atalanta's fate. Defeated in a footrace by Hippomedes, who used a ruse taught him by Aphrodite, she had to break her vow of celibacy and marry the victor. For failing to pay sufficient homage to Aphrodite, the goddess turned them into lions. On the screen we see a bestiary of circus animals and their tamers. The early manuscript of alphabetical words indicates that originally the two-part story of the father and Atalanta fell under the categories of "Seduction" and "Romance," while the bestiary images had been scheduled to appear earlier under "Virginity." Apparently, in the course of making the film Friedrich realized the more powerful irony to be effected by fusing the female erotica with reading mythology in the closet. In either form the associative chain, virginity-utopia-temptation-seduction-romance, dominates these early episodes of the film before the father's cruelty and abandonment come into play.

In several ways, the origins of this film and its range of allusions are overdetermined. Friedrich herself acknowledged that Frampton has been an influence on her, but she attributed her use of the alphabet primarily to the fact that her father is a linguist and an anthropologist. For most of the filmmaker's lifetime he has been a member of the distinguished Committee for Social Thought at the University of Chicago. His works include studies of Indo-European words for trees and kinship names, music in Russian poetry, and agrarian reform in Mexico, although we would not get a clear sense of his professional distinction from his daughter's film. The three poets she says he has studied intensely, Whitman, Sappho, and Ahkmatova, are central to Paul Friedrich's studies of poetry.[14] In fact, he was keeping a dream journal at the same time that she was making *Gently Down the Stream*; in his published study of it, he writes of his "identification" with Whitman.[15] Likewise, we can trace the prevalence of mythology themes in his work. He is the author of a book on Greek goddesses upon which the filmmaker

---

14. Paul Friedrich, *The Language Parallax: Linguistic Relativism and Poetic Indeterminacy* (Austin: University of Texas Press, 1986); Paul Friedrich, *The Meaning of Aphrodite* (Chicago: University of Chicago Press, 1978); chapter 5, "Homer, Sappho, and Aphrodite" offers an extended reading of Sappho's poetry.

15. Friedrich, in *The Language Parallax*, chapter 5, "The Poetry of Language in the Politics of Dreams," interprets the use of language in one of his own dreams and traces the elaboration of the dream into a poem through two drafts. He writes: "the poem (or I, a poet like Walt Whitman) exploits the entire repertoire of aesthetic strategies and devices that I call poiesemes: for example, phonic and visual images that startle; sudden shifts of mood (compassion, outrage); vivid juxtaposition of antithetical forms; metaphors and other analogies (e.g. between surface and projectile points; and, above all, the distillation of gist whereby ethnopolitical conflict is boiled down to a name)" (p. 78).

ironically comments in the section called "Competition." This title refers at once to the opposition of Aphrodite and Demeter in Paul Friedrich's book, *The Meaning of Aphrodite* (1977), and the daughter's competition with the father and with his wives; for she tells us the book, which "argues for the need to reintegrate"[16] the erotic and the domestic goddesses "is dedicated to his third wife." She does not mention that the wife, Deborah Gordon Friedrich, also collaborated on one of the chapters. The images mount a witty opposition between European images of Madonna and Child (often breastfeeding) and Asian erotic woodcuts (including breast sucking), in a parody of art historical discourse.

Friedrich is also in "competition" with the great filmmakers who preceded her within the history of the American avant-garde cinema. Mythopoeia had been central to the work of Deren, Anger, Broughton, Markopoulos, Brakhage, Harry Smith, and others. Several of the major feminist filmmakers of her generation challenged these earlier masters by reworking the serial form most visibly exemplified by Brakhage's *Dog Star Man*, but eschewing his mythological allusions. Abigail Child's *Is This What You Were Born For?* and Leslie Thornton's *Peggy and Fred in Hell* are examples of this. However, in *Sink or Swim* Friedrich directly confronted the mythopoeic mode as a patriarchal inheritance which, she freely confesses, had been a crucial factor in her Oedipal pedagogy. She conflates the scholar Paul Friedrich with the antiacademic filmmakers in this respect. By treating her identification with Atalanta ironically, as if she too had been abandoned by her father because of her gender, she hints that her impressive success as a filmmaker would then be an Atalantan triumph within the tradition that had been dominated by males.

In describing the thesis of *The Meaning of Aphrodite*, she implies that her father's speculation "that there may have been an earlier goddess who embodied the qualities of both Aphrodite and Demeter"(her summary) is a projection of his erotic imagination. So she understands his serial marriages (graphed in the "Discovery" chapter) and his scholarship (described in both "Discovery" and "Competition") as acting out a quest for an idealized woman. In this she stands apart from those feminists (including Carolee Schneemann among filmmakers) who have been inspired by theories of a primal goddess worship anterior to Greek and Hebrew mythology. Her ironies deflate the pretensions of filmic myth making: Neither her cinematography nor her editing evoke the mythopoeic mode; she relegates all allusions to myth to the child's voice-over.

---

16. In *The Meaning of Aphrodite*, p. 190, Paul Friedrich credits Anna Ahkmatova, "who synthesized in her person and projected to her readers both of the complexes dealt with in this chapter as part of a more general image of the artistically creative woman."

As the film progresses, the stories of Paul Friedrich's cruelty and blindness to his daughters deflect attention away from the filmmaker's relationship to the artistic precursors of her metier. For instance, the short narrative of "Pedagogy," in which she tells us that her father taught her chess but would never play with her again after the first time she checkmated him, overshadows the allusion to the chess game near the end of Deren's *At Land*, framed in same way with only the player's hands visible. Friedrich's relationship to Deren is both remote and complex, especially in *Sink or Swim*. Her projection of the figure of the father is so powerful and intricate that her film seems, superficially, to be a work of realism where Deren has pioneered modes of subjective quest romances. In fact, "Realism" is the rubric Friedrich gives the story from which her title derives. There, while we watch "realistic" images of urban children playing, swimming, and eating in some instances with their fathers, the girl narrator tells us that her father taught her to swim by throwing her into the deep end of a pool after a brief lecture on kicking and breathing. Later he terrified her with stories of water moccasins. Nothing could be farther from the magical images of Deren as a version of Aphrodite, emerging from the backward-rolling waves of the sea at the start of *At Land*.

Yet tangentially Deren still informs *Sink or Swim*. The trance film as she perfected it often turned upon fantasies of suicide. In Friedrich's film, by contrast, her mother's suicide threats occur under the chapter title "Insanity." Then, labeling "Ghosts" the long static shot in negative of the filmmaker typing a letter to her father she could not mail (about her mother obsessively listening to Schubert's song, "Gretchen at the Spinning Wheel"), she ironically displaces the spectral effect Deren achieved by using images in negative, in *Ritual in Transfigured Time* and throughout *The Very Eye of Night*. In fact, *ghosts* may be taken as a term for the rhetoric of displacement itself. Within the logic of Friedrich's film it conjures the "Kinship" section in which she had heard the Schubert song. Its lyrics, in German, evoke the anguish of an abandoned woman. To the rhythms and refrains of the song the filmmaker has edited an erotic *periegeton*, intercutting grainy shots of women embracing in a shower with images of travel by airplane, train, and car to Death Valley. The long shots of the solitary female figure in the desert landscape and amid monumental rocks might evoke *At Land* to a viewer familiar with the genre even without the other hints of Deren's haunting of the film. There are echoes of Walt Whitman, too, with both the narrative of "the savage old mother incessantly crying"[17] and in the shots of birds: the two white birds that fly off together near the start of the section and the later images of a solitary dark flyer are emblems from "Out of the Cradle Endlessly Rocking," the great poem of

---

17. Jeffrey Stout reminded me of this allusion.

poetic incarnation where Whitman recuperates his vocation from his identification with the music of "you solitary singer," the bird who lost his mate:

> For I that was a child, my tongue's use sleeping,
> Now that I have heard you,
> Now in a moment I know what I am for — I awake...
> O you demon, singing by yourself — projecting me,
> O solitary me, listening – never more shall I cease imitating, perpetuating
>   you...
> Never again leave me to be the peaceful child I was before what there, in
>   the night,
> By the sea, under the yellow and sagging moon,
> The dusky demon aroused — the fire, the sweet hell within,
> The unknown want, the destiny of me.[18]

As the filmmaker relives her parents', perhaps all parents', erotic tragedy, lesbian love displaces heterosexuality. Significantly, the *periegeton* is ambiguous as to whether she is the deserted lover or the deserter, her father or her mother, Faust or Gretchen, the figure Deren represents or the lovers—male and female—she discards in *At Land*. Placing the Schubert song before its contextual explanation (unless we remember the sad story of the mother's obsession from *The Ties That Bind*) allows Friedrich to make it her own music "projecting me" before it is a sign of her mother's neurotic compulsion. In the letter that concluded "Love. P.S. I wish I could mail you this letter." she wanted to tell her father of her aesthetic revelation: "It's so strange to have so ecstatic a melody accompany those tragic lyrics. But maybe that's what makes it so powerful: it captures perfectly the conflict between memory and the present."

Deren and Whitman fuse with Friedrich's genetic parents in this film of poetic incarnation, haunted by the end of "Out of the Cradle":

> That he was sung to me in the moonlight on Paumanok's gray beach,
> With the thousand responsive songs, at random,
> My own songs, awaked from that hour,
> And with them the key, the word up from the waves,
> The word of the sweetest song, and all songs,
> That strong and delicious word which, creeping to my feet,
> The sea whispered me.[19]

18. Walt Whitman, "Out of the Cradle Endlessly Rocking," *Selected Poems 1855–1892: A New Edition*, ed. Gary Schmidgall (New York: St. Martin's, 1999), pp. 212–13.
19. Ibid., p. 214.

Friedrich's film is one of the many responsive songs arising as if at random, driven by the mother's fantasies of death and the father's displacements of guilt.

Aesthetic issues are inseparable from Oedipal dynamics here. Not only did Paul Friedrich write on music and poetry, he wrote poetry himself. Twice in the film his poetry comes under critical scrutiny for its solipsistic blindness to the "the conflict between memory and the present." The first occasion is the middle of the alphabet: "Memory" is the longest chapter; in the published script it appears in two parts. The first is an evocation of the death of Paul Friedrich's beloved sister when they were children. She had a heart attack jumping into an ice-cold pool. The second part describes a poem he wrote twenty years later when his first child, Su Friedrich's elder sister, was a week old. The filmmaker quotes a passage from it in which she stands in for the lost sister: "But now there is only the quiet face that replaces a drowned sister at last." According to the narrator, "No one blamed him for her death, but he carried the burden of guilt and loss for many years," because she had not waited for him to complete his chores before going to the pool. However, instead of keeping him from extraordinarily abusive punishment of his own children, that guilt may have driven him to reenact a version of that disaster. In the very next section, "Loss," we hear how he held the heads of both the filmmaker and her older sister under the water of a bathtub because they fought with each other and "made [their] mother miserable."

In the course of making the film, Friedrich discovered forgotten home movies her paternal grandfather had taken of his children in the 1930s. So in the first part of the "Memory" chapter we see Paul Friedrich as a boy, playing with his brother and sister and, astonishingly, images of them all swimming in the very pond where the sister died perhaps a year later. (It is one of the ironies of archival footage that we would not know these are actual records of Paul Friedrich's childhood merely by looking at the finished film.) Then, although the discussion of the poem begins "Twenty years later," the home movies go back in time to images of Paul Friedrich playing with his first child when she was a toddler. "Loss," however, uses an utterly different montage strategy: shots of families taking their daughters to their first communion rite counterpoint the account of the father's brutal "baptism" of his daughters.

"Bigamy" offers a different conflict between memory and the present. Friedrich uses the term as an etymological, not legal, category: Two marriages are sequential, not simultaneous. The penultimate chapter of the film proposes a visual self-portrait of the filmmaker as the child voice recounts a meeting, as an adult, with her father and her eleven-year-old half sister:

Just then her father stopped the girl in midsentence to say that
her story didn't interest him. The woman became rigid with fear.

This was her childhood, being played out all over again by the young girl.

By this point, rhyming episodes have drawn an intricate web of connections throughout the film. The trip of the father and this young daughter to visit the now-mature filmmaker recalls a disastrous trip they once took together in Mexico that spans the "Flesh" and "Envy" chapters. The former heading refers to Friedrich's youthful sexuality; she had to be eighteen or nineteen at the time. When she was repeatedly late for meals because of the attentions of a Mexican boy she met on the beach, the father abruptly sent her back to Chicago. "Envy," however, is an interpretive category; for the chapter focuses on the poem he later wrote about the event: "How You Wept, How Bitterly." Criticizing the obtuseness of the poem, the narrator complains, "He still didn't realize that he had been acting like a scorned and vengeful lover, and that hers had not been the tears of an orphaned child, but those of a frustrated teenage girl who had to pay for a crime she didn't commit."

A second *periegeton* of subjective, often handheld, images of Mexico encompasses both sections. The first time we see a receding landscape from the back window of a vehicle, it corresponds neatly to the narrator's description: "She sat by herself at the back of the bus and watched the coastline disappear." The second time it is synchronized to the last line of the father's poem:

Your eyes at our parting condensed all children orphaned by divorce
A glance through a film of tears at a father dwindling to a speck.

Sink or Swim poses the resonances of its own sound and picture nuances against the insensitivity of the father's poetry, which fails to negotiate the play of the ecstatic and the tragic the filmmaker heard in Schubert's song and strives for in her art. That very play, in fact, is at issue in Whitman's "A Voice Out of the Sea" where, as Jeffrey Stout observed, "the bird's song, which both constitutes the mourning of the bird's lost mate and the poet's ecstatic election as one who must sing such songs."[20]

Visually the "Bigamy" chapter is a self-portrait. We see the filmmaker in bed, in the bathtub, watching television, or at her typewriter, smoking or drinking a beer in nearly every shot. Even this wry acknowledgment of addictions caps suggestions from earlier parts of the film. We learn in "Homework" that once her father got a divorce, the taboos were lifted. A television entered the house and the girl spent all her allowance on candy. Significantly,

20. Jeffrey Stout, e-mail letter to author, June 26, 2007.

we see flashes of early 1960s comedies—*Life with Father, The Donna Reed Show, Father Knows Best*—with idealizations of paternal authority, interrupted by a commercial for Lucky Strike cigarettes. Smoking, drinking, and watching television, then, are marked as the obsessive compensations for the lost father. Writing, too, has its refracted history within the film. In this case, the "Journalism" chapter spoke of her diary, a tenth birthday gift from her sister, where she wrote about "punishment assignments, fighting with boys, and playing with her friends," and wrote about the divorce, of which she was so ashamed that she wrote in pencil. (Her mother surreptitiously erased those entries.)

In the last chapter, two women sun themselves on a beach while a naked baby girl plays as if these three females might correspond to the trinity "Athena/ Atalanta/ Aphrodite," which is the final rubric. One of the women is framed remarkably like Maya Deren as she lies on the sand in *At Land.* The camera very slowly zooms out over the lake as the narrator tells a parable of renunciations. Recalling how her mother clung to her father after their divorce, the filmmaker determines not to swim across the lake following him, but to stop. After a hint of fascination with death, which echoes both Deren's scenarios and her mother's speech in *The Ties That Bind*—"The water surrounded her like a lover's arms"—she swims back to her friends.

The compulsion to repeat finds its emblem in the multiple superimpositions of the epilogue; visually a home movie shot of the filmmaker as a preteen is compounded over itself while on the soundtrack we hear her own voice for the first time, in a round in six tracks, chanting the ABC song. Here is how she analyzed the conclusion for Scott MacDonald:

> The conclusion of *Sink or Swim* was more a way for me to acknowledge my absurd ambivalence. A lot of the stories in the film are about doing things to get my father's approval, and then at the end in the last story I decide I'm not going to swim across the lake to please him. I've made a sort of grand gesture of turning back to shore, swimming back to my friends who will hopefully treat me differently than my father has treated me. But then in the epilogue I turn right around and sing the ABC song, which asks what he thinks of me! I believe that, to a certain extent, we can transcend our childhood, but in some way we always remain the child looking for love and approval.[21]

Friedrich seems to have directed the ambivalence she acknowledges toward her parents to her cinematic precursors as well. Although confessional irony is her primary mode, she has never directly addressed in a film her origins as a

21. MacDonald, *A Critical Cinema 2*, p. 314.

filmmaker. Yet, as I have been trying to demonstrate here, in the three strong films in which she "gives birth to [her]self" she inherits the debts of a rich film-making tradition infolded within even richer literary and artistic traditions. Throughout this book, I have stressed the importance of one of those forma-tive contexts, that of Ralph Waldo Emerson, and to a somewhat lesser extent Walt Whitman, for that filmmaking tradition. Since Friedrich, like Abigail Child, gave birth to her filmic persona as an elective heir of Hollis Frampton, who imbibed the Emerson-Whitman lineage by way of its intricate evasions through Ezra Pound, we are not often confronted in her films with the visual spectacle Emerson called "a pictorial air," available to the filmmaker "by mechanical means": rapid movement, detached perspectives, in brief, what I have encapsulated in Emerson's phrase "turning the eyes upside down."[22] In her case, as in Frampton's, we must turn from the sixth short chapter of *Nature* ("Idealism") where that phrase appears, to the fourth ("Language") where we find: "wise men pierce... rotten diction and fasten words again to visible things.... The moment our discourse rises above the ground line of familiar facts and is inflamed with passion or exalted by thought, it clothes itself in images."[23] Friedrich's films repeatedly examine the problematic nature of finding images for her passionate and exalted discourse.

The incongruity between that discourse and images lies at the heart of one of her minor films, *Rules of the Road*, another autobiographical work so thoroughly ironical it might be the satyr play to her major three I have been discussing in this chapter. It also happens to ironize the vehicular theme and perpetual camera movement so often extolled in these chapters. On the soundtrack, the filmmaker for the first time delivers her own monologue, narrating the painful breakup of a relationship with a woman she does not name. The story centers on a car they shared for work, errands, and weekend excursions while they lived together in Brooklyn. As she narrates the history of the station wagon, she interweaves memories of rides from her childhood with accounts of the pleasures and conveniences the car provided her and her lover as well as the fights had while driving. Above all, the voice-over emphasizes her remorse over the breakup. In this account, the automobile gradually becomes an allegorical figure for both the woman she loved and the relationship itself:

> The car seems to collect and hold onto the spirit of those fights in
> much the same way that the brown cloth seats eventually became

---

22. Jeffrey Stout drew my attention to "the trip to Coney Island, wshere the view from the train is like a film strip and the Ferris Wheel is like a film reel" in Friedrich's *Damned If You Don't* as a particularly cogent instance of the Emersonian aesthetic.

23. Ralph Waldo Emerson, *Essays and Lectures* (New York: Library of America, 1983) p. 23.

suffused with the ugly smell of smoke from all the cigarettes we consumed....

I liked to imagine myself driving it many years from now when it became one of the old and familiar things in my life, a part of my small and precious universe of old friends, favorite objects, and her.

There is more camera movement in *Rules of the Road* than in any other Friedrich film. She continually pans, zooms in and out, walks with the camera, nearly always with the goal of finding yet another old beige station wagon parked or moving on the streets of New York or on the highways. The few moments shot from within a moving car express the exhilaration of "the low degree of the sublime" associated with a symbolic break from her parents' severely economical use of the family car ("giddy with relief at leaving behind my parents' Spartan ways") and with erotic euphoria ("When I was doing the driving, I felt as though I was carrying her in my arms—away from the relentless, claustrophobic city towards an unpredictable generous expanse of forest or ocean"). But the euphoria of vehicular movement is merely a foil to the obsessive stalking of similar station wagons in the hope and fear of catching sight of her former girlfriend.

The restless images provide an ironic commentary on the autobiographical monologue, as if they had to stand in for the unfilmed record of the lost relationship. There is no sense that the visual track of *Rules of the Road* would be meaningful as an autonomous poem of movement or travel. In this respect, the film provides a sharp contrast to Stan Brakhage's *Visions in Meditation*, which is the subject of the next chapter. Brakhage's concept of moving visual thinking would locate in his images alone the "discourse...inflamed with passion or exalted by thought."

CHAPTER 15

Brakhage: Meditative Cinema

A t the turning point in his mature career, Stan Brakhage made a series of four films on the theme of Faust, which I have examined elsewhere.[1] Not only did he divorce Jane Collom while making this series and fall in love with Marilyn Jull, whom he would shortly marry, he also formulated the theoretical nexus of ideas to which he assigned the phrase "moving visual thinking" at this time. Furthermore, the Spinozan critique of religion as political theology that had influenced his filmmaking on and off for decades gave way, with one final and brilliant resurgence in *Christ Mass Sex Dance* (1991), to a new fascination with the idea of God and a return to the Christianity of his Episcopalian childhood, in an unorthodox, almost

---

1. See P. Adams Sitney, "Brakhage's Faustian Psychodrama," in *Stan Brakhage: Filmmaker*, ed. David E. James (Philadelphia: Temple University Press, 2005); R. Bruce Elder, "Goethe's Faust, Gertrude Stein's Doctor Faustus Lights the Lights, and Stan Brakhage's Faust Series," *Canadian Journal of Film Studies* 14, no. 1 (Spring 2005), pp. 51–68; Inez Hedges, *Framing Faust: Twentieth-Century Cultural Struggles* (Carbondale: Southern Illinois University Press, 2005), pp. 132–47.

private mode.[2] This gradual change culminated in the 1995 essay "Having Declared a Belief in God" and inflected the titles of the late, hand-painted films *The Lion and the Zebra Make God's Raw Jewels* (1999), *Jesus Trilogy and Coda: The Boy Jesus, In Jesus' Name, Jesus Wept, Christ on the Cross* (2000), *Ascension* (2002), *Resurrectus Est* (2002), and *Panels for the Walls of Heaven* (2002). In this chapter I concentrate on the series of four *Visions in Meditation* he released in 1989 and 1990, utilizing his 1990 lecture "Gertrude Stein: Meditation in Film and Literature" as a guide. Since the ideas and films of Hollis Frampton continued to catalyze Brakhage's thought in the late 1980s and early 1990s, I frequently make reference to them.

Marilyn Brakhage wrote me the following account of the beginning of this astonishingly fecund period in Brakhage's life:

I first met Stan in February of 1987 . . . and moved to Boulder at the end of that summer. That autumn he was still working on the second and third parts of the Faust series (and also finished *Kindering* and *Loud Visual Noises*). At that time he was working as a half-time professor only, teaching during the fall term. The rest of the year he would continue his film work, but also do whatever lecturing he could—to show the work, and to make some more money. An incredibly busy and productive time followed (1988–1990), in which we did a lot of traveling and Stan completed a lot of new work. Early in 1988, I accompanied Stan on a tour of several Canadian cities that I had helped to arrange—Montreal, Toronto, Regina, Vancouver, Victoria. I know he was still showing *Faust's Other: An Idyll* as a work-in-progress at that time. He also shot the film *Matins* while we were in Toronto (on the occasion of Jim Tenney and Lauren Pratt's marriage.) . . . Back in Boulder he was also editing *Marilyn's Window* (also shot in Toronto) and *I . . . Dreaming*, and still working on *Rage Net*.

Around that time (early '88) Stan was also invited to come and give lecture/screenings at the University of Tulsa. Instead of the Tulsa people paying for his flight, I suggested that maybe they would just give him the travel money and we could rent a car and I would drive him there and back. (Stan had by this time given up driving altogether.) So he agreed, I drove, and he took his camera equipment along. Like a typical tourist, I looked up guide books for interesting places to visit along the way, and Stan basically went along with it all, and filmed

2. See Gary Higgins, Rodrigo Garcia Lopes, and Thomas Chadwick, "Grisled Roots: An Interview with Stan Brakhage," *Millennium Film Journal* no. 26 (Fall 1992), pp. 57–58, for a discussion of the filmmaker's religious upbringing. I can find no documentation on Brakhage's reading of Spinoza. However, I recall his mention of the influence of Spinoza as early as 1962.

(sometimes out the window of the car as we drove, sometimes at places where we would stop.)...We went south through Colorado, then East, cutting across a bit of northern Texas, and through Oklahoma to Tulsa. This was in April, 1988. I remember many of the roads were flooded as we drove through northern Oklahoma. The huge golden sculpture...of praying hands that figures prominently in *Faust IV* was also filmed on that trip....On the way back to Colorado, we drove through Kansas, and we stopped in Winfield, where we found Stan's childhood homes (of his mother and of his grandmother.) We went into his old home (the present owners being very friendly and inviting him in when he went to their door) and he remembered the layout of the house (from when he was three or four years old), and the location of what he said was his earliest memory—sitting on the floor playing with blocks, with the sun streaming in through the window. We also visited the cemetery where his father was buried.

That trip was so inspiring to Stan, it seems, that he wanted to do some more traveling around the southwest, and/or he agreed to do so. I can't really remember whether it was more his idea or mine—possibly mine—but I planned another driving trip, anyway, which we did in May of that year, to New Mexico. Around that time, though, Stan also applied for a grant to help finance his proposed *Visions in Meditation* series, which would be filmed around the southwest and which he envisioned as a sort of natural continuation evolving out of *Faust IV*.

The grant application was turned down, but we went ahead with the trip anyway. That second driving trip lasted ten days and we drove south to Taos, Santa Fe, down to the White Sands at Alamogordo, and then to the Carlsbad Caverns in New Mexico's southeast corner, before returning to Colorado. Footage from that trip can also be found in *Faust IV* (the White Sands, for example) as well as in *Visions in Meditation 3* and *4*. (I remember we saw a lot of "dust devils"—little tornadoes—and Stan got out of the car to film one, and as he was filming it, it abruptly changed direction and started coming straight towards us. I called to him to hurry and get back in the car, but he answered, "Just a minute—I'm getting a great shot!"...but managed to get back safely, and it passed us by—but is in the film.)

In June we were in NYC for two weeks, most of the summer back in Boulder, but then we went on a third driving trip, which must have been in August, this time around Colorado—the "painted desert" in the south, west to Mesa Verde, north then, and finally east again across the divide. (This obviously was when he did the shooting for *Visions in Meditation #2*.) When we arrived at Mesa Verde, Stan had a very strong feeling that something terrifying and evil had happened there.

I think we arrived fairly late in the day...stayed overnight nearby, and then returned the following day. He went into a kind of deep filmmaking trance...

So, during the fall of '88, when Stan was teaching again at CU, he was editing *Faust IV*, but not yet the *Visions*...We moved to Toronto in early '89, planning to get married there, and to stay there if possible. However, Stan's search for a position in Toronto did not succeed....Anton was born there in late September...and then we re-located back to Boulder, where Stan continued at CU.

While in Toronto, (early '89), I remember Stan received a print from the lab of the finished *Faust IV*—and in March we went on our fourth and final driving trip together (that is, alone together, before the kids), this time because he was invited to speak at Boston University. We drove from Toronto across New York State and then into Massachusetts. After leaving Boston we drove north through New Hampshire and up the coast of Maine, then cutting inland to Quebec (through deep snow), staying briefly in Quebec City, then, before driving back to Toronto....This trip, however, in March of 1989, was when Stan did the filming for *Visions in Meditation No. 1*. He edited that soon after, while we were living in Toronto (and also did the shooting for *City Streaming*).

Back in Boulder, in the fall of '89, Stan edited *City Streaming*, and made *The Thatch of Night*, as well as beginning his *Babylon Series*. Then 1990: Thinking back on it, I can't imagine how Stan did so much, even though he received a sabbatical from teaching that year....I know he presented the complete *Visions in Meditation* series at CU along with his lecture on "Gertrude Stein: Meditative Literature and Film" in November of 1990. So in that time he edited the next three parts, also finished his *Babylon Series* and made another couple of short films—*Glaze of Cathexis* and *Vision of the Fire Tree*—AND worked on *Passage Through: A Ritual* (which was done before the end of the year), AND shot the footage for *A Child's Garden and the Serious Sea* that summer (which he then edited in 1991.)[3]

In "Gertrude Stein: Meditative Literature and Film," Brakhage declared, "My working process...is to transmogrify (as Stein translates) each vibrancy of unutterably private source into Form." Seizing the occasion of a major address to the faculty of the University of Colorado, he polemically defined the task of cinema while he paid homage to Stein by acknowledging her influence

3. Marilyn Brakhage, e-mail to P. Adams Sitney, December 27, 2004.

on his entire film production but singling out her *Stanzas in Meditation*—"one of the few completed epics of our century"—as the greatest inspiration to his filmmaking and theory during the previous "half-decade or so." Actually, he had championed *Stanzas in Meditation* as Stein's magnum opus since I first heard him speak in 1960. But the commencement of a new series of films, *Visions in Meditation*, and his friendship with the Stein scholar Ulla Dydo, who had published a number of enlightening articles on that epic, may have refocused the long poem of 1932 in the center of his attention.

In 1957, when the Yale University Press first published the 150-page text, with an introduction by Brakhage's future friend Donald Sutherland, John Ashbery, reviewing it for *Poetry*, compared it serially to the paintings of De Kooning, Webern's music, and Henry James's late novels:

> There is certainly plenty of monotony in [the poem], but it is the fertile kind, which generates excitement as water monotonously flowing over a dam generates electrical power.... The poem is a hymn to possibility; a celebration of the fact that the world exists, that things can happen.... *Stanzas in Meditation* is no doubt the most successful of her attempts to do what can't be done, to create a counterfeit reality more real than reality. And if, on laying the book aside, we feel that it is still impossible to accomplish the impossible, we are also left with the conviction that it is the only thing worth trying to do.[4]

Ashbery himself was as marked by his encounter with Stein's epic as Brakhage. He had published his first book, the Stevensian *Some Trees*, the year before. John Shoptaw called Stein "the most urgent of the incitements" to his next book, *The Tennis Court Oath*.[5] In fact, reading *Stanzas in Meditation* in the late 1950s may have been the catalyst for both Ashbery and Brakhage to discover, in their different ways, a modernist recovery of commonplace experience that enabled them each to crystallize their first mature styles. As such, then, Stein was a vehicle for refreshing an Emersonian fascination with the allure of daily life.

Stein achieves so high a level of abstraction in *Stanzas in Meditation* that Ashbery concludes, "it is usually not events which interest Miss Stein, rather it is their 'way of happening', and the story of *Stanzas in Meditation* is a general, all-purpose model which each reader can adapt to fit his own set of particulars."[6] The youthful poet seems to be defining his own program

4. John Ashbery, "The Impossible," *Poetry* 90, no. 4 (July 1957), pp. 250–51, 253–54.
5. John Shoptaw, *On the Outside Looking Out: John Ashbery's Poetry* (Cambridge, MA: Harvard University Press, 1994), p. 51.
6. John Ashbery "The Impossible, p. 251.

while writing of Stein. Thirty-five years later, Brakhage repeats that gesture of poetic fusion when he declares that "literary meditation... eschew[s] Story *altogether*," citing the autonomy of language in Stein's work in order to bolster his assertions that "Film, if it is to be comparable to Literature, must, first, disrupt every literarily logical assumption that Picture is only a container for the variably nameable... Film must eschew any easily recognizable reference... It must give up *all* that which is static, so that even its stillnesses-of-image are ordered on an edge of potential movement."[7]

Ulla Dydo wrote: "In the meditations, consciousness focuses on abstract mental landscapes that do not cohere.... There is trouble in the quibbles but it is not named and not attached to stories. It is as if in meditation Stein 'unhooked' words from events, people, and objects to compose them as efforts of the mind in the act of looking for comprehension."[8]

Brakhage reaffirmed his commitment to Stein and to *Stanzas in Meditation* when filmic representation was in question for him. In the years immediately following the lecture, he would devote himself almost exclusively to hand-painted films. However, the example he cites is the first of his *Visions in Meditation*, which obviously owes its title to Stein's epic but bears no superficial similarities to that source, posing questions to which I shall return shortly. Had he used, say, his earlier film *The Riddle of Lumen* as an example, the studied abstraction of that work might be said to constitute "a freeing of each image (as her each-and-every word) to its un-owned self-life within the continuities (rather than context) of the work";[9] for the film moves from image to image along junctures of visual similarity and antithesis—of color, shape, movement, texture—that undermine overriding categorizations of theme, genre, and narrative voice.

In addition to citing Stein whenever he discussed narration, Brakhage continued to be haunted by Hollis Frampton. In making *The Riddle of Lumen*, Brakhage had been responding to the challenge of Frampton's work, at the height of their friendship. The core of Frampton's *Zorns Lemma* is an extended montage of one-second shots of words found on the streets of New York, arranged in alphabetical order. As the alphabets cyclically repeat, letters are replaced, in inverse order of their frequency as initial letters of English words, by one-second shots of moving objects and molecular events. The film tacitly provokes its viewers to guess the system of its construction and, having done so, to anticipate which letter will disappear next. *The Riddle of*

---

7. Stan Brakhage, "Gertrude Stein: Meditative Literature and Film," in *Essential Brakhage: Selected Writings on Filmmaking*, ed. with a foreword by Bruce R. McPherson (Kingston, NY: McPherson and Co., Documentext, 2001), pp. 195, 199–200.

8. Ulla Dydo, *A Stein Reader* (Evanston, IL: Northwestern University Press, 1993), p. 568.

9. *Essential Brakhage*, p. 201.

Lumen takes its title in allusion to the Latin text of Robert Grosseteste, "On the Ingression of Light," that Frampton translated for a choral reading, one second for each word, over the final, very long, shot of his film. "Lumen" or "light" is the answer to the implicit riddle of Brakhage's film: What is the subject of this work? Or rather, what is the common thread uniting some three hundred discrete shots in approximately a thousand seconds of pure cinema? The shots themselves seem to have been culled from the outtakes of Brakhage's work in several modes over a decade; there are fragments of landscapes, a posed nude, still life details, street scenes, and so on. Local principles of association, such as a series of still round objects, or of contrast, in rhythm, movement, color, depth, or focus momentarily tease us with clues to a pattern; but they veer off into other patterns, frustrating attempts to anticipate any category for the forthcoming shots other than the most general one of a configuration of the light.

In an encomium for Frampton written the year he made the film and published in the very volume in which Frampton's "A Pentagram for Conjuring the Narrative" was written, Brakhage formulated the following, consciously reworking the diction of Charles Olson's "Projective Verse," after insightfully acknowledging the differences between Frampton's relationship to Pound's poetics and his own—the former through direct contact during Pound's "Confucian" period, his own mediated by the Black Mountain school:

> [M]otion pictures permit Hollis Frampton to give us the action of painting both frozen and moving—principally because the experiencing of paint through motion picture projection establishes neither paint'ing' nor paint...the former existing as a series of 'stills' and the latter as an interference with the light. Once one begins to write or talk about 'semblance,' then Film becomes the primary designation of the medium— 24 veils a second, etc. The instant when baby Hollis realized he could have his cake and eat it too was an INSTANTER centering convergent possibilities suddenly taken shape as Thought. The cake was, after all, either 'et' or not on the plate before him. Since then Hollis obviously had it (cake/experience: :Concept) as electrical firing (nerves) in semblances of scene (veils of light) which could USE dichotomies (on-off, yes-no, cake-nocake) in the service of having it all (ALL).[10]

Through its obscurities and convolutions one can discern here the program for *The Riddle of Lumen*: dichotomies organized to foreground the

---

10. Stan Brakhage, "Stan Brakhage on Hollis Frampton," in *Form and Structure in Recent Film*, ed. Dennis Wheeler (Vancouver: Vancouver Art Gallery, Talonbooks, 1972), unnumbered pages.

concept of semblances as veils of light. The antithetical power of primal images (to adapt a title of an important source from Freud) will recur in the Stein lecture and in "Having Declared a Belief in God." Earlier in the text, referring to Frampton's interest in the idea of "blocks of light" resolving wave and particle theories, Brakhage had written "the very machinery of motion pictures function[s] as a perfect (though gross) model of the nature of illumination itself, as Hollis once commented to me 'him'-self."

Likewise, when he writes in "Gertrude Stein: Meditative Literature and Film," "Film must eschew any easily recognizable reference; for reference is always achieved along-a-line of Symbolized Signs," he could be glossing the ironic filming of signs in *The Riddle of Lumen*.[11] Three times, words appear on the screen. First, a child holds a picture book with a few words below each picture. But the book is held upside down, making the reading impossible for the child, and for us as well, because of the brevity of the image. In a film where the norm is a four-second shot, this one takes half a beat, two seconds; very few shots exceed ten seconds. Later, the second and third word images appear as fragments of commercial signs, like those of *Zorns Lemma*. "ROG," perhaps from the name Roger, isolates the Latin root for words of questioning, and "Syste[] & Shoot" elliptically condenses the question of the film: According to what system did the filmmaker shoot (and edit) it?

Furthermore, Brakhage could be thinking of the complex microrhythmic tensions the film establishes between relatively still images and the exhaustive survey of his repertoire of intrinsic and extrinsic movements, each carefully isolated within an individual and clearly demarcated shot, when he proclaims: "It must give-over all senses-of-repetition precisely because Film's illusion-of-movement is based on shot-series of flickering *near*-likenesses of image."[12] Frampton's systemic mode of filmmaking encouraged Brakhage, in that instance, to override his obsession with "the three sisters of Fate: Birth, Sex, Death," and suppressing his usual indicators of theme, genre, and narrative voice, to meditate on "semblances of scene (veils of light)."

In the Gertrude Stein essay, Brakhage paraphrased Frampton's hilarious description of learning the language of birds, which I mentioned in chapter 14. Apparently citing from memory, he unwittingly made a crude story of seduction and abandonment out of it: "The Western emphasis of/on Metaphor is clearly one of Transformation. As such it can be thought of as a passage and ritualized through either story-telling or meditation. There are only five stories (epitomized by filmmaker Hollis Frampton thinking of the five

11. Stan Brakhage, *Essential Brakhage*, p. 200.
12. Ibid.

bird-songs: (1) Good Morning. (2) I found a worm. (3) Love me. (4) Get out. (5) Good Night.)"[13] The original reads:

> One fine morning, I awoke to discover that, during the night, I had learned to understand the language of birds. I have listened to them ever since. They say: "Look at me!" or: "Get out of here!" or: "Let's fuck!" or: "Help!" or: "Hurrah!" or: "I found a worm!" and that's all they say. And that, when you boil it down, is about all we say. (Which of those things am I saying now?)

I take it that the final question is so funny because it points to the self-interested claims the theoretician would make on different readers. This parabolic distillation of linguistic motives prefaces Frampton's reduction of narratives to mythic archetypes, and pairs the archetypes on the bifurcated model of the "I" as speaker and listener. The story of Odysseus narrates the father-son story from the father's point of view; Oedipus tells the same story from the son's.

Frampton returned the compliment to Brakhage in the third chapter of *Circles of Confusion*, "Film in the House of the Word," where he takes up again the theme of cinema and specifically Brakhage's theoretical position, following a chapter on Muybridge in which he suggested that the photographer's time studies emanate from the experience (as if time stopped) of shooting his wife's lover. In an open confrontation with Brakhage's work this time, Frampton aligns Sergei Eisenstein's famous warning about the destructive potential of synchronous sound with Brakhage's opening of *Metaphors on Vision*: "How many colors are there in a field of grass for a crawling baby who has never heard of green."[14] The opposition of visual to verbal puts theoretical writing itself into question. Brakhage had acknowledged this paradox when he punned, "I'm thru writing, thru writing," calling his theoretical endeavor a compulsive form of self-purgation. Yet Frampton saw this as bad faith. He argues:

> Every artistic dialogue that concludes in a decision to ostracize the word is disengenuous to the degree that it succeeds in concealing from

---

13. The text may have been cosmetically corrected for delivery before the faculty of the University of Colorado. In "Poetry and Film" (*Brakhage Scrapbook: Collected Writings 1964–1980*, ed. Robert Haller [Kingston, N.Y.: Documentext, 1982] p. 220) he had cited the same misremembered sequence, but the birds said "fuck me," rather than "Love me." In his deathbed video interview with Pip Chodorov (January 4, 2003) Brakhage, again misremembering the sequence and the diction, cites "Love me." That time he praised Frampton as "great filmmaker, Hollis Frampton, who was a teacher, an aesthetician as I, as God save our souls, as both of us hope to be. He said the whole history of Hollywood movies—any movies, just the movies, was comparable to birdsong."

14. Apparently Frampton was quoting from memory. Brakhage's text asks: "How many colors are there in a field of grass to the crawling baby unaware of 'Green.'"

itself its fear of the word...and the source of that fear: that language
in every culture, and before it becomes an arena of discourse, is, above
all, an expanding arena of power, claiming for itself and its wielders all
it can seize, and relinquishing nothing.[15]

Following the train of Frampton's thought, we watch him set up a hypothetical Eisenstein in opposition to the logophobic Brakhage, an Eisenstein
who may have

glimpsed, however quickly, a project beyond the intellectual montage: the
construction of a machine, very much like film, more effiecient than language, that might, entering into direct competition with language, transcend
its speed, abstraction, compactness, democracy, ambiguity, power...a project, moreover, whose ultimate promise was the constitution of an external
critique of language itself."[16]

Perhaps we need look no further for the reason Brakhage gave the example
of *Visions in Meditation #1* rather than *The Riddle of Lumen* in "Gertrude
Stein..." than to acknowledge that the filmmaker was focusing on his recently completed film of major ambition at the time he wrote the lecture.
Since it was on his mind, it was the obvious work to mention. I quote the full
text of Brakhage's example:

I have made my "Visions in Meditation" in homage to Gertrude Stein's
whole meditative oeuvre epitomized by her *Stanzas in Meditation*.

When this series opens with an image of a white building "whited
out," it is not necessary to know the source of this photograph.

That the structure represented (and over-exposed) is the oldest
church in Maine is not relevant information with respect to the film.

These formal transformations, of this once-church, now exists in a
film that will realize itself through the life of shapes of white.

What it referentially is, was (when photographed) crucial to my
composing of it, my f-stop "take" of it, the rhythms of my gradual
overexposure and, later, editorial juxtaposition of it.

The original cluster-of-shapes generated by this photographed
church ought to cause (through shape shifts throughout) some sense
of The Sacred.

Each viewer, left free of my church-as-such ought to be able to
build each his/her cathedral of the imagination free of architecture
altogether.

15. Hollis Frampton, *Circles of Confusion: Film, Photography, Video, Texts 1968–1980* (Rochester: Visual Arts
Studies Workshop, 1983), p. 83 (ellipsis his).
16. Ibid., pp. 84–85 (ellipsis his).

And if not, then, the integrity of these shapes and orders-of-color—
each shape and tone having a life of its own—could authenticate also
some other level of metaphorical meaning intrinsic to the work
　　...could even inculcate The Antithetical inasmuch as Art, like
Freud's Unconscious, joins opposites as ONE, at once, in Timeless
fusion
　　—though, unlike anything else, each artwork ideally exists as a
paradigm which, *fully* meditated-upon, would present the fullest exac-
titude of meaning imaginable.
It is simply a complex spiritual matter of author *and* reader, or filmmaker and viewer, being true to Source and the fiction of Form at one
and the same time.[17]

　　The argument is very close to Ashbery's view of Stein's "all-purpose model
that each reader can adapt to his own set of particulars." Yet "the fullest ex-
actitude of meaning" in Brakhage's paradigm does not quite correspond to
"each reader['s]...set of particulars." As Stein's reader, Ashbery makes a
poem out of his set of particulars, itself an all-purpose model to which future
readers are invited to substitute their particulars: the poetic spirit dwells in
the discrepancies as if it were an aesthetic game of telephone, which Shoptaw
calls the poetics of misrepresentation. But Brakhage suggests that there is an
irreducible truth in the meditative power of the particularities, or in his own
words, "Let explanation—that after-birth of dramatic assumption—give way
to the complex truths of the *Trans*formative."[18]
　　At stake is a subtle deviation from his earlier claim "that the more personal
or egocentric I would become, the deeper I would reach and the more I could
touch those universal concerns which would involve all man."[19] The *Trans*-
formative, with its pun on the trance state Brakhage believes the artist enters
to receive instruction from the muses, is the alchemy that makes the universal
out of the personal. In an interview, he offered an alternative gloss on what he
learned from Stein's poem:

　　[*Visions in Meditation*] springs directly from *Faust IV*—in fact, the four
　　parts are the fullest possible imaginable extensions of Part 4—what the
　　mind can do as it turns back on itself. The basic inspiration is from
　　the poem in which Stein tries to free words from reference and allows
　　them to exist, each with a life of its own, within the jostling of all the
　　words across the length of the poem. Thus "A" begins to take on a life

17. Brakhage, *Essential* Brakhage, pp. 201–2.
18. Ibid., p. 202.
19. Brakhage, "Introduction," *Metaphors on Vision* (New York: Film Culture, 1964), pages unnumbered.

of its own as the letter "A" or the sound "A" within the poem. You can wring a story from the life of "A" or "THE" or whatever word she introduces and repeats. But Stein didn't merely treat words as sounds. They have very live traits as they evolve, and I tried to create a corollary of that by photographing recognizable landscapes.[20]

Here he smuggles in the idea, foreign to Stein, that narratives inhere even in individual letters, and in definite and indefinite articles. By analogy, stories might be wrung out of film images or even individual frames. Consequently, Brakhage situates all four films on the threshold of narrative, meditating on stories he can't know or tell.

Brakhage's rhetoric in the Stein lecture gives us another key to that difficult and condensed text. Twice he employs the figure of apophasis, assertion by denial. One instance occurs when he tells us that the opening shot shows the oldest church in Maine while declaring that the fact "is not relevant information with respect to the film." Earlier he had prefaced his gloss of the private erotic significance of some of Stein's expressions with "It is not necessary, or even helpful to know that. . . ." It is sufficient to know that she made "translations of daily privacies into corroborative texts . . . texts charged with the energies of personal immediacy and the unfettered passion of the private." While Brakhage continues to affirm the continuity between the personal and the universal, now called "form," he delimits a private space as the source of art—not to be exposed and unhelpful if known—yet requiring strict adherence. The double employment of apophasis and the introduction of fiction (where we would expect Form alone to be in apposition to Source) may reflect an anxiety as if he wanted us to know something about the origins of *Visions in Meditation* that he cannot tell. Therefore, he uses apophasis to affirm an idea of aesthetic autonomy that he suspects is a fiction. Even more fundamentally, he has laid the foundations for an antithetical aesthetics in which texts may be simultaneously autonomous monads and referential narratives, abstract dances of shapes and biographical fictions. Behind his affirmation of *Stanzas in Meditation* as a paradigm lurks Frampton's theory of narrative, Charles Olson's idea of form, and a growing interest in the Sacred as, perhaps, the key to an antithetical aesthetics.

"Form" (a cardinal term for Olson rather than for Stein) is a crucial concept in the lecture:

My working process . . . is to transmogrify (as Stein translates) each vibrancy of unutterably private source into Form.

20. Suranjan Ganguly, "Stan Brakhage—the 60th Birthday Interview," *Film Culture* 78 (Summer 1994), p. 2.

The forms within The Film will answer each other and the form of the paradigm the entirety-of-forms finally is.

And this will axiomatically constitute a meditative art, just as hers is literally thus, inasmuch as integrity-of-form forms Form.[21]

Capitalizing Form, Brakhage acknowledges his flirtation with Plato's metaphysics, which will be relevant to the analysis of *Visions in Meditation #3*. However, the odd phrase "fiction of Form," from the end of the lecture, may be a *figura etymologicae*. A rooter in dictionaries, Brakhage would have found that *fiction*, from Latin *fingere* (to shape, mold, fashion, imagine, feign), and *form*, from Latin *forma* (mold, type, image, beauty), were associated. Where form is an issue, fiction is in play. Charles Olson had troped on the etymology of "Form" in his "Letter to Elaine Feinstein," an important theoretical text for Brakhage:

At the moment it comes out   the Muse ('world'
                                  the Psyche (the 'life'

You wld know already I'm buggy on say the Proper Noun, so much so I wld take it Pun is Rime, all from tope/type/trope, that built in is the connection, in each of us to Cosmos, and if one taps, via psyche, plus a 'true' adherence of Muse, one does reveal 'Form' [22]

In *Webster's International Dictionary* Olson found a speculative etymology relating *Form* to *Morn* through the Greek *morphe* (form) and *marmarein* (to flash, sparkle) and to Sanskrit *marici* (ray of light). Likewise, Webster's etymologists connected *Rime* to *rite* and *rhythm*.

In the lecture, Brakhage points to his invocation of the Sacred in the first of the *Visions in Meditation*. Actually, a quest for the Sacred lies at the heart of every film in the series, as I hope to demonstrate. Such a concern would take him very far from Stein's *Stanzas in Meditation*, or Frampton's work for that matter, but it is consistent with the proof text of antithetical criticism, Freud's essay "The Antithetical Meaning of Primal Words," where the founder of

---

21. Brakhage, *Essential Brakhage*, p. 202.

22. Although Brakhage was thoroughly familiar with Olson's essay (and had in fact first directed my attention to it in 1964), he might have been reminded of the etymologies by my *Modernist Montage: The Obscurity of Vision in Film and Literature* (New York: Columbia University Press, 1990) that he received the year he wrote the Stein essay; see pp. 166–69. The phrase "fiction of Form" suggests Wallace Stevens's "Notes Toward a Supreme Fiction" although Stevens is an unlikely poet for Brakhage to cite, despite the explicit Platonizing in his theoretical book, *The Necessary Angel*. Furthermore, I believe the adverb *axiomatically* reflects the influence of Frampton's diction here, as it does in "Having Declared a Belief in God."

psychoanalysis cites the ambivalence in the root of *sacred*: "'sacer' 'sacred' and 'accursed'; here accordingly we have the complete antithesis in meaning without any modification of the sound of the word."[23]

Brakhage's notion of moving visual thinking encompasses, without being exhausted by, the entangled nexus of Form as fashioning rays of light, revealing the Sacred, in antithetical fictions. If we were to substitute *god* for *form*, the passage in "Gertrude Stein: Meditative Literature and Film" renders a new sense: "The gods within the Film will answer only to each other and the god of the paradigm the entirety-of-god finally is. And this will axiomatically constitute a meditative art, just as hers literally thus, inasmuch as integrity-of-god forms God...It is simply a complex spiritual matter of author and reader, or filmmaker and viewer, being true to Source and the fiction of God at one and the same time." In 1995, when Brakhage tried to elaborate on what he "personally mean[s] by the word 'God,'" he elaborated a series of antitheses: "sheer reception of the entire fiery illumination of the world" and "visual thinking"; "visible-chaos" and "envisioned-meaning"; "stillness" and oneness with "felt radiant particle/waves," the specular microcosm of "I see myself seeing myself infinitely" and "a macrocosm in which one's self-shape didn't exist at all, coexistent with an imagined BEING, larger...2."[24]

Making the four *Faust* films was both a preparation and an exorcism for the four meditations. In the heat of his marital crisis he had reconsidered his use of sound, returned to explore psychodrama, embraced a theme and a myth that had nagged at him for decades, and in the midst of this project sought and found new love. The sudden break recorded in *Faust IV* from psychodrama to travel lyric corresponded to his erotic and emotional revitalization.

Ancient literary criticism called the genre describing what one encounters in travel *periegeten* or rhetorically *topographia* and *topothesis*. The American *periegeten* echoes with reverberations of Whitman's ecstatic inventories of transcontinental wonders: what he calls "my amaze" in the "Proto-Leaf" opening of the 1860 edition of *Leaves of Grass* (later revised as "Starting from Paumanok"):

> Free, fresh savage,
> Fluent, luxuriant, self-content, fond of persons and places
> Fond of fish-shaped Paumanok, where I was born,
> Fond of the sea—lusty-begotten and various...

23. Sigmund Freud, "The Antithetical Meaning of Primal Words, in *The Standard Edition of the Complete Works of Sigmund Freud* , ed. and trans. James Strachey, vol 11, p. 159.

24. Stan Brakhage. "Having Declared a Belief in God," *Telling Time: Essays of a Visionary Filmmaker* (Kingston, N.Y.: Documentext, 2003), pp. 135–36.

Tallying, vocalizing all—resounding Niagara—resounding Missouri,
Or rude in my home in Kanuck woods...
Or withdrawn to muse and meditate in some deep recess,
Far from the clank of crowds, an interval passing, rapt and happy,
Stars, vapor, snow, the hills, rocks, Fifth-month flowers, my amaze,
my love,...
Aware of the mocking-bird of the wilds, at day break,
Solitary, singing in the west, I strike up for a new world.[25]

It may be a mere coincidence that the first of the *Visions in Meditation* shares several loci with Whitman's chant—the sea, Canadian woods, Niagara Falls. These are commonplaces of the North American sublime. The four parts of the series strike up for a new world by musing and meditating on the American landscape in Canada and New England, at Mesa Verde in Colorado, in the Chihuahuan desert and at Taos in New Mexico. That Brakhage was "solitary, singing in the west" is as much a fiction in these works as in *Faust IV*. The unseen presence of Marilyn Jull, at the driving wheel, enabled him to film much of the cycle from a moving automobile.

In the only critical essay I have seen on the series, John Pruitt wrote:

Taken as a whole, the four films in the *Visions in Meditation* series express a vivid sense of traveling across the wide expanse of the North American Continent by car....Throughout the series of four films, the camera emphasizes the great emptiness of continental space with only a faint and fleeting sense of human presence within it, which is,...seen in flashes of cross-cutting. This ultimately unifying visual motif hints that the title of the series plays on the notion of mystical visions in a desert or wilderness...[26]

This is accurate and astute. *Visions in Meditation* lacks any trace of psychodrama; it is a pure example of a filmic *periegeten*, a Whitmanian celebration of travel in quest of symbolic ancestors in the sublime geography and prophetic meteorology of North America. The *topographia* of the series as a whole is an effort "to look at the world with new eyes," in the words of Emerson's *Nature*:

The ruin or blank, that we see when we look at nature, is on our own eye. The axis of vision is not coincident with the axis of things, and

25. Whitman, "Proto-Leaf," *Selected Poems 1855–1892: A New Edition*, ed. Gary Schmidgall (New York: St. Martin's, 1999), p. 177.
26. John Pruitt, "Stan Brakhage and the Long Reach of Maya Deren's Poetics of Film," *Chicago Review* 47/48, no. 4/1 (Winter 2001), pp. 127–28.

so they appear not transparent but opake. The reason why the world lacks unity, and lies broken and in heaps, is because man is disunified with himself. He cannot be a naturalist, until he satisfies all the demands of the spirit. Love is as much in demand as perception.... But when a faithful thinker, resolute to detach every object from personal relations and see it in the light of thought, shall, at the same time, kindle science with the fire of the holiest affections, then will God go forth anew into the creation.[27]

Playing on the etymology of *blank*, Brakhage opens the film with an evocation of the "ancestral theme"—blinding whiteness in order to detach the church, the photographs, the landscape itself "from personal relations and see [them] in the light of thought."

Marilyn Brakhage wrote the catalog entry for the first film in the cycle, quoting from the grant application she mentioned in the letter I cited at length at the beginning of this chapter. The description itself maintains a phenomenological reserve:

This is a film inspired by Gertrude Stein's "Stanzas in Meditation," in which the filmmaker has edited a meditative series of images of landscapes and human symbolism "indicative of the field-of-consciousness within which humanity survives thoughtfully." It is a film "as in a dream," this first film in a proposed series of such being composed of images shot in the New England states and Eastern Canada. It begins with an antique photograph of a baby and ends with a child loose on the landscape, interweaving images of Niagara Falls with a variety of New England and Eastern Canadian scenes, antique photographs, windows, old farms and cityscapes, as it moves from deep winter, through glare ice, to thaw.[28]

The great emptiness of which Pruitt writes takes a different form in each of the four films. The first of the *Visions in Meditation* comes closest to Ashbery's description of Stein's poem. The difficulty of identifying "what is going on" results from the transformation of personal imagery into an oneiric landscape, not so much empty as temporarily abandoned to snow and ice. The shots of a dormant Ferris wheel, particularly, point to a time when the landscape will be reanimated by human activity. The people we glimpse in the film are seen so briefly or so ambiguously that they become glyphs of arrested acts: A few people are walking on the beach; a solitary boy seems to

27. Ralph Waldo Emerson, *Essays and Lectures* (New York: Library of America, 1983), p. 47.
28. *Canyon CinemaFilm/Video Catalog 7* (San Francisco, 1992), p. 57.

be seeking distraction or play in a frozen yard. Ironically, the framed photographs, typical of presumably dead ancestors, offer the film's most sustained visible human presence. Not only do we never learn who they are (or who is walking on the beach or playing in the yard), but it seems as if Brakhage does not know either. The apophasis by which we read of the opening shot "that the structure represented (and over-exposed) is the oldest church in Maine is not relevant information with respect to the film" registers the epistemic ambivalence and uncertainty permeating the film and contributing to its oneiric resonance. In different ways, each film in the cycle tropes the traveling quester's inability to know, making *Visions in Meditation* Brakhage's most mysterious work.

The shots of a stone saint on the facade of a large, probably French Canadian church, and of the isolated steeple cross reiterate religious iconography as a central element in "the field-of-consciousness within which humanity survives thoughtfully." That field of consciousness is a version of time, rhythmically and imagistically refracted in the film as the ice breaks and the snow recedes, emblematically represented by the static Ferris wheel. In one sequence the curvature of the Ferris wheel rhymes with the arc of a rainbow. The rainbow, in turn, joins with the "sacred" buildings and icons to point forward to the fiction of a soteriological future and backward to a myth of origins. From the comparable image of Niagara, enveloped in the mist it creates, a story of geological time can be wrung. Shots of mountains filmed through a twisting anamorphic lens allude to the tropes of *Dog Star Man* and beyond it to the mythopoeic genesis at the heart of that epic's fiction.

Earlier, in *The Book of the Family* Brakhage had filmed photographs of his childhood, his adoptive parents, his grandmother, and Jane's family as indices of his autobiographical endeavor. When he married Marilyn, he decided to abandon that autobiographical strain. Thus, "Gertrude Stein: Meditative Literature and Film" is a manifesto for his future films, in which privacy would be transformed but not directly exposed. Could these old photographs substitute for relics of Marilyn's family? The opening of *Visions in Meditation #1* is similar to that of *Sincerity (reel one)*: After a series of whiteouts of the church in Maine, we glimpse the framed photograph of a child, apparently an image from early in the century. As in *Sincerity*, where he had also made a visit to a place that riveted his attention, photographs evoke a ghostly past. But unlike the autobiography, there is no subsequent accumulation of clues and indices spelling out the meaning of the place and suggesting the relevance of the photographs: no photographs of Brakhage himself nor clips from his earlier films. In this respect alone, *Visions in Meditation #1* resembles Ashbery's pseudoautobiographical accumulation of observational (and in his case conversational) details that, in his description of *Stanzas in Meditation*, "give one the feeling of time passing, of things happening, of a 'plot', though it would be difficult to say what is going on."[29]

In an early version of *Mindfall*, a section of his *Magellan* project, Hollis Frampton included eighteen minutes of epileptic seizures from the library of Congress's Paper Print Collection. Waith G. Chase had made nine documentary films in 1905 to study the movements of epileptics during seizures; he filmed the men naked and the women in long shifts. Frampton planned to subject the filmic relics "to a further fragmentation and sandwiching procedure" in the finished cycle, so they are not included in the one released composite, *Mindfall I & XIV* (1977–80). Brakhage used a fragment of the same footage, one of the male epileptics, in *Visions in Meditation #2: Mesa Verde*.

If the first film of the series evokes a dream in which one fails to recognize people and knows little more than that winter will end, the note to the second suggests a horror story:

This meditation takes its visual imperatives from the occasion of Mesa Verde, which I came to see finally as Time rather than any solidity as Place. "There is terror here," were the first words which came to mind on seeing these ruins; and for two days after, during all my photography, I was haunted by some unknown occurrence which reverberated still in these rocks and rock-structures and environs. I can no longer believe that the Indians abandoned this solid habitation because of drought, lack-of-water, somesuch. (These explanations do not, anyway, account for the fact that all memory of The Place, i.e. where it is, was eradicated from tribal memory, leaving only legend of a Time when such a place existed.) Midst the rhythms, then, of editing, I was compelled to introduce images which corroborate what the rocks said, and what the film strips seemed to say: The abandonment of Mesa Verde was an eventuality (rather than an event), was for All Time thus, and had been intrinsic from the first such human building.[30]

Ostensibly, then, the film records a visit to the ruins the cliff-dwelling Anasazi Indians inhabited from A.D. 500 and mysteriously abandoned around 1300. (Western traders and trappers saw the ruins in the late eighteenth and early nineteenth centuries, but they were not systematically examined until the 1880s. Carefully stabilized since the 1950s, they are now a tourist attraction in Mesa Verde National Park, Colorado.) The site seized Willa Cather's imagination in 1915 and became a central motif of her novel *The Professor's*

29. Ashbery, "The Impossible," p. 251.
30. *Canyon CinemaFilm/Video Catalog 7*, pp. 57–58.

House (1925). Her character, Tom Outland, describes his discovery of the lost cliff city thus:

> Far up above me, a thousand feet or so, set in a great cavern in the face of the cliff, I saw a little city of stone, asleep. It was as still as sculpture—and something like that. It all hung together, seemed to have a kind of composition: pale little houses of stone nestling close to one another, perched on top of each other, with flat roofs, narrow windows, straight walls, and in the middle of the group, a round tower. It was beautifully proportioned, that tower, swelling out to a larger girth a little above the base, then growing slender again. There was something symmetrical and powerful about the swell of the masonry. The tower was a fine thing that held all the jumble of houses together and made them mean something.... I knew at once I had come upon the city of some extinct civilization, hidden away in this inaccessible mesa for centuries, preserved in the dry air and almost perpetual sunlight like a fly in amber, guarded by the cliffs and the river and the desert.[31]

Brakhage's camera is almost in perpetual motion, from the opening shot of the mesa, sighted from a moving automobile. The repetitive probing of his zoom lens, handheld, continues and varies this movement, as he draws nearer to the stone structures and scans their contours. Often they look like small architectural models, because he maintains a distance from them, preferring the virtual closeness of the lens, and because of the absence of a human figure to set the scale. Something unreal, magical, and vaguely frightening possesses the images as a result. Nearly continual superimposition, a canon form of alternate shots of the same sights, does as much to control the rhythm of the film as the camera movement. It modulates between the blue hues of the surrounding landscape and the intense oranges and browns of the cliff houses; flattening and thinning out the cooler layer so that important images, such as a deer or the epileptic man, first dissolve into the compounded film as cinematic petroglyphs, "corroborat[ing] what the rocks said."

As is often the case with Brakhage's work, rhythm determines the form and sense of the whole film. When the epileptic finally appears, midway through, it is as if he were conjured by the rhythm, an embodiment of the genius loci. His spastic gyrations, superimposed upon themselves, constitute a ghostly dance that concentrates within itself the rhythmic tension that has been diffused throughout the film. Brakhage is careful to include a moment

31. Willa Cather, *The Professor's House* (New York: Vintage Books, 1973), p. 201–2.

in which the archaic source of the epileptic image is transparent, so that we recognize the figure at the center of his rhythmic labyrinth as a collage.

Paul Sharits was the first of the major American avant-garde filmmakers to include images of epileptics in his work. However, his two-screen installation *Epileptic Seizure Comparison* (1976) used contemporary footage, rather than Chase's 1907 material, in a color flicker matrix. In his notes on the work, he touches upon the metaphoric range of the imagery: "While the convulsive forms of epilepsy are unfortunate, they are not in themselves painful, despite the fact that the victim appears to be in pain.... Shamans, voodoo practitioners and others, who for purposes of religious ecstasy-catharsis-insight, are known to self-induce physical states which appear similar to epileptic convulsions, often losing consciousness and exhibit muscular spasms."[32]

As early as *Metaphors on Vision* Brakhage associated epilepsy with asthma, from which he suffered intensely. He is both drawn to the quaking figure of his partial invention by an act of identification and repelled by it as the projection of a shamanistic curse guarding a mystery he may describe but not penetrate.

In Cather's novel, Mesa Verde becomes "a sacred spot" (p. 221) and "a religious emotion" (p. 251). The silent stone dwellings seem to require the embodiment of at least one human relic. Outland finds such an emblem:

> At last we came upon one of the original inhabitants—not a skeleton, but a dried human body, a woman.... We thought she had been murdered; there was a great wound in her side, the ribs stuck out through the dried flesh. Her mouth was open as if she were screaming, and her face, through all those years, kept a look of terrible agony.... Henry named her Mother Eve, and we called her that.[33]

Willa Cather's fiction falls just on the borders of the modernist canon, and although the author shares with Brakhage a notion of "the kingdom of art" as a redemptive realm of aesthetic perfection,[34] there is no evidence that Brakhage read *The Professor's House*. Cather seamlessly incorporates Mother Eve within the fictional illusion in order to open a discussion of the abandonment of the cliff dwellings; she even introduces a wise priest to fantasize that she may have been left behind and then killed by an unexpected husband returning to find her in flagrante delicto.

---

32. Paul Sharits, "Filmography," *Film Culture* nos. 65–66 (1978), p. 123.
33. Cather, *The Professor's House*, p. 214.
34. See Bernice Slote, ed., *The Kingdom of Art: Willa Cather's First Principles and Critical Statements, 1893–1896* (Lincoln: University of Nebraska Press, 1966); David Harrell, *From Mesa Verde to the Professor's House* (Albuquerque: University of New Mexico Press, 1992).

Such narrative speculation has no place in Brakhage's modernist construction; for he strives to "eschew Story altogether." Thus Chase's epileptic footage retains something of its archaic autonomy. Following his interpretation of Stein, Brakhage has freed the image "to its un-owned self-life within the continuities (rather than context) of the work." So we recognize it as a cinematic invention, the product of Brakhage's mental association and of the mechanics of the editing table. In order to come to terms with the painful mystery of the site, he juxtaposes the enigma of the anonymous epileptic, and in fusing them suggests a third source of pain and uncertainty not even visualized in the film: the failure of his first marriage. The abandonment of Mesa Verde sublimates the divorce and sale of the Brakhage home in Lump Gulch; the epileptic's seizure allegorizes the spiritual convulsion of that event, now elevated to a work of fate, an "eventuality."

Brakhage's note for *Visions in Meditation #3: Plato's Cave* reasserts the preeminence of "The Antithetical," or "naturally...equivocal...structures":

> Plato's cave would seem to be the *idée fixe* of this film. The vortex would, then, be the phenomenological world—overwhelming, and thus "uninhabitable." The structures of thoughtful meditation are naturally, therefore, equivocal so that, for example, even a tornado-in-the-making will be both "dust devil" and "finger of God" at one with the clockwork sun and the strands of ice/fire, horizon, rock, clouds, so on.
>
> The film is, I believe, a vision of mentality as most people must (to the irritation of Plato) have it, safely encaved and metaphorical, for the nervous system to survive. All the same I hope, with this work, to have brought a little "rush light" into the darkness. The film is set to three movements of Rick Corrigan's *Memory Suite*. Its multiple superimpositions are superbly timed by Louise Fujiki, of Western Cine, as usual.[35]

Brakhage seems to be reading the seventh book of Plato's *Republic* through the optic of Freud's *Beyond the Pleasure Principle*. Plato's paradigm becomes an allegory of the defenses. Consider the following passages from Plato and Freud.

The Republic (Book VII):

At first, when any of them is liberated and compelled suddenly to stand up and turn his neck round and walk and look towards the

---

35. *Canyon CinemaFilm/Video Catalog 7*, p. 58.

light, he will suffer sharp pains; the glare will distress him, and he will be unable to see the realities of which in his former state he had seen the shadows.... Will he not fancy that the shadows which he formerly saw are truer than the objects which are now shown to him?... And if he is compelled to look straight at the light, will he not have a pain in his eyes which will make him turn away to take refuge in the objects of vision which he can see, and which he will conceive to be in reality clearer than the things which are now being shown to him?... And suppose once more, that he is... forced into the presence of the sun himself, is he not likely to be pained and irritated? When he approaches the light his eyes will be dazzled, and he will not be able to see anything at all of what are now called realities.

Beyond the Pleasure Principle:

Let us suppose, then, that all the organic instincts are conservative, are acquired historically and tend towards the restoration of an earlier state of things. It follows that the phenomena of organic development must be attributed to external disturbing and diverting influences. The elementary living entity would from its very beginning have had no wish to change; if conditions remained the same, it would do no more than constantly repeat the same course of life. In the last resort, what has left its mark on the development of organisms must be the history of the earth we live in and of its relation to the sun.[36]

Freud himself turned to Plato, not to *The Republic* but to Aristophanes's speech in *The Symposium*, for confirmation of the conservative or regressive nature of the instincts. In *Beyond the Pleasure Principle* he speculated on the antithetical fusion of self-preservative and death instincts, reconciling them by asserting that "the dominating tendency of mental life, and perhaps of nervous life in general, is the effort to reduce, to keep constant or to remove internal tension due to stimuli...a tendency which finds expression in the pleasure principle."[37]

Recalling that the Gertrude Stein lecture begins with a discussion of metaphor as a vehicle to "resolve Dualities," we might consider how the film represents "a vision of mentality...safely encaved and metaphorical, for the nervous system to survive." We are within the cave when the film begins with

---

36. Sigmund Freud, *Beyond the Pleasure Principle, The Standard Edition of the Complete Works of Sigmund Freud,* trans. James Strachey, vol. 18 (London: Hogarth Press, 1986), pp. 37–38.
37. Ibid., pp. 55–56.

images of Carlsbad Caverns. The subtle superimpositions through most of the film blend nearly continual somatic and vehicular movements. The movements and the superimpositions generate the transformative ground of metaphor so that the interior of the cave seems to open onto a desert landscape with patches of vegetation. But soon the neon illuminations of an amusement park at night and subsequently the display windows of a shopping mall suggest that the "safely encaved and metaphorical" space is a mental theater of facile entertainment and commodity consumption.

Hapax Legomena: Traveling Matte, to which Brakhage had responded so enthusiastically, emerged from a version of the same metaphor. Frampton spoke of the film "as a metaphor for part of the human condition, which is being trapped in this little round bone room (the skull) and trying to see out." In "A Pentagram for Conjuring the Narrative" he had expressed the idea as a metaphor for the self, the "I" which

> lies, comfortable but immobile, in a hemiellipsoidal chamber of tensile bone.... it is certainly alone; and in time it convinces itself, somewhat reluctantly, that it is waiting to die....The presence, in its domed chamber, masters after a while a round of housekeeping and bookkeeping duties. Then it attempts to look outside. Glimpses are confusing: the sensorium reports a fractured terrain whose hurtling bits seldom coalesce, "make sense," as the pregnant idiom has it—and the sense they make is itself fugitive, and randomly dispersed throughout an unguessable volume of nothing in particular.[38]

This "I" proceeds to tell itself stories as it waits to die, a parable Frampton derives from Samuel Beckett.

To Frampton's ironic conceit, Brakhage straightforwardly adds that the Transformation of metaphor "can be thought of as a passage and ritualized through either story-telling or meditation." When the meditation is literary, "[a]ll writers who eschew story altogether are essential [*sic*] aspiring to the philosophical." But cinema has the possibility of approximating moving visual thinking insofar as it offers "a thousand words every 1/48th-of-a-second and, as the mind moves, a corollary of Philosophy."[39] Therefore Brakhage's metaphorical cave would trace its lineage to philosophy while Frampton's would be the symbolic locus of "the genesis of story-telling among the animal necessities of the spirit."[40]

38. Frampton, *Circles of Confusion*, pp. 64–65.
39. Brakhage, *Essential Brakhage*, pp. 194–95.
40. Frampton, *Circles of Confusion*, p. 65.

Perhaps the most important distinction between Brakhage's and Frampton's versions of the cave metaphor would turn on Brakhage's evocation of "most people" where Frampton wrote of a universal "I." Most people, according to Brakhage, do not attempt to look outside; with no wish to change, they instinctually preserve repetitive modes of thought Frampton characterized by a routine of housekeeping and bookkeeping. Eventually Brakhage's camera finds its way to an opening in the cave, flooded with light. As it emerges into that light, with many shots of the sunlit sky as if literalizing Plato's allegory,[41] the rhythmic editing and camera movements rhyme the winter landscape (and lace curtains) of *Visions in Meditation #1* with the southwestern desert. The phenomenon Brakhage films there surprisingly corresponds to Frampton's scenario; the dust devil/finger of God, building a spinning vortex of sagebrush and household trash, creates a "fractured terrain whose hurtling bits [never] coalesce" but are "randomly dispersed throughout an unguessable volume of nothing in particular."

Rick Corrigan's minimalist electronic composition provides one of the most successful of Brakhage's rare soundtracks. When a diminuendo of blurred, abstracted camera movements gradually moves into blackness, the soundtrack alone alerts us that the film continues for a final minute and a half. This termination hints that the topology of ancient philosophy and religion—the cave, the desert, and the whirlwind—is a field of metaphor in which the antithetical images endlessly repeat themselves; for the series Brakhage names—"fire/ice, horizon, rock, clouds"—are all antitheses once we see the horizon as the imaginary locus of the passage of earth to sky, where rock and cloud reflect each other.

When Freud cited Plato, he designated him the "poet-philosopher." Even though Brakhage identifies reservedly with Plato's philosopher-king when he says he "brought a little 'rush light' into the darkness," he was always more comfortable with poetry than with philosophy. If he read D. H. Lawrence's essay "Reflections on the Death of a Porcupine," he would have found a distinction between Platonic idealism and a vitalism close to his antithetical aesthetics:

> Being is not ideal, as Plato would have it: nor spiritual. It is a transcendent form of existence, and as much material as existence is....

---

41. Pruitt, "Stan Brakhage and the Long Reach," p. 131, argued, "The entire 'vision' of the cave is a mental construct resting on nothing except our own human necessity to make such constructs to live within.... Plato's cave is the locus we find ourselves in when we try to get *any* meaning from *any* visual phenomenon, even if we are trying to render utter meaninglessness."

All existence is dual, surging toward a consummation into being. In the seed of the dandelion, as it floats with its little umbrella of hairs, sits the Holy Ghost in tiny compass. The Holy Ghost is that which holds the light and the dark, the day and the night, the wet and the sunny, united in one little clue...

Vitality depends upon the clue of the Holy Ghost inside a creature, a man, a nation, a race...[42]

Brakhage's friend the filmmaker Bruce Elder, an enthusiast of Lawrence's poetics, has argued that Brakhage's films, like Lawrence's poems, "possess a magnificent vitality that comes from being created at electric speed.[43] During the period Brakhage was making *Visions in Meditation*, Elder came to occupy a position similar to the one Frampton had held for him at the height of their friendship. Like Frampton, Elder is an intellectual, both a filmmaker and a writer (on film history as well as theory), and a fervent admirer of Ezra Pound; he even contended with Brakhage on the nature of interior language, maintaining, as Frampton had, that words are an ineluctable accompaniment to thought. Elder may have been an influence on Brakhage when he turned to Lawrence for inspiration in bringing the cycle to its end, as he indicated in his note on the film:

Visions in Meditation #4: D. H. Lawrence. 1990

I've made three pilgrimages in my life: the 40-some-year home of Sigmund Freud in Vienna, Emily Dickinson's in Amherst, and the mountain ranch and crypt, would you call it?, of D. H. Lawrence, outside Taos. I keep returning to the Lawrence environs again and again; and this last time attempted photography in that narrow little building where his ashes were (or were not) deposited (contradictory stories about that). There is a child-like sculpture of The Phoenix at the far end of the room, a perfectly lovely emblem to deflate any pomposity people have added to Lawrence's "I rise in flames..." The building is open, contains only a straw chair (remindful of one Van Gogh painted) and a broom, which I always use with delight to sweep the dust and leaves from this simple abode. I have tried to make a film as true to the spirit of Lawrence as is this gentle chapel in homage to

---

42. D. H. Lawrence, "Reflections on the Death of a Porcupine," *Phoenix* 2 (1925), collected in *Reflections on the Death of a Porcupine and Other Essays* (New York: Cambridge University Press, 1988), pp. 359–61.
43. Bruce Elder, *The Films of Stan Brakhage in the American Tradition of Gertrude Stein, Ezra Pound, and Charles Olson* (Waterloo, Canada: Wilfrid Laurier University Press, 1998), pp. 312–13.

him. I have wanted to make it a film within which that child-Phoenix can reasonably nest.

(Bruce Elder sends me this quote from D. H. Lawrence, which may help explain why *Visions in Meditation #4* is subtitled in his name: "...there must be mutation swifter than irridescence, haste, not rest, come-and-go, not fixity, inconclusiveness, immediacy, the quality of life itself, without dénouement or close." Poetry of the Present, introduction to the American edition of *New Poems*, 1918.)[44]

One would not realize from this note that the crypt at Lawrence's ranch and the objects near it are unrecognizable in the film. In fact, a meticulous viewer would know only that Brakhage passed through Taos, New Mexico (from the brief glimpse of the sign at the La Fonda Hotel); for the fourth is the most elusive of the *Visions in Meditation* and, in that respect, may be the most indebted to its Steinian model, as described by Ulla Dydo:

> In the meditations, consciousness focuses on abstract mental land-
> scapes that do not cohere.... It is as if in meditation Stein "unhooked"
> words from events, people, and objects to compose them as efforts of a
> mind in the act of looking for comprehension.... Their impulse is not
> to tell stories or to explain but to meditate upon what she perceived,
> and as she said, to achieve in their disembodied form an "exactitude of
> abstract thought."[45]

The film builds its oneiric atmosphere from often crepuscular landscapes and probes of indistinguishable objects, as the filmmaker continually shifts focus and exposure values. Its orientation is so predominantly horizontal that an erect silhouette of a man stands out with uncanny emphasis as if it were a ghostly spirit, say, of Lawrence himself. Several shots show the filmmaker's bare feet, suggesting that he was supine when he filmed them. Otherwise, no people can be seen in the whole film. Instead, the dynamics of vehicular movement has blended into the muscular flexing of the eyes as they adjust to focus and intensities of luminosity.

The film seems to have been shot entirely in New Mexico: Sweeping pans of the gypsum dunes of White Sands National Monument; close, caressing movements along the adobe walls of the La Fonda Hotel; and short fades of flat or mountainous horizons, shot from a moving car, periodically help

---

44. The catalogs of Canyon Cinema and the Film-makers' Cooperative misprint dénouement as "de-nouncement." I do not know the point at which the corruption originated. See *Canyon CinemaFilm/Video Catalog 7*, pp. 57. 60.
45. Dydo, *A Stein Reader*, pp. 568–69.

to identify the terrain. The synecdoche of the filmmaker's feet contrasts his state of rest with the dominant propulsion of the film. Here meditation is close to dozing, and perhaps, then, a reconciliation of the opposition between meditation and the open road Lawrence, writing about Walt Whitman, had polemicized:

> Not by meditating. Not by fasting. Not by exploring heaven after heaven, inwardly, in the manner of the great mystics. Not by exalta-tion. Not by ecstasy. Not by any of these ways does the soul come into her own.
>
> Only by taking the open road....
>
> It is the American heroic message. The soul is not to pile up de-fenses round herself. She is not to withdraw and seek her heavens inwardly, in mystical ecstasies. She is not to cry to some God beyond, for salvation. She is to go down the open road, as the road opens, into the unknown, keeping company with those whose soul draws them near to her, accomplishing nothing save the journey, and the works incident to the journey, in the long life-travel into the unknown, the soul in her subtle sympathies accomplishing herself by the way.[46]

Brakhage's fourth meditation is a vision of the open road, a mesh of trav-eling shots punctuated by a few recurring static ones of a suburban street (associated with the images of the filmmaker's feet) and brief images of graz-ing horses. The principles of his antithetical aesthetics are latent in the film and overt in his note. When he said he tried to make the film a nest for the "child-Phoenix"—the child-like sculpture of a Phoenix in the memorial chapel devoted to Lawrence—he was invoking a locus classicus of the an-tithetical image: Ovid calls the nest both the cradle and tomb of the bird (fertque pius cunasque suas patriumque sepulcrum; *Metamorphoses*, xv, 405). Perhaps this antithesis is refracted in the contradictory stories about whether Lawrence's ashes were buried in the crypt, lost, or scattered elsewhere.

Evidently, the elegiac homage to Lawrence played a greater role in the conception of the film than in its manifestation. Lawrence stands in for Bra-khage himself: *Visions in Meditation #4* is a phoenix nest for his own rebirth, a sublimation of his divorce and remarriage. The thematics of renewal hold the four films together: the thaw of the northeastern winter, the resurrection of the epileptic shaman of Mesa Verde and the Library of Congress, the liberated prisoner of Plato's cave, and the phoenix are variations on his "Song of the Open Road." Although Whitman admits he can never escape his demons

---

46. D. H. Lawrence, *Studies in Classic American Literature* (New York: Viking, 1961), p. 172–73.

("Still here I carry my old delicious burdens / I carry them, men and women, I carry them with me wherever I go, / I swear it is impossible for me to get rid of them...") he concludes his chant with an address to his imaginary companion:

> Mon enfant, I give you my hand!
> I give you my love, more precious than money,
> I give you myself, before preaching or law;
> Will you give me yourself? Will you come travel with me?
> Shall we stick by each other as long as we live?[47]

Brakhage's companion was real but by their compact invisible. *Visions in Meditation* was their epithalamium.

---

47. Whitman, "Song of the Open Road," *Selected Poems 1855–1892*, pp. 148–49.

CHAPTER 16

Beavers's Third Cycle:
The Theater of Gesture

In contrast to the astonishing rapidity with which Robert Beavers made the apprenticeship films of his first cycle (1968–70) and the four magnificent and mature works of his second cycle (1971–75), it took him another twenty-six years to finish the seven films of the third cycle of *My Hand Outstretched to the Winged Distance and Sightless Measure*. Of course, this schematic view does not take account of the reediting and new soundtracks he made for all of his early works in the 1990s. Those revisions were integral to the arrangement of the previously autonomous films into the cycles in the first place.

Two central events in the filmmaker's life frame the production of those concluding seven films and account, in part, for the pace of their production: shortly after completing the first version of *Sotiros* in 1978, he and Gregory Markopoulos were hit by a bus in Greece. Beavers was severely injured and almost lost his sight in one eye as a consequence of the accident; then, in 1992, Markopoulos died of a lymphoma. It was only after that that Beavers finished a number of films he had shot in the 1980s and revised the rest of his work. The fleeting presence and hovering absence of Markopoulos hedge the elegiac tone that regularly sounds, fades away, and sounds again throughout the cycle, culminating in the final film.

None of the seven films, *Sotiros* (1976–78/1996), *AMOR* (1980), *Ευψυχι* (*Efpsychi*) (1983/1996), *Wingseed* (1985), *The Hedge Theater* (1986–90/2002), *The Stoas* (1991–97), and *The Ground* (1993–2001), are longer than a half hour. They were made predominantly in Greece, although there are scenes from Austria, Switzerland, and Italy. Hand gestures play a large role in many of them. Although Beavers ceased to pay homage to great artists of the past, allusions to ancient and baroque theater occur throughout the cycle. The theater eventually forms an imaginary backdrop against which simple acts of production and tidying from everyday life take on meaning: the filmmaker highlights shaving, dressing, cutting, sewing, carting, broom making, measuring, stone cutting, and house building.

Sotiros was condensed to twenty-five minutes from three films: *Sotiros Responds* (1975), *Sotiros (Alone)* (1977), and *Sotiros in the Elements* (1977), although there may be nothing of the last in it. "Sotiros," one of the Greek epithets for Apollo, means savior, redeemer, healer; it can be a first name in Greece, the equivalent of Salvador. With Markopoulos, Beavers had visited the temple of Apollo Sotiros (or Epikouros) at Bassae when he started the series. (Nearby, Markopoulos selected a site for the Temenos. The major work of Markopoulos's last fifteen years was the reediting of his entire corpus for screenings in the Temenos; he restructured his work into the twenty-two cycles of *Eniaios*. It would take more than eighty hours to show the approximately one hundred films that comprise the serial work. Beavers' reworking of all of his films and arranging into the three cycles of *My Hand Outstretched* follows the example Markopoulos set with *Eniaios*, who conceived the Temenos project as soteriological on an analogy to the healing cults of Asclepius.)

Uncannily, Beavers sustained the injuries to his leg and to one of his eyes from the bus accident just after he had finished editing the twenty-seven-minute *Sotiros Responds.Sotiros (Alone)*, eleven minutes, took as its theme the filmmaker's subsequent convalescence in Graz. *Sotiros in the Elements*, at seven minutes the shortest of the three, returns to sites and images from the first film with isolated words superimposed on the screen: "When/ return/ there/ He said,/ one/ still. Red./ heal/clouds/ or/ now/ smiling, he said/ step/ open." These words first appear on the right side of the screen, then reappear backward as mirror images on the left side. Ultimately the filmmaker's dissatisfaction with the effect of the words led him to exclude the film from the cycle.

However, he was happier with the use of visible words in *Sotiros Responds*. Therefore, he incorporated its elliptical evocation of speech into the first part of *Sotiros* where the words "He said," and "he said." recur rhythmically on the screen, as if some of the images were the direct discourse of one or two interlocutors. Twenty seconds into the film, after three shots, we read, "He said," in white letters on a black background on the left side of the screen. After another five shots, "he said." appears on the right side, again in white letters against black. This pattern recurs twenty-one times until, after seventeen minutes, a final "He said," appears without the closing counterpart; instead a black pause indicates a transition to the material drawn from *Sotiros (Alone)* where no titles appeared on the screen. These two indications of a speaker frame sequences of up to nine shots, but a few times they merely bracket a single shot. Likewise, after the period and before the next capitalized "He said," there always appears at least one shot and sometimes as many as thirteen. Yet there is no discernible difference between the shots (or the way in which they are edited) within the putative sentence and those outside it; so we cannot separate direct discourse from a framing narrative on the basis of imagery. The film encourages its viewers to read the montage as represented speech while at the same time it resists any systematic mapping of it.

Since the part of the film in which these titles appear continually alternates shots from a hotel room in Bern, Switzerland, with images of several locations in Greece—a shepherd with goats in the countryside, a drunk or "village idiot" in a whitewashed rural town, and street scenes of Athens where we see a blind beggar—we might read the film as a conversation or a monologue in the hotel room about an experience in Greece. Such an intimation of dialogue would align the placement of *Sotiros* at the head of the third cycle with *Winged Dialogue* in the first and perhaps with *From the Notebook Of ...* in the second, according to my reading of its culminating double portrait.

Beavers filmed the hotel room at different hours of the day to record the movement of light around its four walls. Its sparse furnishings include twin beds joined to form a double bed, two desks, and two adjacent sinks. The double furnishings impart to the alternation of "He said," and "he said." a further refinement of the suggested conversation between male companions or the obsessive recollection by one of the speech of the other.

The opening three shots frame an image of the Greek landscape between two glimpses of the empty beds, offering thus a paradigm for a speaker–discourse–speaker (or listener) structure. The frequent matching of camera gestures—a pan to the left after one title card, followed by a pan to the right after the other—reinforces this notion. Rarely do the titles appear without some visual allusion to the hotel room. Finally, one image of Markopoulos in the room supports the notion that he might be the speaker or that the pronouns refer to him and Beavers, although the filmmaker has taken pains to avoid so literal an interpretation. In a conversation at the Temenos Archive in Zurich (June 25, 2002), he glossed the intertitles by reference to Yeats: "Yeats said somewhere that he attended a meeting in which others said everything he thought of saying." He also observed that "Sotiros is the character who plays the role of an idiot in order to say whatever he wants." But when Tony Pipolo asked him if the "he" referred to Apollo, Beavers answered:

> The "he" is left unidentified. It is the voice of Sotiros without Sotiros being shown in the film. In one way "he" is the film. There is also one image of Gregory seated in a chair and the light is resting on his face. Then there was another figure, filmed in Leonidon, and he moved about like a village fool. His name was actually Sotiros. Yet this figure and the blind man are only part of Sotiros.[1]

He reiterated this to me in a letter:

> I am not certain that the He said, & he said. titles are a single he. It might be a dialogue in the third person. At certain points the titles attach themselves to figures in the image, and at other points they appear to be suspended. They are placed in the original *Sotiros Responds* and the silent images that follow or precede the titles have the quality of being a statement... the basic impulse was how to suggest that the film, itself, is a voice. Writing it that way makes it sound very strange. On the other hand I am still thinking about how to present a voice in film and how to place the voice in a particular space. In the case of *Sotiros Responds*, the titles are placed in the space of the hotel room as the sunlight touches various points on the three walls. The name Sotiros, is the actual name of the fellow who does a skip and turning movement while making a gesture to his head with his hand. I associated the name to the light in the room because it also signifies Savior as an attribute of Apollo if I am not mistaken. It leads to the deeper sense in *Sotiros (Alone)* as the film made after the bus accident, the leg injury etc. This is a more personal lyric. I cannot help you with the third title. I was still involved with suggesting a voice and used actual words forwards and backwards and the matte moving at the center of the fold.[2]

If we take "the silent images that follow or precede the titles... [as] a statement," we might conclude that the topic of discussion is the soteriological manifestations of Apollo. The blind man and the village fool represent modes of affliction, often associated in Greek religion and mythology with prophecy. Furthermore, Apollo was both the agent of disease and the savior from it. Georges Dumézil has argued that Apollo was the Greek version of an Indo-European divinity of speech itself, the tripartite patron of prophecy,

1. Tony Pipolo, "Interview with Robert Beavers," *Millennium Film Journal* no. 32/33 (Fall 1998), p. 19.
2. Robert Beavers, e-mail to P. Adams Sitney, April 13, 2005.

power, and social sustenance, and that his patronage of medicine was a secondary formation of his providing nourishment and a means of communication among humans. In this reading, prophecy and the works of the lyre are axial functions: the one reveals to men the thought of Zeus and the other instructs them how to please the gods in return.[3] In the film, however, the "speech" of the village idiot and the blind man take the form of gesture, not words.

The subject of the imaginary conversation or monologue in the hotel room is incidental to the primary force of (unheard) acts of saying, until, in this viewer's mind, the distinctions between saying, gesturing, and filming, just like those between the capital and the lowercase pronouns, expand and collapse. The two *he*s, as pronouns, are substitutes for other signs, empty or hidden names. Furthermore, the past tense—"said"—marks the disappearance of auditory phenomena; as if the hotel room were resonating with the silent reverberations and implications of what *he* (or *He* and *he*) said in it. In contrast to these indications of a lost verbal utterance, the filmic image continually reasserts its equivocal presence in the montage rhythms. When the filmmaker said the "he" speaking is the film itself, he acknowledged, in one way, the Apollonian instructions at the core of his art. Like Markopoulos, who seems to have been one of the vessels of his instruction in this matter, he conceived of his cinema as soteriological: *Sotiros* is a cinematic paean.

Panning seems to play a larger role in *Sotiros* than in any other film by Beavers. Typically, he will cut from a pan to a still landscape with an abrupt shock; sometimes he will hold a shot for a long time only to budge the camera just before cutting to another still image. He seems to be laying bare a syntax of image composition in which filmic frames, camera movements, and ambient sounds take on meaning by resisting the conventions of expression.

After the last occurrence of "He said," there are two shots. In the first an interior shutter closes out light, while the second shows a whitewashed rural building, presumably the same one, with a closed window. When the imagery resumes after a brief black pause, we see and hear a man shaving. Very slowly we come to realize that it is the filmmaker himself, alone, as the parenthesis in the original title for the source of this part of the film had made explicit. In fact, it is not until the very last shot that we can be certain that the figure we have been seeing in close-ups with a large scar on his leg is Robert Beavers: for the final image shows him sitting up in bed projecting shadow figures on the wall with his hand.

Perhaps the first indication that the mode has shifted to self-portraiture would be the synecdoches of a hand turning a tripod in a panning motion, often intercut with pans of a new landscape: a street in an Austrian town and

---

3. Georges Dumézil, *Apollon sonore et autres essais* (Paris: Gallimard, 1982).

the woods surrounding it where we see a burned-out smokehouse. By using
the tripod as the emblem of filmmaking in this work, Beavers may be playing
on the iconography of the three-legged seat of the Delphic oracle. In any case,
it is the trope for the lyre here.

Beavers was convalescing in Graz, where he studied the score of Alban
Berg's *Wozzeck* and read the composer's essays on the subject. He uses the
opera as a crucial intertext in this part of the film, quoting very brief passages
from it seven times. The interconnected auditory fragments operate as the
graphic representations of words had in the first part of the film. *Wozzeck*
becomes the prophetic articulation of the filmmaker's suffering. In fact, it had
been so for Berg himself, who transformed his dismal experience of World
War I and his debilitating asthma into its tragic song.

The opening phrase of the opera, "Langsam! Eins nach dem Andern!"
(Slowly! One after the other!), can be heard over a close-up of the convalescent's ear, as if he were himself listening to Berg's music, but the citation refers
to the previous shots as well, since Wozzeck is shaving Captain Hauptmann
(who sings these lines) as the curtain rises. Each quotation from *Wozzeck* introduces a new voice (aside from the second and third, where Beavers breaks
a short passage from the Doctor into two fragments): Captain Hauptman,
the Doctor, Maria (Wozzeck's unfaithful mistress, whom he murders), a Fool
or Idiot, and Wozzeck himself, as he drowns. Finally a voiceless orchestral
passage ends the film. Each of these citations has links to images in the film
and to Beavers's physical or mental state. Although the first three are keyed to
shots of the ear or blank passages, when the Fool sings, "Ich riech, ich riech
Blut!" (I smell, I smell blood!), we see a close-up of the convalescent's nose,
and when the drowning Wozzeck cries "Das Wasser is Blut... Blut" (The
water is blood... blood), there is an image of a pond in the woods. The progress, then, of the operatic moments not only charts the unfolding of *Wozzeck*
in sequence; it also moves from suggesting the film subject's passive listening
to his imaginative identification.

An allusion to the slow passage of time during convalescence personalizes
Captain Hauptmann's obsession with "the vast stretches of time he sees lying
before him."[4] He cries "Langsam!" to the barber lest he abandon him to empty
time before his next duty. Similarly, the Doctor's inane dietary experiments
with Wozzeck, quoted in the second musical fragment ("Are you carrying on
as usual? Shaving the Captain? Catching lizards? Eating your beans?"), tropes
some of the dubious treatments and operations doctors proposed to Beavers.

Markopoulos told me a harrowing narrative of the events following the
accident. Although I can no longer recall the details, I vividly remember how

---

4. Douglas Jarman, *Alban Berg: Wozzeck* (New York: Cambridge University Press, 1989), p. 25.

impressed I was at the extraordinary efforts he made to get Beavers safely to Austria and the series of sudden, intuitive decisions he made canceling operations and treatments as if he were guided by invisible powers in directing his friend's recovery. Some of that magical thinking can be seen in Beavers's own account of his foreboding before they were hit by the bus:

> While I was still in Switzerland, completing the editing of *Sotiros Responds*, I heard on the radio an extraordinary fragment from Alban Berg's *Wozzeck*, conducted by the great conductor Dimitri Mitropoulos at La Scala. This was nearly impossible to find because it was only a fragment on tape. I sent a letter to the Archivio del Stato in Rome, which had a copy of the tape, and we stopped in Rome on our way to Greece so that I could listen to it. When I came out of the session, I saw a dead bird before me and felt that it was a bad omen. Then we went to Greece and almost immediately afterwards, on Pentecost, we had this accident. Later, in Graz, I had time to read Berg's libretto—which he had written outside of Graz—and his two essays. This entered into my thoughts for *Sotiros (Alone)*. I finally used three or four phrases from *Wozzeck* in the soundtrack and the choice of certain filming locations has an indirect relation to the opera. Much later, after I had fully recovered, I returned to Greece and made the very short film, *Sotiros in the Elements*.[5]

We might read this statement as if the quest for the recording of *Wozzeck* was a fatal lure toward the accident. Such a concatenation of causes and effects would reflect the double nature of Greek religion in which Apollo is both the bringer of disease and its agent of cure. By fusing the three *Sotiros* films into one, Beavers tacitly suggests that the dangerous encounter with Apollonian forces inevitably shaped his film and even used his body as a means of revelation and expression. The film itself, as "Sotiros," spoke first in images and then inflicted the sufferings that became the vehicle for its completion. Thus Berg's *Wozzeck* might be said to have been woven into this process rather than appended as an exterior allusion.

The third musical quotation comes from the prayer of Maria in act 3, scene 1:

> und küsste seine Füsse und netzte sie
> mit Tränen und salbte sie mit Salben.
> [and kissed his feet and washed them
> with tears and anointed them with balm.]

---

5. Pipolo, "Interview with Robert Beavers," p. 18.

Here Maria, driven by sexual guilt for her affair with the drum major, reads from the New Testament description of Mary Magdalen anointing Jesus's feet. In conversation, Beavers spoke of *Sotiros* as "a religious film," pointing out that the German equivalent of the name (and title) occurs in Maria's aria as "Heiland" (Savior):

> Heiland! Ich möchte Dir die Füsse salben! Heiland!
> [Savior! I might annoint Your feet! Savior!]

The filmmaker's acts of identification are complex and obscure here. Although the fragment accompanies a shot of his ear, overtly reconfirming that he is listening to Berg's opera in his hotel room, yet by suggesting a partial identification with the body of Christ, it amplifies the intense narcissism of convalescence; for it follows by two minutes a shot of his bare foot in a pool of light, which initiated a sequence of several shots of the scar on his leg and one of his damaged eye, leading up to the voice of Maria on the soundtrack. Her acknowledgment of the sudden power of sexual fascination might be taken as an oblique commentary on the shots, from the first part of the film, of young bare-chested construction workers on a building site. The later images of the filmmaker's own bare chest, included in the sequence with his wounds, bridge the two vectors of the musical allusion—to the sacrificial body of Christ and to sexual intoxication—in a narcissistic fusion. Freud's discussion of the displacement of "the libidinal cathexis in the ego" brought about by disease, wounding, or hypochondria emphasizes the narcissistic eroticization of corporal ailments:

> Now the prototype of the organ that is painfully tender, that is in
> some way changed and that is not yet diseased in the ordinary sense, is
> the genital organ in its state of excitation. In that condition it becomes
> congested with blood, swollen and humected, and is the seat of a mul-
> tiplicity of sensations.[6]

Light, song, and saying (as showing or revealing) are the crucial thematic elements of *Sotiros*. The Indo-European etymology of the title is particularly rich. It comes from the root *teu which combines many disparate words associated with "swelling": the English words thigh, thumb, thimble, and tumescence; Greek soma (body) and saos (safe, healthy). The filmmaker constructs his art from the saying, song, and light the filmmaker receives and perceives.

6. Sigmund Freud, "On Narcissism: An Introduction," in *The Standard Edition of the Complete Psychological Works of Sigmund Freud*, ed. and trans. James Strachey, vol. 14 (London: Hogarth Press, 1957), p. 84.

The final image allegorizes conjunction by showing the convalescent, unmistakably the filmmaker, making a rudimentary shadow film on the wall beside him by holding his hands in the streaming light.

The next film of the cycle, *AMOR*, is an exquisite lyric, shot in Rome ("Roma" reverses the letters of the title) and at the Heckentheater (Hedge Theater) of Salzburg. The title *AMOR* renders the Greek *eros* into Latin. Beavers had represented that very divinity for Markopoulos in the film *Eros O Basileus* (1967) soon after they first met. Here the filmmaker declares his amor for the craft of filmmaking, for the sounds and surfaces around him, including the clothing on his body. The recurring sounds of cutting cloth, hands clapping, hammering and tapping, emphasize the associations immanent in the montage of short camera movements that bring together the making of a suit and the restoration of a building. There are close-ups of a man, presumably Beavers himself, standing in a new suit, making a series of hand movements and gestures, including clapping. A handsomely designed 10,000-lire banknote suggests the aesthetic economy of the film, in which tailoring points to editing.

In the short essay "La Terra Nuova," Beavers approaches the tropes of Emerson's "Circles" when he discusses *AMOR*:

> This same search leads to the film's individual perspective, which the spectator will enter as the single living participant. Taking an example from Michelangelo's *Sacra Famiglia*, I would suggest that the circular form of the painting is completed by the curved wall and figures in the background that draw the viewer into a "totally rounded orb." Imagine how a film can extend such a perspective in time, bringing it closer to the subjective sense of how we see. It was with such an impulse that I used the full circle of the camera lens in *AMOR*, turning it in front of the aperture to create a movement like the eye turned upwards or cast downwards. I allowed the lens to suggest a rounded field of vision amplified in the form of the film: a "totally rounded orb, in its rotundity joying." (Empedocles)[7]

By the end of the short essay, a mere five paragraphs, the circularity expands to include the rolls of film whose revolutions potentially spin off aesthetic revelation: "Even the simple unwinding and rewinding of film rolls is part of the process and can help to release an insight leading to the film's distinct form."

The movement of the camera lens around the turret, as in *Ruskin*, is one of several manifestations of the circular motif: We see architectural lunettes,

7. Robert Beavers, "La Terra Nuova," *The Searching Measure* (Berkeley: Berkeley Art Museum and Pacific Film Archive, 2004), pages unnumbered.

arches, bowers, sculpted tondos, the rounded image of Andrea del Castagno's *Portrait of a Man* (now in the National Gallery, Washington, DC) on the banknote, prominent buttons on the jacket, spools of thread, as well as the cylindrical shapes of columns, pipes, and sleeves. The moral implications that Emerson draws from the circle may be latent in Beavers's film; for coming fast upon *Sotiros* in the third cycle, *AMOR* is a poem of recovery and expansion:

> The eye is the first circle; the horizon which it forms is the second;
> and throughout nature this primary figure is repeated without end.
> It is the highest emblem in the cipher of the world. St. Augustine
> described the nature of God as a circle whose centre was everywhere,
> and its circumference nowhere. We are all our lifetime reading the copi-
> ous sense of this first of forms.... You admire this tower of granite,
> weathering the hurts of so many ages. Yet a little waving hand built
> this huge wall, and that which builds is better than that which is built.
> The hand that built can topple it down much faster. Better than the
> hand, and nimbler, was the invisible thought which wrought through
> it.... But the heart refuses to be imprisoned; in its first and narrowest
> pulses it already tends outward with a vast force, and to immense and
> innumerable expansions.[8]

Beavers plays the circular motif of *AMOR* off against the molding of space instantiated by forced perspective of the rococo Heckentheater (1704–18) of Salzburg and the elegant Roman Piazetta of St. Ignatius (1725–36). The former is located in the Mirabell Gardens, which were built after the plans of Johann Bernhard Fischer von Erlach and redesigned around 1730 by Franz Anton Danreiter. The tall hedges form a perspectival recession centered on a proscenium, a V shape of trees, standing in for a stage set. As an outdoor theater it recalls the odea of ancient Greece and Rome, but the forced perspective suggests Palladio's Theatro Olympico in Verona with Scamozzi's perspectival set for the Renaissance revival of *Oedipus Tyrannos*. Sebastiano Serlio theorized the use of such perspectives in his *Architettura* (1537–71), where he proposed three different views: a stately vista for tragedy, a street of taverns and brothels for comedy, and a rural backdrop for satyr plays. Although the schema is Serlio's, not Beavers's, a similar distillation of theater and its history resonates through the films of the third cycle; for instance, it follows the noble vista of *AMOR* with a street of prostitutes in Ευψυχι (*Efpsychi*) and a rural location for *Wingseed*.

---

8. Ralph Waldo Emerson, *Essays and Lectures* (New York: Library of America, 1983), pp. 403–5.

The architecture of *AMOR* is theatrical as well. Filippo Raguzzini created the tiny Roman piazza opposite the baroque San Ignazio church for the Jesuits of the Collegio Romano. It is "the only fully rococo planning scheme completed in early 18th-century Rome," according to Dorothy Metzger Habel.[9] Three interlocking ellipses define the exquisite arrangement of curvilinear facades Raguzzini built to articulate the limited space at his disposal.

The recurring shots of cutting and sewing fabric detail the production of the suit worn by the figure whose face we do not see. The attention is on his hands, which he claps, turning the theatrical and architectural space into a sounding board. The scissors cutting the cloth remind us that the hedge theater itself requires continual clipping to maintain its architectural function.

As *AMOR* puts costume and gesture center-stage, *Ευψυχι* (*Efpsychi*) explores the relationship of face to mask and synchronous to nonsynchronous sound. Resembling *Still Light* in some respects, it is a portrait of a young man foregrounded within the static theater of a traditional Greek environment, urban this time rather than insular. In calling the film *Efpsychi*, Beavers chose a title that would be obscure to most of his viewers. It is a Greek word for high spirits or a good soul. In one form it means "to be of good courage" and devolves into a salutation meaning "farewell"; as such it can be read on ancient gravestones.

Paul Arthur has cogently described and interpreted *Efpsychi*:

> Besides providing a densely articulated picture of an urban scene,
> Beavers infuses the exchange among disparate elements with an un-
> dertow of muted drama. It is as if the actor's face, as hub and relay
> for perceptual-emotive anticipation, partakes of a shadow mystery
> play in which isolated representations of artisanal labor acquire
> an affective weight that prods the viewer's desire for discursive, if
> not narrative, coherence.... [T]he reciprocal performances of craft
> manufacture and acting are displayed as vestiges of an earlier cultural
> moment that is not so much "redeemed" by the modern technol-
> ogy of film as graciously recalibrated via the medium's penchant for
> juxtaposition. As embodied in the textures and rhythms of *Efpsychi*,
> the meeting of cinema with traditional craft equally bypasses
> romanticized myths of a Fall, the Machine in the Garden, in order to
> reconcile old and new.[10]

9. Dorothy Metzger Habel, "Piazza S. Ignazio, Rome in the 17th and 18th Centuries," *Architectura* 11, no. 1 (1981), pp. 31–65.
10. Paul Arthur, "Between the Place and the Act: *Efpsychi*," *Millennium Film Journal* No. 32/33 (Fall 1998), p. 58.

Beavers's own note on the film concludes by invoking an Emersonian triad,
if we read "chance," as so many American artists have, as a near synonym for
its apparent opposite, Necessity:

> The details of the young actor's face—his eyebrows, eyes, earlobe, lips
> and chin, etc.—are set opposite the buildings in the old market quar-
> ter of Athens, where every street bears the name of a Classical Greek
> playwright. The nearness of the face and its slightest movements are
> the means of balancing all of the film, from below street level up to the
> rooftops. In this setting, an intense stillness is interrupted sometimes
> by a sudden sound or by a movement in the street. The actor speaks
> a single word, τελευταία, meaning the last one, his features chang-
> ing with each scene and as he repeats the word, each syllable moves
> differently, suggesting a proximity between the erotic, the sacred and
> chance.[11]

All the films of Beavers's third cycle dramatize the problematic status of the
image by repeatedly interweaving and dissecting gestures of signification—
especially hand movements. In *Efpsychi*, one limit of the dissection would
be the attention to individual Greek letters, and small groupings of them,
from street signs. Paul Arthur pointed out that his framing of "'omicron-
delta-omicron' [ΟΔΟ from within the word for *street*, ʿΟΔΟΣ] suggests a
configuration of two eyes and a nose."[12] The analytical fragmentation of the
environment cleanses the filmmaker's instrument of worn-out associations and
habits of emotional reaction in order to examine his feelings with critical rigor.
Having tacitly repudiated the mannerism and mythopoeia of Markopoulos's
cinema, Beavers divested his art of any appeal to originary experience: There
are no staged events or orchestrations of emotion in the third cycle. Accepting
the surface of the world of things and the visible behavior of men as a given,
Beavers probes for signs of hermetic connections; yet for the most part, even
gestures he observes remain enigmatic. Under his persistent gaze, the polished
isolation of solid things and simple acts gives way to the picturing of a restless mind, repeatedly attempting and succeeding as far as possible in defining
the peculiar timbre of a place and finding the measure of his presence in it.
The consequent projection of noetic movement, as the coming into being
and testing of perceptions, associations, feelings, and ideas, invests this work
with lucid serenity. The films themselves affect us so startlingly because the
filmmaker has subtly comprehended the structural impossibility of arriving at

11. Robert Beavers, "On *Efpsychi*," *My Hand Outstreched: Films by Robert Beavers* (New York: Whitney
Museum, 2005), p. 6.
12. Arthur, "Between the Place and the Act," p. 58.

definitions or ends. In *Efpsychi* he may be acknowledging the deferral of any conclusive moment by repeating the Greek word *teleftia* ("the last one") on the soundtrack. Actually, he recorded the word from the shout of a hawker of lottery tickets, advertising that he had only one left to sell. The apocalyptic connotation and the lottery context account for two aspects of the triad, the sacred and chance. The third, eroticism, devolves separately from the location of the film and the manner in which the model is filmed. We see men entering and exiting a brothel, and a couple talking on the street, the woman touching her buttocks and brushing her skirt in a suggestive manner. Quite apart from this commerce in sexuality, the central male figure appears in sensual close-ups of his eyes, eyebrows, chin, cheeks, Adam's apple, neck, lips, torso, and hair. At one point we see him kiss a sacred icon. He is an artisan who makes brooms by hand in a small shop. The montage brings him and his shop in close proximity to a candle maker, a leather cutter, and a stall of fresh fish. The street names in Greek and Roman letters—Eschylou, Sophoklou, Euripidou, and Theatrou—remind us of the centrality of ritual theater for the examination of eroticism, the sacred, and chance in this culture.

In the Temenos Archive in Zurich are volumes of many of the poets Beavers finds closest to his sensibility: Umberto Saba, Stefan George, Wallace Stevens, Rainer Maria Rilke, T. S. Eliot, Elizabeth Bishop, Horace, and Francis Ponge (to whom he once showed his films). Of these, Saba's poems of his native Trieste show some affinities to the moods in which Beavers portrays Athens in *Efpsychi* and *The Stoas*. It is probably a mere coincidence that *teleftea* would translate *Ultime cose* (*Last Things*, 1944), one of Saba's last collections of poetry.[13] More relevant might be the concatenation of self-reflection, lost love, and sacred affection Saba associated with certain Trieste streets and shops and the objects he chanced upon in them, although the explicitly autobiographical aspect of Saba's poetry is foreign to Beavers's work.

Wingseed's lustrous, rich images of a Mediterranean landscape with sheep, goats, and a male nude and its intricate rhythms openly acknowledge the filmmaker's debt to Markopoulos but even more emphatically stake out the ground Beavers has painstakingly secured as his own territory: the fusion of images and image clusters that resolutely maintain their autonomy. One might even see this film as a restatement of his relationship to his lover and teacher.

Wingseed is patently an eclogue: Amid some sheep and many goats we encounter a naked youth, alone aside from the implied attentions of the filmmaker, who observes and directs him. The first glimpse we have of the boy lowering his head on a bed, as if kissing or embracing it, suggests that in this

---

13. Τελευταία is both the feminine singular and neuter plural adjective of τελευταίος.

pastoral he plays the traditional role of the unsatisfied lover, but the cinematic fixation on his body gradually confirms him as an object of erotic fascination, rather than (or perhaps as well as) the subjective core of the film. The relationship of the filmmaker to the young man is both intimate and distanced; it is as if he casts a cold eye on the nature of his desire and, by implication, his own youth.

Even the Pan pipes we hear intermittently on the elegantly minimal soundtrack foster the ambiguity typical of Beavers's art. As an iconographic gesture, the pipes represent the presence of a Poet, of the poetic afflatus. Virgil's *Second Eclogue* (to which I shall return) follows the bucolic tradition in identifying the shepherd as a poet under the protection of Pan:

> mecum una in silvis imitabere Pana canendo [Bucolica, 11, 51]
> [Together with me in the woods you will imitate Pan in singing]

But here Beavers encourages us, at one stroke, to recognize the young man as the persona of a shepherd poet and yet acknowledge that behind him the filmmaker, as the poet-magician, is crafting the whole auditory rhythm with muted goat bells, the wind, a shepherd's guttural call, and panpipes.

Beavers's note for the film moves from commenting on its title to evoking its images and sounds:

> A seed which floats in the air, a whirligig, a love charm. This magnificent landscape, both hot and dry, is far from sterile; rather, the heat and dryness produce a distinct type of life, seen in the perfect forms of the wild grass and seed pods, the herds of goats as well as in the naked figure. The torso, in itself, and more, the image which it creates in this light. The sounds of the shepherd's signals and the flute's phrase are heard. And the goats' bells. Imagine the bell's clapper moving from side to side with the goat's movements like the quick side-to-side camera movements, which increase in pace and reach a vibrant ostinato.[14]

In the representation of sexual longing Beavers took over, and scaled down, the mannerist direction Markopoulos used since his origins in the trance film genre of the later 1940s. The most florid example of his Bronzino-like mode of filming bodies was his portrait of Beavers himself as the incarnation of the nude lover, *Eros O Basileus*. More than twenty years later, Beavers seems to have the earlier film in mind, as he in turn films the young eromenos of *Wingseed*. I use the classical Greek term for the young lover guided by a hint

14. Beavers, note on *Wingseed*. New York Film Festival, October 11, 1999.

embedded in *Wingseed*: in the bedroom there is a momentary pause on the red cover of Gundel Koch-Harnack's *Knabenliebe und Tiergeschenke: Ihre Bedeutung im päderastischen Erziehungssystem Athens* (Boy Love and Animal Gifts: Their Meaning in the Pederastic Educational System of Athens). Koch-Harnack examines the numerous vase paintings in which an older teacher (erastes) gives an animal—most often a hare—to his pupil-lover (eromenos), arguing that the exchange symbolically acknowledges the instinctual drives that bind the pair.

Apparently Beavers conflated the themes of homoerotic teacher-pupil relationship with the bucolic shepherd's lament, traditionally both homosexual and heterosexual, importing from the latter a domesticated animal, a goat, in the place of the wild gift. In Virgil's *Second Eclogue* the shepherd-poet Corydon bewails his hopeless infatuation with the boy Alexis. Dying Daemotas gave Corydon his panpipes,

> et dixit morientes: te nunc habet ista secundum [Bucolica, ii,38]
> [and he said as he died, "Now you will have this as a true successor"]

Beavers's mantle as a second Markopoulos is never so explicit. The bucolic title, *Wingseed*, alone suggests the regermination of poetic—windborne—inspiration. The elaborately artificial conventions of pastoral poetry (here massively imported into cinema) emphasize the continuity of tradition, the succession of poets, and the priority of desire over satisfaction, as if the poetic purpose of desire was to inspire and encourage the crafted artifact.

Along with the seductions of poetic song, Virgil's Corydon offers Alexis gifts of suckling fawns, flowers, and fruit in vain. But Beavers's young protagonist appears to cherish and make a pet of a goat, which according to Koch-Harnack would signal the welcome proffer of the instinctual erotic drive of the erastes. With the acceptance of the gift, if indeed it is a gift, the scene subtly shifts from the rustic landscape to the hedge theater of Salzburg.

The musical structure of Beavers's film sustains its fecund ambiguities in a careful balance. The poem of the mature filmmaker celebrating a perhaps aristocratic youth in the guise of an Arcadian shepherd, and the eclogue of the shepherd, at once the object of desire and suffering from frustrated desire, keep pace with the more submerged, historical resonances of the origins of the filmmaker as eromenos. For even if in some ways *Wingseed* corresponds in Beavers's corpus to *Eros O Basileus* in Markopoulos's oeuvre, it constitutes a chastening of the passionate declaration of the earlier film, as it turns the power of erotic observation and direction into an examination of the inspired continuities of filmmaking and filmmakers.

The Hedge Theater, the last film in the cycle to be completed, follows *Wingseed*, presumably because they were shot in that order. Beavers took fifteen years to give the film its ultimate shape. It is the complement of *AMOR*: they are the two films of the cycle made in Rome and Salzburg, where both use the Heckentheater as an emblem for cinema's perspectival depth and representation of the natural world. In place of the Piazza San Ignazio, Beavers lovingly records details from two churches built by Francesco Borromini. Even the tailoring motif recurs: where *AMOR* shows moments of a suit being made, in *The Hedge Theater* we see a tailor's hand sewing a buttonhole on a white shirt.

The opening montage intercuts details of the church of San Carlo alle Quattro Fontane with bird cages and snares, the sewing of a button, and Beavers operating his camera. The initial parallelism, elaborately unfolded, of Borromini's church and the woodland *rocolo* (filmed in Lombardy) for trapping fowl suggests that the church might be a cage to catch the Holy Ghost or, conversely, the Holy Ghost's snare for human souls. As Leo Steinberg demonstrated, the "S. Carlino" itself is a rigorous iconographic system, "combining octagon-circle-cross-hexagon," symbolically affirming the multifaceted nature of the Trinity. Beavers absorbed this system into his film and amplified it.

Eventually the polarities of the editing alternate between Borromini's St. Ivo delle Sapienza (which Steinberg reads as a symbolic representation of the "*Domus Sapientiae*, the house built by Holy Wisdom"[15]) and the Salzburg hedge theater covered with snow. The editing stresses dead leaves and two stone lions nearly buried in snow. At that point Beavers intercut a shot of himself with a man's arm over his shoulder and brief glimpses of Markopoulos's face, turning the winter vision into a muted elegy for his lover.

Beavers initially planned to complement the film inspired by Borromini with one centered on *San Martino e il povero*, a panel by Stefano di Giovanni, called Sassetta, in the Collezione Chigi-Saracini, Siena. He fused the two projects when he finally found the appropriate form for *The Hedge Theater*. The transition from Markopoulos's gesture of affection to the second part of the film is marked by a sound of fabric ripping as the camera pans up and down Sassetta's poorly preserved panel of St. Martin of Tours giving half of his cloak to a beggar. Beavers alternates glimpses of the painting with images of the hedge theater, now green, in spring or summer. The film ends with an inundation of rain, which we can hear before we see it.

Although the title simply translates the Heckentheater, where much of it was filmed, it harbors a revealing pun; for Beavers's films hedge their theatricality with elegant aesthetic decorum. Consider, for instance, his revision of *The Painting*. By introducing the images of the torn photograph of himself he

15. Leo Steinberg, *Borromini's San Carlo alle Quattro Fontane: A Study in Multiple Form and Architectural Symbolism* (New York: Garland, 1977), pp. xi, xv.

does not abandon the reticence characteristic of his art, but rather inflects it; for the dramatic incident in which Markopoulos ripped up the image (if, indeed, my inference about the significance of those shots is accurate) remains suppressed. Instead, the ripped image anchors the analogy of the filmmaker to the tortured martyr, whether or not we take account of this speculative cause of the defacement of the photograph. Thus, even when he concretizes the personal allusion, Beavers hedges its theatricality. In his lapidary montage the space of the theater suffices, as if that were what the cinema might genuinely offer us, or him. Even the arm draped over the filmmaker's shoulder as he films himself in a mirror is a reticent or understated moment. Whatever it meant to him when he filmed it—perhaps an allusion to the end of *From the Notebook Of...*, that sense has changed with the death of his mentor and lover.

The coda of the film, centered on La Sassetta's panel, becomes a palinode to *The Painting*, the only other locus in his oeuvre where a two-dimensional work of art plays a central role. Again, he hedges the allusion, teasing the viewer to consider the painting an allegory of Markopoulos and himself and at the same time refusing to confirm so bold, so outlandish a leap. The ripping sound that introduces the meditation on *San Martino e il povero* can be an auditory amplification of the severing of the red cloak held taught between the beggar, who grips one end of it with both his hands, and St. Martin, holding the other end with his left hand as he uses the long horizontal sword in his right hand to slice the cloak in half. Just as the Flemish painter of the St. Hippolytus triptych represented the martyr stretched tight above the ground just before his limbs parted from his torso, Sassetta captures the moment when the separation is nearly completed, as the beggar and the future bishop of Tours exchange gazes. St. Martin's horse has turned his head toward the beggar and the cloak, almost as if to see the source of the ripping sound Beavers added to the image.

In the reverberations of that sound, we might imagine the tearing of the photograph from *The Painting*. But now, from the placement of the Sassetta imagery in *The Hedge Theater* right after the shot of the gesture of affection, and by the location of the film itself in *My Hand Outstretched*, the trope reverses and expands to represent the moment death tore Markopoulos's companionship from the filmmaker, without annulling the allusion to the extraordinary generosity of Markopoulos toward Beavers, sharing everything with him, from the beginning of their relationship, and coterminous with the whole of Beavers's artistic career. Alive as well as in his death, he passed his mantle to Beavers. That phrase comes from the Second Book of Kings, where Elijah's cloak symbolized his prophetic election. In leaving it behind for Elisha when the chariot of fire bore him to heaven, he passed on his powers (2 Kings 2:11–14). Elisha expressed his grief in a traditional Hebraic manner by tearing his clothes, but he also accepted Elijah's inheritance with that very gesture. Similarly, the rainfall at the conclusion of the film suggests a hyperbolic metaphor for the tears of mourning and a metonomy of cyclic renewal.

Tearing or ripping is an essential moment in the filmmaking process. The filmmaker tears off a piece of the continuous ribbon of a shot to join it to another piece ripped from a different ribbon of film. Thus the sound of tearing that precedes the first image of La Sassetta's panel is also a sign of the act that brings together the two films Beavers could not complete after shooting them in 1986 and 1987 until he joined them in 2002, even though there is no auditory similarity between the tearing of cloth and celluloid.

Two representations of Athens bracket *Wingseed* and *The Hedge Theater*. *Efpsychi* and *The Stoas* evoke the atmosphere of the city in districts that have survived a century. *The Stoas* is the only film in Beavers's corpus without a significant human presence, aside from a recurring close-up of two cupped hands held apart as if measuring an absent circular object, say, a bowl or a basket. Apparently, Beavers filmed his own hands in a mirror for these shots. For seven minutes we see images from the nearly empty Stoa Ikaros in Athens. Isolated containers indicate that produce—tea, fresh bread—passes through this temporary storage arcade. Idle hand trucks and wagons point to the simple human labor that marks the location with vestiges of a preautomated culture. Then for ten minutes we follow the course and hear the Alpheus River of central Arcadia in shots arranged to reflect the increasing volume and speed of the water as it descends from its source. The final two minutes concentrate on grapes ripening on vines.

Two notes Beavers wrote, at different times, for *The Stoas* may throw some light on the "finality" operating in it and *Efpsychi*:

> I sought in these small industrial arcades the spaces which can be seen first from one side and then from the other, a shape of emptiness, then the divinity of the river—this deep sense of appearance—and finally the grasping of the grape....
>
> In *The Stoas*, there is no figure, and there are no titles. There are only the hands reaching directly into the space of these small industrial arcades, seen from one end and the other, in a light that can still find proportion and finality. The emptiness of the arcades is transformed into the river's movement, which is again stillness. Through the rhythm of the river's image and its sound, a deeper sense of appearance is projected into the space above it. The full length of the stream gathers in the final clusters of grapes.[16]

16. Beavers, note on *The Stoas*, Walter Reade Theater, New York, May 6, 2001.

The language of these notes opens up, or approaches, several of the key elements of Beavers's poetics: the phrases "a shape of emptiness," "the divinity of the river," "[to] find proportion and finality," and "a deeper sense of appearance" strain to articulate the mystery and authority with which he conceives of the cinematic image. The formal terms—proportion, shape, and finality—refer to both the structure of a film and, as emphasized here, the light seized by the camera and attuned in projection. For Beavers this light does not merely reflect or reproduce the world before the camera; it becomes the means for that world to appear, to manifest itself as an image, with a force and a sense of meaningfulness (or finality) that had been occulted previously. Its "deeper sense of appearance" is a form of epiphany, as he indicated in writing of "the divinity of the river" Alpheus. The classical poets, especially Ovid, wrote of this river's passion for the nymph Arethusa, who once bathed in his waters. To escape him she transformed into a fountain, only to occasion their even more profound interpenetration. Something of this myth resonates in Beavers's description of the montage sequence as "[t]he emptiness of the arcades is transformed into the river's movement." The triad of eroticism, the sacred, and chance comes into play when what the filmmaker photographs manifests a "deeper sense of appearance." For that to occur, the film must create an emptiness where the image is no longer "reduced to illustrating a preconception," in the phrase from "La Terra Nuova."

In *The Stoas* this epiphany culminates in the revelation or presentation of grapes. The word "grasping" suggests not only that the hand gestures, gauging the size of a bowl or krater, indicate a Dionysian offering, but that the empty space defined or molded by the hands has become the vessel for epiphany of the divinity of theater and enthusiasm, making the film the Dionysian counterpart to the Apollonian Sotiros as well as the supplement of *Efpsychi*.[17]

The final film, *The Ground*, is the only film in the cycle begun and completed after Markopoulos's death. It was shot in 1995 and finished in 2001. In it Beavers, commingling mourning with serene contemplation, returns to Hydra, the site of *Winged Dialogue*, three years after the death of Markopoulos, who had been the subject of the earlier film. Hydra remains a theater of erotic fascination as it had been in *Winged Dialogue* and *Still Light*, but in *The Ground* the attraction to the eromenos, a bare-chested stonecarver, is restrained almost to the point of melancholy. He is absorbed in his labor, never acknowledging with a look the filmmaker's presence.

The ruined windmill that appears in the first shot of the film and recurs throughout is the same one in which Markopoulos had stood nude in the opening film of the first cycle. Its emptiness now has elegiac implications,

---

17. Beavers, "La Terra Nuova," *The Searching Measure*.

as does the small church where several scenes of Markopoulos had been filmed; in *The Ground* it appears in the distance, on an offshore island of its own.

What, then, is the relationship of the young stonemason to the filmmaker? Varying a trope from *Leaves of Grass*, Beavers identifies his own body with the landscape by intercutting shots of his bare chest with the spare vegetation of the island. In the 1855 version of "Song of Myself" Whitman wrote: "Tenderly I will use you curling grass, / It may be you transpire from the breasts of young men..."[18] Beavers cuts from the hair of his chest to the briars and weeds of a nearly deserted hillside, where we will eventually see a cave. Birds fly into it; a goat is tethered before it. The montage suggests that a donkey stands nearby. These iconic symbols of Hermes, Pan, and Dionysos are manifestations of the "deep sense of appearance" that the filmmaker elicits from "the ground," without reducing them to functions of what he calls an overdetermined intention. The imaginary space his editing rhythms create keep the windmill, the stonecutter, the cave, and the filmmaker's body in ambiguous proximity to each other. Together they instantiate the nodal relations of eroticism, the sacred, and chance; for even if the animals merely happened to be nearby as a consequence of chance, the erotic charge of the editing enhances their sacred associations.

Throughout the film, Beavers cups his hand and turns it toward his breast as if offering a pledge, or makes a fist to beat his chest and then opens his fingers. When I asked him about these gestures, he wrote: "I have placed in this gesture of the hand 5 or 6 different sounds. It is the hollow of the hand and as in *AMOR*, it is a place for sound. In re-reading my notes for *The Stoas* recently, I found that the literal meaning of doron, the Greek word for gift, is 'hollow of the hand.'...I am filming myself, and the gesture is equivalent to 'opening the heart.'"[19]

Allusions to the hand come up again and again in Beavers's texts insofar as he associates the technology of filmmaking with handcraft. Thus we can read the repeated focus on craftsmen in the films as transpositions of his relationship to his art. I have italicized the six allusions to the hand to be found in the ten pages of the short collection of his essays, *The Searching Measure*:

> I memorize the image and movement while holding the film original
> in hand; the memorizing gains a weight and becomes a source for the
> editing.... The editing responds to holding the image *in hand* and to

18. Whitman, "Leaves of Grass," *Selected Poems 1855–1892: A New Edition*, ed. Gary Schmidgall (New York: St. Martin's, 1999), p. 19.
19. Robert Beavers, e-mail to P. Adams Sitney, April 29, 2005.

the weighing of memory and is protected from an overdetermined intention. ["Editing and the Unseen"]

The *same hand* that operated the camera now places each image within the phrases of edited film. Even the simple unwinding and rewinding of film rolls is part of this process and can help to release an insight leading to the film's distinct form. ["La Terra Nuova"]

A filmmaker maintains a continuity in his work; he reaches in one direction and returns in another with something new *in hand....* Harshness, vulgarity, and the continuous opposition of profit may appear to overwhelm, yet a sense within the *eye and hand* maintains its own strength, its own point of origin, and becomes a protection against deceptive choices... ("...without greed, that is most important; no real work can be down without faith and *clean hands.*")— Vitruvius ["Em.Blem"][20]

The emphasis on his hand gestures in *The Ground* underscores the centrality of the filmmaker's body to that film and to the third cycle as a whole, where I have already noted the hands projecting shadows in *Sotiros*, clapping in *AMOR*, signaling and operating the camera in *The Hedge Theater*, and measuring in *The Stoas*. In *AMOR* and *The Hedge Theater* the filmmaker compared his own hands, making the sounds and images of his film, to those of a tailor cutting a suit and sewing a buttonhole. In *The Ground* he edits the movements of the palm and the fist to the work of the young stonecutter chipping at a rock with a mallet and a red, phallic chisel. At times framed and edited as if in proximity to the masonry of a ruined windmill, he represents the continuity of a traditional handicraft, transforming the materials of the ground on which he sits into long-lasting but ultimately impermanent structures. Often Beavers overlaps the sound of the hammering with that of his fist thumping his chest. At other times he lays over the images of his hand gestures the sounds of birds (including a rooster), waves, animals (dogs barking, a braying donkey), the bells worn by goats, and the buzzing of an insect. All of these sounds contribute to the auditory ambience of the island, so they do not appear exclusively in conjunction with the gestural "opening of the heart."

One can read the gestures as the ground from which the images emerge, as if the open palm offered the gift of a sound, say, the braying of the donkey, that brings forth the visible details of the animal's body. Only once does this magic seem unconditioned. In the middle of the film, the filmmaker follows

---

20. Beavers, "La Terra Nuova," *The Searching Measure,*

the opening of the palm with a shot of hands proffering a loaf of baked bread, its brown crust the color of the landscape.

Beavers compares filmmaking to vegetation in a passage that speaks of "the ground":

> Like the roots of a plant reaching down into the ground, filming remains hidden within a complex act, neither to be observed by the spectator nor even completely seen by the filmmaker. It is an act that begins in the filmmaker's eyes and is formed by his gestures in relation to the camera. In a sense he surrounds the camera with the direction of his intuition and feeling. The result retains certain physical qualities of the decisive moment of filmmaking—the quality of light and space—but it is equally surprising how a filmmaker draws what he searches for towards the lens. [La Terra Nuova][21]

In this allegory, "the ground" delineates a division between the visible and the invisible. It hides and protects the fundamental processes of filmmaking from both the artist and his audience. From this ground "a deeper sense of appearance" grows. *Ground* is a Germanic word for which the root *grundus has been postulated meaning "a deep place." It shows up in Old English as *grund*—denoting the bottom of the sea as well as the surface of the earth. In giving his film this title and placing it at the end of *My Hand Outstretched to the Winged Distance and Sightless Measure*, Beavers marks it as both a starting point and the symbolic terminus for the allegories of filmmaking he reiterates, in exquisite variations in the entire series: Its measured rhythms turn us from the ground of the filmmaker and point toward what cannot be made visible.

If stretching out the hand points to the distance receding beyond visibility, that gesture indicates as well the corporeal limitation of the man gesturing. It is a version of Emerson's rhetorical evocation of the transcendence of beauty: "If I could put my hand on the North Star, would it be as beautiful?" In Beavers's title we must configure the hand pointing toward what we can see and indicating what lies beyond our sight. Just as in *Nature* Emerson hypostatizes "the Hand of the Mind" as the consequence of Nature's "discipline of the understanding in intellectual truths ... [in which o]ur dealing with sensible objects is a constant exercise in the necessary lessons of difference, of likeness, of order, of being and seeming, of progressive arrangement; of ascent from particular to general; of combination to one end of manifold forces...—to instruct us that 'good thoughts are no better than good dreams, unless they be executed!' "[22]

21. Ibid.
22. Ralph Waldo Emerson, *Essays and Lectures* (New York: Library of America, 1983), p. 26.

The paradox of Beavers's relationship to Emerson and his tradition is that no filmmaker considered in this book has so thoroughly assumed the weight of European culture (while rejecting the aesthetic mechanisms I have linked to turning the eyes upside down or rushing through space or floating over it in a vehicle). Yet the very notion of the weight of European culture is an American idea—no European filmmaker I know shows the range of Beavers's cultural enthusiasms—linking the filmmaker to Henry James, T. S. Eliot, and Ezra Pound. If the details and references of its films largely evade the Emersonian models, the overall aspiration and achievement of *My Hand Outstretched to the Winged Distance and Sightless Measure* are fundamentally a consequence of the poetics of Emerson and Whitman.

CHAPTER 17

Mekas's Retrospection

Thirty-one years elapsed between the premieres of *Walden* and *As I Moved Ahead Occasionally I Saw Brief Glimpses of Beauty* (2000). During that span of time, Jonas Mekas released twenty-one films and ten videos. Most, or perhaps all, of them are elements in the ongoing sequence *Diaries, Notes and Sketches*. In scale it exceeds any of Brakhage's serial films and even runs longer than Frampton's *Magellan* would have if he had completed it according to his plans. The varieties of its forms, the consistency of its vision, and the range of its affects makes Mekas's film one of the greatest achievements of the American avant-garde cinema. If one of the consequences of the cinematic sequence in the native tradition has been to project and elaborate a world around its central filmmaker-subject, no work—not even the whole corpus of Brakhage's films—has so convincingly populated a filmed world of other beings without sacrificing the intense self-reflection of the filmmaker as *Diaries, Notes and Sketches*.

As I Moved Ahead is Mekas's equivalent to Brakhage's *The Book of the Family*. Astonishingly, an innocent viewer of the nearly five-hour film would not know that the marriage celebrated in it was at its end, despite the unusually persistent allusions that Mekas makes in his voice-over and in the intertitles to very dark moments, apparently in the distant past. While the comparable serial masterpieces consequent to the failure of a marriage, Frampton's *Hapax Legomena* and Brakhage's *Visions in Meditation* (as well as his *Faust* series) never directly allude to the marriage, Mekas's film celebrates it "ecstatically." The adjective *Brief* in its long title indicates that the visions of "beauty" we see through the filmmaker's eyes flickers against a darker, invisible horizon. Similarly, the Dantean title of the diaries he constructed from the footage of the preceding fifteen years, *He Stands in a Desert Counting the Seconds of His Life* (1985) locates the representation of privileged moments in the topos of ascetic withdrawal and ordeals of deprivation. The voice-over, and to some extent the intertitles, of *As I Moved Ahead* are the most explicit reflections Mekas has made about his filmmaking process from within the diaries themselves. Emphasizing that he speaks from the time of editing, many years, even decades, after most of the material was shot, he addresses us as his friends while he sits alone, always late at night, assembling the film.

David James cogently criticized the content of *He Stands in a Desert* shortly after the film was released: "In *He Stands in a Desert* the voiceover lamentation is jettisoned, but the documentation of what is revealed as an astonishingly successful social life still has the desperation of a man shoring against his ruin recollections of his moments in the life-styles of the rich and famous."[1] To this he added a footnote: "Mekas's decision to reserve from this film both the 'personal' and the 'abstract' material from this period is especially unfortunate and, as well as ensuring the discomforting obsession with the famous (especially John Lennon and the Kennedys), it reinstates the separation of public and private whose subversion otherwise marks his work's importance."[2]

When James wrote that, no one could have known, perhaps not even Mekas himself, the scale and ambition of the film of his family life that the filmmaker was nurturing. At nearly five hours, *As I Moved Ahead* is by far his longest diary film. Both *Walden* and *Lost, Lost, Lost* run approximately three hours.[3] Unlike them, it is a film without extended autonomous interludes or episodes.

Astonishingly, on the threshold of his eightieth year, Mekas has given us his most moving and most exuberant film. In some ways it is also his most difficult. He lets us know as he speaks from within the film that, overwhelmed

1. David E. James, "Film Diary/Diary Film: Practice and Product in *Walden*," in David E. James, *To Free the Cinema: Jonas Mekas and the New York Underground* (Princeton, NJ: Princeton University Press, 1992), p. 168.

2. Ibid., p. 168, note 28.

3. Mekas's video works sometimes run even longer. *The Education of Sebastian or Egypt Regained* (1992) is six hours, and the 2003 installation *Dedication to Leger* runs for twenty-four hours.

with the footage he had amassed, he resigned himself to assembling the film largely by chance, putting images of his family life willy-nilly into twelve chapters. Yet one-third of the way through, he advises his viewers to read the film carefully, to interpret what he is showing us, even though later he will contend that these images are immediately transparent, that they mean only themselves. Contradictions of this sort abound in *As I Moved Ahead*; its voice-over text is the richest and most complex the filmmaker ever attempted. Sometimes it gives us crucial hints toward understanding the overall contour of the work; at other times it seems to be responding locally to the memories and emotions evoked by the chance juxtaposition of filmed events; at still other times it depicts the state of mind of the filmmaker, working alone late at night in the last days of the twentieth century. Eventually, the speaking "I" powerfully addresses a sequence of beings he calls "you" over the course of the film. Cumulatively these speeches sketch out a series of triadic relationships (e.g., "I," "you," the film images) that generate the dialectical interactions between chapters.

Play between voice-over commentary and printed intertitles is even more intricate here than in the earlier parts of *Diaries, Notes and Sketches*; for nowhere else in that vast serial film does language play so important a role. In counterpoint to the apparently repetitive structure of the chapters, which make this long element in the grand series a serial film in itself, the titles and spoken texts articulate the temporality of the film, revealing the corrosive power of time by insistently denying it. At several points in this unusually abundant and speculative voice-over commentary, Mekas insists that this is a film about nothing, in fact, "a masterpiece of nothing." The refusal of chronological development, the repetition of intertitles, the voice-over emphasis on both moments of ecstasy and involuntary memories, and the sheer duration of the film deliberately prevent us from quickly grasping its overall form or easily charting its development.

The three longest chapters (8, 10, and 12) run approximately twenty-eight minutes; the shortest (9) lasts only fourteen minutes. They constitute semiautonomous units through which the filmmaker refocuses his interlocking odes to family life and on the relation of cinema to memory. Each chapter reexamines the joys of daily living and wonders at its evanescence; each chapter introduces new material, slightly altering the authorial perspective while asserting a continuity with the previous chapters. Eventually, the rhythmic alternation of chapters articulates the crisis dynamic of the film as a whole.

Usually Mekas speaks on the soundtrack near the start of a chapter to comment on the progress, or the nothingness, of the film so far. Often he laughs at himself and at his self-consciousness as he talks to his viewers. Once, he even tells us he is editing during the last minutes of the twentieth century, waiting for the change of the millennium. The abundant intertitles reinforce the retrospective temporality of the voice-over. In the opening voice-over, Mekas confesses an epistemological skepticism as the ground for his method of editing the film:

> I've never been able really to figure out where my life begins and where it ends. I have never, never been able to figure it all out, what it's all about, what it all means. So when I began now to put all these rolls of films together, to string them together, the first idea was to keep them chronological. But then I gave up and I just began splicing them together by chance, the way I found them on the shelf because I really don't know where any piece of my life really belongs.

Although he repeatedly acknowledges his ignorance, both in speech and in intertitles, just as often he asserts without a doubt that he has "glimpsed brief moments of happiness and beauty" and that these moments are unquestionably real. In fact, he ends the film in his orphic guise, chanting to the accompaniment of his boyan:

> . . . I don't know what life is.
> I know nothing about what life is.
> I have never understood life,
> the real life.
> Where do I really live?
> I do not know; I do not know
> where I come from and where do I go?
> Where am I? Where am I?
> I do not know.
> I do not know where I am,
> and where I am going to
> and where I'm coming from.
> I know nothing about life.
> But I have seen some beauty.
> I have seen some brief, brief
> glimpses of beauty and happiness.
> I have seen, I know
> I have seen some
> happiness and beauty.
> I do not know where I am.
> I do not know where I am.
> I do not know where I am.
> But I know I have experienced
> some moments of beauty,

brief moments of beauty
and happiness
as I am moving ahead, as I am
moving ahead, as I am
moving ahead, my friends!
I have, I know I have
experienced some brief brief
moments of beauty, my friends,
my friends!

While singing this climactic song, he shows again the title of the film, this time handwritten, to which he adds: "Yes, la beauté and it's still beautiful in my memory, as real as then. Yes, as real as this film."

As he clarifies and expands upon the principles of psychological realism that subtend the film (and his earlier diary films as well), he is confident that the events he has filmed are real even if they are colored by his perspective. Fantasy, dreams, and delusion play no significant role in Mekas's cinema. Nevertheless, in chapter 7, he concedes: "I may not be even filming the real life. I may be just filming my memories. I don't care." This concession is of slight consequence insofar as the filmmaker implies throughout the work that memory accurately represents reality. Furthermore, as he describes it, memory's relationship to reality is structurally parallel to that of cinema. This analogy has two consequences: It justifies the representative power of memory while, at the same time, it points to the subjective or personal quality of film imagery. Mekas's images take on the "warmth and intimacy" William James attributed to memories.[4] The other crucial quality James observed, "the past direction of time" or the feeling of pastness inherent in memories, may not be intrinsic to cinema as Mekas conceives it, but he imports that dimension into his film by repeatedly acknowledging the temporal perspective of the moment of editing when all the filming is past—some of it decades old.[5]

The title, reinforced by its punctuating voice-overs, insists that flashes of exhilaration have irradiated the continuous passage of his life, "one epiphany after another," as David James described Mekas's style.[6] The stress on the brevity of these moments not only describes his signature mode of filming but also suggests that the illuminations of beauty and happiness stand out

4. William James, *Principles of Psychology*, vol. 1 (New York: Dover, 1950), p. 650.
5. David E. James recognized the fundamental allegory of *Walden* as the "interplay between the fragments of the past and the present contemplation of them that informs the process of composition." James, "Film Diary/Diary Film," p. 176.
6. Ibid., p. 157. "The constantly voyaging camera creates a continuous stream of visual aperçus, alighting on one epiphany after another—a face, a cup of coffee, a cactus, a foot, a dog scratching itself, another face, a movie camera."

against a background of sustained anguish. In the first chapter we read the intertitle: "about a man whose lip is always trembling from pain and sorrow experienced in the past which only he knows—" Significantly, an image of the filmmaker, playing the boyan, immediately precedes this intertitle. Mekas, as Orpheus, sings a wordless song over these images and over the subsequent shots of rain and lightning. He is still singing when a more anecdotal intertitle follows:

I remember the morning I passed Avignon. The Nice Express was speeding across France. I woke up, and I looked at the window, and I saw the morning. It was the most pastoral, the most peaceful morning I had seen since my childhood. Oh, the lost peace, I thought. Then I fell back into sleep, a tormented, painful sleep with broken bits of memories.[7]

The cause and nature of the filmmaker's pain is not explicit in his film diaries, perhaps it cannot be, insofar as it preceded his acquisition of a camera, or perhaps he cannot bear to speak of it.

The temporal scheme revealed here, of a present joy automatically linked to a childhood memory, shadowing forth the dark tormented time between them,[8] throws retrospective light on an even earlier intertitle: "the beauty of the moment overtook him & he did not remember anything that preceded that moment." The compensation of such intense beauty is oblivion of former agonies; beauty, for Mekas, redeems, or at least dazzles our vision of the Fall. The intertitle appears just before an image of his wife, Hollis Melton, paddling a canoe—from the movement and the camera position it is clear that Mekas must be sitting in the canoe behind her, filming. The shot from the back of the gliding canoe, with low-hanging leaves of trees brushing the camera, is a trope with a long pedigree within the American avant-garde cinema, although the filmmaker does not seem to be trying to evoke Ian Hugo's *Ai-Ye* here. This moment encapsulates the rapturous mood of the opening of the film before the onset of the first crisis. But when, just following the

7. In "Just Like a Shadow" he offers a gloss on this experience: "When you go through what I went through, the wars, occupations, genocides, forced labor camps, displaced person camps, and lying in a looming potato field—I'll never forget the whiteness of the blossoms—my face down on the earth, after jumping out the window, while German soldiers held my father against the wall, gun in his back—then you don't understand human beings anymore." Jonas Mekas, "Just Like a Shadow," *Logos* (Spring 2004), www.logosjournal.com.

8. Here I want to enlarge on David E. James's brilliant analysis of the undercurrents of Mekas's whole diary project. James claims that the impossibility of having film images from the filmmaker's Lithuanian childhood is "the absent center of the entire project" ("Film Diary/Diary Film," p. 168). In a revision of the essay, he calls it "the absent, structuring center." David E. James, *Power Misses: Essays Across (Un)Popular Culture* (London: Verso: 1996), p. 144.

canoe shots, Mekas speaks over scenes that bridge meetings with old friends (dominated by the presence of his daughter, Oona, at different stages of her childhood), he elaborates on his trope of paradise without invoking the Gnostic myth of his 1979 film:

> Without knowing, unknowingly we carry, each of us, we carry with
> us somewhere deep some images of Paradise. Maybe not images—
> some vague, vague feeling, where we have been some place—there
> are places, there are places in which we find ourselves in our lives,
> I've been in such places where I felt, ah, this must be like Paradise,
> this is Paradise, this is how Paradise was, something like that, a little
> fragment of Paradise. Not only the places—I have been with friends,
> many times, and we felt, we all felt some kind of togetherness, some-
> thing special, and we were elated and we felt, ah, we felt like we were
> in Paradise [laughs]
>   ...But we were right here on this, on this earth. But we were in
> Paradise...Forget the eternity, enjoy, yes, we enjoyed those brief
> moments, those moments, those evenings, and there were many such
> evenings, many such evenings, my friends, I'll never forget them, my
> friends—

Here again an epistemological aporia is central to Mekas's theology of memory, where without knowing it, we retain fragments of paradise, as Adam did in the parable of "Paradise Not Yet Lost." This means that, unpredictably, real events can be charged with the resonance of those Edenic feelings of ela-tion, in which we step out of time ("ecstasy"), or compress time. The meta-phor of the "glimpse" in the title locates the compression of time in the realm of vision. Consequently, filmmaking becomes an instrument of discovery of paradise unknown.

For the most part, Mekas follows the usage of his friend, Peter Kubelka, when he speaks of ecstasy as the fundamental aesthetic superlative. At its best, Kubelka claims, cinema induces a state of ecstasy by delivering up to twenty-four "strong articulations" per second. A repeated intertitle in As I Moved Ahead declares "ecstasy of summers & being in New York." So we might be tempted to take his spoken statement in chapter 7, "What an ecstasy just to film," simply as an expression of his joy in shooting film:

> I am obsessed with filming. I am really a filmer...It's me and my
> Bolex. I go through life with my Bolex and I have to film what I see,
> what is happening right there. What an ecstasy just to film. Why do I
> have to make films when I can just film!...I may not even be filming
> the real life. I may just be filming my memories. I don't care!

Or in chapter 8, ecstasy can be understood as the artist's emotional response to the event of his perception and recording:

I am not making films, I am just filming. The ecstasy of filming, just filming life around me, what I see, what I react to, what my fingers, my eyes react to, this moment, now, this moment when it's all happening, ah what ecstasy!

However, I understand the ecstasy of "just" filming as an ontological, as well as a psychological, description of the process. Mekas feels ecstatic when he films and his mode of filming is ecstatic: It reconfigures the temporality of the events before his camera; instead of reducing the image of those events to the mechanical pace for which the machine was designed, his camera ecstatically films them as he sees them; that is, in an intensive, microrhythmic alternation of compression and dilation. The ecstatic temporality of his single-frame spurts and gestural "glimpses" mediates between memory and the paradise of the epiphanic moments. If, as Emerson suggested, etymology unlocks the "fossil poetry" of words, we can read in the word *glimpse* in his title both the oblique, angular *glance* of the eye off its object and the *glimmer* or *glow* of the object attracting the eye: the root g^hlend(h) encompasses words for *shining, gold, sheen,* and *illumination.*

Mekas does not seem at all anxious to resolve the many apparent contradictions in his verbal interventions. For instance, in chapter 7, over a sequence in which his young daughter pulls on his nose, he seems willing to cede the epistemological authority he has been claiming for memory and cinema:

You can call me Romantic.... I do not understand. I never really understood, never really lived in the so-called real world. I lived, I lived in my own imaginary world, which is as real as any other world, as real as the real worlds of all the other people around me. You also live in your own imaginary worlds. What you are seeing is my, is my imaginary world, which to me is not imaginary at all. It is real. It is as real as anything else under the sun. So, let us continue...

The contradictions are central to the meaning of the film. They indicate the large-scale alternations of confidence and despair that sweep across the film in waves. Although each chapter contains moments of affirmation and subtle countercurrents of doubt, the fundamental dynamics of the film occur in the interactions of the chapters. The incessant cascade of vibrant local events obscures these structures.

Throughout Mekas's vast diary project, the crises that structure the rhythms of his moods are repressed rather than directly figured. He is not a filmmaker who forewarns us of the shifts of his thought or outlines the contours of his superstructures, even when he intervenes to tell us how the film was put together. We never know where he is going to take us. The most significant of these unpredictable structuring elements would be the expressions of anguish that counterpoint the joyous imagery of the first three chapters and then suddenly wane, not to return. Since there is nothing within the film itself to account for this shift or to assure us that the narrative of pain will not recur, those early interventions establish the potential for the submerged melancholy to resurface at any moment until the end, giving the final triumphal chant its resonance.

At the start of the film we see, and read, in the first intertitle amid fragmentary images, "The Baptism of Una Abraham" (the daughter of Henny and Raimund Abraham, the architect, who figures prominently in the film). This Roman Catholic rite serves to initiate the sacralization of the film itself. It is to Abraham, in the same reel, that Mekas reveals that his reading of the 1887 preface to Friedrich Nietzsche's *Birth of Tragedy* led him to quit his job and concentrate on making *Guns of the Trees*. In particular, he had been spurred on by the philosopher's retrospective confession that he should have approached his subject as a poet, rather than a scholar, in the first place: "And, indeed, this 'new soul' should have sung, not spoken. What a pity that I could not tell as a poet what demanded to be told!" The filmed baptism and the story of the filmmaker's reaction to Nietzsche's text are tropes for the artistic election of the filmmaker. Between these two epicenters of poetic incarnation, the film focuses its enthusiasm on "[b]eauty of summer heat when you pick wild strawberries" and the subsequent canoe scene. That is the point at which the idea of oblivion alluded to in the intertitle "the beauty of the moment overtook him…" begins to operate in the film as the culmination of the epiphanic style, which set the mood of the opening minutes. The voice-over discourse on paradise would seem to confirm that.

Yet the claims made for this poetic influx are so high that they cannot be sustained. So there is a faint hint of deflation when we see Hollis with her father walking through what Mekas calls, in another intertitle, "the childhood's meadows." But that diminuendo hardly prepares us for the crisis that bursts upon the intertitles, first indirectly identifying the filmmaker as "a man whose lip is always trembling" and then quite explicitly, as the passenger on the train rushing through Avignon, whose morning of extraordinary peace only exacerbated his "tormented, painful sleep." The dialectic that David James so clearly articulated in his study of *Walden* operates here between editing and shooting, language and image, to inscribe a subjective consciousness that not only looks back on the recorded scenes but measures them against past suffering. The first chapter ends without resolving this tension and the second commences without mentioning it. Instead, its first title reassures us, "life goes on."

Three birthday parties—for Almus, an old Lithuanian friend; Sebastian, Mekas's young son; and for Dizzie Gillespie—mark the festive pole of the second chapter, in which Mekas's brother Petras visits from Lithuania. Perhaps more centrally, four formal portraits punctuate this chapter: We see Hollis photographing two of them; a "Soho photographer" shooting a woman all tied up; and Mekas himself in the Chelsea Hotel posing for his cinematic self-portrait. He hesitantly concedes that his creative solitude brings him to reflect about himself:

> So here I am, just myself and the cats and my images and my sounds
> and myself, myself, wondering, wondering about myself. Actually,
> maybe I am exaggerating. I am not really wondering, I am just doing
> my work.

That work turns out to be a version of the ecstasy of shooting film in the thrall of the moment:

> I am not so sure what I am doing. It's all chance. I am going through
> all the reels of sounds... putting it all together by chance, same as
> the images, same, exactly the same as when I originally filmed them,
> by chance, with no plan, just according to the whim of the moment,
> what I felt that moment that I should be filming, this or that, without
> knowing why.

In *whim* Mekas employs a key word from Emerson's vocabulary. In "Self-Reliance" he vaunts: "I shun father and mother and wife and brother when my genius calls me. I would write on the lintels of the door-post, *Whim*." In the moment of shooting, Mekas's genius is upon him; it calls him again when he trusts his editing to chance. But as the amanuensis of Fortuna, Mekas gives himself permission to chant his "song of myself."

As if providing the caption to the formal self-portrait, the filmmaker follows his posed shot with a long intertitle in which he asks "Should I retreat to some silent place and work it all out by myself?" He writes that a "voice" tells him not to retreat but to seek "salvation together with others—." The rapid sequence of images that follows the title glosses "together with others": the banner of Anthology Film Archives, to which he has devoted his energies for more than thirty years, a fire intercut with statues of saints, glimpses of religious texts, a plaster Buddha, a leaping frog, flowers, and a snowball fight briefly recalling Cocteau's *Le Sang d'un poète*. In this montage there are several views of Hollis, both alone and with Sebastian as a baby, and a shot of Oona.

The sequence culminates in the most astonishing intertitle of the film: "Your face was always upon me." Whom is he addressing?[9] The biblical formula suggests that the intertitle is a prayer, as in the Aaronic blessing (Numbers 6:24, "The Lord make his face shine upon thee"). In the biblical metaphor, the face of the Lord is a sun that radiates day and night. If Mekas is acknowledging divine favor here, the "always" indicates extraordinary self-assurance; for, in the following shot, the last of the chapter, we see him playing the boyan, the icon of his orphic election. Pushing the luminous metaphor, we might surmise that he has been sitting before God for his portrait in this chapter. But the addressee might as easily be Hollis, in which case the title could be glossed, "Your image is in my mind all through the making of this film." By hyperbole, the "you" might be his family, who have sustained him in an atemporal dimension. More remotely, we might read "Your face" as a Whitmanesque address to the audience; for Mekas often invokes the viewer in his I-you discourse. In any case, the need to establish a second person, in both the grammatical and epistemological senses, grounds the use of language, printed and spoken, in this film; through the "you," the filmmaker implicitly distinguishes his project from Brakhage's egotistical sublime. Here the mystery and ambiguity of the pronominal adjective allows the three potential references to fuse, granting a sacral air to the compact that binds the filmmaker to divinity, family, and viewers.

Consequently, an epithalamium opens the third chapter, as the voice-over, in high spirits, proclaims the surprise of his marriage. But the real surprise is his identifying Hollis and himself to be the "protagonists of this film." Midway the chapter's focus leaps to the infancy of Oona (her birth will not appear until chapter 6). Yet even this chapter is haunted, on the soundtrack, by a poetry of despair: Angus MacLise (1938–79) drones a lengthy text Mekas wrote in a crisis of 1966:

> The pain is stronger than ever. I've seen bits of paradises and I know I'll be hopelessly trying to return even if it hurts.... Now I want to shoot my own way through myself into the thick night of myself. Thus I change my course, going inwards, thus I am jumping into my own darkness.

In the end, he addresses an unidentified past lover:

> And I sit here alone and far from you and it's night and I am thinking of you.... I saw happiness and pain in your eyes and reflections of the

9. When I asked Mekas about this (October 4, 2004), he said, "That will remain a mystery." He also declined to identify the "you" of the diary text that ends chapter 3.

paradises lost and regained and lost again, that terrible loneliness and happiness.

The ironies of the voiceover are multiple and complex. MacLise, who died at forty-one, substitutes for the then forty-four-year-old Mekas when he reads: "It's at forty that we die, those who did not die at twenty.... I have come close to the end now, it's a question of will I make it or will I not."[10] In a stunning metalepsis, the filmmaker seems overtly to be fusing the 1966 text to the images of his marriage and first child (from the early 1970s) as if to illustrate how he overcame the "terrible loneliness" of the earlier time, while in the shadow of a renewed loneliness he mourns the loss of that marriage and time of child rearing as he edits the film. In this radical reversal of before and after, he deflates the richly ambiguous "you" of the end of chapter 2 to the unknown, distant "you" of 1966, as the reading breaks off against the black screen: "and I reflect upon this and I think about you, like two lonely pilots in outer cold space, as I sit here this late night alone and I think about this—"

Still, Mekas can laugh at himself as he feigns an apology for the fourth chapter: "So, my dear viewers, we have arrived at chapter 4. Sorry that nothing much, nothing extraordinary has so far happened in this movie, nothing much extraordinary. It's all very simple daily activities." The decisive change in the fourth chapter is the dramatic diminution of the undersong of anguish, which structured the first three. It does not quite disappear. There is a moment when he quotes from early written diaries, saying twice: "I have been so totally alone with myself for so long." But this brief declaration of loneliness is merely a feint for the subsequent intervention in which he spells out his relationship to the viewer:

My dear viewers, it's midnight now. I am talking to you and it's very very late in my little room.... These are images that have some meaning to me but may have no meaning to you at all. Then, suddenly I thought [laughs]: there is no image that wouldn't relate to anybody else. I mean, all images around us that we go through our lives, and I go filming them, they are not that much different from what you have seen or experienced ...All our lives are very very much alike...We are all in it and nothing, there is no big difference, essential difference between you and me.

As we hear this declaration of congruence with the viewer, we see Jonas and Hollis at the site of the American sublime par excellence: the Grand

---

10. Mekas would have had no intimation of MacLise's early death when he asked him to record the diary passage, but when he came to edit it into the film he was certainly aware of the significance of the early death in the musician's nearly mythic reputation.

Canyon. At one point they bathe, topless, in a waterfall. Although Mekas had been an outspoken champion of sexual candor in cinema, his films are so lacking in eros or even nudity that this moment and a scene of them waking up in the fifth chapter stand out. In this respect alone he seems to have evaded the heritage of Walt Whitman, who otherwise hovers over the *Diaries, Notes and Sketches*. Even the tone of Mekas's late-night confidences echoes the "afterword" the aged Whitman put on his book in "A Backward Glance o'er Travel'd Roads":

> Perhaps the best of songs heard, or of any and all true love, or life's
> fairest episodes, or sailors', soldiers' trying scenes on land or sea, is
> the resumé of them, or any of them, long afterwards, looking at the
> actualities away back past, with all their practical excitations gone.
> How the soul loves to float amid such reminiscences!
> So here I sit gossiping in the early candle-light of old age—I and
> my book—casting backward glances over our travel'd road.[11]

By the fourth chapter Mekas seems to want the viewers to accept that the film will have no discernible internal development. The repetition of some of the intertitles underscores the similarity of material forming the matrix of the whole film. The titles "home scenes" and "life goes on" appear in nearly every chapter, sometimes more than once. Starting in the fourth chapter, "nothing happens in this film" will appear four times. Yet just as the title cards can stress the repetitive cycles of the film, intertitles that enter later and then repeat can suggest new modulations. Even the dramatic title "the beauty of the moment overtook him & he did not remember anything that preceded that moment" from the first chapter recurs in the fourth between views of the Grand Canyon and the images of the couple showering. However, it is only in the final chapter that the most Proustian title appears; twice we read: "that moment everything came back to me, in fragments," which looks back to the intertitle recurring since the sixth chapter: "a fragment of paradise."

The illusionism of cinema itself might be described as one in which "everything came back...in fragments," since the atomizing mechanism of the camera isolates static fragments of the animate world, so that the apparent movement, and hence the image of the world ("everything"), comes back when the atomized filmstrip is projected. This banal fact becomes significant for Mekas because his ecstatic style entails a hand-crafted attunement of the frame-by-frame atomization. Even when he invokes paradise and plenitude, he cannot evade their fractured mode.

---

11. Walt Whitman, *Selected Poems 1855–1892: A New Edition*, ed. Gary Schmidgall (New York: St. Martin's, 1999), p. 377.

The achronological, repetitive organization of scenes and the insistence that nothing happens in this film serve to repress the recognition of the temporal fate of the marriage, the unstated countersubject of the film. So, when in the final chapter the filmmaker inserts an intertitle hyperbolically affirming this to be "a film about people who never have any arguments and no fights and who love each other," he implicitly admits that his film lays claim to its power in an idealizing ellipsis. This is indeed, in the distinction of "Just like a Shadow," not a film about others but one "all about myself, conversations with my self." In his conversation with himself, Mekas repels the corrosive work of time on his family life. His polemic against "suspense" in chapter 4 is a crucial moment in that conversation, as he struggles against any narrative of time.

With the invocation of "nothing" at the start of chapter 5, the filmmaker abandons the magnificent evasions of the previous four chapters. By baptizing his film "a sort of masterpiece of nothing," and then elaborating instances of nothing as "miracles of every day, little moments of paradise that are here now, next moment maybe they are gone..." just when we begin to see images of "Oona's Baptism June 26, 1975," he sets the stage for a shift of tone that will dominate the celebratory middle chapters. In the final shots of the chapter—a series of self-portraits from the "Chelsea Hotel" (a metonymy for the period just before his marriage)—he quotes an inner voice, advising patience and promising poetic reception: "The voice said: you don't have to go anywhere...your work will come, it will come by itself. Just have trust and knowing and be open and ready."

What is he to receive? What is to come? In the reconstructed logic of As I Moved Ahead, the power of reception is instanced by the magnificent chapter 6, the true center of the film. Its good-humored invocation hides a crucial declaration. I'll quote it in full:

> By the time a viewer, that is you, reaches chapter 6, one expects, that is you, you expect, you expect to find out more about the protagonist, that is me, the protagonist of this movie. So I don't want to disappoint you. All I want to tell you, it's all here. I am in every image of this film, I am in every frame of this film. The only thing is: you have to know how to read these images. How? Didn't all those French guys tell you how to READ the images? Yes, they told you. So, please READ these images and you'll be able to tell everything about me. So, here it is, chapter 6.

If the viewer recalls that the same voice had asserted at the start of the chapter that "Hollis and me" were "the protagonists of this film," it comes as another surprise to hear that there is but one protagonist and he is in every frame and every shot—a shock to hear it stated explicitly even if the viewer had suspected that all along. He challenges us to "read" this change of orientation along with everything else in the film.

At the center of this central chapter, he placed the shots he had taken of Hollis giving birth to Oona. It is the only time in the whole five hours of the film he directly addresses his wife:

> As I was watching you that moment, I thought there cannot be
> anything more beautiful or more important on this earth, between
> heaven and earth, as you were there one with them, one with heaven
> and earth, giving life, giving life to Oona. I admired you that moment
> and I knew that you were completely somewhere else, somewhere
> else I could never be, something I could never totally understand, the
> beauty of the moment, that moment, was beyond any words—

If the epithalamium (chapter 3) temporarily grounded the film in a first-person plural subject, the nativity ode (chapter 6) not only reasserts the single, first-person protagonist, but clarifies a second-person hierarchy, making Hollis now the privileged addressee (transcending the narrator's understanding and assumed into a beauty beyond his language) and making the viewers the secondary interpreters who must learn to read the mediated images (and words) in order to come to know, not the world, but the filmmaker. At this point, Mekas's version of the sublime veers so close to that of Brakhage's precursor birth films (*Window Water Baby Moving, Thigh Line Lyre Triangular, Song 5*, and *Dog Star Man: Part Two*) that he has to shore up his autonomy with virtually synchronous sound and the consequent I-you dichotomy.

Assuming the mantle of poet, he quotes from the *Autobiography* of William Carlos Williams that "the poet's business... [is] in the particular to discover the universal." As if returning to his own myth of poetic origins, he makes the journal entry from 1960 he read in chapter 4 into a title card, "He sits under a tree in the park listening to the leaves," to introduce four shots of a tree, continually changing the exposure of the trunk to capture "what I saw in that tree when I was looking." This time, rather than capturing the wind in the tree or its energy, Mekas's filming reveals the texture and solidity of the trunk, its tender leaves, and its appetite for light, as if it, like Hollis giving birth, mediated between earth and sky (heaven).

The second half of *As I Moved Ahead* struggles to evade the melancholy undersong of the opening chapters, although it is only in the eighth chapter that the threat of a relapse becomes overt. Although he adamantly rejects psychoanalytical categories, he comes close to offering a theory of repression in the crisis of chapter 8. The crucial voice-over passage begins with the only unqualified claim to self-reflection in the whole film: "As I am putting these pieces of film together, this late evening, I am thinking about myself." Then he concedes his discontents: "I have covered myself with layers of civilization, so many layers that now even myself I don't see how easily wounds are being made deep inside.... I know nothing. But I continue moving ahead, moving ahead, slowly, and some glimpses of happiness and beauty come my way."

The depth and invisibility of the wounds make the unexpected glimpses of happiness possible and visible. The most overt repression in his filmmaking is that of a plan or a design. The compensation for repressing the overall schema is the ecstasy of filming. Filming, as he practices it, even severs events and people from their plans and purposes, transporting them to the ecstatic time without past or future he sublimates as "fragments of paradise." In his speech at the beginning of the fourth chapter, Mekas had said: "I do not like suspense." Suspense in cinema is the dominant mode of subjection of the fragmented, ecstatic event to a plan and purpose whose moment is teasingly delayed. Under the pressure of this postponement, the encounter between the filmer and the world before him loses its ecstatic character. Ecstasy and anticipation are irreconcilable. Beauty and happiness come his way "when [he] doesn't even expect it." Yet the deeper repression is the trauma of the past.

The centrality of the traumatic repression significantly distinguishes Mekas's celebration of the present from that of Brakhage, whose youthful polemic against suspense and drama, *Metaphors on Vision*, Mekas published at the time he was turning from narrative to diary filmmaking. In contrast to Brakhage, Mekas stakes his project on the uniqueness and unfathomability of his personal trauma. It does not keep him, at times, from asserting the opposite, that he is just like his viewers, that his experiences are common and ordinary. Even if this fiction were not belied by the overwhelming presence of artistic and social celebrities in his diaries, and the charming idealization of family life both in urban New York and rural Lithuania, the aporia between the incessant, exuberant cascade of visual fragments and the moody haunted voice of the filmmaker, sometimes in despair, sometimes pushing himself to exhilaration, often sounding gleeful even when expressing anxiety,[12] would situate Mekas as an autobiographer in the line of Jean-Jacques Rousseau, a man like no other, rather than that of Augustine, who wrote his life under the theological conviction that he was identical to all other men.

An intertitle confesses: "I envy the others. They seem to be in the very center of gravity. But I seem to live in a permanent flight longing for rest—."

---

12. In chapter 12, he tells us in an intertitle: "when I am nervous I feel great he said."

Between the voice-over and the intertitle, Mekas shows us a boat trip around Manhattan, an affluent variation on Menken's Circle Line voyage in *Excursion*. The Christmas lights and "moonplay" of her *Notebook* will also echo through this chapter, as the filmmaker returns from his concentration on Hollis and Oona to widen again the span of his attention to the streets of New York and to his friends. The "others" of the intertitle are manifestly his fellow humans, perhaps specifically the rich and famous on the boat, rather than poetic rivals. Furthermore, it would be wholly uncharacteristic of Mekas to profess envy of his fellow filmmakers: His consistent mode of self-assertion has been in the promotion and celebration of his peers and influences. On January 4, 1962, he celebrated Menken in his Movie Journal column in the *Village Voice*, in language that would accord with his own cinematic project that was just taking shape at that time:

> Menken sings. Her lens is focused on the physical world, and she sees it through a poetic temperament and with intensified sensitivity. She catches the bits and fragments of the world around her and organizes them into aesthetic unities which communicate to us. Her filmic language and her imagery are crisp, clear, and wonderous....
>
> Does Menken transpose reality? Or condense it? Or does she, simply, go direct to the essence of it? Isn't poetry more realistic than any realism? The realist sees only the front of a building, the outlines, a street, a tree. Menken sees in them the motion of time and the eye. She sees the motions of heart in a tree. She sees through them and beyond. She retains a visual memory of all that she sees. She recreates moments of observation, of meditation, reflection, wonderment. A rain that she sees, a tender rain, becomes the memory of all the rains she ever saw; a garden becomes a memory of all gardens, all color, all perfume, all midsummer and sun.
>
> What is poetry? An exalted experience? An emotion that dances? A spearhead into the heart of man? We are invited to a communion, we break our wills, we dissolve ourselves into the flow of her images, we experience admittance into sanctuary of Menken's soul. We sit in silence and we take part in her secret thought, admirations, ecstasies, and we become more beautiful ourselves. She puts a smile in our hearts. She saves us from our own ugliness. That's what poetry does, that's what Menken does.

Prior to making *As I Moved Ahead*, Mekas went to his archive of footage to excavate an elegy, *Scenes from the Life of Andy Warhol* (1990), which echoes Menken's fast-motion vision of the Pop Art icon, *Andy Warhol*; and just before concentrating on the long film, he made an extraordinary gesture by pulling out shots of nearly every filmmaker and figure in the cinema community he had ever photographed to construct a hymn to his colleagues in catalog form, *The Birth of a Nation*; in chanting this litany of fellow artists, he was preparing the space for his ecstatic ode to family life. Still, Menken and Brakhage may be among the "others...[who] seem to be in the very center of gravity" in their relationship to the orbit of poetic inspiration, enviable insofar as they seemed to receive the afflatus with unqualified authority. Mekas, on the other hand, repeatedly apologizes for his work, even excuses the fragmentary style as a consequence of the "little bits of time" (chapter 9) he can devote to film-making, presumably because of his hectic schedule of work on behalf of other filmmakers.

On the soundtrack of chapter 10, Mekas awaits the turn of the millennium:

I am celebrating all the past years in this footage, this film.... Each of us have our own millenniums, millennia, and they could be longer or shorter, and when I look now at this footage, I look from completely somewhere else, I am completely somewhere else now. This is me, there, here, and it's not me anymore, because I am the one who is looking at it now, at myself, at my life, my friends, the last quarter of the century.

As he speaks, he shows us scenes centering on Oona learning to walk. Reversing the earlier assertion of his own reflection in every image and the necessity of learning to read those images, he now claims: "these images recorded casually at different times, long ago,...mean just what they mean, just what they are, and nothing else beyond themselves." So, as he faces the aporia of the self reflecting on its discontinuous traces, he needs to find a new autonomy in the ecstatic images. An unusual concentration of dated passages—four nearly sequential dates in a little more than three minutes—recovers an illusion of continuity that culminates in the birth of Sebastian, who will come to dominate a central passage in the chapter. The intertitle sequence aligns the birth of Sebastian to the thirtieth anniversary of the Lithuanian pilgrim's arrival in the United States. The projective identification of father and son is intense in this passage. Two shots show Sebastian as a young child pointing beyond the frame to phenomena of interest to him as if directing his father as cameraman. Another superimposes him against the window of a moving train as if we were seeing the landscape through his eyes. Most dramatically, Mekas cuts from a concentrated stare of the baby boy to shots of a circus, thus constructing a shot-countershot exchange in which his son repeats an experience central to Mekas's aesthetic enterprise. The twelve-minute *Notes on the Circus* (1966) was the most ambitious of his early film lyrics and a central sketch in *Walden*.

The penultimate chapter directly addresses Oona, Sebastian, and Hollis:

> As I sit in my room this late night and look at some of the images as
> I am splicing, putting them together, I wonder, I wonder how much
> of yourselves you'll see and recognize in these images. . . . These are my
> memories. Your memories of the same moments, if you'll have any,
> will be very different. . . . I guess, I was filming my own memories, my
> own childhood, as I was filming your childhood. . . . It's you, it's you in
> every frame of this film though it's seen by me. But it is you. . . . I am
> here alone, looking at these images, fragments of my and your lives,
> talking into this mike, by myself, by myself—.

The fundamental dialectic of the film is an often-repeated cycle of isolation, chance, and compensation. Another of the several ways of parsing this
interrelationship would be to call the elements of this dynamic the self, others (friends and family), and ecstasy. Sometimes the filmmaker implies that
the triad is reality, fragmentation, and memory, or even filming, splicing (to
which we must add naming, although he never explicitly acknowledges the
centrality of the verbal action), and reading. These triads alternate and sometimes overlap as they underwrite the oscillating stances the commenting voice
takes toward his unfolding work in successive chapters.

The final chapter is significantly the only one without a dated intertitle.
Instead, it crowns the film with a Proustian declaration of recovered sensoria:

> I am still in Provence, this evening, here, in my editing room, this
> late night. I am in Provence! Feel the sun, I feel the lightness, I see the
> landscape, the trees. The flowers. I can smell the air of Provence and I
> can feel the happiness. . . . Ah, the happiness, the ecstasy of that sum-
> mer. It's still here, now, with me this very moment, and it's stronger
> than anything I have experienced, gone through, today, today, now
> and in New York, it's much stronger and closer and more real.

Although the pathos of the hyperbole figures an intensity of loss, the insistence on the triumph of love, beauty, and happiness is deeply moving.

Throughout his career Mekas has been careful to accumulate images of
himself. Repeatedly, he put the camera on a tripod for a formal portrait. He
also held it at arm's length, even filming his face this way to record his expressions as he sleighed down a snowbank in Central Park. Other times he would
cede the camera to Hollis or another friend to capture his involvement in
the scene at hand. He so loads the final minutes of *As I Moved Ahead* with
stunning instances of these self-portraits that their frequency announces the
imminent closure of the long work.

After the last of three appearances of the intertitle "that moment everything came back to me, in fragments—" he inserts a brief glimpse of Una Abraham at her baptism (the first titled scene of chapter 1), signaling that the span of memory encompasses the whole film. Although the viewer would not know that there will be only eight more minutes to the film, such gestures indicate a formal reorientation insofar as the filmmaker no longer allows chance to play a dominant role in the sequencing of his work. He interrupts the final crescendo with two minutes of meals, birthday parties, and children playing, marked by the familiar intertitles "daily routines" (this time, with irony, a single shot of a roach going around in circles), "life goes on," "wind in the leaves," "home scenes," and "nothing happens in this film." The passage ends in a frenetic dance in which the filmmaker appears to be giving a ride on his shoulders to a child. It is during this scene that he begins to sing the long concluding chant that begins: "I don't know what life is," and adds, "As I am moving ahead, as I am moving ahead, my friends! I have, I know, I know I have experienced some brief brief moments of beauty, my friends, my friends!" [13] The insistence of the song underlies the fragility and brevity of the glimpses of beauty he has equated with happiness.

Finally, there is a radiantly happy shot of Hollis kissing Jonas's cheek as he drinks a glass of wine. He has clearly set his camera upon a tripod to film this intimate image. It is the culmination of the concluding chapter's ode to happiness; evidently the filmmaker withheld it for this capstone position. By placing it where he does, he toasts his wife, their years together, and greets his future viewers. Surprisingly, he follows this with an intertitle seen once before: "the Venetian blinds clank in the wind. I can not sleep. I watch the window, its blackness." At the end of chapter 8, this title card had preceded a pan of Venetian blinds and an image of himself playing the boyan before the blinded windows. But for the finale of the film he followed the quotation with another self-portrait. He took this one when he was finishing the editing; the seventy-eight-year-old poet looks at the camera and, figuratively, at us, and back on the images of his life. By making the final image of himself seemingly twenty years older than those we see in most of the film, he dramatized the leap of time between shooting and editing.

---

13 Although the titles, typed at the beginning and hand-written at the end of the film, are in the past tense (*As I Moved...*), Mekas frequently refers to it as if the title were in the past progressive (*As I Was Moving...*). In the final chant he sings the present progressive line, "As I am moving ahead..." but nowhere within the film does the past progressive appear.

Conclusion: Perfect Exhilaration

Crossing a bare common, in snow puddles, at twilight,
under a clouded sky, without having in my thoughts an
occurrence of special good fortune, I have enjoyed a perfect
exhilaration.

Emerson, *Nature*

Most of the films discussed in the previous pages present us with peaks of perfect exhilaration, often extended passages in which the filmmaker succeeds in conveying his or her rapture with the moment of taking a shot, the ecstasy of camera or vehicular movement, or the perfection of a sequence of shots falling together in a figure of montage. Inevitably these peaks are shadowed by their deflations, sometimes to the point of despair. In "Experience," Emerson writes of "the flux of moods," or alternately of their succession or even "a train of moods like a string of beads," and each colors or shows "only what lies in its focus." The characteristic genre I have been examining, the crisis lyric, takes its shape from the rhythmic alternation of these moods in the succession of their shifting of focus. In Ian Hugo's *Bells of Atlantis*, Anaïs Nin hyperbolically describes this rhythm when she cries: "When human pain has struck me fiercely, when anger has corroded me, I rise, I always rise after the crucifixion, and I am in terror of my ascensions." Generally the moments of pain, anger, and terror are not represented directly in these films. Instead, the tropes of montage or the interactions of picture and sound (especially when speech is involved) figure the negative oscillations against which the refreshed vision, or pictorial air, rebounds. In the exhilaration of filmic discovery, the traumatic sources of aesthetic ecstasy may be nearly erased. William Carlos Williams offers a stunning insight into this reversal in his poem "To a Dog Injured in the Street" when the terrible agony of the wounded animal first "brings me to myself with a start." He recognizes the need to "sing" as a defense against the shock of pain and brilliantly reflects on the pastoral beauty of René Char's lyrics:

> I can do nothing
> but sing about it
> and so I am assuaged
> from my pain.
> A drowsy numbness drowns my sense
> as if of hemlock
> I had drunk. I think
> of the poetry
> of René Char
> and all he must have seen
> and suffered
> that has brought him
> to speak only of
> sedgy rivers,
> of daffodils and tulips
> whose roots they water,
> even to the free-flowing river
> that laves the rootlets
> of those sweet-scented flowers
> that people the
> milky
> way.[1]

The perfect exhilaration of many of the films treated in this book often makes it difficult to capture the subtleties with which their tropes and rhythms assuage occulted pain. In the major cyclic films such articulations often occur between individual films as crucially as within them.

The crisis film employs cinema as an instrument of discovery. The film-maker comes to understand the nature and shape of the crisis by making the film. The film is a surprise and a revelation even to its maker. I know of no passage in Emerson where he writes of a principle of artistic composition

---

1. William Carlos Williams, "To a Dog Injured in the Street." *Collected Poems*, vol. II, (1939–1962), ed. Christopher MacGowan, pp. 255–67.

trusting to the influx of reception and eschewing the predeterminations of design, unless it be in "Self-Reliance," where he proclaims: "let me record day by day my honest thought without prospect or retrospect, and, I cannot doubt, it will be found symmetrical, though I mean it not, and see it not."[2] However, the ethics of surprise articulated centrally in "Circles" and "Experience" (where he insists "All I know is reception") suggests an application in poetics that Emerson's heirs understood. The measure of a work of art would thus be the degree to which it can surprise, and thereby exhilarate, its maker. "The one thing which we seek with insatiable desire," we read at the end of "Circles," "is to forget ourselves, to be surprised out of our propriety, to lose our sempiternal memory, and to do something without knowing how or why; in short, to draw a new circle."[3] "Experience" identifies the revelation of such surprises as "Power" shooting through "the subterranean and invisible tunnels and channels of life," and "the vital force supplied from the Eternal," where "every insight from the realm of thought is felt as initial, and promises a sequel."[4]

In similar terms, Larry Jordan described the process of making his magnum opus, *Sophie's Place* (1983–87) as a serial revelation from the unconscious in which the making of one image promised its sequel:

> [W]hen I did the long 90-minute animation called *Sophie's Place*...
> I held strictly to free-association image. When I finished one image,
> I had to do the next. The first image suggested itself next. I couldn't
> evaluate it and say, "Oh, I could do something better." And I found
> that coming right out of the unconscious like that, I had more
> continuity than any film I'd ever done before.... Human beings
> conduct their lives from much stronger sources than the rational
> mind. Modern psychology is pretty aware that there's a difference
> between the rational mind and another stronger, powerful, larger
> mind, more powerful and archaic from which our drives come, and
> that's what impels our lives.[5]

Over nearly forty engraved background plates, Jordan's cutout figures perform incessant transformations. He actually subtitled the film *An Alchemical Autobiography; Transfiguration and Again Transfiguration*. By calling it an alchemical autobiography, Jordan seems to be aligning himself with C. G. Jung's

2. Ralph Waldo Emerson, *Essays and Lectures* (New York: Library of America, 1983), p. 266.
3. Ibid., p. 414.
4. Ibid., pp. 482–84.
5. Paul Karlstrom, "Interview with Larry Jordan," December 19, 1995, Smithsonian Archives of American Art, www.aaa.si.edu/collections/oralhistories/transcripts/jordan95.htm.

psychological and spiritual readings of alchemical texts, which had considerable influence on American artists once they were translated in the late 1960s. But, perhaps more significantly, he is warning us not to look for the direct unfolding of biographical events in this story of the self, but instead to see an alchemical transformation of that life into an allegory of the temporal progress of his artistic inspiration. In considering the subtitle in this way, I am guided by the model of *The Truth and Life of Myth: An Essay in Essential Autobiography* (1968) by Robert Duncan, one of Jordan's mentors. For Duncan, essential autobiography means the mystical sources of poetic creativity at work in his writing. In that book he dismissed the psychological implications of free association, to emphasize a poetic process channeling what Emerson called "the vital force supplied from the Eternal":

> The meaning and intent of what it means to be a man and, among men, to be a poet, I owe to the workings of myth in my spirit, both the increment of associations gathered in my continuing study of mythological lore and my own apprehension of what my life is at work there....
>
> My purpose...here has been to give some idea how little a matter of "free" association and how much a matter of enduring design in which the actual living consciousness arises, how much a matter of actual times and actual objects the living reality of the myth is for the poet. Just these times, just these objects, just these persons come to mind—at once things-in-themselves and things in ourselves.[6]

Not only does *Sophie's Place* provide a paradigm for the transfiguration of autobiographical material into a powerfully sustained revelation of the design immanent in the spontaneous manipulations of collage cutouts, it culminates in my exhilaration and surprise with an image of eyes turning upside down, atop a hot-air balloon voyage, as if unconsciously interweaving two key elements of the scenario from Emerson I have called up again and again in this book. In his astute discussion of the film, Fred Camper wrote:

> If Jordan's film has a "central character," it is a red-striped balloon, which frequently has eyes, sometimes a hat. It often travels across other images, and appears throughout the film, including at the beginning and the end. Jordan has said that, for him, *Sophie's Place* is a spiritual autobiography, and it is tempting to see the balloon-face as a surrogate

6. Robert Duncan, "The Truth and Life of Myth," in *Fictive Certainties* (New York: New Directions, 1985), pp. 2, 13.

for him and thus, by implication, for the viewer as well, passing as it does through the film's world like a spectator at a vast circus.[7]

In the circular structure of the film, the initial tableau of an English garden with mother and child returns. When the balloon-face manifests itself in that landscape, it rotates completely upside-down. With this concluding gesture the filmmaker redescribes the Emersonian mechanics of achieving the "low degree of the sublime" by which we can be "strangely affected," but he does not essay a mimetic means of inducing it as most of the filmmakers discussed in this book have done (and as Jordan himself had done in other films). The collage animation, together with the incessant series of surprises induced by the filmmaker's discipline of composition, produces a wondrous pictorial air in the alchemical autobiography. Within it compound images of the balloon perspective and the inverted eyes allegorically represent a route to what Jordan calls "spiritual wisdom" in his note on the film:

> A culmination of five years' work. Full hand-painted cut-out animation. Totally unplanned, unrehearsed development of scenes under the camera, yet with more "continuity" than any of my previous animations, while meditating on some phase of my life. I call it an "alchemical autobiography." The film begins in a paradisiacal garden. It then proceeds to the interior of the Mosque of St. Sophia. More and more the film develops into episodes centering around one form or another of Sophia, an early Greek and Gnostic embodiment of spiritual wisdom. She is seen emanating light waves and symbolic objects. (But I must emphasize that I do not know the exact significance of any of the symbols in the film any more than I know the meaning of my dreams, nor do I know the meaning of the episodes. I hope that they—the symbols and the episodes—set off poetic associations in the viewer. I mean them to be entirely open to the viewer's own interpretation.)[8]

The opening background plate—that of the paradisiacal garden—returns in the end, and that is where the balloon-face turns upside down. The other plate mentioned in the note—that of the interior of Hagia Sophia, which gives the film its title—also appears twice, both times early in the film, perhaps corresponding to scenes of formal instruction in the filmmaker's life. During its second appearance we see a magical projection apparatus at work, as if in the alembic of transfiguration the sacred space of Byzantium came

---

7. Fred Camper, "Film of Changes: Larry Jordan's *Sophie's Place*," *Film Culture* no. 76 (June 1992), p. 33.
8. *Canyon Cinema Film/Video Catalog 7* (San Francisco, 1992), pp. 189–90.

to trope the filmmaker's brief enrollment at Harvard University, where he became involved with serious cinema viewing and first started making films. Similarly, the visionary cities and encampments seen in some of the later background plates might refer to his subsequent migrations to San Francisco and New York. Against those backdrops the emerging artificers of transfiguration would symbolically represent his mentors, Robert Duncan, Jess, and Joseph Cornell, although even so general an interpretation is necessarily tentative when the author flatly denies that he knows the "significance of the symbols" arising from his associative process.

The teasing gap between autobiographical narrative and the perfect exhilaration of pictorial invention in *Sophie's Place* suggests a paradigm for the dilemma of my work in this study. My primary effort has been to convey an appreciation for the achievements of eleven filmmakers working in interrelated modes of camera movement, superimposition, associative editing, and the disjunctions of language and image. At the same time I have made liberal use of their writings and interviews, and what I have learned of their biographies, to throw light on the intensities and resonances of those achievements by linking the exhilarations of their cinematic inventions to what Stan Brakhage called "the eccentricities of our personal lives"; for I find two of the three principles he articulated in homage to Andrei Tarkovsky utterly convincing, at least insofar as they apply to the American filmmakers in the heritage of Emerson and Whitman. The first of them, however, is more problematic. Brakhage's triad was:

1) To make the epic, that is, to tell the tales of the tribes of the world.
2) To keep it personal, because only in the eccentricities of our personal lives do we have any chance at the truth. 3) To do the dream work, that is to illuminate the borders of the unconscious.[9]

The centrality of personal life and the illumination of the unconscious are central concerns in these chapters, while the aspiration to make epic forms emerges in surprisingly different ways for many but not all of the filmmakers I have been discussing, if we liberally read the terms *epic* and *tales* as Brakhage apparently does. The epics at issue would be serial films, sequences or cycles of autonomous works, sometimes rigorously delimited as in *Hapax Legomena* or *Is This What You Were Born For?*, sometimes open-ended as in *Diaries, Notes and Sketches* or *The Adventures of the Exquisite Corpse*; and sometimes evolving between those poles as in *The Book of the Family* or *My Hand Outstretched to the Winged Distance and Sightless Measure*. Jeffrey

9. Stan Brakhage, "Brakhage Pans Telluride Gold," *Rolling Stock* 6 (1983), p. 11.

Stout has pointed out that Brakhage's invocation of epic forms opens up an avenue for the examination of the political aspects of these films, which I have evaded. Certainly, in addressing Tarkovsky's achievement, Brakhage was compressing the Russian filmmaker's political position within the category of the epic. Brakhage's own tradition of the American epic that Whitman founded on Emersonian principles entails complex expansions on the political consequences of self-reliance in a massively expanding democracy. However, I have neither the expertise nor the space to unravel the political dimensions of that tradition in the work of the filmmakers discussed here.[10]

In the first generation of these filmmakers, Menken and Hugo generated their strongest films from the Emersonian exhilarations of bodily and vehicular camera movement and superimposition. Their younger contemporaries, Brakhage and Mekas, did the same, but they tended as well to nuance the exhilarations by arranging films into sequences. Whitman's "Song of Myself," the version of the American epic he fashioned from what Emerson called our "flux of moods," was the model for these internally modulated or dialectical serial films, whether or not the filmmakers realized it.

The following generation took the film sequence as an inherited option from the very start of their careers. For Noren, Frampton, and Beavers, the serial organization of films was an index of high aesthetic ambition, the functional equivalent of the epic form. Sonbert flirted with serial organization but ultimately distanced his work from it. Gehr, on the other hand, rigorously clung to the formal simplicity of Menken's clearly delineated parameters of the autonomous lyric. His films are the purest examples of that mode in the tradition.

A third generation, represented here by Child and Friedrich, found in Frampton's ironies, and in his use of language, a productive way to reconfigure

---

10. For alternative views of the politics of the American avant-garde cinema, see David E. James, *Allegories of Cinema: American Film in the Sixties* (Princeton, NJ: Princeton University Press, 1989), *The Most Typical Avant-Garde: History and Geography of Minor Cinemas in Los Angeles* (Berkeley: University of California Press, 2005), *Power Misses: Essays Across (Un)Popular Culture* (New York: Verso, 1997); Paul Arthur, *A Line of Sight: American Avant-Garde Film Since 1965* (Minneapolis: University of Minnesota Press, 2005); Juan Antonio Suarez, *Bike Boys, Drag Queens, & Superstars: Avant-Garde, Mass Culture, and Gay Identities in the 1960s Underground Cinema* (Bloomington: University of Indiana Press, 1996); and Abigail Child, *This Is Called Moving: A Critical Poetics of Film* (Tuscaloosa: University of Alabama Press, 2005). Jeffery Stout suggested that the political dimensions of my argument might be amplified by a consideration of "Emerson's repeated professions of reluctance to engage directly in struggles for political reform; against this, his extensive anti-slavery writings and the central role his ideas played in New England's debate over the Anthony Burns case; the politics of noncomplicity articulated in Thoreau's "Civil Disobedience"; the imaginative effort of re-founding America in Thoreau's *Walden*; the possible echoing of this in Mekas' *Walden*; the centrality of democracy in Whitman's work;...Brakhage's thoughts about the Vietnam War and those protesting it in mass demonstrations; Mekas' "This is a political film"; Mekas' way of treating the theme of exile; the distinction between the characteristic stance of the Emersonian social critic (for example, in Ellison's essays) and the stance adopted by Frampton...and Friedrich;...the politically monitory function of Romantic counter-epics of wandering."

and revitalize two parts of Brakhage's triad while vigorously contesting Brakhage's theoretical perspective and visual rhetoric (and that of his peers). Child sought to make the epic and articulate the unconscious while rejecting the idea of the selfhood behind Brakhage's representation of personal life. Friedrich accepted that selfhood and the oneiric form but turned away from epic or serial forms.

Finally, it needs to be said that this schema does not constitute a hermetic system. Each of the eleven filmmakers have responded to as many and as powerfully formative influences as those I have tried to delineate here. Their films in turn will respond to other contextualizations. But the pervading Emersonian heritage will remain ineluctable. As the liberating god of our native artistic aspirations, Emerson prophesied what these filmmakers realized, that seeing the familiar world with eyes upside down would open fresh channels to the tales of our tribes, the eccentricities of our personal lives, and the borders of the unconscious, in sum, "the axis of primary thought."

Appendix: Chronology of Films

Abbreviations

AC = Abigail Child
AN = Andrew Noren
EG = Ernie Gehr
HF = Hollis Frampton
IH = Ian Hugo
JM = Jonas Mekas
MM = Marie Menken
RB = Robert Beavers
SB = Stan Brakhage
SF = Su Friedrich
WS = Warren Sonbert

1943 *Meshes of the Afternoon* [Deren]
      Geography of the Body [Maas]
1944 *At Land* [Deren]

1945   *A Study in Choreography for Camera* [Deren]
       Visual Variations on Noguchi [MM]

1947   *Fireworks* [Anger]
       Ritual in Transfigured Time [Deren]
       Psyche [Markopoulos]

1948   *Lysis* [Markopoulos]
       Charmides [Markopoulos]
       Earliest material for *Reminiscences of a Journey
       to Lithuania* and *Lost, Lost, Lost* shot [JM]

1949   *The Dangerous Telescope* (shot) [IH]

1950   *Ai-Ye* [IH]

1952   *Interim* [SB]
       Bells of Atlantis [IH]

1953   *Eaux d'artifice* [Anger]

1954   *Jazz of Lights* [IH]

1955   *The Wonder Ring* [SB]

1956   *Glimpse of a Garden* [MM]

1957   *Dwightiana* [MM]
       Hurry! Hurry! [MM]

1958   *The Dead* (shot) [SB]
       Anticipation of the Night [SB]
       Melodic Inversion [IH]
       Arabesque for Kenneth Anger (shot) [MM]
       Bagatelle for Willard Maas (shot) [MM]
       Mood Mondrian [MM]
       The Gravediggers of Guadix (shot) [MM]

1959   *Wedlock House: An Intercourse* [SB]
       Window Water Baby Moving [SB]
       Cat's Cradle [SB]
       Sirius Remembered [SB]

1960   *The Dead* [SB]

1961   *Dog Star Man: Prelude* [SB]
       Thigh Line Lyre Triangular [SB]
       Arabesque for Kenneth Anger [MM]
       Bagatelle for Willard Maas [MM]
       Eye Music in Red Major [MM]
       Notebook [MM]

1962   *Dog Star Man: Part One* [SB]
       Guns of the Trees [JM]
       Rabbitshit Haikus (shot) [JM]

1963   *Dog Star Man: Part Two* [SB]
       Walden (begun) [JM]
       Go!Go!Go! [MM]

1964   *Dog Star Man: Part Three* [SB]
       Dog Star Man: Part Four [SB]
       Songs (begun) [SB]
       Wrestling [MM]

1965   *The Art of Vision* [SB]
       Andy Warhol [MM]

1966   *Spiracle* [RB]
       Acid Man [Cavanaugh]
       Galaxie [Markopoulos]
       Lights [MM]
       Sidewalks [MM]
       Amphetamine [WS, and Wendy Apple]
       Where Did Our Love Go? [WS]

1967   *Winged Dialogue* [RB]
       Scenes from Under Childhood: Section No. 1
       (first film completed of *The Book of the Film*;
       retitled ca. 1989: *The Book of the Family*) [SB]
       23rd Psalm Branch [SB]
       Eros O Basileus [Markopoulos]
       Watts with Eggs [MM]
       The Bad and the Beautiful [WS]

1968   *Plan of Brussels* [RB]
       Early Monthly Segments (begun) [RB]
       Surface Tension [HF]
       Morning [EG]
       Wait [EG]
       Excursion [MM]
       The Adventures of the Exquisite Corpse:
       Huge Pupils [AN]
       Tuxedo Theater [WS]

1969   *The Count of Days* [RB]
       Palinode [RB]
       Walden [JM]

Scenes from Under Childhood: Section No. 2 [SB]
Scenes from Under Childhood: Section No. 3 [SB]
Songs (completed) [SB]
Reverberation [EG]
Still (begun) [EG]

1970 Death of Marie Menken
Diminished Frame [RB]
Still Light [RB]
Early Monthly Segments (shooting completed) [RB]
The Animals of Eden and After [SB]
The Machine of Eden [SB]
Sexual Meditations (begun) [SB]
The Weir-Falcon Saga [SB]
Zorns Lemma [HF]
Field [EG]
History [EG]
Serene Velocity [EG]

1971 *From the Notebook Of . . .* [RB]
The Act of Seeing with One's Own Eyes [SB]
"The Pittsburgh Trilogy" [SB]
The Trip to Door [SB]
Hapax Legomena: Critical Mass [HF]
Hapax Legomena: (nostalgia) [HF]
Hapax Legomena: Traveling Matte [HF]
Still [EG]

1972 *The Painting* [RB]
Work Done [RB]
Sexual Meditations (completed) [SB]
The Riddle of Lumen [SB]
Hapax Legomena: Ordinary Matter [HF]
Hapax Legomena: Poetic Justice [HF]
Hapax Legomena: Remote Control [HF]
Hapax Legomena: Special Effects [HF]
Apparatus Sum [HF]
Shift (shot) [EG]
Reminiscences of a Journey to Lithuania [JM]
Carriage Trade [WS]

1973 *Sincerity (reel one)* [SB]

1974 *The Text of Light* [SB]
SOLARIUMAGELANI: Autumn Equinox, Winter Solstice, Summer Solstice [HF]

Shift [EG]

Eureka (shot) [EG]

The Adventures of the Exquisite Corpse, Part II: False Pretenses [AN]

1975 *Sotiros Responds* [RB]

Ruskin [RB]

Sincerity II [SB]

SOLARIUMAGELANI: Spring Equinox; retitled: *Ingenium Nobis Puella Fecit* [HF]

1976 *Magellan: At the Gates of Death* [HF]

Lost, Lost, Lost [JM]

The Adventures of the Exquisite Corpse, Part III: The Phantom Enthusiast [AN]

Rude Awakening [WS]

1977 *Sotiros (Alone)* [RB]

Sotiros in the Elements [RB]

Soldiers and Other Cosmic Objects [SB]

Otherwise Unexplained Fires [HF]

Untitled [EG]

The Adventures of the Exquisite Corpse, Part IV: Charmed Particles [AN]

1978 *Sincerity III* [SB]

Duplicity [SB]

Duplicity II [SB]

Hot Water [SF]

Earliest material for *As I Moved Ahead Occasionally I Saw Brief Glimpses of Beauty* [JM]

In Between [JM]

Divided Loyalties [WS]

1979 *Creation* [SB]

Roman Numeral Series (begun) [SB]

Gloria! [HF]

Eureka [EG]

Paradise Not Yet Lost a/k/a Oona's Third Year [JM]

1980 *AMOR* [RB]

Arabic Numeral Series (begun) [SB]

Duplicity III [SB]

Sincerity IV–V [SB]

Journeys from Berlin/ 1971 [Rainer]

1981   *Roman Numeral Series* (completed) [SB]
        Is This What You Were Born For?: Prefaces [AC]
        Gently Down the Stream [SF]
        Mirage [EG]
        Untitled—Part One [EG]
        Noblesse Oblige [WS]

1982   *Arabic Numeral Series* (completed) [SB]
        But No One [SF]

1983   *Efpsychi* [RB]
        Hell Split Flexion [SB]
        Is This What You Were Born For?: Mutiny [AC]
        Sophie's Place (begun) [Jordan]

1984   Death of Hollis Frampton
        Tortured Dust (last film completed
        in *The Book of the Family*) [SB]
        Is This What You Were Born For?:
        Covert Action [AC]
        The Ties That Bind [SF]

1985   Death of Ian Hugo
        Signal—Germany on the Air [EG]
        Wingseed [RB]
        He Stands in a Desert Counting the
        Seconds of His Life [JM]

1986   *Confession* [SB]
        Is This What You Were Born For?: Perils [AC]

1987   *The Hedge Theater* (begun) [RB]
        The Dante Quartet [SB]
        Faustfilm: An Opera [SB]
        Is This What You Were Born For?: Mayhem [AC]
        Damned If You Don't [SF]
        Sophie's Place (completed) [Jordan]
        The Adventures of the Exquisite Corpse, Part V:
        The Lighted Field [AN]

1988   *Faust III: Candida Albicore* [SB]
        Faust's Other: An Idyll [SB]
        Is This What You Were Born For?: Both [AC]

1989   *Babylon Series* (begun) [SB]
        Faust IV [SB]
        Visions in Meditation #1 [SB]

Is This What You Were Born For?: Mercy [AC]
Friendly Witness [WS]

1990   *Babylon Series* (completed) [SB]
Visions in Meditation #2: Mesa Verde [SB]
Visions in Meditation #3: Plato's Cave [SB]
Visions in Meditation #4: D. H. Lawrence [SB]
Sink or Swim [SF]

1991   *The Stoas* [RB]
A Child's Garden and the Serious Sea [SB]
Rear Window [EG]
Side/Walk/Shuttle [EG]

1993   *The Ground* (shot) [RB]
Rules of the Road [SF]

1995   Death of Warren Sonbert
Trilogy [SB]
The Adventures of the Exquisite Corpse,
Part VI: Imaginary Light [AN]

1996   *Efpsychi* (revised) [RB]
Sotiros (revised) [RB]

1997   *The Stoas* (revised) [RB]
Ruskin (revised) [RB]
The Birth of a Nation [JM]

1998   *From the Notebooks Of …* (revised) [RB]

1999   *The Painting* (revised) [RB]
Word Done (revised) [RB]

2000   *The God of Day Had Gone Down Upon Him* [SB]
Jesus Trilogy and Coda [SB]
As I Moved Ahead Occasionally I Saw Brief
Glimpses of Beauty [JM]
Plan of Brussels (revised) [RB]

2001   *The Ground* [RB]
The Count of Days (revised) [RB]
Palinode (revised) [RB]
Diminished Frame (revised) [RB]
Still Light (revised) [RB]
Glider [EG]
The Adventures of the Exquisite Corpse,
Part VII: Time Being [AN]

2002 *The Hedge Theater* [RB]
      Early Monthly Segments (edited) [RB]
      Panels for the Walls of Heaven [SB]
      Crystal Palace [EG]

2003 Death of Stan Brakhage
      The Adventures of the Exquisite Corpse,
      Part VIII: Free to Go (interlude) [AN]

2005 *Seeing Red* [SF]

Index